D1254165

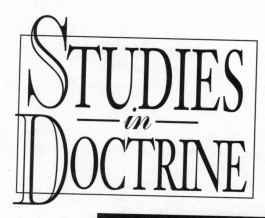

STUDIES
in
DOCTRINE

UNDERSTANDING DOCTRINE

UNDERSTANDING THE TRINITY

UNDERSTANDING JESUS

JUSTIFICATION BY FAITH

Other Books by Alister McGrath:

The NIV Bible Companion, *Zondervan, 1997*
The Sunnier Side of Doubt, *Zondervan, 1990*
Explaining Your Faith, *Zondervan, 1989*
The Intellectual Origins of the European Reformation, *Basil Blackwell, 1988*
Justification by Faith, *Zondervan, 1988*
The Making of Modern German Christology: From the Enlightenment to Pannenberg, *Basil Blackwell, 1988*
The Mystery of the Cross, *Zondervan, 1988*
Reformation Thought, *Basil Blackwell, 1988*
Understanding the Trinity, *Zondervan, 1988*
Understanding Jesus: Who Jesus Christ Is and Why He Matters, *Zondervan, 1987*
Iustitia Dei: A History of the Christian Doctrine of Justification *2 Vols., Cambridge University Press, 1986*
Luther's Theology of the Cross, *Basil Blackwell, 1985*

STUDIES in DOCTRINE

- UNDERSTANDING DOCTRINE
- UNDERSTANDING THE TRINITY
- UNDERSTANDING JESUS
- JUSTIFICATION BY FAITH

ALISTER E. MCGRATH

ZondervanPublishingHouse
Grand Rapids, Michigan

A Division of HarperCollins*Publishers*

Requests for information should be addressed to:

 ZondervanPublishingHouse
Grand Rapids, Michigan 49530

Library of Congress Cataloging-in-Publication Data

McGrath, Alister E.,
    Studies in doctrine / Alister E. McGrath, 1953–
        p.   cm.
    Includes bibliographical references.
    A compilation of the author's previously four, published, separate works: Understanding
doctrine, Understanding Jesus, Understanding the Trinity, and Justification by faith.
    ISBN: 0-310-21326-6
    1. Theology, Doctrinal. 2. Jesus Christ—Person and offices. 3. Trinity.   4. Justification.
I. Title.
BT75.2.M394   1997
230—dc21
                                                      96-53076
                                                      CIP

Printed in the United States of America

97 98 99 00 01 02 03 04 /❖ DH/ 10 9 8 7 6 5 4 3 2

CONTENTS

Understanding Doctrine   227

Justification by Faith   353

FOREWORD

Alister McGrath is an unusual man. A youngish Scotch-Irish English clergyman, he is a much-traveled Oxford academic and a most prolific author. A Thurber cartoon shows grinning felines overrunning two glum men in armchairs, one of whom is saying to the other, "We have cats the way other people have mice" —and McGrath, one might say, writes articles and books the way other people write letters. Sometimes he addresses his fellow professionals, sometimes a wider public, for as well as being technically accomplished, he has a flair for plain communication and a passion for it that not many scholars share. But McGrath, a sometime molecular biologist, is a teacher by instinct, just as he is a Christian by conviction and a theologian by trade.

"A theologian," says someone. "What's that?" It should not surprise us that this question is asked, and asked suspiciously too. Theologians today are classed by some as subversives, undermining rather than strengthening the life of faith, and it is a fact that some Protestant teachers in universities and seminaries during the past century and more have done precisely that. McGrath, however, is a theologian of the older and wiser type, who sees his role as in effect that of a water engineer, supplying God's people with the truth that brings health and straining out the pollution of error. For proof of this, one need only glance at the four primers—on Jesus, on the Trinity, on doctrine, and on justification—that are brought together in this volume.

To whom are they addressed? To those who, intellectually, are Christian beginners. That does not mean that they are beginner Christians chronologically; they may well have been stringing along in the church for many years; but now something has happened to make them aware that their minds are still fuzzy on fundamentals. Maybe it was Jehovah's Witnesses or Mormons at the door, and they did not know how to respond to the visitors' practiced patter. Maybe it was their reaction to a preacher or class teacher; they felt in their bones that something was wrong with what they were hearing, but could not put their finger on the defect. Maybe it was the challenge of having to instruct children, their own or someone else's; they found that they did not know their faith well enough to state it in a child's language. Whatever the cause, they want to get clearer on the basics of their faith and are looking around for help. They will find McGrath's work a godsend.

McGrath identifies himself in print as an *evangelical*, meaning that personal faith in Jesus Christ as Savior, Lord, and God is his focus, and sharing his faith is his purpose. But you could also describe him as *catholic*, in the sense that he seeks to set forth the wisdom of the entire Christian mainstream in a contemporary way; as *Reformed*, in the sense that he endorses the Reformation protest against medieval distortions of the biblical faith and builds on the doctrinal reconstruction of that era; and as *centrist*, in that he positions himself, knowledgeably and skillfully, at the heart of the great intellectual and moral heritage of Christianity over two thousand years. What this means is that, in the best sense of the word, McGrath is an *ecumenical* theologian, and that all Christians, of whatever stripe, who are prepared to think along with him will find that he speaks to both their heads and their hearts. It also means that he is an *evangelistic* theologian (*catechetical* is the word the early Christians would have used), whose account of the basics not only shows inquirers what Christians believe and why, but persuasively invites them into the Christian ranks.

The value of this compendium is great, and so is the enthusiasm with which I commend it.

—J. I. PACKER

UNDERSTANDING
–JESUS–

FOREWORD

One very great weakness in contemporary Christianity is this: Competent communicators of the faith are not very numerous, and are not usually very learned. Those who give their lives to the study of these great truths are often very indifferent communicators. It is rare that you find a man with great erudition who has the ability to distill it in terms which anyone can understand. Alister McGrath is such a man. He is quite brilliant. He got his First in theology at Oxford, while at the same time completing his doctorate in molecular biology! He is one of the major international experts on Luther. He teaches theology at Oxford. And yet he is able to teach total beginners, in language that is clear and untechnical. He is able to write, as he does in this book, on great themes without using long words and heavy footnotes.

So I welcome this book most enthusiastically. It is an excellent example of profundity married to simplicity. And I am sure that Dr. McGrath will write a lot more in this vein, to the great benefit of the general Christian public, as well as producing the major theological works for which he is so well equipped.

But I welcome the book for another reason. England is not a land which breeds systematic theologians. Maybe that is not altogether a bad thing, because no mortal man can get God systematized! But the shortage in systematic theology in this country means that it is not easy for the nonexpert to find a book which explains to him clearly and intelligently who Jesus is and what he has done for us. Within the pages of this book you will find a careful, well-argued explanation of the evidence about Jesus, the nature and purpose of the Gospels, and why it is important to reach clear views about Jesus. You will then be led into a most illuminating investigation of Jesus' person and work, embracing the central tenets of the Christian faith: the incarnation, the cross, and the resurrection. It is a splendid guide through the complexities of these vital doctrines. And it will surely encourage many a reader to go further in his investigations. But above all it gives to the believer a clear reason for the Christian faith which is within him, and to the inquirer a clear understanding of what Christians believe, and why.

I am excited by this book, and shall be surprised if you are not, too!

—MICHAEL GREEN

INTRODUCTION

Christianity has much to say about God and about man. It claims to possess certain crucial insights into the character and purposes of God, and the nature and ultimate destiny of man. It makes claims concerning the meaning of life, and the significance of death. What is particularly distinctive about Christianity, however, is not just these crucial insights themselves, but the way in which we come to know about them in the first place. The Christian faith is ultimately based upon the person of Jesus Christ. Just as a lens may focus the complex elements of a picture into a single point of light, so the many elements of the Christian faith are focused upon the single historical person of Jesus Christ. Who is Jesus Christ? And why is he so important? The Christian understanding of God and man arises from the Christian understanding of the *identity* and *significance* of Jesus Christ. In this sense, Jesus Christ may be said to be the foundation, the center, the focus, and the heart of the Christian faith.

This work is simply an attempt to explain the Christian understanding of the identity and significance of Jesus Christ, and its consequences.

PART ONE

Getting Started

1

Jesus and Christianity

One of the greatest mysteries of life is why some lectures are unspeakably tedious, and others spellbinding. Late in 1899, a series of lectures was given at the University of Berlin by an elderly professor of church history. His subject—the nature of Christianity. His audience—students drawn from every faculty in the university. The lectures were a sensation. Perhaps it was on account of his subject; perhaps it was the fact that the lectures were delivered completely without notes, so that they would have been lost forever were it not for one thoughtful member of his audience who jotted them down in shorthand as they were delivered. The opening sentences of those lectures are memorable:

> The great English philosopher, John Stuart Mill, somewhere observed that mankind cannot be reminded too often that there was once a man whose name was Socrates. That is true—but it is still more important to remind mankind again and again that a man whose name was Jesus Christ once stood in their midst.

At the heart of the Christian faith lies not so much a set of abstract ideas or beliefs but a person. We must resist the temptation to speak about Christianity as if it were some form of "ism," like Marxism, Darwinism, or Hegelianism. These are essentially abstract systems which have become detached from the person of their founder, and reduced simply to sets of doctrines. Although the ideas which we call "Marxism" were originally developed by Marx, the ideas are now quite independent of him. All that Marx did was to introduce them. The relationship between Jesus and Christianity is, however, quite different.

Christians have always insisted that there was something special, something qualitatively different, about Jesus which sets him apart from religious teachers or thinkers, and demands careful consideration. There is a close connection between the person and the message of Jesus—and if anything, it is Jesus' person—what he did, and the impact he made on those who encountered him—which makes his message important. From the outset, Christians appear to have realized that Jesus just could not be treated as an ordinary mortal. As we shall see later, from the earliest of times Christians worshiped and adored Jesus as if he were God. While recognizing the difficulties—and even the dangers—of speaking in this way, the Christian will insist that, in a very real sense, Jesus is the whole of the Gospel message; and that when he speaks of God, he actually means God as he has been revealed to us in the face of Jesus Christ.

In Jesus, the message and the messenger are one and the same. Jesus' message is given weight and status because of who we recognize Jesus to be. As we shall see later, the resurrection of Jesus appears to have been the decisive factor in forcing the first Christians to begin to take the astonishing— but to them necessary and appropriate—step of thinking of Jesus as God, in some sense of the word. We could put this more formally by saying that Jesus Christ is the object of faith, rather than just an example of faith. The challenge posed to every succeeding generation by the New Testament witness to Jesus is not so much, "What did he teach?" but "Who is he? And what is his relevance for us?" Christianity doesn't necessarily claim to possess all truth—but if it loses sight of its central conviction that in Christ it has found access to the deepest truths about God and man, it has lost itself.

The Gospels tell us that as Jesus was walking with his disciples in the region of Caesarea Philippi, he suddenly asked them a question: "Who do men say that I am?" The disciples replied with a variety of answers—they told him that some people thought that he was John the Baptist, others Elijah, Jeremiah, or some other prophet. Jesus then asks his disciples the crucial question, which demands that they speak for themselves, instead of merely reporting the opinions of others. "Who do *you* say that I am?" And Peter replied for them all when he answered: "You are the Christ, the Son of the living God" (Matt. 16:13–16). The central challenge posed to the reader of the New Testament, especially the four Gospels, concerns the identity and relevance of Jesus Christ.

"Who do *you* say that I am?" As we read the Gospels, it is impossible to avoid the impression that we have met a real person. There are many historical characters whom we may know much about—for example, Alexander the Great, Julius Caesar, or Admiral Nelson—yet who fail to make a personal impression upon us. They remain figures from the past whom we do not feel we know by personal acquaintance. Equally, there are many fictional characters who never existed in reality, and yet we feel we "know" them as real people—obvious examples might be Shakespeare's Falstaff, Mr. Pickwick, or Sherlock Holmes.

There are surprisingly few actual historical figures who come over as personalities—people whom we can know personally. An obvious example is Dr. Samuel Johnson, as recorded for us by Boswell, who comes across as a rather grave and melancholy figure who still has a love of fun and nonsense ("The Irish are a fair people—they never speak well of one another").

Another is Socrates, as we find him in Plato's dialogues. But the most important of all is the Jesus we encounter in the Gospel narratives.

Although an historical figure who lived and died in an obscure and uninteresting part of the world two thousand years ago, he comes across as someone we feel we know in the same sense as we know a real and living person—someone whom we can *know*, rather than just *know about*. One of his more reluctant and skeptical admirers once wrote: "We know no one as well as we know Jesus." For precisely this reason, the figure of Jesus Christ exercises a remarkable influence over many who would not dream of regarding themselves as Christians. But what is it about Jesus that causes him to exercise such a remarkable and pervasive influence over men and women some two thousand years after his birth? And how can we make sense of his identity and significance? It is with the unfolding and answering of these questions that this book is concerned.

Who is Jesus Christ? Our first attempt to answer this question might go something like this: Jesus was a first-century Jew who lived in Palestine in the reign of Tiberius Caesar and was executed by crucifixion under Pontius Pilate. The Roman historian Tacitus refers to Christians deriving their name from "Christ, who was executed at the hands of the procurator Pontius Pilate in the reign of Tiberius" (*Annals*, xv, 44, 3).

The historical evidence for his existence is sufficient to satisfy all but those who are determined to believe that he didn't exist, whatever the evidence may be. Indeed, if the existence of Jesus is denied, despite all the evidence we possess which points to the opposite conclusion, consistency would demand that we deny the existence of an alarming number of historical figures, the evidence for whose existence is considerably more slender than that of Jesus.

The historical evidence we possess concerning the origins of Christianity and the character of its early beliefs is most easily explained on the basis of the existence of Jesus as a real historical figure. It involves the most tortuous explanation if he did not exist. Indeed, if Jesus did not exist as an historical figure it would probably be necessary to suppose that someone remarkably like him did in order to explain the evidence in our possession. Thus Paul takes Jesus' existence as a fact which does not require demonstration, and concentrates upon establishing and defending the significance of his life, death, and resurrection.

That Jesus did *not* exist is a dogmatic presupposition quite unacceptable to the unbiased historian, rather than an obvious—or even plausible—conclusion of a detailed study of the evidence. Although there have been, and almost certainly always will be, those who argue that Jesus did not exist, and although they will doubtless continue to provide straws to be grasped by those determined to disprove Christianity, the fact remains that they are simply not taken seriously by disinterested and impartial historical scholarship.

So far, so good. What of the evidence that Jesus was crucified under the procurator Pontius Pilate? One of the earliest literary witnesses to this fact is Paul's first letter to the Christian church at Corinth, probably dating from the early months of A.D. 54. In the first chapter of this letter, Paul lays considerable emphasis upon the fact that Christ was crucified. The subject of his preaching was "Christ crucified" (v. 23); the power lying behind the Gospel proclamation is "the cross of Christ" (v. 17); the entire Gospel can even be summarized as "the word of the cross" (v. 18). If the tradition concerning the crucifixion of Jesus was an invention of the first Christians, we can only conclude that it demonstrates that they were too stupid for words, as the idea of a crucified savior was immediately seized upon by the opponents of the early church as an absurdity, demonstrating the ridiculous nature of Christian claims.

Justin Martyr, attempting to defend Christianity against its more sophisticated critics in the second century, conceded that the Christian proclamation of a crucified Christ appeared to be madness:

> [The opponents of Christianity] say that our madness lies in the fact that we put a crucified man in second place to the unchangeable and eternal God, the creator of the world (*Apology* I, xiii, 4).

For a Jew, anyone hanged upon a tree was to be regarded as cursed by God (Deut. 21:23), which would hardly commend the Christian claim that Jesus was indeed the long-awaited Messiah. Indeed, one of the Dead Sea Scrolls suggests that crucifixion was regarded as the proper form of execution for a Jew suspected of high treason.

It is clear from contemporary evidence that crucifixion was a widespread form of execution within the Roman Empire, and that there was an astonishing variety of manners in which this execution might be carried out. It is impossible to define what form a "normal" crucifixion might take. The victim was generally flogged or tortured beforehand, and then might be tied or nailed to the cross in practically any position, subject only to the ingenuity and perversity of the executioner. Far from being an essentially bloodless form of execution, as some commentators have suggested, the victim would have bled profusely. Only if he had not been flogged or tortured previously, and was bound, rather than nailed, to the cross, would no blood have been spilled.

The punishment appears to have been employed particularly in the suppression of rebellious provincials, such as the Cantabrians in northern Spain, as well as the Jews. Josephus's accounts of the crucifixion of countless Jewish fugitives who attempted to escape from besieged Jerusalem make horrifying reading. In the view of most Roman jurists, notorious criminals should be crucified on the exact location of their crime, so that "the sight may deter others from such crimes." Perhaps for this reason, Quintillian crucified criminals on the busiest thoroughfares in order that the maximum deterrent effect might be achieved.

It is therefore small wonder that the pagan world of the first century reacted with disbelief or disgust to the Christians' suggestion that they should take seriously "an evil man and his cross" (*homo noxius et crux eius*) to the point of worshiping him. Crucifixion was a punishment reserved for the lowest criminals, clearly implying that Jesus was one of their number. Jesus "endured the cross, despising the shame" (Heb. 12:2). The tradition of the crucifixion of Jesus Christ is deeply embedded in the New Testament witness to him at every level. It is impossible to account for this unless it is based upon an historical fact. If the early Christians had based their message upon a fictitious figure or upon a real figure whom they deliberately misrepresented, they would have been fools to portray Jesus as having been calculated to have evoked a more universal negative reaction on the part of their audience as the early Christians proclaimed the Gospel. Were the first Christians *really* that stupid? Would they have invented such a story, which could only be used against them? Once more, there is no reason for any except a dogmatic critic, who is determined to disbelieve each and every statement made by the New Testament concerning Jesus as a matter of principle, to call into question the historical nature of the crucifixion of Jesus.

But it is at this point that we must pause to reflect. The Christian faith certainly presupposes that Jesus existed as a real historical figure and that he was crucified. Christianity is, however, most emphatically not *about* the mere facts that Jesus existed and was crucified. Let us recall some words of Paul:

> Now I would remind you, brethren, in what terms I preached to you the Gospel, which you received, in which you stand, by which you are saved, if you hold it fast—unless you believed in vain. For I delivered to you as of first importance what I also received, that Christ died for our sins in accordance with the scriptures, that he was buried, that he was raised on the third day in accordance with the scriptures, and that he appeared to Cephas [Peter], then to the twelve [apostles] (1 Cor. 15:1–5).

The use of the words "delivered" and "received" is very important. They are drawn from the technical language of tradition, of "handing down," and point to the fact that Paul is passing on to his readers something that had earlier been passed on to him. In other words, Paul was not the first to summarize the Christian faith in terms of these two essential components (Jesus' crucifixion and resurrection)—he had learned this from others. Paul is not relying here on his own memory, but on the collective memory of a much larger group of people. It is widely believed that Paul is reciting a formula, a form of words, which was in general use in the early church and which he himself had received—not just in general terms but in almost exactly the same form as he passes it down to the Corinthian Christians. He is relying not on his own memory but on that of the Christian church in the earliest period of its existence.

Earlier in this letter, Paul had made it clear that the content of his preaching to the Corinthian Christians, upon which their faith was based, was "Christ crucified" (1:17–18; 2:2). It is now clear that two important points must be noted. First, Paul affirms that the Christ who died upon the cross was raised again from the dead. Second, Paul states that not only did Christ *die*, he *died for our sins*. We shall consider each of these two points separately.

Concerning the first of these points, the historical event of the crucifixion was followed by that of the resurrection, and Paul's exposition of the significance of Jesus Christ for mankind is based upon these two events being linked. But whereas it was commonplace for men to be crucified at that time, we possess no account of any other crucified individual being raised from the dead. Indeed, there appears to have been no other case of resurrection in the course of human history. This has prompted some critics to suggest that the event never, in fact, took place. We shall consider this suggestion in chapter four. But it is notable that Paul links Jesus' death and resurrection together as the two elements of his Gospel. Jesus "was put to death for our trespasses and raised for our justification" (Rom. 4:25).

Second, Paul makes a clear distinction between the *event* of the death of Christ, and the *significance* of this event. That Christ died is a simple matter of history; that Christ died *for our sins* is the Gospel itself. Even if it could be demonstrated to the satisfaction of the most biased opponent of Christianity that Jesus Christ really did exist, and that he died upon a cross, this would not prove the truth of the Christian faith. The Christian faith is based upon certain historical events, but is not to be identified with those events alone; rather, it is to be identified with an *interpretation* of these events.

The distinction between an *event* and its *meaning* must be appreciated. Let us take a well-known example. In 49 B.C. Julius Caesar crossed a small river with a single legion of men. The name of that river was the Rubicon, and it marked the boundary between Italy and Cisalpine Gaul. The political significance of that event was that it marked a declaration of war on the part of Caesar against Pompey and the Roman senate. The *event* was the crossing of a river; the *meaning* of that event was a declaration of war.

In many ways, the death of Christ may be said to parallel Caesar's crossing of the Rubicon. The event itself appears unexceptional except to those who know its significance. The Rubicon was a small river and it was not difficult to cross. People had crossed much wider rivers before and have since then. As an *event* it hardly seems significant. Similarly, Jesus died upon a cross. Every man must die at some point. On the basis of contemporary records, we know that an incalculable number of people died in this way at that time. As an *event* it hardly seems important or noteworthy. On the other hand, those aware of the *meaning* of the event saw beyond it, to what it signified, to the reason why it was important. Pompey and the Roman senate were not interested in the mechanics of how Caesar crossed the Rubicon—for them it meant war. Similarly, Paul was not particularly interested in the mechanics of the crucifixion of Jesus—for him, it meant salvation, forgiveness, and victory over death. Thus the "word of the cross" was not concerned with the simple fact that Jesus was crucified, but with the significance of this event for man.

Every now and then books with titles like *Great Moments from English Literature* make their appearance. I think we can safely say that the following lines by Frederick Langbridge will not feature prominently in them!

Two men look out through the same bars:
One sees the mud, and one the stars.

It is quite possible for two observers to be in the same position, and yet see something quite different. In this case, Langbridge draws our attention to the fact that two men, looking out through the same prison bars, see very different things. One looks down and sees the mud; the other lifts his eyes to heaven and sees the stars. The point that Langbridge is trying to make is that some men see nothing but the rut of everyday life ending in death, while others raise their eyes to heaven knowing that their ultimate destiny lies with God. Their situation is identical—but their outlooks are totally different.

Much the same is true of the cross. Two observers may contemplate the cross. One observer may see nothing more than an everyday execution of an unimportant Jew; another may see the Savior of the world dying for him. As we have tried to make clear, Christianity is not just about the *fact* of the cross—it is about realizing its full meaning. That Jesus died is a statement about an historical event—that Jesus died *for us* is a statement about the *meaning* of that event, and is nothing less than the Gospel itself.

This point is so important it needs further discussion. We are not talking about two or more different ways of looking at the same thing. All of us are used to the fact that a painting which seems grotesque to one onlooker appears to be nothing less than inspired to another. Here the object is the same—what is different is that which is seen in it. The cross is somewhat different, and is better understood from the following illustration.

Let us suppose that two observers are standing on the white cliffs of Dover, at some point during the period May 26–June 3, 1940. They see lots of little boats coming and going from the local harbors. For one observer, all that is happening is a relatively unimportant event—the movement of boats. Another observer sees exactly the same events, but is aware of a deeper and more significant truth linked to those events which the other observer misses. He knows that the little boats are engaged in the evacuation of the British Expeditionary Force from Dunkirk in France, and that the success of the operation holds the key to further resistance to Hitler, upon which the outcome of the Second World War will ultimately depend.

Both observers see the same events; one recognizes the crucial significance of what he sees, whereas the other does not. One, knowing the background to what is going on and knowing of the desperate situation in France on account of the astonishingly rapid German advance, recognizes that he is witnessing a moment in history upon which much depends. The other sees nothing but the sea and some boats.

The same is true of the cross. The observer who knew the background, who knew of the mysterious prophecies of the suffering servant and who knew that Jesus had foretold his death, recognized the full meaning of the event. Let us go back to our Dunkirk illustration for a moment. One observer noticed nothing more than lots of boats moving about in the English Channel; another saw the salvation of what remained of the British Army and war effort. So it is with the cross. One observer might notice a man dying on a cross; another sees God working out in a mysterious manner the salvation of mankind.

The same sort of point could be made with reference to the parables. When Jesus told parables, all those listening heard exactly the same words. For example, all those around heard Jesus tell the parable of the Prodigal Son—a story about a boy who leaves home, only to return (Luke 15:11–32). Yet although everyone heard the same story, two quite different reactions to that story can be seen. Some heard a story about a boy who ran away from home, while others heard about the overwhelming and amazing love of God for sinful man. One group heard the story and missed its meaning; the other group heard exactly the same story and realized what it meant. For this second group the penny had dropped. So it is with the cross. To some it is just about the death of a man; to others it is about God entering into his world to redeem those whom he loved.

It is also important to appreciate that a careful distinction must be made between the *truth* and *relevance* of an event. An event may be true, and yet quite without relevance. There will be few who will find themselves even remotely excited by the fact that the capital of Albania is Tirana, or by the accuracy of the annual rainfall figures for the Scottish Highlands. The truth of an event alone is not sufficient to ensure its appeal or relevance. In fact, something may be quite *untrue* and enormously significant. For example, in the mid-1850s new rifles were issued to soldiers of the East India Company. The old "Brown Bess" was replaced with the Enfield rifle which used a different type of cartridge. It was widely believed by the Indian sepoys that the Enfield cartridges were greased with beef fat (which would be defiling to a Hindu) or pig fat (which would be defiling to a Muslim). Although this rumor does not appear to have been based upon fact, it was sufficient to act as a major contributing cause to the Indian Mutiny of 1857. Although not true, it was certainly thought to be relevant!

It will be clear, however, that Paul is making two important statements concerning the crucifixion: First, it is *true*; secondly, it is *relevant*. In other words, the event of the crucifixion really took place and its significance is such that it has continuing relevance for man.

With this point in mind, let us return to the question of who Jesus is. The words of an early German Reformer (Philip Melanchthon) are worth noting here: "To know Christ is to know his benefits." We are actually dealing with two quite different yet closely related questions. One is the question of the *identity* of Jesus: Who is he? The other is the question of the *function* of Jesus: What does he do? If we are going to assess the significance of Jesus, we have to deal with both these questions. Let us illustrate this point with some examples.

It is possible to argue from Jesus' function to his identity. The following argument was used extensively by the early church. First, it was stated that Jesus was the Savior of the world, thus establishing his function (in other words, what he does—he saves). Second, it was argued that the only one who could save man was God. Therefore, if Jesus saved man he must be God. Beginning from Jesus' function, his identity was deduced.

Or the argument could be used the other way around—to work from Jesus' identity to his function. It would be argued that Jesus was God (which is a statement about his identity). Therefore, it is argued, Jesus must reveal God (which is a statement about his function).

For our purposes, it doesn't matter which way around this is argued. The point we want to make is that Jesus' identity and significance are closely related. In establishing who Jesus *is*, we have to bear in mind what he *does*. For Paul, Jesus was the bearer of salvation to sinful man. The "benefits of Christ" were the forgiveness of sins, reconciliation to God, and the hope of resurrection. To "know Christ" thus involves recognizing his significance for us—in other words, recognizing the "benefits" which he brings, making them our own, and subsequently reflecting upon who Jesus must be if he is able to do this for us.

Who is this man through whom the Christian church has always claimed that she has forgiveness of sins? Who is this man whom Christians have worshiped as if he was God? What is so special about this man's death that Christians *celebrate* it where mourning might seem more appropriate?

It is questions like these which come together under the general area of theology known as "Christology," or "the doctrine of the person and work of Christ," and which we shall be considering in the remainder of this book.

2

Why Have Doctrines about Jesus?

Theology is often regarded as idle and pointless speculation about irrelevancies—a harmless, if somewhat pointless, pastime of frustrated academics and bishops with time on their hands. If any area of Christian thought has been characterized by apparently pointless speculation of this sort, it is Christology. Gregory of Nyssa, writing in the fourth century, complained that it was impossible to go out shopping in downtown Constantinople without having to put up with speculation of this sort:

> Constantinople is full of mechanics and slaves, every one of them profound theologians, who preach in the shops and streets. If you want someone to change a piece of silver, he tells you about how the Son differs from the Father; if you ask the price of a loaf of bread, you are told that the Son is inferior to the Father; if you ask whether the bath is ready, you are told that the Son was created from nothing.

There is a widespread feeling inside and outside the Christian church today—as there always has been and probably always will be—that doctrines and dogmas are a waste of time. The Christian creeds all too often appear as arid and dead formulas, bearing little relation to the faith of those who have to repeat them. The great Austrian philosopher Wittgenstein remarked that "Christianity is not a doctrine, not, I mean, a theory about what has happened and what will happen to the human soul, but a description of something that actually takes place in human life." In other words, experience of God and Christ comes before doctrines about them.

The Christian who turns from his real and profound experience of God to the terse and bleak statements of the creeds of the church inevitably feels that they are petty, pedantic, and unreal—totally incapable of capturing his experience or adequately reflecting it. How can the immensity, the richness, the vitality, and the sheer wonder of the Christian's experience of God in Christ be expressed in such clumsy terms? Indeed, why bother with doctrines at all? It is this question which we must consider before going any further, because inevitably we are going to end up talking about doctrines concerning Jesus.

Christians are faced with something of a dilemma. On the one hand, they want to talk about God as the one whom they experience, love, and worship in adoration and wonder. On the other, they are only too painfully aware of the simple fact that God is God, and human language is quite incapable of adequately expressing everything which they would want to say about him. The words of the psalmist are worth recalling: "Be still, and know that I am God." The majesty and wonder of God tends to reduce us to silence. But we must speak of God, despite recognizing the inadequacy of our words, to do justice either to God himself or even to our experience of him.

When I began to study theology at Oxford, one of my tutors was a Jesuit at Campion Hall. As I climbed the staircase leading to his room, I used to pass a gigantic painting of a man and a small boy by the sea. Eventually, I asked someone to explain the painting, and was told the following story. Once upon a time, Augustine of Hippo, a celebrated theologian, was writing a work on the Trinity, exploring the Christian understanding of God. As he was walking along the coast one day, he encountered a small boy pouring seawater into a hole in the ground. Augustine watched him for some time, and eventually asked him what he was doing. "I'm pouring the Mediterranean Sea into this hole," replied the boy.

"Don't be so stupid," replied Augustine, "you can't fit the sea into that little hole. You're wasting your time."

"And so are you," replied the boy, "trying to write a book about God." (It's one of those stories which, if it *isn't* true, certainly ought to be!)

But even with this sobering thought in mind, Augustine still felt it was important to try and speak about God—and inevitably to speak of him in terms of doctrines. In fact, it took centuries for the church to sort out the full significance of its experience of God and Christ and express it—rather clumsily—in the doctrine of the Trinity. But it will be obvious that the Christian experience of God, Christ, and the Holy Spirit was something common to Christian experience long before it was expressed in words or doctrines or wrapped up in some sort of doctrinal formula.

In turning from our experience of God or Jesus to doctrines about them, we are inevitably turning from one thing which is real and authentic to something else which is much less so. But an illustration may help to clarify why this *must* be the case. Let us suppose that you cross the Atlantic Ocean from east to west on a liner. Inevitably, you are overwhelmed by its immensity, by its sheer size, by the sense of being totally insignificant compared with its vastness. Your experience of the ocean makes a deep impression upon you, and although you find it difficult to express in words, you could make a reasonable attempt at describing it to your friends. You then pick up a map of the Western Hemisphere and find the Atlantic Ocean reduced to nothing more than some printed lines on a piece of paper. You may be fortunate enough to find the ocean colored blue and the land masses of America and Europe yellow—but all that you have in your hands is a piece of paper. How on earth does your experience of the Atlantic Ocean relate to it?

First, nobody is going to suggest that the map is a substitute for the real thing. It is an attempt to indicate how various things are related—for example, where Europe and America are situated in relation to each other. It is not even an attempt to scale down the ocean so that you can get the same sort of experience you once had, only on a smaller scale. It is meant to convey certain limited (but important) information, rather than reproduce an authentic experience.

Second, the map is based upon the personal experience of countless others, as they also crossed the Atlantic. Whereas your experience is undoubtedly real and important to you, it represents a single, isolated, and very personal impression of a much greater reality. Taken on its own, your experience of the Atlantic Ocean is unreliable, perhaps providing your friends with as much information about you as about the ocean itself. The function of the map is to combine as many impressions of a greater reality as possible, in order that a more reliable picture may be built up. The other experiences upon which the map is based are just as vivid and real as yours—but the map eliminates the *personal* element of experience of the Atlantic Ocean in order to provide a more generally reliable guide to the same reality.

The parallels between doctrines and maps will be obvious. First, a doctrine about Jesus was never meant to be a substitute for experience of him—it is simply an attempt to state something limited (but important) about him; to relate him to God and to man, as the map relates the Atlantic Ocean to Europe and America. Thus the rather unexciting formula of the creed, which speaks of Jesus as "true God and true man," is really just placing Jesus on the map of human experience. Just as the Atlantic Ocean comes between Europe and America, so Jesus at the very least mediates between God and man. Just as the map told the traveler that the Atlantic would lead him from Europe to America, from the Old World to the New, so the doctrine of the "two natures" of Christ tells us that man encounters God through him.

Refugees fleeing to the United States from persecution or a hopeless economic situation in Europe in the first decades of the twentieth century knew that their hope of a new life lay in crossing the Atlantic Ocean. The deep sense of relief and joy when the New York skyline came into view is well known to us through contemporary films. And so it is with those who are seeking for God, for meaning and hope, in a seemingly dark, meaningless, and hopeless world. Through Christ they encounter the living God—the source of their new life, their hope, and their joy. Nobody is for one moment suggesting that this is everything that could be said about Jesus, or that it adequately describes the deep personal significance which he holds for each and every believer—but it does help us to begin to locate that significance, to be more precise about it than would otherwise be possible.

Second, we all experience Jesus in a different way—he is seen through many eyes, heard through many ears, and loved by many hearts. Inevitably, our attempts to describe this experience are going to be highly impressionistic, probably conveying more information about ourselves than about Jesus. Our backgrounds, our hopes and fears, our understanding of the world—all these things color our impressions of Jesus. But when countless such experiences are taken into account, the personal element may be eliminated to give a more reliable account of the significance of Jesus, reflecting the consensus of the church down the ages, rather than the impressions of a few individuals.

Doctrines are essentially the distillation of the Christian experience of God, in which countless personal experiences are compared and reduced to their common features. Thus the formula "true God and true man" is at the very least an attempt to express the conviction that we only know both God and man through Jesus.

Christianity represents a judicious compromise between two extreme views. Although each of these views is correct and important, each is inadequate on its own. On the one hand is the extreme represented by a purely emotional faith which experiences God and trusts implicitly in him but is unable to express itself coherently. Faith unquestionably has a *content* as well as an *object*—in other words, we don't just believe *in* God, we believe certain quite definite things about him. It is the task of every generation in the history of the Christian church to develop an articulate and authoritative account of its faith. The believer is also a thinker, and can never permit his faith to remain or become a shallow uninformed emotionalism. Emotion is an important element of the Christian faith—and those who despise it have no right to do so—but on its own, it is inadequate, incapable of doing justice to the essence of Christian faith.

On the other hand, Christianity is most emphatically not just a list of intellectual propositions to which the believer's assent is demanded. It is grounded in experience. It is worth remembering that Christian belief in the divinity of Christ did not arise as an intellectual theory, but through the impact of experience. The early Christians were thus faced with the intellectual task of thinking through the implications of their experience of Christ as God, and expressing it in as clear and persuasive a manner as possible. The full-blooded nature of Christian faith can never, as we emphasized above, be adequately expressed as propositions, anymore than the Atlantic Ocean could be reduced to some marks upon a piece of paper. Furthermore, it is possible for Christianity to degenerate into concern for an intellectual system, rather than for a *person* who enters into our experience and transforms it. The intellectual side of Christian faith is important—but once more, taken on its own, it is inadequate. A judicious compromise, therefore, is necessary in order to preserve both what we might call the subjective and objective aspects of faith. In other words, Christian faith is grounded in experience, but its content may still be summarized in propositions such as "Jesus is Lord," "Jesus is the Son of God," or "Jesus is true God and true man." There is no inconsistency involved—both the proposition and the experience relate to the same greater reality which lies behind them both. Faith involves both head and heart!

It is interesting to reflect on the reason why the church started laying down doctrines in the first place. It cannot be emphasized too strongly that doctrines are not a set of arbitrary regulations invented by some committee in an orgy of dialectical wrestling. Far from it—doctrines were hammered out at moments when the very heart of the Christian faith seemed to be under threat through simplification, distortion, or misunderstanding.

Christian doctrines and dogmas became inevitable when disagreement arose within the church about what the Christian experience of God and Christ actually meant. There was every danger that an understanding of God or Christ would arise which made some sort of sense, but could not do justice to the richness of the Christian experience of God. It is much simpler to believe that Jesus was just a splendid example of humanity, with insights and abilities denied to most of us, than to believe that he is (in some sense of the word) God. The difficulty was that this simply didn't seem to tie in with the way in which Christians experienced Christ, which pointed to a rather different way of looking at him. Some words of T. S. Eliot are worth remembering here: "We had the experience, but missed the meaning, but approach to the meaning restored the experience."

Doctrine cannot be isolated from Christian worship and prayer—and the simple fact was that this simpler, neater, more attractive approach to Jesus didn't tie in with the fact that Christians worshiped and adored him, prayed to him, and experienced him in a personal manner. Only by ensuring that doctrine ties in with experience can sense be made of the Christian faith—and once rival theories of Jesus' identity and significance began to appear (such as Arianism), which were so obviously deficient in this respect, the church *had* to make some sort of response. And so doctrines were hammered out and then expressed in creeds. They were never meant to be a substitute for Christian experience—just a sort of "hedge," marking out an area of thought about God and Christ which seemed to be faithful to Christian experience.

Some words of Thomas Carlyle are worth noting here: "If the Arians had won, Christianity would have dwindled to a legend." Experience and meaning would have drifted apart to the point where eventually both were lost. It is simply not true that doctrine is a hopeless irrelevance to the life and work of the Christian church; it is one of the few safeguards by which its identity and relevance have been, and still are, preserved in the face of a disbelieving world.

There is still, of course, widespread reluctance in some quarters to allow Jesus Christ any claim to be God in any meaningful sense of the word. The popular idea of Christianity is still that Jesus Christ was a great moral teacher and that mankind would profit greatly if they took his advice seriously. Of course, there have been other outstanding teachers before Jesus and after him—men like Plato, Aristotle, Confucius, and so on—who have also had some words of wisdom for mankind. The popular idea of Christianity gives Jesus the place of honor among such men, but whatever difference there may be between them is one of degree, rather than kind. They are all basically human beings, enlightened to various degrees, who have contributed to (or at least *tried* to contribute to) the moral education of man.

The first difficulty associated with this view is that it is only too painfully obvious that man has tended never to pay much attention to his teachers. Man has had plenty of good moral advice over the last three or four thousand years, and that given by Jesus is unlikely to make much difference if it isn't followed. Indeed, we might go further and suggest that there appears to be something about human nature which makes it impossible to take good advice. Something more than education is required if man's situation is to be altered for the better.

The second difficulty, however, is even more serious. Christians simply don't view Jesus in this way. They just don't treat Jesus as a super-rabbi. They talk about Jesus being the "Bread of Life," or the "Lamb of God, who takes away the sin of the world." They will undoubtedly make reference to—and value—Jesus' moral teaching, but their main interest concerns the significance of his death and resurrection. Just as with Paul, interest in the crucified and risen Christ has almost completely overshadowed his teaching ministry. Good teachers, after all, are not that difficult to find. People who are crucified, only to be raised from the dead, are somewhat thinner on the ground, and command attention for that very reason.

Christians have never looked back to Palestine to revere the memory of a dead teacher (in other words, a rabbi), but have looked up (if anywhere) to worship a living Lord. However difficult the terms may be, the fact is that Christians have tended to designate the crucified and risen Jesus as "Lord," "Son of God," or "Savior," and have gathered together on the day of the week marking his resurrection to worship him as their Savior and Lord, rather than just learn from him as their teacher.

We can learn much from the history of the Christian church in the first few centuries of its existence. First, it is clear that Christians had no hesitation in worshiping Christ as God. This practice was noted by the younger Pliny in his famous letter of A.D. 112 to the Emperor Trajan, in which he reports that Christians sang hymns to their Lord "as God" (*quasi deo*). The view of one early maverick theologian, to the effect that Christ was merely a rather special man, was answered with an appeal to the universal Christian practice of singing "psalms and songs written from the beginning by faithful brethren, which celebrate the Word of God, that is Christ, and speak of him as God." The heretic bishop Paul of Samosata, deposed in A.D. 268, attempted to stop his congregations worshiping Christ, recognizing that this well-established practice—which, of course, continues to the present day—posed an irrefutable challenge to his own view that Christ was not divine (in any meaningful sense of the word).

The Arian controversy of the early fourth century serves to highlight these points. Arius, while giving Christ precedence over all of God's creatures, insisted that he was still nothing more than a creature, rather than God. Although Jesus was to be treated as the first among men, he was still a man, and nothing more than a man. Two major lines of argument were advanced against him by his orthodox opponent Athanasius. First, he repeated the point we have just noted. Arius, he suggested, was making the entire church guilty of worshiping a creature, rather than God. Only God could be worshiped, argued Athanasius, and as Christians had worshiped Christ from the beginning of the Christian era, this meant that Christ had to be regarded as divine. We can see here an argument from Christ's *function* (as an object of worship) to his *identity* (as God who alone may be worshiped).

Second, Athanasius argued that created beings cannot be saved by another created being. Only God can save—and as Christ saves man (which Arius did not, incidentally, dispute), he must be treated as God. Once more, we can see a direct argument from Christ's function (as Savior) to his identity (as God).

The early Christians, then, worshiped Christ as a fully divine savior, regarding this as the obvious interpretation of the New Testament material. This basic understanding of the identity and function of Jesus Christ has remained characteristic of Christianity since then, despite a number of challenges to this understanding from within, as well as from outside, the Christian church. One such challenge is particularly interesting, and is worth considering in some detail. This is the so-called "Quest for the Historical Jesus" which culminated in the last century.

The period of rationalisms in Europe, usually regarded as having begun in the eighteenth century, showed little taste for ideas such as Jesus being a divine savior. If Jesus was anything, according to the rationalists, he was a good moral teacher. It was argued that ideas such as Jesus being a divine savior were actually due to early Christians misunderstanding or misrepresenting the New Testament, and that it was possible to rediscover the *real* Jesus by approaching the New Testament in a different way. This suggestion should, perhaps, have been viewed with considerably more skepticism than it actually encountered. After all, every week undergraduate theologians, and every year or so some plodding American associate professor of religious studies, "discover" for the very first time exactly what Paul's theology, or the death of Jesus, was *really* about, and find themselves astonished at the lack of excitement and interest their discovery evokes. But the fact remains that some nineteenth-century New Testament scholars felt that it was possible to recover the "real" Jesus from the Jesus of Christianity.

According to these scholars, the early church got Jesus completely wrong. He wasn't God incarnate or a divine savior, but a moral teacher whose views on most things happened—remarkably—to coincide with those of his rediscoverers. Jesus was the teacher of the Fatherhood of God and the Brotherhood of Man—an essentially simple and modern message, for which the first eighteen centuries of the Christian church were totally unprepared and were obliged to leave to modern scholars to take up. The pearl of great price, having only just been dug up, was immediately reburied in the hope that some wise and benevolent professor of theology might rediscover it centuries later. It was nothing less than a matter of divine providence that men, living nineteen hundred years after his death, and sharing nothing of his culture, his background, his language, and his presuppositions, should be able to get Jesus right—when his contemporaries, who shared his culture, background, language, and presuppositions should have got him so terribly wrong. And the fact that the rediscovered Jesus was practically the mirror image of his rediscoverers was purely fortuitous! It just so happened that Jesus actually taught all the right things by the standards of the nineteenth century—the principles which ensure the healthy progress of civilization, morality, and so on.

The possibility that these idealist theologians of the nineteenth century might just have projected their own moral ideas and aspirations onto a distant historical figure, about whom they knew practically nothing, in order to discredit a different understanding of the identity and significance of Jesus, for which they cared even less, never seems to have entered their heads.

Since then, of course, we have been presented with lots of rediscovered Jesuses. He was a freedom fighter, an itinerant Kantian, a hypnotist, a mushroom-eater and a confused prophet, to name but a few. In fact, it is difficult to avoid the impression that there are a lot of people arguing that, whoever Jesus was, he *definitely wasn't* the divine savior of sinful man that Christians have always thought he was. Because Jesus couldn't be God incarnate, they argued, he must have been something else. Curiously, their views on who Jesus really was turned out to be even more unbelievable, although it took some time for this point to be fully appreciated.

In the following chapter we shall look at the nature of the New Testament sources which oblige us to dismiss such "rediscovered Jesuses" as interesting, but quite unjustifiable, products of overactive human imaginations.

3

The Sources of Our Knowledge about Jesus

We are almost totally dependent upon the New Testament, and particularly the first three Gospels, for our knowledge about Jesus. Although there are early documents other than the New Testament writings which make reference to Jesus, or the beliefs of Christians about him, these are of little interest to any except specialist historians. But just what sort of documents are the Gospels?

In the last chapter we met the "Quest for the Historical Jesus" movement which attempted to sift through Christian beliefs about Jesus to find the "real" Jesus who lay behind them. Christianity had got Jesus wrong—it was time to get him right! One of the assumptions made by the movement was that the Gospels, particularly the Synoptic Gospels (that is, Matthew, Mark, and Luke) could be treated as historical sources. In other words, the Gospels were treated as if they were completely impartial documents which merely recorded facts (rather than opinions) about Jesus. It was then up to the individual reader of the Gospels to make sense of these facts as best he could.

In practice, of course, most of those engaged in the "Quest for the Historical Jesus" found themselves turning a blind eye to those facts recorded in the Gospels which they found difficult to cope with. Their desire to discover a simple moral teacher in Jesus led them to ignore, or attempt to explain away, certain facts recorded by the Gospels which didn't fit their preconceived pattern. For example, the Gospel accounts of Jesus' resurrection clearly imply that Jesus was infinitely more than a wandering Jewish moralist—and so these were ignored or rationalized as misunderstandings.

Similarly, the Gospel accounts of Jesus' preoccupation with his forthcoming death at the hands of the leaders of his own people were something of an embarrassment, and were passed over in much the same way. The real significance of Jesus, according to this movement, was his teaching, particularly as expressed in the Sermon on the Mount and the parables, all of which could be expressed morally.

But why were the Gospels written in the first place? And how can we explain the way in which the material is arranged within the Gospels? And, perhaps even more important, what factors determined the material to be included in the Gospels?

All too often, the scholars of the nineteenth century seem to have assumed that the Gospels were written for their convenience; a collection of sayings of Jesus which they could interpret as they pleased. If something didn't appeal to the reinterpreters of Jesus, they felt able to pass over it or explain it away. Since the final decade of the nineteenth century, however, it has become clear that the Gospels simply cannot be treated in this superficial way. The first three Gospels are, indeed, reliable sources of knowledge concerning Jesus. That point has been confirmed, rather than called into question, by responsible New Testament scholarship. But what has become increasingly clear is that this knowledge takes a particular form which cannot be ignored when it comes to interpreting it. So let us look at the broad features of the Gospel accounts of Jesus in order to appreciate this point.

The Gospels weren't written by Jesus himself, nor do they date from his lifetime. It is generally thought that Jesus was crucified about the year A.D. 30, and that the earliest Gospel (probably Mark) dates from about A.D. 65. In other words, there is probably a gap of about thirty years between the events taking place and their being recorded in the form of a Gospel. What happened in between?

It is difficult for the twentieth-century reader to understand why so long a gap existed between the events and their recording. We are used to information being recorded in the *written* form, and easily forget that the primitive world communicated by means of the *spoken* word. The great Homeric epics are good examples of the way in which stories were passed on with remarkable faithfulness from one generation to another.

If there is one ability which modern man has probably lost, it is the ability to *remember* a story or narrative as it is told, and then to pass it on to others afterwards. As one study after another of primitive culture confirms, the passing down of stories from one generation to another was characteristic of the premodern era—including the time of the New Testament itself. Indeed, there are excellent grounds for arguing that early educational systems were based upon learning by rote. The fact that we find it difficult to commit even a short story or narrative to memory naturally tends to prejudice us against believing that anyone else could do it—and yet it is evident that it was done, and was done remarkably well. Indeed, this ability has not been completely lost. I can remember very clearly how a friend described his astonishment when an elderly Jew whom he knew was able to recite the entire Old Testament in Hebrew from memory, while being checked against the printed text!

The period between the death of Jesus and the writing of the first Gospel is usually referred to as the "period of oral tradition," meaning the period in which accounts of Jesus' birth, life, and death, as well as his teaching, were passed down with remarkable faithfulness from one generation to another.

In this period, it seems that certain sayings of Jesus and certain aspects of his life (especially his death and resurrection) were singled out as being of particular importance, and were passed down from the first Christians to those who followed them. Others were not passed down, and have been lost forever. The early Christians seem to have identified what was essential, and what was not so important, among Jesus' words, deeds, and fate, and passed down only the former to us.

An excellent example of this process of transmission may be found in Paul's first letter to the Christians at Corinth, almost certainly dating from the period of oral transmission:

> For I received from the Lord what I also delivered to you, that the Lord Jesus on the night when he was betrayed took bread, and when he had given thanks, he broke it, and said, ". . . Do this in remembrance of me." In the same way also the cup, after supper, saying, "This cup is the new covenant in my blood. Do this, as often as you drink it, in remembrance of me" (1 Cor. 11:23–25).

It is clear that Paul is passing something on to the Corinthian Christians which had been passed on to him, presumably by word of mouth. It is interesting to compare these verses with their equivalents in the Gospels (Matt. 26:26–28; Mark 14:22–24; Luke 22:17–19).

The "period of oral tradition" may thus be regarded as a period of "sifting," in which the first Christians assessed what was necessary to pass down to those who followed them. Thus Jesus' sayings may have become detached from their original context, and perhaps on occasion even been given a new one, simply through the use to which the first Christians put them—proclaiming the Gospel to those outside the early community of faith, and deepening and informing the faith of those inside it. There is every reason to suppose that those early Christians preserved and transmitted faithfully the *substance* and the *meaning* of Jesus' teaching and actions, even if it is conceivable that some slight inaccuracies in the precise wording of Jesus' sayings, or the chronology of his actions, may have arisen. The early Christians weren't parrots—they were preachers.

Although the Gospel writers did indeed pass on to their readers authentic traditions concerning Jesus, those traditions were selected on the basis of the needs of the early Christian church, as it sought to spread the Gospel. Perhaps John's Gospel states this point most clearly:

> Now Jesus did many other signs in the presence of the disciples, which are not written in this book, but these [i.e., the ones that *are* included] are

written that you may believe that Jesus is the Christ, the Son of God, and that believing you may have life in his name (John 20:30–31).

This passage states two things explicitly. First, the principle of *selectivity*. The Gospel writers have been selective in their material (note also John 21:25), following the oral tradition passed down to them. Much information about Jesus has been lost forever, simply because the early Christians did not feel that it was of any relevance to their purposes of evangelization and teaching.

Second, the Gospels were written with a purpose in mind—that of conversion, of generating faith in their readers. To develop this point, we must return to the distinction between *event* and *interpretation* discussed in chapter one.

As we noted in that chapter, Christianity is not primarily concerned with the events associated with Jesus Christ, but with the interpretation of the significance of those events. The Gospel writers were not concerned primarily with recording the events of the life and death of Jesus, but with indicating their significance. We could say that they mingle history and interpretation, in that they indicate the significance of events, rather than merely recording them. Thus in the passage just quoted from John's Gospel, the evangelist is clearly drawing a distinction between "signs" (events) and "believing that Jesus is the Christ, the Son of God" (interpretation). Similarly, we find Paul appealing to an oral tradition which combines the report of events (Jesus' death and resurrection) with the interpretation of these events (forgiveness of sins) in 1 Corinthians 15:3–5 (a passage discussed in chapter one).

Some immortal words from Edmund Clerihew Bentley's *Biography for Beginners* are worth noting here:

> The art of Biography
> Is different from Geography.
> Geography is about maps,
> But Biography is about chaps.

It is, of course, always useful to be reminded of this important point. We may be able to distinguish between geography and biography without too much difficulty, but distinguishing between biography and theology in the Gospels is much more difficult. The Gospel writers were not biographers, or even historians, by our standards, nor were they even remotely interested in giving an exhaustive or totally precise account of everything that Jesus said and did. It did not matter to them at precisely what point in his ministry Jesus told a particular parable, for example—the important thing was that he *did* tell it, and that it was realized to be relevant to the preaching of the early church.

It is obvious that the Gospels of Matthew, Mark, and Luke draw upon common material, although at times we encounter material which is peculiar to one, or two, Gospels. The same material is sometimes presented in one setting in Mark, another in Matthew, and perhaps even a third in Luke. Sometimes the same story is told from different perspectives in different Gospels. Sometimes a story is told at greater length in one Gospel than in another.

It is evident that there is an historical core to the Gospels, underlying the variations encountered in the Gospel accounts. New Testament scholarship has merely clarified the nature of this historical core rather than called it into question. But it is also obvious that the Gospel writers were simply not interested in reproducing precise historical accounts of everything which Jesus said and did. For them, "historical" simply meant "based on historical fact," not "strictly exact chronological account of absolutely everything which Jesus said and did." There can be no doubt whatsoever that the Gospel accounts of Jesus contain a solid base of historical information linked with an interpretation of that information—in other words, biography and theology mixed up to such an extent that they can't be separated anymore. The early Christians were convinced that Jesus was the Messiah, the Son of God and their Savior, and naturally felt that these conclusions should be passed on to their readers, along with any biographical details which helped cast light on them. It is for this reason that fact and interpretation are so thoroughly intermingled in the Gospels. The first Christians had no doubt that their theological interpretation of Jesus was right, and that it was therefore an important fact which should be included in their "biographies."

With this point in mind, let us return to the ill-fated "Quest for the Historical Jesus." The basic assumption which lay behind this movement was that the Gospels were essentially factual accounts of the history of Jesus, which could be interpreted by the reader. Or, to put it another way, the Gospels were treated as raw data which required interpretation. We now know that this is quite unacceptable. The Gospels are not purely factual, but intermingle history and theology, event and interpretation. They are not "raw data" requiring interpretation, but are interpretations of "raw data."

Furthermore, the process of selection which is so important a feature of the "period of oral transmission" means that much information concerning him (which the early Christians thought insignificant for their purposes) is forever lost. As a result, the reader of the Gospels does not have access to the material which he would need if he was to attempt a realistic "reinterpretation" of Jesus. The Gospels are written from the standpoint of faith in the crucified and risen Jesus, and reflect the faith of the early Christians to such an extent that it is actually impossible to distinguish between "event" and "interpretation" at points. The Gospels are written in the light of the fundamental conviction that Jesus is "the Christ, the Son of the living God" (Matt. 16:16), and their content cannot actually be isolated from this conviction.

This point presents no difficulties whatsoever for the Christian reader of the Gospel, who shares the faith of the Gospel writers concerning the identity and significance of Jesus Christ. It does, however, raise certain fundamental difficulties for those who do not share this faith. Basically, the Gospels are out to win their readers over to their point of view about the identity and significance of Jesus by setting the reader alongside the disciples as they come to faith in order that he may share the same experience. But the reader who is convinced that the first Christians were wrong in their understanding of the identity and significance of Jesus—and hence that the Gospels are wrong at certain crucial points—is faced with three possible options.

First, he may argue that the Gospels allow him to develop a different interpretation of the identity and significance of Jesus which he finds more plausible. This is essentially the approach of the "Quest for the Historical Jesus" movement. This approach is initially attractive, but on further reflection is obviously impossible. To reinterpret Jesus requires access to information which is no longer available to us—the *complete* history of Jesus Christ, absolutely everything which he said and did, as well as a total familiarity with the first-century Palestinian culture in which his ministry took place. This history is forever lost to us. All that we possess of it is what we find in the Gospels—and it will be obvious that the Gospel writers have been selective in regard to what they included!

Furthermore, history and theology, event and interpretation, are intermingled to such an extent that they cannot be separated with the accuracy and precision which such a reinterpretation would require. The "reinterpretation" of Jesus *on the basis of the New Testament accounts* is thus a blind alley which leads nowhere.

It is, of course, possible to base a "reinterpretation" of Jesus on something other than the Gospels, such as preconceived ideas about God or man, but this is of little relevance to the Christian understanding of the identity and significance of Christ, particularly as Christians have generally based their understandings of God and man upon Jesus, rather than the other way around. For example, he may say that as God is absolutely beyond this world, he could not have become incarnate. (Anyway, how does he know this? How can he be *sure* that this is what God is really like? Has he access to some source of knowledge denied to everyone else, which allows him to make such certain statements about God?)

The Christian, however, argues the other way around—*because* God *did* become incarnate, we must learn to reject any concept of God which means that he must be thought of as being totally beyond this world, and uninvolved in it. Preconceived ideas about God must be abandoned and replaced with the God whom we see, know, and meet in Jesus Christ.

The argument really concerns how we know about God in the first place. The Christian argues that the person of Jesus is the most reliable source of knowledge about God to be had, whereas others may argue you can learn about him from the night sky, or sunsets, or nice paintings. We shall return to this argument in chapter seven.

Second, he may reject the Gospels completely, and have nothing to do with them. This is an intellectually honest approach, but one which is not likely to commend itself to Christological skeptics!

Third, he may approach the Gospels in the spirit in which they were written, either sharing the faith of the Gospel writers, or allowing himself to be carried along with them. Once more, this approach has the virtue of intellectual honesty. The reader may wish to attempt to restate the convictions of the Gospel writers in terms more comprehensible to the modern reader, but he is still operating within the framework of faith established by the Gospels.

The new understanding of the nature of the Gospels which has developed over the last century thus cannot be said to have eroded confidence in the reliability of the New Testament portrayal of Christ, despite the swashbuckling claims of overenthusiastic critics of Christianity. New Testament scholarship has established that the Gospels are a remarkable, probably a unique, form of writing, and has helped us to understand the purposes, intentions, and priorities of their writers with greater confidence. This new approach does, however, devastate a number of rival approaches to the identity and significance of Jesus.

The father of the modern critical approach to the New Testament was the great Marburg New Testament scholar and theologian Rudolf Bultmann, who emphasized two points. First, the critical approach to the New Testament cut the ground from under liberal Christologies (such as Jesus as just a "teacher" or "moral example"). Second, there was an urgent need to restate the *content* of the New Testament portrayal of Christ in terms that modern man could make sense of. We are particularly concerned with the first of these points here, and will return to the second in a later chapter.

For Bultmann, the New Testament witnessed to an understanding of Jesus as an act of God, totally distinct from anything else. This understanding of the identity and significance of Jesus is deeply embedded in the New Testament, particularly the Gospels, to the extent that it was quite impossible to find any other picture of Jesus portrayed in its pages. Bultmann thus singled out three understandings of the identity and significance of Jesus which could no longer be taken seriously. First, there was the view that Jesus was just a good religious teacher, like Moses. Second, there was the view that Jesus was a religious hero, who died to make some sort of religious point. Third, there was the view that Jesus' significance lay in his religious personality or his consciousness of the presence of God.

The foundations of all these were, according to Bultmann, shattered beyond repair by the rise of a critical study of the New Testament. According to Bultmann, the only understanding of the identity and significance of Jesus which could stand up in the light of New Testament scholarship was that of a unique divine act in human history. How Bultmann went on to explain this divine act does not concern us here, and is actually not relevant to our discussion. What *is* important is the realization that if *any* understanding of the identity and significance of Jesus has been irredeemably discredited by modern New Testament scholarship, it is *not* what we might call the "traditional" picture of Christ as being God and man, but the views of the "rediscoverers of the historical Jesus" and their modern-day followers.

Of course, there are still those who will wish to suggest that Jesus was a religious genius, or hero, or just a lunatic—indeed, there will almost certainly always be views like this in circulation. But what needs to be emphasized is that they cannot be supported by responsible use of the New Testament documents, and particularly the Gospels, as sources. And as we are almost totally dependent upon precisely these sources for our knowledge of Jesus, this virtually amounts to the elimination of such totally inadequate portrayals of the identity and significance of Jesus Christ. It is ironical, to say the least, that some critics of traditional Christianity appeal to Bultmann in support of their views about Jesus being a moral example, or a religious teacher—apparently quite unaware that it was against exactly these views that Bultmann directed his devastating criticisms!

Let us now return to the Synoptic Gospels (Matthew, Mark, and Luke), and look more closely at the way they portray Christ. It is clear that the Gospels are not biographies, although they do indeed contain a hard core of historical information about Jesus. Nor are they religious textbooks spelling out the basics of Christian ethics, although they do indeed contain much teaching concerning morality. Perhaps the most helpful way of thinking of them is to draw a parallel with a somewhat different type of modern literary form—the detective novel.

The essence of every good detective novel lies in engaging the reader in the detective's search for the murderer. In effect, the reader is set alongside the fictional detective as he discovers clues, and gradually builds up a picture of what must have happened in order to uncover the identity of the murderer in an exciting climax. It is only at this point that the reader finds out whether he has noticed all the clues and worked out their significance. Of course, there is always something of a temptation for the author of such novels to introduce so many "red herrings" that it is difficult to distinguish them from real clues. And certain novelists—Agatha Christie comes to mind immediately as an example—even conceal clues from the reader in order to hold his interest to the final chapter.

In several respects, the Gospels parallel this type of writing. The reader of the Gospels is set alongside the disciples as they listen to Jesus preach, as they watch him in action, and as they finally see him die and raised again. But whereas detective novels are basically "Whodunits," the Gospels are "Whowasits." In other words, we are concerned with establishing the identity and significance of their central figure, rather than with picking out a murderer from a number of possible suspects. The Gospel writers allow us to see and hear what the disciples heard, and force us to ask much the same questions which they themselves must have asked before us. Who is this man? And just as the writers of detective novels single out, or draw our attention to, significant things (in other words, clues) which we might otherwise have overlooked, so the Gospel writers do the same. Before we illustrate this with some examples, an important point needs to be made.

It is all too easy to overlook clues, for a number of reasons. For example, something may take place which appears to be insignificant at the time, and yet assumes a much greater significance later, as its full meaning becomes obvious. Thus in Arthur Conan Doyle's story *Silver Blaze*, the full significance of the fact that the dog did *not* bark during the night only becomes evident at a late stage. The *fact* is observed, but its *significance* only becomes apparent later. The author is thus obliged to single out this one apparently insignificant fact (and ignore other apparently equally insignificant facts) because it was later realized to be relevant. He has to be selective, "filtering" out facts which he knows (on account of later developments) to be important, and ignoring others which he knows are not so important (even though this may not have been obvious at the time at which they took place).

There is every reason to suppose that something similar has happened in the case of the Gospels. The first Christians appear to have realized the full significance of some of the things which Jesus said or did after his resurrection, when they suddenly saw things in a completely new light. An apparently insignificant fact thus assumed a new meaning, simply because its full significance was realized—perhaps late in the day, but better late than never. Thus in John's Gospel we find an explicit reference to this process. Jesus makes a remark which appears to refer to the temple at Jerusalem, whereas after the resurrection his disciples realized that it referred to Jesus himself (John 2:19–22).

It is clear that some clues concerning the identity and significance were impossible to overlook—the resurrection itself being the most obvious example. Others, however, appear to have been more subtle—they were only recognized for what they really were after the resurrection when the penny finally dropped for the disciples. This point serves to remind us that the Gospel accounts are meant to be read in the light of faith in the resurrection, which the early Christians evidently took as fundamental to their beliefs about Jesus. And sometimes the fact that something *didn't* happen is important—just as it was important to Sherlock Holmes that the dog didn't bark in the night when the racehorse Silver Blaze was stolen, when it might have been expected to. Thus Mark notes that Jesus was silent before his accusers (Mark 14:61), when he might have been expected to defend himself. The significance of this silence can be seen in the light of the silence of the Suffering Servant (Isa. 53:7) before his accusers. Mark appears to want us to pick up this clue, and draws us on to note other parallels between Jesus and this mysterious Old Testament figure (which we will note in a moment). Let us now return to the Gospel narratives.

It is evident that Matthew initially wants us to draw the conclusion that Jesus was the Messiah, the long-expected descendant of King David who was expected to usher in a new era in the history of Israel. The first part of his Gospel is therefore littered with clues pointing to this conclusion. Thus the Gospel opens with a list of Jesus' forefathers (Matt. 1:1–17) which establishes that Jesus was legally the son of David—as the Messiah ought to have been. We are then given an account of the birth of Jesus in which Matthew makes sure that we don't overlook the remarkable parallels between the circumstances of that birth and the prophecies of the Old Testament. Thus Matthew draws our attention to this point no less than five times (Matt. 1:22–23; 2:5–7; 2:16; 2:17–18; 2:23) in his first two chapters.

Mark's Gospel opens by establishing the credentials of John the Baptist. John is the long-expected messenger who prepares the way for the coming of the Lord (Mark 1:2–3). Having established this point, Mark records John's statement that someone even more significant will come after him (Mark 1:7–8). And who is it Mark immediately introduces to us? "In those days Jesus came from Nazareth of Galilee and was baptized by John in the Jordan" (Mark 1:9). The conclusion Mark wishes us to draw is obvious.

Although some of the clues concerning the identity and significance of Jesus are pointed out with some force, others are left to the reader to pick up for himself. For example, Jesus regularly addresses God as "Father" in his prayers—a very presumptuous practice by the standards of that time. At one point, Mark even gives us the Aramaic original of the word for "Father"—*Abba*, a remarkably familiar term impossible to translate into English ("Papa," "Dad," and "Daddy" often being suggested as the nearest equivalents). The Gospel writers do not bring out the full significance of this practice which clearly points to Jesus understanding himself to have a remarkably intimate relationship to God.

Equally, the remarkable parallels between the righteous sufferer of Psalm 22 and the accounts of Christ's passion are not made explicit, but are left unsaid. Jesus' words "My God, my God, why hast thou forsaken me?" (Matt. 27:46)—The only point, incidentally, at which Jesus does not address God as "Father"—draw our attention to this mysterious Psalm, and particularly to certain of its descriptions of the mode of death of the righteous sufferer. The righteous sufferer is mocked by those who watch him die (Ps. 22:6–8)—as is Jesus (Matt. 27:35). Another remarkable parallel exists between the crucifixion and the account of the suffering servant of Isaiah 53, which only Luke notes explicitly (Luke 22:37). This famous Old Testament prophecy speaks of a suffering servant of God, who was "wounded for our transgressions, [and] bruised for our iniquities" (Isa. 53:5).

Perhaps the most significant part of this prophecy relates to the fact that the servant is "numbered with the transgressors" (Isa. 53:12), which is clearly understood by the Gospel writers to be paralleled in two manners. First, Christ died by crucifixion, which, as we emphasized in chapter one, was a mode of death reserved for criminals. In other words, Christ was identified with sinners by the manner of his death. Second, Christ was not crucified alone, but along with two criminals (Matt. 27:38). In both ways, Christ's death paralleled that of an important Old Testament figure.

Other parallels with this account may be seen in the Gospels, although they are not pointed out by the Gospel writers. Thus Luke notes that Jesus prayed for his executioners (Luke 23:34), paralleling the actions of the suffering servant (Isa. 53:12). In fact, it seems that the first Christians could not help but notice the obvious parallels between the life and death of Jesus and certain significant prophecies of the Old Testament, and take a certain degree of delight in pointing them out to their readers, or allowing them to discover them for themselves.

As we have seen, the evangelists were theologians, rather than biographers, painting a portrait which attempted to bring out the full richness of their impressions of Jesus Christ. When looking at a painting, such as a landscape, we can of course concentrate our attention upon one part of it, examining the small detail underlying the artist's work. The great portrayal of a Flemish landscape may, on closer examination, disclose astonishing attention to detail in individual blades of grass. But it is the overall impression which the picture conveys that is of crucial importance. After marveling at the landscape, our attention may wander to consider the intricacy of the artwork on the blades of grass, as one component of that landscape, of that greater whole of which it is a part. But it is the overall impression and impact which really counts.

Jesus came to those who first knew him as a living man, a totality rather than a sum of small parts. Later, as the first Christians reflected on the astonishing personality of Jesus, they were able to discriminate between the various elements which contributed to the impression he made upon them. But this is something which happened later, after the passage of time allowed such an analysis to take place. The immediate impression which Jesus made upon those whom he encountered is what underlies this analysis. What was it about Jesus that caused those fishermen to drop their nets, leave everything, and follow him into the unknown? What was it that caused people to marvel at his teaching?

With remarkable skill, the evangelists paint for us a portrait of Christ as the King of Israel, the Servant of the Lord, the Friend of Sinners, and the Word Incarnate. This building up of a portrait of Jesus Christ as Savior and Lord was not done in a clumsy or haphazard way, like a child cutting up bits of paper and pasting them into a scrapbook, but in a genuinely artistic process through which material is brought together in the mind of the evangelist as a consistent whole. It is this consistent portrayal of Christ which finds its expression in the Gospels. We must realize that behind the wealth of detail which we find in the Gospels lies an attempt to express the totality of Jesus Christ. The details are like brushstrokes, the landscape for the blades of grass. If you look at a television screen very closely, you will see that the picture is made up of very small colored dots—but to see the picture you have to stand back, losing sight of this detail, as the dots merge to form a picture.

We must learn to stand back from the small details of Jesus in order to grasp him as a whole. The details merge and Christ as Savior and Lord emerges. We will overlook the portrayal of Christ as Savior and Lord as we concentrate upon the parables or the passion narratives. We must learn to see these as pieces of a jigsaw, as intricate detail in a work of art, all combining to disclose Jesus to us as he once disclosed himself to his disciples.

The Gospels portray the gradual dawn of faith in the disciples. Initially, they see in Jesus a great teacher—one who taught with authority, unlike their own teachers (Mark 1:27). Gradually, other insights begin to develop. For example, Jesus performs signs and wonders which arouse enormous popular interest in him throughout the region. Eventually, they have sufficient information at their disposal to come to the conclusion which marks a turning point in the Gospel narratives: the confession that Jesus is the Messiah (Matt. 16:16; Mark 8:29; Luke 9:20). Once the disciples have achieved this basic insight, Jesus tells them that he must be rejected by his own people, suffer, be killed, and rise again (Matt. 16:21; Mark 8:31; Luke 9:22). The emphasis upon the fact this *must* happen, and the use of "be killed," rather than simply "die," indicates that the early Christians regarded Christ's death as an integral part of his ministry and mission—a fact which is perfectly obvious from the remaining writings of the New Testament, even if the Gospels do not choose to emphasize it.

The first Christians did not simply regard Jesus' death as an untimely end to the promising career of a radical rabbi, but as one of the two culminating points of Jesus' mission (the other being his resurrection). Jesus' teaching, important and distinctive though it unquestionably is, assumes its full significance only through the recognition of who Jesus *is*. To put it very crudely: If you have good reason to think that you are dealing with someone who may well be God incarnate, you are likely to take what he says and does a lot more seriously than you would otherwise!

At this point we have sufficient information at our disposal to begin looking seriously at the question of the identity and significance of Jesus. In the second part of this work we shall look at the question of who Jesus is (or "Christology," to give this aspect of Christian theology its proper name).

PART TWO

The Person of Jesus Christ

4

The Resurrection Event

Paul opens his letter to the Christians at Rome by making a crucially important statement concerning Jesus Christ. According to Paul, Jesus "was descended from David according to the flesh and designated Son of God ... by his resurrection from the dead" (Rom. 1:3–4). This brief statement identifies two grounds on which Jesus should be regarded as the Son of God. First, on the physical level, he was a descendent of David. A similar point is made by Matthew as he opens his Gospel (Matt. 1:1). Second, Jesus' resurrection established his identity as the Son of God, clinching other arguments to the same effect, such as those we find in the Gospels. It is obvious that Paul assumes the resurrection really to have taken place, and that the important thing is to establish what it means. Today, however, the suggestion that Jesus might have risen from the dead is treated with skepticism by many. Before we can begin to ask what the resurrection means, we first have to establish the probability that the resurrection took place at all. So let us begin this chapter by looking at the evidence.

The first point to be made is that the theme of the resurrection occurs throughout the New Testament, and in the preaching of the early church in the period after the completion of the New Testament writings. This obviously doesn't prove that the resurrection took place; what it does prove beyond any reasonable doubt is that the first Christians—indeed, the first *generations* of Christians—regarded the resurrection as an essential, and in some cases perhaps even the central element of the Christian faith. But why? Why should the suggestion that Jesus was actually raised from the dead have become universally accepted among the first Christians?

After two thousand years, Christians have become used to the idea of Jesus being raised from the dead—but the idea is actually very strange. Indeed, by the standards of the first century, it was an extraordinary belief. A much more plausible idea would be that God had exalted Jesus to heaven.

As is well known, there was a widespread belief within Jewish circles in the resurrection of the dead at the time of Jesus. Indeed, Paul was able to exploit the differences between the Pharisees and Sadducees on this point during an awkward moment in his career (see Acts 23:6–8). But this belief concerned the *future* resurrection of the dead, at the end of time itself. The Christian claim was that Jesus had been raised *now*, before the end of time.

When Paul refers to Jesus as the "first-fruits" of the resurrection (1 Cor. 15:20–23), he means that he was the first of many to rise from the dead—that Jesus had, indeed, been raised before anyone else. This is quite different from Jewish ideas about the resurrection.

So there was something quite distinct and unusual about the Christian claim that Jesus had been raised from the dead, which makes it rather difficult to account for. Why should the first Christians have adopted what was by the standards of their time such a strange belief? The first Christians didn't adopt a widespread Jewish belief, as some have suggested—they altered it dramatically. What the Jews thought could only happen at the end of the world was recognized to have happened in human history, *before* the end of time, and to have been seen and witnessed to by many. This was a startlingly new belief, and its very novelty raises the question of where it came from. Why did the first Christians adopt this belief? The event of the resurrection of Jesus, it would seem, caused them to break with the traditional belief concerning the resurrection. There can be no doubt that the first disciples *did* believe that Jesus had been raised by God. What we must ask is whether they were right in believing this.

Second, the tradition concerning the empty tomb is so important an element in each of the four Gospels (Matt. 28:1–10; Mark 16:1–8; Luke 24:1–11; John 20:1–10) that it must be considered to have a basis in historical fact. The story is told from different aspects, and includes the divergence on minor points of detail which is so characteristic of eyewitness reports.

Curiously, all four Gospels attribute the discovery of the empty tomb to women. At that time the testimony of a woman was virtually worthless. In first-century Palestine this would have been sufficient to discredit the accounts altogether. If the reports of the empty tomb were invented, it is difficult to understand why their inventors should have embellished their accounts of the "discovery" with something virtually guaranteed to discredit them. Were the first Christians really that stupid? Why not attribute this discovery to *men*, if the story was just invented?

The most obvious explanation is that it was such a widely accepted tradition within the early church that the discoverers of the empty tomb were women that the idea could not be modified, even to make the story of the discovery more plausible.

Furthermore, we know something about the common practice of "tomb veneration"—returning to the tomb of a prophet as a place of worship. This practice appears to have been widespread at the time of Jesus. Matthew 23:29–30 almost certainly refers to this. In fact, the practice continues to this day—the tomb of David in Jerusalem is still venerated by many Jews. But there is no record whatsoever of any such veneration of the tomb of Jesus by his disciples—an unthinkable omission, unless there was a very good reason for it.

That reason appears to be the simple fact that Jesus' body was missing from its tomb. There seems to have been no dispute about this at the time—indeed, the rumor of Jesus' resurrection could have been put down without the slightest difficulty by the authorities simply by publicly displaying the corpse of Jesus.

It is of the greatest importance that the New Testament does not contain so much as the slightest trace of an attempt to reconcile belief in Jesus' resurrection with the existence of his corpse in some Palestinian grave. Nor is there any hint—in the New Testament or anywhere else—that the Jewish authorities either produced, or attempted to produce, the corpse of Jesus. Had this been done, the preaching of the early church would have been discredited immediately. But the intriguing fact remains that no such move was made to discredit the first Christians' proclamation of the resurrection and its implications—and the simplest explanation of this remarkable omission is that the corpse was disquietingly absent from its tomb. All the evidence indicates that the tomb was empty on the third day. The controversy at the time concerned not the *fact* of the empty tomb, but the *explanation* of that emptiness.

Matthew records one explanation advanced by one group of critics of Jesus—the disciples had stolen the body at night (Matt. 28:13–15). But it is clear that the disciples believed in a somewhat more exciting explanation—that Jesus had been raised from the dead.

Once more, we must emphasize this point: There can be no doubt that the first disciples *did* believe Jesus had been raised by God. The reports concerning the empty tomb are completely consistent with this belief, and must be regarded as being at least as historically accurate as any other reported event from that time. Our task is simply to account for this belief, and ask whether it is likely to be correct.

Some recent thinkers have argued that the empty tomb is actually irrelevant because it does not prove that the resurrection took place. It is difficult to follow the logic of this argument. It is certainly true that, taken by itself, the empty tomb does not prove that the resurrection took place. What we are talking about, however, is not a *single* piece of evidence but the *cumulative force* of a number of pieces of evidence which combine to give an essentially consistent picture of what happened on the first Easter Day and its significance for believers. If the resurrection did indeed take place, one would expect the tomb to have been empty. It is therefore important to note the unanimous tradition of all four Gospels to the effect that this was the case. It certainly does not prove that Christ was raised—but taken in conjunction with other pieces of evidence, it is seen to be of importance in establishing an overall picture of the event of the resurrection.

Third, there are persistent accounts in the New Testament documents of Jesus appearing to his disciples (such as Matt. 28:8–10, 16–20; Luke

24:13–43; John 20:11–29; Acts 1:1–11). Whatever we may make of these accounts, it is clear that the first Christians realized that the same person who had been crucified and buried was very much alive. Although he had unquestionably died, in some way—and the New Testament accounts of the resurrection appearances suggest that those who experienced Christ in this way found it difficult to put their experience into words—he still encountered men and women and made himself know to them. Paul's references to this are of particular importance (1 Cor. 15:3–8), in that Paul believed it was the *risen* Christ who had appointed him as an apostle. We shall return to the importance of the resurrection for Paul later in this chapter.

Fourth, we have to account for the transformation of the first Christians and the remarkable advances which Christianity made in the period immediately after Christ's death. It is clear from the Gospel accounts of Jesus' betrayal that the disciples were devastated by his arrest and execution. The fact that Peter was moved to deny Jesus at this point is particularly significant (Mark 14:66–72). It is clear that the disciples were demoralized to the point of despair by the betrayal and crucifixion. Indeed, the Gospels do not record the presence of any of the leading disciples at Calvary. Mark notes the presence of three women in particular at the scene (Mark 15:40–41), but his attention appears to be mainly directed toward the reaction of the Roman centurion to Jesus' death. Mark also fails to note the presence of the disciples at Christ's burial (Mark 15:42–47). Indeed, Mark appears to go to some lengths to emphasize that the only witnesses present at Jesus' death and burial (Mary Magdalene and Mary the mother of James) were also those who first discovered the empty tomb (Mark 15:40, 47; 16:1–8). John notes that the disciples met secretly in the aftermath of the crucifixion "for fear of the Jews" (John 20:19).

But this all changes remarkably suddenly. If the accounts of the early church recorded in Acts are anything to go by, the disciples appear to have undergone a remarkable transformation. They were transformed from a band of cowering and demoralized disciples to potential martyrs who proclaimed the resurrection of Jesus with remarkable boldness. An early Christian sermon recorded in Acts makes clear the understanding of what happened underlying this remarkable change:

> This Jesus, delivered up according to the definite plan and foreknowledge of God, you crucified and killed by the hands of lawless men. But God raised him up, having loosed the pangs of death, because it was not possible for him to be held by it (Acts 2:23–24).

Note the emphasis upon the necessity of the crucifixion—the possibility that it was an accidental end to Jesus' ministry is excluded in favor of the view that this seemingly appalling and senseless event was part of God's intention for Jesus, possessing a deeper meaning and significance.

It is, of course, possible that the disciples were deluded idiots who were content to be martyred for a myth. There is little doubt that many of the early Christians were subjected to various forms of unpleasantness, and some executed, for reasons directly related to their faith. The book of Revelation, the final (and most enigmatic!) work in the New Testament, appears to have been written with this situation in mind. A similar situation may underlie 1 Peter. In both cases, appeal is made to the resurrection of Jesus as a ground for hope in the face of such opposition, even when death is seen as the inevitable consequence.

Later, the practical results of martyrdom came to be more fully appreciated—the African Christian theologian Tertullian, writing in the early third century, remarked that "the blood of the martyrs is the seed of the church." In other words, martyrdom has useful propaganda value.

The early Christians, however, appear to have been content to accept this fate on the basis of another consideration—the belief that those who suffered with Christ would one day be raised from the dead, just as he had been. They may have been completely deluded in this confident expectation—but there is no doubt that they firmly believed in it, and thus force us to account for the origins of their belief. As a piece of circumstantial evidence, it unquestionably points to something or other which gave rise to this belief—and the resurrection of Jesus is totally consistent with it.

Acts also records a remarkable growth in the church at this early stage: A growth which continued after the New Testament period. Early Christianity was not spread at the point of the sword, by force, but through the persuasiveness of its preaching (and Acts may well give us insights into the nature of that preaching). By the early fourth century, Christianity had become so widespread and influential that it was recognized as the official religion of the Roman Empire. From this point onward its successes must be attributed at least in part to its new official status. But before this point it had nothing to commend it except its beliefs.

Of these beliefs we know that the idea of resurrection was considered essential and appears to have been a leading feature of early Christian preaching. Despite hostility on every side, early Christianity possessed a vitality which kept it going and kept it spreading. This vitality was unquestionably a reflection of a belief in the resurrection of Jesus. Once more, it is necessary to note the possibility that the early Christians were wrong in this belief—although some of the alternative explanations of the origins of this belief are more improbable than the idea of resurrection itself! But the fact still remains that this idea was central to the worship and preaching of the first Christians, and it remains so to this day.

Fifth, we must consider the remarkably exalted understandings of Jesus which became widespread within Christian circles so soon after his death.

Jesus was not venerated as a dead prophet or rabbi—as we have already seen, he was worshiped as the living and risen Lord. The use of the word "Lord" in the New Testament is worth noting, and we shall discuss it in the next chapter. At some points in the New Testament, Jesus appears to be explicitly identified with God himself, and some sort of implicit identification along these lines is widespread and would become normative in the following centuries. At several points in the New Testament, words originally referring to God himself are applied to Jesus. Two examples are especially interesting. In Romans 10:13 Paul states that "everyone who calls upon the name of the Lord [Jesus, in this case] will be saved"—yet the original of the Old Testament quotation (Joel 2:32) is actually a statement to the effect that everyone who calls upon the name of *God* will be saved.

In Philippians 2:10 Paul alters an Old Testament prophecy to the effect that everyone will one day bow at the name of God (Isa. 45:23) to refer to Jesus. Of course, Paul regarded this identification of Jesus and God as perfectly legitimate on the basis of the resurrection. John established the basic practice of referring to Jesus as "Lord and God" (John 20:28)—a title which Thomas gave to Jesus, according to John, after being convinced that the resurrection really did take place.

Thus Gregory Nazianzen, writing in the fourth century, stated that Christians believed in a "God who was made flesh and put to death in order that we might live again." The term *Theotokos* ("Bearer of God," or perhaps "Mother of God") came to be used to refer to Mary in the fourth century, and was basically an expression of the belief that her child was (in some sense) none other than God himself.

But how could this remarkable transformation in the perceived status of Jesus have come about? He died as a common criminal. But even as a prophet or martyr the most this would merit would be veneration of his tomb (see Matt. 23:29). Of course, we have already noted that there was a problem about Jesus' tomb which was found to be empty so soon after his death. But the point still remains important: Why did the early Christians start talking about a dead rabbi as if he were God? And, perhaps even more interesting, why did they start talking about him as if he were *alive*, praying to him and worshiping him?

Once more, we must note that it is possible that they were the victims of a hysterical delusion which has continued to this day. But there is another explanation: that they believed Jesus to be raised from the dead by God, thus establishing or demonstrating the unique relationship between God and Jesus. And it was on the basis of their understanding of this unique relationship that the early Christians based their views of Jesus.

Sixth, we must consider the way in which the first Christians worshiped. We know that two sacraments or rites became normative within the church in a remarkably short period, both being witnessed to in the New Testament itself. These are baptism and what is now known variously as the "breaking of the bread," "communion," or "Eucharist." Both reflect a strong belief in the resurrection. Thus Paul states that baptism calls to mind the death and resurrection of Jesus (Rom. 6:4–5). It is interesting to note that the early church baptized its converts on Easter Day to bring home fully the significance of the resurrection to the sacrament.

Equally, a strong belief in the resurrection has always led to the Eucharist being seen as a celebration of the living presence of Christ in his church, rather than a veneration of a dead teacher. Baptism and Eucharist alike are essentially celebrations of Christ's Easter *victory*, rather than solemn memorials of the debacle of Good Friday. The belief that the Jesus who was crucified is now alive and present within his church has exercised an enormous influence over Christian worship down the ages, going back to the earliest of times.

Seventh, we must consider the Christian experience of Jesus down the ages. This is a very difficult thing to assess, because it is so subjective. However, it is clear that Christians have *experienced* Jesus in such a way that they refuse to speak of him in any way other than that of a living Savior and Lord. Jesus does not come across as a dead teacher or a past historical figure, but as a present and living reality.

The experience of Paul with the risen Christ on the road to Damascus (described in Acts 9:1–9; 22:4–16; 26:9–18, and referred to in 1 Cor. 15:8–9; Gal. 1:11–24) has been paralleled in the Christian experience down the centuries to the present day. Whatever we may make of this fact, the point simply is this: Christians find it easy to believe in the resurrection of Jesus basically because they feel they *know* or *experience* him here and now. This evidence would not stand up for one moment in a court of law but it reminds us that Christianity is grounded in experience and that the Christian experience of Jesus is consistent with the idea of his resurrection.

In an earlier chapter, we suggested that the Gospels were rather like detective novels. In her famous detective novel *The Unpleasantness at the Bellona Club*, Dorothy L. Sayers opens the chapter describing Lord Peter Wimsey's breakthrough in the mystery surrounding the death of General Fentiman with the following words:

> "What put you on to this poison business?" [Detective Inspector Parker] asked.
>
> "Aristotle, chiefly," replied Wimsey. "He says, you know, that one should always prefer the probable impossible to the improbable possible. It was possible, of course, that the general should have died off in that neat way at the most confusing moment. But how much nicer and more probable that the whole thing had been stage-managed."

Inevitably, we are faced with a similar dilemma in dealing with the resurrection of Jesus. There are a number of perfectly possible explanations of the evidence we noted above. Jesus may possibly just have fainted on the cross, and revived in the tomb, to wander off into the unknown; the first Christians may possibly have been the victims of hysterical delusions; the "resurrection" may possibly have been an invention of the disciples to cover up their own theft of Jesus' corpse from the tomb. These are all possibilities—but somehow, they seem terribly implausible. They simply don't have the "ring of truth" about them. They are "improbable possibles," to use Wimsey's terms. And so we begin to consider the "probable impossible"—the astonishing suggestion that Jesus really did rise from the dead, and that this simple assumption more than adequately accounts for the evidence in our possession.

But an objection may well be raised that the resurrection is simply an impossibility, and therefore cannot have happened, no matter what the evidence may be for suggesting that it did. This point is important, and we shall illustrate its fundamental weakness by looking at the famous debate between two German scholars over precisely this point. Ernst Troeltsch, writing at the turn of the twentieth century, argued that what he called the "principle of analogy" must govern our thinking about Jesus. In other words, we should ask whether present-day analogies exist in the case of the events reported in the Gospels. If they do exist, we may conclude that a reasonable foundation has been laid for establishing that these events actually did take place—obviously, it doesn't *prove* that they did take place. To give an example: Jesus was executed by crucifixion. There were countless analogues of the process of crucifixion as a form of execution at the time, for which we have excellent archaeological and literary evidence. The idea of "execution" still has present-day analogues, although not in the more civilized parts of Western Europe. We may therefore conclude that there is a real possibility that Jesus was executed by crucifixion. Now we must establish whether this possibility did, in fact, take place—and on the basis of the evidence available from the Gospels, we may conclude with reasonable certainty that it did.

But what if an event recorded in the Gospels is without a present-day analogue? To give an example: Jesus was raised from the dead. This is claimed to be a unique event—no one has ever been raised from the dead before (despite the occasional insignificant references to something possibly along the same lines in Egyptian or Nordic mythology, and despite resuscitations [not resurrections to a new kind of life] as with Lazarus and others). No one presently alive has ever witnessed a resurrection—indeed, the Christian claim that Christ's resurrection is unique suggests that this is impossible anyway. Therefore, Troeltsch argued, we must conclude that the resurrection probably did not happen.

It is interesting to reflect on the following point. Let us suppose that something absolutely unique, which has never been repeated, took place about two thousand years ago, in an obscure part of the civilized world. (Perhaps a bloody corpse, fresh from an expert execution, and obviously dead, came back to life?) Accounts of it, ultimately going back to eye-witnesses, were written down shortly afterwards, and preserved to the present day. Would a present-day observer be inclined to believe that the event has actually happened? He would probably not, unconsciously allowing his methods of investigation to dictate his view of what could and what could not have happened. There are excellent reasons for thinking that, on the basis of the methods and presuppositions of some contemporary historians, unique and extraordinary events simply cannot be thought of as ever happening. So what happens if one actually did take place?

Although Troeltsch's point was taken seriously by scholars for several decades, it is now regarded as somewhat old-fashioned. The most important criticism of it to have been made recently is due to the brilliant and greatly respected German theologian Wolfhart Pannenberg. Pannenberg criticized this approach along the following lines. The "principle of analogy" is basically a useful tool for historical research—but Troeltsch has turned it into a dogmatic view of reality. In other words, Troeltsch is saying that because we have no present-day analogues of something, it simply can't have happened in the first place. A unique event is therefore excluded from the outset, because it doesn't have any parallels today. What Troeltsch is saying is that the resurrection can't have happened because dead men don't rise. In other words, resurrections don't happen, so the resurrection of Jesus can't have happened. But, as Pannenberg emphasizes, all that Troeltsch is doing is to exclude the resurrection as a possibility altogether, no matter what the evidence in favor of it may be. According to Pannenberg, we should abandon this unjustified dogmatic view of what can happen and what can't, and simply concentrate on the evidence for the resurrection with open minds about its possibility. And, according to Pannenberg, the evidence in favor of the resurrection being a real historical event is decisive. Like Lord Peter Wimsey in Dorothy Sayer's tale, we must abandon our preconceived ideas about what can happen and what can't, and be open-minded about the evidence.

Christ, then, was raised from the dead. But so what? We remember the difference between an event and its meaning—what is the *meaning* of the resurrection? The New Testament gives us several answers to this question. First, it shows us how the resurrection was good news *personally* to certain individuals. Second, it explores the significance of the resurrection for the identity of Jesus. We begin by looking at the more personal aspects of the resurrection, before considering its second aspect in the following chapter.

The resurrection transformed individuals. John 20:11–18 is an account of how the resurrection was recognized to be good news by Mary Magdalene, who is presented to us as a grieving and distraught individual, convinced that she has lost her Lord forever: "they have taken away my Lord, and I do not know where they have laid him" (John 20:13). The moment of recognition, in which Mary suddenly realizes who it is who is addressing her, is often regarded as one of the more tender moments of the New Testament. The moment of recognition, and the simultaneous dawning of hope and joy, are adequate testimony to the personal relevance of the Gospel of the resurrection in this case. In the case of Peter, we encounter a betrayer, a failed apostle who denied Christ when he was convinced he would have given his life for the privilege of confessing his name. Peter was called to be an apostle by the lakeside (Luke 5:1–11). The scene of his failure was the "charcoal fire" (John 18:18) in the courtyard of the High Priest. With great skill, John's Gospel draws our attention to the fact that Peter and the disciples' final encounter with the risen Lord incorporates both these elements (John 21:1–19) in a new commissioning of Peter and the disciples by the risen Christ. The symbols of calling and failure are there, reminding them of the past— but the risen Christ is also there, the symbol of hope, forgiveness, and a new beginning, summed up in the new commissioning of the disciples. Peter will not fail to confess Christ again—and, in an aside, we are reminded of the price he finally paid for that confession (John 21:19). Today, in the bread and wine of the eucharistic celebration, we are fed and nourished by the body and blood of the risen Christ, and reminded that the risen Christ is present among us, encountering us, calling us, and claiming us as his own.

An illustration may help to bring this point out. The full impact of the horror of the First World War upon the British people can never be fully appreciated by those who didn't go through it themselves. The most appalling carnage and suffering was seen on the battlefields of Flanders, on the banks of the Somme, and elsewhere. And, as people looked back on this war, it was hoped that it would be the war to end all wars—that the death and suffering of so many might not be in vain. A symbol was chosen to express this hope of peace arising from the carnage of war—the poppy. In the blood-drenched ground of Flanders, poppies sprang up—and were seen as symbols of hope, of new life in the face of death. And so the poppy was worn on the anniversary of the ending of the First World War, to remind all of the carnage of war and the hope that sprang up in its aftermath. All too soon, of course, it became clear that this was probably a vain hope.

In many ways, the bread and wine of the Eucharist symbolize something very similar to those poppies—life through death, hope in the face of apparent despair. The bread and wine are the poppies of the cross, symbolizing the Christian hope of eternal life in the midst of a world of death and decay, established on the basis of the crucifixion and resurrection of Christ. It is this element of hope—in the Christian sense of a sure and confident expectation that God will raise us up as he once raised Christ—that underlies the eucharistic celebration of Christ's death and resurrection. In the words of George Herbert:

> Rise, heart, thy Lord is risen. Sing his praise
> Without delays,
> Who takes thee by the hand, that thou likewise
> With him mayst rise.

The resurrection means that the limitations of space and time are abolished. We do not need to be born again as first-century Palestinians to encounter Christ, in that the risen Christ finds us and calls us, whatever our situation. Christ breaks down historical and cultural barriers—and ultimately the barrier of death itself—precisely because he is risen and alive. For man, death means a severing of relationships, in that he is cut off from those whom he knew and loved. In the case of Jesus, we find that his death had exactly the opposite effect on account of the resurrection—it restored him to fellowship with those whom he loved (Mary Magdalene being a good example) and opened up the possibility of fellowship with those whom (so to speak) he had never known—like us.

Many of us have read the memoirs of dead statesmen. I remember once hearing a recording of some of the wartime speeches of Winston Churchill. As I listened to them, I became conscious of three things. First, that the man had a remarkable grasp of rhetoric, a way of using words to great effect, denied to lesser mortals like myself. Second, he was dead, and that I was listening to a voice from the past, preserved only in the form of magnetic imprints. Third, that the situation which he was addressing was no longer of any particular relevance. The Second World War was long since over, and there was no immediate danger of hordes of hostile armies surrounding my room. The Battle of Britain was something I read about in history books, rather than a crucial struggle under way at this very moment, with its outcome uncertain. The contrast with Jesus is obvious. Christians simply cannot think of Jesus as a distant voice from the past, in that he is so obviously experienced as a present reality. Man's situation is more or less the same as it ever has been—confronted with his mortality, he needs a reason for hope and meaning in the face of death and extinction. The resurrection of the one who was crucified, and the assurance that those who suffer with Christ will one day be glorified with him (Rom. 8:15–18), is potentially precisely such a reason.

To take this point a little further: All of us, especially those interested in the history of ideas, are only too painfully aware of the way in which intellectual fashions change. Philosophical ideas which were adopted by one generation are often just abandoned (rather than actually disproved) by another. The astonishingly rapid collapse of Hegelianism in Germany in the nineteenth century is a case in point. It is almost as if mankind wanders from one set of "isms" to another, only to turn, dissatisfied, to yet another. Although Christianity can be stated (though not entirely satisfactorily) in terms of philosophical ideas of one sort or another, it is basically about the identity and significance of a *person*.

We emphasized earlier that in Christ, the messenger and the message coincide. When addressing the Christians at Corinth (1 Cor. 1:17–2:5), Paul emphasized that the Gospel was not about human wisdom, but about the power of God demonstrated in the cross of Christ. Despite all the changes in the world of ideas that the last two thousand years have seen, the Gospel has not become irrelevant in the way that so many philosophical systems—each of which was modern and relevant in its own day—have done. Why not? Because what is passed down from one generation to another is the experience of the presence of the crucified and risen Christ. One generation may attempt to explain its significance in Hegelian terms, and another in existentialist terms—but the death of Hegelianism, for example, did not bring with it the death of Christianity. Each generation may (and, indeed, must) try to explain the identity and significance of Jesus in ideas or terms which make sense to its contemporaries—but what is passed on from one generation to another is not so much these ideas or terms, but the living reality which lies behind them. To take the resurrection seriously is to realize that the living and risen Christ is— to put it crudely—much bigger than any one generation's apprehension or understanding of him, and that he will be equally really present to future generations, despite differences in culture or intellectual outlook.

Our attention now turns to the New Testament understandings of the identity of Jesus. In what ways did the first Christians understand Jesus? Who did they think he was? We shall consider these questions in the following chapter.

5

The New Testament Witness
to the Person of Jesus

The witness of the New Testament to Jesus Christ is complex. At times it explicitly refers to him as God. At others it uses highly suggestive titles to refer to him—Messiah, Son of God, Lord, Savior, and so on. In the present chapter we are going to look at some of these titles and attempt to make sense of them before looking at the most powerful and profound way of thinking about Jesus—that of the Incarnation—in the chapters which follow. But before we do this, we must remember that the New Testament witness to Jesus concerns far more than the titles it uses to refer to him. It concerns the claims which he made, the things which he did, the impact he made on those who encountered him, the worship that was paid to him, and his resurrection from the dead.

We are presented with a complex overall picture and we cannot really isolate fragments of it. The remarkable feature of the New Testament is actually not so much that it refers to Jesus as "Lord," or that he was worshiped by the early Christians, or that he was raised from the dead—but that *all* these things, and many more besides, are true *of the one and the same man*. These may be seen as the development of perfectly legitimate insights into the identity and significance of Jesus, rather than as inventions or serious distortions of the evidence. The facts about Jesus were, from the beginning, such that it was—sooner or later—appropriate to refer to him in the way that we actually find in the New Testament. There is every reason to suppose that there was a direct, continuous, and unbroken line between the historical figure of Jesus of Nazareth and the church's Christological interpretation of his identity and significance. What was it, we must ask, about Jesus that caused the first Christians to speak about him in these ways?

It is clear that the first Christians regarded Jesus as both the source and the object of their religious experience—in other words, their experiences were understood to depend on him and to derive from him. They didn't experience the same sorts of things (such as God) in the same way that Jesus experienced them—they clearly understood their experience of God to derive from Jesus the Lord, and only to make sense when this was realized.

The conviction that Jesus was a present and living reality, the source of authentic experience of God, is deeply embedded in the New Testament. Jesus is simply not understood as an example of how we experience God, but as the source of our experience of God—and even as the *object* of our experience of God, so that Jesus may be said to be experienced in the same way as God. This important point illustrates how appallingly inadequate it is to suggest that Jesus relates to Christians in much the same way as a rabbi relates to his disciples, or the founder of a university to his students. Indeed, it is tempting to suggest that those who speak of Jesus in this way have never really experienced the profound and vital impact of Christianity, perhaps overlooking—and certainly minimizing—the emotional aspects of faith in Christ. Certainly Jesus is revered and imitated—to the somewhat limited extent that is possible—but the Christian experience of Jesus far transcends this. Once more, we must pause and reflect upon the impact of the resurrection upon the first Christians, and their understanding of its relevance for their relation to the crucified Jesus.

The complex New Testament witness to Jesus Christ is probably best understood as a gradual drawing out of something which was always there from the beginning. In other words, the first Christians were confronted with something so exciting and novel in the life, death, and resurrection of Jesus that they were obliged to employ a whole range of images, terms, and ideas to describe it. There was simply no single term available which could capture the richness and profundity of the first Christians' impressions and experience of Jesus. They were thus forced to use a whole variety of terms, one of which might illuminate one aspect of their understanding of him, another of which might illuminate a different aspect—and, taken together, combined to build up an overall picture of Christ. At times they may even have borrowed ideas from paganism to try and build up this picture—for example, it is often thought that John 1:1–18, with its emphasis on the "Word" (Greek: *logos*), is trying to show that Jesus occupies the same place in the Christian understanding of the world as the idea of the *Logos* occupies in secular Greek philosophy—it just means that they noticed an analogy or parallel, and saw the obvious advantages to be gained by exploiting it to express something which they already knew (and, of course, to make Christianity more understandable to Greek philosophers).

We know that the early Christian church exploded (there is no other word which really describes the impact which it made) into the first-century Mediterranean world. In the course of this astonishingly rapid advance, it encountered both Jewish and Greek cultures. The Jews already knew all about ideas like "Messiah" and "Son of God," which made it easy for the Christians to explain their understanding of Jesus to them. It was merely necessary to persuade them that Jesus was indeed the fulfillment of the Old Testament prophecies, the long-promised Messiah. Matthew's Gospel seems to have been written with this sort of audience in mind—in an earlier chapter, we noticed how often he points out the parallels between Jesus' ministry and Old Testament prophecies.

In the case of the Greeks, it was more difficult. After all, the Christians could hardly have expected their Greek audience to have read the entire Old Testament before they could have the Gospel explained to them. And so they used analogies and ideas which would express their understanding of the identity and significance of Jesus in terms that their Greek readers could understand—Acts 17:16–34 describes Paul's "Areopagus sermon" at Athens, in which exactly this can be seen happening. Terms like "Savior" or "Redeemer" could be used, which didn't totally depend upon the Old Testament for their meaning. But all that the Christians were doing was expressing something they already knew, something that was already there, in new and different ways, in order to get their message across. The fact that Christianity found it so easy to cross cultural barriers at that time is a remarkable testimony to the effectiveness of the first Christians' attempts to express their beliefs in ways that made sense outside a Jewish context.

Let us begin our examination of some of the titles used by the New Testament to refer to Jesus by looking at the title "the Christ," or "the Messiah"—the two are the same, the former being the Greek version, the latter the Hebrew. (The two words are found together in John 1:41.) Thus when Peter recognizes Jesus as "the Christ, the Son of the living God" (Matt. 16:16), he is identifying Jesus with the long-awaited Messiah. It is, of course, very easy for the modern reader to assume that "Christ" was Jesus' surname, and to forget that it is actually a title—in other words, "Jesus the Christ." The term "Messiah" literally means "the anointed one"—in other words, someone who has been anointed with oil. This Old Testament practice indicated that the person anointed in this way was regarded as having been singled out by God as having special powers and functions—thus 1 Samuel 24:6 refers to the king as "the Lord's anointed." The basic sense of the word could be said to be "the divinely appointed King of Israel." As time passed, the term gradually came to refer to a deliverer, himself a descendant of David, who would restore Israel to the golden age she enjoyed under the rule of David.

It must be remembered that at the time of Jesus' ministry, Palestine was occupied and administered by Rome. There was intense nationalist feeling at the time, and this appears to have become linked with the expectation of the coming of the Messiah. For many, the Messiah would be the deliverer who expelled the Romans from Israel and restored the line of David. It is clear that Jesus refused to see himself as Messiah in this sense. At no point in his ministry do we find any violence against Rome suggested or condoned, nor do we find even an explicit attack on the Roman administration. Jesus' attacks are directed primarily against his own people. Thus after his triumphal entry into Jerusalem (Matt. 21:8–11), which gives every indication of being a deliberate messianic demonstration or gesture, Jesus immediately evicts the merchants from the temple (Matt. 21:12–13).

Interestingly, Jesus was not prepared to accept the title "Messiah" in the course of his ministry. Mark's Gospel should be read carefully to note this point. When Peter acclaims Jesus as Messiah—"You are the Christ!"—Jesus immediately tells him to keep quiet about it (Mark 8:29–30). It is not clear what the full significance of the "Messianic secret" is. Why should Mark emphasize that Jesus did not make an explicit claim to be the Messiah, when he was so clearly regarded as such by so many? Perhaps the answer lies later in Mark's Gospel, when he recounts the only point at which Jesus explicitly acknowledges his identity as the Messiah. When Jesus is led, as a prisoner, before the High Priest, he admits to being the Messiah (Mark 14:61–62). In other words, once violent or political action of any sort is no longer possible, Jesus reveals his identity. Jesus was indeed the deliverer of the people of God—but not, it would seem, in any political sense of the term. The misunderstandings associated with the term, particularly in Zealot circles, appear to have caused Jesus to play down the messianic side of his mission.

It is also clear that the Jews did not expect their Messiah to be executed as a common criminal. It is worth noting that, immediately after Peter acknowledges Jesus as the Messiah, Jesus begins to explain to his disciples that he must suffer, be rejected by his own people, and be killed (Mark 8:29–31)—hardly an auspicious end to a messianic career. Indeed, Paul made it clear to the Corinthian Christians that the very idea of a "crucified Messiah" (or "a crucified Christ") was scandalous to a Jew (1 Cor. 1:23). From a very early stage, it is clear that Christians recognized a link between Jesus' messiahship and the destiny of the mysterious "Suffering Servant":

> He was despised and rejected by men; a man of sorrows, and acquainted with grief; and as one from whom men hide their faces he was despised, and we esteemed him not. Surely he has borne our griefs and carried our sorrows; yet we esteemed him stricken, smitten by God, and afflicted. But he was wounded for our transgressions, he was bruised for our iniquities; upon him was the chastisement that made us whole, and with his stripes we are healed. All we like sheep have gone astray; we have turned every one to his own way; and the Lord has laid upon him the iniquity of us all (Isa. 53:3–6).

A second title which claims our attention is "Lord" (Greek: *kyrios*). The word is used in two main senses in the New Testament. First, it is used as a polite title of respect, particularly when addressing someone. When I write a letter to my bank manager, beginning "Dear Sir," I am not for one moment implying that he has been knighted—I am just being polite. Similarly, when a pupil addresses his teacher as "Sir," he is also being polite. The same principle applies in several passages in the New Testament. Thus when Martha speaks to Jesus and addresses him as "Lord" (John 11:21), she is probably—although not necessarily—merely treating Jesus with proper respect.

Of infinitely greater importance, however, are the frequent passages in the New Testament in which Jesus is referred to as "the Lord." The confession that "Jesus is Lord" (Rom. 10:9; 1 Cor. 12:3) was clearly regarded by Paul as a convenient statement of the essential feature of the Gospel. Christians are those who "call upon the name of the Lord" (Rom. 10:13; 1 Cor. 1:2). But what is implied by this affirmation? It is clear that there was a tendency in first-century Palestine to use the word "Lord" (Greek: *kyrios*; Aramaic: *mare*) to designate a divine being, or at the very least a figure who is decidedly more than just human, in addition to its function as a polite or honorific title for a person of importance. But our attention is particularly claimed by the use of this Greek word *kyrios* to translate the four letters used to refer to God in the Old Testament.

The Old Testament writers were reluctant to refer to God directly, and on occasions where it was necessary to make reference to God, they tended to use a cipher of four letters (often referred to as the "Tetragrammaton"). This group of letters, which lies behind the English Authorized Version's references to God as "Jehovah," and the Jerusalem Bible's references to God as "Yahweh," was used to represent the sacred name of God. When the Old Testament scriptures were translated from Hebrew into Greek, the word *kyrios* was used to translate the sacred name of God. Thus Josephus tells us that the Jews refused to call the Roman Emperor *kyrios*, because they regarded this name as reserved for God alone.

It is therefore important to notice that the New Testament on occasion transfers an Old Testament reference to "the Lord" (in other words, God) to "the Lord Jesus." Perhaps the most striking example of this tendency may be seen by comparing Joel 2:32 with Acts 2:21. Joel refers to a crucial period in the history of the people of God, in which the Spirit of God will be poured out upon all men (Joel 2:28). On this "great and terrible day of the Lord" (that is, God) (Joel 2:31), "everyone who calls on the name of the Lord will be saved" (Joel 2:32)—in other words, everyone who calls on the name of God will be saved. This prophecy is alluded to in Acts (2:17–21), in the context of the day of Pentecost, ending with the assertion (Acts 2:21) that "everyone who calls on the name of the Lord will be saved." It is then made clear, in what follows, that the "Lord" in question is none other than "Jesus of Nazareth," whom God has made "both Lord and Christ" (Acts 2:36).

A further interesting example may be found in the use made of Isaiah 45:23 in Philippians 2:10–11. According to Isaiah, "the Lord" (that is, God) states that "every knee shall bow" to him. Paul, possibly taking up a tradition going back to an earlier stage, identifies "the Lord" as Jesus in the following passage:

> Therefore God has highly exalted him and bestowed on him the name which is above every name, that at the name of Jesus every knee should bow ... and every tongue confess that Jesus Christ is Lord, to the glory of God the Father (Philippians 2:9–11).

A further example is to be found in Hebrews 1:10, which alters the reference of Psalm 102:25 from God to Jesus. This practice of transferring from one Lord (God) to another (Jesus) is known to have infuriated Jews at the time. Thus in the second-century dialogue between Trypho the Jew and Justin Martyr, Trypho complains that Christians have "hijacked" passages referring to God in order to refer them to Christ. There was, of course, no suggestion that there were two "Lords" (in other words, two Gods)—simply that Jesus had to be regarded as having a status at least equal to that of God, which demanded that he be addressed and worshiped as God. The use of the term "Lord" to refer to Jesus may therefore be seen as a recognition of his exalted status, arising from his resurrection.

A further title used by the New Testament to refer to Jesus is "Son of God." In the Old Testament, the term is occasionally used to refer to angelic or supernatural persons (Job 38:7; Ps. 82:6; Dan. 3:25). Messianic texts in the Old Testament refer to the coming Messiah as the "Son of God" (2 Sam. 7:12–14; Ps. 2:7). The New Testament use of the term seems to mark a development of its Old Testament meaning, with an increased emphasis upon its exclusiveness. Although all men are sons of God in some sense of the word, Jesus is *the* Son of God. Paul distinguishes between Jesus as the *natural* Son of God and believers as *adopted* sons—their relationship to God is quite different from Jesus' relationship to him, even though both may be referred to as "sons of God." Similarly, in 1 John, Jesus is referred to as the Son, while believers are designated as "children." There is something quite distinct about Jesus' relation to God as expressed in the title "Son of God."

The New Testament understanding of Jesus' relationship to God, expressed in the Son-Father relationship, takes a number of forms. First, we note that Jesus directly addresses God as "Father," with the very intimate Aramaic word "Abba" being used (Matt. 6:9; 11:25–26; 26:42; Mark 14:36; Luke 23:34, 46). Second, it is clear from a number of passages that the evangelists regard Jesus as the Son of God, or that Jesus treats God as his father, even if this is not stated explicitly (Mark 1:11; 9:7; 12:6; 13:32; 14:61, 62; 15:39). Third, John's Gospel is permeated with the Father-Son relationship (John 5:16–27; 17:1–26), with a remarkable emphasis upon the identity of will and purpose of the Father and Son, indicating how close the relationship between Jesus and God was understood to be by the first Christians. At every level in the New Testament—in the words of Jesus himself, or in the impression which was created among the first Christians—Jesus is clearly understood to have a unique and intimate relationship to God, which the resurrection demonstrated publicly (Rom. 1:3, 4).

We could continue this examination of the various titles which the New Testament employs to refer to Jesus, to illustrate the many facets of its complex witness to his identity and significance. There is, however, a danger that by doing this we may miss seeing the forest for the trees—in other words, we will fail to see that these titles, together with the New Testament accounts of the impact Christ had upon those whom he encountered, build up to give a pattern. It is clear that the New Testament witnesses to Jesus as the embodiment of all God's promises, witnessed to in the Old Testament, brought to fulfillment and fruition. The statements made about Jesus may be broadly listed under two classes. First, we have statements about Jesus' *function*—statements about what God has done for man in Jesus. Second, we have statements about Jesus' *identity*—who he is. The two are, of course, closely connected. Just as a collection of pieces of a jigsaw puzzle build up to give a pattern which no single piece can show on its own, so the New Testament "Christological titles" build up to give an overall picture which no single title can adequately disclose. Taken collectively, they build up into a rich, deep, and powerfully persuasive portrait of Christ as the divine Savior and Lord who continues to exercise an enormous influence over and appeal to mankind.

What we are going to do now is to examine one way of looking at Jesus, of making sense of him, which has proved particularly helpful and illuminating, and greatly influenced the Christian church down through the ages.

6

The Incarnation: The Doctrine

Jesus was a man. Of that, the New Testament leaves us in no doubt. He was thirsty, he was tired, he suffered, and he died. It also leaves us in no doubt that he was more than a man. The question is: How are we to make sense of the manner in which Jesus was more than just a man? The approach which we are going to consider in the following chapters is summarized in the prologue to John's Gospel (John 1:1–18), and culminates in the following remarkable statement: "the Word became flesh and dwelt among us, full of grace and truth; we have beheld his glory, glory as of the only Son from the Father, full of grace and truth" (John 1:14). The *Word* (the term used for one who is living, imperishable, creative, and divine) *became* (in other words, entered into human history) *flesh* (the term used for what is creaturely, perishable, finite, mortal, and human). The idea of "incarnation" simply means God taking on flesh, humbling himself to take upon himself the entire experience of existence as man in all the conditions of humanity. The one who was there from the beginning, the one who was God, became man. As one of the better-known Christmas carols states:

> Veiled in flesh the Godhead see,
> Hail the incarnate Deity!
> Pleased as man with man to dwell, Jesus our Emmanuel!

The full force of this idea, its meaning for our understanding of God and ourselves, will become clear in the following chapter. In the present chapter, we are going to ask whether this idea is a reasonable summary of the New Testament evidence concerning Jesus, and look at the ways in which the Christian church has tried to express it.

As we saw in an earlier chapter, the resurrection exercised a decisive influence upon Christian thinking concerning the identity and significance of Jesus. The theme of the risen life pervades the New Testament, and governs much of the early Christian proclamation. Thus Paul states that the resurrection established that Jesus was the Son of God (Rom. 1:3–4). But did Jesus *become* the Son of God at his resurrection, or did the resurrection *disclose* something which had always been true? Did the resurrection change Jesus' status, or did it just make clear what that status had always been?

It is clear from the New Testament that Jesus was regarded as having the same status disclosed by his resurrection (in other words, his being Son of God) in his lifetime. Thus Paul clearly regards Jesus as having this status at the time of his death, speaking of the "Son of God, who loved me and gave himself for me" (Gal. 2:20). The Synoptic Gospels indicate that Jesus enjoyed this status at least from the time of the beginning of his ministry (Mark 1:11). At some points it even seems to be suggested that Jesus possessed this divine status from the beginning of time (John 1:1–14; Phil. 2:6–11; Col. 1:15–20). At the very least, we may say that the New Testament indicates that there never was a time in his life that he was not already what the resurrection disclosed him to be—the Son of God. In other words, the resurrection demonstrated or proved Jesus' divine status in his lifetime, the clue to his identity and significance which clinched the case for his claim to a unique relationship to God. Let us look at some ways in which the New Testament expresses the divinity of Jesus.

In an earlier chapter, we noted the difference between a *functional* and an *ontological* Christology. A functional Christology is basically a way of thinking about Jesus which is primarily concerned with establishing what Jesus *did*—his "function," to put it crudely. An ontological Christology is primarily concerned with establishing who Jesus *is*—his identity. Of course, it is obvious that these two ways of thinking about Jesus are virtually the same in terms of their practical results. If Jesus *is* God, then he *acts as God and for* God. And if Jesus *acts as God and for* God, then to all intents and purposes he *is* God. But there is a difference, and it is important to note it at this point. The New Testament writers seem to have begun their reflection concerning the identity and significance of Jesus by reflecting on what he did for man, and then gone on to ask who Jesus must be if he is able to act in this way. Of course, there are cases in which direct statements are made about this identity—a good example is the one we've just been looking at in which Jesus is recognized as being the Son of God on account of the resurrection. But what did Jesus *do*? And what does it tell us about him? There is, it must be emphasized, no tension between "functional" and "ontological" Christologies in the New Testament—rather, there seems to be an obvious progress from the functional to ontological in the New Testament. The first Christians found themselves obliged to speak of Jesus in divine terms, or at least terms which implied divinity, and thus were obliged to go on from there and think through the consequences of these ways of speaking about Jesus for their understanding of the relationship of Jesus to God. Let us look at some important New Testament statements on such matters.

1. Jesus Saves

In the third part of this book we shall be exploring this theme in more detail, looking at some of the questions which it raises. For example, what does "save" mean? And how is "salvation" related to Jesus' life, death, and resurrection? However, we can make a very important statement even at this earlier stage: *Only God can save!* This great theme is echoed throughout the Old Testament. Israel is reminded time and time again that she cannot save herself, nor can she be saved by the idols of the nations around about her. It is the Lord, and the Lord alone, who will save:

> Who declared it of old? Was it not I, the Lord? And there is no other god besides me, a righteous God and a Savior; there is none besides me. Turn to me and be saved, all the ends of the earth (Isa. 45:21–22).

In the full knowledge that it was God alone who was Savior, that it was God alone who could save, the first Christians had no hesitation in affirming that Jesus was Savior, that Jesus could save. Perhaps it is worth remembering how the fish came to be a symbol of faith to the early Christians—the five letters spelling out "fish" in Greek came to represent the slogan "Jesus Christ, Son of God, Savior." In the New Testament, Jesus saves his people from their sins (Matt. 1:21); only in his name is there salvation (Acts 4:12); he is the "pioneer of ... salvation" (Heb. 2:10); he is the "Savior, who is Christ the Lord" (Luke 2:11). In these affirmations and countless others, Jesus is understood to *function as God*, doing something which, properly speaking, only God can do.

2. Jesus Is Worshiped

Within the Jewish context within which the first Christians operated, it was God and God alone who was to be worshiped. As Paul reminded the Christians at Rome, there was a constant danger that men would worship creatures, when they ought to be worshiping their creator (Rom. 1:23). We have already noted the fact that the early Christian church worshiped Christ as God—a practice which is clearly reflected even in the New Testament. Thus 1 Corinthians 1:2 suggests that Christians are those who "call on the name of our Lord Jesus Christ," using language which reflects the Old Testament formulas for worshiping or adoring God (Gen. 4:26; 13:4; Ps. 105:1; Jer. 10:25; Joel 2:32). Jesus is clearly understood to *function* as God, in that he is an object of worship. Within the strict monotheism of the Jewish context within which this worship took place, it is clear that an important statement concerning Jesus' identity and significance is being made.

3. Jesus Reveals God

"He who has seen me has seen the Father" (John 14:9). These remarkable words, so characteristic of John's Gospel, emphasize the belief that the Father speaks and acts in the Son—in other words, that God is revealed in and by Jesus. The Christian claim that God is most fully and authentically revealed in the face of Jesus Christ is simply a summary statement of the kaleidoscope

of New Testament descriptions of the intimate relation between the Father
and the Son, between God and Jesus. To have seen Jesus is to have seen the
Father—in other words, Jesus is understood, once more, to *function* as God.

4. Jesus Represents God

One of the great New Testament themes is that the promises of the Old
Testament are fulfilled in the coming of Christ. The promises made by God
to his people are seen to have been honored. But it is clear that the New Tes-
tament also contains promises, made by Jesus himself on behalf of God. For
example, at the heart of the proclamation of the Gospel as we find it in John's
Gospel lie the great promises of salvation: "He who believes has eternal life"
(John 6:47); "He who eats my flesh and drinks my blood has eternal life, and
I will raise him up on the last day" (John 5:54). According to this Gospel,
Jesus makes promises on behalf of God. In many respects we may see this as
a statement to the effect that Jesus is the plenipotentiary, the authorized representative, of God. This idea is expressed particularly well by the Hebrew
concept of the *shaliach* ("plenipotentiary"). When a king sends his *shaliach* to
negotiate with someone, that *shaliach* is empowered to act on his behalf—to
enter into agreements, to make promises, and so on. Although the king is not
himself physically present in these negotiations, to all intents and purposes
he might just as well be. The promises made are made on his behalf and will
be honored by him. It is important to notice how often we find reference in
John's Gospel to the total unity of purpose of Father and Son (John 17:20–
25): The Son is sent by the Father (John 5:30). Jesus is clearly understood to
make such promises on behalf of God, and at the desire of God, and is thus
unquestionably understood as *functioning as God and for God* in this respect.
Jesus functions as God's *shaliach*, his plenipotentiary representative, in whom
and through whom God has pledged himself to act.

We could go on and consider other New Testament understandings of
the manner in which Jesus' function and identity are closely interrelated. But
it will be clear, on the basis of our discussion so far, that the New Testament
at the very least understands Jesus to *act as God and for God* in every area of
crucial relevance to Christianity. In short, we must—in the words of a first-
century writer—learn to "think about Jesus as we do about God" (2 Clement
1:1–2). We are thus in a position to take the crucial step which underlies all
Christian thinking on the incarnation—that, as Jesus *acts as God and for God
in every context of importance*, we should conclude that, for all intents and purposes, *Jesus is God*. Thus when we worship Jesus, we worship God; when we
know Jesus, we know God; when we hear the promises of Jesus, we hear the
promises of God; when we encounter Jesus, we encounter none other than
the living God. The idea of the incarnation is the climax of Christian reflection upon the mystery of Christ—the recognition that Jesus revealed God;

that Jesus represented God; that Jesus speaks as God and for God; that Jesus acted as God and for God; that Jesus *was* God.

Let us return once more to the resurrection. We have already seen that the New Testament recognizes that Jesus was always what the resurrection disclosed him to be. The resurrection established his divine status as Son of God. But where did this status come from? It is at this point that the close relationship between the resurrection and incarnation becomes clear. If Jesus Christ always possessed his unique status, that status must be traced back to his birth, and even further. The incarnation may thus be seen as the logical conclusion of Christian thinking concerning the significance of the resurrection.

Recently there has been some discussion about the logical order of the incarnation and resurrection. One of the disadvantages of not being God is that we see things the wrong way around, looking at things from man's standpoint rather than God's. The order in which things actually exist (the "order of being" as it is sometimes called) is usually exactly the opposite of the order in which we come to know about them (the "order of knowing"). We come to *know* about Christ's divinity through the resurrection, and as a result we arrive at the idea of the incarnation. So we could say that the resurrection comes before the incarnation in the "order of knowing." But it will be obvious that, once we know about the incarnation, we realize that it must take precedence over the resurrection in the "order of being." We could summarize this by saying that Christ *was* divine before the resurrection *discloses* that he is divine. But this argument is not particularly important: All that we need to note here is that there is a very close relationship between the incarnation and resurrection.

The problem that the Christian church had to deal with now was simply this: How can Jesus be both God and man? We have already seen the thinking which lay behind this conclusion—the problem was to make sense of it! The first four or five centuries saw this question being debated at great length throughout the Christian world. In many respects the debates are of little interest, concerning technical matters of Greek philosophy of little relevance for today. But they are important in one respect—they show how well aware the church was that the Gospel itself was at stake in these debates. For the early fathers, Jesus had to be both God and man if salvation was to be a possibility. If Jesus was not God, he could not save; if Jesus was not man, man could not be saved. The affirmation that Jesus was both God and man came to be seen as a means of safeguarding the Gospel proclamation of the redemption of mankind in Christ. The early Christians were actually far more interested in *defending* this insight, rather than trying to *explain* it! We must never fall into the trap of suspecting that the fathers thought that they were explaining how Jesus could be both God and man—it is clear that they were simply trying to find ways of making sense of a *mystery*, something which in the end defied explanation. But it was no mystery invented just to give bishops or theologians something to do with their spare time—it was the central mystery of the Christian faith, upon which Christianity would stand or fall. To illustrate this point, let us leave the first five centuries of the Christian era behind for a moment, and move to a very different situation— Berlin in the early nineteenth century.

Like many people at the time, Friedrich Schleiermacher, one of the more important Christian thinkers of the last two centuries, found the "two natures doctrine" (the doctrine that Jesus was both God and man) rather heavy going. On the one hand, it seemed very difficult to understand; on the other hand, it seemed to him that something very much like it was necessary. Why? Let us follow his reasoning through. Let us agree that Christians believe that man is saved only through Jesus Christ. That is a rather bald summary of the many statements of the New Testament on the matter, but it is good enough for our purposes. What does this actually imply? The first point that Schleiermacher makes is this. It is obvious that Jesus is a man. That point does not really need to be emphasized, but it is a good point to start our thinking from. But if he is *just* a man, like all other men, we find ourselves faced with a problem. That means he shares man's need for redemption, so he cannot possibly redeem us. There must be some essential difference between Jesus and man if Jesus is indeed to be our redeemer. After all, Christianity has always insisted that Jesus is the solution to man's problem, rather than part of that problem!

Perhaps we can avoid this problem by dropping the idea that Jesus is man altogether, and simply state that he is God. But then he has no point of contact with those who need redemption. How can he relate to them? There must, then, be some point of difference between Christ and God which allows Christ to make contact with those whom he is meant to redeem. And so we eventually move toward the recognition that Jesus must be God *and* man if he is to redeem man. This simply states the basic principle which lies behind the idea of the incarnation.

We could develop the same idea along different lines. Let us suppose that we have two people—let us call them "A" and "B." A and B enjoy a close relationship, which breaks down completely over some misunderstanding. A is convinced that it is the fault of B, and B is sure that A is in the wrong. So strongly do they hold their views that they refuse to speak to each other. The situation is, unfortunately, all too familiar from everyday experience— whether it is a matter of personal relationships, or industrial relations. We all know situations where this has happened, and may even have been unfortunate enough to have been involved with them ourselves. But how can the situation be resolved? How can A and B become reconciled? It is clear that the situation demands a *mediator*, a *go-between*. Let us reflect on the qualifications such as a mediator might need.

It will be obvious that the best mediator or go-between is someone whom both A and B know and respect, but who will be impartial. Let us call this mediator "C." C must represent A to B, and B to A. He must not be identified with either A or B, yet he must have points of contact with both if he is to be accepted. This situation is familiar to us all—it's just a question of working out who C must be. To give an example: Late Victorian novels often portray a crisis arising between a father and his son, with the mother acting as the mediator between them. Although she is not identical with either father or son, she has relationships with both of them which establish her credentials as a go-between. She is close enough to both of them to represent them both, and yet sufficiently different from them both to prevent her being identified with either. The relevance of this little digression for our understanding of the identity of Jesus Christ will be obvious.

The idea of Jesus being the one and only go-between or mediator between God and man is deeply ingrained in the New Testament. "For there is one God, and there is one mediator between God and men, the man Christ Jesus" (1 Tim. 2:5). Paul talks about God "reconciling" us to himself through Jesus Christ (2 Cor. 5:18–19). What is particularly interesting is that Paul uses the same Greek word to refer to the restoration of the relationship between God and man which he had used earlier to refer to the restoration of the relationship between a man and his wife who had fallen out (1 Cor. 7:10–11). Christ is understood to act as the mediator or go-between in restoring the relation between God and man to what it once was. And now we can start applying the ideas we discussed in the previous paragraph. This mediator must represent God to man, and man to God. He must have points of contact with both God and man, and yet be distinguishable from them both. And so on. In short, the traditional idea of the incarnation, which expresses the belief that Jesus is both God and man, portrays Jesus as the perfect mediator between God and man.

How, then, may the idea that Jesus is God be *understood*? The exhaustive discussion in the first five centuries of the precise relationship between Christ, God, and man was brought to an end by the Council of Chalcedon (A.D. 451). Just as the chairman of a committee finally feels obliged to bring a debate to an end when all the issues appear to have been raised and exhaustively discussed (only to be raised again!), so the Council of Chalcedon brought the debate within the early church on the identity of Jesus Christ to an end. Over five hundred bishops met to hammer out an agreement which would do justice to the various points which had been raised during the debate. The Christian church in Alexandria (in modern-day Egypt) had laid stress upon the importance of the divinity of Christ, whereas the church in Antioch (in modern-day Turkey) had laid much greater emphasis upon the humanity of Christ. All sorts of theories had been put forward to explain the way in which God and man were united in Christ. Which would the Council adopt?

What the Council actually said is very significant. It didn't lay down one specific way of thinking about the relationship between Jesus, God, and man. It stated that it was necessary to regard Jesus Christ as fully divine and fully human. In doing this, the Council was simply restating what was widely agreed within the church: that if Jesus was not God, he was of no relevance to any thought about God and eternal life; that if he was not man, he was irrelevant to any experience of human life. It merely restated a crucially important insight—it didn't explain it, or lay down some specific way of making sense of it. But this was all that the Council wanted to do—to identify the essential point at issue.

The Council of Chalcedon was content to reaffirm a fact without attempting to interpret it—and it was wise to do so. Interpretations vary from one age to another, depending upon the time and place. Platonism might be used to interpret the incarnation in third-century Alexandria, Aristotelianism in thirteenth-century Paris, and Hegelianism in nineteenth-century Berlin. But Chalcedon attempted to safeguard an essential fact which could be interpreted in terms of ideas which make sense at any particular point in history, provided these explanations do not deny or explain away any part of the fact. Every explanation must, in the final analysis, be recognized to be inadequate, and Chalcedon merely stated with great clarity what the essential fact which required explanation and interpretation was: Jesus really is both God and man. So long as Jesus was recognized as being both God and man, all was well. So long as man knows that he really does encounter God, and not some demigod or deluded egomaniac, in Jesus, he knows that Jesus has a unique position in relation to both God and man, and may base his faith upon it. So long as he knows that in Jesus he really does encounter a man, he may rest assured that God is involved in human history and experience—and, specifically, in his own history and experience.

To make this point absolutely clear, the Council used a technical term already well established by this time. This is the term which is usually translated into English as "of one substance" or "of one being." Jesus is "of one substance" with God, just as he is "of one substance" with man. In other words, Jesus is the *same* as God; it really is God himself whom we encounter in Jesus, and not some messenger sent from God.

In the early church there was a remarkably heated debate over two Greek words which differed only by one letter. One means "of a similar substance" (*homoiousios*), the other means "of the same substance" (*homoousios*). We could translate them more simply as "being like" and "being the same as." In his famous book *The Decline and Fall of the Roman Empire* Gibbon pointed out that never before had so much fuss been made over a single letter of the alphabet. But there is all the difference in the world between the two ideas. Let us take the idea of Jesus being "similar to" God. That means that in Jesus we encounter someone who is like God in some way. It isn't God himself whom we encounter, but his surrogate or representative. God sends his troubleshooter and keeps out of things himself. God remains aloof from human history and human experience—he experiences us at second hand, and we experience him at second hand. How unsatisfactory this would be.

Imagine having to communicate with someone we knew and loved through third parties all the time! No human personal relationship can work like that. God does not know what it is like to be frail, weak and mortal—in short, he does not know what it is like to be man, like ourselves. We can only approach God as someone whom we know indirectly, and who knows us indirectly.

At Chalcedon, the church opted conclusively for a different understanding of the relation of Jesus and God. In Jesus we encounter God at first hand, directly. To encounter the risen Christ is to encounter none other than the living and loving God. To put this in a dangerously crude way: God knows what it is like to be human. Although only a single letter separates *homoiousios* ("being like God") from *homoousios* ("being the same as God"), a world separates the views of Jesus which they represent. In English, the difference might be brought out by saying the former corresponds to "Jesus is good" and the latter to "Jesus is God." Chalcedon made no attempt to explain the mystery with which we are confronted as Christians, and we totally misrepresent and misunderstand it if we think it did—it just identified the central point at stake, and made crystal clear the Christian point of view.

To many, the Chalcedonian definition is unspeakably tedious and practically unintelligible. It reads like a legal document, rather than a statement conveying the excitement and vitality of faith. It is, of course, the job of a preacher to translate Chalcedon into everyday language. In the following chapter we're going to do this. But a few thoughts at this stage might be helpful. Chalcedon simply states in a form of a definition what the first five centuries of Christian reflection on the New Testament had already established—the sorts of things which we have been discussing in this chapter. It isn't an arbitrary invention, the product of confused minds, but an attempt to sum up a long and important debate and declare its result. Although turgid and unexciting to read, the definition established the basis upon which faith depends—the *sine qua non*.

No one would dream of confusing a marriage certificate with a marriage—yet the certificate declares the essential basis upon which a marriage rests. It is the starting point for building and development, not an end in itself. Chalcedon defines the point from which we start—the recognition that, in the face of Christ, we see none other than God himself. That is a starting point, not an end. But we must be sure of our starting point, the place at which we begin, if the result is to be reliable. Chalcedon claims to have established that starting point, and whatever difficulties we may find with its turgid language and outdated expressions, the basic ideas which it lays down are clear and crucial, and are obviously a legitimate interpretation of the New Testament witness to Jesus Christ. But now we must ask: What happens when we go on from this starting point? What does the incarnation tell us about God and about ourselves? What does it tell us about the nature of God and the destiny of man? In short, what is the cash value of the incarnation? Let us go on and see.

7

The Incarnation: Its Significance

Jesus is God—that is the basic meaning of the incarnation. It is a remarkably profound and exciting idea which has enormous consequences for the way in which we think about ourselves and about God. In this chapter we are going to "unpack" the meaning of the belief that Jesus is both God and man. Some of the ideas it involves are simple, others are more complex. Let us begin with a simple idea.

What is God like? This is a crucial question and we shall be exploring it further in a moment. But first we need to ask a penetrating question: *How do we know what God is like in the first place?* Before we start thinking about the results, we need to think about the means we will use to get them. When the Christian speaks of God, he means God as he has been revealed in Jesus Christ—the God who became incarnate. What can we say about God? He is immortal, invisible, infinite, and so on—but that is hardly very informative. All that we are actually saying is that God is *not* mortal, God is *not* visible, God is *not* finite. While all this may well be true, it is hardly very exciting or interesting. What can we say *positively* about God? It is here that the incarnation establishes a crucial principle: God is Christlike. These three simple words can totally alter our way of thinking about God. Let us look at an example to bring out the importance of this principle.

What can we say about the love of God for man? We could say that it is infinite, boundless, beyond human telling, and so on—but, once more, all that we have done is to speak of it *negatively*, explaining what it is *not*. In fact, we are virtually saying that, whatever the love of God may be like, we can't say anything about it. But the love of God is a rather important and exciting aspect of Christianity, something which we would clearly very much like to be able to talk about! Surely we can say something clear, intelligible, positive, and exciting about it—unless we are doomed to have to keep quiet about it forever! On the basis of the incarnation, we may make a very positive and simple statement about the love of God for man. The love of God is like the love of a man who lays down his life for his friends (John 15:13). Immediately, we are given a picture, an image, drawn from human experience—something concrete and tangible, something we can visualize and relate to. A picture is worth a thousand words—and in the picture of a man laying down his life, giving his very being, for someone whom he loves, we have a most powerful, striking, and moving statement of the full extent of the love of God for sinful man. We can talk about the love of God in terms of our own experience, and supremely in terms of the tender image of Jesus Christ trudging to Calvary, there to die for those whom he loved. It is a moving, poignant, and deeply evocative image which we can easily imagine and identify with—in short, it is a statement about the love of God which speaks to us, which appeals to us and which brings home exactly what the love of God is like. No longer need we be at a loss for words to speak about God. We are given a handle to attach to God in order that we may get hold of him. One of the early church fathers, Origen, compared the incarnation to a small statue—a scaled-down model of the real thing which allows us to discern its features more clearly.

We may go further than this. Until Christ came, every image of God may be said to have been an idol—something which we ourselves constructed and worshiped. In Christ we are given an image of God—something we can visualize, imagine in our minds, and relate to. Without the death of Christ, there is every danger that our conception of the love of God will be soft and sentimental. But the cross brings home the deep relationship of severity and kindness, already known to every parent, which is so characteristic of God's dealings with us. The appalling cost of forgiveness to God is shown in the cross. God does not simply say, "Never mind," to the sinner, pretending that sin never happened or that it is of no significance. We wouldn't accept that concept of forgiveness for ourselves, so why should we force it on God? True forgiveness involves facing and recognizing the great pain and distress caused by the offense—a process for which the cross is perhaps the most powerful illustration known. The love of God for his people is expressed, not in a soft and sentimental way, but in the context of the seriousness of God's hatred for sin. The cross sets forward the full and tremendous cost of *real* forgiveness— a forgiveness in which the full seriousness of sin is met and dealt with, in order that love may triumph. The cross confronts us with the knowledge that man's sin wounds God to the heart, causing more hurt that we can ever imagine. Yet God offers man forgiveness—a *real*, if painful, forgiveness in which all is faced and all is forgiven in order that man may go forth into eternal life with his God. Recognition of sin is a humiliating, painful, and healing process. The incarnation helps us to realize that God humbled himself to meet us, and that we too must humble ourselves if we are to meet him.

The incarnation makes God tangible. It helps us think about God. It is quite astonishing how the question, "Is Christ divine?" is discussed as if we had an excellent idea about what God was like, while Christ himself remained something of an enigma. But exactly the opposite is so obviously the case! Christ confronts us through the Gospel narratives and through experience, whereas we have no clear vision of God. As John's Gospel reminds us: "No one has ever seen God; the only Son, who is in the bosom of the Father, has made him known." (John 1:18). God is Christlike—in other words, we learn to think of God as we see him in Christ. For the Christian, it is Christ who provides us with the basis of the most reliable knowledge of God available.

We could further unpack the meaning of the incarnation by thinking about two pieces of glass. The first is a window. Suppose you are in a room which is completely dark, without any means of letting light in. Then someone knocks a hole in the wall and makes a window. The light is let in and the room illuminated. But we can also now see the outside world through the window—a world which was always there but which we couldn't see properly before. Jesus is a window into God; he is the light of God who has come into the world to illuminate it, and who lets us see God. Perhaps the window is not as large as we would like and perhaps the glass is less clear than we would like (1 Cor. 13:12 is worth noting here), but God is suddenly made available for us in a new way. Many of us know what it is like to get up early in the morning, stepping out of bed into a dark room—when we open the curtains, the room is suddenly flooded with light and the outside world beckons to us. The same sense of excitement, like a dark room being flooded with light, or a beautiful landscape opening up before our eyes, can perhaps be felt when reading the prologue to the fourth Gospel (John 1:1–18).

The second piece of glass is a mirror. As we look in a mirror, we see ourselves reflected. As we look at Christ, we see ourselves reflected as we shall finally be—man in a perfect relationship with God. Jesus discloses to us what it is like to be truly human, to live with God and for God. As we look at him, we are made painfully aware of just how far we have to go before we're anything like him! But the vision of restored and redeemed humanity presented to us in Jesus Christ gives us a foretaste of the New Jerusalem, an encouragement as we try to grow more like him and a challenge to our commitment to the Gospel which alone can transform us in this way. Two pieces of glass; two aspects of Jesus Christ.

All too often, critics of the incarnation dismiss the idea because it seems inconsistent with their understanding of God. These critics, however, seem to know *exactly* what God is like, and on the basis of this idea of God, reject the incarnation. But on what basis do they establish this idea of God? What source of knowledge do they possess which is denied to everyone else, and which is more reliable than the knowledge of God to be had in Jesus Christ? All too often, criticisms of the incarnation boil down to the simple, and not very significant, statement that someone somewhere has an idea of God which is inconsistent with the idea of the incarnation. But so what? Unless he can prove, beyond all reasonable doubt, that God is *really* like that, his criticism is not important. And the simple fact is that mankind has been unable to reach much in the way of agreement on what God is like. For the Christian, God is to be known and seen most reliably as we encounter him in Jesus Christ. That is the

Christian view of God. It may be inconsistent with somebody else's view of God—but that doesn't entitle them to say that the Christian view of God, expressed in the incarnation, is *wrong*. All statements about God are ultimately a matter of faith (even those of the atheist), and the most that this critic can do is register his *disagreement* with the Christian viewpoint. To do more is to go far beyond the limited evidence available at his disposal.

Man has tried to think about the nature of God for some considerable time, without reaching much agreement. A philosopher in the classical theist tradition would regard the word "God" as referring to some supreme absolute, about which man could say little. It was against this idea of God that the French philosopher Pascal protested when he wrote his famous words: "the God of Abraham, Isaac, and Jacob, not of the philosophers." The deist would regard God as a heavenly watchmaker who, having wound up the universe and set it going, left it to its own devices. A Hindu would feel able to say, without the slightest sense of impropriety, "I am God"—meaning that the one unchanging reality is spread among all existing things to such an extent that it can't be separated from any of them. The atheist would treat the word "god" as referring to a distant supernatural ruler (who doesn't exist anyway) who hurls down arbitrary dictates to mankind from his Olympus, and imprisons man's spirit in time and space. And so on. We could give an exhaustive list of the various ideas about God which man has toyed around with since he began to think, but there would be little point in doing so. All that we want to make clear is that the word "God" can mean any number of things. In countries within which Christianity has been dominant, of course, this difficulty may be less important than we have suggested, due to the influence of Christianity. But it obviously raises the question: What God are we actually talking about? How do we know what "God" is like? Where can we find out?

All sorts of answers have, of course, been given to questions like these. God may be seen in a glorious sunset, in the night sky, in the ordering of the universe, to name but three answers to one of them ("Where can we see God?"). But the Christian insists that God is to be most reliably and completely known as he is revealed in the person of Jesus Christ. This is not to say that God may not be known, in various ways and to various degrees, by other means—it is simply to say that Christians believe that Jesus Christ is the closest encounter with God to be had in this life. God makes himself available for our acceptance or rejection in the figure of Jesus Christ. To have encountered Jesus is to have encountered God. Paul refers to Jesus as the "image of the invisible God" (Col. 1:15). In the letter to the Hebrews, we find Jesus described as the "stamp" of God's nature (Heb. 1:3)—the Greek word used could refer to an image stamped upon a coin, conveying the idea of an exact likeness. The God with whom we are dealing is the "God and Father of our Lord Jesus Christ" (1 Peter 1:3), the God who seeks us, finds us, and meets us in Jesus Christ.

What sorts of things does the incarnation tell us about the "God and Father of our Lord Jesus Christ?" Perhaps most obviously, it tells us that the God with whom we are dealing is no distant ruler who remains aloof from the affairs of his creatures, but one who is passionately concerned with them to the extent that he takes the initiative in coming to them. God doesn't just reveal things *about* himself—he reveals *himself* in Jesus Christ. Revelation is personal. It is not given in a set of propositions, a list of statements which we are meant to accept, but in a person. It is to Christ, and not to the creed, that the world must look for redemption. The creed points away from itself to the one hope of redemption, to Jesus Christ. It is not the creed but the astonishing act of God in history to which it bears witness which is the source of the saving power underlying the Christian proclamation. Christianity has always insisted that man can *know*—not just *know about*—God. God does not encounter us as an *idea*, but as a *person*. We may know much *about* the President of the United States, or the British Royal Family—but that doesn't mean that we *know* them. For someone to be *known* means that they want to *be known*—there must be a willingness on their part to let us know them. But God goes further than this. He takes the initiative in approaching us, in disclosing to us that he wants us to know him. God reveals himself to man, and by revealing himself, discloses his love for man and his desire to enter into a relationship with him. Just as the waiting father encountered the returning prodigal son, so God encounters us.

The incarnation speaks to us of a God who *acts* to demonstrate his love for us. That "God is love" (1 John 4:8) is a deep and important truth—but far more important is the truth that God *acted* to demonstrate this love. "In this the love of God was made manifest among us, that God sent his only Son into the world, so that we might live through him" (1 John 4:9). Actions, as we are continually reminded, speak louder than words. That "God is love" could be misunderstood as a static timeless universal truth; that "God so loved the world that he gave his only Son, that whoever believes in him should not perish but have eternal life" (John 3:16) makes it clear that God is dynamic, a living God, who acted in order to reveal the full extent of his love for us.

The incarnation speaks to us of God humbling himself in order to make himself known to us, to call us back to him, to reveal the full extent of his love toward us. The words of Emily Elliott are memorable:

Thou didst leave thy throne and thy kingly crown
When thou camest to earth for me.

Christianity does not teach that man has to climb a ladder into heaven in order to find God and be with him—rather, it teaches that God has come down that ladder in order to meet us and take us back with him. We don't have to become like God before we can encounter him, because God became *like us* first. God meets us right where we are, without preconditions. A very famous saying of Athanasius is worth noting here: "God became man so that we might become God." By this, he simply meant that God became man in order that man might enter into a relationship and fellowship with him. The personal relationship which Christians presently enjoy with God through Christ is a foretaste of the fuller and deeper fellowship we will one day enjoy.

The theme of the humility of God is expounded with great feeling in a famous passage, usually thought to be a Christian hymn going back even before the writings of Paul, which Paul quotes in much the same way as I have been quoting from hymns in this chapter:

> Though [Jesus Christ] was in the form of God, [he] did not count equality with God a thing to be grasped, but emptied himself, taking the form of a servant, being born in the likeness of men. And being found in human form he humbled himself and became obedient unto death, even death on a cross (Phil. 2:6–8).

This passage brings to mind a vast range of images of great men humbling themselves in order to bring about something worthwhile. God stoops down in order to meet us where we are. We all know the story of the ancient king who chose to leave his life of luxury in his palace and live as a peasant among his people, in order to understand them and thus rule them better on his return.

A similar thought is expressed by Mrs. Cecil F. Alexander in her famous Christmas carol:

> He came down from earth to heaven,
> Who is God and Lord of all,
> And his shelter was a stable,
> And his cradle was a stall:
> With the poor and mean and lowly
> Lived on earth our Savior holy.

God himself enters into the world, the vale of soul-making, full of darkness and tragedy. It is this "far country" into which the Father enters to call his lost children home. Let us remind ourselves of that celebrated statement of John: "The Word became flesh and dwelt among us" (John 1:14). The word translated by "dwelt" could be translated more accurately as "pitched his tent." This translation presents us with a powerful image, undiminished by the passage of time. The image is that of a wandering people who dwell in tents (as Israel once did in the period looked back to by the prophets as a time when she was close to God). One day they awake to find a new tent pitched in their midst—God himself has come to dwell among them as they wander. God is with them.

"God is with us." This great theme of the incarnation is summed up in the name *Emmanuel* (Matt. 1:20–23). We must appreciate the importance of names for the biblical writers. Not only does a name disclose something of the personality of the individual, but being allowed to give someone a name establishes your authority over them. In the creation accounts, it is man who is allowed to name the animals (Gen. 22:19–20) and thus to establish his authority over them. But man is not allowed to name God—it is God who reveals his name to man (Ex. 3:13–15). Man is not allowed to establish authority over God. So it is with Jesus. Mary and Joseph are told what the name of their child shall be—they didn't choose it themselves: "You shall call his name Jesus, for he will save his people from their sins" (Matt. 1:21). The name "Jesus" literally means "God saves," just as "Emmanuel" means "God with us" (Matt. 1:23). What, then, does "God being with us" mean? Two main meanings may be identified. First, God is on our side; second, God is present with us. We will look at these now.

"If God is for us, who is against us?" (Rom. 8:31–32). "God is with us" means "God is on our side." The birth of the Son of God demonstrates and proclaims that God is on our side, that he has committed himself to the cause of the salvation of sinful mankind. In the birth of the long-promised Savior, in his death on the cross of Calvary, and in his resurrection from the dead we have a demonstration, a proof, a guarantee that God stands by us. Christmas tells us that the God we are dealing with, the God and Father of our Lord Jesus Christ, is not a God who is indifferent to our fate but one who is passionately committed to our salvation, to redeeming us from sin, and to raising us to eternal life on the last day.

Second, "God is with us" means that God is present among us. We are not talking of a God who stands far off from his world, aloof and distant from its problems. We are dealing with a God who has entered into our human situation, who became man and dwelt among us as one of us—who knows *at first hand* what it is like to be frail, mortal and human, to suffer and to die. We cannot explain suffering, but we can say that God took it upon himself to follow this way. God became the man of suffering, so that he could enter into the mystery of death and resurrection. God knows what it is like to be human—an astonishing and comforting thought. We are not talking about God becoming *like* man, just as if he was putting on some sort of disguise so that he could be passed off as a man—we are talking about the God who created the world entering into that same world *as* man and *on man's behalf* in order to redeem him. God has not sent a messenger or a representative to help the poor creatures that we are—he has involved himself directly, redeeming his own creation, instead of getting someone else to do it for him. God is not like a general who issues orders to his troops from the safety of a bombproof shelter, miles away from the front, but one who leads his troops from the front, having previously done all that he asks them to do in turn.

The suffering and pain of the world simply will not go away, and we have every right to dismiss those who tell us that one day all will be well—

after we have adopted their particular solution to the world's ills. Realism now demands that we work toward the alleviation of misery and suffering, recognizing that the vision of its total elimination is utopian. The idea of a political revolution which will eliminate human misery and suffering has lost what little credibility it once had, and has probably caused just as much misery where it has become a dogma. What, then, may one say about God and suffering? Can anything be said which is of comfort? In the history of the world, four answers have been given. First, suffering is real and will not go away, but death comes as the end, and in death there is an end of suffering and eventual peace. Second, suffering is an illusion. It simply is not there, but is imagined. Third, suffering is real, but we ought to be able to rise above it and recognize that it is of little importance. The Christian has the fourth answer: God suffered in Christ.

God knows what it is like to suffer. The letter to the Hebrews talks about Jesus being our sympathetic high priest (Heb. 4:15)—someone who suffers along with us (which is the literal meaning of both the Greek word "sympathetic" and the Latin word "compassionate"). This thought does not explain suffering, although it may make it more tolerable to bear. For it is expressing the deep insight that God himself suffered at first hand as we suffer. We are given a new perspective on life. Christianity has always held that it is the suffering of Christ upon the cross which is the culmination, the climax, of his ministry. God shares in the darkest moments of his people.

There is a famous saying about the medical profession worth remembering here: "Only the wounded physician can heal." Whether this is true or not is a matter for debate. But it does highlight the fact that we are able to relate better to someone who has shared our problem, who has already been through what we are going through now—and triumphed over it. As many already know from experience, it is often difficult to relate to someone who hasn't shared our problem. One way of getting around this is the idea of empathy. You empathize with the other person's problems and fears. Even though you haven't shared them—and may not even be able to understand them—you let them think that you have and that you understand exactly how they must be feeling. It works splendidly—provided the person you're trying to help doesn't see through it! The incarnation speaks of God *sympathizing* with our sufferings—not *empathizing*, as if he himself hadn't experienced them at first hand. God sympathizes in the strict sense of suffering alongside with us. In turning to God, we turn to one who knows and understands.

There is a splendid story once told about shepherds in East Anglia, formerly the center of England's wool trade. When a shepherd died, he would be buried in a coffin stuffed full of wool. The idea was that, when the day of judgment came, Christ would see the wool and realize that this man had been a shepherd. As he himself had once been a shepherd, he would know the pressures the man had faced, the amount of time needed to look after wayward sheep and would understand why he hadn't been to church much! The story does, however, make an important point which we must treasure as one of the greatest of the many Christian insights into God. We are not dealing with a distant God who knows nothing of what being human, frail and mortal means. He knows and understands, and so we can "with confidence draw near to the throne of grace" (Heb. 4:16).

Who was Jesus? In this part of the book, we have been looking at questions about the *identity* of Jesus. But Christianity has much to say about the *significance* of Jesus—about what he *did*. In this part, we have been looking mainly at the birth and resurrection of Jesus Christ. In the next part, our attention moves to the cross. Why did Jesus have to die? And what are the implications for us, living some two thousand years after that event? Why is the cross universally recognized as the symbol of the Christian faith? Let us now move on to deal with questions like these.

PART THREE

The Work of Jesus Christ

8

The New Testament Witness
to the Work of Jesus

A
s I have emphasized throughout this book, Christianity is not the religion taught or preached by Jesus. It centers on the great drama of
redemption accomplished by his death and resurrection. Nor is it primarily
concerned with the life of a holy man or hero who serves as an example to
his followers, but with a series of events in history which are recognized as
acts of divine redemption. From the time of the New Testament onward, the
Christian church has always proclaimed the necessity, the possibility and the
actuality of redemption through the death of Christ. Thus the New Testament witness to the identity and significance of Jesus Christ culminates in
his death and resurrection, rather than in his moral teaching. This is most
evident in the New Testament letters, although, as we saw earlier, the same
concentration on his death and resurrection may be seen as underlying the
Gospels as well. It is evident from the New Testament that Jesus' death was
not seen as an accident, the untimely or premature end to the career of a
promising rabbi, but something through which God was working to achieve
some definite purpose.

At some point, however, we have to turn from facts to interpretations of
their significance. The death and resurrection of Jesus may, as we have
insisted, be regarded as historical events. But what do they *mean*? Why are
they significant? We have already emphasized the important distinction
between an event and its interpretation: There is all the difference in the
world between the statements "Jesus died" and "Jesus died for me." The former refers to an event, the latter to its interpretation. In this part of the work,
we are going to look at *interpretations* of the significance of the death and resurrection of Jesus Christ. These are sometimes called "theories of the atonement" (although this phrase is not particularly helpful or illuminating). The
previous part dealt with the question of the *person* of Christ; we are now concerned with the *work* of Christ.

The New Testament uses a wide range of images to express the richness
of its understanding of the work of Christ. We may describe these images as
analogies, models, or metaphors—but the important point to appreciate is

that we are attempting to explain or interpret what was going on between God, man, and Christ in the crucifixion and resurrection in terms of ideas we are already familiar with from everyday life. The New Testament writers did exactly what every good preacher is meant to do—use illustrations and analogies drawn from their experience to help "unpack" their theology. What happened on the cross cannot be reduced to a single statement or image. We have to build up a picture of what was going on by using a wide range of illustrations, each of which casts light on one particular aspect of our subject. It may well be that one individual finds one illustration more helpful than another—but this does not entitle him to argue that it is this illustration, and this illustration alone, which is good enough to stand on its own as a description of what was going on. Let us begin by looking at seven images the New Testament uses to bring out the meaning of the death and resurrection of Jesus Christ.

1. Ransom

The idea of Jesus giving his life as a ransom is found on the lips of Jesus himself in the Synoptic Gospels. Jesus came "to give his life as a ransom for many" (Mark 10:45). If Jesus spoke Aramaic—which seems highly likely—it is possible that we could translate this as "give his life as a ransom for *all*," because it is impossible to distinguish between "many" and "all" in Aramaic. The idea is also found elsewhere. First Timothy 2:5–6 is particularly important: "For there is one God, and there is one mediator between God and men, the man Christ Jesus, who gave himself as a ransom for all." A ransom is, of course, a price which is paid to achieve someone's freedom. In the Old Testament, however, it is evident that the emphasis falls upon the idea of being freed, of liberation, rather than speculation about the nature of the price paid, or about the identity of the person to whom it is paid. Thus Isaiah 35:10 and 51:11 refer to the liberated Israelites as the "ransomed of the Lord." The basic idea is that God intervenes to deliver his people from captivity, whether from the power of Babylon (Isa. 51:10–11) or death (Hos. 13:14).

The early fathers were intrigued by the question of to whom the ransom was paid. Some developed the idea that Christ's death was a ransom paid to the devil, so that the satanic dominion over man might be broken and man might be freed. However, as we all know only too well from experience, analogies break down very quickly! The important thing to remember when dealing with an analogy is that the crucial point which the analogy illustrates must be identified. A similar point applies to metaphors. For example, an enthusiastic gardener might survey his magnificent display of blooming half-hardy annuals swaying in the wind, and refer to them as a "sea of color." By that, he means that the observer is confronted with a vast expanse of moving color, similar to the impression created by the sea. He does not mean that they are wet or salty! The point which he is trying to make by the analogy must be identified and appreciated. To ask: "To whom is the ransom of Jesus' life paid?" is rather like asking: "Are the half-hardy annuals salty and wet?" We have failed to appreciate the point which is being made, and have concentrated our attention on something we weren't meant to think about at all. For the New Testament, "ransom" means "freedom"—and beyond this point the analogy breaks down. Fortunately, however, we have other analogies which we can use to explore the meaning of Christ's death. Let us go on to another image similar to the one we've just been looking at.

2. Redemption

The basic idea expressed here is that of "buying back." An example all too familiar from English life in the nineteenth and early twentieth centuries is provided by the pawnbroker. After pawning an item, it is necessary to redeem it—to buy it back from the pawnbroker—to reestablish possession of the item. A similar idea underlies the practice of redeeming slaves, a familiar event in New Testament times. A slave could redeem himself by buying his freedom. The word used to describe this event could literally be translated as "being taken out of the forum [the slave market]." As with the idea of ransom, we are dealing with the notion of restoring someone to a state of liberty, with the emphasis laid upon liberation rather than upon the means used to achieve it. It is thus interesting to notice how the words "redeemed" and "ransomed" are used side by side at points in the Old Testament, for example, Isaiah 55:10–11; Jeremiah 31:11; Hosea 13:14 (RSV).

In the Old Testament, God is often said to redeem his people (Deut. 7:8; 2 Sam. 7:23; Hos. 7:13; Zech. 10:8). Once more, it is necessary to note that the emphasis falls upon the act of divine deliverance or liberation, rather than upon any money used to achieve this liberation (Isa. 52:3 even makes it clear that money is not involved). The New Testament can use the term in the sense of being liberated from bondage—for example, bondage to the law (Gal. 3:13; 4:5). More often, however, the word is used in the more general sense of simply being set free (Rev. 5:9; 14:3–4). Here, as with the image of ransom, we are dealing with the idea of Christ's death and resurrection setting man free from his bondage to sin and death. Paul's repeated emphasis that Christians are slaves who have been "bought with a price" (1 Cor. 6:20; 7:23) does, however, remind us that we cannot overlook the fact that our present liberty is somehow related to the death of Christ.

3. Justification

The idea of justification—which became especially important within the church at the time of the Reformation in the existent century—is used frequently by Paul. "We are justified by faith" (Rom. 5:1), and thus have peace with God. The notion of justification is based upon the idea of being "put right," rather than being "made righteous" or "declared righteous." Perhaps the English word "rectification" expresses its meaning better. Man is put right with God, rather than being made morally righteous. Justification is about "rightness" rather than "righteousness." When Paul speaks of "justi-fication by faith," he is expressing the idea that man becomes right with God through faith. It may be that Paul is saying that it is faith itself which puts man right with God, or that it is through faith that man receives something which puts him right with God, or that faith *is* the right relationship to God. This isn't actually terribly important for our purposes. The important thing is that man is understood to be placed in a right relationship with God through the death and resurrection of Christ (Rom. 4:24–25).

There are two possible ways of drawing out the meaning of the word "justification." In the Old Testament, the idea often has forensic overtones—in other words, it can refer to legal proceedings. If an accused man is justi-fied, he is declared to be in the right, or vindicated, by a judge in court. This idea can be transferred to the New Testament without difficulty. The idea that man is justified by the blood of Christ (Rom. 5:9) may be understood to mean that a sinner is vindicated by God on account of the death of Christ.

A second way of approaching the concept of justification is to see it as referring to a personal relationship. Justification may then be understood as the establishment or reestablishment of a right relationship between God and man, in much the same way as a right relationship might be established or reestablished between two people. "Justification by faith" could be inter-preted as meaning that faith *is* the right relationship between man and God. Genesis 15:6 is interpreted by some Old Testament scholars to mean that Abraham, by believing God, placed himself in a right relationship with him.

4. Salvation

This idea is used frequently in the New Testament (Acts 13:26; Eph. 1:13; Heb. 1:14). The way in which the idea is used in the New Testament (the verb is generally used in the future tense) suggests that it should be thought of as a future event—something which is still to happen, although it may have begun to happen in the present. The basic idea is that of deliverance, preservation, or rescue from a dangerous situation. The verb is used outside the New Testa-ment to refer to being saved from death by the intervention of a rescuer, or to being cured from a deadly illness. It can also refer to being kept in good health. The word "salvation" is thus used by the Jewish historian Josephus to refer to the deliverance of the Israelites from Egyptian bondage.

Two ideas are thus suggested by the concept. The first idea is that of being rescued or delivered from a dangerous situation. Just as the Israelites were delivered from their captivity in Egypt at the time of the Exodus, so

Christ is understood to deliver man from the fear of death and the power of sin. The name "Jesus" means "God saves," and it is clear that the New Testament means "saves from sin" (Matt. 1:21 is interesting here).

The second idea is that of "wholeness" or "health." There is a very close relation between the ideas of salvation and wholeness. In many languages, the words for "health" and "salvation" are one and the same. Thus it is sometimes difficult to know whether a passage should be translated in terms of salvation or wholeness—for example, should the Greek version of Mark 5:34 be translated as "Your faith has made you whole" or "Your faith has saved you"? This close association of ideas was also found in the English language until the time of the Norman Conquest in 1066. The Old English word for salvation, *hoel* (note the similarity to the modern English words "heal" and "health"), was replaced by the Latin form "salvation" at that time, so that the English-speaking world has lost this close association of both words and concepts. But in other modern languages, this close association remains. Let us explore its meaning.

When someone who has been ill is healed, he is restored to his former state of health, of wholeness. The creation stories of Genesis make it clear that God created man in a state of wholeness and that this wholeness was lost through the Fall. Just as healing involves restoring man's health, so salvation involves restoring man's wholeness, restoring him to the state in which he was first created by God. Paul draws attention to the relation between the first and the second Adam (Christ): Through Adam, man lost his integrity before God; through Christ, that integrity can be regained and restored. In many respects the Gospel is like a medicine—something which heals us, even though we don't understand how it works. It doesn't matter that we do not fully understand exactly how God is able to work out our salvation through the death and resurrection of Christ. The point is that Christians have always believed that God could and did save man in this way, even if they couldn't quite understand how or why (although they were certainly prepared to speculate over these questions).

Let us develop this medical analogy a little further, to bring this point out. When I was very young I developed a bad infection which had to be treated with antibiotics. I took my penicillin, as directed by the doctor, and the infection cleared up. I hadn't the slightest idea what the drug was or how it worked—I just trusted the doctor's diagnosis and the cure he prescribed. Many years later, as an Oxford undergraduate studying biochemistry, I learned how penicillin actually worked, the way in which it destroyed bacteria. Yet, I remember thinking at the time, it worked perfectly well without my understanding exactly what was happening! In many ways there is an obvious parallel with the Gospel proclamation of salvation in Christ which diagnoses our problem (sin) and offers us a cure (Christ). We don't know exactly how Christ overwhelms sin—although in this part of the book we'll be looking at some suggestions—but we firmly believe, on the best authority, that he *does*. The theologian may fuss over the details, but the crucial thing is our belief that Christ somehow provides a solution to the problem of the human situation.

"Your faith has made you whole"—by restoring man to fellowship with God, and beginning the long and painful process of learning to live with God and for God. Why should it be painful? Because for so long we have tried to live without God, when we finally come to adjust our lives to make room for him, we find it very difficult to make the adjustment. Many of us know only too well what happens when the blood circulation is cut off from an arm or leg. When the circulation is restored it is acutely painful as the limb tries to readjust to the presence of the life-giving fluid. Yet that pain comes about through the limb coming to life again. So it is with coming back to God. It is painful, but it is also coming back to life.

5. Reconciliation

"In Christ God was reconciling the world to himself" (2 Cor. 5:19). This famous statement draws our attention to the idea of "reconciliation." The word and the idea are all too familiar to us all. The world in which we live cries out for reconciliation—reconciliation of employers and employees, of husband and wife, of parents and children. Paul uses the word in another context to refer to a reconciliation of an estranged husband and wife (1 Cor. 7:11). The idea of reconciliation is fundamental to human experience, especially in the area of personal relationships. The parable of the prodigal son (Luke 15:11–32) is perhaps the supreme illustration of the importance of reconciliation in the New Testament. It illustrates vividly the reconciliation of father and son, and the restoration of their broken relationship.

The parallel between the reconciliation of two individuals and between man and God will be obvious. God is treated as a person, someone to whom man can relate. Their relationship, once close (as in Eden), has been seriously disrupted to the point where it exists in name only. Man is, and will always remain, a son of God—it is God who has created him and it is God who continues to love him, despite man's journey into the far country away from God. It must be emphasized that the prodigal son remained the son of his father even when he set off to live independently, confident that he could live without his father's continual presence and oversight. But that relationship exists in name only—one party to the relationship acts as if it was not there. Reconciliation takes place when both parties to a relationship take the relationship with full seriousness, and acknowledge their mutual love for each other and the obligations which they have toward each other. The son returns to his father and they embrace—the relationship becomes *real*.

Reconciliation involves someone taking the initiative. If there are two persons who once enjoyed a close relationship but now have drifted apart, that relationship will remain broken unless someone attempts a reconciliation. Someone—usually one of the two parties to the relationship—has to take the initiative and approach the other party, acknowledging that the relationship has gone wrong, recalling how precious and important that relationship once was, affirming their love and concern for the other and asking them to restore the relationship. If the other party is not prepared to restore the relationship, no progress has been made. If reconciliation is offered but not accepted, the relationship remains unaltered. There is simply no such thing as a "legal fiction" in personal relationships. If, and only if, both parties agree to restore the relationship will reconciliation be achieved. All this is evident from our experience of the niceties of everyday personal relationships. By making an appeal to personal relationships—and the parable of the prodigal son makes this appeal with remarkable power—the New Testament grounds our relationship with God in everyday experience.

"In Christ God was reconciling the world to himself." How is Christ understood to be involved in the reconciliation between man and God? There are two ways of looking at this question. First, the phrase "In Christ God was" is taken as a reference to the incarnation. In other words, God incarnate makes his reconciling appeal to man. Christ, as God incarnate, takes the initiative in proclaiming the overwhelming love of God for man and the divine wish that man should be reconciled to him. In proclaiming the need and possibility of reconciliation to God, Christ addresses us as God and on behalf of God.

Second, the phrase "in Christ" is understood to reflect a Hebrew grammatical construction with which Paul would have been familiar, which would be better translated as "through Christ." In other words, "Through Christ God was reconciling the world to himself." Christ is understood as the agent of divine reconciliation, the one through whom God reconciles us to him, the mediator or go-between. The following remarks from the letter to the Colossians are instructive: "And you, who once were estranged and hostile in mind ... he has now reconciled in his body of flesh by his death" (Col. 1:21–22). The ideas of "estrangement" (or "alienation," as it could also be translated) and "hostility" are used to refer to man's initial relationship with God, which is transformed through the death of Christ into reconciliation.

A further idea associated with the reconciliation of God and man through the death of Christ is peace. Reconciliation means the end of hostility and the beginning of peace. Through Christ, God was pleased "to reconcile to himself all things ... making peace by the blood of his cross" (Col. 1:20). Here Christ is seen as a mediator between God and man, pleading God's case to man and man's case to God, abolishing the hostility between them and establishing a new relationship of peace and harmony. Christ makes an appeal to us on behalf of God that we should be reconciled to him. Paul continues his discussion of the reconciliation of man to God as follows: "In Christ God was reconciling the world to himself, not counting their trespasses against them, and entrusting to us the message of reconciliation. So we are ambassadors for Christ, God making his appeal through us" (2 Cor. 5:19–20). The idea here is that believers are representatives of Christ in the world, just as an embassy is the representative of a country or monarch in a foreign land.

The emphasis upon the divine initiative is important: It is *God* who reconciles us to him—not the other way around. God approaches us, and it is up to us to respond. It is God who takes upon himself the pain and the anguish of broaching the situation of human sin, attempting to let us know of the great distress which sin causes him and the barrier it places between him and us. "Your sins have made a separation between you and your God," in the famous words of the prophet (Isa. 59:2). It is God who discloses to us the full extent of his love for us, despite the fact that we are sinners. Our love of God is a result of his love for us, not the other way around: "In this is love, not that we loved God but that he loved us and sent his Son to be the expiation for our sins" (2 John 4:10).

6. Adoption

The image of adoption is used by Paul to express the distinction between sons of God (believers) and *the* Son of God (Jesus Christ). The most important passages are Romans 8:15, 23; 9:4; Galatians 4:5; Ephesians 1:5. It is clear that this is a legal image. A father would be free to adopt individuals from outside his natural family and give them a legal status of adoption, thus placing them within the family. Although a distinction would still be possible between the natural and adopted children, they have the same legal status—in the eyes of the law they are all members of the same family, irrespective of their origins.

Paul uses this image to indicate that, through faith, believers come to have the same status as Jesus (as sons of God), without implying that they had the same divine nature as Jesus. Faith brings about a change in man's status before God, incorporating him within the family of God, despite the fact that he does not share the same divine origins as Christ.

7. Forgiveness

This is perhaps the most powerful and familiar image used to explain the significance of Christ's death and resurrection. The image can be interpreted in two ways: as a *legal* concept and as a *personal* concept. The legal use of the term is probably most familiar from the parable of the merciless servant

(Matt. 18:23–35). Here forgiveness is understood in terms of the remission of a debt. The servant is so heavily in debt to his master that he cannot pay it—and as an act of compassion, the master forgives him the debt. In other words, he writes it off, cancels it. The idea of "forgiveness of sins" may thus be regarded as a legal concept, involving the remission of penalty.

The second sense of the term is probably more familiar, and clearly is closely related to the idea of reconciliation. Forgiveness is here understood as something necessary for a personal relationship to be restored to its former state after a hurtful disagreement or misunderstanding. Once more, it is necessary for one party—in this case, the offended party—to offer the other forgiveness. Once more, it is necessary for him to broach a difficult and painful situation in order to restore the relationship. If it is not accepted, the relationship remains unaltered. Forgiveness offered, yet not accepted, does not transform a relationship. As with the idea of reconciliation, we are presented with the concept of a personal, and greatly hurt, God offering to man his forgiveness.

We have now looked at seven analogies or illustrations of what Christ achieved on the cross. Perhaps it is worth noting that they broadly fall under three categories.

1. *The commercial or transactional approach*—Here Christ's death is understood as the basis of a transaction by means of which man is transferred from bondage to liberty. Obvious examples are the ideas of ransom and redemption.

2. *The legal approach*—Here Christ's death is understood as the means by which a change in man's legal status is achieved—for example, being vindicated of guilt, being adopted into a family, or being forgiven a debt.

3. *The personal approach*—Here Christ's death is understood as the means by which a personal relationship between God and man is restored—for example, being made "right with God," reconciliation and forgiveness.

It would be possible to extend this list considerably and give an exhaustive list of ideas, analogies, or metaphors used to explain what it was that Christ achieved on the cross. This exercise would probably be interesting, but is not particularly relevant to our purposes. In the following three chapters we propose to look at three main "theories of the atonement"—ways of making sense of the significance of the death of Christ—which have been influential over the last two thousand years of Christian history. These theories are basically attempts to develop insights contained in the New Testament in a more systematic manner. We begin with the theory that Christ's death is a demonstration of the divine love, sometimes called the "moral" or "exemplarist" theory of the atonement.

9

The Loving God

The death of Jesus Christ demonstrates the overwhelming love of God for sinful man. Perhaps the most famous statement of the extent of this love may be found in John's Gospel: "God so loved the world that he gave his only begotten Son, that whoever believes in him should not perish, but have eternal life" (John 3:16). But how does the death of Christ demonstrate this love of God for man?

The theme of the love of God for his people is deeply embedded in both the Old and the New Testaments. One of the great themes expounded by the Old Testament prophets is the love of God for Israel which he demonstrated by delivering her from bondage in Egypt and leading her into the promised land. The eighth-century prophets in particular portray God reflecting with sadness on the way the child whom he loved so dearly has wandered away from him. One of the most powerful statements of this theme may be found in the prophet Hosea: "When Israel was a child, I loved him, and out of Egypt I called my son. The more I called them, the more they went from me. . . . Yet it was I who taught Ephraim to walk, I took them up in my arms; but they did not know that I healed them. I led them with cords of compassion, with the bands of love" (Hosea 11:1–4). Israel is portrayed as the wayward child of God, whom God brought into being, cared for and supported while still incapable of looking after herself, and finally led into the promised land. Just as a mother can never forget the child to whom she gave birth, so God can never forget his people (Isa. 49:14–15). Even though Israel abandons and rejects her God, God continues to love her (Hos. 14:4). God is frequently portrayed as musing over the delight he will feel when Israel returns to him to dwell under his protection (Hos. 14:4–7). The great covenant formula—"You will be my people, and I will be your God"—is seen as establishing a relationship between God and his people which nothing can destroy. It may be threatened by the great empires of the world, or by the disobedience of Israel herself, yet God, in his love, remains faithful to his people.

This theme is taken up and developed in the New Testament, perhaps most powerfully in the parable of the prodigal son (Luke 15:11–32). We all know this story far too well to need to tell it again here. The son goes off into the far country, only to realize his stupidity, and longs to return home to his father. Yet he is convinced that his father will have disowned him, will no longer wish to acknowledge him as his son. Every age has its own "far country," and is thus able to identify with the parable with remarkable ease. But it is perhaps worth noting that the title traditionally given for the parable is not quite right. It is certainly true that the parable deals with a prodigal (the word means "wasteful") son—but it also deals with a waiting father.

In this parable we see a reflection of the relationship between man and God. And the remarkable feature of the parable is the picture of God which it gives us. The father sees the returning son—he has been waiting—long before the son notices him, and rushes out to meet him. Although the parable indicates that the son had come to his senses and wanted to admit his stupidity to his father, he isn't given a chance to do this. The father embraced him before he could say a word, and made abundantly clear the full extent of his love for the son whom he thought he had lost.

The New Testament takes this idea of the overwhelming love of God for sinners a stage further by specifically linking it with the death of Christ. As Paul puts it: "God shows his love for us in that while we were yet sinners Christ died for us" (Rom. 5:8). In this passage, Paul reflects upon the sort of people we might feel prepared to die for. Perhaps we could think of some remarkable, outstanding person who is clearly so good that we would have no hesitation in giving our lives in order to save theirs (Rom. 5:7)—but it might be difficult to think of someone like this. For Paul, this thought just brings home still further the immensity of the love of God for sinners. Even while we were still sinners—before we repented or improved ourselves—Christ died for us. In human terms, the greatest demonstration of love a human being can manage is also his last—he gives the greatest thing which he has, his own life. "Greater love has no man than this, that a man lay down his life for his friends" (John 15:13).

Examples of this behavior are quite rare in everyday life, and are all the more memorable when we encounter them. All too many date from the time of the First World War, with its previously unimagined horrors. The story is often told of a soldier in the trenches who saw his comrade fall wounded some distance from the safety of his own lines. Rather than leave him to die, he crawled the considerable distance to where the man lay, and brought him back. As he tried to lower his friend into the trench, he himself was hit by a sniper's bullet and mortally wounded. As he lay dying, he was told that his friend would live, and he was able to die with that knowledge. He had given his life for a friend. Doubtless many other—and even more pathetic—examples of this sort of behavior could be given. It illustrates human love forced to its absolute limits, in that the man who gives his life for his friend does not even enjoy the satisfaction of his future company. All is given, and nothing received—except, perhaps, an all too brief satisfaction that something worthwhile has been achieved.

It is clear that the New Testament writers regarded Christ as giving his life for a purpose. Equally, there can be no doubt that they understand it to represent a most powerful demonstration of the love of God for his people. But it is also far more than that, and implies far more than meets the eye. In the last two centuries there has been a growing tendency in some quarters to insist that the death of Christ is a demonstration of the love of God for us—and nothing more than that. The image of Christ loving, suffering, and finally dying evokes a deep response in man, causing him to love God in return—and nothing more. There is no need to involve the idea of an incarnation of God, the resurrection, original sin, or vicarious suffering—simply the idea of love begetting love. What traditionally had been seen as one aspect of a greater whole is treated as if it were all that could be said about the meaning of the death of Christ. It is this theory which is sometimes referred to as the "moral" or "exemplarist" theory of the atonement, and has achieved some popularity in the more rationalist sections of the Christian church. There are, however, certain serious difficulties which must be noted in connection with it.

First, we must ask exactly how we know that the death of Christ represents a demonstration of the love *of God* for man. For traditional Christian belief there is no difficulty about this whatsoever. Christ is God incarnate, and in the image of the dying Christ we see God himself giving himself up for his people. The great hymn of Charles Wesley exults in this thought:

Amazing love! How can it be
That thou, my God, shouldst die for me?

The great paradox of the immortal God giving himself up to death on behalf of the people whom he loves is nothing less than amazing, and is the theme of much reflection within the Christian tradition. To return to Wesley:

'Tis mystery all! The Immortal dies:
Who can explore His strange design?
In vain the first-born seraph tries
To sound the depths of love divine!

By giving himself up to death, the incarnate God demonstrated the full depths of his love for mankind. It is indeed the love *of God* which we are dealing with, in that it is none other than God himself who loved us and gave himself for us.

But is it actually possible to get rid of the idea of Christ being God incarnate, as many of those inclined toward rationalism think? Christ is now seen as a man—a very special man, to be sure—but a man none the less. Christ is therefore to be thought of as making the greatest sacrifice which man can make—giving his life for others. But is this the love *of God*? Clearly it is not. It represents the height of human love—what the love of God might well be *like*. But in that Christ is not God incarnate, it is not the love of God which we are dealing with. If Christ is not God in any meaningful sense of the word, the best we can look for is information about what the love of God is (or might be) like—and not a demonstration of what the love of God actually is. A messenger or delegate can tell us that—but only God himself can show us. The soldier we mentioned above demonstrated exactly this love in giving his life for his friend—and we would not dream of suggesting that this was the love of God.

Why are we justified in singling out Christ as the supreme demonstration of the love of God? For the traditional Christian, the answer is evident: Christ is God incarnate, and thus commands our attention for that very reason. But if he is not God incarnate, we must justify his uniqueness in some other way. This actually proves to be remarkably difficult. Outstanding human acts of love are certainly rare—but in the course of human history, so many such acts have taken place that the best we could manage is to identify Jesus as one among many. And is there not some truth in the suggestion that the idea of the uniqueness of Christ is actually a doctrine of traditional Christianity, based upon the idea of the incarnation, which rationalism has inherited and tried to reinterpret in terms which would not establish that uniqueness in the first place? In other words, the traditional Christian ideas about Christ are retained by rationalists, yet reinterpreted in such a way that they lose their force (even if they become more credible to the skeptical mind)?

Let us take this point a little further. There are certainly those who would suggest that the idea of Jesus showing the love of God is a perfectly adequate statement of the Gospel. But, in reply, we must make an historical point: This version of Christianity would hardly have survived in the world into which Christianity first exploded. It may be that this is a reinterpretation of the Christian understanding of what happened on the cross which makes sense to modern man—but it certainly would have cut no ice in the past. It is difficult to see why this idea should catch the imagination of man. Man has always shown himself remarkably ungrateful for even the most interesting pieces of information—and that is all we are dealing with in this view of the death of Christ: the information that God loves us. But so what? After all, why should Christ's sufferings be regarded as such overwhelming demonstrations of divine love? Unless mankind was involved in some terrible predicament, and unless Christ's death could be shown to be directly related to that predicament, it is difficult to see why man should be even remotely interested in, or grateful to, Jesus. And once we start talking about "man's predicament," we are moving on to rather different understandings of the significance of the death of Christ!

The "moral" or "exemplarist" theory of the atonement seems to presuppose that man's basic problem is that of ignorance—he doesn't know what God is really like. Thus he may think that God doesn't love him. The death of Jesus on the cross educates him—it informs him that God really does love him. The theory appeals to those inclined to rationalism because it seems to eliminate ideas which they find difficult, such as the incarnation, resurrection, or human bondage to sin. But it just isn't that simple. Let us ask some reasonable questions. Is it *really* the love of God which is revealed? A more credible interpretation is that it is a splendid example of *human* love—man's love for man—which is revealed. And what point did it serve? None—except possibly Barabbas—can be said to have benefited directly from his death. The idea of Jesus dying to make some sort of theological point also strains the imagination somewhat. Why did God reveal that he loved man in such a strange way? Why did it take the death of Jesus to prove this? Why couldn't God just have told us that he loved us, instead of going about conveying exactly the same information in such a complicated and ambiguous way? Ambiguous? Yes—because it is far from clear what information, if anything, is being revealed about God.

Let us develop this point about the ambiguity of the cross. Traditional Christianity has always insisted that the cross represents, among other things, the disclosure of the full extent of God's love for sinful mankind. Working on the basis of a theology of the incarnation—in other words, the belief that it is God incarnate who is himself dying on the cross—this idea makes perfect sense. But if the theology of the incarnation is discarded in order to make way for a simpler view of the death of Christ, what are we left with? What reasons do rationalists have for suggesting that it is the love of God which is being revealed? Why can rationalists reject the idea that the death of Christ shows that God is totally uninvolved in his world? Why can rationalists reject the idea that the cross is completely meaningless? Why can rationalists reject the idea that the cross reveals the terrible wrath of God? Why can rationalists reject the idea that the terrible death of a wonderful man like Jesus shows that God is an arbitrary tyrant who enjoys inflicting suffering on the innocent? In short—why can rationalists reject all these ideas in favor of the idea that the cross reveals the love of God? It is not the most obvious of explanations. It is far from clear what, if anything, this theory tells us about God. The answer would seem to be that traditional Christianity has, on the basis of its understanding of the incarnation and resurrection, rightly insisted that the cross reveals the love of God—and this idea has been taken over by rationalism, although the theological framework which gave and guaranteed this explanation is discarded. If this is so, we are entitled to make an important observation: This theory of the atonement is ultimately dependent upon a theology of the incarnation and resurrection, and logical consistency demands that this be recognized. In other words, this rationalist theory of the atonement is actually much more complicated than might at first be thought.

A further point we might consider is the following: God can be left out of this theory with the greatest of ease, and apparently without making much difference. As we have seen, if Jesus is not God incarnate, we are not talking about a revelation of the love of *God* but the love of *man*. And if Jesus shows us the limits of man's love for man, and inspires us to imitate his example, why do we need to bring God into the theory? It works perfectly well without him. It is simply moralism, providing us with information about the way in which we ought to behave, rather than with reliable information about God. Christ is treated as a moral example, showing man what he is capable of. In other words, Jesus is an example of what every man could be. He is different in degree, and not in kind, from the rest of mankind. But why, then, is Jesus special? Mankind has been fortunate enough to have lots of splendid moral and religious teachers in the course of history, showing in their lives the principles which they taught. Why should Jesus be special?

The traditional answer to this question is perfectly straightforward: The resurrection demonstrates Jesus' identity as the Son of God, expressed in the idea of the incarnation. Jesus is special because of his unique relationship to God. If this view of the identity and significance of Jesus is abandoned, the special place which Christians give Jesus will have to be justified on some other grounds. But what grounds might these be? The excellence of his moral teaching? But Christians have tended to treat Jesus' teaching with great respect on account of who they knew he was, rather than working out who he was on the basis of what he taught. And Christians simply do not follow Jesus as you might follow Socrates or Gandhi (people whose lives and views do indeed deserve to be respected) in the way this theory suggests. Once more, we see that this theory of the atonement is simply derivative or parasitic—it actually depends upon insights drawn from the framework of traditional Christianity which rationalism prefers to discard. Whether they can actually do this is open to serious question.

Finally, it must be asked whether this theory of the atonement has a realistic view of man. Is man really capable of recognizing the death of Christ as a revelation of the love of God, and responding to it? What happens if man's will is so corrupted that he is incapable of making a response like this?

Tennyson's famous words in his great poem *In Memoriam* seem hopelessly idealistic:

We needs must love the highest when we see it.

The more cynical observation of antiquity seems much closer to our experience: We see the good and approve of it—but we actually go and do something worse.

Earlier, we noticed how Christians worshiped and adored Jesus as their Savior and Lord, praying to him and praising him as if he were God himself. The view of Jesus expressed in the "moral" or "exemplarist" theory of the atonement doesn't fit in with this at all. It is certainly true that the death of Christ demonstrates the love of God for man—nobody is going to deny that.

But this love of God is grounded in the idea of the one who was rich beyond all splendor, becoming poor for our sake. As the Nicene Creed puts it: "For us men, and for our salvation, he came down from heaven." We might go back to Charles Wesley's famous hymn:

> He left His Father's throne above,
> So free, so infinite His grace;
> Emptied Himself of all but love,
> And bled for Adam's helpless race.

The full wonder of the love of God for man can only be appreciated when we recognize what the incarnation and crucifixion really mean. God humbles himself and stoops down to meet man where he is. The first Christians believed, as we still believe, that Jesus was the embodiment of God, God incarnate, God giving himself to mankind. In the incarnation we see God giving his own self. At Calvary, God took upon himself the suffering, the pain, and the agony of the world. God showed the full extent of his love by coming and suffering himself—not by sending a messenger or a substitute. It helps to know that in the seemingly senseless and pointless suffering of Jesus, God himself is present, sharing in the tragedies of the human race. Jesus did not come to explain away or to take away suffering—he came to take it upon himself, to assume human suffering and lend it dignity and meaning through his presence and sympathy. It is *this* which is the full-blooded meaning of the love of God, rather than the anemic travesty of this idea to be found in the "moral" theory of the atonement.

In contemplating the appalling spectacle of Jesus dying on the cross, we come to see none other than God taking upon himself the agony of the world which he created and loves. It is *this* which is the "love of God" in the full-blooded sense of the word. John Donne expresses this thought:

> Wilt thou love God, as he thee? then digest
> My soul, this wholesome meditation,
> How God the Spirit, by angels waited on
> In heaven, doth make his temple in thy breast.
> The Father having begot a Son most blessed,
> And still begetting (for he ne'er begun)
> Hath deigned to choose thee by adoption,
> Coheir to his glory, and Sabbath's endless rest;
> And as a robbed man, which by search doth find
> His stol'n stuff sold, must lose or buy it again:
> The Son of glory came down, and was slain,
> Us whom he had made, and Satan stol'n, to unbind.
> T'was much, that man was made like God before,
> But, that God should be made like man, much more.

In its deepest sense, the love of God for man is that of a God who stoops down from heaven to enter into the world of men, with all its agony and pain, culminating in the grim cross of Calvary.

We could extend the parable of the prodigal son to say that God himself went into the far country to meet us and bring us home. Earlier we noted the story from the time of the First World War of the soldier who went out into No-Man's-Land—the "far country"—from the safety of his trench in order to bring his beloved comrade home. He did—but it cost him his life. We left out one part, the final part, of that pathetic story. As the soldier lay dying, knowing that he had saved his friend, he whispered, "I brought him through." The Son of God went into the far country and brought us through, brought us home, though it cost him his life. It is this astonishing love of God which lies at the heart of the Gospel proclamation:

> Love so amazing, so divine,
> Demands my soul, my life, my all!

Why is this overwhelming love of God for man so important? Love gives meaning to life in that the person loved becomes special to someone, assumes a *significance* which he otherwise might not have had. There is every danger that man will feel lost and overwhelmed in the immensity of the world. What place does he have in it? Is he in any way special? Christianity makes the astonishing assertion—which it bases upon the life, death, and resurrection of Jesus Christ—that God is profoundly interested in us and concerned for us, despite our apparent indifference to him. Furthermore, God is understood to give the fullness of his loving attention to each and every one, the totality of his own personal interest. The experience of love is perhaps one of the deepest and most important that human existence knows. Let us take two people, one of whom cares passionately for the other, yet keeps quiet about it. Then the other finds out, perhaps by chance, and realizes that he means something special to someone else, that a new relationship is possible, that at least in the eyes of one other person he is important and precious. That moment of recognition can be devastating, and from that moment, life may be seen in a very different light. So it is with God. The realization that we mean something to God, that Christ died *for us*, that Christ came to bring *us* back from the far country to our loving and waiting father, means that we are special in the sight of God. In the midst of an immense and frightening universe, we are given meaning and significance by the realization that the God who called the world into being, who created us, also loves us and cares for us, coming down from heaven and going to the cross to prove the full extent of that love to a disbelieving and wondering world.

10

The Victorious God

The theme of God's victory over hostile forces is often encountered in the Old Testament. Creation itself is frequently regarded as a divine victory over the forces of chaos (Job 26:12–13; Ps. 89:9–10). This great theme of God's victory over sin, evil, and oppression is, of course, most obvious in the Old Testament accounts of the exodus from Egypt. God is seen as having delivered his captive people from their captivity, as having gained a great victory over the forces of oppression and darkness. The great song of triumph in Exodus 15 exults in this victory: "I will sing to the Lord, for he has triumphed gloriously; the horse and his rider he has thrown to sea. The Lord is my strength and my song, and he has become my salvation" (Ex. 15:1–2). It was through this historic act of divine deliverance that Israel was brought into existence as a people, and it is obvious that Israel never forgot its importance. Time and time again the Psalms recall that great act of divine victory and deliverance, and look forward to similar divine victories in years to come (Pss. 135 and 136 are worth reading at this point).

If the exodus from Egypt is viewed by the Old Testament as a divine victory marking one turning point in the history of Israel, the exodus from Babylon is viewed as the second. In the sixth century before Christ, Jerusalem was besieged and captured by the Babylonians, and many of the inhabitants of Jerusalem deported to a life of exile in Babylon. It is this long period of exile which lies behind the deep sense of nostalgia found in Psalm 37: "By the waters of Babylon, there we sat down and wept, when we remembered Zion. On the willows there we hung up our lyres. For there our captors required of us songs . . . saying, 'Sing us one of the songs of Zion!' How shall we sing the Lord's song in a foreign land?" (Ps. 137:1–4). That captivity lasted half a century, and the exiles seem to have given up hope of ever seeing Jerusalem again. As that captivity wore on, a new prophet rose among the exiles, declaring that God would soon deliver his people from Babylon, just as he had once delivered them from Egypt (Isa. 40–45). In a great moment of vision, the prophet sees God acting decisively to redeem his people:

Awake, awake, put on strength, O arm of the Lord;
Awake, as in days of old, the generations of long ago.

Was it not thou that did cut Rahab in pieces, that didst pierce the
     dragon?
Was it not thou that didst dry up the sea, the waters of the great deep;
that didst make the depths of the sea a way for the redeemed to pass
     over?
And the ransomed of the Lord shall return,
and come to Zion with singing (Isa. 51:9–11).

The theme of the "Lord [baring] his holy arm before the ... nations"
(Isa. 52:10), which runs throughout this great prophecy, is a theme of divine
victory and divine deliverance. It is this vision of the great and mighty acts
of God in history, by which his people are delivered and preserved, which is
summed up in one of the most famous passages in this prophecy:

> How beautiful upon the mountains are the feet of him who brings good tid-
> ings, who publishes peace, who brings good tidings of good, who publishes
> salvation, who says to Zion, "Your God reigns." Hark, your watchmen lift
> up their voice, together they sing for joy; for eye to eye they see the return
> of the Lord to Zion. Break forth together into singing, you waste places of
> Jerusalem; for the Lord has comforted his people, he has redeemed
> Jerusalem (Isa. 52:7–9).

This theme of the victory of God in delivering his people from captivity became deeply embedded in the hopes and expectations of Israel as the
centuries passed. Israel once more came to be under foreign rule, first by the
Greeks, then by the Romans. But the great theme of deliverance continued
to be celebrated in the feast of the Passover.

The feast of the Passover celebrated—as it still celebrates today—the
events leading up to the exodus and the establishment of the people of Israel.
The Passover lamb, slaughtered shortly before, and eaten at the feast, sym-
bolizes this great act of divine redemption. It is thus very significant that the
Last Supper and the crucifixion of Jesus took place at the feast of the
Passover. The Synoptic Gospels clearly treat the Last Supper as a Passover
meal, with Jesus initiating a new version of this meal. While Jews celebrated
their deliverance by God from Egypt by eating a lamb, Christians would
henceforth celebrate their deliverance by God from sin by eating bread and
drinking wine. Passover celebrates the great act of God by which the people
of Israel came into being; the Eucharist celebrates the great act of God by
which the Christian church came into being.

John's Gospel seems to work with a slightly different date: Jesus is crucified at exactly the same moment as the slaughter of the Passover lambs
begins. It is not quite clear if or how the differences between the Synoptic
and Johannine accounts can be resolved. But what is important here is the
point which John's Gospel wants to make: The *real* Passover lamb is not

being slaughtered in the temple precincts, but on the cross—"Behold the Lamb of God, who takes away the sin of the world!" (John 1:29).

The very timing of the Last Supper and the crucifixion, and the close parallels with the Passover feast, make it clear that the Gospel writers see a close connection between the exodus and the death of Christ. Both are to be seen as acts of divine deliverance. Both are to be seen as acts of divine victory. But it is in the New Testament letters, especially those of Paul, that this idea is fully developed. Here, the death and resurrection of Christ are often reaffirmed as a decisive act of divine deliverance by which man has been liberated from the tyranny of sin and death. Paul draws on images of conflict taken from the battlefield, the amphitheater, and the athletic stadium to bring out the full significance of this theme of victory. "Thanks be to God, who gives us the victory through our Lord Jesus Christ" (1 Cor. 15:57). For the writers of the New Testament, the forces of evil are as real as the forces of good. Despite the fact that they have little to say to explain its origins, they never attempt to explain it away. For Paul, God "disarmed the principalities and powers and made a public example of them, triumphing over them in him [Christ]," (Col. 2:15). In John's Gospel, we also find the cross interpreted as a symbol of victory—victory over darkness, death, and the world (John 12:31–33 is particularly interesting). Thus the final words of Jesus from the cross—"It is finished" (John 19:30)—should not be seen as a cry of hopeless defeat—"It is all over"—but as a shout of triumph—"It is accomplished!" What had to be done, had been done, and done well.

The idea of God's victory over the forces of sin, death, and evil in the cross has always had enormous dramatic power, making a strong appeal to man's imagination. The New Testament writers are content to indicate that, somehow, God achieved a great victory through the death of Christ and that this victory affects believers here and now. But Christianity soon exploded into the first-century Mediterranean world, and Christian preachers found that this way of looking at the death of Christ seemed to lack something— it didn't explain why Christ had to die, for example. And so they developed the idea along lines somewhat different to those found in the New Testament. An illustration from the works of Gregory the Great, writing in the sixth century, will make this clear.

According to Gregory, the devil had managed to gain rights over man on account of man's sin, and God was not in a position to violate those rights in order to deliver man from the power of the devil. Therefore God devised a cunning plan by which the devil might be trapped. God sent into the world someone who looked like sinful man but who was actually sinless—in other words, Jesus Christ. The devil, not realizing that Jesus was sinless, naturally assumed that he could claim his rights over him, and eventually took his life. Gregory likens what happened next to a great fish being caught on a baited fishhook. The devil saw only the bait (Christ's humanity) and not the hook (Christ's divinity), and so found himself trapped. Having overstepped his authority, the devil's rights over man were forfeited, and God was thus able to deliver man from the power of the devil. Other writers suggested that the cross was more like a mousetrap than a fishhook, but the same basic ideas were still used. It need hardly be added that the New Testament was quite innocent of this type of speculation!

Another way of approaching the New Testament's emphasis upon victory over sin and death through Christ may be found in a famous eleventh-century Easter hymn by Fulbert, Bishop of Charters:

> For Judah's Lion burst his chains
> Crushing the serpent's head;
> And cries aloud through death's domain,
> To wake the imprisoned dead.

This highly imaginative hymn takes up the image of Jesus Christ as the conquering lion of the tribe of Judah, developed in the book of Revelation (Rev. 5:5), who fulfills the great promise of redemption made to Adam that he will trample the serpent under his feet (Gen. 3:15). The tyranny of death over man is broken by Christ's death and resurrection. It is interesting to note that Christ uses death to defeat death—a point often made during this period by preachers. An appeal was often made to the story of David and Goliath—just as David killed Goliath with the giant's own weapon, so Christ defeated death with its own weapons.

The idea of Christ "wakening the imprisoned dead" reflects the belief that Christ's death and resurrection were important, not only for those alive at the time and in years to come, but also for those who had come before. The basic idea is that Christ's victory over death is retrospective as well as prospective, and is thus good news for those who have already died. These are understood to be prisoners held captive by death, and through the defeat of death by Christ they are delivered from their bondage and set free. In the Middle Ages, this idea was developed as the "harrowing of hell"—an interesting idea worth looking at briefly.

The idea of the harrowing of hell is loosely based upon some New Testament passages which could be interpreted as suggesting the Christ went down to the place of the departed—in other words, hell—between his crucifixion and resurrection (Matt. 12:39–40; Acts 2:27–31; Rom. 10:7; Col. 1:18; and especially 1 Peter 3:18–22). The basic idea is that Christ descended into hell, with the cross of victory, and took the castle of hell by storm, setting free all those held prisoner. In the great portrayals of this scene dating from the fourteenth century, Christ tends to appear like a medieval knight, using his cross as a lance to break down the castle doors. But perhaps the most familiar portrayal of this powerful image for the modern reader is to be found in the religious allegory *The Lion, the Witch and the Wardrobe* by C. S. Lewis.

In this work we encounter the White Witch who keeps the land of Narnia covered in wintry snow. In the midst of this land of winter stands the witch's castle, within which many of the inhabitants of Narnia have been imprisoned as stone statues. In the fourteenth chapter of the book, Lewis describes the killing of Aslan, perhaps the most demonic episode ever to have found its way into a children's story. The forces of darkness and oppression seem to have won a terrible victory—and yet, in that victory lies their defeat. Aslan surrenders himself to the forces of evil, and allows them to do their worst with him—and by doing so, disarms them. In the famous words of William Cullen Bryant, "Truth crushed to earth will rise again." The description of the resurrection of Aslan is one the book's more tender moments, evoking the deep sense of sorrow so evident in the New Testament accounts of the burial of Christ, and the joy of recognition of the reality of the resurrection. In the sixteenth chapter of the book, Lewis graphically describes how Aslan—the lion of Judah, who has burst his chains—breaks into the castle, breathes upon the statues, and restores them to life, before leading the liberated army through the shattered gates of the once-great fortress to freedom. Hell has been harrowed—it has been despoiled and its inhabitants liberated from its dreary shades.

It will, however, be obvious that the struggle between good and evil continues to this day. So how can we talk about the cross as a decisive victory over evil? The crucifixion and resurrection are seen by the New Testament writers as a turning point, a decisive battle, in God's war against the evil powers that enslave and incapacitate man. This war was not begun with the birth of Christ, nor was it ended with his resurrection. The war has been going on since the beginning of time, and continues to this day. But the death and resurrection of Christ mark the dawn of a new and a decisive phase in this struggle, in which victory has been gained and yet not gained. To illustrate this point, let us consider a modern example.

On a fateful day in June 1944, the Allied forces managed to establish a bridgehead in Europe on the beaches of Normandy. This momentous day was called "D-Day," and historians have emphasized that it marked a decisive turning point in the history of the Second World War. The war was not won on that day—victory did not come until the following year, on "VE-Day." But, in a sense, the war *was* won on that day—because from that moment onward, the war entered a new phase, a phase of victory. Looking back on the history of the Second World War, the great turning point may be identified as the seizing of a bridgehead, a small pocket of Allied land in the midst of hostile territory, in June 1944.

So it is with the incarnation, death, and resurrection of Jesus Christ. In the incarnation, God established a bridgehead in hostile territory from which to begin the reconquest of his own world. In Christ's death and resurrection, we may see the age-old conflict between good and evil entering a new phase. It has not yet been won, but it is as if we have been granted a preview of the end of history, and can know that, in the end, evil will be destroyed. And from that standpoint, the cross and resurrection are seen as the turning point, the moment in which victory was gained and yet not gained. The cross and resurrection are to D-Day as the end of history is to VE-Day. We know that sin and death are defeated, even if the battle goes on around us.

A final point may be considered. Does not the emphasis upon the victory given in the cross diminish the place of the suffering of Christ in obtaining this victory? That this is a real danger may readily be conceded—but it is easily avoided. One of the most powerful pieces of reflection upon the meaning of the cross was written before 750 in Old English, and is widely known as the *Dream of the Rood* ("Rood" is the Old English, or Anglo-Saxon, word for "cross"). In this poem, the writer tells of how he dreamed "the best of dreams," in which he saw a cross studded with the jewels and richness of victory:

> It was as though I saw a wondrous tree
> Towering in the sky, diffused with light.

Yet as he wonders at this "glorious tree of victory," it changes its appearance before his eyes, becoming covered with blood and gore. How can it be that this strange tree should have two so very different appearances? As he wonders, the cross begins to speak for itself, telling him its story. It tells of how it was once a young tree, growing in a forest, only to be chopped down and taken to a hill. When it had been firmly put in its place, a hero came and voluntarily mounted it:

> Then the young hero (who was God almighty)
> God ready, resolute, and strong in heart.
> He climbed onto the lofty gallows-tree,
> Bold in the sight of all who watched,
> For he intended to redeem mankind.

Before his eyes, the young hero is pierced with dark nails. The tree is penetrated by those same nails and drenched with the blood which pours from their wounds—and yet it is through this appalling suffering that victory is gained and man set free. And so the poet tries to show how the gloriously jeweled cross of victory—perhaps an allusion to the crosses carried in processions in churches at the time—is actually pierced with nails and drenched with blood. Christ suffered on the "gallows-tree," and yet was "successful and victorious" in his mission. The cost of this victory was high and must never be forgotten:

> May God be friend to me
> He who suffered once upon the gallows-tree

Here on earth for men's sins. He redeemed us
And granted us our life and heavenly home.

And if this seems to amount to triumphalism, it must be remembered
that the victory won is not that of force but of tenderness: The symbol of victory, which goes forth conquering and to conquer, is the figure of a lamb as
if it has been slain.

Why is this theme of the divine victory over sin, death, and evil so
important? Perhaps the most convincing answer to this question is given by
Martin Luther King in his famous sermon *The Death of Evil upon the Seashore*
(the title of the sermon derives from Exodus 14:30: "And Israel saw the
Egyptians dead upon the seashore"). The belief that God has already entered
into battle with the forces of evil gives hope to man as he attempts to wrestle with evil in his own day. As we struggle to defeat the forces of evil, we
know that God is struggling with us. At the very moment when evil seems to
gain its greatest victory, it is defeated with its own weapons. The faith that
God has entered into man's conflict against his enemies, on his side, sustains
him in his struggle to escape from the bondage of every evil Egypt. The great
theme of the "victorious God" gives hope where otherwise there would be
despair, and sustains man in his endless, and seemingly unwinnable, fight
against evil. The darkness and despair of Good Friday must give way to the
triumph of Easter Day. As Martin Luther King so wisely observed, "Without such faith, man's highest dreams will pass silently to the dust."

11

The Forgiving God

The great theme of a God who forgives his wayward people is touchingly portrayed in the parable of the prodigal son. The waiting father, as we have seen, rushes out to greet the returning son and forgive him for his waywardness. The parable draws our attention to the love of the father for his son. It also, however, raises a question for many people: How can the father just forgive the son like that? It seems rather superficial, almost as if the father is suggesting that the past may be forgotten, set aside as if it never happened. Our sympathies often actually lie with the second son who is outraged by his father's behavior!

It is, however, unfair to expect a single parable to bring out the many aspects of the Christian understanding of the nature of forgiveness. This particular parable focuses our attention upon the love of the father. Parables usually just make one point, and the point which this parable makes is that a loving God eagerly awaits the return of his wayward children. This is one aspect of the Christian understanding of God, but it is quite ridiculous to suppose that this is all that there is to it. It is an insight which is to be treasured, to be sure, but it is by no means all that has to be said about God. It is quite improper to single out this parable as if it presented the Gospel in a nutshell, as if we could dispense with the remainder of the New Testament. There are many passages in the New Testament which draw attention to the seriousness with which God takes sin, and the great cost of true forgiveness.

The Lord's Prayer draws a direct comparison between God's forgiveness of our sins and our forgiveness of other people's sins (Matt. 6:12, 14–15), and makes it clear that if we don't forgive the sins of others, God won't forgive ours. Yet we all know from our own experience, only too painfully, how very difficult it is to forgive someone. It is easy to forgive someone for something unimportant, but when it is something really important, something which means a lot to us, we find it very difficult. It is here that the difference between real and false forgiveness becomes clear. It is very easy to say "I forgive you" to someone who has deeply hurt us, and not mean it. Resentment against that person remains, and we have "forgiven" them in word only and not in reality. Real forgiveness mean confronting the hurt which has been caused, recognizing its full extent and importance. It means going to the person who has caused such hurt and pain, and explaining the situation to him. It means telling him that, despite the great hurt and injury which has been done, his continued friendship is of such importance that you want him to accept your offer of forgiveness. And that is a difficult offer to accept—because it involves a deeply humbling admission, that injury has been caused. It may even be that we are unaware of the hurt and pain we cause to those whom we love by our actions. Forgiveness is an essential aspect of human personal relationships, just as love and trust. Without real forgiveness, our relationships with others would be false and superficial.

So it is with our relationship with God. The cross brings home to us the deep hurt and pain which our sin causes God. In Christ, God makes clear how painful and costly true forgiveness really is. And it is a real forgiveness which God offers us in Christ—a forgiveness which, if accepted, will transform our relationship with God. The offer of forgiveness of our sins is both deeply humiliating and deeply satisfying. It is humiliating because it forces us to recognize and acknowledge our sin; it is satisfying because the very offer of forgiveness implies that God treats us as important to him. God offers us forgiveness because, despite our sin, he loves us and wants us to return to him, to relate to him as we are meant to. God created us in his image and likeness (Gen. 1:26–27), thus we have an inbuilt capacity to relate to God which sin threatens to frustrate and which forgiveness offers to restore.

The theme of the "image of God in man" is an important one and worth thinking about a little more. When I was at school, we used to enjoy playing around with chemicals in the school laboratory. One of the more amusing tricks was to get a really old copper coin and drop it in a beaker of diluted nitric acid. The acid would turn blue and rather unpleasant brown fumes would be given off—and the coin would appear as if it were new. The acid had dissolved the dirt and grime which had obscured the features of the coin. The interesting point is this: The coins we used for this experiment were old British pennies which had the image of Queen Victoria stamped upon them. This image would, however, be quite invisible on account of the accumulated dirt. Although the image was there, it could not be seen. The acid restored the image so that it was clearly visible. Christianity has always insisted that although the image of God in man is obscured and hidden through sin, it remains there nevertheless. It just needs something to restore it—a theological equivalent of diluted nitric acid, in fact. The Gospel could be seen as restoring the image of God, man's ability to relate to God, by removing the obstacles to this relationship. Forgiveness does not necessarily mean that *sin* is eliminated—it means that the *threat sin poses to man's relationship to God* is eliminated. There is all the difference in the world between being sinless and being forgiven!

So far, however, we have just been talking about personal relationships. What about the wider consequences of forgiveness? What about its effect upon a group of people, upon the community? The distinction that we are about to draw is well known, and in English law is summed up in the difference between a *tort* and a *crime*. A tort is a personal injury, something which somebody does to me (like being rude to me in the absence of witnesses) which has no effect on anyone else and which I can forgive without involving anyone else. A crime is something which someone does to me (like robbing me or murdering me) which has wider effects upon the community. Robbing and murdering injure the community and not just me as an individual—and as a result, have to be dealt with by the community. If anyone can be said to "forgive" these actions, it is the community against which they have been committed, and not just me as an individual. And it is here that we are forced to recognize that human sin has consequences not just for the relationship of an individual with God, but for the relationship of people in general. This point is particularly clear in the Old Testament, where the destructive effects of sin upon the community of Israel are emphasized. Sin is about self-centeredness (how often it has been pointed out that the center of "sin" is "I"), which means that we ignore both God and our neighbor in our actions. The impact of sin is felt at both the private and the communal level. The question of how God can forgive sin thus comes to concern the *justice* of this forgiveness. How can God forgive sin when it has such consequences for society? Will this forgiveness not encourage man to commit sin?

The legal theory of the atonement attempts to meet these objections by demonstrating that God acts in complete justice in forgiving sin through the death of Christ. Although the roots of this idea are deeply embedded in both the Old and New Testaments, the first systematic development of the theory is to be found in the works of Anselm, the eleventh-century Archbishop of Canterbury. This idea has since become so influential that it is worth examining in some detail.

Anselm expresses his dissatisfaction with the understanding of the death of Christ as a victory over sin, death, and evil, because it does not really explain why Christ is involved in this victory in the first place. Why could God not have gained this great victory in some other way? How does Christ's death come into the picture? Anselm therefore sets out to develop a theory of the meaning of the death of Christ which firmly established its necessity as the means by which God worked out the salvation of the world.

His argument goes like this. God made mankind in order that he might have eternal life, but unfortunately man's sin intervened to make it impossible for him to gain eternal life unaided. So if man is going to have eternal life, God will have to do something about it. God cannot just pretend that sin doesn't exist or dismiss it as unimportant. Anselm then draws an analogy from the feudal outlook of the period. In ordinary life, an offense against a person can be forgiven, provided that some sort of compensation is given for the offense. Anselm refers to this compensation as a "satisfaction." For example, a man might steal a sum of money from his neighbor: In order to meet the demands of justice, he would have to restore that sum of money, plus an additional sum for the offense given by the theft in the first place—and this additional sum of money is the "satisfaction." Anselm then argues that sin is an offense against God, for which a satisfaction is required. As God is infinite, an infinite satisfaction is required. But as man is finite, he can't pay this satisfaction. And so it seems impossible that man shall ever have his eternal life.

Anselm then makes the following point. Although man ought to pay the satisfaction, he cannot; and although God is under no obligation to pay the satisfaction, he clearly could if he wanted to. And so, Anselm argues, it is quite clear that a God-man would be both able and obliged to pay this satisfaction. Therefore, he argues, the incarnation and death of Jesus Christ may be seen as a means of resolving this dilemma. As man, Christ has an obligation to pay the satisfaction; as God, he has the ability to pay it. And so the satisfaction is paid off, and man is able to regain eternal life.

Anselm's theory was important because it showed that a good case could be made for involving the death of Christ in the scheme of the divine forgiveness of sin without contravening justice. The theory has, of course, been very heavily criticized—for example, on account of its feudal ideas. But Anselm was just doing what every good preacher tries to do—use contemporary analogies to make a theological point. In a feudal society, like Anselm's, you would use feudal analogies. We can hardly expect him to have imagined what life would have been like in the sixteenth or twentieth centuries! The basic point which Anselm made is still of crucial importance—and that is that God does not act in an arbitrary or unjust way in redeeming mankind, but is totally faithful to his righteousness. God is not involved in questionable actions (like deceiving the devil) nor does he pretend that sin is insignificant and can be overlooked. For Anselm, God is just and acts in accordance with that justice in redeeming mankind. It is this authentic New Testament insight which Anselm has so vigorously upheld, even if his defense of the insight takes him far from the cautious statements of the New Testament on the matter.

A useful distinction which may be made here is between "justice" or "law," and "laws." The words "law" or "justice" express the basic principle of not acting arbitrarily but in accordance with generally accepted standards, whereas "laws" are various expressions of what those standards might be. Thus practically everyone agrees that "law" is a good thing, but when it comes to defining what it means, disagreement arises. "Law" is recognized as essential, while the "laws" which express it are a matter for debate. Thus Anselm justifies the idea of redemption by *law* by an appeal to eleventh-century *laws*, just as Calvin made an appeal to sixteenth-century laws—but the fact that those laws no longer apply today doesn't actually invalidate the basic principle he is trying to establish. The legal approach to the death of Christ is concerned with *law*, rather than with *laws*—in other words, with the basic conviction that God acts justly in dealing with sin and redeeming mankind. The cross demonstrates that the guilt of sin is really forgiven, and makes clear the full cost of this forgiveness.

The New Testament itself is not particularly concerned with the mechanics of the death of Christ—how it is that God is able to forgive the sins of man through the death of Christ. Of course, by drawing analogies with the Old Testament sacrificial system and the Suffering Servant of Isaiah 53, it gives us hints about ways in which we might relate Christ's death to our forgiveness, and these hints have been developed in the various legal theories of the atonement. All these theories make the same point expressed so simply by Mrs. Cecil F. Alexander:

> There was no other good enough
> To pay the price of sin;
> He only could unlock the gate
> Of heaven, and let us in.

But the New Testament's real concern lies elsewhere—in the emphatic assertion and proclamation that God really has dealt justly with human sin through the cross of Christ. It was through the cross of Christ, and through this alone, that real forgiveness of real sins became possible. How this was done is of relatively little importance in comparison with the fact that it was done. The guilt and the power of sin were broken through Christ. But it is worth noticing that the New Testament does not portray God as a cruel tyrant who arbitrarily demands the suffering and death of an innocent victim in order that the guilty party may escape his anger. The idea of a bloodthirsty, vengeful God has no place at all in the New Testament, which affirms that God himself entered into history in order to suffer for offending sinners. If *anyone* suffers, it is God himself who suffers on man's behalf and in man's place in order that justice and mercy might both be satisfied. It is the judge himself who suffers in order that his own law may be upheld and man truly and justly forgiven.

Forgiveness, then, if it is to be real forgiveness, is a costly business. Just how much it cost God to forgive man his sin is shown in the cross—the torment of the dying Christ, the incarnate God, gives us a most vivid and distressing insight into the nature and extent of God's forgiving love. As the *Dream of the Rood* puts it so powerfully:

> This is the tree of glory
> On which God Almighty once suffered torment
> For the many sins of mankind, and for the deeds
> Of Adam long ago.

It is God who suffers in order to bring home to man how precious real forgiveness can be. And although forgiveness is a difficult offer to accept

because of the clear implication that we are at fault, the thought of the crucified God makes this an offer we may find easier to accept than might otherwise be the case. The love and compassion shown in God's forgiveness
make the gentle chiding of our faithlessness more bearable. Christ is the only
man in history to see sin through the eyes of God, to see sin for what it really
is. And in the crucifixion we are shown the full horror of the consequences
of sin, and the urgency of the call to repent, to turn away from it to the one
who alone may break its hold upon us. The cross reveals both the seriousness of sin, and the purpose and power of God to overcome it.

How, then, are we involved in this process of forgiveness? Three main
ways of dealing with this question have been suggested. The first is that of
substitution—Christ, the righteous man, takes our place on the cross. It is
we who should have been crucified, yet Christ took our place, removing from
us the penalties due for sin. This idea is suggested by several passages in the
New Testament. "For our sake he [God] made him [Christ] to be sin who
knew no sin, so that in him we might become the righteousness of God"
(2 Cor. 5:21). The second is that of participation—man participates in the
forgiveness which Christ won upon the cross. This view draws upon many
New Testament passages, particularly Romans 8, in which the constant
involvement of the believer with all that Christ has done is constantly emphasized. The believer participates in whatever Christ has done: We share in
Christ's suffering, death, and final glorification. The third is that of representation—Christ represents man to God, just as he represents God to man.
And as the representative of man, Christ wins forgiveness for him on his
behalf. Christ is thus understood to suffer on the cross on behalf of, but not
instead of, sinful man. But whichever of these models the reader finds most
helpful in dealing with the New Testament statements on the involvement
of the believer in the death and resurrection of Christ, the fact that he *is*
understood to be involved in some way is not questioned. In some way, each
of us may be said to have been present at Christ's crucifixion, just as in some
way, each of us may be said to share in his resurrection.

Why is the idea of forgiveness so important? Man needs to know that,
despite his sin, he may enter into fellowship with God. One of the most
remarkable features of the Gospel is the assertion that man is brought to God
through God being brought to man. There are many religions which teach
that God does not welcome man until he ceases being a sinner—in other
words, man must become righteous before he can enter into fellowship with
God. God in Christ first welcomes man, and in that way brings about a *real*
transformation in man. Forgiveness imparts, rather than demands, newness of
life. It is the offer of forgiveness, so powerfully and tenderly embodied in the
dying incarnate God, Jesus Christ, which brings home to man his need for
repentance and amendment. Man can come to God, just as he is, knowing that

the offer of pardon and forgiveness carries with it the promise of transformation and renewal:

> Just as I am, without one plea
> But that Thy blood was shed for me,
> And that Thou bidst me come to Thee,
> O Lamb of God, I come.

PART FOUR

Conclusion

12

The Identity and Significance of Jesus Christ

Who is Jesus Christ? And why is he so important for Christians? These are the questions which have dominated this book. As we emphasized at the beginning, there is a very close connection between the person and the work of Jesus Christ—between who Jesus is and what he did. Although we have actually been more interested in the question of the identity of Jesus, we have also tried to show some of the ways in which Christians have understood the meaning of Christ's death. In the late seventeenth century, Isaac Newton discovered that a beam of white light, when passed through a glass prism, was split into a beam containing all the colors of the rainbow. The prism didn't create those colors—they had always been there in the beam of light—it just enabled them to be separated from each other and seen individually. Much the same sort of process leads to the formation of a rainbow, with raindrops acting as prisms. And so it is with our reflections on Jesus Christ. Just as the prism showed up the many components of a beam of white light, so we have tried to show the many ideas and insights which are contained in the death and resurrection of Jesus Christ, and look at them individually. They haven't been invented—just uncovered. But in the end we must remember that they are all part and parcel of one and the same thing—the person of Jesus Christ.

The cross is the central symbol of the Christian faith. It is the sign which is made at our baptism, when we bind ourselves to the God and Father of our Lord Jesus Christ. It is the sign which adorns our churches. It was in this sign that the first Christian Roman Emperor, Constantine, went forth to conquer. As we have seen in this work it is the cross which establishes the distinctively Christian understanding of the nature of God, and brings home to us with some force the full implications of God's love and forgiveness. The identity and significance of Jesus Christ are fully disclosed through the cross—first by his being crucified upon it, and then by his being raised from the death which it brought. The empty cross, as much as the empty tomb, reminds us of the strange and mysterious way in which God is at work in the world. To end this book, we are going to bring together some of the thoughts which have been developed here and which have relevance to both the individual believer, as he attempts to understand his own faith better and explain it to others, and to the life of the Christian church in general.

Let us begin by looking at the relevance of what has been said so far to the individual believer. The impact and relevance of the cross could be summarized very simply in four familiar images or pictures which help illustrate the meaning of the cross and draw on ideas we have already discussed. There is much more that could be said about the cross, as we have tried to show, and it could be said a lot better and more profoundly than this—but these four points should be helpful as "discussion starters." The reader who has had any difficulty in following the discussion in the earlier part of this book may find it helpful to treat them as "pegs" on which to hang the various points we have been making.

1. The Cross as the Place Where God and Man Meet

Imagine that you are driving along a country road, perhaps at night. As you drive along, your headlights pick up a sign at the side of the road. It has a cross on it. What does it mean? It means that there is a crossroads ahead, and that means oncoming traffic. Unless you are careful, you may find yourself in collision with another vehicle. The cross here means "a point of meeting." And so it is with the cross of Christ. God and man meet in the cross. It is through the cross that God discloses himself to us, calls to us, and meets us. Christianity is about coming to the foot of the cross, recognizing that in some strange and mysterious way the same God who made heaven and earth makes himself available for us at this very place. In the cross and resurrection of Jesus we recognize that Jesus is none other than God himself, humbling himself, even to death on a cross in order to bring us home from the far country.

Let us remember once more that very powerful parable of the prodigal son. It is a very moving and vivid illustration of the love of the father for his wayward son. Perhaps the thought of Jesus dying on the cross suggests that we might develop this parable slightly to bring out the full-blooded meaning of the death of Christ: The father goes after the son into the far country and brings him home, despite the appalling cost of this venture to himself. It is God who comes to meet us, who searches us out and finds us, to bring us home to him. In that dreadful image of the dying crucified Christ, we are presented with the sight of God, raised up high upon the cross, drawing men to himself. "Behold, my servant . . . shall be exalted and lifted up" (Isa. 52:13)—only now do we realize the full significance of those prophetic remarks. The servant was indeed exalted and lifted up—not exalted in status, by being made a king, but by being exalted and raised up upon the cross in order that all men might see and wonder (John 3:14–15; 12:32–33).

2. The Cross as the Demonstration of Man's Sin

Now imagine that you are back at school. You are doing some arithmetic—a very simple sum: 5 + 7 = ? is the problem you have to solve. After much thought (remember, you're very young again!) you write the answer with a flourish: 5 + 7 = 13 and the teacher promptly scrawls a symbol by the sum to show that you are wrong—a cross. A cross means wrong, not right. In a similar way, the cross means that we are not right with God. It tells us that we are sinners, men and women who need his grace and forgiveness. Can you see what a costly thing forgiveness is for God? God is loving, as we have seen, but he is also holy and righteous. How, then, can he *really* forgive us sinners? He can't just say, "Never mind, we'll pretend it never happened"—even we couldn't accept that idea of forgiveness. In the cross of Christ, we are talking about the *real* forgiveness of *real* sins, not some sort of pretend, fairy-tale stuff. God's forgiveness of sin comes about through the death of Christ on the cross—*real* forgiveness of *real* sin—in which we come face to face with both God's total condemnation of sin and his incredible and overwhelming love for us sinners:

> We may not know, we cannot tell,
> What pains He had to bear;
> But we believe it was for us,
> He hung and suffered there.

Christ died upon the cross to take upon himself our sin. Through his suffering and death upon the cross, perhaps in a way we shall never understand, God was able to forgive our sin. This astonishing fact should make us get down on our knees in wonder, rather than rush to speculate about the mechanics of the process!

The Gospel tells us that we are far from God, lost in a dark world and desperately needing hope, meaning, and love. The feeling of "lostness" might make us wonder if there is, in fact, anyone who is ever going to meet us and find us. The cross of Christ tells us that, even though we are sinners, God has not forsaken us but has taken the initiative in meeting us and finding us. Christ's suffering and death upon the cross were *for us*—he died to show us how far we are from God and at the same time to open the way back to God. The cross exposes sin and shows how its power and guilt can be broken. The cross stands at the center of the Christian faith, revealing both the seriousness of human sin and the purpose and power of God to deal with it. If you think of sin as guilt, think of Christ as bearing our sin upon the cross; if you think of sin as despair, reflect upon the hope we have set before us in Christ's victory over death; if you think of sin as being far from God, rejoice in the fact that God has met us in Christ and offered to bring us home. Jesus said, "I am the way, and the truth, and the life" (John 14:6). He did not merely show us the way and then leave us to make our journey unaided. Like the shepherd, he guides us along that way, traveling with us (Psalm 23 is worth reading again in this connection).

The cross, then, brings judgment—but we must not think of this judgment as something that is purely negative in which God just blames us or shows us how inadequate we are for the fun of it. Perhaps another everyday situation in which judgment is given may help bring this point out. When a doctor diagnoses an illness, he is passing a judgment on you—he is telling you what is wrong with you. But he is telling you what is wrong with you in order that you may be cured. And in order to be cured, you need to know what is wrong with you. It is remarkable how many people who are ill are quite unaware of the fact—they just accept their situation as normal, unaware that something is wrong and that something can be done about it. The first step in the process of healing is identifying what the problem is. And so it is with judgment passed upon us in the cross of Christ—a judgment which identifies that something is wrong with man and thus opens the way to healing, transformation, and renewal. The idea of Christ as the "light of the world" (John 8:12) is useful here—light shows up things for what they really are, bringing everything to light and making clear the dilemma with which man is faced. Perhaps we could say that the cross offers a diagnosis of the human situation as the first step toward transforming it.

3. The Cross as the Demonstration of God's Love

Imagine that you are writing a letter to someone very dear to you. Perhaps you are sending a Valentine card or a very personal letter. You write it, sign it and then indicate your affection for the person who will receive the letter by placing crosses at the bottom. Crosses mean love. The cross brings home to us the full extent of God's love for his people. "God so loved the world that he gave his only Son" (John 3:16). "God shows his love for us in that while we were yet sinners Christ died for us" (Rom. 5:8).

It is an astonishing thought that God—when the full meaning of this world is grasped—actually loves us personally. It seems strange and impossible. There is simply no limit to the love of God for us. As Christ was dying upon the cross, those around him made fun of him. "Come down from the cross," they screamed. "Save yourself!" But he didn't—he stayed where he was and died, showing that there was no limit to his love for us. There was simply nothing more that could be given than his own life. "Save yourself," the crowd shouted, and yet Jesus died in order to save us instead. The words of a famous Christmas hymn are enlightening here:

O may we keep and ponder in our mind
God's wondrous love in saving lost mankind.
Trace we the Babe, who hath retrieved our loss,

From his poor manger to his bitter cross;
Treat in his steps, assisted by his grace,
Till man's first heavenly state again takes place.

4. The Cross as a Decision

Let us now turn to a fourth way in which we might use a cross in everyday life. Placing a cross against a name on a ballot paper means you are voting for them; it means that you are making a decision. The cross of Jesus Christ also demands a decision. As we have seen, God offers man love, forgiveness, and reconciliation through the cross. And this offer forces us to make a decision: Will we respond to it or not? Forgiveness or reconciliation offered and not accepted does not transform a relationship. In effect, God has given us the immense privilege of saying "No" to his offer of love. He knocks on the door, gently, seeking admission (Rev. 3:20–21) but we must open the door. A favorite analogy for this in the Middle Ages was the opening of a shutter. Let us suppose that you are in a dark room and want it lit up. The shutter is closed and the sunlight is beaming down upon that shutter, yet the light will not enter that room and illuminate it until you open that shutter. So it is with the forgiving grace of God—like the sunlight, it is always there at our disposal. But a decision, an action, is required if it is to influence us or affect us. Opening that shutter to let the light in is just like saying "Yes" to God's offer of grace.

A famous German poem by Angelus Silesius has been quoted much in the present century by theologians. The important lines go like this:

Were Christ a thousand times to Bethlehem come,
And yet not born in you, it would spell your doom.
Golgotha's cross, it cannot save from sin,
Unless for you that cross is raised within.
I say, it helps you not that Christ is risen,
If you yourself are still in death's dark prison.

In other words, the incarnation, crucifixion, and resurrection are of little relevance to anyone unless they are received and appropriated by faith. Christ was born in Bethlehem, but he must be born in *us* if he is to do us any good. Christ died on the cross of Calvary, but unless we make that cross our own, unless we accept and receive its power of faith, it remains a distant, remote, and not particularly relevant event. The great gap of space and time which separates us from the death and resurrection of Jesus Christ is bridged by faith in order to grasp and appropriate what is on offer. Faith, to use John Calvin's famous analogy, is like an empty, open hand stretched out toward God, with nothing to offer and everything to receive. Faith is the final step in the process begun by the cross of Christ—we recognize its meaning, we realize its relevance, and finally we receive its benefits.

The cross, then, is central to the faith of the individual believer. Like John Bunyan's *Pilgrim* he may lay his burdens at its foot and go forward into a new life. But an important part of that new life is the community of faith, the Christian church, which has been called out from the world as the people of God. What is the relevance of the cross to that church?

First, the cross must be allowed to function as the foundation and the criterion of the church's understanding of its identity and its mission. It is through the strange and mysterious events which culminate in the crucifixion and resurrection of her Lord that she came into being, and it is recalled, rehearsed, and reenacted in the service variously known as the Eucharist, communion, or breaking of bread. Here the church is reminded of something which she must never be allowed to forget—that whatever social, political, or cultural situation she may find herself in, her distinctive identity lies in the fact that she has been called from the world by the series of events leading up to and then away from the cross. It is the "word of the cross" which she must proclaim and by which she must judge first herself and then others. The essential and vital *distinctiveness* of Christianity can all too easily be lost: All that then remains is a church which retains its structure but has lost both meaning and experience. In an age where society has taken over most of the social functions once exercised by the church, there is an increasingly urgent need for that church to rediscover the vitality and authenticity of the original function of the church—there is no sadder sight than a church seeking for a meaning which was once given to it and which it has now lost.

In the light of the cross, and the grim spectacle of the crucified Christ, we realize the futility of the world's values and ideals. In the famous words of Thomas à Kempis, "The glory of the world fades away" (*sic transit gloria mundi*). In the eyes of the world, "might is right"—but the church must learn to conquer in weakness. The sign in which she will conquer is that of a lamb who has been slain. Yet in her weakness lies her greatest strength. The dying Christ who, counter to every expectation was raised from death in power and glory, is the model by which the church must gain and exercise authority. There is no room for triumphalism or self-confidence: simply a recognition of the need to return continually to the foot of the cross, there to reflect upon the mysterious way in which God works in his world and in his church. Perhaps it is significant that the church tends to be at its weakest spiritually when it possesses its greatest temporal strength. In the eyes of the world, a system of beliefs must be sophisticated and subtle if it is ever to gain acceptance, but the church must learn that her only wisdom is the foolishness of the cross and the proclamation of Christ crucified. This proclamation seems hopelessly weak and foolish, and there is every temptation to embellish it with what our day and age accepts as wisdom—yet which another generation will regard as discredited. In the cross, we are confronted with a set of values different from

those of the world—what the world sees as folly and weakness and humilia-
tion is recognized by those with the insight of faith as the wisdom and the
strength and the glory of the living God (1 Cor. 1:17–31). The passionate
concern of the Christian and the church for the affairs of the world in which
they live must be accompanied by a critical attitude toward its standards,
expectations, and hopes.

We must also note a temptation to which the church is prone in her
preaching and her reflection upon the Gospel message which has been
entrusted to her. That temptation is to treat Christianity as primarily a set of
interesting moral or religious *ideas* which can be conveyed by teaching or
argument. Unfortunately, people cannot be argued into the kingdom of God,
because what is entrusted to the church is not so much a set of ideas as the
living reality which lies behind them. It is the crucified and risen Christ who
stands at the center of the Christian faith—a *person*, not a set of *ideas*.

There is a story which is told (in a number of versions!) about the
philosopher Bertrand Russell. One day, he was walking down a road when
he suddenly stopped and said to himself, "the ontological argument is right
after all!" (In other words, that a certain philosophical proof for the existence
of God was valid.) On another day, somewhat earlier in human history, Saul
of Tarsus was walking down a different road when he encountered the risen
Christ. Russell had encountered an idea; Saul had met a person—and there
is all the difference in the world between the two experiences. That
encounter with the risen Christ certainly gave rise to a set of ideas—but lying
behind them as their source and origin was the risen Christ. We are often
told that faith is "caught, not taught," and the point which this statement
makes is simply that there is far more to Christianity than a set of ideas, rules,
or beliefs, and that assent to these isn't the same as the experience of encountering Jesus Christ. The cross reminds us that the central question we were
once forced to ask ourselves, and which we must subsequently force others
to ask, is not, "Do you believe *this* idea or *that* idea?" but, "Who do *you* say
Jesus Christ is?"

In this book we have been concerned with exploring the various ways of
understanding the full significance of Jesus Christ and his relevance for us.
There are many matters which have been discussed all too briefly, and an
embarrassingly large number of questions which haven't been discussed at
all! It is, however, hoped that this book will stimulate its readers to begin to
think further for themselves on the full relevance of Jesus Christ. But now
we must conclude.

The "word of the cross" (1 Cor. 1:18) is the story of a God who loved
his wayward children to the point where he stooped down from heaven to
meet them and suffered and died upon the cross to demonstrate the full
extent of his overwhelming compassion and care for those whom he loved.

God journeyed into the far country, enduring its suffering, pain, and agony, to meet us and embrace us. Like a great beacon, the cross stands as a sign summoning men to discover the "God and Father of our Lord Jesus Christ," the God of the cross, who counted us worthy of so great a sacrifice. Why should God love sinful man? Why did the cross have to happen? In the end, these questions are not terribly important. The important point is that the cross did happen, and that "the word of the cross" is that, astonishing and incredible though it may seem, God loves us and gives himself for us. Like a beacon on a hill, the cross stands as a symbol of hope in despair, life in the midst of death, light in the darkness. "When I am lifted up, I will draw all men to myself" (John 12:32). Then, as now, the cross is charged with the power, love, and compassion of God. It is the bread of life waiting to satisfy the hunger of men. In the words of Thomas à Kempis:

> There is no salvation of soul, no hope of eternal life, except in the cross. Therefore, take up the cross, and go forward into eternal life. Christ has gone there before you, bearing his cross. He died for you upon the cross, that you may bear your cross, and die on the cross with him. For if you die with him, you will live with him; if you share his sufferings, you will share his glory.

Through the cross, God meets us in our lostness and finds us, setting us on the road which leads home—a road on which Christ has gone before us, blazing a trail in which we may follow, knowing that by doing so, we pass from death to eternal life.

UNDERSTANDING
—the—
TRINITY

PREFACE

If you can understand it, it's not God!" (Augustine of Hippo). Augustine rightly pointed out that no human mind could ever fully comprehend God, but we must at least *try* to understand who God is and what he is like. The Christian understanding of God, culminating in the doctrine of the Trinity, is remarkably deep and rich, and the reader must be warned from the beginning that the best that this book can do is to scratch the surface. But it is written in the belief that it may be helpful to those who find difficulty in thinking about God, and especially the doctrine of the Trinity. I hope that it will cast at least a little light on these areas, and perhaps even stimulate the reader to think more about them. The reader who found my earlier book *Understanding Jesus* helpful may well find that the present book will further help him both in understanding his own faith and explaining it to others. If it manages to do either of these, it will have served its purpose well.

All too often, books dealing with the doctrine of the Trinity assume that their readers already know *why* they believe in the doctrine, so that all that needs to be done is to explain the doctrine. The present book is written in the belief that the best way of understanding what the doctrine of the Trinity is all about is to wrestle with why Christians believe in this doctrine in the first place—and shows how the idea of God as a Trinity is presupposed even at this stage. As the book progresses, it will become increasingly clear that the doctrine of the Trinity is simply the believer's final word about the God whom he knows, loves, and adores.

—ALISTER MCGRATH

1

God and His Critics

Every newspaper dreads publishing an obituary before its subject has actually died! The story is told of a famous London newspaper which published the obituary of a noted politician. Later that morning, the editor received an outraged phone call from the man himself. "I've just read my own obituary in your paper," he told the unfortunate editor. "I see," came the reply. "And may I ask where you are speaking from?" And we all know of Mark Twain's famous cable from Europe to the Associated Press: "The report of my death was an exaggeration."

In the 1960s a whole host of articles and books appeared, announcing that "God was dead." Looking back on those days, it rather looks as if this death was an event engineered by the media. The power of the media—both press and television—to change, rather than just report, what happens is legendary. For instance, a well-known newspaper editor is once alleged to have told his staff to get busy covering the war in Cuba. "But there isn't a war in Cuba!" his astonished staff replied. "Well," he riposted, "we can soon change that." Publicizing John Robinson's book *Honest to God* (S.C.M. 1963), the *Sunday Observer* declared, "Our image of God must go." Robinson's book was little more than a confused sketch of what he thought some modern theologians were saying—but by the time the *Observer* had finished with it, the very existence of Christianity seemed overnight to depend upon it. A similar situation developed in the United States. *Time Magazine*, soon to be followed by *The New Yorker* and the *New York Times*, looking for a suitable headline to a report in its religion section on the ideas of a few angry young theologians, reached for the nearest cliché and declared the existence of the "death of God" school. The curious American public were treated to intense, somber discussion of the course theology would take "after the death of God."

These reports of the death of God, however, turned out to be a little premature. The "death" was, in fact, something of a nonevent, and the whole "death of God" debate is now generally regarded as telling us much more about North American and European society in the 1960s than about God. "God is dead"—the slogan so familiar to those who lived in the 1960s—really means "I don't find God a personal reality anymore," or "the society in which I live doesn't need God anymore." But if this is the criterion which determines whether God is "dead" or not, it is obvious from the expansion of Christianity since then that God is very much alive. The talk about "a world come of age" which doesn't need God anymore, seems strange and out of place in the sober realism of today, so different from the optimism of the 1960s. Similarly, we hear much from the "death of God" school about the inability of "modern man" to make sense of the word "God." But just who is this "modern man?" All too often he seems to be some Oxford don pontificating over a glass of port in his senior common room about the meaninglessness of words—someone who has never experienced God at first-hand, but just reads about him at second-hand in books. It is remarkably difficult for anyone who has first-hand experience of the living God to think of him as being "dead."

God obstinately refuses to show any signs of *rigor mortis*. There is just no way that the church can be described as finding itself stuck with the corpse of God on its hands: Indeed, the resurgence and growth of faith throughout the worldwide church points to his vitality. God is *alive*. God's obituary has been frequently penned since the dawn of the Enlightenment of the eighteenth century by those who believed that they had finally killed him off. But just like the boy who cried "Wolf!" so often that everyone stopped listening to him, so we need to be more than a little skeptical about these declarations of God's demise. "What—is God dead *again*?" we might well ask. In reply we are assured that God is *really* dead this time around—that is, until the next time. The impression given is that God is in some sort of coma, so that it's just a matter of time before he dies—but the reality is that God gives every indication of being very much alive. In fact, the indications are that the obituary of the "death of God" school has already been written and published, while a far from dead God continues to excite and arouse a new generation of believers. "God is dead" is dead.

What do we mean when we talk about "God" anyway? There is a tendency on the part of many—especially those of a more philosophical inclination—to talk about God as if he was some sort of *concept*. But it is much more accurate to think of God as someone we *experience* or *encounter*. God isn't an idea we can kick about in seminar rooms—he is a living reality who enters into our experience and transforms it. Our experience of God is something which we talk about with others, and our encounter with him is something which we can try to put into words, but behind our ideas and words lies the greater reality of God himself. A visitor to the Taj Mahal may try and describe what he saw, putting it into words; however, what is important to him is not so much the words he uses but what he is trying to describe in those words. Let's develop this point a little.

Suppose you were with Napoleon Bonaparte as he began his triumphant Hundred Days in France, after escaping from exile in Elba. From all the accounts we possess of that remarkable period in modern French history, it is clear that Napoleon exercised a remarkable influence over all whom he encountered. It is probable that he would have made an equally deep impression upon you. You then try to put that experience, that encounter, into words, and—like so many biographers—find yourself constantly unable to express fully the greatness of that person. Although you try, you are always painfully aware that you are unable to describe adequately your experience of the personal reality of Napoleon. Words can neither capture nor convey your experience in a complete and satisfactory way. But let us suppose you then meet someone else who had also been with Napoleon during those eventful Hundred Days. Now, suddenly, you are able to share a common experience. No longer do you need to describe it to each other, because you both share the experience of the encounter with this individual. You can develop what you already have, swapping stories about what happened and helping each other further to understand what went on at the time. Now words can *recapture* that experience—an experience they couldn't really *capture* in the first place.

It's the same with all the great experiences of life—the experiences that really matter, that change people. You can share them with others, but it is very difficult to describe them. I remember once asking an older friend what it was like living in London during the blitz in the Second World War. After several attempts to describe what it was like, he gave up, saying, "It's no use—unless you actually lived through it, you can't understand what it was like." Encountering and experiencing God is exactly like this: It is something exceptionally difficult to describe, but it is something which is very easy to share with someone who has already had that experience. It is for this reason that talking about God is so difficult. Christians find it difficult to describe their experience of God to their non-Christian friends simply because there is no point of contact, no common ground, on which they can build.

Many of us have been subjected to what is probably one of the most subtle of modern tortures—having to listen to someone describe their holiday experiences, or look at somebody else's vacation photographs. It's just one of those things that you have to put up with if you don't want to spoil your friendship. And so you listen to them as they ramble on at great length about the Tower of London, or show a color transparency of the Great Pyramid: "Sorry it's out of focus—you can just see me behind that camel there." There is no point of contact between you and your friends, and you find yourself becoming increasingly bored. But then the situation suddenly changes: They start talking about the Oxford colleges—and you were there as a student. As you realize that you share a common experience or encounter, that you have something in common, the situation is transformed.

Again, it's like being at a party and finding yourself trapped with someone and having to talk to them. You've never met them before, and after a few minutes you rather wish it had stayed that way. The conversation falters somewhat as you each try to think of something to talk about. Then you discover that you both know the same person well—and suddenly conversation becomes a lot easier. Each of you may see him in a different light, but it's the same person you're both talking about. What the other says ties in with what you already know about that person, and may even help you understand or know him better.

And so it is with God. When Christians talk about God, they're not discussing an idea or a concept, but an encounter, an experience, which they share. It's like talking about a friend they have in common. Even though they may perceive God in slightly different ways, there's no doubt that they're talking about the same person, the same experience, the same encounter—and what one says may help someone else gain a deeper understanding of what God is like.

Perhaps we ought to clear up a possible misunderstanding at this point. When we talk about "experiencing God," we're not saying that our present experience—whatever that may be like—*is* God. What we are saying is that it is possible to experience God, not that God is to be identified with our experiences. Liberal theology has a tendency not merely to *discover* but also to *define* God in terms of present experience. Thus the nineteenth-century theologian Schleiermacher spoke of God as the origin of a "feeling of absolute dependence," while the noted American liberal Paul Tillich referred to God as "the experience of the unconditioned." Recently a New York theologian suggested that his experience of an "energy that has no name" on stepping out of his bath was an experience of God (rather than of the undoubtedly high quality of New York City water).

How can—and how dare—this theologian identify God with his experience on getting out of his bath? In saying that, he and others make the existence of God virtually dependent upon present experience and private judgment. And when such liberal theologians fail to experience such "energy that has no name" on getting out of their bath, they start writing about the "death of God" or the "experience of the absence of God," when what they really ought to be writing about is the total inadequacy of liberal thinking about who God is and what he is like! For God's existence is prior to and independent of our experience of him. Psalm 42 is a deeply moving account of the psalmist's conviction that God *is there*, even though he does not *experience him as present* here and now. Scripture affirms that God encounters us and we experience that encounter, but not that our everyday experience defines what God is like. Our experience of encountering God is not a private experience either, but one shared with others—their experience confirms and extends ours. An illustration will help bring this point out.

I remember once reading a book about the British scientific intelligence network during the Second World War. It was a rather entertaining book, and I enjoyed reading it. Even though I knew next to nothing about the scientific principles at stake, I could follow the book and learned a lot from it. At one point the author describes how he had to travel by air from one part of England to another to attend a special meeting—and I suddenly began to read the book more carefully, for I realized that I knew the pilot of the plane. After the war he had taken up a university post at Oxford, and I knew him as a delightful but slightly scatterbrained academic. The author described several of the crazy things this pilot did, and I can remember thinking, "He's *still* just like that!" Two points stood out for me. First, the book suddenly became more interesting because it was talking about someone I knew. Second, what was said both confirmed and extended my knowledge of that person: It was consistent with what I already knew, and told me more about him.

In many ways this little episode illustrates how Christians think about God. As they read the Bible they encounter someone they *know*, someone who stands out from its pages as a living reality in their experience. And what they read extends and develops their knowledge of that person. It is worth noting that Christians have always talked about *knowing* God—not just *knowing about*, but *knowing*. We may know a lot about someone, and yet not know him—just as we may know someone, but not know very much about him. I can open the *Encyclopedia Britannica* and find out an enormous amount about some important historical figure, like Napoleon Bonaparte or George Washington, but that doesn't mean that I know them. Many of us have had the experience of meeting someone at a party and getting to know them as a person, yet managing to find out very little about them. And it's surprising how little husbands really know about their wives, as I keep discovering.

We can identify two main ways in which we get to know a person. First, we may be told a lot about this person, so that when we meet him we already know exactly who he is and can develop the relationship from that point. Second, we may meet someone about whom we know nothing or very little, and discover that we can relate to them as a person—and as that relationship develops, so we discover more about them. And so it is with God. Many people know a lot about God—they may read their Bibles or talk to individuals who have had a deep and real experience of God. But they have yet to have this experience for themselves—they have yet to *encounter* God. Then, when that encounter occurs, they know exactly what has happened and who it is that they have encountered, and can take the relationship on from that point. "Knowing" means encountering and experiencing someone. Knowledge *about* God and knowledge *of* God are combined, as factual knowledge and encounter together make up our knowledge of and relationship with the person of God.

Alternatively, we may encounter God and yet not realize quite what has happened. When I was a child I can remember being told the story of Cinderella, who goes to Prince Charming's ball incognito. There, she and the prince fall in love. Although the prince doesn't know who she is, there is no contradiction involved: Falling in love doesn't depend upon knowing everything about someone, but upon the way in which you experience that person. And that is very often what happens with God. We encounter him, perhaps very suddenly, and our relationship with him begins. As is often the case, "faith is caught, not taught." After this initial encounter, we then start to learn more about God.

Let's go back to our Cinderella story for a moment. After the prince had fallen in love with her, despite her midnight flight from the ball, he was determined to find out more about her—such as who she really was, for a start. He needed a name to put to the girl he'd fallen in love with. This sort of experience is recounted in both the Old and New Testaments. Someone experiences something, encounters someone and then realizes that this is none other than God himself. Thus Samuel hears the call of the Lord, but doesn't realize what it is (1 Sam. 3:1–18). He has to be told that this is the Lord who has spoken to him (1 Sam. 3:8–10). To take another famous example, Saul of Tarsus has a remarkable experience on the road to Damascus (Acts 9:1–6), but has to be told who it is that had met him on that road: "I am Jesus, whom you are persecuting" (Acts 9:5). Many people have had the experience of encountering someone or something which they know is real in their personal experience, yet need to be told that this is none other than the living God. And then they start to find out more about him.

This point needs to be remembered in relation to the endless—and remarkably unproductive—arguments about whether the existence of God can be proved. Like a rather tedious game of chess, some of these arguments usually end in a permanent stalemate. Anyhow, it's important to realize that there's a difference between constructing a totally watertight argument for the existence of God and being convinced that God exists. Many of the world's greatest philosophers think that God's existence can be proved without any real difficulty, but ultimately God's existence doesn't depend upon these arguments. Being convinced that God exists may come about through a variety of factors—such as personal religious experience, reading scripture, or reflection upon the resurrection—of which rational argument is only one.

In the end, however, the Christian's faith in God doesn't depend upon any argument but upon an experience. This is not to say that no reasons for the existence of God may be given, of course. It is simply to point out that a lot of people have the idea you have to prove that God exists before you can start taking him seriously, or experience or encounter him. As most of these arguments about whether God exists or not often end in this permanent stalemate, both the atheist and the Christian alike take their positions as a matter of faith. It is worth emphasizing this point, because it is too often overlooked. The atheist believes that there is no God, but his position is a matter of faith rather than fact. He cannot prove beyond all reasonable doubt that God does not exist, just as the Christian cannot prove with total conviction that God does exist: Both are positions of faith. Any philosophy of life which is based upon the belief that there is no God (such as Marxism in its many forms) is as much a matter of faith as Christianity itself.

We could take this point a little further. As we shall see later, one of the reasons why Christians believe in God is their conviction that he has revealed himself, supremely in Jesus Christ. This ground of faith in God is in addition to any argument which may possibly prove God's existence. But the atheist's position is based solely upon such arguments—after all, if there is no God, the possibility of this nonexistent God actively revealing his nonexistence is somewhat remote. Atheism is, in fact, no more scientific than Christian faith, despite the attempts of atheists to convince us otherwise. Both atheism and Christianity are, then, matters of faith—whereas agnosticism is just a matter of indifference.

A number of arguments have been used by atheists in the present century to attempt to discredit Christianity. None of them is particularly convincing, although some are quite important in terms of their influence. In the following pages we shall examine two of the main arguments for atheism currently in fashion.

1. God Is a Projection of Human Ideals and Desires

This idea is particularly associated with the early nineteenth-century thinker Ludwig Feuerbach, who is known to have influenced Karl Marx. According to Feuerbach, "God" is basically nothing more than the projection of human ideals and desires onto an imaginary plane. In other words, we "project" our desire for eternal life, meaning, love and so forth *ad infinitum*, and call the imaginary result "God." God doesn't really exist—but we do. To use the technical Hegelian language which Feuerbach employs to develop this theme: "God" is the *objectification* of our own desires and longings. Thus whereas orthodox Christianity has always argued that "God is love" (1 John 4:8), Feuerbach argues that "love is God," meaning that the human ideal of love is objectified to give the idea of God.

Developing these ideas, Feuerbach argues that atheism is the only way of liberating human beings from their delusion. If only we would realize that there is no God, we could recognize that it is we ourselves who are God— because it is our ideals and desires which we mistakenly think of as God. For this reason, Feuerbach argues that atheism is the true basis of humanism. In order to value humanity properly, it is necessary to deny the existence of God.

This argument was remarkably influential in some circles in the nineteenth and twentieth centuries. For instance, Sigmund Freud's dismissal of religion as some sort of "wish fulfilment" is simply a psychological adaptation of Feuerbach's ideas. However, it is clear that there are certain outstanding difficulties with this view, the most obvious being: How can Feuerbach *prove* that his account of how we think of God is right? Basically, Feuerbach is arguing that we invent God because we need him. But this is just a hypothesis, a suggestion, which—by its very nature—cannot be proved. The suggestion that "God exists because Christians want him to" is just as logically plausible as the suggestion that "God doesn't exist because atheists don't want him to." This is no *proof* that God doesn't exist, it is simply an *assertion* that he doesn't.

A second difficulty to be noted is that Feuerbach's argument for atheism seems to rest on a rather elementary logical error. Feuerbach's argument, as has often been observed, runs like this:

1. Nothing exists, or needs to exist, just because we want it to exist.
2. We want God to exist.
3. Therefore God doesn't exist.

The conclusion just doesn't follow from the premises—it is an excellent example of a *non sequitur*. Things don't exist just because we want them to—but from the fact that we *do* desire their existence, it hardly follows that they *don't* exist! The correct conclusion is simply that God cannot be proved to exist just because we want him to exist.

Furthermore, it is absurdly simplistic to think that the existence of God can be regarded simply as a consolation in life, something which makes things easier for us to bear. Time and time again, scripture represents God as making considerable demands of us, even the surrender of our lives. The historical fact that there have been so many Christian martyrs who knew that God was calling them to lay down their lives for him, should alert us to the naïvety of this argument. This God isn't the sort of sugar-coated God we might like to dream up. As we saw a moment ago, the same faulty logic can lead to the following argument:

1. Nothing does not exist, nor needs not to exist, just because we don't want it to exist.
2. Atheists don't want God to exist.
3. Therefore God exists.

Wishful thinking is hardly the most reliable guide on the basis of which to decide whether God exists or not.

Similarly, Freud's version of the argument simply adds psychological theory to the "projection theory" which he uncritically accepted as correct.

Yet, like Feuerbach, all that Freud succeeds in doing is establishing as a hypothesis the suggestion that religion is an illusion based upon neurosis or immaturity—and proof for this hypothesis is wanting. According to Freud, religious ideas are the fulfillment of the oldest, strongest, and most power-ful wishes of humanity—but that doesn't mean that religion is a delusion. Simply because we want something to exist, we can hardly conclude that it doesn't exist. And here, of course, Christian theology has a major insight to bear: We are created in the image of God (Gen. 1:26–27), so that some sort of correspondence between our wishes and reality in relation to God *is to be expected*. Freud, of course, had no time for what Christianity had to say on the matter: Historically, his own atheism was well established before he developed his psychological theory of religion to support it. It wasn't as if he gave up Christianity because of his psychology—rather, he shaped his psy-chology to buttress his rejection of Christianity. But logic and theology alike allow the Christian to treat his dismissal of God with exactly the same lack of respect which he himself earlier showed for Christianity.

Finally, a more pragmatic point may be made. Feuerbach was writing in the early nineteenth century at a time when optimism in human nature and potential was considerable. The development of evolutionary theory later that century heightened this optimism. For Feuerbach, man is his own God, and atheism provides a means by which he may be liberated from the false God of Christianity. But Feuerbach did not foresee the horrors of the First World War, of Auschwitz, of human atrocities against fellow humans on a larger scale and with an intensity hitherto undreamed of. More than a cen-tury of experience with his man-turned-God demonstrates that he is simply not capable of the responsibilities which being God lays upon him. Having "liberated" ourselves from one God, we find ourselves enslaved to another lesser God of much more questionable moral character. This pragmatic point confirms the theoretical weakness of Feuerbach's atheism by drawing atten-tion to its practical consequences.

What remains of this atheist argument for the nonexistence of God? Not much. Christians can hardly be expected to give up their faith in God just because of an unproven and unprovable suggestion, which ultimately rests upon an elementary logical error, and ignores Christian insights into both God and ourselves. The atheist argument is no proof for the nonexis-tence of God: Like arguments for the existence of God, it is at best merely suggestive (how suggestive being a matter for some debate) and most emphatically not conclusive. Not to believe in God on the basis of this argu-ment requires a leap of faith at least as great as that involved in believing that he does exist through the argument from design. In fact, Feuerbach's real sig-nificance lies in the influence he had upon the atheism of Karl Marx, to which we now turn.

2. God Is the Opiate of the Masses, Serving the Vested Interests of Society

Karl Marx's critique of Christianity has had a powerful influence upon both secular and Christian Western thought, but has not itself been subjected to the rigorous criticism that it so obviously needs. Earlier, we noted Feuerbach's idea that "god" was the projection of our desires and ideals. Marx develops a slightly different but clearly related idea: Our religious ideas, such as God, result from our social and economic situation. In other words, it is the nature of society itself—its social conditions and the economic system which supports it—which governs our thinking about God and so forth.

For Marx, Western European society was the product of the capitalist economic system. This system, particularly the privatization of property, deprived individuals of their proper social rights—it *alienated* them, to use Marx's key term. That alienation has a number of consequences, according to Marx, and one of them is religious belief in God. Faith in God is thus one result of unjust social conditions—and if those conditions are changed, faith in God can, in principle, be eliminated. Underlying Marx's communist vision is a fundamentalist atheism—the critical and dogmatic assertion that the coming revolution will eliminate religious belief along with unjust social conditions.

Rejecting the view that there is anything inherently wrong with humanity that causes self-centeredness or "egoism," to use Marx's term, Marx argues that it is capitalism which is the source of humanity's problems. Eliminate capitalism, and human alienation, and hence religion, is eliminated with it. Through socioeconomic engineering, the human dilemma may be overcome. At this point, it is worth noticing how Marx locates the problem at the social rather than the individual level—it is society which must be changed if the individual is to be liberated.

Marx thus regards Christianity as the "opium of the people": A means of alleviating the social misery of the oppressed masses (and hence delaying the inevitable revolution) which is a direct result of their social and economic conditions. Once those socioeconomic conditions are altered through the communist revolution, there will no longer be any need for Christianity: It will become redundant.

However, Marx never shows any interest in Christianity as such—he is simply concerned with the social function of religion, whether it is Judaism or Christianity. At no point do we find Marx attempting to criticize any specific doctrines of Christianity or its claims to truth in general: His criticism is based upon his understanding of religion as at best a symptom of human alienation, and at worst a way in which the status quo can be maintained by oppression. Thus Marx's hostility to Christianity occasionally appears to derive from his observation of the behavior of certain pastors whom he regarded as oppressing the masses, rather than any attempt to come to terms with what Christianity itself has to say.

Marx's criticisms of Christianity never penetrate, or even make the slightest attempt to penetrate, to the essence of the Christian faith. Religion is at best useless and at worst positively harmful, Marx asserts ("argues" is hardly the right word)—and as Christianity is a religion, these criticisms apply to it. We find no attempt to wrestle with the question of the identity of Jesus Christ, or the relevance of the cross and resurrection to the world. Christianity is to be rejected because it stands in the way of Marx's vision of the communist society. It delays the inevitable revolution. For Marx, socialism was an historical inevitability, therefore the elimination of Christianity was equally inevitable—but, as with so many early nineteenth-century theories, the gulf between theory and reality proved to be unbridgeable. The passage of time causes the late twentieth-century reader to have the most serious doubts concerning the reliability of Marx's social judgments, let alone the religious views he based upon them. The "historical inevitability of socialism" has been discredited by much recent social scientific research.

The view of Christianity as opium handed out to the masses by their masters to dull their awareness of their situation—paralleling the modern situation in which psychiatric patients are heavily sedated to prevent them from becoming troublesome in the hospital—was developed by Lenin (Vladimir Ilyich Ulyanov). Lenin's absurdly hostile attitude to Christianity as a "spiritual intoxicant" is based on his conviction that Christianity deceives workers and inhibits the communist revolution. Only by eliminating Christianity and establishing an atheist state may communism be achieved.

We now have enough information about the Marxist critique of Christianity to indicate its obvious weaknesses. First, it is clear that Marx does not directly criticize the specific doctrines of Christianity, such as the existence of God, or the Christian understanding of what God is like. Religion in general, and Christianity in particular, is to be criticized on account of its social functions. The existence of God is not disproved—it is simply declared to be an obstacle to the achievement of Marx's political and economic vision. The plausibility of that vision is itself seriously called into question by the simple fact that Marx's vision of a religionless society is increasingly being recognized as utopian. The fundamental dogma that religion is the consequence of social alienation is seriously undermined by the all-too-obvious fact that religion is nowhere in decline in communist societies. In an effort to make theory and reality converge, forcible suppression of Christianity has been attempted within such societies, but is increasingly being recognized as counterproductive. Even in these societies, human beings remain the fundamentally sinful human beings they always have been and always will be, with human self-interest proving totally resistant to the social cures offered.

Marxism is an example of the countless theories which try to account for the tragic history and situation of humanity in terms of the influence of some external factor—social or economic conditions, poor education, or sexual repression, to give some obvious examples. But is it not the reality that there is some fatal flaw within human nature itself; that there is something inherently wrong with us, which no amount of tampering with external matters will alter? Marxism, like so many other failed remedies of the past for the human predicament, confuses causes and effects, leaving the real source of human misery untouched—and the real source of that misery lies within us, as human beings. It is here that Christianity addresses a fundamental challenge to Marxism, arguing that it is the regeneration and renewal of humanity which is needed if the *real* source of alienation is to be dealt with at its root. Like an amateur physician, Marxism deals with a symptom, thinking it is the disease itself.

What remains of the Marxist criticism of Christianity? Perhaps the important insight that all too often the church has uncritically supported the ruling classes, ignoring its responsibilities to the poor and oppressed. That, however, remains a criticism of how Christianity is applied, rather than of Christianity itself. The church needs to be challenged, both from inside and outside its bounds, to demonstrate that it has social and ethical relevance and does not merely buttress those who exercise power. Marx, however, consistently demonstrated the most superficial understanding of Christianity throughout his life, criticizing Christianity on account of its social role rather than its specific beliefs. The nonexistence of God is simply treated as an axiom, a self-evident proposition, by Marx, and is nowhere backed up by arguments which can be thought of as proofs. For Marx, God does not exist in a socialist society, and does not need to exist. But, as history has shown, no amount of socioeconomic engineering has achieved the voluntary and self-evident atheism Marx presupposes. It is all too obvious that God will outlive his morticians, Freudian and Marxist alike.

God, then, has taken something of a battering in the last two centuries or so. But, in the words of William Cullen Bryant: "Truth crushed to earth will rise again." The alleged "proofs" of the nonexistence of God turn out to be like spiders' webs which collapse when touched, despite looking so attractive and permanent in the early morning mist. For the Christian, the living God is present and active in his world, quite irrespective of whether his existence is recognized or denied. In the end, the Christian doesn't believe in God because someone has argued him into believing that he's there, but because he has experienced, has encountered, the reality of the living God. In the following chapter, we're going to develop this point further.

2

Encountering God

Most people approach Christianity with preconceptions which prevent them from realizing what it's all about in the first place. One of these preconceptions is that you have to believe in God already before Christianity makes any sort of sense. Underlying this is the idea that Christianity basically concerns knowledge about God: Given that he exists, we can say this and that about him. But all that this leads to is a conception of God, an idea about him. When reading history books (as almost all of us are forced to do at some stage in our lives!) we can begin with the assumption that Admiral Nelson or George Washington or Napoleon Bonaparte existed, and go on to find out more about them. And much the same idea persists about Christianity: You start from the assumption that God exists, and then go on to find out something about him by reading the appropriate textbooks, such as the Bible.

What sort of arguments might be advanced to suggest that the assumption that God exists is reasonable? Before we even ask this question, however, it is worth pointing out that for many people, this whole business is a waste of time. God is there, and that's all there is to it. He is experienced as being present and real. Why bother trying to prove that God is there when we already know this from our experience of him? After all, no scriptural writer bothers to give proof of God's existence, of which they were all only too aware. These points must be conceded. But in reply it may be pointed out that these arguments are not directed to those who already know and experience God as a personal reality, but to those who are finding difficulty with the idea of God in the first place. To some, they are helpful starting-points in their thinking about God, and they are useful for that very reason. In what follows, we shall briefly outline three lines of reasoning which point to the existence of God. We shall call these "the argument from morality," "the argument from rationality," and "the argument from desire."

1. The Argument from Morality

All of us make moral judgments at times. Even if we find moral philosophy hopelessly bewildering, there are times when we are forced to make judgments about what is right and what is wrong. When the first photographs of what had happened at the concentration camp at Auschwitz were released to an unsuspecting world, most people were sincerely horrified and outraged at what had taken place. They just knew it was wrong intuitively, without the need for any moral guidelines or arguments. But where do these intuitive moral ideas come from? And are they valid, of any significance, to understanding what is right and what is wrong? Or are they simply instincts from the distant past, or inhibitions which arise from society—both of which, when recognized for what they are, may be overcome? After all, we overcome other inhibitions when they get in the way of what we want to do.

However, the simple fact is that we don't regard the executioners of Auschwitz as having overcome inhibitions or as having liberated themselves from the primitive forces of instinct—we believe, quite forcefully, that they did something which is *wrong*, something which quite definitely ought not to have been done. Similarly, some would argue that "right" means "in accord with the laws of the land." Yet all of us know only too well that laws can be unjust, can be wrong. The executioners of Auschwitz were, after all, acting legally in what they did—yet that hardly makes what they did "right." Again, some would argue that the basis of morality is "the greatest good of the greatest number." And the executioners of Auschwitz would agree: They were simply liquidating minority groups such as the Jews in order that the well-being of the majority would be enhanced. And so we could go on through the various "naturalist" explanations of morality. But in the end they fail to satisfy us because they all carry with them the suggestion that morality is arbitrary, something which humans have invented.

Deeply embedded in human nature are ideas of "right" and "wrong" which cannot be explained away in this manner. It is almost as if there are certain definite ideas about the way in which we ought and ought not to behave built into human nature. But where do they come from? What lies behind these natural ideas of "right" and "wrong?" Perhaps it is nothing— simply the blind and irrational forces of evolution. In which case morality is the law of the jungle, the instinct for survival, and it is robbed of its force. In this view, "right" and "wrong" are simply biological behavior patterns. But the picture is actually more complex than this. Knowing what is right, we often do what is wrong. All of us, when we attempt to live up to our moral ideals (wherever these ideals come from in the first place), find ourselves unable to do so. We *recognize* them, but cannot *actualize* them. There seems to be something about human nature which allows us to recognize what is right, and yet at the same time causes us to fail to do it.

The ability of the Christian understanding of both God and human nature to explain these observations will be obvious. God is the ground and basis of the moral order, the one who created human beings in his own image (Gen. 1:26–27). We should therefore expect some traces of the mind of God to remain stamped upon us as part of our nature. Yet, through sin, our ability to live up to the moral law is compromised (Rom. 7:15–25 is worth reading at this point). It is through the realization that we know what is right, and yet are unable to achieve it, that we begin to understand the need for redemption. The coherence of the Christian understanding of God and human nature—which is not based upon such arguments in the first place—is remarkable.

2. The Argument from Rationality

In assessing whether God exists or not, we are obliged to use our minds, to use reason. This is the tool we regard as appropriate for the task in hand. The reliability of reason to determine whether God exists or not is an inevitable assumption of any argument about whether God exists or not. But this assumption actually implies far more than might at first be thought. Let us suppose that you program a computer to analyze various pieces of data, and arrive at a conclusion—perhaps to determine the estimated population growth of a country from recent census returns. The accuracy of the relation between the data and the conclusion is determined totally by the way in which you program the computer. Program the computer at random, and the results are unreliable, to say the least. Confidence in the ability of the computer to handle data is ultimately confidence in the computer program, and hence the programmer. If an army of monkeys were to be given access to personal computers, there is a genuine possibility (however slight!) that, given enough time and enough monkeys, one of them would write a program which could handle such data reliably. But it is still very improbable. A good program results from a good programmer.

In turning to deal with the human mind, we are faced with a similar situation. Without pressing the similarity between the mind and a computer too far, it will be obvious that we are faced with a comparable situation—the ability to handle data in order to reach a conclusion. But what is the basis of our trust in reason to do this? It is obvious that all knowledge depends upon the validity of our reasoning process, and any elements of irrationality at any stage in that process of reasoning could potentially invalidate it. It is possible that human reason came into existence by chance, perhaps through the blind forces of evolution, in much the same way as any army of monkeys might write a computer program. Alternatively, we might suggest that underlying *our* reason is *somebody else's* reason, in much the same way as human intelligence lies behind a good computer program. Earlier, we noticed how the Christian understanding of human nature assumed a direct continuity between God and ourselves—and what is true in the field of morality is also true in the field of rationality. Human rationality derives from the divine rationality, and its ability to understand nature is ultimately a reflection of the fact that both were created by the same rational God.

Once more, it is necessary to point out that this doesn't prove that God exists. It simply points out that there is a coherent Christian understanding of the basis of rationality which is perfectly adequate to deal with what we know by experience. It is suggestive, not conclusive.

3. The Argument from Desire

Most of us are aware of experiences of longing, of desire, for something which requires satisfaction. Hunger is an experience which we all know, and it corresponds to a physiological need within us and something which is objective outside us (food). The feeling of thirst is a parallel case: Something natural within us points to a need which can be met by the appropriate external substance (water). A similar point could be made in relation to sexual desire. All these longings within us correspond to a real human need which may satisfy them. It reflects our physiological makeup, the way we are.

A further deep longing within most individuals is well known, but difficult to put into words. Perhaps its most eloquent analysis may be found in the writings of C. S. Lewis, especially his famous sermon "The Weight of Glory." It is a deep longing for something which no finite object can ever satisfy: A spiritual restlessness, a desire for immortality, a search for meaning—we could extend this list at great length. The basic feeling is, however, known to most of us, even if we find it difficult to describe. It is a sense of spiritual emptiness, an awareness that physical things cannot satisfy part of our nature. This feeling is well known to many, and existentialist philosophers have glorified it with the rather clumsy label "thrown-out-ness." It is as if we are all in a "distant country" (Luke 15:13), cut off from a joy which we have never really known, yet which we somehow seem to remember. It is like the echo of a tune which we have never really heard, or news from a country which we have never visited yet which we feel that we somehow already know. But what does this longing point to?

It is, of course, possible to argue that it points to nothing, being simply a by-product of evolution. It might be pointed out in reply that this would be to dismiss or invalidate an alarming number of human emotions. The Christian would say that this deep-felt longing within human nature is a consequence of the way we are made. We are created, as we have seen, in the image of God, with an in-built capacity to relate to God; and these spiritual longings within us point to the absence of that relationship. As Pascal put it, "There is a God-shaped gap within us"—a gap which really exists and which nothing except God himself can fill. Just as hunger points to the need for food, so these spiritual longings point to the need for God. The full force of this point is obvious to Christians, who find it virtually impossible to think of life without God. Without God, there would be an emptiness, a void, in human existence of such magnitude that life would hardly seem worth living. But even for the non-Christian, the force of this point should be clear. Unless we are to invalidate our experiences, we must ask what this sense of spiritual emptiness means. Perhaps it means nothing and is insignificant; perhaps it is pointing toward a real need which can be met by none other than the living God; perhaps it is pointing towards our spiritual homeland, the distant country, to which we are being called home.

At this point, it is worth noting how often scripture compares experiencing God with satisfying physical needs. "Taste and see that the Lord is good," says the Psalmist (Ps. 34:8). Jesus Christ is variously referred to as the "bread of life" or "the living water." "I am the bread of life. He who comes to me will never go hungry, and he who believes in me will never be thirsty" (John 6:35); "Whoever drinks the water I give him will never thirst" (John 4:14). The awareness of spiritual hunger and thirst, by analogy with physical hunger and thirst, raises the question of whether this hunger and thirst may be satisfied—and Christianity proclaims that they may indeed be more than satisfied through an encounter with the living God.

Once more, it is necessary to point out that such an argument is suggestive rather than conclusive. But here, as with the other two arguments, it is worth noticing how the Christian understanding of the relation of God and ourselves ties in perfectly with experience. Faith illuminates experience, and is in turn validated by experience. Christianity interprets our experiences in terms of the need to enter into a relationship with God, and proclaims that this relationship is a real possibility through the death and resurrection of Jesus Christ.

What is the relevance of arguments such as these, which suggest that God exists but do not prove it? Ultimately, the only meaningful proof is encounter with and experience of God as the reality toward which such considerations point. Let us illustrate this point by considering two similar situations, both concerning the heavens, one drawn from the New Testament and the other from the world of astronomy.

As even the most casual reader of the New Testament and practically everyone who sends or receives Christmas cards knows, shortly after his birth Jesus was visited by the wise men, the mysterious night visitors from the East (Matt. 2:1–12). (Actually, we don't know how many of them there were, even though the traditional number is three. What we do know is that they brought three gifts [Matt. 2:11], and we always assume that they brought one each!) What was it that brought them to Jesus? All too often the impression is given that the wise men, who were almost certainly the astronomers of their day, were led directly to Bethlehem by the appearance of the famous star, whereas what actually happened was rather different. They saw the star at its rising, which alerted them to the existence of a newborn king, and traveled to Jerusalem in order to be given more specific directions; and it was from Jerusalem that they were directed to Bethlehem. An event in the world of nature—the star—led them to begin the search for the Messiah, and took them part of the way to finding him. But for the final part of that search, they relied upon the great Old Testament prophecies as to where this individual would be born (Matt. 2:2–8). Scripture confirmed what nature suggested—that the newborn king was to be found in Bethlehem.

The parallel with arguments for the existence of God will be obvious. Like the star of Bethlehem, they point to something, but do not take us all the way; they indicate the existence of something, but do not disclose exactly what it is or where it may be found. The important thing is to go on from there, inquiring as to where God may be found. Like the wise men, we too are led to scripture if we are to find out more about this God and where he may be found. And, as Christianity has always insisted, God is most reliably to be found and known in precisely the same place in which those wise men first found him—in the person of Jesus Christ. Arguments for the existence of God, like the star of Bethlehem, can bring us part of the way to finding God, but for the final part of that journey we need guidance from those who already know where he may be found, or who have already found him. We shall return to this point shortly. Let us turn from the star of Bethlehem to another, more recent, event relating to our knowledge of the heavens.

In the year 1781, the English astronomer, William Herschel, caused considerable excitement by discovering the mysterious green planet, Uranus. Up to this point it had been generally assumed that the entire solar system was already known, and the discovery of this mysterious new member of the solar system called many of the traditional presuppositions about that system into question. By the year 1820, however, it was observed that this new planet behaved in an unusual way. Its orbit was not exactly what was expected. Several explanations were advanced to explain these perturbations to its orbit: Perhaps the planet Saturn was heavier than had generally been assumed, or perhaps there was a still unknown planet lying beyond Uranus which was distorting its orbit through gravitational attraction. It was far from clear exactly how the evidence was to be interpreted, but it was certainly highly suggestive.

In 1843, John Couch Adams at Cambridge and August Leverrier at Paris began to explore the hypothesis that there was a trans-Uranic planet. Although it had not been seen and recognized by anyone up to this point, they were able to work out roughly where this planet should be found in the night sky. In England and in Berlin, telescopes began to search the skies for this hypothetical planet—until the Berlin observatory finally reported its discovery. The new planet was named Neptune. In due course, it was found that perturbations to the orbit of this new planet suggested the existence of a planet lying still further from the sun, eventually leading to the discovery of Pluto in 1930.

The point we want to make is obvious. On the basis of data which suggested, but did not prove, the existence of a planet lying beyond Uranus, the search for this planet was undertaken with seriousness and commitment, eventually leading to its discovery. So it is with God. The evidence for his existence is real and highly suggestive, but not conclusive. The existence of God is one possible way of explaining the evidence of experience, but not the only way. Just as the trans-Uranic-planet hypothesis was only finally verified by taking it seriously, and looking for that planet where the evidence suggested it might be found, so the "God hypothesis" can be verified by taking it seriously and looking for him where Christianity has always suggested he may be found. And where is God to be found? Like the planet Neptune, in the night sky? Perhaps (see Pss. 8:3; 19:1). But the Christian points to the biblical record culminating in Jesus Christ, especially in his death and resurrection, as the supreme demonstration of the existence and character of God. It is here that Christianity has always insisted that God is most reliably disclosed and revealed: It is here that he may be found. To develop this point, let us consider how the biblical witness to God both confirms and extends any knowledge of God available from nature itself.

An example may help to make this point clearer. The idea that God is the creator of the world in which we live, including ourselves, is often argued by some philosophers to be obvious from nature itself. This theme is familiar to most readers of classical philosophical works. On the other hand, as Cicero pointed out in his *De natura deorum* ("On the nature of the gods"), the ideas of God which were obtained from nature were fragmentary and often inconsistent. There was a limit to what could be known about God from nature—for example, that he was the creator, and that he was good and wise. This point was developed further in the eighteenth century by Bishop Butler in his famous work *The Analogy of Religion*. Butler underscored the ambiguity of nature as a source of knowledge of God: After all, nature was littered with violence, waste, and carnage; "red in tooth and claw," and with the moral code "eat or be eaten," it was hardly the best place to look for God! If reliable knowledge of God is to be had, a more reliable source than nature is required.

At this point, the Christian will point out that scripture endorses these insights drawn from nature—for example, that God is the creator, and that he is good and wise—as well as developing them. There is a hymn by Isaac Watts which deserves to be known better than it is:

The heavens declare thy glory, Lord!
In every star thy wisdom shines;
But when our eyes behold thy word,
We read thy name in fairer lines.

The basic point being made is that the scriptural witness to God is consistent with and endorses what we already know, or think we know, by experience, and that it both states this more clearly and develops it further. Scripture establishes a reliable framework for thinking and talking about God, which goes far beyond the very modest knowledge of God which it is possible to derive from nature. And scripture constructs this framework around the central event to which it bears witness: the life, death, and resurrection of Jesus Christ.

The importance of the scriptural testimony in relation to any discussion of God which claims to be *Christian* cannot be overestimated. We need to be told what God is like—left to ourselves we would just end up with a bewildering and contradictory collection of ideas about what God might be like. Scripture authorizes us to talk about God in certain very definite ways: It lays down the framework for our discussion of God. As we shall see in later chapters, it is scripture which bears witness to God as he has revealed himself to us. Christians have always recognized that they are responding to God's revelation of himself, and not just inventing ideas about who God is and what he might be like. God's revelation of himself, culminating in the death and resurrection of Jesus Christ, is mediated to us through the scriptural testimony. And so it is scripture which is the primary source of Christian reflection on who God is and what he is like. As we have seen, the scriptural witness to God ties in with experience—but it goes far beyond it, adding important insights which otherwise we could not hope to have.

Thinking about God is difficult for many people because it seems terribly abstract. We can't see, hear, or touch God in the way that we can experience other objects around us. Often we feel that we need something more concrete, more tangible, on which to base our discussion of God. One of the most powerful insights which the Christian religion has to offer concerns the way in which we know about God in the first place. According to Christianity, the most reliable knowledge of God which we have in this life is to be found in the person of Jesus Christ. In *Understanding Jesus*, I spent some time exploring this very important insight, and we shall return to this point in later chapters. But the history of Jesus is also of importance in connection with the question of the existence of God. The resurrection of Jesus immediately forces us to ask: Who or what lay behind this remarkable event?

As we saw in *Understanding Jesus*, the first Christians were completely convinced that the resurrection did not merely demonstrate the existence of God, but represented God's endorsement of Jesus' mission. His words and deeds were, so to speak, stamped with the seal of divine approval through the resurrection. The resurrection overturned the judgment of the world—that Jesus was a failure—and established in its place the judgment of God upon all that Jesus said and did. The resurrection demonstrated that God endorsed and vindicated Jesus, whereas the world had thought God condemned him. Important though the resurrection is in answering the question of exactly who Jesus was, and why he is so important, we must realize that the resurrection is also of importance in relation to our knowledge of God. For the Christian, the existence of God is confirmed by the resurrection of Jesus Christ.

This point is also of relevance to those who find arguments about the existence of God hopelessly abstract. Instead of thinking about abstract ideas like morality or reason, we can start thinking about something very specific and very definite: Exactly what was it that happened on the first Easter Day? What was it that transformed the experience of the disciples? What was the meaning of the empty tomb? These are all historical questions, not abstract philosophical questions. The Christian answer is that God raised Jesus Christ from the dead. Alternative explanations seem so improbable that we are continually forced back to the Christian answer as the most satisfying. The reality of God is expressed in the transformation of the situation of Good Friday into the situation of Easter Day, in which death gave way to new life, despair to joy, and darkness to light. And in the same way the Gospel holds out the promise of the transformation of our own situation here and now. The same God who raised Jesus Christ from the dead makes himself available for us, promising to transform our death to new life, our despair to joy, our darkness to light. And the Christian experience of God is that he has done and still does precisely this to those who come to him.

These lines of argument, however, may suggest that the only way to become a Christian is to arrive at belief in the existence of God, and then go on to ask what extra facts Christianity has to add to this belief. In fact, this is not correct. To go back to our history book analogy, the Christian view of God is best compared to a historical figure who steps out of the pages of a history textbook and meets us right where we are. The idea that we have to discover who God is, and what he is like, is quite foreign to Christianity, which is based on the recognition that God has taken the initiative and come to meet us in history. What is offered to us is not just information about God, but the living God himself. This point is very important, and we shall explore it a little further before moving on to other matters.

Many people seem to think that a precondition for becoming a Christian is belief in God, and that Christianity just supplements this belief by adding one or two extra bits to this basic belief, such as ideas about how we should behave, and so on. In fact, most people seem to disregard or reject Christianity on the basis of what they think it ought to be about, rather than what Christianity actually has to say. But Christians don't think in this way. They don't think of themselves as *searching for God*—they think of themselves as *having been found by God*, waiting for the God who comes to them. Both the Old and the New Testaments speak of a God who seeks us out, who comes to meet us where we are and take us home with him. The Bible inverts the scheme many of us are used to working with—our search for God—and invites us to think instead of God's search for us. God comes to search for us, to meet us where we are, to make himself available for our acceptance or our rejection. It is this step which many find difficult to take, largely because they are still working with the idea of God as a concept, something which exists in the world of ideas. Christians, as I emphasize throughout this book, work with the idea of God as a person, some*one* (not some*thing*) who is able to take the initiative in making himself known to us and establishing a relationship with us.

To encounter God is to encounter a personal reality, not just to have an interesting (if unoriginal) idea. The idea of God needs to be supplemented by a personal encounter with the living God to which it points and bears witness. For some people the idea of God is an end in itself, whereas for the Christian it is one possible starting-point for the real objective—a personal relationship with the living and loving God. Thus Christian faith is not so much about *belief* in the *idea* of God, as *trust* in the *person* of God. Of course, it is obvious that we can't dispense with the idea of God—and nobody is suggesting for one moment that we could. The point we're trying to make is that the Christian experience of God is infinitely more rich and profound than a mere idea!

Let us take this one stage further. We can encounter a person of whose existence we were quite unaware up to that point. Every now and then, you come across a magazine article or news item about someone being reunited with a long-lost brother or sister of whose existence they were quite unaware. You may read about someone, such as the President of the United States, and then meet him—but all of us know that it is perfectly normal to meet someone whom we have never heard of before. After all, that's how many friendships develop. And so it is with God. It is not just possible, but positively routine, for individuals to meet God, to encounter him, even though they hadn't believed in him previously. Just as a new and hitherto unknown person may suddenly enter into our lives, so God is able to do exactly the same.

Encounter with God and belief in God's existence may come about simultaneously. It is part and parcel of the Christian experience of God that he acts in this way. It may be that their encounter with God is not recognized for what it really is—and the case of Samuel may be noted again (1 Sam. 13:1–10)—but there are remarkably few individuals who have not, at some time in their lives, felt something strange, something awesome, something disturbing, something inexplicable, at work within them, challenging their perceptions of reality and enlarging their mental horizons. This feeling, deeply embedded in human religious experience down the ages, was addressed by Paul in his famous sermon at the Areopagus in Athens (Acts 17:16–34). "Now what you worship as something unknown I am going to proclaim to you," he declared (Acts 17:23)—in other words, Christianity puts a name to this reality of which we are aware, and opens the way toward a full appreciation of the richness and profundity of the experience of God.

In this chapter, we have been exploring ways in which we come to a knowledge of God. The basic idea is that of a partial and imperfect awareness of the existence and nature of God from nature itself, which is confirmed, supplemented and developed through the scriptural witness, culminating in Jesus Christ. The word of God *was spoken* by the prophets, but the word of God *became incarnate* in Jesus Christ. The same God who spoke through the law and the prophets became like one of us, a mortal and frail human being, in order to speak to us directly. "In the past God spoke to our forefathers through the prophets at many times and in various ways, but in these last days he has spoken to us by his Son" (Heb. 1:1–2). Real knowledge of God is not just a list of points about God, but a real and redeeming encounter with the living God, in which God—so to speak—steps out of the pages of scripture to confront us and challenge us with his presence.

When I was doing research in molecular biology some time ago, there was considerable excitement about the development of new techniques which allowed us to examine animal or plant cells without disturbing them in any way. These techniques were known as "noninvasive", because they didn't involve disturbing or intruding upon the system being studied. And most people like to work with a "noninvasive" concept of God—a God who doesn't disturb us or affect us in any way at all. God is treated like a book on a shelf, which may be lifted down when needed, and ignored the rest of the time. John Owen's witty lines, written in the seventeenth century, are still as relevant as ever:

> God and the doctor we alike adore,
> But only when in danger, not before;
> The danger o'er, both are alike requited,
> God is forgotten, and the doctor slighted!

Nobody can be argued into the kingdom of God, for the very reason that Christianity does not concern ideas but a living reality. To persuade someone that God exists is not necessarily to make him a Christian, but for someone to encounter the living God and respond to him—now that is something very different. After all, I could persuade a male friend of mine that a certain female exists—but there is all the difference in the world between that and my friend meeting this girl, discovering that they can relate to each other, and falling in love. Christianity is not like some sort of religious education lesson in which facts are pumped into our heads; rather it is like a love affair—something powerful, challenging, and possessing real meaning to those involved. And it is this knowledge of God to which the Christian faith bears witness. It isn't a "knowledge" for which a relatively high IQ and a university degree are required, but a personal knowledge of God which lies within the grasp of everyone. It is a knowledge which involves our hearts, not just our heads. It is a knowledge which arises through meeting someone, through encountering the living God, not through reading dry and dusty textbooks.

This point is so important that one final illustration will be given. All of us admire someone greatly—it may be an historical figure from the past or someone who is still alive. Suppose you identify one person like this. You could find out a lot about him. You could study all the right books and magazine articles, and listen to all the right TV and radio programs, and you'd soon know a lot about that person. My approach to Martin Luther, one of my own favorite people, is rather similar. I've read just about everything he wrote, and even more that has been written about him. But Luther is a dead figure from the past, someone whom I will never know as a person, someone with whom I could never establish a personal friendship. It may be the same with the person you're thinking of as well. That person remains someone distant, someone you know a lot about but don't know personally.

Now, imagine there's a knock at your front door, and you discover that the person you admire so much is there, asking to be let in so that he or she can meet you and get to know you. Can you see that there's all the difference in the world between this situation and knowing about the person from books? Now you're meeting a living reality, where before you were just learning facts. You come to know that person in a new, a qualitatively different, way. And so it is with the Christian experience of God. There is a quantum leap between these two ways of knowing someone. If you must, you can learn all about God from books. But the Christian experience of God is that he's knocking at the door of your life, asking to be let in so that he can get to know you and relate to you (Rev. 3:20–22). He isn't breaking the door down with a sledge-hammer, but gives you the privilege of saying no. Real knowledge of God comes about through opening that door and letting him in, and in no other way. Afterwards you read about him in a new light and a new way, because now you can relate to him in a completely different way.

Here, then, is no shallow and superficial textbook knowledge of God, but something vital and dynamic, something exciting, something which gives meaning to life. This is no dead letter, but a living reality. To know God is to encounter the living and loving God, and really to live and really to love as a result. Christianity is about a meeting which becomes a love affair between us and the living God who comes in search of us and takes the initiative in meeting us. The full extent of God's love for us is revealed in the cross of Jesus Christ (John 3:16; Rom. 5:8). To be a Christian is to take God's proffered hand and go forward into eternal life, not quite knowing what this will involve, but being certain that, wherever we go and whatever happens as a result, he will never let us go.

3

Thinking about God

The nineteenth-century poet Tennyson is reported to have said that most Englishmen pictured God as an enormous clergyman with a long beard. Whether this is a helpful way of thinking about God is open to question, but it does draw attention to the fact that we need to visualize God in some sort of way. How often have we been reminded that a picture is worth a thousand words? Some theologians prefer to talk about God in terms of abstractions, often giving the impression that this is the only respectable way for intelligent human beings to think about God. Many of us have had to wade our way through their somewhat turgid discussions of "the ground of our being," "ultimate being," and so on, often not realizing that it is God they're trying to talk about. It is thus something of a relief to turn back to the world of scripture, which offers us a series of highly effective pictures of God (such as God as a father, and God as a shepherd) drawn from everyday life, building up to give us a comprehensive view of what God is like. Although none of these images is adequate in itself, together they give a consistent and satisfying picture of what God is like.

In the next chapter, we'll be looking at these pictures or models of God, and seeing how, individually and collectively, they help us think about God. Before we do that, however, we must deal with some questions which arise from using these pictures or models in the first place. Perhaps the most obvious of these is the simple question: Why do we need to use these models at all? Why can't we just give an exact description or a precise definition of what God is like, and dispense with all these ideas? After all, they are somewhat elementary, and surely we ought to be able to dispense with them and get on to more sophisticated ways of thinking about God.

The first point that should be noted is human finitude and sinfulness. How can mortal, fallen humans ever expect fully to appreciate or understand what God is really like? When we consider what the word "God" actually means, it is absurd to suppose that we can ever fully describe or define him. God is someone of whom we catch glimpses, as seen through dark glass (1 Cor. 13:12, AV). For the human mind to capture God in his fullness is about as probable as being able to pour the entire Atlantic Ocean into a bucket!

The early fathers of the Christian church used to compare understanding God with looking directly into the sun. The human eye is simply not capable of withstanding the intense light of the sun. And just as the human eye can't cope with the brilliance of the sun, so the human mind can't cope with the glory of God. The well-known words of Bishop Reginald Heber are relevant here:

Holy, Holy, Holy, though the darkness hide Thee,
Though the eye of sinful man
Thy glory may not see.

The story of the pagan emperor who visited the Jewish rabbi Joshua ben Hannaniah is also of relevance. The pagan emperor asked to be shown Joshua's god. The rabbi replied that this was impossible, an answer which failed to satisfy the emperor. So the rabbi took the emperor outside and asked him to stare at the midday summer sun. "Impossible!" replied the emperor. "If you can't look at the sun, which God created," replied the rabbi, "how much less can you behold the glory of God himself."

As every amateur astronomer knows, however, it is possible to look at the sun through dark glass, or in the early morning through a mist, both of which greatly reduce the brilliance of its disc to manageable proportions. In these ways the human eye can cope with an object which is otherwise completely beyond its capacities. In much the same way, it is helpful to think of the scriptural models or pictures of God as revealing God in manageable proportions so that the human mind can cope with him. The great reformer John Calvin is often thought of as being a rather stern theologian, but he has his tender moments as well. One of those moments lies in his famous assertion that "God accommodates himself to our weakness"—in other words, God knows the limitations of our intellects and deliberately reveals himself in such a way that we can cope with him.

It is in this respect that the doctrine of the incarnation is of such importance. (See my book *Understanding Jesus*, pp. 91–119, for a discussion of the incarnation and the insights into God which it allows us.) We could say that Jesus is God "scaled down to size," or in Charles Wesley's famous words, "our God contracted to a span." The basic idea is that something or someone who is vast and complex is presented to us in such a way that we can grasp him and begin to make sense of him. God came to us in a way appropriate to our human condition, in the form of something which we could see, touch, and handle (see 1 John 1:1–3).

When I was young, I can remember trying to understand what numbers meant. What does the concept of "three" mean, for example? The way I had to conceptualize "three" was by looking at three counters, or three chairs, or three tables, and learning that the concept of "three" was being embodied in each case. As I got used to this way of thinking, I soon learned to think of the idea of "three" without needing to think about chairs or tables at the same time. And in many ways, this is a helpful way of thinking about the incarnation. Abstract ideas are difficult for us to cope with, and God knows this, and so he reveals himself in a form we can cope with. God reveals himself in the form of a person, in the form of someone whom we can identify with, visualize, and relate to. And just as I, when I was young, had to think of "three" in the specific form of three chairs or three tables, so we learn to think of "God" in terms of Jesus Christ. To quote the famous words of a second-century writer, "We must learn to think of Jesus as of God" (1 Clement 1:1). Of course, the incarnation is far more than a way of helping us to grasp truths which would otherwise be difficult or inaccessible, as we saw in *Understanding Jesus*, but one of its several functions is to enable us to begin to think about God in a thrilling and exciting way which would otherwise be denied to us.

In many areas of life we come across the problem of trying to express or portray something rich and profound, and find ourselves seriously restricted by the medium we're using. An obvious example brings this point out very well. Let's suppose that you are out walking one day and come across a magnificent view, a panorama which holds your attention and which you want to record in some permanent form. Back at home, you get your pencil and drawing-pad out and sketch the scene. Immediately you find yourself limited and restricted by having to represent a three-dimensional world on a flat sheet of paper. There is an extra dimension to reality which you simply can't reproduce on the two dimensions of the paper. You may, by skillful use of perspective, manage to create the illusion of dimension, but the fact remains that it cannot be captured adequately. And although you may be able to convey shadows and highlights by skillful use of your pencil, the fact remains that you are sketching in black pencil on a white background, producing a monochrome version of a multicolored reality. Once more, we find it impossible to convey color adequately through monochrome, even though we may be able to make the best possible use of the materials and techniques we have at our disposal.

So it is with our thinking about God. God has an extra dimension which we cannot really accommodate properly. Just as we cannot adequately convey a multicolored object in monochrome, so we cannot adequately express God's nature in human words. The Austrian philosopher Ludwig Wittgenstein pointed out that human words were completely incapable of describing something as mundane as the aroma of coffee. How much more difficult it is, then, to describe God! No way of representing God can ever do justice to him as he really is, and we must learn to do the best with what we've got.

Let's develop our sketch-pad analogy further, in order to make an additional important point. Let us suppose that you lived in a dungeon all your life and were cut off from all contact with the outside world. You know nothing of trees, the sun or the sky—all you know about is the dark room in which you've been trapped all your life. Then one day a newcomer arrives in the cell and tells you that there's a world outside that dungeon of which you were hitherto totally unaware. You may have argued that there must be a better world than the one which you already know, but you couldn't be sure. The arrival of this individual with news of this world intrigues and excites you. Perhaps the first question you ask is: What is it like?

In reply, the newcomer takes out a pencil and sketch-pad and starts to draw. He draws a picture of a landscape with sun, trees, and sky; he sketches animals, plants, and rivers. You are bewildered, for all you see is pencil lines on paper. You find it difficult to understand that you are dealing with a black-and-white, two dimensional representation of a colored, three-dimensional reality. The idea that you are being presented with a reduced or scaled-down version of the reality outside your dungeon is virtually impossible for you to comprehend. The breakthrough only really takes place when you realize that the sketches are inadequate and partial representations of a greater reality which itself simply cannot be adequately represented through the medium in question. Of course, if you yourself were able to break free from your dungeon and see the outside world, you'd be able to realize how the sketch related to the reality. But let's suppose you can't break free, and that you remain trapped. Your knowledge of that outside world remains given and embodied in the form of those sketches.

In many ways this analogy captures the situation we find ourselves in as we try to think about and picture God. The basic problem is that we, who have never penetrated beyond our own world of time and space, possess certain highly suggestive insights pointing to the existence of another world lying beyond us. But our knowledge of that world is given to us in the medium of human words—a medium which is the best we possess, but one that cannot portray it adequately. Our knowledge of God takes the form of verbal pictures, of sketches in words. And we must learn that these verbal sketches, while never adequately conveying the glory, majesty, and beauty of God, can nevertheless give us an inkling of what he is like, just as the newcomer's pencil sketches would give the inhabitant of the dungeon an idea of what the outside world was like.

This is another way of saying that the medium we are forced to use is inadequate to convey the fullness of both trees and God. A black-and-white sketch of a tree points to what the real thing is like and allows us to identify the real thing when we encounter it. But there is just no way in which those gentle pencil strokes can ever adequately represent every aspect of that tree. Let's consider two situations. Let's suppose that you show this sketch to someone who's seen a tree already. He will recognize your sketch immediately—he shares your experience of a tree and knows what it is that you are drawing. Now suppose you've never seen a tree in your life, like the prisoner in the dungeon. When you encounter a tree for the first time, you realize what it is. You can see the obvious resemblance between the pencil sketch and the real thing.

Similarly, the medium we have to use to describe God is human words. There is just no way that these words can do justice to everything we'd like to say about God. In fact, it's difficult even to know where to start. But what we can do is give a verbal equivalent of a pencil sketch, building up a picture of what God is like. We could use parables, or the sort of models we'll be talking about later in this chapter. And someone who already knows God will recognize that we're talking about the same God that he knows and experiences. Our words ring true to his experience—he can make the connection between our words and his experience.

Now suppose you talk to someone who has never experienced God before. He gets a "feel" for what God must be like, even though he has never encountered or experienced him. And when he encounters God, he realizes who and what it is that he has encountered. He can make the connection: "This experience I have just had corresponds to what you were talking about." The important point here is that although human words are inadequate fully to express the richness and depth of the Christian experience and knowledge of God, they point to God in much the same way as a sketch of a tree points to the tree itself.

We could develop our dungeon analogy still further. Christianity has always insisted that Scripture contains insights into the nature of God which are confirmed and developed through God himself coming to us. In the birth, life, death, and resurrection of Jesus Christ we can see God himself coming to us, in our human situation, in much the same way as the newcomer arrived in the dungeon. God "visits" (see Luke 1:68, AV) his people, giving them insights concerning himself. Those insights take the form of verbal pictures, models of God in the form of words, which enable us to begin to visualize who God is and what he is like. In addition to these is one picture or model of God which towers over the rest: The person of Jesus Christ, whom faith recognizes to be none other than God incarnate, the living God coming to live among us as one of us.

Now, we have been left these verbal pictures in scripture and in the memory of the church in order that we may, in our own day and age, begin to think about God on their basis. Of course, they cannot do justice to the reality of the living God, but they point us in the right direction and begin to help us think about God in ways which would otherwise be denied to us. One day, Christians believe that they will see God face to face, as he really is, so that all these partial ways of thinking about him may be left behind forever. But until that day dawns, we must rely upon the richness of the biblical witness to God, confirmed in Christian experience, as the basis for our thinking about him. We must recognize its limitations, but rejoice that we have these verbal sketches on which to base and build our understanding of who God is and what he is like.

How, then, may we best use these verbal sketches or models of God? We can take our understanding of "models" of God much further by thinking about the way in which models are used in scientific thinking in order to advance our knowledge of the natural world. For the scientist, models are partial, conceivable ways of imagining or mentally picturing something which is not itself observable. In other words, it is a way of thinking about something which we otherwise have considerable difficulty in visualizing, which allows us to gain insights into the world of nature. In fact, so successful have some of these models become that many people think that they are to be identified with the real thing. This point is so important that we must think about it in more detail, especially for the benefit of anyone who has found this paragraph difficult reading.

Let's begin by thinking about a situation familiar to many people who study science at high school. If you compress gas in a container, you find that the volume the gas occupies gets smaller as the pressure you apply gets greater. This observation, stated in a more mathematical form, is known as Boyle's Law. If you think of the molecules of gas as billiard or pool balls continually bumping into each other, you find that you can predict this law. The smaller the space in which the billiard balls are forced to move (in other words, the volume), the more they collide with each other and the sides of the container (in other words, they exert more pressure). This model is sometimes known as the kinetic theory of gases.

Now, nobody is saying that gas molecules are identical to billiard balls—for a start, they're billions and billions of times smaller. What we are saying is that billiard balls are a good model for gas molecules, and for two reasons. First, they allow us to picture what molecules are like. We can't see the molecules—they're far too small—but the model allows us to visualize them, to form a mental picture of what they're like. It's not ideal, but it allows us to think of the molecules, to form a picture of them, where otherwise we couldn't picture them at all. Second, it allows us to understand and explore at least one aspect of the behavior of those molecules. Obviously, it doesn't allow us to explain every aspect of their behavior, but it does help us understand at least part of what's going on, and allow us to try and predict some other properties of the system. It's like an analogy—and we all know that analogies are helpful, providing we remember that every analogy breaks down at some point. And so it is with models—they help us think about things which we otherwise couldn't visualize at all, and allow us to understand at least part of what's going on. Going back to the kinetic theory of gases for a moment, it will be obvious that we are saying that "the complex behavior of gases can be partially understood if we think of gas molecules as being like hard inelastic spheres such as billiard or pool balls."

One of the many interesting things about university Christian groups is that many of their members—indeed, often the majority of their members—are studying natural sciences rather than arts. Why is this? Perhaps one reason might be that they are aware of the handiwork of God as they see it in nature, whereas arts students tend to study the work of other human beings. But perhaps another, and more important consideration is that scientists are used to talking and thinking about reality in terms of models, in terms of partial and conceivable representations of reality, and thus have little difficulty in handling the same tools when speaking and thinking about God.

We could go on and give many more examples of the scientific use of models, but the basic point we're trying to make is clear. It will also be obvious that we use much the same sorts of models to think about God. For example, we could model God on a shepherd, just as we model gas molecules on billiard balls. Here we take something which we are already familiar with and know something about (the shepherd), and say that it gives us a useful mental picture of God, and helps us understand the way in which he behaves. In the following chapter, we'll be looking in some detail at the biblical models of God and what they have to tell us about him. But first, we need to note several important points about models if we are to avoid making some elementary mistakes when we use them.

First, we may accidentally identify the model with what is being modeled. To go back to the kinetic theory, we might accidentally assume that gas molecules *are* billiard balls. Remember, what is being said is that in certain respects gas molecules behave *as if they were* billiard balls. Similarly, when we suggest that a suitable model for God is a shepherd, we are saying that in certain respects God may be thought of as being like a shepherd—for example, in his care for and guidance of his sheep. We must always remember that a model is both like and unlike what is being modeled—the important thing is to identify what the points of likeness are.

It is amazing how many people reject Christianity because they confuse the mental pictures or visual aids with the reality they're trying to describe. These models, however, are not the real thing which Christians believe in—most Christians are only too painfully aware of the enormous difficulties faced in trying to describe God, and are profoundly grateful that God has "accommodated himself to our weakness" (Calvin) by giving us such helpful and memorable ways of thinking about him. However, we can only use these pictures properly when we understand that they themselves are not what Christians believe, but that Christians believe in God, to whom these pictures point. We may often hear people saying, "I can't believe in some sort of shepherd up in the sky," or "You can't expect me to take all this nonsense about an old man sitting on a heavenly cloud seriously." These people, however, are simply confusing a way of picturing God with the reality of God himself. To bring out this crucial point, let's consider another analogy.

Let's suppose that we ask three artists to paint a picture of a bowl of fruit. We invite them into our studio, put a bowl of fruit in front of them, and leave them to get on with it. Later we come back and discover three very different paintings. One is a very straightforward representation of a bowl of fruit, which is immediately recognizable as such. The second is rather more difficult to recognize as a bowl of fruit: All the fruit has inexplicably taken on the shape of cubes, and the colors of the fruit have been transformed into various shades of blue. The third painting is totally unrecognizable: The artist belongs to one of the more abstract schools of interpretation, and the painting vaguely resembles a patchwork quilt. Now, we invite some friends around to look at the paintings. First they look at the third painting, and then we ask them what it represents. After several minutes' baffled silence, we take them to the next painting. Here the silence is shorter, as some of the group begin to see the outlines of the bowl of fruit. When they come to the first painting they have no difficulty in recognizing what is being portrayed—and so when we show them the original bowl of fruit, they have no difficulty in recognizing it as what the first painting was based on.

Let's take this analogy a stage further. Does the fact that the third picture was not recognized as an adequate representation of the bowl of fruit mean that the bowl of fruit didn't exist in the first place, or that it was not a representation of that bowl of fruit? Both of these conclusions are clearly incorrect. We might be tempted to draw them, but they are not logically valid. The only valid conclusion is that the painting was not immediately recognizable as a representation of the reality of the bowl of fruit. Very much the same situation exists with models or visual pictures of God. We may find them difficult to understand, and even be tempted to dismiss them, but this has no bearing whatsoever on the reality which they represent. We could tear up that third painting and consign it to a rubbish bin, but the bowl of fruit would still exist. When dealing with either paintings of bowls of fruit or models of God, therefore, we must avoid confusing the representation of reality with that reality itself.

Second, we must remember that complicated things may need more than one model to explain them. An excellent example of this is light. In the early twentieth century it became increasingly clear that the behavior of light was such that it could only be explained by assuming that certain aspects of that behavior had to be explained by treating it as a wave, and others by treating it as a particle. In other words, two different (and contradictory) models had to be used if the full complexity of the behavior of light was to be explained. In fact, a theory was later developed (the famous "Quantum Theory") which enabled these models to be reconciled. Each of these models illuminated some aspects of the behavior of light, and failed to clarify others. But they were complementary, rather than contradictory. Broadly speaking, the more complex the situation, the greater the number of models needed to explain it. Every now and then, books with titles such as *Models of Humanity* appear, making it clear just how many different models have to be used even to begin to account for the complexity of human beings. And so when we come to deal with models of God, we should hardly be surprised to find that there are many models given in scripture, each of which illuminates one aspect of God, and which together combine in a complementary manner to build up a powerful and evocative picture of God.

Third, it may be assumed that something which is necessary for the model is also necessary for whatever is being modeled. We could put this more formally by saying that the logical necessity of some of the features of the model are improperly projected onto the system being modeled. An example will help bring out the relevance of this difficult but important point. In the second half of the nineteenth century it became increasingly clear that light could, in some respects, be treated as if it was a wave motion. One example of wave motion was already well-known—sound. Sound was thus treated as a model of light. In many ways this was helpful: It allowed scientists to understand various aspects of the behavior of light on the assumption that light behaved just like sound. Now, sound requires a medium for its propagation—in other words, it needs to travel through something like air or water. An experiment I remember being shown at high school demonstrated how making a vacuum around a ringing bell stopped its sound traveling. The ringing bell was placed inside a large glass container, and the air was gradually pumped out. As this was being done, the sound of the bell became fainter and fainter until eventually we could no longer hear it. And so we realized that sound needed to travel through something.

It was therefore assumed that light also needed to travel through something and the word "aether" was coined to describe the medium through which light waves traveled. If you read old radio magazines, or listen to old radio programs, you'll sometimes find people referring to "waves traveling through the aether." But by the end of the century it had become clear that light did not seem to need any medium to travel through. What had happened was simply that the logical necessity of one aspect of the model (sound) had initially been assumed to apply to what was being modeled (light), and this assumption was gradually recognized to be incorrect as the experimental evidence built up.

And so it is with models of God. For example, we often use "father" as a very helpful model of God, emphasizing the way in which we are dependent upon God for our existence. But for every human child there is a human mother as well as a human father. This would seem to imply that there is a heavenly mother in addition to a heavenly father. But this assumption rests upon the improper transfer of the logical necessity of an aspect of the model (father) to what is being modeled (God), in just the same way as the necessity of one aspect (the need for a medium of propagation) of the model (sound) was transferred to what was being modeled (light). This is a difficult point, but well worth grasping, as it enables us to avoid making many of the mistakes which commonly arise through the biblical use of models to talk about God. Perhaps it is as well to ask ourselves what a given model, such as "God as King," is *not* saying as much as it *is* saying.

One final point needs to be made. In this chapter we have emphasized how the full complexity of the nature and character of God can be at least partially mediated through simple visual images, images which are often so simple that a child can understand them, just as scientific truths can often be mediated in the same way. Yet people very often seem unable to cope with this way of thinking about reality. You say to them, "Why don't you think of an atom as a sort of gold ball?" and they respond, "That's far too simple. I can't believe that. Surely you can give me something more sophisticated than that?" And so you try a different way of representing that atom. You take a piece of paper, write down a complicated mathematical function, and say, "That's another way of representing an atom." And they then respond. "That's far too complicated. You're just blinding me with your science. Surely you can explain it in more simple terms that that?"

In many ways, this just goes to show that you can't please everyone all the time. But it also indicates the genuine difficulty that many—indeed, probably most—people have in understanding the way in which complicated things are described and portrayed. A gold ball and a wave function (the "complicated mathematical expression" in the last paragraph) are both perfectly legitimate and proper ways of describing atoms, each with its own uses. And so it is with God. When we say that "God is like a father—both severe and kind to his children," we very often get the response, "I can't believe that. It's far too simple. I'm not a child aged six—give me something more sophisticated." And so you talk about "the need to recognize a creative dialectic between severity and kindness within the economy of salvation," only to be told, "That's far too complicated. If there really is a God, I'm sure he would have made it more simple than all this abstract nonsense." It's almost as if Christianity is something which was invented by human beings, and which stands or falls depending upon whether it is sophisticated in a simple way! But the reality of the situation is that we are trying to describe God as best we can at a number of levels. The little child can think of God as a loving shepherd, and the university professor as "the ground of radical creativity"—

but they are both thinking about the same God, only in different ways and at different levels.

One of the most exciting things about Christianity is that it allows God to be portrayed and conveyed in these very different ways, each of which allows genuine and helpful insights to be gained. The critic who won't believe Christianity either because it's too simple or because it's too complicated (depending upon which of these two objections you've just met) has probably already made his mind up about Christianity and doesn't want his prejudices disturbed. But for those for whom this is a genuine difficulty, the use of models in the world of science is an extremely helpful way of illustrating how simple pictures and models can mediate the most profound insights.

In the following chapter, we shall turn to look at the richness, vividness, immediacy and dramatic force of the biblical models of God in order to begin our discussion of God as a person.

4

Biblical Models of God

Let's suppose you're watching a drama on television. Perhaps it's a play, like *Arsenic and Old Lace* or *Romeo and Juliet*. The individual characters come onto the screen and you can see what they look like. You can also see the settings in which the action takes place. Your mental picture of the characters and the settings is given to you through the medium of television. Now imagine that you're listening to that same drama, except that it's being transmitted by a radio station. There is no picture to see, the only medium being presented to you is sound. You have to imagine what the characters look like; you have to imagine what the settings look like. Many people actually prefer the medium of radio because they find it more stimulating for this very reason.

In many ways, the biblical witness to God is very like a radio play. You are given a picture of God in words, not a series of photographs. You must sit down and think about God in terms of the verbal images which you are given, each of which is capable of giving several invaluable insights into God. And just as you have to try and wonder what the person behind the voice is really like, so we have to try and think what the reality behind these verbal images may be. Both the Old and New Testaments use models to stimulate and guide our thinking about God—verbal pictures of God which we can remember and reflect upon.

Before we examine some of these models, two points ought to be made. First, in the last chapter we pointed out how models were "partial and conceivable representations of reality." Does this not suggest that the Bible is giving us only a partial, and hence inadequate, picture of God? Certainly not! Scripture gives us a rich range of models which, like a child's toy bricks, build up to give a comprehensive and reliable picture of God. Each of these models, taken on its own, is certainly inadequate. God is a shepherd, for example—but there is a lot more that can and should be said about God than that. The biblical models of God are the building-blocks which combine to give a comprehensive picture of God.

Second, we need to note that we are authorized to use only certain models of God—those given in scripture. As we have stressed, the primary source of our knowledge of God is scripture. Indeed, we could say that God lays down the ways in which he wants us to think about himself. This means that we cannot just choose any old model and argue that it adequately represents God; we need to concentrate on those which we are given, and work out what it is that they are telling us about God. On the basis of these insights, we may well be able to come up with modern equivalents which mediate the same insights—for example, God as a probation officer, or a managing director. But we must remember that our attempts to devise contemporary models are always secondary to, and dependent upon, the scriptural testimony. The best preacher and communicator will be the person who, steeped in a knowledge of the biblical models of God, finds the most helpful contemporary analogies for them by reading the newspapers and watching television—but these are simply contemporary restatements of the original models. They do not have the same status as the God-given and authorized models which we find in scripture. The preacher must therefore continually seek to relate the biblical models to the modern world, while never allowing the latter to supersede the former.

In the present chapter we're going to examine some of the biblical models of God in order to see how they combine to build up an overall portrayal of God. The biblical models for God are fresh and vivid, drawn from the everyday life of the period. These models include forces of nature, inanimate objects and human beings—all of which allow us to begin to think of God in a tangible manner. Although the passage of time has made some of these less vivid than they once were, it requires remarkably little effort to bring out their full force and vitality. We begin with one of the most familiar of all the biblical models of God.

1. God as Shepherd

One of the most familiar verses in the Bible is Psalm 23:1—"The Lord is my shepherd." This image of God as a shepherd is encountered frequently in the Old Testament (e.g., Ps. 80:1; Isa. 40:11; Ezek. 34:12), and is taken up in the New Testament to refer to Jesus, who is the "good shepherd" (John 10:11). But what does this model tell us about God?

First, we encounter the idea of the loving care of the shepherd for his sheep. The shepherd was committed to his flock of sheep on a full-time basis. Indeed, the shepherd tended to be regarded as a social outcast in Israel on account of the enormous amount of time he was obliged to spend with his flock, which prevented him from taking part in normal social activities. The idea of God as a shepherd thus conveys the idea of the total commitment of God to his people. The idea is developed very powerfully in the New Testament, especially in the parable of the lost sheep (Luke 15:3–7). Here the shepherd actively seeks out the lost sheep in order to bring it home. The final intensification of the image is found in John's Gospel, where it is emphasized that the good shepherd—who is immediately identified as

Jesus—will willingly go so far as to lay down his life for the safety of his sheep (John 10:11–16).

Second, thinking of God as a shepherd speaks to us of guidance. The shepherd knows where food and water are to be found and guides his sheep to them. It is he who finds the green pastures and quiet waters (Ps. 23:2) for his sheep. I was brought up in the Irish countryside where flocks of sheep wander aimlessly around, giving every impression of being lost. Left to their own devices, sheep have a habit of getting lost and wandering off into dangerous countryside, becoming stranded on hillsides. It is the shepherd who keeps the sheep on safe ground and ensures that they have food and drink. To liken God to a shepherd is to emphasize his constant presence with his people, and his gentle guidance as he tries to protect them from the dangers of life and bring them to a place of plenty and safety. "He tends his flock like a shepherd: He gathers the lambs in his arms and carries them close to his heart; he gently leads those that have young" (Isa. 40:11).

Third, the image of God as shepherd tells us something about ourselves. We are the sheep of God's pasture (Pss. 79:13; 95:7; 100:3). Like sheep, we are incapable of looking after ourselves and we continually go astray. We are not self-sufficient: Just as the sheep rely upon the shepherd for their existence, so we have to learn to rely upon God. We may like to think that we are capable of looking after ourselves, but realism demands that we recognize just how totally dependent upon God we are from the moment of our birth to our death.

Human sinfulness is often compared with running away from God like a stray sheep: "We all, like sheep, have gone astray, each of us has turned to his own way" (Isa. 53:6; cf. Ps. 119:176; 1 Peter 2:25). Just as the shepherd goes to look for his lost sheep, so God came to find us in our lostness and bring us home. The parallels with the parable of the prodigal son (Luke 15:11–32) will be obvious. In fact, in Luke 15 we find three stories of "lostness," all illustrating the idea of our being lost, then someone looking for us, and then rejoicing when they find us and bring us home. The shepherd finds his lost sheep (Luke 15:3–7); the woman finds her lost coin (Luke 15:8–10); the father finds his lost son (Luke 15:11–32). And in all these analogies we find the same constant emphasis of the Gospel: We are lost but God has come into the world in his Son Jesus Christ in order to find us and bring us home rejoicing.

A final point which the model of God as shepherd makes with particular clarity concerns the nature of the relationship of the believer with God. The shepherd doesn't point his sheep in the right direction leading to the "quiet waters and green pastures," but takes them there, carrying those who are too weak to make the journey unaided (Isa. 40:11). Christianity is not about God telling us where to go and what to do if we want salvation, and then leaving us to get on with it—it is about God graciously accompanying, supporting, and sustaining us as he journeys with us and guides us. Similarly, Jesus tells us that he is "the way and the truth and the life" (John 14:6). He doesn't just show us the way that leads to eternal life, but sets us on that path and journeys with us as we travel. The great theme of "Emmanuel"—God is with us (Matt. 1:23)—resounds throughout the Christian life as we remember that God is with us, even in life's darkest moments, guiding us to our eternal rest.

2. God as Spirit

"God is spirit" (John 4:24). But what does this tell us about God? In dealing with this model we need to remember that the English language uses at least three words, "wind," "breath," and "spirit," to translate a single Hebrew word, *ruach*. This important Hebrew word has a depth of meaning which it is virtually impossible to reproduce in English. This has the obvious result that if we want fully to understand the depths of meaning associated with the model of God as spirit, we need to try and understand the richness of this important model. Furthermore, we need to remember that by translating the Hebrew word *ruach* by "spirit," many English versions of the Old Testament lose much of the richness of the original image. In the present section, we're going to try to unfold the richness of this very helpful way of thinking about God.

First, the idea of spirit is associated with life. When God created Adam, he breathed into him the breath of life, as a result of which he became a living being (Gen. 2:7). The basic difference between a living and a dead human being is that the former breathes and the latter doesn't. This led to the idea that life was dependent upon breath (and we recall that "breath" is one of the senses of the Hebrew word *ruach*). God is the one who breathes the breath of life into empty shells and brings them to life. Just as God brought Adam to life by breathing into him, so God is able to bring individuals and his church to life through his spirit today. The famous vision of the valley of the dry bones (Ezek. 37:1–14) also illustrates this point: The bones only come to life when breath enters into them (Ezek. 37:9–10). So the first idea that the model of God as spirit suggests is that God is the one who gives life, perhaps even the one who is able to bring the dead back to life.

The second idea that the model of God as spirit helps us understand is that of power. Here we are thinking especially of the wind (remembering that the Hebrew word *ruach* also has this meaning). All of us are used to seeing things being moved by an invisible force—the wind does it all the time. We often see papers blown across the road by the wind, or trees bending before its force. And in those areas of the world where hurricanes are common, entire towns may be destroyed by the power of this invisible force which we call the wind. The Old Testament writers, noticing the way in which the wind acted, could hardly fail to notice an obvious parallel with the way in which God acted. God is like the wind—an unseen force which acts upon things and people. I remember once being blown over by the wind while crossing a street, and feeling rather stupid about it afterwards!

We could develop this idea further. Let's suppose that you're starting a fire the hard way—by striking a spark onto some tinder which then begins to smoke. If you blow on the tinder, that little pile of smoldering tinder begins to glow and then catches fire, setting the whole pile of wood alight. So God breathes upon our faith in order to establish it and set us on fire with a love for himself. If you've been stupid enough to light that campfire in the middle of a forest while there's a strong wind blowing, the sparks from your fire could end up setting the whole forest ablaze. Yet it was only a little spark which started it off—with the help of the wind. In the same way, God is able to turn the spark of our faith into a burning fire which can set the world alight in much the same way as our campfire could set a forest alight. Thinking about God as the wind helps us understand how God is able to do so much with so little.

Wind is something which we know by its effects, rather than something which we know in itself. If we were pressed hard enough, we could probably give some sort of description of what the wind is—"air molecules in high-speed motion" perhaps. But we all find it much easier to speak about the wind in terms of what it does, rather than what it is. The wind is whatever it is that's blowing that piece of paper about. The wind is what's making that plume of smoke bend in that direction. The wind is the force that's blowing that enormous tree over. And so it is with God. Many people find it much easier to talk about God in terms of what he does, rather than in terms of what he is. God is whoever transformed my friend's life by bringing him to faith. God is whoever raised Jesus Christ from the dead.

We could develop this point a little further. Let's suppose that there have been high winds in your area recently, and as you walk around afterwards, when the wind has stopped blowing, you come across an enormous tree lying on the ground. It has been torn up from the ground with its roots still intact. How did it come to be there? It is almost certain that it has been blown down by the wind. We have got so used to seeing things being blown down by the wind, however, that we rarely reflect on how strange an event this is. How is it that infinitesimally small air molecules can knock an enormous tree down? After all, air is what we're breathing here and now, and it's not doing anybody any harm. We can't feel the wind anymore, because it is calm. Yet the fallen tree stands as a witness to the presence and activity of the wind in the past. The fact that the wind is not blowing now does not mean that it didn't blow in the past and won't blow again in the future. The uprooted tree is a symbol of the unpredictability and power of the wind.

The parallels with the way in which God is present and at work within his world will be obvious. There may be moments when God seems to be present in our lives or in history in a powerful and exciting way, yet this may be followed by a period of calm, a period in which God does not give any indication of his presence. Like a sailing ship, we may find ourselves becalmed in the spiritual doldrums. Yet this may suddenly give way to renewed divine activity as the wind of God blows again in our lives and in history. The very unpredictability of the wind points to the fact that God acts in a way which we do not fully understand and cannot predict.

A third way in which the model of God as spirit is helpful concerns the various ways in which God's activity is experienced. Sometimes God is experienced as a judge, one who breaks us down in order to humble us; at other times he is experienced as one who refreshes us, like water in a dry land. The biblical writers were already familiar with the fact that one and the same thing could be experienced in different ways on account of their experience of the wind. To understand this, let us consider the two main types of wind known to the Old Testament writers.

Israel, we must remember, bordered the Mediterranean Sea on the west and the great deserts on the east. When the wind blew from the east, it was experienced as a mist of fine sand which scorched vegetation and parched the land. Travelers' accounts of these winds speak of their remarkable force and power. Even the light of the sun is obliterated by the sandstorm thrown up by the wind. This wind was seen by the biblical writers as a model for the way in which God demonstrated the finitude and transitoriness of his creation. "The grass withers and the flowers fall, because the breadth of the Lord blows on them" (Isa. 40:7). Just as the scorching east wind, like the Arabian Sirocco, destroyed plants and grass, so God was understood to destroy human pride (see Ps. 103:15–18; Jer. 4:11ff.). Just as a plant springs up, fresh and green, only to be withered before the blast of the hot desert wind, so human empires rise only to fall before the face of God.

Thus, at the time when the prophet Isaiah was writing, Israel was held captive in Babylon. To many it seemed that the great Babylonian Empire was a permanent historical feature which nothing could change. Yet the transitoriness of human achievements when the "breath of the Lord" blows upon them is asserted by the prophet as he proclaims the pending destruction of that empire. God alone is permanent, and all else is in a state of flux and change. "The grass withers and the flowers fall, but the word of our God stands forever" (Isa. 40:8). The rise and fall of the Roman Empire, and more recently the British Empire, must remind us of this point, so powerfully developed through the model of God as the scorching desert wind.

The western winds, however, were totally different. In the winter, the west and south-west winds brought rain to the dry land as they blew in from the sea. In the summer, the western winds did not bring rain but coolness. The intensity of the desert heat was mitigated through these gentle cooling breezes. Just as this wind brought refreshment, by moistening the dry ground in winter and cooling the heat of the day in summer, so God was understood to refresh human spiritual needs. In a series of powerful images, God is compared by the Old Testament writers to the rain brought by the western wind (Hos. 6:3), refreshing the land. A friend of mine, who had spent some time working in East Africa, told me that one of the most remarkable sights he had seen was the effect of rain upon the dry land. What had been arid and barren ground suddenly turned green as all sorts of plant life seemed to appear from nowhere. In many ways this brings out the importance and meaning of the biblical model of God as the gentle west wind which brings rain to the thirsty land. We are like travelers through a dry land who suddenly discover an oasis. In the midst of our weariness and anxiety, God refreshes us.

3. God as Parent

The image of a human parent is used to a considerable extent by both the Old and New Testament writers as a model of God. Although the strongly patriarchal structure of society at the time inevitably meant that emphasis was placed upon God as father (e.g., Jer. 3:19; Matt. 6:9), there are several passages which encourage us to think of God as our mother (e.g., Deut. 32:18). We shall be considering these two images together, and ask what they tell us about God.

The first, and most obvious, point is that God is understood as the one who called us into being, who created us. Just as our human parents brought us into being, so God must be recognized as the author and source of our existence. Thus at one point in her history, Israel is chided because she "forgot the God who gave [her] birth" (Deut. 32:18; cf. Isa. 44:2, 24; 49:15).

The second point which the model of God as parent makes is the natural love of God for his people. God doesn't love us because of our achievements, but simply because we are his children. "The Lord did not set his affection on you and choose you because you were more numerous than other peoples, for you were the fewest of all peoples. But it was because the Lord loved you" (Deut. 7:7–8). Just as a mother can never forget or turn against her child, so God will not forget or turn against his people (Isa. 49:15). There is a natural bond of affection and sympathy between God and his children, simply because he has brought them into being. Thus God loved us long before we loved him (1 John 4:10, 19). Psalm 51:1 refers to God's "great compassion," and it is interesting to note that the Hebrew word for "compassion" (*rachmin*) is derived from the word for "womb" (*rechmen*). God's compassion toward his people is that of a mother toward her child (cf. Isa. 66:12–13). Compassion stems from the womb.

The Old Testament in particular often compares God's relationship with his people to a father's relationship with his young son. When the son is very young, he is totally dependent upon his father for everything, and their relationship is very close. But as the son grows older, he gradually comes to exercise his independence and break away from his father so that relationship becomes more distant. The prophet Hosea uses this illustration to underline how Israel has become a virtual stranger to the God who called her into existence:

> When Israel was a child, I loved him, and out of Egypt I called my son. But the more I called Israel, the further they went away from me. They sacrificed to the Baals and they burned incense to images. It was I who taught Ephraim to walk, taking them by the arms; but they did not realize it was I who healed them. I led them with the cords of human kindness, with ties of love (Hos. 11:1–4).

This image is, of course, developed with enormous skill in the parable of the prodigal son (Luke 15:11–32). The point being made is that the natural love of the father for his son is wounded by the growing independence and alienation of the son. Like the prodigal son, we choose to go our own way, ignoring God. Yet the same God who created us also redeems us as he enters into human history in the person of Jesus Christ in order to find us, meet us, and bring us back to him. In many ways, the entire Bible can be read as the story of God's attempt to bring his creation back to him.

The third aspect of this model which is of interest concerns prayer. In the Sermon on the Mount, Jesus compares the believer's act of praying to God with a child's act of asking his father for something he wants (Matt. 7:7–11). The basic idea underlying this comparison is that even human fathers, despite being sinful, wish the best for their children. The child may ask for something outrageous, which the father refuses to give him, in the child's best interests. I can remember asking my father for a hunting knife when I was quite young. My father, being alarmed at what I might do with it, quite naturally refused—an action which I thought was quite unreasonable at the time. A few months later, a relative (knowing that I wanted such a knife) gave me one—and I promptly managed to cut myself very badly with it.

The parallels between the father and God, and the child and ourselves, are very clear. The child has a somewhat distorted and unrealistic view of what his own capabilities and needs are, and his requests to his father reflect this immaturity. The father tries to help his child become more realistic and mature by his responses to such requests. He may give the child something which the child would never have thought of asking for. But the fundamental assumption is that the relation of asking and giving between father and son is governed by the father's love for his child, and his passionate desire for the child's well-being.

A similar relation exists between God and the believer. Our requests to God all too often reflect our immaturity and our unrealistic estimation of our needs. Like a wise father, God tries to help us become more realistic and mature by his responses to those requests. But his total love for and dedication to us is not called into question by his failure to meet all our requests.

4. God as Light

"God is light" (1 John 1:5). The imagery of light and darkness is often employed in both Old and New Testaments to help us understand what God is like. But what does the model of God as light tell us about him?

Let's begin with an image which occurs several times in the Old Testament—that of watchmen waiting for the dawn (e.g., Ps. 130:6). The night was seen as a time of potential danger when watchmen had to be posted throughout the city of Jerusalem in order to warn of any threat to the city which developed under the cover of darkness. The arrival of the dawn was seen as marking the end of this threat—at least, for the time being. Dawn thus came to be associated with hope, or with a sense of relief. "I wait for the Lord, my soul waits, and in his word I put my hope. My soul waits for the Lord more than watchmen wait for the morning" (Ps. 130:5–6). The ending of the night was often seen as an image of the end of a period of despair or misery, the dawning of a new period of life and light, and particularly the dawning of the "Day of the Lord," the messianic era.

The rising of the sun marks that dawn, and it was natural that the sun should be seen as an analogy of God (although it must be remembered that the Old Testament always played this point down in case it led to sun-worship). Thus Malachi, the final prophetic work in the Old Testament, looks forward to a time when God will come to visit and redeem his people (Mal. 3:1–4; 4:1–2). The coming of God to his people is then compared to the rising of the sun: "The sun of righteousness will rise with healing in its wings" (Mal. 4:2). This verse has been made famous through the Christmas carol "Hark! the herald angels sing," even though the Hebrew is probably better translated as "risen with healing in its *rays*":

Hail, the heav'n-born Prince of Peace!
Hail, the Sun of Righteousness!
Light and life to all He brings,
Ris'n with healing in His wings.

The same idea lies behind the famous messianic passage in Isaiah: "The people walking in darkness have seen a great light" (Isa. 9:2). The idea can, of course, be developed in other directions. For example, in an earlier chapter we saw how trying to get a direct glimpse of God was like staring into the sun—an impossibility, something which we simply are not capable of.

Second, light exposes things for what they really are. When I was a college student at Oxford, I was given a rather dilapidated room to live in during my second year. The walls were badly in need of painting, the carpet was worn through, and the windows were so dirty it was virtually impossible to see through them! In the daytime the room looked dreadful, but I soon discovered that you couldn't see any of this at night! By using subdued lighting, the room took on an almost magical quality. I couldn't see the dirty walls or windows, and the holes in the carpet were very difficult to spot unless you knew exactly where to look for them. It was the same room, but the absence of any strong light prevented all these things being noticeable. Of course, when daylight returned, I could hardly help noticing them again!

Light, then, shows things up—warts and all—for what they really are. When the shadows and half-lights are removed, we discover that they have been hiding the real state of things from our sight. In the light of the word of God (Ps. 119:105), we are shown up for what we really are—lost sinners, far from home, who need to return to God. The word of God is like a spotlight which picks us out and exposes us. It judges us simply by showing us up as we really are, scattering the shadows and darkness of our illusions of what we are like. In John's Gospel we find Jesus being identified as the "light of the world" (John 8:12; cf. 12:46). Jesus is the one who shows things up for what they really are, just as light does. "If I had not come and spoken to them, they would not be guilty of sin. Now, however, they have no excuse for their sin" (John 15:22). In the light of Jesus, we realize how far short of God's standards we have fallen, and how much we need the grace of God if we are to be redeemed.

We can take the idea of Jesus as the "light of the world" a little further. Let's suppose that you are in a small boat off a rocky coastline. As night falls, you realize that you cannot see the coast any longer, and are unsure how to navigate back to your home port. And then you see a light in the distance, flashing regularly—a lighthouse. While the Old and New Testament writers didn't know much about lighthouses, they had an equivalent—the city on the hill, lit up so that wayfarers could find their way to safety from the perils of the night (Matt. 5:14). Here we have the idea of a light showing us the way home. John's Gospel in particular develops the idea of Jesus himself being the light which guides us home to God. Jesus is the "light of the world" (John 8:12), just as he is "the way and the truth and the life" (John 14:6) leading us to the Father.

This way of thinking about God also helps us understand how we, as Christians, are meant to be the "light of the world" (Matt. 5:14). We all know what it is like to try and find our way out in the country at night, when there is no artificial light of any sort. It makes us realize how much we rely on the light of the sun. But not every night is dark. The light of the full moon, though much fainter than that of the sun, illuminates the night landscape and allows us to find our way. It may not show up every feature of the landscape—for that we have to wait for the sun. The moon is, in fact, simply reflecting the light of the sun—it has no light of its own. Taken by itself it is just a lifeless, barren, cold ball of moon-rock. Having no light, no source of power, of its own, it can still cast light on the earth by reflecting the brilliance of the sun.

So it is with us as Christians who, as "the light of the world," reflect the glory of "*the* light of the world." It isn't as if we possess some independent source of illumination—our light is based upon an external source which we reflect. Taking this a little further, we might recall that the moon shows phases—a process that used to be called "waxing and waning." The more of the moon that is illuminated, the greater the light it reflects to earth. The amount of light reflected depends upon the relative positioning of sun, earth, and moon. And so it is with Christians—we must learn to place ourselves in the right position with both God and our fellow human beings if we are to be most effective witnesses.

5. God as a Rock

The Old Testament frequently refers to God as a rock (e.g., Pss. 18:2; 28:1; 42:9; 78:35; 89:26; Isa. 17:10). In many ways it may seem quite inappropriate to model God on an inanimate object such as a rock. However, the image is actually very helpful, conveying one simple and very powerful idea—security and reliability. Psalm 42:7, for example, develops a very vivid picture of the psalmist being beaten down by a powerful flood continually threatening to overwhelm and destroy him. And yet, in the midst of this sea of surging water, there is a place of security—the rock which is God (Ps. 42:9). A rock is something firm and immovable which can survive storms, floods, and heat alike. It is a place of refuge. Thus Moses, when criticizing the Israelites for worshiping false gods, points to the close relation between God, rocks, and safety: "Where are their gods, the rock they took refuge in?" (Deut. 32:37).

There is a story which is told about the eighteenth-century English hymn-writer Augustus Toplady. Once Toplady was out walking in the Malvern Hills, in south-western England, when a heavy rainstorm developed. Toplady is reported to have rushed to find shelter from the storm, eventually sheltering in a fissure in the rocky hills. As he sheltered in the rock from the storm, he began to reflect on the parallels between escaping from a rainstorm and escaping from the forces of sin, death, and decay—and so he came to write his famous hymn:

> Rocks of ages, cleft for me,
> Let me hide myself in Thee.

In thinking about God as a rock, we can think of him as a secure place of shelter from the storms of life, a place of refuge from sin and evil.

The famous hymn by John Newton makes this point well, and takes the imagery a little further:

Dear name! the rock on which I build,
My shield and hiding place.

Both the Old and New Testaments also encourage us to think of a rock as a secure foundation upon which we may build. This idea, of course, is developed most vividly in the Sermon on the Mount, with its famous parable of the house on the rock (Matt. 7:24–27). The basic idea being developed is that any construction, whether a house or an attitude to life, must rest upon a secure foundation if it is to survive. It cannot be built upon shifting sands, but must rest upon something permanent and enduring. In thinking of God as a rock, we are invited to reflect upon the fact that it is God, and God alone, who is unchanging and permanent, despite all the changes we see going on around us. It is on the rock of God alone that we must build our house of faith, knowing that only in this way can we weather the storms and floods of life.

The idea of God as a rock, then, conveys the important fact that God is something permanent and secure in a rapidly changing and unstable world: "Who is God besides the Lord? And who is the Rock except our God?" (2 Sam. 22:32–33). God is our place of refuge, our hiding place, the firm foundation upon which we base our lives and our faith. All these ideas are vividly captured by the model of God as a rock.

In this chapter we have looked at some of the biblical models of God in order to show how useful they can be. The everyday world gives us "pegs" on which we can hang our thoughts about God, allowing us to avoid using highly abstract language about him. In many ways models are like parables, but whereas a parable is "an earthly story with a heavenly meaning" (as every Sunday school student knows), a model is basically something drawn from everyday life which gives us insights into God. A parable is about a story, but a model is something from the world around us.

All of us know how difficult it can be to talk about God, and how hard it often is to find words which even begin to describe him adequately. In scripture, however, we are given a way around this problem through a whole series of rich and powerful images which stimulate our imagination. For example, we are told by the biblical writers that God is like a rock, and immediately we begin to try and draw out the points of comparison. These simple, everyday images stimulate our thinking by forcing us to ask questions such as, "In what way is God like a rock?" They are like discussion starters or conversation pieces—things which get us thinking and stop us being too abstract about God. They are pregnant with meaning and insights. It's very easy to Westerners, who are used to a conceptual way of thinking, to talk about God in hopelessly abstract ways. The biblical models of God bring us back to the concrete world of everyday things, and tell us that we can talk about God perfectly well without having to indulge in highly conceptual ways of thinking. Instead of talking about God as a "creative and dynamic power" (a temptation to which theologians are prone), we can say that "God is like the wind"—a much more vivid and creative way of talking, which immediately invites us (and anyone who happens to be listening) to start thinking about the ways in which God is like the wind.

In this chapter we've been looking at some of the biblical models of God, trying to draw out some of the insights they give us into what God is like, and the way which he is present and active in his world. It may be that, as you read this chapter, you began to get some insights in addition to those here—if this happened, it just goes to prove how powerful and stimulating these models of God can be. Of course, we've only been able to look at a very limited number of models due to pressure on space. You might like to think about some additional models of God, not discussed here, and see what insights they give. Here are four you might like to try thinking about: God as king; God as friend; God as judge; God as fire.

In the following chapter we're going to look at what is often regarded as the most powerful of all biblical models of God—God as a person. What does it mean to talk about God as person? What insights do we gain from talking about a "personal God?" Are we justified in talking about a "personal relationship with God?" It is to questions such as these that we now turn.

5

A Personal God

One of the most important Christian insights is that we are made in the image of God (Gen. 1:26–27). There is a basic likeness between ourselves and God which makes it possible for God both to present a picture of himself to us in human terms and to enter into a meaningful relationship with us. Both Old and New Testaments therefore draw extensively on language and ideas drawn from our own personal lives in order to help us understand what God is like. Personal language is the most helpful and reliable medium available for communicating the nature, character, and purposes of God. Theologians often describe this way of thinking about God as *anthropomorphisms* (descriptions of God based upon human analogies, such as "the arm of the Lord" [Isa. 51:9]) and *anthropopathisms* (descriptions of God based upon human emotions, such as "the love of God").

For some, this way of thinking about God is very crude and primitive. It suggests to them that God is basically an old man in white robes enthroned on a cloud, which is far too unsophisticated an idea for the modern period. They would much rather think of God in more abstract terms, regarding him as a force or power behind the universe. Although this criticism may seem plausible initially, it actually rests upon a misunderstanding. The picture of an old man sitting on a cloud is simply a mental picture of what God is like, and not the reality of God. In an earlier chapter we pointed out that one of the simplest mistakes to make when using models, is to identify the model with what is being modeled. In other words, the image of an old man sitting on a cloud is just one way of thinking about God, just as the image of a gold ball is one way of thinking about atoms.

The basic point to realize is that anthropomorphic ways of thinking about God are concessions to our weakness. In other words, God knows how difficult it is for us to think about him, and so he gives us vivid learning aids in order to help us picture him in our minds. After all, we are always told that a picture is worth a thousand words! It is perfectly obvious from the biblical material that it is impossible to capture the richness and profundity of God in human words. As a result, a whole range of pictures, models, images, and metaphors have to be used, each of which casts light on one or two aspects of God's being and nature. None of them in itself is even remotely adequate to do justice to who and what God is. As we saw in the last chapter, we can gain invaluable insights into God by thinking of him as a shepherd or a rock.

This point is so important that it deserves an illustration to bring it out. Let us take the biblical image of God as a rock and look at two ways of understanding it. The person who has completely missed the point of this way of thinking about God might say something like this: "You are asking me to believe that God *is* a rock. I can't believe that. There are lots of rocks in my garden, but I don't worship them. How can you identify God with a lump of stone in this ridiculously unsophisticated way? I just can't believe in a God like that." This person has made the elementary mistake of identifying the model (a rock) with what is being modeled (God). The person who understands the biblical ways of speaking about God would say something very different: "So God is *like* a rock, is he? I suppose this means that in some way or other, a rock helps us understand what God is like. Now, when I think of a rock, I think of something that is permanent and secure, the sort of place you might build a castle on. And so God also represents a place of security and permanence, something on which I can build." Do you see the crucial difference between these two ways of approaching the biblical ways of speaking about God?

One of the most remarkable things about the biblical way of speaking about God is that it is able to use the most unsophisticated starting-points to build up a remarkably sophisticated picture of God. Thus we could begin with the idea of a shepherd—something which is grounded in the everyday life of individuals, and which doesn't require any intellectual brilliance to grasp. Or we could begin from the idea of the wind, or our father or mother, or any of the many biblical models of God drawn from everyday experience. We then ask what these models tell us about God, and gradually build up an understanding of God. Although this understanding of God is based upon shepherds, rocks, the wind and so on, it completely transcends them.

We could take this idea a little further by thinking about an artist and his pictures, for example, Leonardo da Vinci and the *Mona Lisa*. As he paints, the artist applies colors to his canvas so that in one sense the resulting picture is nothing more than a mixture of colors. Yet the image which this mixture of colors conveys to us is the enigmatic face of the Mona Lisa. And it is this image that we see and which holds us spellbound. But behind this image stands a woman. We know virtually nothing about her. She is the reality behind the painting, the one who inspired the image which has intrigued generations of curious onlookers. Now, on the basis of this analogy, we have identified two different levels of representation of reality. First, we have a mixture of colors on a canvas. Second, we have the haunting image of the Mona Lisa which those colors combined to give. And third, we have the Mona Lisa herself, the real creature of flesh and blood who is represented in that portrait. She is not identical with that portrait, but it corresponds to her, echoing her and capturing her likeness.

Those same three levels can be seen in the models of God we use. First, they are collections of words—and how can human words adequately capture the greatness of God? Second, we have the image which those words combine to create in our minds: Images of God as a shepherd, as a father, and so on. And third, we have the reality of God himself. He is not identical with these verbal pictures, but they correspond to him, they echo him, and they capture his likeness.

Our response to the critic who dismisses God because he can't believe in an old man (or an enormous bearded nineteenth-century English clergyman!) sitting somewhere up in the clouds is therefore very simple. Everybody knows that the image of an old man sitting on a cloud is a totally inadequate representation of God, but this has no bearing on whether God exists or not, or what he is actually like. The same critic might refuse to believe in atoms because he finds it impossible to think of a world in which billions and billions of gold balls are flying around the place. He might refuse to believe that the Mona Lisa existed as a real person, because real persons are three-dimensional, not two, and move about, while the Mona Lisa has never altered her facial expression in centuries. But all he has actually done is drawn attention to the fact that both atoms and God—neither of which can be seen by the naked eye—are rather difficult to visualize without using models of some sort, and that the models used are sometimes not quite as good as we would like them to be. The question of the existence of God is quite independent of the difficulties we have in adequately understanding and visualizing him.

With these points in mind, let us begin to think about the idea of a personal God. What does it mean to speak of God as a person? The first point to make is that we are not saying that God is a human being. This point is obvious from our discussion of some of the models of God: When we say that God is our shepherd, we aren't saying that God is a human being surrounded by sheep, but what we are saying is that God is like a shepherd in various ways. In much the same way, we are saying that a human person is a good model for God. But in what way is God like a person?

The fundamental point behind the idea of a personal God is this: *God is able to enter into a personal relationship with us.* In other words, our relationship with other persons (our personal relationships) are analogous to our relationship with God. We don't relate to God in an abstract way, as if he was some diffuse cosmic force or moral principle, but in a personal way. We experience God in a personal manner, and our own personal relationships give us insights into our relationship with God. To give one very obvious example: When we talk about God as "love," we are using a concept directly derived from the sphere of personal relationships. This fact is acutely embarrassing for some theologians, who want to abandon belief in a personal God on the basis of their questionable belief that the modern world can't cope with it. Thus John Robinson, in his once-famous book *Honest to God*, declares that our image of a personal God must go—and yet insists that our most profound experience is of God as love!

What insights, then, does the idea of a personal God allow us to gain? How is our understanding of the nature and character of God illuminated by human personal relationships? Space allows us to consider only a few.

The first insight is well-known, and requires little discussion. We have already seen how there is a world of difference between *knowing about* a person and *knowing* a person. To know about someone or something is simply to produce a list of facts we know about them—the color of their hair, their height, their weight, their family history, and so on. To know someone, on the other hand, is to experience them in a personal manner. It is to enter into a relationship with them in which they know us and we know them. It is a mutual, shared experience. The concept of *reciprocity* is central here: A personal relationship involves A knowing B, and B knowing A, whereas it is quite possible for A to know an enormous amount *about* B without B even knowing that A exists. For example, I know something about the President of the United States, but that doesn't mean that he knows the first thing about me. The Christian understanding of our relationship with God is that this is a mutual relationship—it is not just a matter of us knowing something *about* God, but of us *knowing* God and *being known by* God.

Second, personal relationships establish the framework within which words such as "love," "trust," and "faithfulness" have their meaning. Both the Old and New Testaments are full of statements concerning the "love of God," the "trustworthiness of God," and the "faithfulness of God." "Love" is a word which is used of personal relationships. Furthermore, the great biblical theme of promise and fulfillment is based ultimately upon a personal relationship, in that God promises certain definite things, such as eternal life and forgiveness, to certain individuals. One of the great themes which dominates the Old Testament in particular is that of the covenant between God and his people, by which they mutually bind themselves to each other: "I will be their God, and they will be my people" (Jer. 31:33). The basic idea underlying this is that of the personal commitment of God to his people, and of his people to their God.

This context of a personal relationship between God and his people also allows us to make sense of some biblical ideas which otherwise might seem rather strange. For example, we often find reference to God being jealous (Num. 25:11; Deut. 4:24; 32:16; 1 Kings 14:22; Pss. 78:58; 79:5; Ezek. 8:3–5; Zech. 1:14). Does it not seem rather strange to think of a good God being jealous? However, when we consider the background to this term, its meaning and relevance become obvious. God is the one who loves his people. He is the one who brought them into being, delivering them from Egypt and leading them into the promised land (Hos. 11:1–4). He loves his people so much that he is prepared to give his only Son up for them (John 3:16). Just as a husband and wife swear that they will love and stand by each other no matter what the future holds, so God and his people declare in the covenant that they will be faithful to each other. God is totally committed to the safety and well-being of his people. And it is clear that this love relationship is precious to God, that it means everything to him.

Imagine that you have fallen in love with someone, and have done everything you can to further their well-being and safety, even to the point of risking your own career or life. And this person, in turn, falls in love with you, and a permanent relationship results. You swear eternal love to each other. How many romantic novels have been written on this very theme. But then someone else comes along and seduces this person who means everything to you. Your relationship seems to be in ruins. How would you feel about it? Again, countless romantic novels have been written on this theme as well. One of the Old Testament books, Hosea, explores this theme with great skill and compassion.

Hosea draws a parallel between the situation of a man and his faithless wife and that of God and Israel. Although God loved Israel passionately and totally, the fact remained that Israel preferred to follow other gods in his place. God said, "I cared for you in the desert, in the land of burning heat. When I fed them, they were satisfied; when they were satisfied, they became proud; then they forgot me" (Hos. 13:4–6). The work ends by portraying God musing over the delight he will experience when he welcomes his wayward people home (Hos. 14:4–7).

It is within this context that we are to understand the jealousy of God. It is no bitter, wounded pride, but the result of total mutual dedication and commitment being shattered through the infidelity of one party, while the other party remains totally committed and dedicated. As scripture continually emphasizes, God's faithfulness is not canceled by our faithlessness. Two illustrations, both drawn from the world of personal relationships, are used to make this point. First, there is the rupture of the relationship between husband and wife through adultery. Second, there is the alienation of a son from his father, so powerfully described in the parable of the prodigal son. Both can be restored through repentance and forgiveness. To speak of the jealousy of God is not to imply that his pride is wounded through our infidelity, but simply to emphasize the full extent of his love and commitment to us. God made us for himself in order that both might enjoy the resulting relationship, and he is grieved, both for himself and for us, through our lack of faithfulness to him. God's jealousy is an expression of his love for and commitment to us, his burning desire that we shall be his and he shall be ours.

The personal framework which establishes the meaning of the word "love" is of importance in another context—one which is all too often overlooked. The doctrine of universalism is taken seriously in several of the more rationalist sections of the Christian church, largely because it is held to be inconceivable that a God of love should not wish to save everyone. It is argued that God will save everyone on account of his loving character—but this is so obviously wrong. The doctrine of universalism is actually a denial of God's love. To see why this is so, let us look at the question more closely. Love is about the reciprocal free response of two individuals. A loves B freely, and B loves A freely. To talk about being forced to love someone is something of a contradiction in terms. How many romantic novels have been written with the following basic plot: A loves B, but B loves C, and C loves B. A discovers that the father of B has committed some dreadful secret sin, and threatens to expose and ruin him unless B marries him. So B marries A—but she still loves only C.

The problem about universalism is that it requires that everyone—whether they like it or not—is forced to love God and be loved by him in return. A fundamental and God-given human freedom is completely compromised. The essence of the Gospel is that God proclaims and demonstrates his love for us by sending his Son Jesus Christ to die for us, but does not force us to respond to him. We are given the enormous privilege of saying no to God if we do not wish to return that love. Faith is basically saying yes to the love of God, allowing a love relationship to develop. In no way does God force us to respond positively to him.

Now, let us suppose that an individual decides that he simply does not want to love God or be loved by him: He wants to say no to God. Universalism, however, declares that he *must* be saved: Even though he does not *want* to be saved, he *must* be. His personal freedom and rights, given by God, are to be violated in the name of a dogma. Universalism declares that what this person wants is of no consequence: he *must* be saved. The most dreadful and distressing image results—one of God forcing this individual to abandon his own wishes, demanding that he respond to him, and refusing to take no for an answer. This is a sub-Christian view of God. The Christian view is of a God who offers his love to individuals in order that they may respond; the universalist view is of a God who forces his love upon individuals, irrespective of their integrity and wishes. God's love is something offered, not something imposed. To put it in a manner which some may find offensive, but which corresponds exactly to what is being said: Christianity speaks of God *loving* us, but universalism speaks of God *raping* us. Neither scripture nor the Christian tradition knows anything of so repulsive a doctrine, which it has rightly and consistently rejected as sub-Christian and unworthy of the God whom we know and meet in Jesus Christ.

Third, thinking of God as a person helps us understand the powerful appeal which Christianity has always had, and enables us to avoid blunting its force through misrepresenting or misunderstanding it. Christianity is not about a set of interesting ideas but about a person. If it were about a set of interesting ideas, we would find ourselves confronted with a number of serious difficulties. Christianity would be perverted into a form of intellectual élitism which most of humanity is disqualified from grasping. And ideas, as anyone who has worked in the field of history knows, have a habit of going out of fashion, often never to make a comeback. It would be remarkable if some ideas originating in first-century Palestine were found to be of continuing relevance in the modern world, which faces a completely different cultural, social, and intellectual situation. And anyway, having an interesting idea may be exciting at the time, but the excitement soon wears off. I can remember my excitement at first encountering some interesting ideas as a student, including the Quantum Theory, but once the novelty of the ideas wore off, I found myself getting bored by them. It's like reading a very short book: The first time around, it's quite interesting, but each time you read it, it gets less and less interesting until eventually it gets boring. We need more than interesting ideas about God to keep us going for the rest of our lives.

Thinking of God as a person immediately overcomes this difficulty. Suppose that you meet someone at a party—let's call this individual John Smith. After talking to him for a while, you learn the following things about him: He is male, aged twenty-five, likes French cookery, went to Switzerland on holiday last year, and plays the piano. Next time you meet him, you might learn more about him. But what is also happening is that you are getting to know—not just know about—John Smith. You begin to relate to him as a person, as John Smith, and not just the individual who is male, aged twenty-five, who likes French cooking, went to Switzerland last year, and plays the piano. You discover you like him, and a relationship begins to develop between you in which *facts about* John Smith increasingly become less important, and *John Smith himself* becomes increasingly important. All of us know about this from experience.

Let's take this a little bit further. As you get to know and like John Smith better, you find that he comes to exercise an increasing influence over you. You start to take his ideas seriously, and so on. Of course, this process may well be mutual, in that you will influence John Smith as well. We change through the influence of other people—they affect us. In other words, personal relationships are *transformational*: We are changed through the influence of other people. And so it is with God. Knowing God and having a relationship with God means being changed by God. Many of us know by personal experience that our lives are changed when we meet God. We try to become better people, to become more like God himself.

Another point that ought to be made concerns preaching. Let's suppose that you are convinced that a friend of yours would benefit greatly from getting to know John Smith. You try to persuade them of this fact. How would you do it? You could say something like this: John Smith is male, aged twenty-five, likes French cooking, went to Switzerland for a vacation, and plays the piano. In other words, you're just telling them facts about him. You are helping your friend to *know about* John Smith. But what you really want to do is not to tell them about John Smith, but to set up a situation in which they can meet and encounter each other, in which your friend can get to *know* him. You want to point him in the direction of John Smith, and suggest that he can and should meet him. You could tell him that John Smith is to be found at such-and-such a place, and that he's a really nice person.

Much the same applies to preaching about God. We could tell someone a lot about God, perhaps even giving him several textbooks to read, but what we really want to do is to point him in the right direction, and allow him to discover God for himself. In effect, what we are saying is: This is how *I* came to meet God, and I can assure you I am profoundly grateful that I did. Why don't you try to meet God in the same way, and see what happens? Preaching the Gospel is basically pointing away from ourselves to the person who lies behind our faith, and proclaiming that this person makes himself available for those who seek him. The preacher is like a signpost, pointing toward God and declaring that he's a lot nearer than we might think.

In John's Gospel we read of how Philip tells Nathanael about Jesus, declaring that the long-awaited Messiah has finally come: "We have found the one Moses wrote about in the Law, and about whom the prophets also wrote—Jesus of Nazareth" (John 1:45). Nathanael argues that this is impossible—how can the Messiah come from Nazareth of all places? Philip, however, avoids the trap that all too many preachers fall into—getting stuck in dead-end arguments. Instead of launching into a long and rather pointless speech about the origins of the Messiah, he simply says, "Come and see" (John 1:46), and Nathanael goes and looks—and is convinced by who and what he finds: "Rabbi, you are the Son of God; you are the King of Israel" (John 1:49). In many ways this illustrates perfectly the chief function of any preacher: to announce that God is near at hand, and then invite his hearers to "come and see," allowing God to take over the situation from that point onward. His hearers encounter a living person, not a lifeless and abstract idea. When we suggest that our friends meet John Smith, our job is simply to point them in the right direction—John Smith may be relied upon to do the rest, simply because of who and what John Smith is. Likewise, our preaching is primarily concerned with setting up the conditions under which our audience may encounter God—by proclaiming their need for God and pointing them in the right direction in order that they may encounter him.

Another point which ought to be made concerns the way in which we experience people. When someone important dies, there are usually lots of TV interviews with people who knew him. And one of the most interesting things that usually emerges from these interviews is that these people all knew the dead person from different angles, seeing him in a different light. Sometimes it's difficult to believe that they're all talking about the same person! However, it was the same person they knew, in every case—they just knew and experienced him in different ways. There is something very personal about each of their recollections, reflecting the simple fact that the dead person related to each of them individually, in different ways. They may all have known roughly the same things *about* this dead person—when he was born, who his family were, what his achievements were, how he died, and so on. But they still *knew* him in different ways.

It will be obvious that we encounter a similar situation with God. We may all know roughly the same things *about* him, but we all *know* him in different ways, for he relates to us as individuals, just as any other person. God isn't like some sort of inanimate object, such as a block of wood, which is passive and static—he is active and dynamic, relating to each and every one of us in different ways. This point is probably easy enough to understand, but it does have a very important result which we all too often overlook.

When we talk about God, we are partly talking about *the way in which we know God*. And the way in which each of us knows God is rather personal. The way I know God and experience him is probably rather different from the way you know and experience him. Now, suppose I was trying to persuade someone that it would be a good idea for him to come to know God. I would probably explain to him the way in which I knew and experienced God, and imply that he could know and experience God in the same way. But God might relate to this individual in a totally different way. I might even put this person off wanting to know God, simply because of what attracted me personally to God. This individual might be attracted to God for reasons which are very different from my own. It is for reasons such as these that preaching must be recognized as pointing *away* from the faith of the individual believer and *toward* the basis and content of that faith—the living God himself.

A further point concerns the way in which we know other persons—a way which distinguishes them from objects. This point has been discussed considerably during the present century, particularly by philosophers such as Martin Buber. We shall introduce this point by considering an analogy. Let's contrast the way we know another person from the way in which we know a table or a chair. The table or chair remains static as we investigate it: It is passive, and we are active. We can treat it as an object, and we always retain the initiative in studying it. What we know about it can be expressed in terms of statements such as "the weight of this table is such-and-such," or "the dimensions of this chair are such-and-such."

But when we come to study another person, we find that a very different situation develops. The other person is active, not passive. Although we may start to try and find out about them, the situation can be reversed very quickly: The other person can take the initiative away from us by starting to question us before we have a chance to question them. Interviewing people can be very easy, provided they let you ask all the questions and just confine themselves to answering. In this way you can find out about them without letting them find out very much about you. But sometimes the person who is being interviewed turns the tables and starts questioning his interviewers. And unless the interviewers regain the initiative very quickly, the situation can become chaotic. Persons are active subjects, not passive objects. Martin Buber thus distinguishes between *experience* (in which we are dealing with a passive object like a table) and *encounter* (in which we are dealing with an active subject, such as another person). We experience a chair, but we encounter a person.

When we try to describe our knowledge of a person, we find it difficult to do in exactly the same way as we might with a table. We can give their weight and dimensions in each case, and give a good physical description of what they looked like. But there is something about a person which we cannot describe—we cannot just reduce them to a set of statistics or a system of descriptive terms. Imagine someone very close to you who means a lot to you. Now think of all the things you know about them—their age, their weight, their height, the color of their eyes, and so on. Perhaps you could make a list on a piece of paper. But when you have finished—no matter how long that list is—you will soon realize that you haven't been able to describe that person properly. You could give that list to someone else and ask them if they feel that they *know* that person on the basis of what you've said about them. The answer will be no—they may now know a lot *about* this person, but they won't *know* them. Why not? Partly because you just cannot describe something so complex as a person in this way. But also partly because knowing is a *two-way process*, in which we are known by someone else. If A knows B, then B knows A. It is this important insight which Buber tried to get across with his idea of "encounter," which points to a mutual meeting of two persons.

The relevance of these insights to our discussion of God as a person will be obvious. First, we can't treat God as an object, something which we can examine at our leisure and under conditions of our choosing. Many nineteenth-century theologians in particular seemed to treat God as some sort of biological specimen, held captive in a cage, which they could examine in any way they pleased. This view of God fell out of fashion after the First World War, with the growing realization that God must be recognized as God, and cannot be treated in this demeaning way. He is someone active, someone who takes the initiative away from us and seeks us before we seek him. The Bible emphasizes the initiative of God in seeking us, and has little time for any idea of religion as our seeking after God. We are placed in the position of responding to God. It might well be that we would like to be in the position of interviewers who can ask God all the questions, keeping him under our control—but unfortunately it is God who is conducting the interview, under conditions which he has chosen. We have lost the initiative to God, and must learn to respond to him as he has disclosed himself.

It will also be clear that Buber's philosophy (sometimes referred to as "dialogical personalism"), with its idea of an encounter between God and man modeled on an encounter between two human persons, lends added weight to the crucial distinction between *knowing about* God and *knowing* God—a distinction which we have already drawn attention to in this book. Any understanding of God which forbids us to speak of *knowing* God condemns itself as inadequate and inauthentic, and is simply sub-Christian. Christian prayer, for example, with its emphasis upon petition (that is, asking God for things), is modeled on the relation between two human persons, as we have seen (note especially Matt. 7:7–11). If an understanding of God is not capable of explaining why Christians pray to God in this way, it is once more to be rejected as simply incapable of bearing the crucial insights of the Christian faith. It may seem to make more sense to some modern souls to speak of God as "the ground of our being," "ultimate reality," or some similar abstract way of speaking, but it doesn't make much sense of the practice of Christian prayer. And how can we *know* "ultimate reality" anyway? Isn't it really something (note the deliberate use of the word "thing"!) which we can at best *know about*?

Thinking about God as a person, then, illuminates and safeguards many essential Christian insights about the nature and character of God. The supreme illustration of God as a person, however, is to be found in the incarnation. In Jesus Christ we encounter none other than God in the embodiment of a human person. In the following chapter we shall explore how the recognition that Jesus Christ is none other than the living God himself both confirms and develops the idea of God as a person, and lays the foundation for the distinctively Christian insights into God safeguarded by that most enigmatic of Christian doctrines—the doctrine of the Trinity. Curiously, it is through recognizing the full implications of affirming that God is a person that we are set on the road which leads to the recognition that God is *three* persons.

6

The Incarnate God—Jesus Christ

In an earlier chapter I asked you to imagine that you had lived in a dungeon all your life, with no knowledge of the outside world at all. And then someone who knew that world arrived and began to draw sketches of it. Although your knowledge of that outside world would be fragmentary and a little confused, you would at the very least become aware that there was something beyond the walls which held you captive. Now imagine that you are in that situation—in a dungeon, *knowing* that there was something beyond those walls, and excited by rumors and hints of what it was like. For a long time, you wonder what it is like, perhaps lying awake at night and imagining what you might be able to see one day.

And then you hear something. There is a noise coming from one of the walls, about halfway up. It starts off as a gentle scraping, and you have to listen carefully to work out whether your ears are playing tricks on you or not. Then it becomes louder, and you know that something is happening. Then suddenly a hole the size of your hand appears in the wall, and you realize that someone has drilled through the wall. As the dust subsides, a brilliant beam of light dazzles your eyes. You have lived in darkness for so long that your eyes have become accustomed to the gloom, and they have to readjust to the new situation. Then, anxiously, you creep up to the hole and look through it. And there, beyond the thick stone wall, you catch a glimpse of the world outside—a world of light and color, of motion and sound. The hole isn't large enough to allow you to see everything, and the sound is distorted by the echo of the hole in the wall. But you have suddenly been presented with a new, direct vision of the world beyond.

You had been prepared for what you now see by the drawings you had once been shown, but now you realize for the first time the full significance of those two-dimensional static sketches. You see a tree, gently swaying in the breeze, gloriously green against a blue sky, and you realize that this is what the static two-dimensional monochrome sketch represented. Perhaps the subtle fragrance of fresh air, charged with the perfume of the flowers, begins to permeate and refresh the stale atmosphere of your prison. And suddenly a new perspective on your situation begins to dawn as you realize that there is an exciting new world outside, beckoning to you, calling you, inviting you to participate in it. It is *there* and you are *here*—but somehow it seems much nearer at hand than you could ever have imagined.

The parallel between this analogy and the Christian understanding of the incarnation is clear. "In the past God spoke to our forefathers through the prophets at many times and in various ways, but in these last days he has spoken to us by his Son [who] . . . is the radiance of God's glory and the exact representation of his being" (Heb. 1:1–3). In the Old Testament prophets, law, and writings, we learn of God's gradual revelation of himself to his people. Like people trapped in a dungeon, they gradually realized that there was more to reality than what they could see—that the bounds of time and space did not exhaust a description of reality. Initially, they learned "in various ways" of what God is like, through the verbal pictures they were given by the prophets. Each stage of this revelation laid the foundation for the next, until finally the scene was set for the great breakthrough. This was not a breakthrough which men made from their side of the walls of time and space, but one which God made from his side. The Old Testament prepared the way for this breakthrough, giving us inklings of what the world on the other side was like, and encouraging us to await and listen for the sound of the tunneling.

And then, when the breakthrough came, the verbal pictures of God we had been given were seen in their true light. We were able to understand, perhaps for the first time, what they really meant. Those hints of the coming of the suffering servant (Isa. 53), those rumors of the vindication of the righteous sufferer (Ps. 22), those promises that the Lord would suddenly come to his temple (Mal. 3:1)—all are suddenly seen in a new light as the reality to which they bear witness is seen for the first time. No longer are we dependent upon descriptions of what God is like, passed down from one generation to another—God himself "has come and has redeemed his people" (Luke 1:68). God himself comes to us, in the form of a person—Jesus Christ. Setting aside his glory, power, and majesty, God humbled himself and stooped down in order to meet us where we are, in a form with which we could identify. Jesus reflects, echoes, and embodies what God is like—in short, Jesus is God in the flesh, God incarnate.

Our imaginary prisoners in that dungeon might pick up their two-dimensional monochrome picture of a tree, and compare it with the three-dimensional colored image which they saw through the hole in the wall, and suddenly declare, "So *that's* what this was all about! Now we can see that these pencil strokes here represent those branches, and these the leaves, but before we weren't quite sure exactly what they were meant to represent." What had been slightly unclear before, perhaps even enigmatic, is suddenly recognized for what it really represents. And so it is for the Christian reading the Old Testament in the light of the coming of God in Jesus Christ. The Old Testament law and prophets are illuminated, are seen in a new light, because what they are representing and pointing to is suddenly made available. Thus Matthew takes a certain delight in taking his reader through a gamut of Old Testament prophecies (e.g., Matt. 1:22–23; 2:5–6, 15, 17–18, 23; 3:3), effectively saying, "Now we know what these prophecies are really all about."

Through Jesus Christ, whom we recognize to be God incarnate, a direct and personal encounter between ourselves and God is made possible. The one who the great Old Testament figures knew indirectly and incompletely takes the initiative and comes to us as one of us. One of the most powerful passages dealing with the relation between the faith of the great Old Testament heroes and those of the Christian era in the New Testament is Hebrews 11:1–12:2. In this great passage the writer points out how the Old Testament figures knew what the promises of God were leading up to, even though they themselves did not live to see it happen. "All these people were still living by faith when they died. They did not receive the things promised; they only saw them and welcomed them from a distance" (Heb. 11:13; cf. 11:39–40). The same theme can be seen in Luke's account of the encounter between the infant Jesus and Simeon (Luke 2:25–35). Here Luke rather tenderly allows us to witness the reaction of an old man who realizes that the moment he and countless others had waited for expectantly—the coming of God to his people—had finally happened (Luke 2:29–32).

Why do Christians believe that Jesus *is* God? (For a discussion of this point, see *Understanding Jesus*, pp. 63–119.) It must be emphasized that this was not an eccentric conclusion reached by some single misguided early Christian thinker, rather it represented the considered judgment of the whole Christian community as it reflected on the evidence they either knew at first hand—the life, and supremely the death and resurrection of Jesus Christ— or the witness to this evidence contained in the New Testament documents. In the long period of debate in the early church over this matter, no other explanation of the identity and significance of Jesus Christ was found to be adequate to do justice to the Christian experience of God through Jesus Christ, or the New Testament evidence itself. This was the collective conclusion of the Christian community over a period of centuries, not the unilateral decision of an autocratic and eccentric theologian! In Jesus Christ we encounter none other than the living God. If Jesus Christ was just a human being, then he is no more relevant to our thinking about God than any other human being who has put his mind to the question down the ages. But on the other hand, the church was equally insistent that if Jesus Christ was to be identified with God in a simplistic manner, so that his humanity was denied or neglected, he would be entirely irrelevant to human life. The danger of thinking of Jesus as God, and God alone, however, only arose once the fact that he *was* God in the first place had become generally established.

In the modern period, of course, we have seen a number of challenges to the idea that Jesus is none other than God incarnate. One of the most frequently heard complaints concerning the doctrine of the incarnation is that it is illogical. Some recent theologians have asserted that to say that Jesus is God is just as logically inconsistent as saying that a circle is a square. Being human excludes being divine. But is this really right? Let's look at this carefully.

Circles and squares belong to the world of shapes, and are mutually exclusive—in other words, being a circle means *not* being a square, a triangle, or any other shape. The common logical world that both squares and circles occupy is that of *shapes*. To say that something is "both a circle and a square" is first of all to say that this "something" is a *shape*. When we go on to ask what sort of shape it is, we find a logical contradiction involved: We are told that it is two different and mutually incompatible shapes at one and the same time. And so a logical contradiction results. A similar situation arises within the world of colors. Red and blue occupy mutually exclusive territories in the common world of colors—a color may be red or blue or something else, but not both red and blue. Once more, a simple logical contradiction results if we say that such and such a color is red and blue at one and the same time.

But what is the common logical world occupied by God and man? Why are God and man logically incompatible? A circle and a square are two different shapes; red and blue are two different colors; God and man are two different—well, two different *what*? The simple fact is that they are just *different*, and not in any way logically incompatible. Let's go back to our colors and shapes. Something cannot be both a circle and a square, but something can be a *red square*. There is nothing logically inconsistent about something being both red and a square—the two ideas are drawn from different logical worlds. "Red" and "square" are different ideas, to be sure, but the idea of something which is both red and square certainly involves no contradiction. Similarly, "God" and "man" are drawn from different logical worlds—and thus in asserting that Jesus is both God and man, no logical contradiction of any sort is involved.

A more sophisticated analysis of the question of the logical relationship of "God" and "man" in the incarnation is due to perhaps the greatest of all English theologians, William of Ockham. In the fourteenth century Ockham demonstrated, with considerable logical rigor, that no inconsistency of any kind was involved in the concept of the incarnation—and then went on to demonstrate how this helped us better understand the nature of the incarnation. But the basic point we are emphasizing is obvious: The assertion that the idea of Jesus being divine is absurd because it involves "logical contradiction" is not to be taken too seriously.

We are also told by some modern theologians that the doctrine of the incarnation is irrelevant to the modern situation, and that everything that needs to be said about Jesus can be said, and said well, without the need to involve the idea of the incarnation. In fact, however, this is not the case. Let's look at some examples to bring this point out.

First of all, let's ask why we are talking about Jesus Christ at all. Why is he so special? Why has Christianity singled out this person, and this person alone, as supreme among human beings? The traditional answer has always been that the resurrection from the dead demonstrates that Jesus Christ is divine, and thus establishes that he has a unique status and identity which distinguishes him from all other human beings. There may well have been other human beings whose conduct and personality distinguished them—people such as Socrates in the ancient world, or Gandhi in more recent history—but we rightly respect these people as fellow human beings, not as God incarnate. Jesus' uniqueness is, for the Christian, ultimately grounded in *who he was* rather than *what he said and did*. In other words, Christians have always tended to regard Jesus' teaching and lifestyle as of importance because of who they knew him to be, rather than because of what this teaching and lifestyle were in themselves.

Let's suppose that we eliminate the idea of Jesus being God incarnate, as some modern thinkers suggest we can. How, then, are we to justify the unique position which Jesus has always possessed for Christians? The answer, simply stated, is that it cannot be justified. What conceivable relevance can the teachings of a first-century Palestinian male have for us today, in such a totally different cultural setting? There is an enormous gulf separating first-century Palestine from the twentieth-century West, and anyone who has failed to realize this has probably not even begun to wrestle with the enormity of the problem. For example, many feminists argue that Jesus' teaching is compromised by his very masculinity, as well as the patriarchalism of his social context. So why should we pay any attention to Jesus? How can we justify his uniqueness with reference to his teaching? The answer seems to be that we cannot, unless we recognize that Jesus *was* someone very different from the rest of us, and that this point of difference is of central importance.

For traditional Christianity, the incarnation demonstrates that God has come among us as one of us, addressing us and calling us personally. It does not matter greatly *when* this happened in history—the important point is that it *did* happen, and that it thus tells us something important about who God is and what he is like. But if the idea of the incarnation is abandoned, we are left with the picture of a Jewish rabbi, distant in time, whose teaching and lifestyle may have singled him out in his own day, but who has little relevance in ours. It becomes difficult, to say the least (and many would simply acknowledge that it is utterly impossible), to justify the unique position which Jesus has always had for Christians. Far from being the center of the Christian faith, he becomes relegated to the margins.

For, as even many critics of the incarnation are prepared to admit, Christians simply do not relate to Jesus as a distant figure from the past, but as the present and living Lord. They do not regard him as a distant teacher from the past, a long-dead rabbi or guru—they know him as their risen Lord, one whom they worship and through whom they know the living God. The doctrine of the incarnation preserves these central insights, without which Jesus sinks into near-oblivion as the historical founder of a religion which now seems content to do without him. To abandon faith in the incarnation is to lose sight altogether of the centrality of Jesus to the Christian faith.

A second point which may be made concerns the rise of a particular form of atheism in the twentieth century. This movement is sometimes known as "protest atheism," on account of the fact that it "protests" against a certain concept of God. The twentieth century has witnessed human cruelty and ferocity rarely paralleled in the history of the world. The horrors of the First World War in Europe, of the Stalinist purges in the Soviet Union, of the Nazi extermination camps, and of the programs of genocide in South East Asia—all have raised the question in the minds of many people concerning how God is involved in this world of suffering. Protest atheism is directed against the image of a God who stands aloof from his world while such suffering continues. To abandon the incarnation is to abandon the crucial Christian insight that God in Christ subjected himself to the cruelty and evil of the world.

A playlet entitled *The Long Silence* brings out this insight with remarkable force.

The Long Silence

At the end of time, billions of people were scattered on a great plain before God's throne. Most shrank back from the brilliant light before them. But some groups near the front talked heatedly—not with cringing shame, but with belligerence.

"Can God judge us? How can he know about suffering?" snapped a pert young brunette. She ripped open a sleeve to reveal a tattooed number from a Nazi concentration camp. "We endured terror, beatings, torture and death!" In another group, a Negro boy lowered his collar. "What about this?" he demanded, showing an ugly rope burn. "Lynched—for no crime but being black!" In another crowd, there was a pregnant schoolgirl with sullen eyes. "Why should I suffer?" she murmured. "It wasn't my fault."

Far out across the plain there were hundreds of such groups. Each had a complaint against God for the evil and suffering he had permitted in his world. How lucky God was to live in heaven where all was sweetness and light, where there was no weeping or fear, no hunger or hatred. What did God know of all that man had been forced to endure in this world? For God leads a pretty sheltered life, they said.

So each of these groups sent forth their leader, chosen because he had suffered the most. A Jew, a Negro, a person from Hiroshima, a horribly deformed arthritic, a thalidomide child. In the center of the plain they consulted with each other. At last they were ready to present their case. It was rather clever.

Before God could be qualified to be their judge, he must endure what they had endured. The decision was that God should be sentenced to live upon earth—as a man!

"Let him be born a Jew. Let the legitimacy of his birth be doubted. Give him a work so difficult that even his family will think him out of his mind when he tries to do it. Let him be betrayed by his closest friends. Let him face false charges, be tried by a prejudiced jury, and convicted by a cowardly judge. Let him be tortured. At the last, let him see what it means to be terribly alone. Then let him die. Let him die so that there can be no doubt that he died. Let there be a host of witnesses to verify it."

As each leader announced his portion of the sentence, loud murmurs of approval went up from the throng of people assembled. And when the last had finished pronouncing sentence, there was a long silence. No one uttered another word. No one moved. For suddenly all knew that God had already served his sentence.

It is quite possible that we can express sorrow or regret through someone else. Sending someone else, however, to apologize for something, to send your condolences, is hardly anything like actually entering into the situation of suffering yourself. The incarnation declares that God suffered in Jesus Christ. God knows, therefore, what it is like to suffer at firsthand; God took human suffering upon himself, lending it meaning and dignity through his presence. To abandon the incarnation is to abandon the idea of a God who enters the world of suffering and sorrows, only to return to a sub-Christian view of God which is an easy target for the criticisms of protest atheism.

In an earlier chapter we noted the impact of the publication in England of John Robinson's book *Honest to God* in 1963. The book was publicized in a newspaper article with the striking headline *Our Image of God Must Go!* It was probably this headline, rather than the somewhat turgid and unoriginal book itself, which caused the greater impact. The image of God which had to go, according to Robinson, was that of an old man in the sky. We have already seen how simplistic and superficial this criticism is. But in the face of the deadly serious criticisms of protest atheism, there is one image of God which *must* go in the modern period—and that is any view of God which sees him as detached from and uninvolved with this world of suffering: In short, a nonincarnational view of God. For traditional Christianity, God suffered in Christ upon the bitter cross of Calvary—he took upon himself the suffering and sin of his creation in order to redeem it. The deadly barbs of protest atheism, which so easily destroy the nonincarnate God of modernism, are impotent against this God—the God who revealed himself to us through Jesus Christ, the *real* God of the Christian faith and not the invented God of modernism. The words of the First World War Christian poet G. A. Studdert-Kennedy evoke this authentic understanding of God with tender insight:

> God, the God I love and worship, reigns in sorrow on the Tree,
> Broken, bleeding, but unconquered, very God of God to me.

The concept of God which results from abandoning the incarnation is simply not a viable option in the twentieth century—it is against precisely this concept of God that the deadly barbs of protest atheism are directed. If this is what God is like, declares this influential movement, we cannot believe in him or take him seriously. Protest atheism has an understandable tendency to select soft targets, and there are few targets softer than a nonincarnational view of God. And the abandonment of such a sub-Christian view of God need not be mourned, for in its place arises the authentically Christian understanding of the God who became incarnate in Jesus Christ. Once more, the crucial importance of the incarnation is evident.

A third point concerns the interpretation of the cross. For some modern theologians, the cross is to be interpreted as nothing more than a demonstration of the love of God. The concept of the incarnation is to be abandoned, we are told, as a logical contradiction. The idea of the death of Jesus Christ upon the cross (and note that these modern theologians do not regard that death as reversed or overturned by the resurrection!) as demonstrating the love of God for us, however, is regarded as acceptable to a "world come of age." Unfortunately, it is obvious that this idea is dependent upon that of the incarnation. Let us follow this argument through.

The tender and authentically Christian insight that the death of Jesus Christ upon the cross reveals the full extent of the love of God for us is ultimately grounded in the recognition that it is none other than the Son of God who is dying upon the cross (John 3:16; Gal. 1:4; 2:20; Titus 2:14). Jesus Christ, the incarnate God, loved us and gave himself for us upon the cross of Calvary. While we were still sinners, God stooped down and gave himself up to the nails of the cross—all for the love of sinful humanity (Rom. 5:8). The words of William Blake in *Jerusalem* capture this point rather well:

> Jesus said: Wouldst thou love one who never died
> For thee, or ever die for one who had not died for thee?
> And if God dieth not for man and giveth not himself
> Eternally for Man, Man could not exist; for Man is love
> As God is love.

But what remains of the cross if we deny that it is God incarnate who died upon its outstretched arms? We are told by these modern theologians that

Jesus was no more than a splendid example of humanity—a human being, better in degree than us, but a human being nonetheless on that account. On the cross, therefore, we see a man losing his life. He did not give his life in the place of anyone else, except possibly Barabbas (Matt. 27:15–26). He was unjustly executed, like all too many before him and all too many after him, as a criminal. It might well be possible to speak of his death as demonstrating, in some rather obscure way, the love of one man for his fellow human beings. But God is not involved. It is not God who is nailed to the cross. It is not something which affects God directly in any way. In short, it is quite improper to speak of the cross showing the love of God for humanity. If anything, it merely illustrates one possible way (and certainly not the only or the best way) in which one human being may demonstrate his love for others. Is this really the foundation of a faith which goes out to conquer the disbelief of the world? It may be easier to believe this than to believe in God incarnate giving himself for us upon the cross—but, in comparison, it is hardly worth believing.

Many critics of the incarnation seem to think that the idea of Jesus being God and man is an arbitrary and irrational dogma invented by some mentally defective thinkers in a period which saw some fairly lousy thinking in the first place. For some modern writers, the demand for belief in the divinity of Jesus is seen as an absurd entry condition for church membership—should not church membership be open to everyone? Why should they be forced to believe in such an irrational and arbitrary edict before they can join a church? No other club or society makes such absurd demands of potential members. The Christian response to this outburst is simply that it rests upon an elementary misunderstanding. Let's illustrate this by looking at a less theological illustration.

Let's suppose you're about to make an omelet. You go into the kitchen, and there you discover three notices, each of which lays down conditions you must observe if you're going to make an omelet. The first declares that you may only make omelets if you are wearing black leather shoes. The second insists that you must stand with one hand behind your back and recite the Declaration of Independence as you make the omelet. The third demands that you break the eggs before you are allowed to make the omelet. How would we respond to those three? The first two we would dismiss as arbitrary, perhaps invented by the manufacturers of black leather shoes or misguided patriots—they bear no relation to the process of making omelets. The third, however, is simply a recognition of the realities of omelet-making—you can't make an omelet without breaking eggs. No amount of arguing is going to change that—it will merely delay the production of the omelet.

Critics of the incarnation seem to think that it's in the same class of arbitrary edicts as the first two omelet regulations. But more enlightened thinkers will realize that it's simply a statement of the way things are. Just as the relation of egg shells, egg contents and omelets demands that the eggs be broken to make an omelet, so the relation of God, humanity, and Jesus is such that we are obliged to recognize that Jesus is both God and man. It is an insight into the nature of things, a statement of the nature of reality as Christianity has grasped it. The reasons for making this assertion are excellent, and cannot be dismissed on the basis of such flimsy criticisms. The Christian church affirms that, in the end, everything it stands for rests upon the recognition of the divinity of Jesus—it is not making an arbitrary demand for membership, but stating the crucial and fundamental insight with which it stands or falls.

The Christian Gospel proclaims and affirms that God—the living God, the same God who created the universe and us—went to the cross of shame for love of us, sinners though we are. The incarnation gives and guarantees the meaning of the cross as the demonstration of the love of God for us. Deny the former and the latter is denied along with it. All too often, many modern critics of Christianity seem to assume (for they rarely trouble themselves to prove) that they can eliminate elements of Christian faith which they find objectionable, leaving what remains virtually untouched. They seem to assume that there is some sort of religious equivalent of precision surgery that can cut out one small part of the body without affecting the rest. Now, this is fine with an organ like the appendix which serves no useful purpose, but what about the heart or the brain? Cut these out and the body ceases to function. These organs are essential to the well-being of the body, so closely are they related to other organs, and so many are the organs which depend upon them. It is obvious that the doctrine of the incarnation is like the human heart, rather than the appendix. Eliminate it, and the fabric of the Christian faith unravels; the powerhouse of the faith ceases to pulsate. When a human heart stops beating, it is merely a matter of time before death occurs. It may be possible to delay that moment through artificial means such as life-support systems, but a state of suspended animation, leading only to death, is the inevitable result.

So it is with any form of Christianity which abandons faith in the incarnation—it is merely a matter of time before it dies. It may retain the outward signs of life for some time, but an irreversible and fatal process of decay has set in. One of the more curious features of criticisms of the doctrine of the incarnation is that they tend to be self-defeating. Those who criticize the incarnation all too often seem to end up with a dull, bookish form of Christianity, lacking any real vitality and excitement, incapable of converting anyone. A theology which is pure and abstract means the end of any living knowledge and a complete detachment from human existence, as the Russian thinker Nicolas Berdyaev so convincingly argued. As a matter of history, it seems that where Christianity is spreading actively and forcefully, it does so on the basis of a firm and convinced faith in the resurrection of Jesus Christ, the incarnate God. To reject that faith—for example, by becoming a

Unitarian—is to follow a road which has proved historically to be a spiritual and theological dead end, leading nowhere.

In this chapter we have been looking at the importance of the incarnation—the recognition that Jesus Christ is none other than God himself. This crucial insight can be justified on both the basis of the New Testament evidence and the Christian experience of God in the risen Christ. It is also essential to the fabric of the Christian faith. Remove or deny this insight, and the Christian faith, like a woolen garment, begins to unravel, lose its shape, and become of no significance. The alternatives offered by those who would have us become "modern" are not merely unjustified—they are totally inadequate, incapable of coherently conveying Christian insights which even many "moderns" recognize as essential. They may be of interest to bookish people who like reading Proust and listening to Shostakovich, but they are of no relevance to, they possess no vitality or power for, the vast majority of humanity who know their need for redemption but see in the "modern" understanding of Jesus no more than an academic moralist incapable of understanding, let alone redeeming, their situation. But for Christianity, God meets people precisely where they are—because he has already been there himself.

The doctrine of the incarnation allows—indeed, it demands—that we recognize that the only really accurate and reliable picture of God which the world has ever been shown is in Jesus Christ. One of our difficulties in thinking about Jesus as God is that we tend to bring our own ready-made ideas of God (wherever we may have found them) to the person of Jesus, and then try to make him fit in with our concept of God. But if we take the idea of a revelation of God in Jesus Christ with the seriousness it demands and deserves, we must be willing to have our understanding of God changed, even revolutionized, by what we find. God, as C. S. Lewis so frequently pointed out, is the Great Iconoclast—the one who breaks down our preconceived idea of what he's like so that he can make himself known to us as he really is. And our simple view of God is wrecked by the insight that Jesus is God.

Given that Jesus *is* God, doesn't this say something very important about God himself? Doesn't it mean that God is to be identified with Jesus? How, then, can we avoid suggesting that Jesus is a second God? After all, did not Jesus pray to God? And was not God in heaven during the earthly ministry of Jesus? In asking questions like this, we immediately begin to trace the path which leads to the distinctively Christian understanding of God—the Trinity. We have a long way to go before we arrive there, but by recognizing that Jesus Christ is none other than God incarnate, we have set our feet firmly upon the road that leads to this the most enigmatic of all Christian doctrines. In the following chapter we shall begin to move slowly and carefully down that road as we begin to sketch the outlines of the Christian understanding of the God who revealed himself in Jesus Christ.

7

The Road to the Trinity

To many people, the doctrine of the Trinity is a piece of celestial mathematics—and bad mathematics at that! Why, complained the great rationalist thinker, should we think of God in so clumsy and complicated a way? Why not just eliminate all this nonsense about "three-in-ones" and so on, and deal with God instead? After all, the New Testament doesn't talk about God in this way—it talks about God in beautifully simple terms. Thomas Jefferson, third president of the United States, stated this feeling rather well:

> When we shall have done away with the incomprehensible jargon of the Trinitarian arithmetic, that three are one, and one is three; when we shall have knocked down the artificial scaffolding, reared to mask from view the very simple structure of Jesus; when, in short, we shall have unlearned everything which has been taught since his day, and got back to the pure and simple doctrines he inculcated, we shall then be truly and worthily his disciples.

Jefferson's words will strike a chord of sympathy with many a reader, as they once did with this writer. Surely Christianity is a very simple religion: the assertion that God loves us and redeems us through Jesus Christ. But the nagging question underlying the more critical reader of these words is this: Is God really so simple that we can understand him, that we can capture him in such simple terms as Jefferson suggests? The wise and challenging words of Augustine are worth remembering: "If you can understand it, it's not God."

An illustration will help us think about this. Imagine an iceberg, chillingly white on a cold blue polar sea, majestically drifting toward warmer latitudes, there to melt. Its rugged features are there for all to see, contrasted against the sea. And yet, as we contemplate this iceberg from a passing ship or aeroplane, it is all too easy to overlook something about that iceberg—the simple fact that what we can see is only a fraction of its bulk. Perhaps as much as nine-tenths of it is hidden from our view beneath the waterline. It really is there—it is unquestionably part of that iceberg—but it cannot be seen from above the waterline: All that is presented from our view is its tip.

Perhaps another illustration will help us as we begin to explore the doctrine of the Trinity. Imagine that it is a cold and frosty winter night, and the features of the landscape are picked out by the light of the moon. As you look toward the moon you wonder what it is like. From one night to another you sketch the features you can see, perhaps aiding the naked eye with field glasses or a telescope. And as you sketch, night by night, you begin to realize that part of the moon is permanently hidden from your view—only half of its face can ever be seen from earth. You later discover that this is because of the similarity of the rotational period of the moon about its own axis and about the earth, so that the moon more or less keeps the same face presented to the earth—an unhappy celestial accident which meant that the far side of the moon was a mystery until orbiting satellites photographed its hidden features and relayed them to earth. Even though the far side of the moon could not be seen from earth, it was known to be there—the satellites merely told us what it was like.

A final example is worth noting. Let's suppose you plant a seed in the ground—a bean, say. You then watch the ground carefully for signs of action (like Mr. Pooter watched his mustard and cress in *Diary of a Nobody*). Initially nothing seems to happen at all (notice how Jesus draws out the implications of this in Mark 4:26–29). Even though nothing can be seen from the surface of the ground, however, the seed is growing in secret. If we were to dig up the ground at the point where the seed was planted, we would be able to see the root and stalk developing. Eventually, the shoot breaks through the surface of the earth. But there is more to the growing plant than that shoot. Beneath the surface, hidden from view, lies the root system—a central part of the plant which remains unseen from the surface

In all these examples, we have seen one common factor: The vantage point of the observer stops him from seeing whatever he's looking at it in its totality. In other words, the point from which we have to look at something determines how much of it we can see. If you're in a boat on the surface of the sea, you only see the tip of the iceberg—but there's a lot more to that iceberg than what you can see. If you're on the surface of the earth, you can only see half of the surface of the moon—the far side remains hidden from your gaze. And if you're looking at a plant from the surface of the ground, you can only see the bit which is above ground—the root system remains hidden. And for human beings like us, who live on the surface of the world, we can only apprehend a fraction of the reality of God. There is simply far more to God that meets the eye.

Let's develop this point with reference to the iceberg. The bit of the iceberg which we notice, which attracts our attention, is its tip. It is the tip of the iceberg which stands out. Some might be tempted to conclude that this is all there is to the iceberg—the bit that we can see. But, as can be shown without too much difficulty, the vast bulk of the iceberg is there to be discovered. Similarly, what we know about God seems very simple—the great affirmation that God loves us, meets us in Jesus Christ, and takes us home to him. But this is just the tip of the theological iceberg. If we begin to explore what God must be like if he is able to act in this superficially simple way, we discover that what seemed to be very simple on the surface is actually much more complicated. The great declaration that "God was reconciling the world to himself in Christ" (2 Cor. 5:19) turns out to be the tip of the iceberg, and the doctrine of the Trinity the bit which is hidden beneath the surface. In other words, "God was reconciling the world to himself in Christ" is the shoot of the plant whose root is the doctrine of the Trinity. We shall develop this point shortly. Our attention is first claimed by a useful distinction which can be introduced at this stage—the distinction between *kerygma* and *dogma*.

Between *what*? Let's use two English words instead: "proclamation" and "doctrine." *Kerygma* is a Greek word used frequently in the New Testament meaning "proclamation," the sort of thing that a herald (Greek: *keryx*) would declare. But what is being proclaimed? In the Old Testament, the proclamation is that God has acted in history to redeem his people. An excellent illustration of *kerygma* is the following passage:

> How beautiful on the mountains are the feet of those who bring good news, who proclaim peace, who bring good tidings, who proclaim salvation, who say to Zion, "Your God reigns!" Listen! Your watchmen lift up their voices; together they shout for joy. When the Lord returns to Zion, they will see it with their own eyes. Burst into songs of joy together, you ruins of Jerusalem, for the Lord has comforted his people, he has redeemed Jerusalem (Isa. 52:7–9).

The "proclamation" is the good news of God's redemptive action in history, and so it is hardly surprising to find that the New Testament is full of the proclamation of God's saving activity in the death and resurrection of Jesus Christ (Acts 5:42; 17:23; Rom. 10:8; 15:19; 1 Cor. 11:26; Col. 1:28; 4:4; 1 John 1:1). According to Acts, the apostles "never stopped teaching and proclaiming the good news that Jesus is the Christ" (Acts 5:42).

Doctrine is something rather different, however. It is basically concerned with correlating all the aspects of Christian faith and bringing them together into a coherent unity. Doctrine is to proclamation what wine-skins are to wine—something to contain it, to give it shape and strength. It is like a trellis upon which a climbing rose might be grown, or the steel mesh of reinforced concrete—something which creates a framework, a *structure*, which supports something else. Doctrine is about exploring the consequences of Christian faith, making sure that every aspect hangs together properly. To develop this point, we must consider the relation between "doctrine" and "proclamation," between *dogma* and *kerygma*.

Let's consider something which you might hear a preacher declare in a sermon, as he unfolds the importance of Christianity for his audience: "We come to God through Jesus Christ—he is the way back to God for us. If you want to find God, here is where you look—right in the face of Jesus Christ. Here is God, coming up to meet us right where we are, here and now. And through the death and resurrection of Jesus Christ, the way back to God is opened up." It shouldn't be too difficult to improve on this, but it allows us to make a point. What the preacher is concerned with is *proclamation*: the setting out of the relevance and importance of Jesus for his hearers. Now consider what the theologian would say: "Jesus Christ is both God and man: He is God incarnate."

Now, what the theologian is saying seems much less attractive and exciting than what the preacher has to say. But can you see that what the theologian is saying is really something like this: "Look, preacher, what you are saying depends upon recognizing that Jesus is both God and man—that he is God incarnate. If he isn't God, then he is entirely irrelevant to any thought about God; and if he isn't human, then he is entirely irrelevant to any experience of human life. In other words, the challenging message you were rightly delivering makes certain presuppositions about Jesus which we have to make sure we can justify and defend." And here we see the basic relation between doctrine and proclamation, between *dogma* and *kerygma*. Doctrine is taking the trouble to think through the implications of the proclamation, and making sure that these implications are understood by those whose business it is to defend Christianity against its critics.

This point is difficult but important. Once it is understood, the way is open to grasping the distinctive role that the doctrine of the Trinity plays in Christian thinking. What we are leading up to is simply this: The *proclamation* is that "God was reconciling the world to himself in Christ"; the *doctrine* is that the "God" in question has to be thought of as a Trinity if this proclamation is valid. Or, to go back to our iceberg analogy: The tip of that iceberg is the proclamation—the bit which we first encounter. But on further exploration, we discover the doctrine, the part which is already there, but which we didn't realize was there until we began to explore further.

Let's put this in another way. When you are explaining what Christianity is all about to your interested friends, you needn't mention the word "Trinity" at all. You speak to them about God, and about the way in which God has revealed himself to us and reconciled us to himself through Jesus Christ. But if you were to sit down and start thinking about the question "What must God be like if he is able to act in this way?" you will end up with the doctrine of the Trinity. In other words, the doctrine of the Trinity is the end result of a long process of thinking about the way in which God is present and active in his world. It is the result, not the starting-point, of a long process of thinking which can be seen going on in the first four centuries of the Christian era, as Christian theologians wrestled with God's self-revelation in scripture and tried to understand it. The *proclamation* is that God redeems us in Jesus Christ—the *doctrine* is that God *must* be like this if he acts in the way in which Christians know that he does.

An illustration may help bring this difficult but important point out. Centuries ago it was noticed that pieces of amber, if rubbed with a dry cloth, suddenly began to attract dust or small pieces of paper. Nobody was quite sure why it behaved in this way, but it unquestionably did behave in this way. As the centuries passed, and studies on this curious phenomenon proceeded, it was realized that this was an instance of the generation of static electricity through a process of ionization. In other words, beginning with the fact that amber did behave in this way, the implications of this observation were unfolded scientifically. The scientific basis of the observation was established. Now it will be obvious that we can make a distinction between two things:

1. the fact that amber, when rubbed with a dry cloth, attracts bits of paper
2. the general principles of static electricity, as these are now understood

The first is the observation, the second is the theoretical framework within which this observation is set.

Applying this illustration to the doctrine of the Trinity, we can make a distinction between two things:

1. the fact that "God was reconciling the world to himself in Christ"
2. the doctrine of the Trinity

The first is the proclamation of the fact that God acts in this specific way; the second is the theoretical framework within which this observation is set, the understanding of the nature of God which follows on from the recognition that he acts in this specific way. This insight also helps us with a slight difficulty which is sometimes emphasized by some modern theologians, anxious to discredit the doctrine of the Trinity. If you look at the doctrine of the early church during the first two-and-a-half centuries or so, you find that the doctrine of the Trinity has yet to be developed. The theologians of the period are well on the way to developing the doctrine, but it hasn't yet appeared in its definitive form. That development took place in the third or fourth century. And so, argue critics of the doctrine, this proves that it's not an essential element of Christianity.

Our response to this argument is quite simple. As we have seen, the doctrine of the Trinity is basically an attempt to bring together the incredible richness of the Christian understanding of God. It is the distillation of the kaleidoscopic Christian experience of God in the light of its scriptural foundations. The scriptural witness to and Christian experience of God came first, and reflection on it came later. In view of the complexity of that experience, it is little wonder that it took so long for the theologians of the church to wrestle with the implications of their faith, and find the best way of describing the God whom they knew in so rich and diverse a fashion. The basic facts (such as the biblical witness to the action of God in history) and the fundamental experiences (such as the experience of an encounter with God through the risen Christ) which *gave rise* to the doctrine had always been known—what was still in a process of development over the first few centuries was the investigation of the *implications* of these facts and experiences.

Let's look at another historical example to bring this point out—a mathematical example, this time. How do you go about working out the area enclosed by a curve, or the volume enclosed by an irregular shape? The classical period saw a number of ingenious geometrical ways of doing this being developed. In the late seventeenth century, however, Newton and Leibniz independently developed the mathematical science of *calculus* which allowed these problems to be analyzed directly, without having to go through the complicated classical procedure. The story of this development is known to just about everyone who has ever studied mathematics. But what did Newton and Leibniz actually *do*? Basically, they discovered a new tool for handling numbers. They were able to bring together in a single method what the classical period had treated as a number of problems. What they invented was a sophisticated way of bringing together and developing methods which were already known. Now the older methods were not wrong—they were just shown to be rather clumsy and inelegant compared with the new method.

The parallels with the doctrine of the Trinity will be obvious. The doctrine of the Trinity is a tool which enables the remarkably complex biblical witness to God to be brought together in a more sophisticated whole. It is a way—in fact, really the only way—of making sense of the biblical witness to God. It takes what is already there, what is already known, and shows how it is all related together as a consistent whole. It is a tool, a method, for handling the kaleidoscope of biblical affirmations about the nature and character of God, and bringing them together. And as it took thousands of years to develop the method of calculus, we can hardly complain that it took the Christian church a mere few centuries to bring together in a single and consistent whole the profundity and richness of the Christian experience of God.

In the following chapter, we shall begin to consider precisely what this Christian experience of God which leads to faith in the Trinity might be.

8

God as Three and God as One

Once upon a time there was a committee. It had three members. Now committees are things which exist to find something to do. And so they set up a project. It was a complicated and long-term development project which took a long time to get off the ground. But it eventually got going, and the committee was pleased with the way it seemed to be working. The project was a long way from the committee's offices, however, so communication was something of a problem. Soon the project developed some teething problems, so the chairman paid occasional visits to it, firing some of its directors and hiring new ones. But things got worse, and the committee realized that it would have to monitor the project on a more long-term basis. So the three of them decided that one of them would have to spend some time living and working on the project, and put things right. But which one would it be? "Not me!" said the chairman. "Someone has to stay back at the office and keep an eye on things here." And so the other two committee members drew straws, and the short straw was drawn by Mr. Davidson. So Mr. Davidson was sent off to the project. "Don't forget to keep in touch—and we'll expect a full report from you on your return" were the parting words of the chairman.

This is really a rather pointless story, except that it illustrates only too well the way in which a lot of Christians think about the Trinity! In their thinking, Jesus is basically one member of the divine committee, the one who is sent down to earth to report on things and put things right with the creation. Earlier we looked at biblical models of God (chapter 4), but nowhere in scripture is God modeled on a committee. The idea of an old man in the sky is bad enough, but the idea of a committee somewhere in the sky is even worse! What, we wonder, might be on their agendas? How often would the chairman have to cast his vote to break a tie between the other two? The whole idea is ludicrous. But how did it develop? Why do some Christians think in this way? The answer is simply that they have been taught about the Trinity so badly that this gross misunderstanding is virtually inevitable. In the remaining chapters we propose to explore *why* it is that Christians believe in the Trinity, and *what* it is that they believe about it.

Where must our discussion start? Perhaps from the most obvious of all places—the conviction of both Old and New Testament writers that there is only one God, and that is the God of Abraham, Isaac, and Jacob. "Hear, O Israel: The Lord our God, the Lord is one" (Deut. 6:4)—a theme taken up, endorsed and echoed by the New Testament writers (Mark 12:29; 1 Cor. 8:6; Eph. 4:6; 1 Tim. 2:5; James 2:19). The four points in the Old Testament in which God speaks of himself in the plural (Gen. 1:26; 3:22; 11:7; Isa. 6:8) are usually understood as "plurals of majesty," or "the royal we," although many Christian writers, such as Augustine, argued that these verses already contained hints of a Trinitarian way of thinking. At no point in the New Testament is any suggestion made that there is any God other than he who created the world, led Israel to freedom, and gave her the Law at Sinai. The God who liberated his people from their captivity in Egypt is the one and the same God who raised Jesus Christ from the dead.

The New Testament emphasizes that there is only one God (Matt. 23:9; Mark 10:18; 12:29; John 5:44; 17:3; Rom. 3:30; 1 Cor. 8:4, 6; Gal. 3:20; Eph. 4:6; 1 Tim. 1:17; 2:5; James 2:19; 4:12; Jude 25). It is also clear that God is not *identified* with Jesus: for example, Jesus refers to God as someone other than himself; he prays to God; and finally he commends his spirit to God as he dies. At no point does the New Testament even hint that the word "God" ceases to refer to the one who is in heaven, and refers solely to Jesus Christ during the period of his earthly existence. This may seem a trivial observation, but it is actually rather important.

Let's pause for a moment and see how far we've got. What we have seen so far is that both Old and New Testaments are united in their assertion that there is only one God, and that "God" is to be distinguished from Jesus Christ. So far, so good. Earlier we noted Thomas Jefferson's complaints about the "incomprehensible jargon of the Trinitarian arithmetic," but so far we haven't encountered any difficulties at all.

The difficulties really begin with the recognition of the fundamental Christian insight that Jesus is God incarnate: that in the face of Jesus Christ we see none other than the living God himself. Although the New Testament is not really anything like a textbook of systematic theology, there is nothing stated in the great creeds of the church which is not already explicitly or implicitly stated within its pages. Jesus is understood to act *as God and for God*: Whoever sees him, sees God; when he speaks, he speaks with the authority of God; when he makes promises, he makes them on behalf of God; when he judges us, he judges as God; when we worship, we worship the risen Christ as God; and so forth. The New Testament even hints that he was active in the process of creation itself (John 1:3; Col. 1:16; Heb. 1:3). Jesus is the one who can be called God and Lord, who acts as creator, savior, and judge, who is worshiped, and to whom prayers are addressed.

It will now be obvious that we are beginning to wrestle with the real problem at issue: In one sense, Jesus is God; in another, he isn't. Thus Jesus is God incarnate—but he still prays to God, without giving the slightest indication that he is talking to himself! Jesus is not *identical* with God in that it is obvious that God continued to be in heaven during Jesus' lifetime, and yet Jesus may be *identified* with God in that the New Testament has no hesitation in ascribing functions to Jesus which, properly speaking, only God could do. One way of dealing with the problem was to refer to God as "Father" and Jesus as "Son" or "Son of God" (e.g., Rom. 1:3; 8:32; Heb. 4:14; 1 John 4:15), thus indicating that they had the common stock of divinity, but that they could be distinguished, with the Father being thought of as being in some way prior to the Son.

The situation is made still more complex, rather than resolved, through the New Testament's insistence that the Holy Spirit is somehow involved in our experience of both God and Jesus, without being *identical* to either of them (John 16:14; 20:22; Acts 5:9; 8:39; 16:7; Rom. 8:9, 26, 34; 1 Cor. 3:16–18; 1 John 4:2; 5:8). In some sense, Jesus Christ *gives*, or is the *source of*, the Spirit, but the Spirit and Jesus cannot be directly *identified*. The Spirit of God, which the Old Testament recognized as being present in the whole of creation, is now experienced and understood afresh as the Holy Spirit of the God and Father of our Lord Jesus Christ.

Before we continue any further, we must consider the relation between God and Jesus in more detail. The main point that requires careful discussion is this: If Jesus *is* God, does this not imply that God *is Jesus*? In other words, if Jesus Christ is God, must we not draw the conclusion that God is to be identified totally with Jesus Christ? And yet, as we saw above, it is obvious from Jesus' own teaching that he thought that God was still very much in heaven! The paradox we're beginning to wrestle with is expressed well by St. Germanus in his famous seventh-century Christmas hymn:

The Word becomes incarnate
And yet remains on high!

But does not this call into question the traditional Christian affirmation that Jesus *is* God? Perhaps some illustrations may begin to cast some light on the basic problem we're facing here.

Let's suppose that you are on a liner as it crosses the Atlantic Ocean from Europe to America. The journey makes a deep impression upon you as you watch the great ocean swell bursting against the ship and covering it with salty spray. You can feel the great untamed power of the ocean as it tosses the liner to and fro. You are overwhelmed by its sheer immensity as day after day passes without any sight of land. But have you actually experienced the Atlantic Ocean? Your immediate answer would be an indignant "Of course I have!" But on reflection, you might begin to realize the difficulty which lies behind this simple question.

Think of how vast the Atlantic Ocean is: its untold depths, its enormous span from North America to Europe, from one icy polar sea to another. Think of the enormous volume of water which goes to make up its bulk. Did you *really* experience and encounter *all* that water? After all, your liner cut a remarkably narrow and shallow path through that ocean. In terms of the sheer bulk of the ocean, you probably experienced an infinitesimally small percentage of that ocean. So your claim to have experienced it would have to be called into question. You may have sampled a tiny fragment, but you didn't experience the whole thing. While accepting this point, you would, however, have every right to insist that you *did* experience the Atlantic Ocean. You know what it is like through encountering it at first-hand. There is just no way that you could have encountered every single molecule of North Atlantic water, but you did have a real first-hand experience of what that ocean is like.

Let's take another example to make this point clear. Like many people, I vividly remember the moment when a human being set foot on the moon for the first time. It was astonishing to think that history was being made before our very eyes as we watched the television pictures being relayed from the moon, showing Neil Armstrong setting foot on alien ground for the first time. And that same Apollo team brought back samples of moon-rock from that mission, so that they could be analyzed on earth. Now, through the analysis of that rock we came to know more about the moon. True, it was only a sample of the moon that was brought back to earth (to bring the whole moon back would not have been a particularly realistic possibility), but it allowed us a *direct* encounter with the substance of the moon. It really was the moon which was being studied in laboratories throughout the world after the Apollo mission.

With these illustrations in mind, let's come back to the question of the relation between Jesus and God. The doctrine of the incarnation affirms that it really is God who we encounter in Jesus Christ, but that this does not allow us to assert that Jesus and God are identical. In the illustrations we find the same difficulty being experienced. On the one hand, the moon-rock *isn't* identical with the moon (after all, the moon is still there in the night sky); on the other, it *is* identical with the moon in that it lets us find out what the moon is like—it is a representative sample of what the moon is like.

Let's develop this moon-rock illustration further. Until about 1950 we knew the moon only as a distant object. It was something far away which we could only find out about by looking at it through our telescopes. But when the first samples of moon-rock were brought back, we suddenly knew about the moon in a new and direct way. In a way God is like the moon. Before Jesus Christ came, we knew about him in a rather distant way. And then suddenly, on account of the incarnation of Jesus Christ, we knew him in a new, direct, and exciting way. Of course, this new advance didn't come about because of some human technological advance, but through God's decision to become incarnate, to make himself known to us in Jesus Christ. And so where before God could have seemed to be little more than a distant idea, he now becomes a person. And just as people were excited about holding the first moon-rock, and knowing that they held in their hands a bit of the same moon which illuminated the night sky, so the first Christians got excited about being able to touch the one who was none other than God incarnate. (1 John 1:1–4 conveys this excitement well.) We don't need to figure out who God is and what he is like, because he has taken the initiative and told us.

Let's suppose that you are back at high school, and you are asked to find out what gases are present in air. How would you go about doing this? Perhaps the most obvious way would be to take a sample of the air in a small container, and then submit this sample to chemical or physical analysis. And on the basis of the analysis of that small sample, you could say what gases are present in the air. Now, what is the relation of that small sample of air to the earth's atmosphere? Obviously, they aren't identical. All the earth's atmosphere hasn't been compressed into your small container. But on the other hand, that sample *really is air*—it allows you to find out what the air is like. It doesn't exhaust the earth's atmosphere, but it does allow you to find out what it is like.

Jesus allows us to sample God. This is a remarkably helpful way of beginning to think about the incarnation. It really is God whom we encounter, but this doesn't mean that God is *localized* in this one individual, Jesus Christ. Because Jesus *is* God, he allows us to find out what God is like, to have a direct encounter with the reality of God. And because God is not totally identical with Jesus, he remains in heaven, in much the same way as the earth's atmosphere remains there, despite the fact that we've taken a small sample of it. As we have already emphasized in an earlier chapter, God is just too big, too vast, for us to handle—and so God, knowing our weakness and accommodating himself to it (to use Calvin's helpful phrase again), makes himself available for us in a form which we can cope with. The doctrine of the incarnation affirms that it really is God whom we encounter directly in Jesus Christ, just as it affirms that God remains God throughout. A similar situation exists in relation to the Holy Spirit. Again, Christianity rightly insists that in the Holy Spirit we really encounter none other than God himself, but that this doesn't mean that God can be said to be *identical* with the Holy Spirit.

How, then, are we to make sense of the complicated New Testament witness to God, Jesus Christ, and the Holy Spirit? The situation is clarified if we ask two simple questions. First, when we talk about God, which God do we mean? Second, how do we encounter this God? These questions are both of considerable importance in evangelism and preaching, and allow us to begin to gain important insights into the complex biblical witness to Father, Son, and Holy Spirit. We begin with the first of these two questions.

Who is the God of Israel? Of course, one answer might be that he is God—there just isn't any other God, and that is all that there is to it. But a more helpful answer to the question would go something like this. The God of Israel is the God who revealed himself to Abraham, Isaac, and Jacob; the God who led the people of Israel out of Egypt and into the promised land with great signs and wonders. In other words, we tell a story about God which helps us understand who he is.

We might do the same sort of thing when trying to identify a person. Your conversation with someone might go like this. "You know John Brown? You don't. Well, do you remember reading about a man who managed to row a boat all the way across the Atlantic Ocean about a year ago? The boat nearly sank at one point. And when he finished the journey, he wrote a book about it. Ah! You *do* know who I mean." What you are doing here is telling a story which centers on John Brown—you are identifying him in this way. John Brown is the person at the center of the story—the story is told about him. And so it is with God and the Old Testament. The Old Testament identifies God from the history of his people. The great stories of Abraham, Isaac, and Jacob, of the Exodus from Egypt, and so on, are told in order to identify God. The God of Israel is the one who acted in this way.

This is made clear in a number of Old Testament passages (e.g., Ex. 19:4–5; Deut. 26:5–9; Ezek. 20:5–26). Question: Who is God? Answer: Whoever got us out of Egypt! Of course, God has a name as well—a name which proves difficult to translate into English, "Yahweh," "the Lord," and "Jehovah" being three of the best-known translations. But the fact remains that God is usually thought of in terms of what he did, rather than in terms of his name.

Now we turn to the God whom Christians worship and adore. Who is this God? To answer this question, the New Testament tells a story—perhaps the most famous story in the world—the story of Jesus Christ. And as that story reaches its climax in the account of the resurrection of Jesus from the dead, we learn that God, for Christians, is the one who acted in this way to raise Jesus. Question: Who is the God whom Christians worship and adore? Answer: Whoever "raised Jesus our Lord from the dead" (Rom. 4:24). Of course, the New Testament writers make it abundantly clear that the God who "raised Jesus our Lord from the dead" is the same God who got Israel out of Egypt, but the New Testament emphasis falls upon the resurrection of Jesus.

This idea can be taken further without difficulty. The resurrection of Jesus and the pouring out of the Holy Spirit at Pentecost are treated as closely related by the New Testament writers. The complexity of their statements concerning the relationship of God, Jesus, and the Holy Spirit defies neat categorization, but it is clear that "God" is the one who raised Jesus from the dead, and is now present in his church through the Holy Spirit. In many ways, the Christian formula "Father, Son, and Holy Spirit" (Matt. 28:19; 2 Cor. 13:14) corresponds to the Old Testament formula "the God of Abraham, Isaac, and Jacob"—it *identifies* the God in question. Question: What God are you talking about? Answer: The God who raised Jesus Christ from the dead, and is now present in the church through the Holy Spirit. The Trinitarian formula is a shorthand way of identifying exactly what God we are talking about—it is almost a proper name, in fact. Christianity packs into this one neat phrase the high points of salvation history, the big moments (resurrection and Pentecost) when God was so clearly present and active. It specifically links God with these events, just as Israel specifically linked God with the Exodus from Egypt. It focuses our attention on events in which God's presence and activity were concentrated and publicly demonstrated.

The doctrine of the Trinity is thus a summary of the story of God's dealings with his people. It narrates the story of how God created and redeemed us. It hits the high points of this story, affirming that it is the story of the one and the same God throughout. If you were talking about a great modern statesman, such as Winston Churchill or John F. Kennedy, you would concentrate upon the high points of their careers, the moments when they stepped onto the stage of history in order to change its direction. Similarly, the doctrine of the Trinity identifies those great moments in the history of salvation when God was active *and was seen to be active*. It affirms that God is active in his world, that he is known by what he does, and points to the creation, the death, and resurrection of Jesus Christ, and Pentecost as turning points in his dealings with us. The doctrine of the Trinity thus spells out exactly who the God we are dealing with actually is.

The second question follows on from this: How do we *encounter*, how do we *experience*, this God? Where and how may he be found? The New Testament gives two main answers to this question. First, he may be found in Jesus Christ. Second, he may be found through the Holy Spirit. Jesus Christ, as we have seen, is God incarnate: To have seen him is to have seen God; to have encountered him is to have encountered God. But, we might reasonably ask, how do we encounter or experience *Jesus*? The New Testament gives the answer: through the Spirit. The Spirit represents Jesus Christ to us in order that we may gain access to the Father through him.

This idea is developed with great skill in John's Gospel. According to John, the Spirit was given after the resurrection with the explicit purpose of glorifying Jesus and revealing the truth about him (John 14:16–17; 16:13–14). Jesus gives the Spirit to his disciples, emphasizing the close personal link between them (John 20:22). The Spirit leads individuals to a knowledge of Jesus and fellowship with him—and through that knowledge of and fellowship with Jesus comes knowledge of and fellowship with the Father. The close link between Father, Son, and Spirit is emphasized in a number of ways. Just as the Father sends the Son (John 5:23), so it is he sends the Spirit in the name of the Son (John 14:26). Or, as another passage suggests, it is the Son who sends the Spirit (John 16:7). This is given added weight by the encounter between Jesus and his disciples after the resurrection, in which the Son bestows the Spirit upon them (John 20:22). The Son comes from God (John 16:27) just as the Spirit comes from God, sent by the Son (John 15:26).

We could summarize this complex network of relationships like this:

1. The Father sends the Son in his name, and the Son is subject to the Father.
2. The Father sends the Spirit in the name of the Son, and the Spirit is subject to the Father.
3. The Spirit is sent by the Son, and is subject to the Son.

It will be clear that this set of relationships can be represented in the following manner:

Father	Son
Father	Spirit
Son	Spirit

There is a continuity of relationships between Father, Son, and Spirit, thus establishing an unbreakable link between encounter with or experience of the Spirit, the Son, and the Father. Incidentally, there is a long-standing (and, it must be said, rather unproductive) disagreement between the Eastern and Western churches over whether the Spirit proceeds from the Father alone, or from the Father and the Son. The intricacies of this debate cannot concern us here.

It is also important to realize that the New Testament tends to think of the Holy Spirit as the Spirit of Christ as much as of God. The Spirit is understood to stand in the closest of possible relationships to Christ, so that his presence among the people of Christ is equivalent to the presence of Christ himself, just as the presence of Christ is treated as being that of God himself. In other words, to encounter the Son is really to encounter the Father and not some demigod or surrogate. To encounter the Spirit is really to encounter the Son and hence the Father. The enormous importance of this is obvious: The believer of today can encounter the living God at first-hand, not through semidivine or created intermediaries. To affirm the divinity of Father, Son, and Spirit is not to suggest that there are *three* gods, but simply that the one God can be encountered in these different ways, all of which are equally valid. It means that God makes himself available, here and now, directly and personally. There is no point in history which stands outside the saving purposes of God.

The doctrine of the Trinity does not *explain* how it is that God is able to be present in this remarkable way—it simply *affirms* that God *is* present and available in this manner. Any understanding of God which makes it inconceivable that he should be personally present here and now is simply inadequate to do justice to the richness of the biblical witness to and Christian experience of God. The doctrine of the Trinity, like the doctrine of the incarnation, is not some arbitrary and outdated dictate handed down by some confused council—it is the inevitable result of wrestling with the richness and complexity of the Christian experience of God.

We can now see why Christians talk about God being a "three-in-one." One difficulty remains, however, which must be considered. How can God be three persons and one person at the same time? This brings us to an important point which is often not fully understood. The following is a simplified account of the idea of "person" which may be helpful, although the reader must appreciate that simplifications are potentially dangerous. The word "person" has changed its meaning since the third century when it began to be used in connection with the "threefoldness of God." When we talk about God as a person, we naturally think of God as being *one* person. But theologians such as Tertullian, writing in the third century, used the word "person" with a different meaning. The word "person" originally derives from the Latin word *persona*, meaning an actor's face mask—and, by extension, the role which he takes in a play.

By stating that there were three persons but only one God, Tertullian was asserting that all three major roles in the great drama of human redemption are played by the one and the same God. The three great roles in this drama are all played by the same actor: God. Each of these roles may reveal God in a somewhat different way, but it is the same God in every case. So when we talk about God as one person, we mean one person *in the modern sense of the word*, and when we talk about God as three persons, we mean three persons *in the ancient sense of the word*. It is God, and God alone, who masterminded and executes the great plan of salvation, culminating in Jesus Christ. It is he who is present and active at every stage of its long history. Confusing these two senses of the word "person" inevitably leads to the idea that God is actually a committee—which, as we saw earlier, is a thoroughly unhelpful and confusing way of thinking about God. The books suggested for further reading will help clear up this point.

9

God and the Trinity

Most Christians rarely talk about the Trinity—but they talk about God rather a lot. This simple observation is all too often overlooked, for it actually contains an important insight into the purpose and place of the doctrine of the Trinity. For when the Christian talks about "God," the concept of God he is working with, on being fully unpacked, is found to be Trinitarian. In other words, the Christian idea of God is *implicitly* Trinitarian, and all that theologians have done is to make *explicit* what is already *implicit*.

Let's look at some examples to bring this out. Christians pray to God almost as a matter of instinct—it seems to come to them naturally. As they kneel down to say their prayers, they are aware that in some way (which is very difficult to express) God is actually *prompting* them to pray. It is almost as if God is at work within them, creating a desire to pray, or to turn to him in worship and adoration. Yet God is also the one to whom they are praying! A similar situation arises in worship. Although it is God whom we are praising, we are aware that it is somehow God himself who moves us from within to praise him. Theologians have captured this mystery (but certainly not *explained* it) in the formula "to the Father, through the Son, and in the Holy Spirit." In prayer and worship alike, we seem to be brought before the presence of the Father, through the mediation of the Son, in the power of the Holy Spirit.

Now, there is no reason whatsoever why the ordinary believer should want to become a theologian, despite all the protests of those who think that academic theology is a good, splendid, and necessary thing. The ordinary believer wants to keep his faith simple, and this wish must be respected. But *underlying* this simple faith is a far from simple concept of God! When the theologian begins to unpack the idea of God which underlies the New Testament witness and Christian experience, a remarkably complex idea, which strains the limits of human reason, begins to emerge. Earlier, we suggested that an iceberg was a helpful illustration of this point: Only part of it is seen from the surface, and when you begin rummaging around beneath the surface, you discover there is far more to it than meets the eye. And so it is with God. The God in whom the believer puts his simple faith turns out, on closer inspection, to possess hidden depths.

An illustration may make this point clearer. Suppose you turn on your radio or television. Immediately it starts to receive transmissions, snatching the radio waves from the transmitter and converting them to sound and vision. Now, your simple action was merely that of flicking a switch. But *underlying* this simple action which enables the equipment to receive these signals are things like the theory of electromagnetic radiation and integrated circuit technology, about which most of us know nothing. Yet we don't *need* to know about them in order to use our television receivers. If we were to go into the details of how our television works, so that we can *understand* what happens when we turn it on, we would have to face these complicated things. Now, faith in God is to the doctrine of the Trinity what flicking that switch is to the theory of electromagnetic radiation and integrated circuit technology. We can keep our faith simple, or we can explore its depths—and if we opt for the latter, we'll find that the doctrine of the Trinity is already there, perhaps undetected, in our simple faith in the God who raised Jesus Christ from the dead.

The simple believer may well wish to rest content with affirming that God has redeemed him through Jesus Christ, and that he prays to and worships the God who has redeemed him in this wonderful way. But underlying this deceptively simple confession of faith is a very complicated idea of God. Now, if this *idea* of God is simplified, we don't end up with the simple faith of the believer—we end up with no faith at all! To illustrate this point, let's take a simple view of God—the view which is sometimes referred to as "classical theism," which thinks of God as the immortal, invisible, omnipotent and omniscient being who brought this world into existence but is not part of it. This sort of idea of God underlies much classical Greek and Roman thinking, and also some modern ways of thinking about God (such as Deism and Unitarianism). It will be obvious that this view of God presents no real intellectual problems—it is easy to grasp, and involves no difficult ideas such as the divinity of Christ or the doctrine of the Trinity. It is exactly the sort of way of thinking about God which so appealed to Thomas Jefferson, as we noted earlier (p. 195).

But what view of God does this imply? It implies a God who is outside space and time, and cannot become involved with it. It implies a God whom we have to discover, rather than a God who makes himself known. It implies a God who is always beyond us, and not a God who comes to meet us where we are. It implies a static, rather than a dynamic, God. It implies a God who created, but cannot redeem. In short, this view of God bears virtually no resemblance to the God who makes himself known to us through scripture, through the death and resurrection of Jesus Christ, and through Christian experience. And, as a matter of historical fact, it was against precisely this view of God that the early church had to develop its doctrine of the Trinity—in order to prevent the "God and Father of our Lord Jesus Christ" (1 Peter 1:3) becoming confused with this inadequate and deficient view of God. The Christian church was faced with a choice: It either adopted a God who could be *understood*, but could not *redeem*, or a God who could *redeem*, and yet not be *understood*. Rightly, as events proved, it adopted the second of these two options. For history has shown that there was no third option available.

The view of God which we loosely termed "classical theist" is thus easy to understand but totally inadequate to account for the biblical witness to and Christian experience of God. Christians know of God as a dynamic, pulsating activity, something or someone who is alive, and not a static thing "out there." Simple faith knows of a God who is active, who makes himself known to us, who comes to us and meets us—and there just isn't any simple way of describing or portraying this God. In other words, once we try to *conceptualize* this simple faith, we discover just how complex and rich the Christian understanding of God really is. We can develop this point by considering a related theological problem.

In the sixteenth century, a very helpful way of thinking about the identity and relevance of Jesus became widespread (although the ideas involved go back to Eusebius of Caesarea). This is often referred to as the "threefold office of Christ." Jesus' identity and relevance can be summed up in the Trinitarian formula "prophet, priest, and king." The *prophetic office* concerns Jesus' teaching and his miracles; the *priestly office* concerns his offering made for the sin of humanity upon the cross, and the continued intercession of the risen Christ for his people; the *kingly office* concerns the rule of the risen Christ over his people.

These three categories were seen as a convenient summary of all that Jesus Christ had achieved in order to redeem his people. Jesus is prophet (Matt. 21:11; Luke 7:16), priest (Heb. 2:17; 3:1) and king (Matt. 21:5; 27:11), bringing together in his one person the three great offices of the Old Testament. Jesus is the prophet who, like Moses, would see God face to face (Deut. 34:10); he is the king who, like David, would establish his reign over the people of God (2 Sam. 7:12–16); he is the priest who will cleanse his people of their sins. Thus the three gifts brought to Jesus by the Magi (Matt. 2:1–12) were seen as reflecting these three functions.

What, then, is being said when Jesus is spoken of as "prophet, priest, and king?" That there are three individuals called Jesus? Certainly not! What is being said is that the one individual, Jesus Christ, assumes the functions of these three great Old Testament offices or institutions. We can put this more precisely by going back to our discussion in chapter four where we looked at biblical models of God. When we talk about Jesus being "prophet, priest, and king," we are basically saying that there are *three essential models* which must be used if the full significance of Jesus for us is to be brought out. If only one or two of these is used, a deficient and inadequate understanding of the identity and relevance of Jesus Christ results.

For example, if Jesus is thought of as being a prophet, but not a priest or king, we find his identity and significance reduced to that of a religious teacher. If we think of him as both prophet and king, but not a priest, we find him being portrayed as an authoritative religious teacher who rules over those whom he teaches—but whom he doesn't redeem. Only by bringing all three models together do we build up the authentic Christian understanding of the identity of Jesus: The one who redeems his people, who instructs them, and who rules over them with authority.

With this illustration in mind, let us return to talking about God as "Father, Son, and Holy Spirit." A helpful way of looking at this is to say that *three essential models* must be used if the full depth of the Christian experience and understanding of God is to be expressed adequately. No one picture, image or model of God is good enough—and these three models are essential if the basic outlines of the Christian understanding of God is to be preserved. The first model is that of the transcendent God who lies beyond the world as its source and creator; the second is the human face of God, revealed in the person of Jesus Christ; the third is that of the immanent God who is present and active throughout his creation. The doctrine of the Trinity affirms that these three models combine to define the essential Christian insights into the God who raised Jesus Christ from the dead. None of them, taken on its own, is adequate to capture the richness of the Christian experience of God.

A helpful distinction may be introduced at this point to avoid a misunderstanding (technically, "Sabellianism"). We need to draw a distinction between God as he actually is, and the way in which God acts and reveals himself in history. In scripture, we find particular attention being directed to the way in which God acts in history—for example, in creation, redemption, and the giving of the Holy Spirit at Pentecost. Now, this might give the casual reader the impression that God is Father at *this* point in time (for example, at creation), and is Son at *that* point in time (for example, on the cross of Calvary). In other words, to put it very crudely, the impression might be given that God is Father until the birth of Jesus, that he is Son until Pentecost, and that thereafter he is the Holy Spirit. In fact, the doctrine of the Trinity affirms that *all* of God's actions reflect the fact that God is eternally what his revelation in history demonstrates him to be—Father, Son, and Holy Spirit. It may be that certain actions emphasize that God is Father, just as others may emphasize that he is Son—but God acts as a Trinity throughout all his works. Thus even at creation itself we find reference to the Father, the Word, and the Holy Spirit (Gen. 1:1–3).

If God was just "Father," we would have to think of him as the distant and far-removed creator of this world who never becomes directly involved in its affairs. He would govern it from the safety of heaven, far removed from its problems and dangers, rather like a general directing his frontline troops from the safety of a far-distant, bombproof bunker. But Christians know that God just isn't like that. If God was just "Son," we would have to think of God as being identical with Jesus Christ: Jesus is God, and God is Jesus. All of God is concentrated in Jesus, like a billion quarts in a pint-pot. But Christians know that God just isn't like that. Jesus wasn't talking to himself when he prayed. And the New Testament is most careful to insist upon a distinction between Father and Son, as we have seen: God and Jesus cannot just be identified. If God was just the Holy Spirit, we would have to think of him as just part of the world of nature, caught up in the natural process, or in terms similar to nineteenth-century idealist philosophies. But, once more, Christians know that God just isn't like this. He is not reduced to being part of the natural process, but also stands over and against it.

And so we are forced to recognize the need to bring these three models or ways of visualizing God together, if an authentically Christian view of God is to result. Any one of them is only a starting-point—the other two add perspective and depth. To talk of God as Father is really to talk about a one-dimensional God; to talk about God as Father and Son is really to talk about a two-dimensional God; but to talk about God as Father, Son, and Holy Spirit is to talk about a three-dimensional God; God as we encounter him in the real world. Father, Son, and Holy Spirit are the essential building-blocks of the Christian understanding of God.

It would certainly be much simpler if God could be totally described using just one of these models instead of all three. Unfortunately, Christians have to deal with God as he is rather than as they would like him to be. Our little intellectual systems find themselves groaning under the strain of trying to accommodate God, like old wineskins trying to contain new wine. In an earlier part of this book we saw how difficult it is for human words to capture God. If human words cannot adequately describe the aroma of coffee, to use Wittgenstein's famous analogy, how much less can they describe God! Those who complain about the "illogicality" of the doctrine of the Trinity seem to work on the assumption that if you can't understand something, it is wrong for that very reason. They cry, "Contradiction!" and expect everyone to abandon whatever it is that is alleged to be contradictory there and then. But reality just isn't like that.

Much modern science recognizes the fundamental mysteriousness of reality, and that the best we can hope to get is a partial apprehension or grasp of what it's like. Simply because we can only gain a partial glimpse into the way things are, it is inevitable that contradiction of some sort will arise. An example of this from the world of science concerns the nature of light. By the first decade of the twentieth century, it was clear that light behaved in a very strange way—sometimes it seemed to behave as if it was a wave, and sometimes as if it was a particle. It couldn't be both at once, and so the cry "contradiction!" was raised. How could it be two totally different things? But eventually, through the development of the Quantum Theory, it was found that this contradiction expressed a fundamental difficulty in grasping what the nature of light really was. In other words, the contradiction did not arise on account of light, but on account of our difficulties in conceiving it.

To put this another way, we could return to the idea of a model, discussed in an earlier chapter. The nature of light was such that two contradictory models had to be used to account for its behavior. No one model was good enough to explain it, and so two—the models of "wave" and "particle"—had to be used. The difficulty arose because of the way in which we "picture" or conceive light, not on account of the nature of light itself. Now, the relevance of this illustration to the doctrine of the Trinity will be obvious. Basically, we are suggesting that God, like light, is very difficult to "picture." The difficulty arises simply on account of the way in which we think about God. And where *two* contradictory models of light were needed to account for its behavior (prior to the development of Quantum Theory), *three* "contradictory" models of God are required to account for the way in which Christians encounter and experience him.

Let's take this illustration a little further. Most of us know what light is without needing to think about waves, particles, or Quantum Theory. Light is what we need in order to see, to do our everyday business, to read and write. It is what comes out of the sun, and to a lesser extent from the moon. It is what we get when we switch on electric light bulbs or strip lighting. If we were physicists, we might want to think about light in much more detail and go into the full complexities of it—and so we might start talking about waves, particles, and Quantum Theory. But we don't need to do this in order to make use of light or to recognize it when we see it.

Similarly, most of us know who and what God is without needing to think about the Trinity. God is the one who created this world and us. He is the "God and Father of our Lord Jesus Christ." He is the one who raised Jesus Christ from the dead. He is the one who knocks at the door of our life, gently asking to be admitted. He is the one whom we worship and adore, and to whom we pray, and so on. Now, if we were theologians we might like to think about God in more detail, and that thinking would eventually lead to the doctrine of the Trinity—and so we would start talking about Father, Son, and Holy Spirit. But we don't *need* to do this in order to encounter or experience him, any more than we need to be experts on the nature of light to switch on car headlights. It is not the *doctrine of the Trinity* which underlies the Christian faith, but the living God whom we encounter through Jesus Christ in the power of the Holy Spirit—the God who *is* the Trinity.

How, then, are we to bring these three models of God together? Probably because I'm Irish, one of my favorite people is St. Patrick, patron saint of Ireland. Patrick's analogy for the relation between God and the Trinity was provided by the shamrock—a three-leafed plant looking rather like clover, Lucerne or alfalfa. Each of the three portions of the leaf is an essential part of that leaf, but the leaf itself is greater than its parts. It is the leaf itself which models God, and the three parts of the leaf which model the individual persons of the Trinity. A similar analogy is provided by a triangle, with its three sides, or by a family of two parents and their child. The individual persons of the Trinity—Father, Son, and Holy Spirit—combine to create a whole in which their individualities are transcended to give a higher unity. Thus when we think of God, we don't think of three *individual gods*, but of one God whom we experience and encounter in a threefold manner.

The following analogy may help bring out the distinctive role of the doctrine of the Trinity. Imagine a river—perhaps a great river, like the Nile or Mississippi—as it enters the sea, maybe through a great estuary. You wonder what the source of the river is like and where it might be. Let us suppose that you own a small boat which you launch into the estuary and begin the journey upstream to trace the river to its source—perhaps like the great expeditions of the last century which set out in search of the source of the Nile. You begin from where the river rushes in to embrace the sea, and follow the course of its stream until finally (maybe a very long time later!) you realize that the great lake which you have just entered has no other streams entering or leaving it—you have traced the river to its source.

The first point to make is the following. The estuary, the stream, and the source are all part of the same thing—the river. All three collectively make up the totality of that river, and the absence of any of them is unthinkable. A river must have a source, a flux or stream, and a place at which it enters the sea or another lake. The eleventh-century theologian Anselm of Canterbury used the analogy of the River Nile to make a very similar point.

It is, however, the second point which is more important. We began the search for the source of that river at the point at which it met the sea—the point at which its flux, its stream or flow, entered the sea. It was this point which allowed us to gain entry to the flux of the stream itself. And it was the stream itself which both guided us to its source and provided the means by which we might get there. It pointed the way and gave us the medium on which the boat could travel safely. And finally its source was reached—it is here that we found our journey's end. Can you see that it was the river itself—from estuary, to stream, to source—which both pointed the way to and provided the means of reaching our objective? At every point in the journey, the river itself helped us in our search, providing both directions and the medium of transport. Although our interest was really in the source of the river, every point on that river—whether estuary or stream—derived from that source. We were already encountering the water from that source as we entered the river estuary. Perhaps it was not immediately recognizable as the water from that source, but the fact remains that it was the same water.

Let us use this illustration to help us understand the doctrine of the Trinity. The doctrine of the Trinity affirms that, even as we begin our search for God, it is God who helps us to find him. It is God who sets us on the right path, directs us, and provides us with the means we need to find him. God is involved from the beginning to the end of our search for him, of our encounter with him. It may be that we do not recognize God fully for what he is and what he is doing, but the fact remains that he is involved. God is both the goal of our journey and the means by which we find him. We come to the Father through the Son in the power of the Holy Spirit. At every stage, God is already there. And it is insights such as these that the doctrine of the Trinity is meant to safeguard, by preventing us from adopting inadequate views of God.

In the end, however, it is very difficult to find illustrations for the doctrine of the Trinity—simply because the doctrine is in a class of its own. There is really nothing which can illustrate it adequately, although we can hope to cast light on it in various ways. Earlier we drew attention to the danger of confusing a *representation* of God with the *reality* of God. There is every danger that we will fall into the same trap with the Trinity, by confusing a representation of the doctrine (such as a shamrock leaf or a river) with the Trinity itself, perhaps rejecting the Trinity because we aren't convinced by the illustrations used to represent it. Perhaps it is necessary once more to emphasize the mysteriousness of God—not to discourage thinking about him, but simply to draw attention to the fact that we are never going to be able to describe him adequately.

In this book we have been exploring the Christian understanding of God: the way in which we speak and think about him, the idea of a "personal God," and finally the doctrine of the Trinity. There is undoubtedly much more that could be said about these, and it could unquestionably be said much better as well. However, it is time to draw the great themes of this book together, as we prepare to conclude.

10

The Strong Name of the Trinity

What sort of animal, my wife and I wondered, should we buy for our son as a pet? Eventually, our thoughts turned to rabbits, and we bought a little book on the subject of . . . rabbits. It was most helpful, describing breeds of rabbits which we had never heard of before, including Flemish Giants. As I read about these enormous rabbits, some words seemed to stand out from the page: "Caution: these rabbits are too big to be handled by children." And the book went on to recommend dwarf rabbits—which can be held in the palm of the hand—as ideal children's pets. Isn't this just the way we try to treat God? We try to make him into something which we can handle, something which we can control when in fact God is just too big and too great to be handled by human beings. As Martin Luther once remarked, "It is God who handles us, and now we who handle God!" We tend to treat God as if he were some kind of pet, something which we can tame, something which we can domesticate.

In the end, the doctrine of the Trinity represents our admission that we cannot tame God to fit our tidy little systems. God just will not fit into the palm of our hands so that we can hold him down! Like the wild West wind in Shelley's *Ode*, he is uncontrollable. Far too many thinkers regard God as some sort of biological specimen, something which can be pinned down beneath a microscope slide to be studied at our convenience and under conditions of our own choosing. Perhaps the famous opening words of Hannah Glasse's eighteenth-century recipe for Hare Soup may show up the basic problem here: "First catch your hare!"

As we have been arguing throughout this book, the Christian theologian isn't in the position of a geologist studying rocks or a paleontologist studying fossils—all they have to do is go out and find their rocks or fossils. Perhaps it is more helpful to think of the theologian as being like a student of rare butterflies—he has to find *and capture* his specimens. Unlike rocks and fossils, butterflies are very much alive, and are not enthusiastic about being captured! The theologian is forced to admit that the initiative lies with God. We may see things and hear rumors of God's existence and nature from the world around about us, but the full self-disclosure of God is something which happens on his terms. In other words, God lets us see him in a particular way, and we must take him as and where we find him. God, as we have said before, is not a concept or idea which we can kick around at leisure in our seminar rooms—he is the living God who created the world and us, and who obstinately refuses to surrender himself to our theological dissecting tables.

The doctrine of the Trinity is the response of the Christian community down the centuries as it has responded to and reflected upon God's revelation of himself. Everyone likes simple religions, and there is always a temptation to make Christianity as easy as it possibly can be. But there's a limit to how much you can simplify something which is already very complicated. Try to imagine something very complicated which you're familiar with, and work out how you would explain it in very easy terms to someone else. You will almost certainly find yourself oversimplifying it—as you explain your subject, you will probably find yourself thinking, "It's not really like this at all, but unless I explain it like this, you'll never understand it." It is so much easier to think of God in very simple terms—perhaps as the great heavenly ruler of the universe, far removed from this world. But the problem with this is obvious: This isn't just an oversimplification of the Christian understanding of God, it's a serious distortion of this understanding. The really simple religions are actually ones which have been *invented* by human beings.

Christians, then, respond to God as he has revealed himself in scripture, in Christian experience, and in the life, death, and resurrection of Jesus Christ. If Christians had just invented their idea of God, of course, they could simplify it enormously—but the point is that they haven't. They don't have control over God and the way in which he has revealed himself. This is something which is "given," something which is already there even before we begin to think about it. In the eleventh century, Anselm of Canterbury came up with a formula which is very helpful in understanding this point— "faith seeking understanding (*fides quaerens intellectum*)." In other words, faith comes first—and *then* we have to try and understand it.

Imagine an iceberg suddenly floating toward you. In some senses, encountering God's revelation of himself is rather like encountering an iceberg—it's already there, and once we encounter it, we can explore it and find out what it's like. But we can't lay down what that iceberg ought to be like—we have to take it as it comes. Nor is it something we've invented—it is something already there, independent of us. An image of God which we invent is nothing more and nothing less than an idol, and that is why it is so important for the New Testament writers that Jesus Christ is the God-given image of God (see Col. 1:15). In other words, we are *authorized* by God to use this image of himself. It is an image which has been given to us by God, rather than one which we have invented or made up.

When thinking about God, we can do one of two things. We can invent an idea of God, laying down what God ought to be like in the light of what everyone has said about God during human history, or we can respond to God as he has revealed himself. The difficulty with the former option is that it isn't a realistic option at all. If you look at the ideas of God which human beings have had in history, they have virtually nothing in common. Western philosophy has been obsessed with the idea of God which is sometimes called "classical theism"—but this bears little relation to the idea of God associated with Hinduism, Buddhism, or African tribal religions.

All too often, Western philosophers seem to work on the assumption that they know exactly what God is like, through thinking intelligent thoughts about the universe and reading Platonic dialogues, and that they are thus in a position to pass judgment on what everyone else (such as Christians) says about him. It is as if they have access to some sort of infallible source of knowledge about God which allows them to lay down what God is really like and criticize anyone whose views happen to differ from theirs as being "philosophically naïve." The truth of the matter, however, is that God has always proved to be something of an enigma to human reason. All human statements about God, whether made by the Christian believer or a professional philosopher, are matters of faith. That is one of the reasons why the self-revelation of God is such good news.

Against the tendency of human beings to invent or construct their own idea of God and then worship it (which is idolatry) or declare that it's not worth worshiping (which is rationalism), we may set the exciting and deeply disturbing Christian insight that God has taken the initiative in revealing himself to us. Who God is and what he is like—these are matters on which God himself has decided to have the final word. Christian thinkers thus attempt to wrestle with God as he has revealed himself in scripture, particularly in its testimony to Jesus Christ. And they have every right to resist the criticism of those who suggest that they are being "philosophically naïve" in doing so. After all, philosophers—who have some difficulty in even reaching any agreement on whether God exists—do not have access to some private and infallible knowledge of God which is denied to everyone else.

For some modern critics of the doctrine of the Trinity, it is obvious that it rests upon a series of the most appalling mistakes, including (to name only the more obvious) mathematical confusion and philosophical unsophistication. Some of these critics seem to think that some early Christian committee had sat down to shape their understanding of God, and—being unable to agree upon how many bits of God there were—thought of a number between one and ten and agreed upon three as a judicious compromise. Like the White Queen in Lewis Carroll's *Through the Looking Glass*, who made a habit of believing six impossible things each day before breakfast, they took a certain pleasure in the absurdity of their ideas. The idea of the God of Christianity being just one, according to some of these critics, was found to be rather demeaning to God, and so it was thought necessary to expand God somewhat to emphasize his greatness and superiority over other gods. Now the early Christians were, of course, very primitive people and, as the latest scholarship had just discovered, primitive peoples could count no higher than three. In other words, they understood "three" as we would understand "infinity," so that the statement that "God is three" really meant "God is infinite." And so the idea of God being three, instead of just one (or in addition to being one), came into being as an expression of the infinite superiority of the Christian God over all other gods.

Scholarship has, however, moved on since the 1890s! Primitive peoples, it was discovered, could cope with numbers far in excess of three. Anyway, it was perfectly obvious that the doctrine of the Trinity had nothing to do with mathematics, but was an attempt to express the fullness and richness of the Christian experience and understanding of God. It attempts to capture the mystery of God in a form of words, to distill a host of insights into a formula. It is "bones to philosophy, but milk to faith" (John Donne). The doctrine of the Trinity is to the Christian experience of God what grammar is to poetry—it establishes a structure, a framework, which allows us to make sense of something which far surpasses it. It is the skeleton supporting the flesh of Christian experience. The Christian experience of God was already there, long before the doctrine of the Trinity was formulated, but the doctrine casts light on that experience and helps us understand *who* it is that we are experiencing. It *interprets* our experience of God *as experience of God*. It eliminates inadequate and unsatisfactory ideas of God which stand in his way—just as we might dredge a channel to allow the current to flow more freely, so the doctrine of the Trinity dredges the channels of our minds, removing obstacles (such as sub-Christian ideas of God) which stand in the path of God as he moves to encounter us.

The doctrine of the Trinity, then, is the Christian's last word about God. It is not something which we begin with, but something we end up with. When you're trying to explain Christianity to someone, the last thing you'd want to talk about is the Trinity. Instead, you might begin by talking about Jesus Christ, about his death on the cross and resurrection, or you might talk about the possibility of encountering or experiencing God here and now. But even as you begin to talk about God in such ways, you are working within the framework established by the doctrine of the Trinity. You could say that the doctrine of the Trinity is latent within the way you're talking about God, and all that theologians have really done is to draw out something which is already there. The doctrine of the Trinity wasn't *invented*—it was *uncovered*. It is something implicit within all Christian thinking about God, and all that theologians have done is to make it explicit. It's like someone drawing a map which shows all the features of the country, thus allowing you to establish how they relate to each other. Those relations are already there—the map just helps make them clearer.

What, then, is the importance of the doctrine of the Trinity? Someone once asked Louis Armstrong what jazz was. "If you gotta ask what it is, you'll never know!" he replied. And people often ask who or what God is, and expect a slightly more helpful answer. The doctrine of the Trinity is a summary of the Christian's answer to who God is and what he is like. It is like the synopsis of a story—the story of our redemption through the death and resurrection of Jesus Christ. It hits the high points of that story, talking about our creation, our redemption and our renewal. But it is the story of the one and the same God who stoops down to meet his creatures where they are in order to bring them back to him. It is a summary of God's relevance for us, of what God does for us. It is a declaration that the same God who so wonderfully created us has acted even more wonderfully to redeem us.

One of the most powerful of all the Christian church's many hymns is the ancient Irish hymn usually ascribed to Patrick, the patron saint of Ireland, and generally known as "St. Patrick's Breastplate." In this hymn, the believer is constantly reminded of the richness and the depth of the Christian understanding of God, and that it is this God who has been bonded to the believer through faith:

> I bind unto myself today
> The strong name of the Trinity,
> By invocation of the same,
> The Three in One and One in Three.

It is the power and presence of *this* God which allows the Christian to hold his head up high in a world of darkness and sin.

The hymn then moves on to survey the vast panorama of the works of God in history. The believer is reminded that the God whom he has dared to make his own through faith is the same God who brought the earth into being, and as the believer contemplates the wonders of nature, he may grasp the astonishing insight that the God whose presence and power undergirds the world of nature is the same God whose presence and power is channeled into his individual existence:

> I bind unto myself today
> The virtues of the star-lit heaven,
> The glorious sun's life-giving ray,
> The whiteness of the moon at even,
> The flashing of the lightning free,
> The whirling wind's tempestuous shocks,
> The stable earth, the deep salt sea,
> Around the old eternal rocks.

Our attention then turns to the work of God in redemption. The same God who created the world—the earth, the sea, the sun, moon, and stars—acted in Jesus Christ to redeem us. In the history of Jesus Christ, from his incarnation to his second coming, we may see God acting to redeem us, an action which we appropriate and make our own through faith:

> I bind this day to me for ever,
> By power of faith, Christ's incarnation;
> His baptism in the Jordan river;
> His death on cross for my salvation.
> His bursting from the spicèd tomb;
> His riding up the heavenly way;
> His coming at the day of doom:
> I bind unto myself today.

The believer is invited to reflect upon the history of Jesus Christ: his incarnation, baptism, death, resurrection, ascension, and final coming on the last day. And all these, Patrick affirms, are the actions of the same God who created us, as he moves to redeem us through Jesus Christ. All these were done for us, for the sinful creatures upon whom a gracious God took pity.

Finally, the God who called the universe into being and redeemed us through the great sequence of events which is the history of Jesus Christ is also the God who is with us here and now, who meets us and stays with us:

> I bind unto myself today,
> The power of God to hold and lead,
> His eye to watch, his might to stay,
> His ear to hearken to my need;
> The wisdom of my God to teach,
> His hand to guide, His shield to ward,
> The word of God to give me speech,
> His heavenly host to be my guard.

This is the God who is witnessed to in scripture and encountered in human experience—the God who broke the mold of human thinking, forcing us to stretch our ideas and categories to their limits in order even to begin to accommodate him. This is no God who wound the world up, like a clockwork mechanism, and then left it to run on its own; this is no God who hurls down dictates from the safety of the Olympian heights; this is no God who is dissolved into, and indistinguishable from, the natural process; this is the God who makes himself known to us and available for us through the death and resurrection of Jesus Christ, "the God and Father of our Lord Jesus Christ."

In this book we have been laying the foundations for the Christian understanding of the Trinity. We have been discovering the doctrine of the

Trinity as we have reflected on the way in which Christians think and speak about the God who meets us and gives himself to us in Jesus Christ. The reader who wishes to develop his thinking on this doctrine further should consult the books recommended for further reading at the end of this book. The foundations which we have been laying in this book may be built upon, and there is much more that could be said about the doctrine than has proved possible in these pages. It is, however, hoped that the reader will have been stimulated to think about this difficult doctrine of the Christian faith with more confidence than might otherwise have been the case.

The doctrine of the Trinity, then, sums up the astonishingly rich and hard-won insights of Christian believers down the ages into the nature of God. For the theologian, it is a safeguard against inadequate understandings of God; for the Christian believer, it is a reminder of the majesty and mystery of the God who gave himself for his people upon the cross. It does not really help us to understand God, but it does enable us to avoid inadequate ways of thinking about him. Faced with the choice between an invented God who could be understood without the slightest difficulty, and the real God who couldn't, the church unhesitatingly chose the latter option. The believer will still find it easier to talk about "God" than to talk about "the Trinity," and need hardly be criticized for doing so. But when that believer begins to reflect upon who this God whom he worships and adores really is, his thoughts will move toward the "strong name of the Trinity." It is here that the long process of thinking about God comes to a stop, as we realize that we can take it no further. And it is here that thought gives way to worship and adoration.

> Holy, holy, holy, Lord God Almighty!
> All Thy works shall praise Thy name
> In earth, and sky, and sea;
> Holy, holy, holy, merciful and mighty,
> God in three Persons, blessed Trinity!
>   (Bishop Reginald Heber)

BIBLIOGRAPHY

For an introduction to the insights concerning the identity of Jesus Christ which underlie the doctrine of the Trinity, see Alister McGrath, *Understanding Jesus* (Eastbourne, Kingsway Publications, 1987).

The remaining books suggested for further reading are generally of a more academic nature, but they will allow the interested reader to develop further the arguments found in the present book.

For a discussion of proofs and alleged disproofs of the existence of God, see:

Hans Küng, *Does God Exist?* (London, Collins, 1980).
Richard Swinburne, *The Existence of God* (Oxford, Clarendon Press, 1979).

For further discussion of "models," see the following:

Ian T. Ramsey, *Models and Mystery* (Oxford, Oxford University Press, 1964).
Ed. F. W. Dillistone "Talking about God: Models, Ancient and Modern," *Myth and Symbol* (London, SPCK, 1966), pp. 76–97.

For excellent discussions of aspects of the doctrine of God, see:

J. I. Packer, *Knowing God* (London, Hodder and Stoughton, 1973).
Ronald H. Nash, *The Concept of God: An Exploration of Contemporary Difficulties with the Attributes of God* (Grand Rapids, Mich., Zondervan, 1982).

For Further discussion of the doctrine of the Trinity, see:

E. Calvin Beisner, *God in Three Persons* (Wheaton, Ill., Tyndale Press, 1984). This short work gives an excellent account of the biblical foundations of the doctrine.
Eds. Carl E. Braaten and Robert W. Jenson, *Christian Dogmatics* (Philadelphia, Penn., Fortress Press, 1984), vol. 1, pp. 83-191. This important essay explores the place of the doctrine in systematic theology.
Royce Gordon Gruenler, *The Trinity in the Gospel of John*, (Grand Rapids, Mich., Baker Book House, 1986). A careful study of the Trinity as it is presented in John's gospel. Dr. Gruenler has promised to supplement this work with two further books on the Trinity, to which we may look forward.
Alasdair Heron, *The Holy Spirit* (London, Marshall, Morgan and Scott, 1983). This useful book includes a particularly helpful discussion of the differences

225

between the Eastern and Western churches on the role of the Holy Spirit within the Trinity.

Two influential twentieth century discussions of the doctrine are:

Karl Barth, *Church Dogmatics* I/1 (Edinburgh, Clarke, 1936).

Jürgen Moltmann, *The Trinity and the Kingdom of God: The Doctrine of God* (London, SCM, 1981).

UNDERSTANDING
—DOCTRINE—

INTRODUCTION

Doctrine! The very word sends shivers down a lot of spines. The mental journey between "doctrine" and "doctrinaire" is all too short and easy for comfort. Doctrine suggests something petty and pedantic. It conjures up images of hard-bitten theologians, scrabbling furiously and pointlessly over words. It even evokes painful memories of the Spanish Inquisition, when men and women suffered for not accepting the right ideas. Doctrine seems like a relic of a bygone age. It may have been important once upon a time. But not now. There is a widespread feeling that doctrine is an irrelevance to modern Christian faith and Christian life. One influential Christian writer once remarked that some of the works he read on Christian doctrine made as much sense and were just about as exciting as mathematical tables!

This attitude is perfectly understandable. Many people who have had a profound experience of God find that doctrines seem somehow terribly *unreal*. Take a woman who has felt herself overwhelmed by the closeness of God at the birth of her first child. Or a student who experiences an awesome sense of God's forgiveness as she prays. Or someone who, like the present writer, has been out alone in the Arabian desert in the depths of the night, and caught a sense of the immensity of God amidst the splendor of the starry heavens. All these have felt the presence of God. And if they turn from this experience to consider Christian doctrines, they often feel a sense of anticlimax. The doctrines seem stale and frigid in comparison with what they know of God. They just don't measure up to the real thing. They seem like mathematical equations, cold and impersonal. Surely God's not like that! What conceivable relevance can they have? Why bother with them? Surely doctrine has no relevance for the ordinary believer.

Now that I've sketched the problems people have with doctrine, I suppose you expect me to say something like this: "Well, you're wrong! Doctrine is vitally important, and you ought to accept this as a fact, and stop complaining." However, I want to say nothing of the sort. You are right. I feel exactly the same way myself. Doctrine *does* seem something of an irrelevance. It does seem more than a little pedantic. And it does seem strange to be concerned with precise neat little formulas about God. All these are real, not imagined, problems. *Christianity is not, and never has been, about finding the right combination of words! It is about encountering the living and loving God.*

But there is more to doctrine than you might think. And, curiously, doctrine actually deals with exactly the same problems just noted. If we want to talk about God, to share our experiences of him, or to try and explain why Jesus Christ is so important, we end up making doctrinal statements. Without fully realizing it, every Christian believer is concerned with doctrine. In this book, I want to try to explore what doctrine is, and why it matters. Thinking about doctrine is actually an excellent way of deepening our understanding of our faith. And it is certainly not an irrelevance! But that is to skip ahead to the conclusion of this book. Let's begin somewhere more suitable.

1

Getting Started

Commitment is fundamental to any but the most superficial forms of human existence. In his famous essay "The Will to Believe," the celebrated psychologist William James makes it clear that there are some choices in life which cannot be avoided. To be human is to make decisions. We are all obliged to choose between options which are, in James' words, "living, forced and momentous." In matters of morality, politics, and religion, we must make conscious choices—and, as James stresses, our whole life hangs upon the choice made.

Every movement which has ever competed for the loyalty of human beings has done so on the basis of a set of beliefs. Whether the movement is religious or political, philosophical or artistic, the same pattern emerges—a group of ideas, of beliefs, are affirmed to be, in the first place, true, and in the second, more important. It is impossible to live life to its fullness, and avoid encountering claims for our loyalty of one kind or another. Marxism, socialism, atheism—all alike demand that we consider their claims. The same is true of liberalism, whether in its religious or political forms. As Alasdair MacIntyre demonstrated so persuasively in his *Whose Justice? Which Rationality?* liberalism is committed to a definite set of beliefs, and hence to certain values. It is one of the many virtues of MacIntyre's important work that it mounts a devastating critique of the idea that liberalism represents some kind of privileged and neutral vantage point from which other doctrinal or religious traditions (such as evangelicalism) may be evaluated. Rather, liberalism entails precommitment to liberal beliefs and values. Liberal beliefs (and thus values) affect liberal decisions—in ethics, religion, and politics.

Time and time again, life-changing decisions are demanded of us. How shall I vote at the next election? What do I think about the riddle of human destiny? What form of educational system do I consider to be best? Is the use of deadly force justifiable to defend democracy? What rights do animals have? All these questions force us to think about our beliefs—and make a choice. You cannot sit on the fence throughout life, as William James demonstrated with such remarkable clarity. To suspend judgment on every question which life raises is to be trapped in an insipid agnosticism, where all the great questions arising out of human experience receive the same shallow response: "I don't know—and I don't care."

Thinking people need to construct and inhabit mental worlds. They need to be able to discern some degree of ordering within their experience, to make sense of its riddles and enigmas. They need to be able to structure human existence in the world, to allow it to possess meaning and purpose, and to allow decisions to be made concerning the future of that existence. In order for anyone—Christian, atheist, Marxist, or Moslem—to make informed moral decisions, it is necessary to have a set of values concerning human life. Those values are determined by beliefs, and those beliefs are stated as doctrines. Christian doctrine thus provides a fundamental framework for Christian living.

Christianity is not a set of woolly and ill-defined (but vaguely benevolent) attitudes to the world in general and other human beings in particular. It is not an unstructured assortment of emotions or feelings. Rather, it centers on beliefs about Jesus Christ, which give rise to specific religious and moral attitudes to God, other human beings, and the world. Jesus Christ is the beginning, the center, and the end of the Christian message of hope. At the heart of the Christian faith stands a person, not a doctrine—but a person who gives rise to doctrine the moment we begin to wrestle with the question, "Who is Jesus Christ?" The idea that we can somehow worship, adore, or imitate Jesus Christ without developing doctrines about him is indefensible.

The novelist Dorothy L. Sayers is perhaps best known as the creator of Lord Peter Wimsey, a distinguished aristocratic amateur detective. She was also no mean amateur theologian, who was thoroughly impatient with those who declared that doctrine was "hopelessly irrelevant" to the life and thought of the ordinary Christian believer. "Ministers of the Christian religion often assert that it is, present it for consideration as though it were, and, in fact, by the faulty exposition of it make it so." She was especially—and rightly—scornful of those who argue that it is principles, not doctrines, which distinguish Christianity from paganism. Writing in the depths of the Second World War, she declared:

> That you cannot have Christian principles without Christ is becoming increasingly clear, because their validity depends upon Christ's authority; and, as we have seen, the totalitarian states, having ceased to believe in Christ's authority, are logically quite justified in repudiating Christian principles. If "the average man" is required to "believe in Christ" and accept his authority for "Christian principles," it is surely relevant to inquire who or what Christ is, and why his authority should be accepted.... It is quite useless to say that it doesn't matter particularly who or what Christ was or by what authority he did those things, and that even if he was only a man, he was a very nice man and we ought to live by his principles: for that is merely Humanism, and if the "average man" in Germany chooses to think that Hitler is a nicer sort of man with still more attractive principles, the Christian Humanist has no answer to make.

Why do Christians take the teachings of Jesus Christ so seriously? Why do they attribute such authority to him? Underlying the authority of Jesus is the Christian understanding of who he is. Christians regard Christ as authoritative because, in the end, they recognize him to be none other than God himself, coming among us as one of us. The authority of Jesus Christ rests in his being God incarnate. His teaching is lent dignity, weight, and authority by his identity. And that identity can only be spelled out fully by the doctrine of the person of Christ. Christian principles thus rest on Christian doctrine.

Some writers have suggested that the authority of Christ rests upon the excellence of his moral and religious teaching. This position initially sounds attractive; on closer inspection, however, it turns out actually to undermine that very authority. By what standards do we judge his teaching? The argument rests on knowing in advance what moral or religious teachings are to be regarded as outstanding. Jesus Christ is then regarded as authoritative, to the extent that he echoes these already existing standards. He is judged by a higher authority—what these writers regard as morally and religiously acceptable. For classical Christian thought, it is existing human religious and moral ideas which are to be challenged and judged by Jesus Christ; for these modern writers, it is existing notions of morality and religion which are to judge Jesus Christ. Christ is thus placed firmly under human authority, denied any role of challenging and overturning accepted human ideas and values.

It may seem very attractive to see Jesus as some sort of projection or validation of our own standards and aspirations. Yet if we allow that Jesus has authority simply because he echoes what we happen to believe to be right, we are setting ourselves above him in judgment. It is our own concepts of morality, our own standards (wherever they come from) that are judging him. And all too often those standards are little more than the prejudices of our own culture. By judging Jesus in this way, we lock ourselves into our own situation. We are prisoners of our culture, unable to see its limitations. We are unwilling to accept criticism from outside it. If Jesus echoes our own values and aspirations, we gladly accept this support; if Jesus should happen to challenge them, we dismiss him, or choose to ignore the challenge. Jesus is thus denied any possibility of transforming us, by challenging our presuppositions. We are reluctant to hear him, where he does not echo our own voices. If Jesus has any authority in this way, it is simply as a passive echo of our own ideas and values. "I happen to buy most of what Jesus said, but not because it's in the Bible or because he said it, but rather because I find it existentially valid. And I have to be candid enough to say that there are a few things Jesus said that I can't buy" (Thomas Maurer).

It is for this reason that doctrine is of central importance. Christianity does not assert that Christ has authority on account of the excellence or acceptability of his teaching; rather, the teaching of Christ has authority and validity on account of who he is—God incarnate. The New Testament provides ample justification of this point; throughout his writings, Paul begins by making doctrinal affirmations, and then proceeds to draw moral conclusions. Doctrine comes first; moral and religious principles follow. For example, the doctrine of the resurrection leads to an attitude of hope in the face of adversity; the doctrine of the incarnation of Christ leads to an attitude of humility on the part of believers; the doctrine of the reconciliation of believers to God through Christ leads to a plea that believers should be reconciled among themselves.

Doctrine about Christ arises from the need to tell the truth about Christ; to explain who he is, and his significance for the human situation. To fail to develop doctrines about Jesus Christ is to reveal a dangerously shallow commitment to him, and to the unremitting human quest for truth. Doctrine reflects a commitment to truth on the one hand, and to the centrality of Jesus Christ to the Christian faith on the other. It is no good to mumble vague generalities about Jesus being "the moral educator of mankind" or "a good man who deserves to be imitated." It is necessary to spell out, as precisely as possible, what it is that Christians have found, and continue to find, so profoundly attractive, authoritative, and challenging about him.

Doctrine is the Christian church giving an account of itself, as it answers to the call of God in Jesus Christ. It is the response of the human mind to God, as love is the response of the human heart. The nucleus of the Christian faith is the mystery of the person of Jesus Christ. What does his crucifixion and resurrection tell us about ourselves? About God? About the world? In what way can they change our situation? What must we do if we are to appropriate, to make our own, the new possibilities and opportunities opened up by this most dramatic manifestation of the power of God at work in human history?

If doctrine at times seems to be little more than a barren repetition of ancient words and formulas, approaching a mindless ritual, it is because we have failed to appreciate its vitality and relevance. The failure of human language to capture the richness of experience has long been known and lamented. The Austrian philosopher Ludwig Wittgenstein pointed out that it was impossible to describe the aroma of coffee using words; imagine how much worse it must be when trying to describe something as profound as the Christian experience of being redeemed from sin. Doctrine is an attempt to spell out in human words something which cannot really be expressed in words. Hilary of Poitiers, one of the more perceptive Christian writers of the fourth century, captured this dilemma perfectly: "We are compelled to attempt what is unattainable, to climb where we cannot reach, to speak what we cannot utter. Instead of the bare adoration of faith, we are compelled to entrust the profound matters of faith to the perils of human language." Doctrine may seem to be excessively preoccupied with the details of verbal formulas—but this reflects the basic Christian conviction that, if the truth about Jesus Christ is proclaimed and accepted, the human situation can be transformed. Doctrine aims to provide a springboard to propel us into a personal response to the truth and the love of God, revealed in Jesus Christ. "To know Christ is to know his benefits," as the sixteenth-century theologian Philip Melanchthon wrote. Properly understood, doctrine may be continually rediscovered as something newly meaningful for our own day and age.

In practice, most Christians probably do not need to be persuaded that doctrine is important. Most realize the importance of doctrine to their faith, and some may have found the arguments presented in this chapter unnecessary. In his comedy *Le Bourgeois Gentilhomme*, the seventeenth-century French playwright Molière tells of the astonishment of Monsieur Jourdain on being told that, when he asked for his slippers and nightcap, he was speaking prose. "Good Lord!" he exclaimed. "I have been speaking prose for more than forty years without knowing it." In much the same way, most Christians make doctrinal statements without realizing it. Every time a hymn is sung, the creed is recited, sermons are heard, or a scriptural passage is discussed—matters of doctrine are involved.

Nevertheless, many Christians do have difficulty with doctrine. They may be puzzled over why it should have caused so much controversy. They may occasionally have wondered if it might be possible to abandon doctrine, without doing any real harm to the Christian faith. And for some, certain doctrines cause considerable bewilderment—such as that most mysterious of all doctrines, the Trinity. The remainder of this book aims to deal with those questions. We begin by considering in more detail precisely what doctrine is.

PART ONE

Doctrine: What It Is

Christian doctrine is the response of the Christian church to God, as he has revealed himself, especially in scripture and through Jesus Christ. It is an obedient, responsible, and faithful attempt to make sense of the cluster of astonishing and exciting possibilities opened up by the coming of Jesus Christ. As the following chapters will make clear, doctrine is a complicated matter, which is not adequately described simply as "Christian teachings." Doctrine serves four major purposes. It aims:

1. to tell the truth about the way things are.
2. to respond to the self-revelation of God.
3. to address, interpret, and transform human experience.
4. to give Christians, as individuals and as a community, a sense of identity and purpose.

We shall explore each of these aspects of the nature of doctrine in the chapters which follow.

2

The Way Things Are: Doctrine and Description

Relevance" and "meaningfulness" were words which captured the imagination of a recent generation. Unless something was "relevant" or "meaningful," there was no point in bothering with it. Christian doctrine, many suggested, was outdated and irrelevant. The brave new world that was dawning could manage very well without such relics of the past.

The danger of all this is clear. Beneath all the rhetoric about relevance lies a profoundly disturbing possibility—that people may base their lives upon an illusion, upon a blatant lie. The attractiveness of a belief is all too often inversely proportional to its truth. In the sixteenth century, the radical writer and preacher Thomas Müntzer led a revolt of German peasants against their political masters. On the morning of the decisive encounter between the peasants and the armies of the German princes, Müntzer promised that those who followed him would be unscathed by the weapons of their enemies. Encouraged by this attractive and meaningful belief, the peasants stiffened their resolve.

The outcome was a catastrophe. Six thousand peasants were slaughtered in the ensuing battle, and six hundred captured. Barely a handful escaped. Their belief in invulnerability was relevant. It was attractive. It was meaningful. It was also a crude and cruel lie, without any foundation in truth. The last hours of that pathetic group of trusting men rested on an utter illusion. It was only when the first salvoes cut some of their number to ribbons that they realized that they had been deceived.

To allow "relevance" to be given greater weight than truth is a mark of intellectual shallowness and moral irresponsibility. The first, and most fundamental, of all questions must be: Is it true? Is this worthy of belief and trust? Once this has been established, the relevance of the belief in question may be considered. It is quite possible that most readers will find the contents of the *Annual Yearbook of Statistics* for 1965 utterly tedious—yet they may rest assured that those contents are reliable. They chronicle the way things were. They are a record of facts. Truth is certainly no guarantee of relevance—but no one can build their personal life around a lie.

Christian doctrine aims to describe the way things are. It is concerned to tell the truth, in order that we may enter into and act upon that truth. It is an expression of a responsible and caring faith—a faith which is prepared to give an account of itself, and give careful consideration to its implications for the way in which we live. To care about doctrine is to care about the reliability of the foundations of the Christian life. It is to be passionately concerned that our actions and attitudes, our hopes and our fears, are a response to *God*—and not something or someone making claims to divinity, which collapse upon closer inspection.

Perhaps the German church struggle of the 1930s highlights the importance of doctrine in the modern world. When Adolf Hitler came to power, he demanded that he and the Nazi government of the Third Reich should have authority over the church and its preaching. The German church polarized into two fractions: the "German Christians," who believed the church should respond positively to National Socialism, and the "Confessing Church"—including such writers as Karl Barth and Dietrich Bonhoeffer—who believed that the church was answerable to Jesus Christ, and him alone. Representatives of this "Confessing Church" met at Barmen in 1934, where they issued the famous "Barmen Declaration," perhaps one of the finest statements of the Lordship of Jesus Christ over his church and its implications:

> "I am the way, and the truth and the life. No one comes to the Father except through me" (John 14:6). "I tell you the truth, the man who does not enter the sheep pen by the gate, but climbs in by some other way, is a thief and a robber.... I am the gate; whoever enters through me will be saved" (John 10:1, 9).

> Jesus Christ, as he is attested for us in Holy Scripture, is the one Word of God which we have to hear and which we have to trust and obey in life and in death. We reject the false doctrine, that the church could and would have to acknowledge as a source of its proclamation, apart from and besides this one Word of God, still other events and powers, figures and truths, as God's revelation.

In other words, the church cannot and must not substitute anything (for example, the state government or German culture) or anyone (such as Adolf Hitler) for Jesus Christ. If the church ever loses her faithful obedience to her Lord, she has lost her life and her soul.

Doctrine thus defines who we are to obey. It draws a firm line of demarcation between a false church, which answers to the pressures of the age, and a true church, which is obedient and responsible to God, as he has revealed himself in Jesus Christ. "True knowledge of God is born out of obedience" (John Calvin). Inattention to doctrine robs a church of her reason for existence, and opens the way to enslavement and oppression by the world. The German Christians, through well-intentioned but muddled attitudes toward the world, allowed that world to conquer them. A church which takes doctrine seriously is a church which is obedient to and responsible for what God has entrusted to it. Doctrine gives substance and weight to what the Christian church has to offer to the world. A church which despises or neglects doctrine comes perilously close to losing its reason for existence, and may simply lapse into a comfortable conformity with the world—or whatever part of the world it happens to feel most at home with. Its agenda is set by the world; its presuppositions are influenced by the world; its outlook mirrors that of the world. There are few more pathetic sights than a church wandering aimlessly from one "meaningful" issue to another in a desperate search for relevance in the eyes of the world.

To speak of obedience may seem to represent some sort of lapse into mindless authoritarianism, or degeneration into blind servility. Obedience may take the form of such slavishness; it need not, and should not. To be a slave to the truth is to maintain intellectual rigor and integrity; to take liberties with the truth is to prefer an imagined and invented state of affairs to reality. If I were to insist that the American Declaration of Independence took place in 1789, despite all the evidence which unequivocally points to the year 1776, I could expect no commendations for maintaining my intellectual freedom or personal integrity. I would simply be obstinately and stubbornly *wrong*, incapable of responding to evidence which demanded a truthful decision.

An obedient response to truth is a mark of intellectual integrity. It marks a willingness to hear what purports to be the truth, to judge it, and, if it is found to be true, to accept it willingly. Truth demands to be accepted, because it inherently deserves to be accepted—and acted upon. Christianity recognizes a close link between faith and obedience—witness Paul's profound phrase, "the obedience of faith" (Rom. 1:5; see p. 281)—making it imperative that the ideas which underlie and give rise to attitudes and actions should be judged, and found to be right.

Beliefs are important because they claim to describe the way things are. They assert that they declare the truth about reality. But beliefs are not just ideas absorbed by our minds, which have no further effect upon us. They affect what we do and what we feel. They influence our hopes and fears. They determine the way we behave. A Japanese fighter pilot of the Second World War might believe that destroying the enemies of his emperor ensured his immediate entry into paradise—and, as many U. S. Navy personnel discovered to their cost, this belief expressed itself in quite definite actions. Such pilots had no hesitation in launching suicide attacks on American warships. Doctrines are ideas—but they are more than mere ideas. They are the foundation of our understanding of the world and our place within it.

Doctrine is not, however, something which we have invented. It is our response to the action of God. Doctrine is a human mental reaction to the historical action of God. It is not some sort of speculative guesswork about

God or Christ. Rather, it is rational reflection upon the death and resurrection of Jesus Christ, in the full awareness of the newness and mystery of this event. To use a marvelous turn of phrase from Paul, it is our "reasonable service (*logike latreia*)" to God (Rom. 12:1; note that translations of the Greek vary). It is responsible, in the sense that it answers and is answerable to someone. It *answers* to God, in that it arises in the aftermath of our awareness of being called, being summoned, by God, through Jesus Christ. We need to be told what God is like; left to our own devices—as history makes abundantly clear—a myriad of contradictory and inconsistent ideas of God would arise, all the products of human imagination and guesswork. It is *answerable* to God, in that it purports to speak of him, to describe him, and to lead to him. For a human to dare to speak about God in this way is potentially presumptuous, even fatuous—unless we have reason to believe that we are *authorized* to speak in this way by God himself.

The notion of "authority" evokes negative reactions from many people. It is frequently confused with "authoritarianism." In 1950, a work was published entitled *The Authoritarian Personality*, arguing that authoritarianism was the hallmark of a basically weak and dependent individual, lacking any personal strengths of character, who compensates for his or her near-total inadequacy by imposing a mindless authority. "Authority" is thus often understood as a demand for blind obedience, characteristic of the weak. But authority is not the opposite of freedom. Indeed, rightly understood, authority can actually establish freedom. The real contradiction of authority is *an absence of any accountability for our actions*. Authority is about being called to answer for one's freedom. Authority is about *accountability*, about being *answerable* to others outside our situation for whatever course of action we freely choose. To speak of the "authority of God" in this doctrinal context is to stress that we are accountable for the manner in which we respond to him and represent him. We are free to speak about God in whatever way we choose—but *responsible* talk about God is grounded in an awareness of our need to answer to God for what we speak about him.

In part, Christian doctrine seeks to tell the truth about God by exposing false ways of thinking and speaking about God. It shows up much human thinking of God as intellectual Towers of Babel—things which humans have created, in defiance of God. It condemns as false and untrue our sentimental views of Jesus, our cozy ideas about human nature, and slick and too-easy concepts of God. These are exposed as our own creations; we are asked instead to consider God as he has made himself known, however disturbing and disruptive this may prove to be. If doctrine is not grounded in the truth of God, it is to be ridiculed and rejected. Yet the obstinate fact remains, that doctrine claims to be grounded in God's revelation of himself, in the scripturally-mediated account of the coming of Jesus Christ. It declares that it is not a human invention, but a response to the revelation of God. God, it affirms, has permitted—has *authorized*—us to speak about him in this way.

To speak about Jesus Christ is to speak about newness. Far from providing some useful comments on the way things are, Jesus Christ opens up a new way of being. It is this new wine, this new creation, which demands a new way of speaking about God, and what he has done for us. The life, death, and resurrection of Jesus Christ brings us a new *knowledge* of God and of ourselves, set firmly in the context of a new *relationship* to God, made possible through faith in Christ. As Christians seek to share with the world their experience of the redeeming and liberating love of God, they are forced to give an account of this experience. How did it happen? What effects did it have? And what are its consequences?

Doctrine thus arises from the passionate commitment of the Christian church to tell the truth about God, and show up the weakness and poverty of non-Christian understandings of who God is and what he is like on the one hand, and who human beings are on the other. Doctrine confronts the world in judgment, and provides a basis for resistance to its oppression. Its starting point was not a smoke-saturated committee room, filled with academics arguing endlessly and pointlessly over their ideas about God. Rather, it begins from a realization of what God has done for us in Jesus Christ. It begins from an awareness that Christ confronts us, as he confronted his contemporaries, with divine judgment and, in its wake, the possibility of divine renewal. Jesus Christ brings judgment and conversion; in short, he is the Savior.

And this must have puzzled the first Christians. Indeed, there is every reason for thinking that they were overawed, astonished, and perplexed (as well as overjoyed) at what God had done in and through Jesus Christ. They were acutely aware that there was only one God, and that he jealously reserved use of the word "savior" for himself (see, for example, Isa. 45:21–22). Only God can save. The New Testament, however, proclaimed Jesus Christ as Savior. New Testament texts making this suggestion include Matthew 1:21 (which speaks of Jesus saving his people from their sins), Luke 2:11 (the famous Christmas message of the angels: "Today in the town of David a Savior has been born to you"), Acts 4:12 (which affirms that salvation comes through Jesus), Hebrews 2:10 (which calls Jesus the "author of salvation"). Titus 1:3–4 speaks of "God our Savior" at one point, and "Christ Jesus our Savior" at another. A contradiction seemed to have developed.

Nevertheless, the first Christians obviously felt that it was vitally important to remain faithful to their experience of salvation through Jesus Christ. Instead of shrugging their shoulders and avoiding facing the issues raised, they asked a crucial question. "What must be true of Jesus Christ if this is possible?" If Christ is our Savior, yet salvation is something which God, and God alone can do, it is clear that a very important insight into the identity of Jesus Christ lies to hand. They were determined to tell the truth about Jesus Christ; part of that truth involved wrestling with the implications of what God was acknowledged to have done through him. The doctrine of the incarnation—the declaration that Jesus Christ is both God and man—may be regarded as the climax of the Christian attempt to tell the whole truth about Christ. And this doctrine undergirds the basic Christian conviction that to tell the truth about Jesus Christ is to tell the truth about God—and about ourselves.

This might seem to raise an alarming possibility. Is this emphasis upon Jesus Christ justified? Surely God may be known in other ways? Can God not be seen in a beautiful sunset? Can he not be known through our being deeply impressed by the star-spangled heavens? Can we not sense his presence in the glory of great music, or discern him through a great work of art? But this emphasis upon Jesus Christ is not intended to imply that God is to be known definitively, most reliably, and most fully through Jesus Christ. The doctrine of the incarnation lends weight to this central Christian insight: that God has chosen to reveal himself supremely and definitively—to the point of becoming incarnate—in Jesus Christ.

To put this another way: Jesus Christ is the authoritative self-revelation of God. The word "authoritative" is helpful here. Sometimes people speak of a particular performance of a drama (shall we say, Shakespeare's *Macbeth*) or a musical composition (perhaps a Beethoven symphony) as *authoritative*. What is meant by this? The basic idea is that, in some way, this performance conveys what the writer or composer intended far more accurately than its rivals. It is more authentic than the alternatives. It is more reliable. This is not to say that all other performances fail totally to convey anything of what Shakespeare or Beethoven intended—it is to suggest that they fail to convey it in its fullness. They are overshadowed by the authoritative version. They are judged in relation to it. Where they are seen to echo and fulfill his intentions, they are to be praised; where they fail to do justice to them, they are found wanting. By defining one version as authoritative, a benchmark or standard is being established by which all others are to be evaluated.

In the same way, Jesus Christ is an authoritative revelation of God himself. God may indeed be discerned elsewhere—in the wonders of his creation, or in the heights of human artistic creativity. But these are subordinate to the supreme focus of God's self-revelation in Christ. Every now and then, someone suggests that a piece of sixteenth-century verse, or a hitherto obscure drama of the period, was written by none other than Shakespeare himself. And such claims have to be put to the test. How is this done? By examining works which were unquestionably written by Shakespeare, in order that points of similarity may be identified. The works which are known to be authentic are the standard by which others are evaluated. In the same way, Jesus Christ is the authentic revelation of God, by which other alleged revelations can be judged.

Doctrine makes truth-claims. To speak of doctrine as "truth" is rightly to draw attention to the fundamental Christian conviction that doctrine claims to make significant and justifiable statements about the order of things, about the way things are. Nevertheless, it is also concerned with maintaining the possibility of *encountering* the truth, which the Christian tradition firmly locates in Jesus Christ as the source of her identity. At the outbreak of the Second World War, William Temple—then Archbishop of York—identified the tension between these concepts of truth in his remark, "our task with this world is not to explain it, but to convert it." Although Temple's phrase is clearly derivative (borrowing from Karl Marx), the point he scores is important. Doctrine does not merely describe the way things are—it opens up the possibility of changing them. It is not a static representation, but an invitation to the dynamic transformation, of the human situation. Doctrine is able to effect what it signifies.

Doctrine describes what Christians believe to be true; it also invites those outside the Christian church to believe in this truth. In his *Unscientific Postscript*, the nineteenth-century Danish philosopher Søren Kierkegaard stressed that "the possibility of knowing what Christianity is without being a Christian must be affirmed." In other words, it is possible to *know about* Christianity without being a Christian. For Kierkegaard, doctrine is not just a description of what Christianity is. It is also a challenge to *become* a Christian.

Doctrine arises within the community of faith, as it seeks to make sense and give order and structure to its experience of and encounter with God through the risen Christ. Doctrine is thus an "insider" phenomenon, reflecting the faith of Christian believers in Jesus Christ. Outside this context, doctrine may seem barren and lifeless, in that its vital links with the death and resurrection of Jesus Christ are not fully understood. To those outside the community of faith, what requires explanation and elaboration is not actually specific *doctrines*, but what doctrine attempts and purports to represent—the Christian experience of the risen Christ. It is difficult to explain the doctrine of the incarnation (to take a particularly important example) to those who are not Christians, because they find it difficult to understand *why* anyone should want to speak of Jesus as both God and man in the first place. The pressures which lead to the doctrine are not fully grasped. Doctrine must therefore be and become a stimulus to evangelism—that is, an attempt to enable those outside the Christian faith to share in its experience and knowledge of God in Jesus Christ.

The foundation of Christian doctrine is thus—and always has been—Jesus Christ. He *is* the truth which sets us free (John 14:6; 8:32). But how do we know about him? How do we have access to this foundational resource of Christian belief? To ask such questions is to move on to deal with the relation of doctrine to scripture.

3

Responding to God: Doctrine and Revelation

Christian faith and Christian doctrine are both a response to God. They are a reaction to the action of God. For Christian theology and spirituality, that action of God culminates in the coming of Jesus Christ. One of the most cherished insights of Christian theology is that Jesus Christ represents God addressing us as human persons in and through a human person. Faith is a response to the call of God—an awareness of being called, and a willingness to respond to that call.

"Scripture is the manger in which Christ is laid" (Martin Luther). With these words, Luther points to the centrality of scripture: There is no other witness to the call of God through the life, death, and resurrection of Jesus Christ than this. If Christian doctrine is the response of the Christian church to Jesus Christ, the centrality of scripture to Christian faith and doctrine will be evident. There is no other way of gaining access to the history of Jesus Christ. The authority of scripture thus rests partly in its witness to Jesus Christ. But scripture contains more than an account of the history of Jesus Christ. It tells us how the first Christians understood him—who they thought he was, and what effect they believed this must have on their lives.

The coming of Jesus Christ did not take place in a vacuum. It was not some kind of bolt from the blue, a totally unexpected event. The Old Testament provides us with vital clues about the sort of expectations the people of God had concerning their future Messiah. It allows us to get a feeling of the sense of anticipation felt by the Jewish people as they awaited the coming of their deliverer. The Old Testament writers speak powerfully and movingly of a God who created the world, who called the people of Israel into existence to be his witness to the Gentiles, and who would come again to visit and redeem his people. It is a moving testimony to the active presence of God in the life of a people, and to their conviction that this presence would assume new and more powerful forms in the future. The Old Testament thus matters profoundly to Christians, partly because it sets the coming of Jesus Christ in its proper context. It sets the scene for understanding what the titles applied by the New Testament to Jesus, such as "Savior" and "Messiah," actually mean. To stress that doctrine is a response to the coming of Jesus Christ is thus in no way to set aside the Old Testament. To understand Jesus Christ is to view him against the pattern of divine activity and fidelity established by the Old Testament.

Scripture witnesses to the revelation of God. As such, it is the central resource of Christian faith and doctrine. This stress upon the doctrinal authority and importance of scripture is the common heritage of all Christians, not merely those who approve of the sixteenth-century Reformation. The Second Vatican Council's dogmatic constitution on divine revelation may be regarded as summarizing a consensus amongst responsible Christian theologians concerning the importance and authority of scripture:

> Since everything asserted by the inspired authors or sacred writers must be held to be asserted by the Holy Spirit, it follows that the books of Scripture must be acknowledged as teaching firmly, faithfully and without error that truth which God wanted put into the sacred writings for the sake of our salvation.

But what, it may reasonably be asked, of other resources for Christian doctrine? What about tradition? Isn't it somehow very *Protestant* to place such emphasis upon the importance of scripture? These questions demand to be considered before we go any further.

DOCTRINE, TRADITION, AND SCRIPTURE

Tradition, rightly understood, is not a source of revelation in addition to scripture, but a particular way of understanding scripture which the Christian church has recognized as responsible and reliable. For Irenaeus, a second-century writer especially concerned with the threat posed by Gnosticism, the idea that God could reveal himself authoritatively apart from scripture was irresponsible. If this was the case, anyone (especially Gnostics!) could claim that they had access to special insights, directly given to them by God. For Irenaeus, God had revealed himself perfectly well in scripture, and no additional resources were necessary.

But then there was the question of how scripture was to be interpreted. The Gnostics had a habit of interpreting certain biblical passages in a thoroughly unchristian manner. To combat this, Irenaeus laid down a basic principle. The Christian church interpreted these disputed passages in certain specific ways, which were "traditional." In other words, there was a traditional way of reading and interpreting scripture, reflected in the creeds. To be a Christian was to accept the authority of scripture in the first place, and in the second to accept that it had to be read in certain ways. Scripture and tradition are thus not two alternative sources of revelation, as suggested in some quarters; rather they are (to use a word favored by scholars) *coinherent*. Scripture cannot be read as if it had never been read before. There are certain ways of reading scripture which are more authentically Christian than others.

Tradition is thus rightly understood (as it was understood by both the Reformers and the Second Vatican Council) as a history of interpreting and wrestling with scripture. (Reacting against the growing influence of Protestantism in the sixteenth century, some Roman Catholic theologians at this time developed the idea that there were two sources of revelation—scripture, and unwritten traditions, possessed only by the true church. This has not, however, found sympathy with many twentieth-century Catholic writers.) Tradition is a willingness to read scripture, taking into account the ways in which it has been read in the past. It is an awareness of the communal dimension of Christian faith, which calls shallow individualism into question. There is more to the interpretation of scripture than any one individual can discern. It is a willingness to give full weight to the views of those who have gone before us in the faith.

It may be objected at this point, that this seems to contradict the Reformation scripture principle—that it is scripture alone which is authoritative. But this principle was never intended by writers such as Luther or Calvin to mean that scripture is read individualistically. It was in no way intended to elevate the private judgment of the church (although it was interpreted in this way by certain radical reformers, outside the mainstream of the Reformation). Rather, the scripture principle affirms that traditional ways of reading scripture must, in principle, be open to being checked concerning their reliability. It is possible that the church may occasionally get scripture wrong (as the Reformers believed that it had been misunderstood at a series of points)—and at these points, it is essential that scripture be examined in depth to ascertain its true meaning. But that is a matter for the community of faith, not some private individual acting on his or her own behalf.

Tradition, then, is the corporate historical reflection upon scripture, not a source of revelation in addition to scripture. It is a process of responsible and obedient reflection upon the meaning of scripture for the community of faith, in whatever situations it may find itself. It is one of the major achievements of both theological scholarship and the ecumenical movement to demonstrate that this emphasis upon the priority of scripture is not a Protestant obsession, but is rather a common feature of responsible Christian thought.

DOCTRINE AND THE INTERPRETATION OF SCRIPTURE

Scripture is thus the primary source for doctrinal reflection within the Christian church. There is no other access to the self-revelation of God in Jesus Christ. Many eighteenth-century writers believed that reason was a sort of omnipotent and objective human ability to discover God, and lay down what he is like, and what he can and cannot do. Revelation, it was argued, was thus quite irrelevant and unnecessary: Human reason could find out all it needed to know about God without such external aids. That view is now seriously discredited, with the real limitations placed upon human reason being better understood. There are certain things that human reason is very good at—the field of mathematics, for example. Equally, there are certain things it is not so good at. Unaided reason is no longer regarded as having anything especially helpful to say about who God is and what he is like—although it is invaluable in making sense of God's revelation of himself.

Doctrine interprets scripture. There is, however, a real danger that biblical interpretation and doctrine will become detached from one another, with doctrine being seen as having an independent existence. This is a seriously deficient understanding of the nature of doctrine. Doctrine claims to interpret scripture, and is to be judged in that light. It is a framework for the interpretation of scripture which claims to be based upon scripture, itself. If doctrine is understood as a way of interpreting scripture on the basis of scripture, the great Reformation principle, *scriptura est suipsius interpres* ("scripture is its own interpreter"), is upheld. The sixteenth-century Reformation is a classic case of doctrine being subjected to radical examination, to see whether it was, in fact, firmly based in scripture. Reformers such as Martin Luther and John Calvin were, in principle, prepared to abandon doctrines which could not be shown to be securely grounded in scripture.

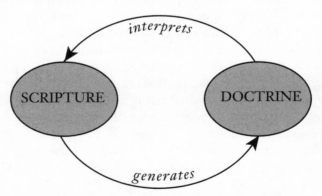

The Interaction of Scripture and Doctrine
Figure 1

Perhaps the best way of summarizing the relationship between doctrine and scriptural interpretation is shown in Figure 1. The starting point for doctrinal reflection is an attempt to make sense of the scriptural witness to God's saving action toward us, culminating in the coming of Jesus Christ. The resulting doctrines are not an end in themselves; rather, they are themselves a framework for the interpretation of scripture. There is a process of feedback between doctrine and scripture, as they mutually complement one another. The primary purpose of doctrine is to allow a more reliable interpretation and application of scripture. This basic approach can be found in John Calvin's famous *Institutes of the Christian Religion* (1559), in which the distinguished reformer sets out to provide his readers with a volume of Christian doctrine which will aid them as they read scripture.

> Although the Holy Scriptures contain a perfect doctrine, to which nothing can be added (our Lord having been pleased to unfold the infinite treasures of his wisdom therein), every person who is not intimately acquainted with them needs some sort of guidance and direction, as to what he or she ought to look for in them. . . . Hence it is the duty of those who have received from God more light than others to assist the simple in this manner and, as it were, give them a helping hand to guide and assist them to find everything that God has been pleased to teach us in his word. Now, the best way of doing this is to deal systematically with all the main themes of Christian philosophy.

In other words, a systematic presentation of the main themes of Christian doctrine is an excellent guide to scripture. It provides a sort of route map by which the various scriptural landmarks may be located and identified, and related to each other. Doctrine, to use a phrase due to Calvin, is like a pair of spectacles through which scripture may be properly read. It stresses the unity of scripture, which might otherwise seem like a series of unconnected stories and sayings.

A helpful way of thinking of the relation of doctrine to scripture, probably suggested by a growing Victorian public interest in botanical gardens, was put forward by the nineteenth-century Scottish writer Thomas Guthrie. Guthrie argued that scripture is like nature, in which flowers and plants grow freely in their natural habitat, unordered by human hands. The human desire for orderliness leads to these same plants being collected and arranged in botanical gardens according to their species, in order that they can be individually studied in more detail. The same plants are found in different contexts—one of which is natural, the other of which is the result of human ordering. Doctrine represents the human attempt to order the ideas of scripture, arranging them in a logical manner in order that their mutual relation can be better understood.

Doctrine integrates scriptural statements. It brings together the kaleidoscope of scriptural affirmations about God, Jesus Christ, and human nature. It discerns common patterns underlying the wealth of scriptural statements and illustrations. It distills the essence of these statements into as compact a form as possible. Doctrine is thus a summary of scripture. Suppose you were asked to explain what Christians believed about Jesus Christ. You might well find that this might take you some time. You would probably want to talk about the main New Testament titles used to refer to Jesus—such as "Son of God," "Son of Man," "Savior," and "Lord." You would find yourself trying to explain what each of them meant, and what it told us about Jesus. You might want to take a series of key scriptural verses, each making an important affirmation about the importance of Jesus—such as Romans 1:3–4, with its succinct explanation of what the resurrection tells us about this identity. Yet you could not summarize the entire biblical witness to Jesus Christ in a single proof text.

After a while, you might find yourself wondering if there was an easier way of doing this. Is there any way in which the rich (and very extensive) scriptural witness to the identity and importance of Jesus Christ could be summarized in a sentence or two? The doctrinal statement "Jesus is God and man" aims to do this. It provides a neat outline of the key features of the Christian understanding of the identity and significance of Jesus Christ. It is a summary of the scriptural teaching, and not a substitute for it.

As an example, let us consider the doctrine of the incarnation—the idea that God became man in Jesus Christ. What scriptural elements does it integrate? Even the briefest of lists of such scriptural elements would include:

- the belief that God has acted decisively for human salvation through Jesus Christ.
- the belief that God has revealed himself definitively in the person of Jesus Christ.
- the practice of the worship of Jesus, already found within the New Testament, and a key feature of Christian devotion thereafter.

The doctrine of the incarnation distills the common features of each of these elements. It asks the question: What must be true about Jesus Christ if these beliefs and practices are justified?

A second example might be the doctrine of the Trinity, which attempts to bring together into a single formula the richness of the Christian understanding of God. For example, it holds together the following central elements of the biblical witness to the nature and purposes of God:

- God created the world.
- God redeemed us through Jesus Christ.
- God is present in his church through the Spirit.

The doctrine of the Trinity affirms that these all relate to the same God. It is not as if one god created the world, while another redeemed it, and a third is present thereafter. Rather, the same God is present and active throughout the history of redemption. The doctrine integrates these three elements into a greater whole. Each is declared to be an essential aspect of the Christian understanding of God. It is not meant to explain how God can be like this; it simply affirms that, according to the biblical witness, he *is* like this. It insists that the biblical statements about God be seen as an integrated whole, rather than a series of loosely collected items.

Seen in this way, doctrine is not—and was never meant to be—a substitute for scripture. Rather, it is a learning aid for reading scripture. (A learning aid, it may be added, that can be corrected in the light of scripture, if it can be shown to be out of line with it.) Like a pair of spectacles, it brings the text of scripture into focus, allowing us to notice things which might otherwise be missed. Doctrine is always under scripture, its servant rather than its master. Doctrine stands or falls with the Word of God, revealed in scripture, in that this Word of God precedes, creates, and criticizes all doctrinal statements.

DOCTRINE AND THE NARRATIVE OF SCRIPTURE

Recent discussion on the relation between doctrine and scripture has highlighted a problem which, despite its difficulty and technicality, demands to be considered in the present chapter. The following quotation from *Believing in the Church*, published in 1981 by the Doctrine Commission of the Church of England, identifies this problem:

> The form of Scripture is not such that we can easily deduce from it general statements of what it is that we believe. Its most characteristic mode of writing is that of narrative . . . it contains relatively little of the kind of doctrinal statement from which a reasoned presentation of the Christian faith could be logically deduced. . . . The characteristic mode in which Scripture conveys to us the things concerning God, Jesus and man is not (in this sense) "doctrinal" at all. It is mainly (though not exclusively) *narrative*.

In other words, scripture is primarily concerned to tell us the story of God's redeeming engagement with the world, culminating in the life, death, and resurrection of Jesus Christ. It relates a history.

So how do we make the transition from history to doctrine? How do we convert a story into a belief? Two questions are of central importance. First, how can a story, a narrative, be *authoritative*? And second, how can a narrative or story be converted into doctrine? We begin with the first of these two questions.

To see how a story can be authoritative, let us turn to the late Renaissance, and the city of Florence. Florence went through a series of political and social difficulties in the late Renaissance, with a resulting loss of morale. It found itself plagued by internal factionalization and external threat. How could it make sense of what was happening to it?

The answer lay in noticing parallels between the history of Florence and that of ancient Rome. The Florentines noticed that Rome seemed to suffer from much the same difficulties as they did. The story of Rome seemed to tie in with the story of Florence. It cast light on what was happening. Gradually, the story of Rome began to be recognized as being authoritative for Florence. The story of ancient Rome was seen as the best way of making sense of what was happening in modern Florence. In trying to understand their present problems, the pattern of the past was seen to be helpful.

In a similar way, the story of Jesus Christ is held to be authoritative for Christians. It is this story, and no other, which helps to make sense of the riddles of human faith and experience. And whereas Florence had to invent its links with ancient Rome, the Christian church stands in an unbroken line with the story of Jesus—a story which is recalled regularly in the eucharistic celebration. The character of the Christian community arises from the fact that it came into being as a response to Jesus Christ. The narrative of Jesus is recognized as authoritative by the Christian church. Its attitudes to power, to pride, to loss, to death, to grief, to despair—all are governed by the narrative of Jesus Christ. It evokes a deep sense of "happening," the memory of a foundational narrative and its present significance for the community whose identity is tightly bound up with it. It provides a focus of identity for the community. The New Testament affirmation of the conformity of the believer to Christ—that, through faith, those who believe in Christ are somehow caught up in him, so that *his* history becomes *their* history—provides a significant theological foundation for this correlation of narratives. His death is their death, his life is their life—and the narrative of Jesus gives some specification to Christian existence by aligning that existence with a lived life, with a specific historical person.

The story of Jesus Christ controls the Christian self-understanding. Especially in the Pauline writings, participation in Christ points to a conformity of the believer's existence to his. Through faith, the believer is caught up in a new outlook on life, a new structure of existence, embodied in Jesus Christ. Through faith, we come to share in Christ. His story becomes our story. The believer is one who is "in Christ." For Paul, the believer repeats the story of Jesus Christ in his or her own life, sharing in that story: We share in his sufferings, in order that we may share in glory (Rom. 8:17). The story of Jesus Christ gives some shape, specification, and substance to what human outlooks on life, what forms of action, what moral motivations, are appropriate expressions of our own sharing in the life of Christ.

In this way, the history of Jesus Christ is authoritative within the Christian church. It is this story, and no other, which controls our understanding of God, Jesus Christ, and ourselves. It is the story of Jesus, for example, which governs Christian ethics: in the life of Jesus, we see a pattern of faithful and obedient response to God which is the goal of all believers.

This line of argument helps us see how a story can be authoritative. We must now turn to the second problem. How can a story give rise to doctrines? To deal with this question, let us go back to Ancient Greece. Early Greek thinkers tended to use stories as a way of making sense of the world, and discovering more about it. The Greek myths are basically stories or narratives (whose truth content, it may be added, was virtually nonexistent; the gospel story, on the other hand, is thoroughly grounded in history). To explain things, you told a story. A decisive shift appears to have taken place shortly before the time of Plato. A conceptual way of thinking now gained the upper hand. Ideas took the place of stories. In the modern period, conceptual ways of thinking tend to dominate western culture, while narrative ways of thinking are dominant in native African cultures.

These ways of thinking are not inconsistent. The gospel is capable of being stated in both forms—the story of Jesus Christ, and the interpretation of this story in terms of doctrines. The story of Jesus takes priority, however. Doctrine provides the framework by which the scriptural narrative is interpreted. It is not an arbitrary framework, however, but one which is suggested by that narrative, and intimated by scripture itself. It is to be discerned within, rather than imposed upon, that narrative. The narrative is primary, and the interpretative framework secondary. The New Testament includes both the narrative of Jesus of Nazareth and interpretation of the relevance of that narrative for the existence of the first Christian communities. Doctrine represents the extension of the doctrinal hints, markers, and signposts to be found within the New Testament, especially in the Pauline writings.

Narratives need interpretation. The scriptural narrative is no exception. The Old Testament could be read as a story of the quest for identity among a nomadic people of the Ancient Near East. The gospels could be read as the story of a misguided Galilean revolutionary or a radical Jewish rabbi. But these would not be especially reliable ways of reading the scriptural story. Doctrine lays down the right way of reading this story. It affirms the particular interpretation, or range of interpretations, of the scriptural narrative appropriate for the Christian community. Thus the assertion "Jesus is the Christ" is a doctrinal statement which allows the story of Jesus to be read and understood in a particular way—the *right* way, according to Christianity. Other ways certainly exist (for example, reading the story of Jesus as the story of a purely human political figure)—doctrine declares that these are at best inadequate, and at worst wrong.

As we noted earlier, Calvin suggested that doctrine was like a pair of spectacles for reading scripture. Doctrine, like spectacles, brings things into focus and allows a clearer vision of things than the unaided eye. Doctrine is thus a way of reading scripture, suggested by scripture itself, which brings the text into focus, and allows us to read it with greater clarity. For example, Romans 1:3–4 justifies Paul's claim that Jesus is the Son of God by appealing to the story of Jesus. Two crucial elements of that story—his descent from David, and his resurrection—are seen as establishing that Jesus is the Son of God. Once this doctrinal insight has been reached, the scriptural story can be read again *in the light of that insight*. This pattern is repeated throughout Paul's writings. The story of Jesus allows insights into the nature of God, Jesus, and humanity, which can then be used to make further sense of the scriptural narrative. The crucial point is this: The doctrines which interpret the story of Jesus are themselves based upon that story. They are not plucked out of thin air.

An example may make this point clearer. The doctrine of the incarnation affirms two vital insights: "Jesus is God" and "Jesus is man." Whatever else these insights may mean, they mean that, within the scriptural story of Jesus Christ, Jesus may be seen playing two quite different roles—the human and the divine. Two roles which had hitherto been regarded as mutually exclusive, demanding different actors, are held by the narrative to be intimately related and focused on the single person of Jesus. Within the context of the narrative, Jesus acts as God (for example, by forgiving sin: Mark 2:5–7), as well as man (for example, by weeping or by becoming tired). The doctrine of the two natures provides a means of interpreting the scriptural narrative, and ensuring its internal consistency. There is thus a dynamic relationship between doctrine and the scriptural narrative. There is a process of interaction, of *feedback*, between doctrine and Scripture, between the interpretative framework and the narrative itself.

The only major difficulty which could result from going over from a narrative to a conceptual framework of thinking would arise if the original narrative were lost. Suppose that the story of Jesus Christ, having been allowed to generate a doctrinal specific framework, were forgotten. The doctrines remained, but the narrative was forgotten. Had this occurred, serious anxiety would necessarily have resulted concerning the reliability of this framework. It would have been left suspended without visible support. There would be no way of checking whether the doctrines were reliable interpretations of the story of Jesus Christ. However, the foundational narrative of Jesus has been preserved by the community of faith, and accorded primary status in doctrinal reflection (particularly within the churches of the Reformation). The Scripture principle is basically an assertion of the primacy of the scriptural narrative of Jesus over any doctrines which it may generate. The scriptural narrative remains, and we thus continue to have access to a means of testing the reliability of doctrines. Doctrine does not have an existence which is independent of scripture; rather, doctrine is always under scripture. In principle, doctrines will always continue to be judged on the basis of whether they reliably interpret the biblical witness to Jesus Christ.

Earlier, we noted a misgiving many people have about doctrine. Doctrines may at times seem abstract, and not firmly located in the reality of everyday life. Yet the realization that doctrine is basically the interpretation of a story—the story of Jesus Christ—brings home the fact that doctrine is firmly grounded in the realities of life. Doctrine is a bridge, which seeks to link our lives with the life of Jesus Christ. It aims to connect the realities of our existence with the realities of *his* existence. It interprets *our* story in the light of *his* story. Doctrine is only to be dismissed as an abstract irrelevance if its purpose and place are seriously misunderstood.

The parables of Jesus also make doctrinal statements in the form of stories. A story is told, and the doctrine is explained. What might be seen as abstract and unreal (the doctrine) is shown to be grounded in the concrete events of human existence. For example, the Pauline doctrine of justification by faith seems to many to be something of an unintelligible abstraction. Yet this doctrine merely states in a conceptual form the same basic point made so memorably and so powerfully in the parable of the Pharisee and the Publican (Luke 18:9–14). The utter paradox of grace is here stated with supreme clarity. It is not the morally upright Pharisee but the repentant sinner who is justified before God. (Note that there is not a hint of hypocrisy here; the Pharisee would have done all that he claimed to have done. To suggest that the Pharisee was a liar is to lose sight of the point of the parable.) The doctrine of justification by faith makes much the same point as the parable. Yet the neatness and conceptual clarity of the doctrine is offset by the vividness of the parable, and its firm location in the world of human life. Perhaps we need to recapture the ability and will to restate doctrines in terms of stories, if their power, relevance, and vitality are to be fully appreciated.

This, then, is a very brief sketch of how the story of Jesus Christ can give rise to doctrine. There is no inconsistency or major difficulty involved. Indeed, there is an enormous advantage to this relation of narrative and doctrine: It means that Christianity can make sense to anyone, whether they use narrative (for example, in many modern African cultures) or conceptual ways of thinking (for example, in modern Western cultures). The gospel can be stated in ways appropriate for all, whether their worlds are shaped by stories or by ideas.

This chapter may have conveyed the idea that doctrine is primarily about ideas—ideas derived from scripture, to be sure, but ideas nevertheless. This might create the impression that doctrine is rather stuffy and dull, having no bearing upon human experience. In fact, Christian doctrine is a vital resource in understanding and transforming human experience. We shall explore how in the following chapter.

4

Intellect and Feelings: Doctrine and Experience

Christianity represents a judicious compromise between two extreme views, one subjective, one objective. On the one hand, there is the extreme represented by a purely emotional faith, which experiences God and trusts implicitly in him—but is unable to express itself coherently. This approach is totally subjective, reducing faith to little more than a muddled bundle of emotions. This view is inadequate, rather than wrong; it needs to be supplemented with a stress on the objective side of faith. We don't just believe in God, we believe certain quite definite things about him. In other words, faith has a content as well as an object. It claims to tell the truth (see chapter 2). It is the task of every generation in the history of the Christian church to develop an articulate and authoritative account of its faith. The believer is also a thinker, and can never permit his faith to remain or become a shallow uninformed emotionalism. Emotion is an important element of the Christian faith, and those who despise it have no right to do so—but on its own, it is inadequate, incapable of doing justice to the essence of Christian faith.

On the other hand, there is the view that Christianity is a list of intellectual propositions to which the believer's assent is demanded. This severely objective approach needs to be corrected by recognizing that Christian faith is grounded in experience. Faith does not merely concern beliefs; it concerns life, in every one of its rich aspects. The "God of the Christians" (to borrow a phrase from the third-century writer Tertullian) is no intellectual abstraction, but a God who is known in and through personal experience. The distinguished theologian Rudolf Bultmann made the point that doctrine without experience is little more than a dead letter:

> If someone says that he cannot find God in the reality of his own existence, and if he tries to make up for this by the thought that God is nevertheless the final cause of everything that exists, then his belief in God is the intellectual speculation of a dogma. No matter how strongly he may hold this belief, it will never be true faith—for faith can only be the recognition of the activity of God in his own life.

Experience of God provides the stimulus to develop doctrines about God. Thus the Christian belief in the divinity of Christ did not arise as an intellectual theory, but through the impact of *experiencing* Jesus Christ as God. The early Christians were thus faced with the intellectual task of thinking through the implications of their experience of Christ as God, and expressing it in as clear and persuasive a manner as possible. The full-blooded nature of Christian faith can never be adequately expressed as propositions.

Although each of these views is correct and important, each is inadequate on its own. It is possible for Christianity to degenerate into little more than an intellectual system, rather than a relationship with a person, who enters into our experience and transforms it. The intellectual side of Christian faith is important—but once more, taken on its own, it is inadequate. A judicious compromise, therefore, is necessary in order to preserve both the subjective and objective aspects of faith—in other words, Christian faith is grounded in experience, but its content may still be summarized in propositions such as "Jesus is Lord," "Jesus is the Son of God," or "Jesus is true God and true man." There is no inconsistency involved—both the proposition and the experience relate to the same greater reality, which lies behind them both. Faith involves both head and heart. Objective and subjective aspects of faith are like two sides of the same coin—they may be different, but they are both essential aspects of the same thing. They both represent the same thing, viewed from different angles.

There is, however, something of a tension between the objective and subjective aspects of faith. On the one hand, we want to talk about God as the one whom we experience, love, and worship in adoration and wonder. On the other, we are only too painfully aware of the simple fact that God is God, and that human language is quite incapable of adequately expressing everything that we want to say about him. The majesty and wonder of God tends to reduce us to silence. Our experience of him is virtually impossible to put into words. But we must speak of God, even though we recognize the inadequacy of our words to do justice either to God himself, or even to our experience of him. How else can we share our experience of him with the world? Words are the only means we have of talking about God.

Suppose that you were to cross the Atlantic Ocean on one of the great liners that still work the transatlantic routes. You would probably find that you were overwhelmed by the immensity of that ocean—by its sheer size, by the sense of being totally insignificant in comparison with its vastness, as you spent day after day without seeing land. Your experience of the ocean would make a very deep impression upon you. Suppose that you subsequently were to pick up a map of the western hemisphere, and find the Atlantic Ocean reduced to nothing more than some printed lines on a piece of paper. You might be fortunate enough to find the ocean colored blue, and the land masses of America and Europe green—but all that you would have in your hands would be a piece of paper. How would your experience of the Atlantic Ocean relate to this small area of blue color on that paper?

Two points may be made. First, nobody in their right mind is going to suggest that the area of blue color on that map is meant to be an exact representation of the Atlantic Ocean. The map is not *identical* with that vast ocean. Rather, the map is an attempt to indicate how various things are related to one another—for example, where Europe and America are situated in relation to each other, and to the Atlantic Ocean. It is not even an attempt to scale down the ocean so that you can get the same sort of experience you once had, only on a smaller scale—it is meant to convey certain limited (but important!) information, rather than reproduce an authentic experience in all its fullness.

Second, the map is based upon the personal experience of countless others, as they also crossed the Atlantic. Whereas your experience is undoubtedly real and important to you, it represents a single, isolated, and very personal impression of a much greater reality. Taken on its own, your experience of the Atlantic Ocean is unreliable, perhaps providing your friends with as much information about you as about the ocean itself.

Furthermore, all of us tend to dismiss the experience of others. We are often unwilling to accept anything on the authority of others. We are very reluctant to allow that others might experience more than we do, or have insights which we overlooked. The noted theologian A. E. Taylor made this point very clearly.

> Authority and experience do not stand over against one another in sharp and irreconcilable opposition. Authority is the self-assertion of the reality of an experience which contains more than any individual has succeeded in analyzing and extricating for himself. It is indispensable for us as finite historical beings who need a safeguard against our inveterate tendency to supplement the statement "this is what I can make of this situation" by the perilous addition, "and this is all there is to it."

In other words, one individual's experience is unlikely ever to sound the full depths of reality—but *many* such individuals might, by pooling their experiences, give rise to a much more reliable picture of reality.

The function of the map of the Atlantic Ocean is to combine as many impressions of that ocean as possible, in order that a more reliable picture may be built up. The experiences of others, upon which the map is based, are just as vivid and real as yours—but the map eliminates the personal element of experience of the Atlantic Ocean, in order to provide a more generally reliable guide to the same reality. The parallels between doctrines and maps will be obvious. Doctrines are essentially the distillation of the Christian experience of God, in which countless personal experiences are compared and reduced to their common features. Thus the formula "true God and true man" is at the very least an attempt to express the conviction that we only know both God and man through Jesus.

Christian doctrine cannot be—and anyway was never meant to be—a substitute for experience of the living God. It is an attempt to relate Jesus Christ to God and to us, as a map relates the Atlantic Ocean to Europe and America. It aims to put Jesus on the map between God and ourselves, in order to allow us to experience God through Jesus. Thus the formula of the creed, which speaks of Jesus as "true God and true man," is really placing Jesus on a theological map. Just as the map told the traveler that the Atlantic would lead him from Europe to America, from the Old World to the New, so the doctrine of the "two natures" of Christ tells us that we encounter God through Jesus Christ.

Refugees fleeing to the United States from persecution or a hopeless economic situation in Europe in the first decades of the twentieth century knew that their hope of a new life lay in crossing the Atlantic Ocean. The deep sense of relief and joy when the New York skyline came into view is well known to us through contemporary films. And so it is with those who are seeking for God, for meaning and hope, in a seemingly dark, meaningless, and hopeless world. Through Christ, they encounter the living God, the source of their new life, their hope and their joy. Nobody is for one moment suggesting that this is everything that could be said about Jesus, or that it adequately describes the deep personal significance which he holds for each and every believer—but it does help us to begin to locate that significance, to be more precise about it than would otherwise be possible.

Doctrine thus addresses and interprets experience. It aims to make sense of human feelings, by explaining what they mean and what they point to. One such feeling has been explored with considerable brilliance by the great English literary critic and novelist C. S. Lewis, and deserves special attention. Lewis was aware of certain deep human emotions which pointed to a dimension of our existence beyond time and space. There is, Lewis suggested, a deep and intense feeling of longing within human beings, which no earthly object or experience can satisfy. Lewis terms this sense "joy," and argues that it points to God as its source and goal (hence the title of his autobiography, *Surprised by Joy*). Doctrine interprets this experience as a longing after God. It gives shape and meaning to what might otherwise seem a meaningless aspect of human existence. Doctrine interprets the sense of longing as a pointer towards its fulfillment in a relationship with God.

To understand Lewis at this point, the idea of "joy" needs to be explained in a little more detail. From the windows of his family home in Belfast, Northern Ireland, the young Lewis could see the distant Castlereagh Hills. The sight of these distant hills, often wrapped in mist, seemed to him to symbolize something which lay beyond his reach. A sense of intense longing arose as he contemplated them. He could not say exactly *what* it was that he longed for;

merely that there was a sense of emptiness within him, which the mysterious hills seemed to heighten, without satisfying. In his novel *The Pilgrim's Regress*, Lewis uses the image of these hills as a symbol of the heart's unknown desire.

Lewis describes this experience (perhaps better known to students of German Romanticism as *Sehnsucht*) in some detail in his autobiography *Surprised by Joy*. He tells his readers how, as a young child, he was standing by a flowering currant bush, when—for some unexplained reason—a distant and poignant memory was triggered off.

> There suddenly arose in me without warning, as if from a depth not of years but of centuries, the memory of that earlier morning at the Old House when my brother had brought his toy garden into the nursery. It is difficult to find words strong enough for the sensation which came over me; Milton's "enormous bliss" of Eden ... comes somewhere near it. It was a sensation, of course, of desire; but desire for what? Not, certainly, for a biscuittin filled with moss, nor even (though that came into it) for my own past ... and before I knew what I desired, the desire itself was gone, the whole glimpse withdrawn, the world turned commonplace again, or only stirred by a longing for the longing that had just ceased. It had only taken a moment of time; and in a certain sense everything else that had ever happened to me was insignificant in comparison.

Lewis here describes a brief moment of insight, a devastating moment of feeling caught up in something which goes far beyond the realms of everyday experience. But what did it mean? What, if anything, did it point to?

Lewis addressed this question in a remarkable sermon entitled "The Weight of Glory," preached at Oxford University on June 8, 1941. Lewis spoke of "a desire which no natural happiness will satisfy," "a desire, still wandering and uncertain of its object and still largely unable to see that object in the direction where it really lies." There is something self-defeating about human desire, in that what is desired, when achieved, seems to leave the desire unsatisfied. Lewis illustrates this from the age-old quest for beauty.

> The books or the music in which we thought the beauty was located will betray us if we trust to them; it was not *in* them, it only came *through* them, and what came through them was longing. These things—the beauty, the memory of our own past—are good images of what we really desire; but if they are mistaken for the thing itself they turn into dumb idols, breaking the hearts of their worshipers. For they are not the thing itself; they are only the scent of a flower we have not found, the echo of a tune we have not heard, news from a country we have not visited.

The paradox of hedonism—the simple, yet stultifying, fact that pleasure cannot satisfy—is another instance of this curious phenomenon. Pleasure, beauty, personal relationships: All seem to promise so much, and yet when we grasp them, we find that what we were seeking was not located in them, but lies beyond them. There is a "divine dissatisfaction" within human experience, which prompts us to ask whether there is anything which may satisfy the human quest to fulfill the desires of the human heart.

Lewis argues that there is. Hunger, he suggests, is an excellent example of a human sensation of needing something, which corresponds to a real physical need. This need points to the existence of food by which it may be met. Thirst is an example of a human longing pointing to a human need, which in turn points to its fulfillment in drinking. Any human longing, he argues, points to a genuine human need, which in turn points to a real object corresponding to that need. A similar point is made, although a little cryptically, in relation to human sexual desire. And so, Lewis suggests, it is reasonable to suggest that the deep human sense of infinite longing which cannot be satisfied by any physical or finite object or person must point to a real human need which can, in some way, be met. Human desire, the deep and bitter-sweet longing for something that will satisfy us, points beyond finite objects and finite persons (who seem able to fulfill this desire, yet eventually prove incapable of doing so); it points *through* these objects, and persons towards their real goal and fulfillment in God himself.

This point is made clearly in a letter to his brother, dated October 31, 1931.

> The "idea of God" in *some* minds does contain, not a mere abstract definition, but real imaginative perception of goodness and beauty, beyond their own resources, and this not only in minds which already believe in God. It certainly seems to me that the "vague something" which has been suggested to one's mind as desirable, all one's life, in experiences of nature and music and poetry, even in such ostensibly irreligious forms as the "land east of the Sun and west of the Moon" in Morris, and which arouses desires that no finite object even pretends to satisfy, can be argued *not* to be any product of our own imagination.

In other words, the sense of "desires that no finite object even pretends to satisfy" corresponds to a real human need, and the fulfillment of that need—but how?

Lewis argues that this sense of longing points to its origin and its fulfillment in God himself. In this, he echoes a great theme of traditional Christian thinking about the origin and goal of human nature. "You have made us for yourself, O Lord, and our hearts are restless until they find their rest in you" (Augustine of Hippo). We are made by God, and we experience a deep sense of longing for him, which only he can satisfy. Although Lewis' reflections on the desire he calls "joy" reflect his personal experience, it is evident that he (and countless others) consider that this sense of longing is a widespread feature of human nature and experience. An important point of contact for the proclamation of the gospel is thus established.

Lewis' insights also bring new depth to familiar biblical passages concerning human longing for God. "As the deer pants for streams of water, so my soul pants for you, O God. My soul thirsts for God, the living God" (Ps. 42:1–2).

Note the great sense of *longing* for God expressed in this passage—a sense of longing which assumes added meaning if Lewis' reflections on "joy" are allowed. Note also the biblical parallel between a sense of need—in this case, animal thirst—and the human need of and desire for God.

Perhaps the finest statement of the theological implications of this deep sense of longing is to be found in *Till We Have Faces*, Lewis' brilliant retelling of the classic Greek love story of Cupid and Psyche. In one passage, Lewis has Psyche tell her sister (who here relates the story) of her longing for something which she senses lies beyond the world as she experiences it.

> "I have always—at least, ever since I can remember—had a longing for death."
>
> "Ah, Psyche," I said, "have I made you so little happy as that?"
>
> "No, no, no," she said. "You don't understand. Not that kind of longing. It was when I was happiest that I longed most. It was on happy days, when we were up there on the hills, the three of us, with the wind and the sunshine... Do you remember? The color and the smell, and looking across at the Gray Mountain in the distance? And because it was so beautiful, it set me longing, always longing. Somewhere else there must be more of it. Everything seemed to be saying, Psyche come! But I couldn't (not yet) come and I didn't know where I was to come to. It almost hurt me. I felt like a bird in a cage when the other birds of its kind are flying home."

Psyche's experience of a sense of longing for something indefinable, evoked by the beauty of the world, ends in frustration; nothing in the world can satisfy her longing. It is only by being set free from the limitations of the world itself that Psyche can experience the fulfillment of her sense of longing. And so our hearts are also restless, until they find their rest in the God who created us for fellowship with him.

Doctrine aims to interpret experience, in order to transform it, through an encounter with the risen Christ. It is like a net which we can cast over the experience, in order to capture its meaning. It interprets the human sense of "longing" as "longing *after God*," and thus opens up the way for this longing to be satisfied, and thus transformed.

Sometimes doctrine interprets experience by declaring that it can be unreliable and misleading. Experience appears to suggest one thing; doctrine interprets it to suggest something rather different. One of the most important writers to deal with this point is the great German reformer, Martin Luther. Luther's characteristic approach to the interpretation of experience is often known as "the theology of the cross." He suggests that we attempt to imagine what it was like for the disciples on the first Good Friday. They had given up everything to follow Jesus. Their whole reason for living centered on him. He seemed to have the answers to all their questions. Then, in front of their eyes, he was taken from them and publicly executed. You can feel an immense sense of despair as you read the Gospel accounts of the death of Jesus. The moment of Jesus' death would probably have been the darkest point in the lives of the disciples. It must have seemed as if their entire world had collapsed, shown up as a fraud and an illusion.

Of course, we know how that story ended. We know how the disciples' sorrow was transformed to joy and wonder, as the news of the resurrection of Jesus became known. But try to imagine yourself standing among the disciples as they watched Jesus suffer and die—*without* knowing that he would be raised again from the dead. Set aside your knowledge of what happens later, and try to imagine what it must have been like to watch Jesus die on the cross. Where was God in all this? Why didn't he intervene? It was all enough to make anyone doubt whether God existed in the first place. It is easy to get a feel for the sense of despair and bewilderment on that sad day. God was experienced as being absent. There was no way in which anyone experienced his presence on that dreadful day. Even Jesus himself seems to have had a momentary sense of the absence of God—"My God, my God, why have you forsaken me?" (Matt. 27:46).

This way of thinking brings home to us how unreliable experience and feelings can be as guides to the presence of God. Those around the cross did not experience the presence of God—so they concluded that he was absent from the scene. The resurrection overturns that judgment: God was present in a hidden manner, which experience mistook for his absence. Doctrine interprets our feelings, even to the point of contradicting them when they are misleading. It stresses the faithfulness of God to his promises, and the reality of the resurrection hope—even where experience seems to suggest otherwise. Doctrine thus gives us a framework for making sense of the contradictions of experience.

It is to his credit that C. S. Lewis also considered the way in which words can *generate* experience. In *Surprised by Joy*, he comments on the effect of a few lines of poetry upon his imagination. The lines were from Longfellow's *Saga of King Olaf*:

"I heard a voice that cried,
Balder the beautiful
Is dead, is dead."

These words had a profound impact upon the young Lewis.

> I knew nothing about Balder; but instantly I was uplifted into huge regions of northern sky, I desired with almost sickening intensity something never to be described (except that it is cold, spacious, severe, pale and remote) and then ... found myself at the very same moment already falling out of that desire and wishing I were back in it.

Words, Lewis discovered, have the ability to evoke an experience we have not yet had, in addition to describing an experience we are familiar with. In his essay *The Language of Religion*, he made this point as follows:

> This is the most remarkable of the powers of Poetic language: to convey to us the quality of experiences which we have not had, or perhaps can never have, to use factors within our experience so that they become pointers to something outside our experience—as two or more roads on a map show us where a town that is off the map must lie. Many of us have never had an experience like that which Wordsworth records near the end of *Prelude XIII*; but when he speaks of "the visionary dreariness," I think we get an inkling of it.

Doctrine shares this characteristic of poetic language, as identified by Lewis—it tries to convey to us the quality of the Christian experience of God. Doctrine is able to offer some pointers for the benefit of those who have yet to discover what it feels like to experience God. It uses a cluster of key words to try to explain what it is like to know God, by analogy with human experience. Let us take forgiveness: If you can imagine what it feels like to be forgiven for a really serious offense, you can begin to understand the Christian experience of forgiveness. Or reconciliation: If you can imagine the joy of being reconciled to someone who matters very much to you, you can get a glimpse of what the Christian experience of coming home to God is like. It is like coming home after being away and alone for a long time. Doctrine uses analogies like these to try to signpost—like roads leading off Lewis' map to an unseen town—the Christian experience of God, for the benefit of those who have yet to have this transforming experience.

Those who have experienced the reality of God in Christ find that they have been called out of the world. It is true that Christians continue to live in the world, but not *of* the world. This brings us to the fourth aspect of Christian doctrine to be considered in this present work: Doctrine marks believers off from the world. It gives Christian individuals and communities a sense of identity in the world. We shall explore these themes in the chapter which follows. If the present chapter is concerned with the relevance of doctrine to the individual (as he or she attempts to make sense of personal experience), the following chapter is especially concerned with the relevance of doctrine to the Christian church. Doctrine shapes corporate identity.

5

Believing and Belonging: Doctrine and Christian Identity

Doctrine is there to help the church to be what it is called to be. It shapes the vision of the world associated with the body of Christ. It could be said that doctrine gives Christians a sense of identity, at both the personal and the communal level. It explains what Christianity is all about. But this suggestion is open to a misunderstanding—that doctrine somehow invents a corporate identity. In fact, the Christian church has already been given its identity by the God who called it into being. The Christian church did not come into being of its own accord. It is a response to the calling of God. The initiative lies with God, who has called the church out (the root meaning of the Greek word *ekklesia*) of the world—called it out of darkness into his wonderful light.

JESUS CHRIST AND CHRISTIAN IDENTITY

In calling the church out of the world through the life, death, and resurrection of Jesus Christ, God has given the church its identity. Its reason for existence is the proclamation of Jesus Christ, which is seen to be charged with the potential to transform the world, to bring about a new creation. Christians, as a body and as individuals, are called to affirm the judgment of the world in Christ. They witness to the new creation which lies on the other side of this judgment. A new life and a new lifestyle result from faith in the death and resurrection of Jesus Christ. God interrupts our lives and offers to change them through the transforming presence and power of Christ.

The fundamental reason for the church being there is thus Jesus Christ. At first sight, this may seem an astonishingly naïve and blinkered statement. Surely the church is there to bring about fair social conditions? Surely Christians are called to transform society, to bring about a new and more just world? Yet, on reflection, the wisdom of the statement becomes clear. Christian values—the values which must govern our understanding of what "justice" means—arise in the wake of Jesus Christ. As John Rawls stressed in his *Theory of Justice*, there is little to be gained from asserting the need for justice, unless it can be given some shape and specification. It needs to be earthed, unless it is to remain an abstract and unusable concept. The Christian cannot simply baptize secular ideas of justice. Many such ideas of justice rest upon profoundly unchristian ideas about the nature and destiny of humanity. Ideas of justice reflect worldviews and values. The pressure for the Christian to transform the world is the result of our vision of what God wishes his world to be like, a vision of the new creation in Christ. To insist that Christianity centers on Jesus Christ is to declare that, in him and through him, we have access to ideas and values which govern the Christian vision of how the world should be.

Doctrine thus seeks to preserve the identity of the church. It enables the Christian church to remain faithful to its calling, and to the one who called it into being. It does this partly in a negative way, by declaring that Christians cannot simply baptize secular ideas of justice, integrity, and morality. It is unquestionably much easier for Christians to accept secular views of justice, such as those developed until recently with vigor and conviction by Marxist social analysts. It is much easier to gain a hearing by endorsing existing secular political attitudes. Yet these views and attitudes rest upon theories of the nature and destiny of human beings which generally profoundly contradict those of the Christian faith. Marxist values rest upon Marxist doctrines, such as the nonexistence of God and the inevitability of socialism— just as Christian values ultimately rest upon Christian doctrines. A failure to realize the extent to which values, attitudes, and actions rest upon *doctrinal* foundations explains much of the moral shallowness of Christian liberalism in recent years.

The belief which appears to underlie this liberalism—that all cultural values and attitudes are somehow "God-given," and thus to be respected— is alarmingly naïve. It ignores, for example, the significant extent to which they are shaped and manipulated by powerful groups within society for their own ends. Culture can be little more than successful politics. Sexual domination, racial exclusivism, the perpetuation of the dominance of one social grouping over another on religious grounds (one of the most crippling aspects of the Hindu caste system), the belief that profits justify exploitation of individuals—all are examples of profoundly unchristian cultural attitudes which have been created and molded by power groups, eager to preserve their own privileged positions. Doctrine passes judgment on these attitudes by destroying the delusions about human nature and destiny, and about the nature and purposes of God himself, upon which they are ultimately based.

Doctrine also serves a positive function. It affirms what is distinctive about Christianity. It identifies what is unique, what is identity-giving, about the gospel. It criticizes the church and individual believers when they lapse into vague generalities about the gospel, or lose sight of its uniqueness and

God-given relevance to the world. It affirms that God has called the Christian church into existence for a reason.

Doctrine presupposes the existence of the church—not a doctrine of the church, but a historical community of faith which confesses Jesus Christ as Lord. The common life of prayer, reading of scripture, and worship of this community provides the stimulus for doctrinal reflection. Doctrine arises within the community of faith, as it seeks to make sense and give order and structure to its experience of and encounter with God through the risen Christ. Doctrine is thus an "insider" phenomenon, reflecting the hopes and beliefs of the Christian community of faith—above all, its experience of forgiveness and new life through Christ. Outside this context, doctrine may seem barren and lifeless. It may seem little more than a collection of hairsplitting distinctions. But what needs to be explained to such people is not specific *doctrines*, but what doctrine attempts to represent—the redemptive communal experience of the risen Christ as Lord. What moves Christians to make doctrinal statements is the wish and need to give substance and expression to their experience of God in Christ. The impulse which animates the genesis of doctrine is thus prior to any specific doctrinal formulations as such—yet, paradoxically, requires precisely some such doctrinal formulation if it is to be transmitted from one generation to another.

This allows us to make an important distinction between "doctrine" and "theology." "Doctrine" implies a reference to the ideas of a community, whose members value and are committed to them. "Theology" more properly refers to the views of individuals, not necessarily within this community or tradition, who seek to explore ideas without any necessary commitment to them. Doctrine possesses a strongly representative character, attempting to describe or prescribe the beliefs of a community. Of course, Christian communities include some theologians within them—but those theologians do not speak *on behalf of* that community. The community is not committed to the ideas of its theologians. The community is at liberty to appropriate or reject their speculation. Doctrine entails a sense of *commitment* to a community, and a sense of *obligation* to speak on its behalf, where the corporate mind of the community exercises a restraint over the individual's perception of truth. Doctrine is an *activity*, a process of transmission of the collective wisdom of a community concerning its experience of Jesus Christ. The views of theologians can be doctrinally significant—if they have won acceptance within the community (a process generally referred to as "reception"). The concept of "reception" is of central importance to the concept of doctrine, in that a community is involved in the assessment of whether a decision, judgment, or theological opinion is consistent with their corporate understanding of the Christian faith. Doctrine is communally authoritative teachings regarded as essential to the identity of the Christian community.

DOCTRINE AND CHRISTIAN IDENTITY

We can now begin to explore the theme of "doctrine and Christian identity" in more detail. Two basic principles govern this vital aspect of Christian doctrine.

1. Doctrine distinguishes the Christian church from the world, including non-Christian religions and Western secular culture.
2. Doctrine distinguishes one Christian denomination from another.

The recent rise of the New Age movement has highlighted the crucial importance of doctrine in the modern Western world. For doctrine allows one religious group to be distinguished from another—including the New Age movement from orthodox Christianity. Occasionally, religious groups seem to be very similar to each other—yet, on closer inspection, they prove to have radically different ideas about such crucial matters as the character and purposes of God, and human nature and destiny. To understand this crucial aspect of Christian doctrine further, let us consider four different situations in the history of the Christian church.

1. The Early Church

Initially, Christianity had to define itself over and against Judaism. After all, Christianity emerged from within Judaism, yet regarded itself as distinct from it. So how could continuity with the great Old Testament tradition be affirmed, while at the same time making clear that Christianity was not Jewish? Paul's doctrine of justification by faith is an excellent example of a doctrine which, on the one hand, *affirms* the continuity between the Old and New Testaments, and on the other, *distinguishes* Christianity from Judaism. The doctrine affirms that the great promises made by God to Abraham and his successors now apply to Christian believers—without in any way implying that they required to be circumcised, or observe the Jewish law, as a result.

As Christianity expanded into the Mediterranean world of the second century, however, the question of its relation to Judaism became increasingly distant and irrelevant. Christianity now had to define itself over and against a number of key movements in the world of this period. One of these movements was Gnosticism. The central problem with Gnosticism was that, in many respects, it seemed virtually identical to Christianity. Gnostic beliefs (which, incidentally, bear more than a passing resemblance to those of modern New Age movements) seemed very close to those of Christianity. Gnostic writers appealed to Christians to join them, arguing that they basically believed the same things.

This precipitated a crisis of identity within Christianity during the second century. It became increasingly obvious that Christian groups would have to pay much more attention to thinking through what they believed. It meant that thought had to be given to developing criteria by which the claims of groups to be "Christian churches" could be tested. Gnosticism posed a powerful challenge to the Christian church, in effect forcing the latter to clarify its boundaries. The Gnostics argued that they had received a secret tradition, directly from the apostles, to which Christians did not have access. They had access to secret saving knowledge (the word "Gnostic" comes from the Greek word *gnosis*, "knowledge"). The Christian church vigorously denied this, arguing that everything necessary for salvation was openly available through scripture. Yardsticks—such as the canon of the New Testament, or adherence to the apostolic rule of faith, summed up in the Apostles' Creed—were agreed by which the claims of religious communities to be Christian churches could be checked out.

One of the most important Christian writers to deal with this emerging problem was Irenaeus (c.130–c.200), a bishop in the southern Gallic city of Lyons. Irenaeus insisted that the basic elements of the Christian faith were public knowledge, and not some secret tradition available only to the few. He drew up a number of short statements of faith, which summarized the basic Christian teaching on certain key subjects. Christians believe

> in one God, the maker of heaven and earth, and of all the things that are in them, through Jesus Christ the Son of God, who, on account of his overwhelming love for his creation, endured the birth from the Virgin, uniting man to God in himself, and suffered under Pontius Pilate, and rose again, and was taken up in majesty, and will come again in glory, the savior of those who are saved and the judge of those who are judged.

This statement (which is basically a prototype of the Apostles' Creed) served to distinguish Christians from non-Christians, such as Gnostics. It created a sense of identity among the Christian churches, which were often geographically isolated in the far-flung Roman Empire. All Christian communities and believers, Irenaeus stressed, shared the same faith. Although the church was scattered from one end of the earth to the other, it shared common doctrines deriving directly from the apostles through scripture.

Doctrinal formulations began to become particularly important in this way towards the end of the second century. Nevertheless, this does not appear to have been understood as an attempt primarily to define what individual Christians believed; rather, it seems to have been intended as a means by which the credentials of a community or movement claiming to be a Christian church might be tested. To allow Christianity to be confused with Gnosticism would result in the gospel becoming diluted and confused, losing sight of many central insights of the New Testament.

2. Medieval Christendom

With the conversion of the Roman emperor Constantine (AD 312), a new situation began to develop. Under the Edict of Milan (AD 313), Christianity assumed a new status as the official religion of the Roman Empire, eventually leading to the development of medieval "Christendom." The Roman Empire was officially Christian, and there was thus no longer any need to distinguish Christians from their neighbors. With this development, doctrine lost its identity-giving function. "Church" and "society" were regarded as more or less the same thing. Doctrine was no longer of importance, in that Christianity no longer felt any need to distinguish itself from society. Society, it was argued, *was* Christian.

This is not to say, of course, that the medieval church had no interest in doctrine whatsoever. It is simply to note that doctrine was not seen as a criterion of identity in the period, except in the specific area of combating heresy. "Christendom" was sufficiently stable and well-defined to allow the need for doctrinal self-definition to become of little relevance. It is precisely this lack of interest in doctrine which is widely held to underlie the origins of the Reformation: Doctrinal confusion and vagueness on certain key issues (such as justification by faith) in the first two decades of the sixteenth century led Luther to feel that the church of his day had lost sight of the true gospel. Medieval European Christendom, through losing interest in doctrine, had also lost touch with the gospel.

3. The German Reformation

With the advent of the Reformation, however, the situation changed significantly. Martin Luther's program of reform at Wittenberg in the late 1510s and early 1520s centered on a specific doctrine—justification by faith alone. It was on the basis of this doctrine that Luther and his colleagues, eventually to become the Lutheran church, would take their stand against the papacy and the world. Germany became the arena of confrontation between two rival groups—Lutheranism and Roman Catholicism—each claiming to be authentically Christian. They had to distinguish themselves from one another. And the easiest and most reliable way of distinguishing themselves was through doctrine.

The Roman Catholic Church responded to Lutheranism at the Council of Trent, which defined Catholic ideas on doctrines such as justification with unprecedented clarity. Trent provided a remarkably comprehensive statement of Catholic doctrine, thus providing an explicit definition of the boundaries of the Roman Catholic Church. The Reformation thus restored the identity-giving function of Christian doctrine.

The situation in Germany became even more complicated during the 1560s and 1570s, as Calvinism began to make major inroads into previously

Lutheran territory. Three major Christian denominations were now firmly established in the same area—Lutheranism, Calvinism, and Roman Catholicism. All three were under major pressure to *identify* themselves. Lutherans were obliged to explain how they differed from Calvinists on the one hand, and Roman Catholics on the other. And doctrine proved the most reliable way of identifying and explaining these differences: "We believe this, but they believe that." The period 1559–1622, characterized by its new emphasis upon doctrine, is generally referred to as the "Period of Orthodoxy."

Lutheranism and Calvinism were, in many respects, very similar. Thus both claimed to be evangelical, and rejected more or less the same central aspects of medieval Catholicism. But they needed to be distinguished. And doctrine proved to be the most reliable way of distinguishing two otherwise very similar bodies. At most points of doctrine, Lutherans and Calvinists were in broad agreement. Yet there was one matter—the doctrine of predestination—upon which they were radically divided. (Lutherans held that predestination referred to God's general decision that anyone who came to faith would be saved; Calvinists argued that it referred to his specific decisions concerning which individuals would be saved.) The emphasis placed upon the doctrine of predestination by Calvinists in the period 1559–1662 partly reflects the fact that this doctrine distinguished them from their Lutheran colleagues.

4. The English Reformation

The sixteenth-century English Reformation under Henry VIII bore little relation to its German equivalent. The historian F. W. Powicke remarked that "the one thing that can be said about the Reformation in England is that it was an act of State . . . the Reformation in England was a parliamentary transaction." There is enough truth in Powicke's generalization to draw attention to a key difference between the German and English Reformations. In Germany, there was a protracted struggle between Lutheran and Roman Catholic, as each attempted to gain influence in a disputed region. In England, Henry VIII simply declared that there would only be one national church within his realm. By royal command, there would only be one Christian body within England. The reformed English church was under no pressure to define itself in relation to any other Christian body in the region. The manner in which the English Reformation initially proceeded demanded no doctrinal self-definition, in that the church in England was defined *socially* in precisely the same way before the Reformation as after, whatever political alterations may have been introduced. This is not to say that no theological debates took place in England at the time of the Reformation; it is to note that they were not seen as being of decisive importance. They were not regarded as identity-giving.

The Lutheran church in Germany was obliged to define and defend its existence and boundaries by doctrine because it had broken away from the medieval Catholic church. That church continued to exist around Lutheran regions, forcing Lutheranism to carry on justifying its existence. The Henrician church in England, however, regarded itself as continuous with the medieval church. The English church was sufficiently well defined as a social unit to require no further definition at the doctrinal level.

The situation remained much the same under Elizabeth I. The "Elizabethan Settlement" (1559) laid down that there would only be one Christian church in England—the Church of England, which retained the monopoly of the pre-Reformation church, while replacing it with a church which recognized royal, rather than papal, authority. The phrase "Church of England," as defined legally in Halsbury's *Laws of England*, makes no reference to its doctrine: The "Church of England" is regarded as continuous with the church established in England during the period 597–686. Roman Catholicism, Lutheranism, and Calvinism—the three Christian churches fighting it out for dominance of the continent of Europe—would not be tolerated within England. There was thus no particular reason for the Church of England to bother much about doctrinal questions. Elizabeth ensured that it had no rivals within England. One of the purposes of doctrine is to divide—and there was nothing for the Church of England to divide itself from. England was insulated from the factors which made doctrine so significant a matter on the mainland of Europe in the Reformation and immediate post-Reformation periods.

Indeed, the need to ensure that all English Christians (whether inclined toward some form of Protestantism or Roman Catholicism) felt reasonably at home in the Church of England led to the importance of doctrine being played down: An emphasis on doctrine might lead to divisions within the new church, and hence to internal weakness. As Elizabeth tried to ensure England's safety in the dangerous world of the late sixteenth century, the last thing she wanted was an England torn apart by doctrinal differences. A divided English church would be a divided England; and a divided England would be a weak England, vulnerable to foreign subversion or invasion from France or Spain.

That situation, however, has now changed completely. Today, the Church of England is no longer the only significant Christian body in England, on account of the growth of evangelicalism, the rapid expansion of the house-church movement, and the new confidence evident within English Roman Catholicism; the notion of the "establishment" of the Church of England has degenerated into little more than a legal fiction. English society as a whole is now not merely non-Christian (due, amongst other factors, to the extensive immigration of Moslems and Hindus from the Indian subcontinent), but is even at points aggressively secularist. In addition, there is a new threat from religious groups which—like Gnosticism in the early church period—bear a superficial resemblance to Christianity, yet are actually profoundly unchristian. The New Age movement is a case in point. There is thus a growing need for self-definition on the part of the Church of England, if it is to survive as a distinctive Christian body—and an inevitable part of that process of self-identification is a new attention to matters of doctrine. We argued above that the traditional marginalization of doctrine within the Church of England partly reflects the specific social, religious, and political situation of sixteenth-century England, now radically altered through a process of historical erosion. A new social situation demands a new—and more positive—attitude to doctrine. The twentieth century cannot be fettered with obsolete hangovers of the sixteenth century. The new interest in doctrinal matters evident among younger English Anglicans reflects this point, and echoes a wider recognition of the importance of doctrine within many other churches.

A HIERARCHY OF DOCTRINES

Doctrine, as we have seen, divides Christianity from the world, giving Christian denominations a unity over and against secular culture and other religions; it also, however, divides denominations from one another. There is thus a tension in the function of doctrine. On the one hand, it unites Christians against non-Christians; on the other, it divides one Christian from another. Once this fact has been recognized, an important conclusion may be drawn: Not all Christian doctrines are of equal importance. This insight has been explained and justified using two different, though related, models—that of a hierarchy on the one hand, and a concentric series of circles on the other. We shall explore both.

Christianity possesses a hierarchy of doctrines. By this is meant the following. Doctrines are not all of equal importance. At the top of the hierarchy is a cluster of fundamental doctrines, the denial of which involves setting oneself outside the Christian church. Beneath this cluster of doctrines are to be found a group of nonessential doctrines, of varying degrees of importance. While all Christians are (or ought to be) united on the fundamentals of faith, disagreement is to be accepted on secondary matters.

In the sixteenth century the German Lutheran writer Philip Melanchthon introduced a new word into the vocabulary of theologians. The word Melanchthon coined is *adiaphora*—"matters of indifference." For Melanchthon, the gospel consists of a central core, centering upon the gracious redemption of sinners in Jesus Christ. This central core is surrounded by a concentric ring, containing doctrines of secondary importance. Disagreement upon these matters among Christians might be tolerated, provided the doctrines in the central core region were not called into question or denied. To affirm the doctrines in the core region is to be a Christian; to affirm the doctrines in the outer circle is to be a particular kind of Christian.

Both these models raise the same question: What are the fundamentals, and what are the secondary doctrines, or "matters of indifference?" Modern ecumenical discussions have centered upon identifying which doctrines are essential to Christian belief, and which are open to debate. On the basis of these discussions, some illustrations of each type of doctrine could be given.

Fundamental doctrines, essential to Christian identity:

- the divinity of Jesus Christ
- the humanity of Jesus Christ
- the existence of God
- the doctrine of salvation by grace through faith
- the Trinity

Secondary doctrines, upon which disagreement may be permitted within Christianity:

- whether, and in what way, Christ is present in the sacraments
- whether baptism signifies or causes believers to be born again
- whether "justification" means "declaring righteous" or "making righteous" (or something in between?)
- in what precise way Jesus is both God and man

Thus, on the basis of this analysis, Christians ought to be united on the fact that Jesus is both God and man, but at liberty to disagree on the most appropriate way of making sense of this mystery. In other words it is the fact, rather than any particular theory, of the incarnation which is fundamental to the Christian faith. Doctrine thus attempts to define what is essential and fundamental to Christianity, while at the same time mapping out areas in which debate is possible. It encourages Christians throughout the world and across doctrinal divisions to value and affirm the fundamentals which they have in common, rather than dwelling upon the differences which divide them. It affirms the common identity and purpose of Christians, to enable them to be faithful to their calling in the world.

This process of reflection has been encouraged by the rise of the ecumenical movement, probably one of the most important developments in modern Christian history. There is a new willingness on the part of many denominations to build bridges, and to attempt to overcome the division of the churches. A central feature of this process of drawing together is engagement with doctrinal matters. The heritage of doctrinal disagreements between denominations has been subjected to critical examination concerning its biblical foundations, and its originating historical circumstances. This has helped to identify on the one hand a common core of central and essential Christian doctrines, shared by all Christian believers, and on the other hand, a number of areas in which genuine disagreement may be accepted.

For many Christians, these divisions are painful. It hurts when Christians disagree amongst themselves. Why should the church be disunited in this way? Why can't Christians be agreed upon everything? If you feel like this, remember that all Christians share a central core of faith. What they have in common far outweighs their differences. It is natural to concentrate upon differences, and forget how much Christians have in common with one another. Yet it is far more important that a person should know the risen Christ, than that they should express their faith in him in some particular way. Forms of words, ways of expression, and patterns of worship vary between Christians in one part of the world and another—but underlying them all is the same Lord. So learn to be positive, and concentrate upon what Christians have in common, over and against the world.

Doctrine, then, is there to help the church become what it has been called to be. It achieves this goal, in part, in a defensive manner. An illustration may help to summarize this crucial function of doctrine. Consider a medieval English castle, with an inner keep and outer defensive fortifications, such as a wall and a moat. The real hub of the castle is the keep. The life of the castle centers upon it. The walls and other fortifications are there merely to defend the keep in times of danger. So it is with doctrine. The real lifeblood of the Christian faith is not doctrines as such, but the real and transforming presence of Jesus Christ in the life of individuals and the church. Doctrines are there to defend that presence.

In times of peace, the castle walls could be allowed to fall into a certain amount of disrepair. There was no need for them to be permanently manned. No threat was posed to the keep. In the Middle Ages, there was no particular need for any emphasis upon doctrine—no real threat existed to the Christian faith. But that situation changed. The moment a dangerous situation developed, the castle walls had to be repaired. They were manned constantly, in order to defend the keep against new threats. And so the church must be prepared to rediscover the importance of doctrine, where the Christian gospel is under threat. It is under threat in the western world, not least because of the new and aggressively secular attitudes of Western society. Other factors underscore the need for Christianity to rediscover its identity, and state it in doctrinal terms—for example, the rise of militant Islam worldwide, and the birth of the New Age movement. Doctrine matters more now than it has mattered for a long time.

Doctrine thus aims to keep the church faithful to the God who has called it into being, and to the proclamation of the good news of Jesus Christ. It summons the church to a contemplative and obedient receptivity to the challenge and judgment of Jesus Christ. We must be prepared to yield to this challenge and judgment, in that Christian identity is not determined by human agents, but by the God who called the Christian church into being, and defined its tasks. This is no call to a blind obedience to authority, but a faithful and obedient response to truth. Doctrine is no intellectual straight-jacket, imposed to silence discussion within the church. Rather, it is the out-come of a loving and committed process of reflection on the central symbol of the Christian faith—the cross of Christ. Here lies the true identity of the Christian individual and the Christian community—and doctrine is an attempt to spell out that identity, in order that it may be preserved in the pre-sent and transmitted to the future. It is an attempt—a bold and necessary attempt—to keep the "salt of the earth" salty. For if that salt "loses its salti-ness, how can it be made salty again? It is no longer good for anything, except to be thrown out and trampled" (Matt. 5:13).

In the last four chapters, we have been considering what doctrine is. It will be clear that doctrine serves a number of vital purposes. The second part of this work consolidates these impressions, by explaining in more detail why doctrine is of such importance to the Christian church.

PART TWO

Doctrine: Why It Matters

6

Doctrine and Faith

Christianity is about coming to life in all its fullness. One of the reasons why Christianity has been so powerful a force in world history for so long is that it possesses the ability to change human lives. This ability is not some sort of add-on extra, an option or extension which can be added to the basic package. It is fundamental to the nature of the Christian gospel itself. Let three twentieth-century people relate how this happened to them.

> I had been running away from God for a long time. I just knew he was there. And then I came home to him. I just gave up running away from him, and asked him to come into my life. I knew he was real, and I knew he wanted me. I've never looked back on that moment.

> You must picture me alone in that room at Magdalen, night after night, feeling, whenever my mind lifted even for a second from my work, the steady unrelenting approach of Him whom I so earnestly desired not to meet. That which I greatly feared had at last come upon me. In the Trinity Term of 1929 I gave in, and admitted that God was God, and knelt and prayed: perhaps, that night, the most dejected and reluctant convert in all England.

> There might be no certainty that Christ was God—but, by God, there was no certainty that he was not. This was not to be born. I could not reject Jesus. There was only one thing to do once I had seen the gap behind me. I turned away from it, and flung myself over the gap toward Jesus.

These three people—an Oxford student, C. S. Lewis, and the American writer Sheldon Vanauken—are describing how they came to faith. The pattern is slightly different in each case. They express themselves in different ways. Yet there is a common core to them. Each discovered the reality of God. Countless others could tell similar stories of how they made that same discovery.

"Now that's what Christianity is *really* about!" some may say. "It's got nothing to do with doctrinal nit-picking and hair-splitting. It's about making a personal discovery of God. It's about wanting to serve him in the world. It's about praising and adoring him. How on earth can something so real, something so pulsating with life, have anything to do with the drab and dreary statements of the creed or doctrine textbooks? We can do without those very well."

This is a powerful criticism. It reflects the feeling of some, especially those who have had a dramatic conversion experience, that the reality of God is somehow compromised by doctrinal statements. God is real; doctrines, however, often seem abstract and unreal. Take "justification by faith." Most people don't understand what this doctrine means, let alone what its relevance might be. The words are strange; the idea seems unintelligible. Doctrines often create a bad impression on outsiders, who come to think of Christianity as little more than a list of things you have to believe. The creeds often seem like little more than checklists of beliefs. And a serious misunderstanding of Christianity can come about as a result—the idea that Christian faith is just accepting certain things as true. But it is through exploring the nature of faith that we can begin to gain a preliminary understanding of why doctrine is of such central importance to the Christian believer and the Christian church.

THE NATURE OF FAITH

Faith, in the full-blooded Christian sense of the word, is a complex notion, bringing together a cluster of key ideas. Its basic sense, as found in the New Testament, could be summarized as "the new way of existence made possible through the death and resurrection of Jesus Christ." The English word "belief" is, unfortunately, quite incapable of bringing out the full meaning of the New Testament concept of faith. It seems to suggest that the life, death, and resurrection of Jesus changes our ideas—but not our lives. The New Testament word for faith, *pistis*, seems to embrace all of the following ideas.

1. Faith as Assent

Faith believes that certain things are true. "I believe in God" means something like "I believe that there is a God," or "I think that God exists." Faith assents belief in the existence of God. This is an essential starting point. After all, before we can begin to say anything about what God is like, we need to assume that there is a God in the first place. It is interesting to note that many people outside the Christian faith have the impression that there is nothing more to Christian faith than assent to God's existence. Christian belief is little more than running through a checklist of propositions—such as those contained in the creeds. That is why it is essential to realize that Christian faith, for the New Testament writers, includes the idea of trust.

2. Faith as Trust

When I declare that "I believe in God," I am not just saying that I believe that God exists. I am affirming my trust in him. Faith cannot be equated with knowing. It is not something purely intellectual, enlightening the mind while leaving the heart untouched. Faith is the response of our whole person to the person of God. It is a joyful reaction on our part to the overwhelming divine love we see revealed in Jesus Christ. It is the simple response of leaving all to follow Jesus. Faith is both our recognition that something wonderful has happened through the life, death, and resurrection of Jesus Christ, and our response to what has happened. Faith realizes that God loves us, and responds to that love. Faith is saying "Yes" to God.

Christians don't just *believe*—we believe *in someone*. Faith is like an anchor, linking us with the object of faith. Just as an anchor secures a ship to the ocean floor, so our faith links us securely with God. Faith is not just believing that God exists; it is about anchoring ourselves to that God, and resting secure in doing so. Whatever storms life may bring, the anchor of faith will hold us firm to God.

Perhaps the clearest exposition of this aspect of faith may be found in Hebrews 11:1–12:3. This famous passage opens with a definition of faith (11:1) as "being sure of what we hope for and certain of what we do not see." What this means is illustrated by the trust of the individuals mentioned in the remainder of the chapter. Abraham was called to go to a strange land to receive his inheritance (11:8)—and he trusted God, and went. All believed that God could be trusted, and acted on the basis of that faith. This great passage closes (12:1–3) by urging us to consider all these great men and women of faith, to learn from their example, and to trust God as they did.

The story is told of the great French tightrope walker Blondin, who crossed the Niagara Falls on a tightrope. One of the American onlookers congratulated him on his achievement. "Do you believe I could do it again?" the Frenchman asked him. "Certainly!" came the unhesitant reply. "Well, why don't you let me carry you across?" Blondin replied. The American blushed, and hastily melted into the waiting crowd. He might have been prepared to believe that something could be done—but he wasn't prepared to put himself at risk on the basis of his belief. Many individuals believe that God exists, and that he is able to forgive the sins of those who trust in him—but are not prepared actually to take that step of faith. That is why commitment is so important an element of Christian faith.

3. Faith as Commitment

Time and time again, scripture encourages us to think of our faith as a personal relationship with God. God is one who has publicly demonstrated his commitment to and love for us in the cross of Jesus Christ; he will not abandon us. He will be with us, wherever we go. Faith is our commitment to God, our decision to allow him to be present with us, to guide us, to support us, to challenge us, and to rule us. It is a joyful and willing self-surren-

der to God. It is a throwing open of the doors of our lives, and inviting God
to enter, not merely as our guest, but as our Lord and master. God's commitment to us demands a commitment from us in return. Just as God humbled himself on the cross to meet us, so we must humble ourselves in ·
repentance to meet him.

It is helpful to remember the close links between the creed and baptism
in the early church. When Christian converts declared that they believed in
God, in Jesus Christ, and in the Holy Spirit, they were declaring publicly
their commitment to the gospel. They were not just telling the world *what*
they believed about Jesus Christ; they were telling the world *that* they
believed in Jesus Christ. At the time, this was a risky business: To admit to
being a Christian was to open yourself to ridicule, discrimination, victimization, and possibly much worse. To "come out" as a Christian was a matter of
real courage. "I believe in God" means "I have committed myself to God."
To believe in God is to belong to God. It is also to obey God.

Writing to the Christians at Rome, Paul mentions "the obedience that
comes from faith" (Rom. 1:5). At one point, he gives thanks to God that the
faith of the Roman Christians is being reported all over the world (Rom. 1:8);
at another, that their obedience is being reported everywhere (Rom. 16:19).
Faith, then, leads to obedience. It is a willingness to trust and obey the God
who has called us to faith in him. We are called to be doers, rather than just
hearers of the Word of God (James 1:22; 2:14–20).

These elements of trust and commitment are of central importance to
the Christian understanding of faith. Suppose you are on a walking holiday
by the coast. As you walk along the shoreline one day, you notice a small
island a short distance from land. The receding tide has uncovered a sand
causeway leading to the island. Intrigued, you walk out, and begin to explore
it. The first object you notice is a small rowing boat, moored to a rock. As
you clamber over the rocks of the island, your attention is drawn to the richness of its animal and plant life. The receding tide has left behind countless
rock pools, filled with sea life of every kind. This brings out the amateur
marine biologist in you, and you spend hours happily identifying types of
molluscs.

When you next look up, you realize that the tide has begun to come in.
The sand causeway is already submerged. A thought flashes through your
mind. *If things get really dangerous, that boat would be a way of escape.* As you
clamber down the rocks to the waterline, you discover that the tide has
already reached a dangerously high level, and that it would be impossible to
wade back to the shore. You scan the shoreline in desperation, hoping that
there is someone within earshot who might be able to help you. But you are
utterly alone. As the tide rises further, you remember that an exceptionally
high tide is due today. There is every chance that you will be swept away by

its current. Your only hope of escape lies with the boat. You jump in, cast off, and row for the safety of the shore.

In the course of this adventure, your attitude to the boat passes through three quite different stages. Initially, you see the boat as little more than a feature of the landscape. It exists. It is there. But it has no particular relevance to your situation. You are perfectly prepared to affirm that it exists—but whether it exists or not is of little importance. As you become aware of the danger of your situation, however, a new attitude to the boat emerges: It is a potential means of escape. It is seen as a way in which you—or anyone else in the same situation—could escape from danger. You may not yet have reached the stage where you want to make use of it. You might want to explore other ways of getting out of this jam. But you are prepared to believe that the boat could be a way out. And finally, you come to the point where you decide to trust the boat. Your faith expresses itself in action and commitment, as you get into it, and put to sea.

The same three stages can be seen with attitudes to God. First, there is the attitude which is prepared to admit that he exists. The statement "There is a God" is accepted intellectually. The second stage involves accepting that God could be of some relevance to anyone who was in trouble. This still lacks personal application, however: God may be of relevance and importance to someone else—but not (yet) to me. Finally, there is the stage at which God becomes important at a personal level. He is of direct relevance to *me*. A new element enters into the equation—that of trust and personal commitment.

THE IMPORTANCE OF DOCTRINE: CAN WE TRUST GOD?

All the words used in the previous section—trust, commitment, and obedience—need qualification. Who or what do we trust? Why do we trust them? Who do we commit ourselves to? Who do we obey? Christian faith is not blind obedience. If people demand that we obey them, we naturally want to know why. What is it about them that gives them the authority to demand our obedience? If people demand that we trust them, we have every right to ask whether they are worthy of that trust. Why should I put my trust in Jesus Christ? Why should anyone base his or her entire life upon him? Earlier, we quoted Sheldon Vanauken's words concerning his leap of faith: "I could not reject Jesus. There was only one thing to do once I had seen the gap behind me. I turned away from it, and flung myself over the gap toward Jesus." Vanauken here describes making a leap of faith, as he committed himself to Jesus Christ. But why? What grounds did he have for making this commitment? As many Germans discovered to their horror in the 1930s, it is perfectly possible to put your trust in someone who, like Adolf Hitler, eventually turns out to be something approaching the devil incarnate. It is equally possible to commit yourself to someone or something profoundly evil and destructive, as the story of Dr. Faust's pact with the devil brings out. It is perfectly possible to believe in the authority and reliability of something which, like the Book of Mormon, turns out to be a crude forgery, a human invention. In all these cases, faith is shattered by reality; such a faith can only survive by blindly, doggedly, and obstinately ignoring the truth. How could Vanauken be reasonably sure that his faith would not be shattered like this? How could he know he was not flinging himself into an abyss, a bottomless pit, an empty void?

This point is brought out clearly by Francis Schaeffer in his much-admired book, *He Is There and He Is Not Silent*. Schaeffer suggests that we imagine a group of mountaineers, high up in the Swiss Alps. As they scale the bare rock, they are suddenly engulfed by fog. Their position becomes dangerous, as ice begins to form. One of the climbers suggests that they take a "leap of faith"—letting go of their hold on the rock, in the hope that they will land safely on an unseen ledge some short distance below. There is, however, no evidence that such a ledge exists. None of them knows the area, or has any idea what lies beneath them. To trust in their colleague's advice would be a blind leap of faith, a shot in the dark. The mountaineers would be fools if they trusted him blindly in this manner.

Then, Schaeffer continues, the climbers hear a voice calling to them through the fog. The unseen speaker tells the climbers that he is an experienced guide, a veteran mountaineer who knows the area like the back of his hand. He tells them that, although they cannot see it, there is indeed a place of safety just below them. By letting go of the rock, they will save themselves. The mountaineers are in a position to challenge the reliability, competence, and truthfulness of the speaker. They are not being asked to trust blindly in his judgment. They are being invited to verify the trustworthiness of the speaker before obeying him. They have the opportunity to know something about him before committing themselves to him.

It is this vital need to know *about* God which underlies the importance of Christian doctrine. Doctrine is concerned with defending and explaining the utter trustworthiness, integrity, and truthfulness of God, as we know him in scripture and through Jesus Christ. It is vital that Christians rest assured that the God in whom they have put their faith is profoundly worthy of that trust. One example will help to bring out this point. The doctrine of salvation through Christ assures us that God redeems us in a way in which his integrity and ours is preserved. We are not redeemed by exploiting some legal loophole, by ignoring our sin, or by compromising God's own righteousness.

Why did God have to redeem us through the death of Christ on the cross? Why couldn't he have done something much simpler? For example, why could he not have simply declared sin to be forgiven and forgotten?

After all, God is merciful—why can't he just show that mercy by overlooking sin, or telling us that it doesn't matter? There are many things that can be said about God. For example, he is merciful; he is wise; he is righteous. All of these can be determined without any difficulty from scripture. But these qualities, or attributes, of God cannot be considered in isolation from each other. God isn't merciful on Mondays and Tuesdays, wise on Wednesdays and Thursdays, and righteous on Fridays and Saturdays. He is all of these things, all of the time.

God's mercy and his justice are both involved in the redemption of humanity. God's tender mercy makes him want to redeem us in the first place; his justice determines the way in which he redeems us. Both mercy and justice are thus involved in redemption—but they are involved in different ways. God's mercy leads to the *decision* to redeem; God's justice leads to the particular *method* of redemption chosen. Neither God's mercy nor his justice are suspended—they are both in operation.

Now if God just declared that sin was forgiven, his mercy would indeed be satisfied—but what about his justice? God's implacable hostility to sin would be compromised. God would give the impression of having done some shady deal, by which his own principles were compromised. One of the more spectacular episodes in American politics of the late 1980s was President Reagan's arms deal with Iran. Ronald Reagan—perhaps the most popular president of the United States in recent years—constantly affirmed his total opposition to terrorism. Terrorists should be isolated. President Reagan regarded the Iranians as terrorists, holding American hostages against international law. They should be quarantined. Nobody should do any deals with them.

And then it turned out that President Reagan had authorized the sale of military equipment to Iran. The same man who had used all his moral authority to oppose dealing with Iran was seen to have compromised his own principles. He was being inconsistent. Some even suggested that he was being dishonest. His popularity slumped. A new word—"Irangate," by analogy with the Watergate scandal which brought down President Richard Nixon—briefly entered the political vocabulary of American journalists. The moral of this incident is clear: If you condemn something, don't compromise your principles by doing that thing yourself!

You can see how this applies to God and the redemption of humanity. As scripture makes abundantly clear, God is totally opposed to sin. He loves the sinner, certainly—but the sin, he detests. If God were to be seen to act in such a way as to condone sin, his integrity would be compromised. If God were to pretend that sin didn't really matter, the scriptural condemnations of sin would be seen to be hollow. If God can act in such a way as to tolerate sin, failing to condemn it, why should we not behave in the same way? It is not enough that God *is* just—he must be *seen* to act in a just manner. The redemption of the world thus becomes a test case. Will God act publicly in the righteous manner that his condemnations of sin suggest? Or will he continue to condemn sin, while doing some kind of deal with it behind our backs, along the lines of Ronald Reagan and Iran?

Now Ronald Reagan was able to explain his action in dealing with Iran along the following lines: There were American hostages held by groups sympathetic to Iran. By doing a deal with Iran, it would be possible to speed up the release of these hostages. The end thus justified the means. But, as the opinion polls soon made clear, the American public was not impressed. The end *and the means* both had to be consistent with moral principles. The redemption of the world is admirable, as an end or goal—but the means by which this is attained must be seen to be principled. God has publicly to demonstrate his justice, his determination to deal with sin firmly and fairly, in the way in which he redeems the world. The Christian doctrine of redemption affirms that God demonstrates total integrity and trustworthiness in this central aspect of his dealings with us. He—unlike President Reagan—may be trusted. Faith trusts in a God whom doctrine affirms to be worthy of trust, and whom doctrine declares may be known and encountered through Jesus Christ.

Having encountered God through Jesus Christ, the Christian life is begun. And, once more, doctrine plays a major role. It shapes Christian attitudes towards God and the world, as we shall see in the chapter which follows.

7

Doctrine and the Christian Life

A common complaint about doctrine runs along the following lines. "Doctrine is out-dated and irrelevant. What really matters is our attitudes to other people, and our morality. Doctrine doesn't matter." Dorothy L. Sayers reacted as follows to this suggestion in a lecture of 1940:

> The one thing I am here to say to you is this: That it is worse than useless for Christians to talk about the importance of Christian morality, unless they are prepared to take their stand upon the fundamentals of Christian theology. It is a lie to say that dogma does not matter; it matters enormously. It is fatal to let people suppose that Christianity is only a mode of feeling; it is virtually necessary to insist that it is first and foremost a rational explanation of the universe. It is hopeless to offer Christianity as a vaguely idealistic aspiration or a simple aspiration of a simple and consoling kind; it is, on the contrary, a hard, tough, exacting and complex doctrine, steeped in a drastic and uncompromising realism.

Attitudes depend on doctrine. Granted that Christian attitudes—as expressed, for example, in morality—are of central importance, the fundamental importance of doctrine will be obvious. But how does doctrine affect attitudes? To explore this theme, we will consider two key areas of Christian life: spirituality and ethics.

CHRISTIAN SPIRITUALITY

"Spirituality" is a poorly defined word. Nevertheless, it refers to one of the richest aspects of the Christian faith—the way in which we lead a "spiritual life." "Spirituality" is about ways of deepening our knowledge and love of God, of leading a more authentically *Christian* life. In part, spirituality concerns adopting right attitudes towards God and his creation. Once more, those attitudes are shaped and informed by doctrines. Two examples will illustrate this point.

1. The Doctrine of Justification by Faith

Modern Western society, especially in the United States of America, is very achievement-orientated. "You are what you make of yourself" is a key slogan of the enterprise culture. You have to lift yourself up by your own bootlaces. Many are deeply influenced by the secular values of success instilled into us by our families and peers. And these secular attitudes have important spiritual spin-offs. Many feel that they must *do* something or *achieve* something before God can love them. The gospel proclamation of the *unconditionality* of God's love for us can be difficult for such people to accept—because it so obviously contradicts the standards of Western culture. Surely they must do something before God can accept them? Many are taught that dependency on others is to be discouraged. As a result, they believe strongly in the cult of independence: Personal fulfillment is based on not being dependent on anyone or anything. The idea that God loves us, however, is an invitation to learn to depend on God. This clashes with the set of values we have absorbed from secular culture, which asserts that the way to get ahead in the world is through being independent.

The Christian doctrine of justification by faith mounts a powerful challenge to these attitudes. We are asked to believe that we have been accepted by God through Jesus Christ, despite being unacceptable. Our status before God is something given, not something earned. As Martin Luther—whose name is especially associated with this key doctrine—put it: "Sinners are attractive because they are loved; they are not loved because they are attractive." God's love for us is not dependent upon our achievements. We can never earn our salvation. We do not need to be high achievers to become Christians; it is God, not us, who achieves things. The tranquillity of faith—so powerful a theme of Luther's spirituality—rests upon recognizing that God has done all that is necessary for our salvation in Jesus Christ, and has done it well. We are asked to accept what God has done for us in Jesus Christ, and act upon it.

Luther died in the early hours of Thursday, February 17, 1546. His last word was "*Ja*—Yes," muttered as he lay dying, in response to one of his friends, who asked if he was "willing to persevere in the Christian faith and doctrine that you have preached." Shortly after his death, his friends found a note lying on a table in the same house. It was Luther's final written statement. Its last six words read, "*Wir sind Bettler. Hoc est verum*"—"We are beggars. This is true." For Luther, Christians are spiritual beggars, incapable of achieving anything unaided, and dependent totally upon the generosity of a God who gives. The doctrine of justification by faith could be summed up in Luther's final six words. God gives; we receive—gladly and gratefully.

2. The Doctrine of Creation

Many people feel frightened and lonely in the world. They are overwhelmed by the thought of the immensity of the universe. The stars studded in the night sky seem to emphasize the brevity and unimportance of human life. After all, even the nearest of those stars are billions of miles away, and become further from us with each moment that passes. The light from them now reaching us may have begun its journey centuries ago, long before we were born. The light from the sun takes a mere eight minutes to reach us; that from one of the nearer stars (Betelgeuse, in the constellation of Orion) takes nearly two hundred years. Every year, astronomers report the discovery of new and more distant galaxies. It becomes increasingly clear that the universe is a vast and lonely place. We can very easily feel alienated from it.

The doctrine of creation defuses this sense of loneliness. It allows us to feel at home in the world. It reminds us that we, like the rest of creation, were fashioned by God (Pss. 19:1; 102:25). We are here because God wants us to be here. We are not alone, but are in the very presence of the God who made and owns everything. We are in the presence of a friend, who knows us and cares for us. Behind the apparently faceless universe lies a person. The stars in the night sky are then no longer symbols of despair, but of hope—the same God who made *them* also *made us* and cares for us (Ps. 8). They are even reminders of God's promises, and their fulfillment (Gen. 15:1–6). This central doctrine affirms that we are here because we are meant to be here, in the presence of the God who created us and redeemed us.

The doctrine also disarms the threat of astrology—a particular concern for the Israelites while in exile in Babylon, who seem to have felt intimidated by Babylonian astrology. The stars, the Babylonians suggested, had a secret and baleful power over human destiny. To realize that the stars have been created by God is to understand that they are under his authority. He has called them by name (Ps. 147:4). The stars are under the same constraints of createdness as everything else. They cannot exercise a sinister power over us. It was not merely Babylonian astrology which taught some form of astral fatalism; similar ideas can be discerned within the modern New Age movements. the doctrine of creation allows these ideas to be set to one side; all of creation is under the authority, whether acknowledged or not, of the one who created it—and who makes himself known to and available to us in Jesus Christ.

Doctrine does more than generate and inform Christian spiritual attitudes. It also allows crucial insights concerning the shape and pattern of the Christian life. The doctrine of prevenient grace illustrates this point particularly well.

3. The Doctrine of Prevenient Grace

Many Christians, looking back on their lives, are aware that God appears to have been somehow guiding them toward conversion. The doctrine of prevenient grace addresses this feeling ("prevenient" means "going ahead of," or "going in advance"). The doctrine is firmly grounded in scripture. For example, Paul was aware that, long before his conversion, God was somehow preparing him for his mission to the Gentiles (Rom. 1:1–3). The doctrine was given new importance by Augustine of Hippo in the late fourth century.

Augustine was born in modern-day Algeria on November 13, 354. His mother was a Christian and very much wanted her son to share her faith. Augustine had, however, other ideas. While his mother was praying for him, he slipped on a boat leaving North Africa for Rome. The story of Augustine's subsequent conversion at Milan several years later is well known. In his autobiography (the *Confessions*), Augustine tells how in August 386 he sat under a fig tree in the garden of his house at Milan, and heard some children playing in a neighboring garden. They were singing as they played, and the words they sang were, "Take up and read! Take up and read!" Augustine rushed indoors, opened his New Testament at random, and read the verses which stood out from the page: "Clothe yourselves with the Lord Jesus Christ, and do not think about how to gratify the desires of the sinful nature" (Rom. 13:14). He closed the book, and told his friends he had become a Christian. On his return to North Africa, Augustine would assume responsibilities which marked him out as one of the greatest Christian leaders and thinkers of all time.

But as Augustine looked back on the events leading up to his conversion, he could not help but notice that God had been preparing him for this great moment. Somehow, God had gone before him, and prepared him for the crucial step of confrontation and conversion. Two episodes which Augustine recalled from his time in Italy bring out this point.

On his arrival at Milan, Augustine discovered that the local Christian bishop had a reputation as a splendid orator. As Augustine himself had ambitions to become a public orator, he decided to find out whether the reputation was merited. Perhaps he could pick up some tips which might come in useful later. Each Sunday, he slipped into the cathedral and listened to the bishop preach. Initially, he took a purely professional interest in the sermons as pieces of splendid oratory. But gradually, their content began to take hold of him. He developed an interest in Christianity. "I had yet to discover that it taught the truth," he later remarked, "but I did discover that it did not teach the things I had accused it of."

Later, Augustine began to go through a spiritual crisis. He broke off his relationship with his mistress—a relationship which had lasted fifteen years, and had given every appearance of stability to his colleagues. He developed a sense of spiritual lostness. But how could he change his ways so late in life? Surely he was too set in his ways to change? In the midst of this crisis, God seemed to speak to him. Augustine had long been attracted to the writings of the author Marius Victorinus: He now discovered that this writer had become a Christian late in life. A visitor to Augustine's residence told him of how Victorinus had been converted by studying the scriptures, and had insisted on going to church and making a public declaration of faith. The visitor relished the story as a superb piece of gossip; for Augustine, however, it seemed to be the voice of God addressing him in secret. If Marius Victorinus could do it, so could Augustine. Another fundamental psychological block to conversion had been removed. Yet again, God had seemed to be speaking to him and guiding him, even before the great moment of conversion.

The importance of this doctrine to Christian spirituality will be obvious. God prepares a way for his coming into our hearts. Just as John the Baptist prepared the way for the coming of the Lord in the wilderness, so God is at work, in the hearts and minds of men and women, preparing them to recognize and receive him. This does not represent an overriding of human freedom; rather, it amounts to a gentle breaking down of the barriers which naturally come between us and God. God is at work, perhaps in unknown and mysterious ways, among those who have yet to come to faith. Perhaps this may pass unnoticed at the time. But, as countless Christians—Augustine included—can testify, once people come to faith, it is very often possible to discern the ways in which God guided, prepared, and challenged them, even before the moment of faith dawned.

CHRISTIAN ETHICS

Not so long ago, there was a movement within liberal theology which argued that there existed a universal morality which Christianity reflected. It was not necessary to know anything about Christian theology to make ethical judgments. This universal morality, it was argued, was adequate in itself. The Christian, Buddhist, Hindu, Moslem, humanist, and atheist were all, it was argued, committed to much the same set of moral principles (with unimportant local variations). In his essay *The Abolition of Man*, C. S. Lewis described these as "the ultimate platitudes of Practical Reason." That view is now regarded as so seriously vulnerable as to be virtually defunct. Works such as Jeffrey Stout's *Ethics after Babel* destroyed the credibility of the idea of a "universal morality." Christian morality—like every other form of morality—is something special and distinct, and not just a subspecies of some nonexistent "universal morality." With the passing of the myth of a "universal morality," Christian writers have begun to write with much greater confidence on the theme of "Christian morality," in the knowledge that there *is* a distinctively Christian outlook on many matters. And this outlook, it is increasingly being stressed, is based upon Christian doctrine.

To make this point, we may consider two highly acclaimed recent works on the theme of Christian ethics, Oliver O'Donovan's *Resurrection and Moral Order*, and John Mahoney's *The Making of Moral Theology*. Despite differences between the two authors, one theme emerges as of major importance: Ethics rests upon doctrine. To give but one example: For O'Donovan, Christian ethics rests upon a proper understanding of the objective order imposed upon creation by God. To *act* in a Christian manner rests upon *thinking* in a Christian manner.

But how does doctrine affect Christian morality? To illustrate the importance of doctrine, we shall consider the way in which four major Christian doctrines have a direct impact upon the way we act.

1. The Doctrine of Justification by Faith

What is the motivation for ethics? Why should we want to do good works of any sort? The doctrine of justification by faith makes two central points of relevance here. First, it stresses that there is no way that our moral actions can earn our salvation. They have no purchasing power in respect to salvation. Second, works are done as a response to our justification. They are a natural expression of thankfulness to God. The *gift* of our justification lays upon us the *obligation* to live in accordance with our new status. We are *made* children of God through our justification as an act of free grace—and now we must act in accordance with this transformation. The slogan "become what you are!" neatly summarizes this situation, and encapsulates the essence of Pauline ethics with some brilliance. In justification we are made to be the light of the world (Matt. 5:14–16): Therefore we must shine out as lights in a dark world, as a city on a hill (Matt. 5:14; Phil. 2:15). We *are* the light of the world; therefore we must *become* the light of the world. Our justification brings about a new obedience—an obedience which would not be conceivable before our justification, and which ultimately rests upon the grace of God.

There is thus an "automatic" or "natural" connection between the justification of the sinner and his or her desire and ability to perform good works. The New Testament analogy of the tree and its fruits expresses the fundamental idea that the radical transformation of individuals (and it is worth remembering that the English word "radical" comes from the Latin *radix*, meaning "root") is prior to our ability to produce good works. In the Sermon on the Mount, Jesus points out that a good tree bears good fruit, and a bad tree bad fruit (Matt. 7:16–18). The nature of the fruit is biologically determined by the plant itself. Thus grapes don't grow on thorn-bushes, nor do figs grow on thistles. These are just the biological facts of life. If you want to get figs, you have to establish a fig tree, and get it to fruit.

Underlying these remarkably simple analogies is profound theological insight. The transformation of humanity is a prerequisite for its reformation. Or, as Martin Luther put it, "it isn't good works which makes an individual good, but a good individual who does good works." The New Testament, particularly in the Pauline writings, emphasizes that this transformation is to be understood as *God's transformation of us*, rather than our own attempt to transform us: Thus Paul speaks of the "fruit of the Spirit" (Gal. 5:22), drawing attention to the fact that this "fruit" is the result of God's action within us, rather than of our action independent of God. Whereas secular ethical systems tend to discuss moral acts in terms of their goal (in other words, what they achieve, or are intended to achieve), a theological ethical system based upon the doctrine of justification by faith will therefore discuss moral acts in terms of what they *presuppose* or *are intended to express* (in other words, the individual's radical transformation through his conversion). The starting point of an authentically *Christian* ethics is the recognition that the conversion of the individual leads to a new obedience, a new lifestyle, and a new ethic.

2. The Doctrine of Original Sin

A central insight of an authentically Christian morality is its realism concerning the limitations of human nature. Where some secular moral thinking degenerates into little more than a blind utopianism, Christian morality addresses the human situation with an informed realism about its strictly limited possibilities. In arguing against an unrealistic reliance upon human reason in ethics, the distinguished Roman Catholic moral theologian Charles Curran remarked that "the disrupting influence of sin colors all human reality," including human reason itself. Reinhold Niebuhr, perhaps one of the greatest Christian ethical thinkers of the twentieth century, poured scorn on the "perfectionist illusions" which so confused and misled many liberal Christian thinkers in the 1930s. The doctrine of original sin destroys naïve views of human perfectibility. There is, according to this doctrine, something inherently *wrong* with human nature, which makes it self-centered, rebellious, and disobedient. There is simply no point in informing sinful humanity that the world would be a better place if everyone stopped doing things that are wrong. What is required is a transformation of the human situation so that the motivation for doing wrong is eliminated or reduced. Underlying both the view that the human predicament arises from ignorance and the view that Jesus Christ is nothing more than a good teacher is a remarkably shallow understanding of the nature of humanity itself. As Niebuhr emphasized, all too many modern thinkers tend to work with a remarkably naïve view of human nature—probably reflecting the fact that their middle-class intellectual backgrounds tend to inhibit them from encountering and experiencing the darker side of human nature.

The radical realism of the Christian view of sin, and its devastating consequences for our understanding of human beings as moral agents, is captured in the words of Robert Browning, in *Gold Hair*:

> 'Tis the faith that launched point-blank its dart
> At the head of a lie; taught Original Sin,
> The corruption of man's heart.

The bland assumption of the natural goodness of human nature, so characteristic of much Western liberal thought, is called into question by this doctrine. The myth of human perfectibility and inevitable progress has been shown up for what it is by the savagery and cruelty of the twentieth century. If ever there was a period in human history when human evil was evident, it was the twentieth century. How many outrages such as Auschwitz must we experience before the naïve assumption that all human beings act out of the best of intentions is exposed for what it is—a cruel and seductive lie? Even those who are reluctant to call this inborn and inbuilt discord "sin" are prepared to recognize its reality—witness the famous words of the atheist poet A. E. Houseman:

> The troubles of our proud and angry dust
> Are from eternity, and shall not fail.

The doctrine of original sin brings a breath of refreshing realism to Christian ethics. It allows us to understand that human beings are fallen, with an alarming degree of ability to do evil, knowing that it is evil. The implications of human self-centeredness for political institutions (for example, evident in the way in which they can be manipulated and exploited) and moral action will be obvious. Niebuhr's argument for democracy—an excellent example of the political application of a Christian doctrine—was quite simple: It was just about the only way of controlling human self-centeredness, and forcing national leaders to respect the needs of others. Put very simply, the doctrine of original sin tells us that morality concerns weak, self-centered, and exploitative human beings—in other words, *real* humans, not the perfectible angels of wishful liberal thinking. Power, capital, and force—all can be, and will be, abused and exploited for personal ends, unless the political and moral will exists to control them.

Charles Curran also pointed out some central ethical consequences of the Christian doctrine of original sin. Even human reason, the central resource upon which so much secular ethical theory rests, must be regarded as compromised by sin. "In the total Christian horizon the disrupting influence of sin colors all human reality ... sin affects reason itself." Furthermore, sin is so deeply embedded in human nature and society that there are points at which it is impossible to adopt a course of action which avoids sin. The Christian is obliged to choose between two decisions, each of which is sinful. "In some circumstances the Christian is forced to do something sinful. The sinner reluctantly performs the deed and asks God for forgiveness and mercy." As Helmut Thielicke argued in his *Theological Ethics*, human society is so thoroughly saturated with sin that Christian ethical decision-making must learn to come to terms with compromise, adjusting to the sinful realities of the world, rather than pretending that an ideal situation exists in which it is possible to draw a clear-cut decision between "right" and "wrong." To pretend that it is possible to make ethical decisions without coming to terms with the severe limitations placed upon human reason and will by sin, is to live in a Walter Mitty world of unreality and dreams.

Curran and Thielicke are excellent examples of Christian writers on ethics who are concerned to develop genuinely *Christian* approaches to ethical questions, rather than just rehashing secular ideas and values. Time and time again, these writers show the importance of doctrine to ethics. Christian ethics is simply too important to be left to those whose values are determined by the world, rather than by the gospel.

3. The Doctrine of Creation

Recognition that the world was created by, and now belongs to, God has important consequences for understanding our own responsibilities within that world. We have been placed within God's creation to tend it and take care of it (Gen. 2:15). We may be superior to the remainder of that creation, and exercise authority over it (Ps. 8:4–8)—but we remain under the authority of God, and responsible to him for the way in which we treat his creation. We are the stewards, not the owners, of creation. We hold it in trust. There is a growing realization today that past generations have seriously abused that trust, exploiting the creation and its resources. There is a real danger that the "goodness" of creation, including its delicate ecological balances, will be shattered through human greed.

Fortunately, there has been a growing awareness recently of this need to take a more responsible attitude toward creation. Reflecting on our responsibilities as stewards of God's creation is the first step in undoing the harm done by past generations. It matters to God that vast areas of our world are made uninhabitable through nuclear or toxic chemical waste. It matters that the delicate balance of natural forces is disturbed by human carelessness. Sin affects the way we treat the environment as much as it does our attitude toward God, other people, and society as a whole. This Christian doctrine is the basis of a new—and overdue—attitude toward the creation, and our place within it.

4. The Doctrine of the Incarnation

Some Christians dismiss the suggestion that Christianity involves political or social action. Surely, they say, Christians ought to be concerned about the hereafter rather than the here and now. What reasons may be given for suggesting that Christian ethics, with its vigorous concern for human beings and the creation, is of any importance? Some pointers have already been given in the material already presented; nevertheless, more can be said. Perhaps the doctrine of the incarnation is of supreme importance in this respect.

The doctrine of the incarnation speaks to us of God becoming man. God redeemed his creation from within that creation. He delivered his creatures as one of them. God lodged himself firmly within his creation, in order to redeem it. That same pattern of involvement should be evident in the lives of those redeemed through the coming of Jesus Christ. "Be imitators of God" (Eph. 5:1).

This phrase serves to emphasize the importance of the incarnation. If we are to be "imitators of God" (and what a challenging phrase that is!), we need to know what God is like. The doctrine of the incarnation affirms that Jesus Christ tells us in his words, and shows us in his actions, what God is like. For example, Christians are urged to "love one another" (1 John 4:7–11). This is clearly of some importance for Christian morality. But what does this word "love" mean? Unless we can spell out what it means and implies, we are left in some doubt about what is required of us.

The doctrine of the incarnation allows us to say what the "love of God," which we are meant to imitate, looks like. In the image of Jesus Christ, trudging to his lonely place of execution, we are given a model of the love of God. His act of total self-giving, even to the point of death, is the model for true Christian love. He thought not of himself, but of others.

We could take this idea further. Throughout his ministry, we notice Jesus Christ accepting individuals, being prepared to associate with those who were regarded as socially acceptable as much as those who were regarded as social outcasts. The good news of the kingdom was for all, without distinction. That same pattern of divine acceptance should be ours as well. To recognize that Jesus Christ is God incarnate is to recognize that he maps out patterns of behavior that ought to be characteristic of Christians. Yet we are not saved by imitating Christ; it is by being saved that we are moved to be conformed to his likeness, as we seek to be imitators of God through him.

This brief survey has attempted to show the major impact which doctrine can and must have upon Christian living. The Christian who prays, thinks, and worships cannot avoid engaging with matters of doctrine—and the Christian who is doctrinally informed will bring new insights and depth to all these activities. A lack of doctrinal awareness leads to a shallow spirituality and potentially misguided ethics. This point naturally brings us to consider the question of whether it is possible to have "Christianity without doctrine" in the first place.

8

Is Christianity Possible Without Doctrine?

Many find themselves attracted to the idea of "Christianity without dogma." Christianity, they might argue, is a practical religion. The Sermon on the Mount, they might suggest, lies at the center of the Christian faith, rather than Paul's theology or its development in the Christian tradition. The gospel is moral, or it is nothing. Christianity is about bringing into the modern world the same breadth of spirit, the same compassion and care, the same depth of spiritual awareness, that was first shown to the world in the person of Jesus of Nazareth. Christianity is about action and attitudes, not about the cold, barren, and outdated world of dogmas. Especially in the late nineteenth century, there were many writers who argued that Christianity was basically nothing more and nothing less than the personal religion of Jesus. We were called to share his faith in God. We should not believe *in* Jesus, but *with* Jesus.

There will be many who will feel sympathy with such views. Indeed, if I may be allowed to share a personal memory, I once held them strongly myself. I no longer do so, and believe that I was seriously (but sincerely) mistaken in accepting this radical devaluation of doctrine. Like many a young man, I found the romantic image of a "Christianity without doctrine" profoundly attractive. It seemed to represent the best of all possible worlds, combining a rhetorical appeal to the great Western liberal deities of intellectual freedom and personal integrity with an unashamed, almost mystical, sentimental fascination, focused upon the distant hero-figure of Jesus himself. Here was a living person, whose gospel consisted in the simplicities of commitment and obedience. The demand to follow him was a call to imitate him in his relation to God and to others. We are called to imitate him, to copy him, to pattern ourselves upon him.

Simple solutions are attractive, yet seductive. As I reflected upon my early understanding of Christianity, I began to appreciate how intellectually shallow it was. "Christianity without doctrine" seemed to me increasingly untenable. In the remainder of this chapter, I shall outline some of the difficulties which persuaded me to abandon my belief in this idea. Inevitably, ideas and arguments which have been deployed earlier in this work may reappear, in slightly different forms, in this chapter; it is, however, important that they should be marshaled together in dealing with this important question. Some of these arguments are mutually related, others are not. They seem to me, however, to build up to give a decisive cumulative case against the possibility of a "Christianity without doctrine."

1. Believing in Jesus—Not with Jesus

It is impossible to speak about Christians copying the private relationship of Jesus to his Father (a classic belief of the "Christianity without doctrine" school) without noting that Jesus spells out, in sermon and parable, what that relationship presupposes, expresses, and demands.

If Christianity is simply about Christians imitating Jesus' relation to God, we are confronted with two major obstacles. First, we are told remarkably little about it in the New Testament itself. What form did it take? The Gospels are silent, apparently reflecting a silence on the part of Jesus himself. Jesus withdrew from the crowd to be with his Father in prayer, and if we were ever meant to know the full details of his personal relationship with the Father (which is highly unlikely), that knowledge has been denied to us. In the second place, what we do know about Jesus' relationship with his Father puts it beyond us. It is not transferable to believers. We cannot share in its fullness. Jesus' relationship with the Father reflects who Jesus is—and we can never share his unique identity and thus his relationship.

In any case, the history of Christianity shows no evidence of Christians ever believing that they were called to mimic the faith of Jesus. Rather, we find faith in and worship of a risen, redeeming, and glorified Christ. Christ is someone in whom we can trust, but one whom we can only imitate very poorly—and in his relationship to God, we cannot imitate him at all. If we are the children of God, it is not in the same sense as Jesus was the Son of God. The gospel is not about copying Jesus, or repeating his experiences—it is, as it always has been, about appropriating Jesus. We come to God in Christ and through Christ—not with Jesus.

This view of Christ as a religious example is closely linked with a deficient view of human nature, which does not—or *will* not—come to terms with the sheer intractability of the fact of human sin, and the strange and tragic history of humanity in general, and the Christian church in particular. As Bishop Charles Gore pointed out incisively a century ago:

> Inadequate conceptions of Christ's person go hand in hand with inadequate conceptions of what human nature wants. The Nestorian conception of Christ ... qualifies Christ for being an example of what man can do, and into what wonderful union with God he can be assumed if he is holy enough; but Christ remains one man among many, shut in within the limits of a single human personality, and influencing man only from outside. He can be a Redeemer of man if man can be saved from outside by bright example, but

not otherwise. The Nestorian Christ is logically associated with the Pelagian man.... The Nestorian Christ is the fitting Savior of the Pelagian man.

In other words, a Nestorian Christology (that is, a view of Jesus Christ which regards him primarily as a human example worthy of imitation) is linked with a Pelagian doctrine of human nature (that is, the idea that human beings are perfectly capable of attaining salvation without divine aid, except in the general area of being provided with guidance and examples of what is required of them).

Jesus must be more than just a religious teacher to account for his position within Christianity. C. S. Lewis expressed this point clearly and trenchantly:

> We have never followed the advice of great teachers. Why are we likely to begin now? Why are we more likely to follow Christ than any of the others? Because he's the best moral teacher? But that makes it even less likely that we shall follow him. If Christianity only means one more bit of good advice, then Christianity is of no importance. There's been no lack of good advice over the last four thousand years. A bit more makes no difference.

In fact, however, Christians do not speak of Jesus in this way, as Lewis stresses. They speak of being "saved" through him. They speak about encountering God through him.

In any case, the teaching of Jesus himself carries us beyond the idea that Jesus is only a teacher. The outrage provoked by Jesus among his Jewish audience when he declared that the paralytic's sins were forgiven (Mark 2:5) was utterly genuine. Their theology was utterly correct: "Who can forgive sins but God alone?" (Mark 2:7). Jesus' words point back to himself. If they are to be taken seriously, they amount to a remarkable statement concerning Jesus himself. His identity and status become part of this message. His statements about God are mingled with statements concerning himself, even to the point where the reliability and trustworthiness of the former come to depend upon the latter. The statements concerning what Jesus believes himself to be called and able to do require clarification of the relationship between Jesus and God, between the Son and the Father—and thus point to the need for doctrines, such as that of the incarnation.

2. The Authority of Jesus Rests Upon Doctrinal Beliefs Concerning Him

To allow that Jesus is a religious teacher is to raise the question of his authority. Why should we take him seriously? We have been fortunate enough to have had the advice of countless moral and religious teachers in human history—what makes Jesus different? What singles him out as commanding attention? As we have already seen (pp. 232–234), it is untenable to suggest that Jesus' authority rests upon the excellence of his moral or religious teaching. To make this suggestion is to imply that Jesus has authority only when he happens to agree with us. We thus would have authority over Jesus.

In fact, however, the teaching of Jesus has authority on account of who Jesus is—and the identity and significance of Jesus can only be spelled out in doctrinal terms. "We cannot go on treating and believing in Jesus Christ in a way in which it would be wrong to treat and believe in another man, without a theory of his person that explains that he is something more than man" (Charles Gore). It is doctrine which explains why and how Jesus' words and deeds have divine, rather than purely human, authority. It is doctrine which singles out Jesus Christ, and none other, as being God incarnate. To pay attention to Jesus Christ reflects our fundamental conviction that God speaks through this man as through no other. Here is no prophet, speaking on God's behalf at secondhand; here is God himself, speaking to us. "We have to do with God himself as we have to do with this man. God himself speaks when this man speaks in human speech" (Karl Barth). Quite contrary to the Broad Church liberals of the nineteenth century (who believed it was possible to uphold the religious and ethical aspects of Christianity, while discarding its doctrines), the authority of Jesus' moral and religious teaching thus rests firmly upon a doctrinal foundation.

This point is made with care and persuasion by the distinguished Oxford philosopher of religion Basil Mitchell. In his essay "Is there a distinctive Christian ethic?" Mitchell stresses that ethics depend upon worldviews—and that worldviews in turn depend upon doctrine.

Any worldview which carries with it important implications for our understanding of man and his place in the universe would yield its own distinctive insights into the scope, character, and content of morality. To answer the further question, "What *is* the distinctive Christian ethic?" is inevitably to be involved to some extent in controversial questions of Christian doctrine.

The "Christianity without doctrine" school thus finds itself in something of a quandary. If Christianity is primarily about certain religious or moral attitudes, it seems that those attitudes rest upon doctrinal presuppositions. Doctrine determines attitudes. It is utterly pointless to argue that we all ought to imitate the religious and moral attitudes of Jesus—that is a demand for blind and unthinking obedience. The question of *why* we should regard these attitudes as being authoritative demands to be considered. And that means explaining what it is about Jesus Christ as singling him out as authoritative—in short, developing doctrines about Jesus.

This point was made clearly and prophetically by William Temple. Writing against the "Religion without Dogma" movement in 1942, he declared that:

You would hardly find any theologian now who supposes that Christian ethics can survive for half a century in detachment from Christian doctrine, and this is the very last moment when the church itself can come forward with outlines of Christian ethics in the absence of the theological foundation which alone makes them really tenable. Our people have grown up in a generally Christian atmosphere, and take it for granted that all people who are not actually perverted hold what are essentially Christian notions about human conduct. But this is not true.

(Temple then goes on to illustrate this point with reference to the rise of Hitler and Stalin in the 1930s.) Although many liberal and radical writers of the 1960s suggested that Christian ethics could be divorced from doctrine, and maintain an independent existence, the wisdom of Temple's words is once more apparent. Distinctive *ethics* (whether Marxist, Christian, or Buddhist) are dependent upon *worldviews*, which are in turn shaped by *doctrines*, by understandings of human nature and destiny.

What we might call the "common-sense-Christianity" school will probably continue to insist that faith is a "practical and down-to-earth matter," having nothing to do with "airy-fairy theories" (if I might use phrases I was fond of myself at one time). The famous economist J. M. Keynes came across similar attitudes among industrialists and politicians. "We're practical people," they declared, "who have no need for abstract theories about economics." Yet these people, Keynes scathingly remarked, were little more than the unwitting slaves of some defunct economist. Their allegedly "practical" outlook actually rested upon unacknowledged economic theories. They lacked the insight to see that what they regarded as obvious was actually based upon the theories of some long-dead economist. Without knowing it, "common-sense-Christianity" rests upon quite definite doctrinal foundations. The man who declares, in the name of common sense, that "Jesus was simply a good man," may genuinely believe that he has avoided matters of doctrine—whereas he has actually echoed the doctrines of the Enlightenment. The study of Christian doctrine is thus profoundly liberating, as it exposes these hidden doctrinal assumptions. Every version of Christianity that has ever existed rests upon doctrinal foundations; not every version of Christianity has grasped this fact. The genuine question of importance is quite simple: Which of those doctrinal foundations is the most authentic and reliable?

3. The Gospel Itself Rests Upon a Doctrinal Framework

Why is Christianity good news? In part, because it proclaims the reality of the love of God to the world. It points to Jesus Christ upon the cross, and declares, "God loved the world this much" (see John 3:16). But the death of Jesus Christ upon the cross is only good news if it is interpreted in a certain way.

Doctrine defines how the cross of Christ is to be interpreted. To put it another way, it provides an interpretative framework for understanding the events of Calvary. It is not good news if a man, after a life of self-giving and care for his fellows, should be harried, tortured, mocked, and finally executed in a triumphant display of barbarity. It is no gospel if this man reveals the love of one human being for another, far far away and long long ago. It only becomes good news if it is interpreted in a certain way. It becomes good news if it is the Son of God himself who gives himself in order that we might come to newness of life. It becomes good news if these events are interpreted in terms of a sufficiently high profile of identity between Jesus and God, such as that set out by the doctrine of the incarnation.

Doctrine aims to explain what it is about the life, death, and resurrection of Jesus Christ which is good news. It aims to explain and justify the vital connection between the "there and then" of Calvary and the "here and now" of our own situation. It is an interpretative bridge between history and faith, between the past and the present. It relates the events of Calvary to our own experience, interpreting the latter in terms of the former.

4. Doctrine Defines What Manner of Response Is Appropriate to the Gospel

What must we do to be saved? What sort of response is appropriate to the gospel? What conditions must be met before the renewal promised in Jesus Christ can be actualized in our lives? To answer these questions—even if the answer proposed is "nothing"—is to make vitally important doctrinal statements. Enormous decisions, affecting our manner of life, depend upon these doctrinal presuppositions.

To illustrate this point, we shall consider the events surrounding a small group of Italian noblemen in the early sixteenth century. The group, all of whom were educated at the University of Padua, met regularly, to discuss the question of how they might be saved. They were confused—hardly surprisingly, as the church had gone through a long period of confusion in relation to the doctrine of justification. No one could say, with any great degree of certainty, what an individual had to do in order to be saved. This alarming degree of uncertainty was reflected in Martin Luther's anxieties about his own spiritual situation, which would eventually boil over into the Lutheran Reformation.

In the year 1510, the small group of Italian noblemen split into two. They had been unable to reach agreement on what their response to the gospel ought to be. One section of the group (the larger), centering on Paolo Giustiniani, entered a local monastery, there to work out their salvation under conditions of the utmost austerity. Only in this way, they believed, could they be sure of gaining salvation. The smaller section, centering on

Gasparo Contarini, believed that they could gain salvation while remaining in the everyday world. It was only later that the confusion was resolved, in the aftermath of the Reformation: It was possible to be saved through responding to the gospel in faith, while remaining active in the world.

The doctrine of justification by faith spells out what response is required of individuals, if they are to benefit from the death and resurrection of Jesus Christ. This doctrinal framework is essential: We must know what is demanded of us, if we are to be reconciled to God and receive newness of life. As the Reformation made abundantly clear, to be vague in this respect is disastrous, both spiritually and theologically. It is of no value to be able to give a full account of all the benefits and challenges the gospel brings, without being able to explain how that gospel may be received. Doubts about whether one has made the appropriate response to the gospel will inevitably lead to spiritual paralysis through doubt and confusion.

A similar point was made by the philosopher Immanuel Kant, in his work *Religion within the Limits of Reason Alone*. Kant stressed that, unless an individual could know that past sins had been forgiven and moral guilt canceled, it was virtually impossible for him or her to live a moral life. It was only when this individual knew that the guilt of the past had been canceled that moral improvement could begin. Doubts about whether forgiveness had *really* been granted could thus completely wreck an individual's life. They would bring about a form of moral paralysis. For such reasons, Kant insisted that individuals should be able to *be assured* of the forgiveness of their past sins, in order that they might get on with the business of leading new lives.

Precisely the same point must be made in connection with faith. The believer must know that he or she has been forgiven, and accepted by God. It is only when we are sure that we really have begun the Christian life that we can begin to pay full attention to what the Christian life demands. Our personal living out of the gospel depends on being able to rest secure that we stand within the gospel. A doctrine which makes clear what we must *do* in order to begin the Christian life is thus an essential and proper precondition for all Christian morality and spirituality.

5. Doctrine Is the Proper Outcome of Reflection on Faith

Human beings are rational creatures. They ask questions—questions like "Why?" As Plato stressed, there is a natural human desire to "give an account of things." Why are we being asked to accept the teachings of Jesus Christ? Why is he singled out among other human beings? Psychologists have pointed out that there seems to be some basic human need to *attribute* meaning to events. "Attributional processes" seem to be a normal part of human reflection upon the puzzles of human existence, in an attempt to make sense of it all. This need to make sense of things applies equally to matters of

Christian faith. For example, the crucifixion and resurrection are things which need to be explained. Why did they happen? What do they mean?

In his 1891 Bampton Lectures, delivered at Oxford University, Charles Gore pointed out that this natural human inquisitiveness has its religious outcome in doctrine.

> Christians found themselves treating Jesus Christ, believing in Jesus Christ, as they had never treated or believed in any other man. . . . Because they were rational they must have asked themselves "Why is he to be so treated? What is his relation to God whose functions he exercises? Why are we not idolaters if we yield him such worship?" They must have asked these questions because they were men endowed with reason, and could not therefore go on acting without giving some account of their action.

Doctrine is nothing other than the attempt of rational believer to make sense of every aspect of their experience of Jesus Christ. If conversion involves the mind as well as the soul, doctrine is its inevitable outcome, as the believer brings his or her mind to bear on the implications of faith.

The eleventh-century writer Anselm of Canterbury had a neat way of expressing this. He spoke of "faith seeking understanding." Once you come to faith, you aim to understand what you have believed. Faith comes first, and is followed by understanding. Doctrine results from this attempt to understand what has been believed. It attempts to make explicit the implicit assumptions of faith. For example, faith believes that we have been saved through Jesus Christ; doctrine asserts that this belief implies that Jesus must be both God and man if this is to be possible. Doctrine is basically the outcome of taking rational trouble over the mysteries of faith. To prohibit this rational reflection in order to develop a "Christianity without doctrine" is to deny Christians the right to think about their faith. Doctrinal reflection is the product of a passionate search for truth, combining intellectual curiosity and honesty.

This chapter has outlined in the briefest of manners some of the reasons for thinking that doctrine is a proper and necessary element of Christianity. The idea of a "Christianity without Doctrine" may, on first inspection, seem both plausible and attractive. On closer examination, however, this proves to be a profoundly misleading impression. Even the very brief points made in the present chapter must go some way toward suggesting that doctrine serves a vital purpose.

This is not to say that Christianity is only about doctrine. As we have stressed throughout this book, an experience of God through Jesus Christ lies at the heart of the Christian faith. Doctrine is only one aspect of that faith. It is, however, a vital aspect. It is like the bones which give strength and shape to the human body. It is like the steel rods which reinforce concrete structures. Without doctrine, faith becomes shapeless, weak, and vulnerable. Doctrine addresses, interprets, and transforms human experience, in order that a dynamic, living, and resilient faith may result.

In a later chapter, we will look at one of the more helpful ways of getting to grips with doctrine in this way. It is by studying the creeds that a new appreciation of the depths and richness of the Christian faith can come about. However, another question demands to be considered more pressingly. Any volume which deals with the subject of doctrine ought to deal with one of the great taboo areas of modern Christian theology—heresy. What *is* heresy, and why is so much importance attached to it? It is this difficult and sensitive subject, hardly even touched upon in modern theological writings, which we shall consider in the next chapter.

9

The Coherence of Doctrine and the Challenge of Heresy

The very word "heresy" is unfashionable. It rarely enters the vocabulary of many modern Christian writers. Even to suggest that an individual's views are "heretical" is to risk being scorned for holding on to thoroughly outdated ideas. Even to mention the word "heresy" is to court the charge of being "medieval" or "authoritarian." It must be said that these charges have much to commend them. Many of the more recent heresy trials have been little less than disgraceful, often showing up the prosecutors as dogmatic and small-minded individuals, with little real understanding of the Christian gospel.

An example might be given to make this point. One of the greatest works of Scottish theology in the nineteenth century was John McLeod Campbell's *Nature of the Atonement*, published in 1856. Yet this same individual had been tried for heresy by the Church of Scotland a quarter of a century earlier. While minister at the village of Rhu on the Gare Loch, Campbell had preached that God's saving grace is offered to all, and not just to the elect. Some members of his congregation took notes of these sermons. Among Campbell's statements thus recorded was "The person who knows that Christ died for every human being is the person who is in a condition to go forth to every human being and say, 'Let there be peace between you and God!'" This clearly taught that Christ died for all sinners, and not just for the predestined few—and thus contradicted the Westminster Confession of faith, a sixteenth-century document whose statements were at that time rigorously upheld within the Scottish kirk.

The note-takers complained with "detestation and abhorrence" that their minister was preaching heresy. The case finally came to the General Assembly of the Church of Scotland in 1831. After an all-night sitting, the Assembly declared, by a majority of 119 to 6, that he had taught "doctrines at variance with the Word of God and the standards of the Church of Scotland." It imposed the most severe penalty at its disposal. He was to cease to be a minister of the church. Needless to say, the Church of Scotland would later relax its strict views on this particular doctrine (often known as "limited atonement"), which is not explicitly stated in scripture. By then, however, Campbell was dead. This welcome development was too late to be of any interest to him.

Countless other such cases could be instanced. The notion of heresy, and all the apparatus of heresy trials to which it gave rise, seem to be firmly erased from much modern Christian thinking. I wish to suggest, however, that the idea of heresy remains important for the Christian churches. Neither the word nor the ideas should be allowed to be abolished or forgotten, as if they were of purely antiquarian interest. This is not for one moment to suggest that legal action, criminal or civil, should be taken against individuals who might be regarded as heretical. Rather, it is to affirm that the theological notion of heresy can still be of considerable service in maintaining the faithfulness of the Christian church to her calling.

Let us begin by considering what the term originally meant. The Greek word *haeresis*, as used within the New Testament, can have the more or less neutral sense of "party" or "faction" (Acts 5:17; 15:5; 26:5). However, the word can also have a developed meaning—a party or faction which arises through a defective understanding of the Christian faith (1 Cor. 11:19; Gal. 5:20). It is not simply doctrinal disagreement which made a heresy; it is the threat which it posed to the unity of the Christian church. By the fourth century, however, the word had acquired a developed meaning, more or less equivalent to the present-day meaning of the word. "Orthodoxy" (that is, "holding right views") became established as the opposite of heresy.

What does the word heresy designate? To begin with, let us draw a distinction between *unbelief* and *heresy*. Unbelief, it must be stressed, is not a heresy. Walter Kaufmann entitled his personal atheistic manifesto *The Faith of a Heretic*. In fact, the title is quite inappropriate. Atheism is no heresy; it is simply a non-Christian belief. To understand the importance of heresy, and the particular challenge and difficulties is poses for Christianity, it is necessary to realize that heresy is a form of belief. Orthodoxy and heresy are both subcategories of Christian faith. Heresy is something which arises within the context of faith. We could represent the situation diagramatically as in Figure 2.

It is thus quite incorrect to suggest that atheism, agnosticism, Islam, or Hinduism are in any way heresies. (It is certainly true that the Spanish Inquisition regarded Moslems and Protestants alike as heretics—but this reflects the politicized idea of heresy associated with the Middle Ages. We are here concerned with reclaiming the authentically theological sense of the term, which involves setting to one side such distortions of the notion as are associated with the Inquisition.)

As the diagram indicates, unbelief could be defined as the rejection of the central cluster of Christian beliefs centering on the redemptive action of God through Jesus Christ. To deny that God redeems us through Jesus Christ is not strictly heresy; it is more a form of unbelief. Heresy arises through accepting the basic cluster of Christian beliefs—yet interpreting them in such a way that inconsistency results. A heresy is thus an inadequate or deficient form of Christianity. By its very deficiency, it poses a threat to the gospel.

Figure 2

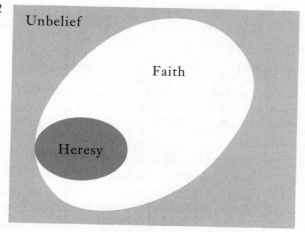

The Relation of Unbelief, Faith and Heresy

This difficult point needs illustration. Let us consider the statement: Human beings are reconciled to God only through Jesus Christ. This is a central insight of the New Testament. To deny it is to place oneself outside the boundaries of the Christian church. It is to identify oneself as a non-Christian. This is not to make any moral judgment about the person wishing to do this, nor to make any statement concerning the intellectual merits of the case. It is simply to say that the holding of certain views inevitably means declaring that one does not share central Christian presuppositions and, for that reason, cannot in all integrity be regarded as a Christian. The word "Christian" cannot be allowed to become so vague that it allows anyone, irrespective of his or her views, to be considered a Christian. As we stressed in an earlier chapter (pp. 265–76), doctrine functions as a social demarcator, laying down criteria for determining who is a member of the Christian community, and who is not.

To accept and act upon this belief, that human beings are reconciled to God only through Jesus Christ, is to declare that one stands within the community of faith. But there now arises the question of how this statement is to be interpreted. Heresy arises through inadequate understandings of central Christian beliefs. An example, arising from the belief just mentioned and centering upon the identity of Jesus Christ, may prove helpful.

Suppose you held that Jesus Christ is just a good man, like any other human being. He might be a particularly fine teacher, or a morally outstanding individual. Nevertheless, he is *only* a man, differing from us in degree, rather than kind. What is the result of this belief? The answer is that it makes the belief, that human beings are reconciled to God only through Jesus Christ, internally inconsistent. There is a fatal contradiction within it. For if Jesus is just a human being like us, he shares our common condition.

He is not so much the solution to our problem, as part of it. Either he cannot do anything about the situation, or else he can only change it to the extent that any other human being can. But the emphasis upon the fact that our situation *has* been changed, and *only* changed through Jesus Christ, is inconsistent with this belief concerning the identity of Jesus. If Jesus Christ is only human, we cannot be reconciled to God through him. And so doubt is cast over a central premise of the Christian faith. Why? Because it is shown to be inconsistent with another belief. Either one or the other is wrong. They cannot both be right. To maintain that both are correct is impossible. There is a serious deficiency somewhere along the line.

Heresy arises through inconsistency. It arises through beliefs which are in conflict with the central Christian affirmation of redemption in Jesus Christ. All the major heresies of the Christian faith center upon precisely this principle. Let us consider two classic fourth-century heresies to make this point clearer.

ARIANISM

This heresy declared that Jesus Christ was a creature, not God incarnate. In many ways, Arius was forced to this conclusion by his acceptance of the classical Greek view of God as unchangeable, which he found to be irreconcilable with the Christian doctrine of the incarnation. Despite what is often said about him, Arius was a reluctant heretic, forced to make a momentous choice between Christian and classical Greek views of God—and feeling obliged to opt for the latter. Arius affirmed that it was possible to refer to Jesus as "Son of God," but in a purely honorary manner. To do this was just a way of being polite about Christ. Jesus is preeminent among all God's creatures—but is still a created being. He is not, and cannot be thought of, as being God incarnate.

This caused a radical inconsistency within the Christian doctrine of salvation, as Arius' opponent, Athanasius, was quick to point out. It meant that one creature (Jesus Christ) was held to be able to redeem other creatures (sinners). Yet only God could save. Either salvation was thus an impossibility, or there was something radically wrong with Arius' understanding of the identity of Jesus Christ. It was fatally flawed at some point. Yet, as Arius was perfectly prepared to accept that we are redeemed only through Jesus Christ, the fault had to lie with an inadequate understanding of the identity of Jesus Christ. It was only through allowing that Jesus Christ was both God and man that redemption could be safeguarded. Arius' ideas posed a serious threat to the Christian doctrine of salvation.

APOLLINARIANISM

Apollinarius felt that the dignity of Jesus Christ was compromised by the suggestion that he was fully human. If Jesus Christ was totally human, he argued, he would have a normal human mind, subject to all the temptations and unpleasant thoughts that human beings are prone to have. This was unthinkable. So, in a thoroughly well-intentioned effort to preserve the dignity of Christ, Apollinarius argued that Jesus must have had a divine, rather than a human, mind. This was vigorously challenged by his opponent, Gregory of Nazianzen. On the basis of his maxim "the unassumed is the unhealed," Gregory argued that Christ must have had a human mind. Otherwise, the human mind was unredeemed. Part of our human nature (and a very important part of that) would have been left unaffected by the incarnation. A vital section of our humanity would have been unredeemed. Once more, heresy was seen to be an inadequate statement of the Christian faith.

Heresy is thus clearly seen to be a defective version of Christianity. It is a version of Christianity, in the sense that it accepts the major premises of faith—which distinguishes it from unbelief, or non-Christian beliefs. But precisely because it is inadequate, it poses a threat to Christianity. Thomas Carlyle once wrote that, "if Arianism had won, Christianity would have dwindled to a legend." There is much truth in the old Latin proverb, *corruptio optimi pessimum est*, "there is nothing worse than the corruption of the best."

Heresy is simply second-rate Christianity. Heresy might be good in comparison with unbelief—but it had to give way to something which was better. As Voltaire remarked, "the best is the enemy of the good." And, if Christianity is to survive, let alone to prosper, it must confront a hostile world with all its resources fully available. The early church was so concerned about the threat posed by heresy, on account of its perilous situation. It felt itself to be continually under threat from an aggressive pagan culture. Its future depended upon its intellectual credibility on the one hand, and its internal unity on the other. Heresy destabilized the church, both intellectually and socially.

It is right that every age should reconsider the classic heresies, in order to establish whether they really are fatally flawed. Orthodoxy is not something which demands to be believed on blind trust—it has a theological case to make, by demonstrating its superiority over heretical versions of Christianity. Each generation will wish to convince itself of the rightness of the evaluation of heresies and orthodoxy made by previous generations. But all the indications are that the classical heresies will continue to be considered deficient and inadequate versions of the gospel.

This analysis also draws attention to the importance of internal consistency. Doctrines are not stated or developed in isolation. They interact with one another. Rightly understood, there is a wonderful coherence to Christian doctrine. We could explore this further by returning to the principle which we explored earlier, that human beings are reconciled to God only through Jesus Christ. Let us briefly consider this further.

We have already seen how this principle necessitates certain central beliefs concerning Jesus Christ. He must be fully human and fully divine; otherwise, radical inconsistency arises within the principle. This shows the close connection between the doctrine of salvation and the doctrine of the two natures of Jesus Christ. It also provides a vital stimulus, which eventually leads to the doctrine of the Trinity. If Jesus is God, any simple idea of God is shown to be inadequate. The Christian doctrine of God must be capable of doing justice to the divinity of Christ. Considerations along these lines eventually lead to the classic Christian statement on the nature of God—the doctrine of the Trinity. The principle also necessitates important insights concerning human nature. For example, the assertion that Jesus Christ is the savior of all human beings naturally implies that all human beings need to be saved. Latent within the doctrine of the universal redemption of humanity through Jesus Christ is the doctrine of the universal sinfulness of humanity—in other words, the basis of a doctrine of original sin.

This analysis could be extended. However, the basic point is clear. Consistency and coherence are vitally important to Christian doctrine. Doctrines cannot be considered in isolation; they must be considered in relation to other doctrines, and in relation to the central reality which they claim to interpret to the best of their ability—Jesus Christ. It is not as if this consistency has to be invented; it is already given. It is not as if the coherence of Christian doctrine is imposed upon that doctrine; it is already inherent within it. It is the task of responsible doctrinal reflection to ensure that this coherence is not disrupted or compromised through inadequate or deficient statements of key doctrines—such as Arianism. It is probably impossible to get rid of all the unhelpful associations of the word "heresy." But it continues to be an important and usable concept—if it is rightly understood.

We may summarize the present discussion in this way. Heresy is an inauthentic and inadequate account of the Christian faith, whose inauthenticity and inadequacy are disclosed by critical comparison with orthodoxy. Orthodoxy is not, and never must become, something which is enforced by law or by force. It is something which, like truth itself, commends itself by its inner coherence and credibility. The history of the Christian faith suggests that it cannot risk being weakened by allowing inadequate versions of the gospel to pass as authentic. There is a need for each and every generation to reclaim the concept of heresy, in its legitimate form, having the courage to suggest that certain presentations of Christianity are just not good enough.

This means that Christians must be encouraged to wrestle with matters of doctrine, and to see why certain versions of Christianity are unnecessarily weak. In an earlier chapter, we mentioned that wrestling with the creeds is perhaps one of the best ways of coming to grips with doctrine. We shall now turn to consider how these central Christian declarations of faith can help in this way.

10

Wrestling with Doctrine: Discovering the Creeds

The creeds are well known to most Christians, not least through having become incorporated into various set forms of worship. During the twentieth century, the creeds have gained new importance, as they have increasingly become seen as stressing the unity that exists between Christians. In 1920, the Lambeth Conference recognized the Apostles' Creed as one of the four pillars of Christian unity. In 1927, the World Conference of Faith and Order, meeting at Lausanne, declared that this creed could be used wholeheartedly by Christians of all persuasions. Whatever may divide one group of Christians from another, the creeds provide a summary of the points which unite them.

The oldest and simplest creed of the church is generally known as the Apostles' Creed. All Christian churches recognize its authority and its importance as a standard of doctrine. To study the Apostles' Creed is to investigate a central element of our common Christian heritage. It is an affirmation of the basic beliefs which unite Christians throughout the world and across the centuries. Its text runs as follows:

> I believe in God, the Father almighty, creator of heaven and earth. I believe in Jesus Christ, his only Son, our Lord. He was conceived by the power of the Holy Spirit, and born of the Virgin Mary. He suffered under Pontius Pilate, was crucified, died and was buried. He descended to the dead. On the third day he rose again. He ascended into heaven, and is seated at the right hand of the Father. He will come again to judge the living and the dead. I believe in the Holy Spirit, the holy catholic church, the communion of saints, the forgiveness of sins, the resurrection of the body, and the life everlasting. Amen.

The Apostles' Creed, however, was not the only creed to come into existence in the period of the early church. Two major controversies in the early church made it necessary to be more precise about certain matters of doctrine. The first controversy (the Arian controversy of the fourth century) centered on the relationship of Jesus and God. In order to avoid inadequate understandings of the relation of the Father and the Son, the Council of Chalcedon (AD 451) endorsed a creed now generally known as the "Nicene Creed." This creed, roughly twice as long as the Apostles' Creed, begins with the words

"We believe in one God." In its efforts to insist upon the reality of the divinity of Jesus Christ, this creed speaks of Jesus as "being of one substance with the Father." It includes important amplifications of the Christian doctrine both of the person of Christ and of the person and work of the Holy Spirit.

A second major controversy shortly afterwards centered on the doctrine of the Trinity. In order to avoid inadequate understandings of the relation of the Father, Son, and Spirit, the formula generally known as the "Athanasian Creed" was drawn up. This creed, which opens with the words "Whoever wishes to be saved . . . ," is by far the longest of the three creeds, and is nowadays rarely used in any form of public worship.

THE ORIGINS OF THE CREEDS

The origins of the creeds may be found within the New Testament itself. There are frequent calls to be "baptized in the name of Jesus Christ" (Acts 2:38; 8:12; 10:48), or "in the name of the Lord Jesus" (Acts 8:16; 19:5). In its simplest form, the earliest Christian creed seems to have been simply the declaration that "Jesus is Lord!" (Rom. 10:9; 1 Cor. 12:3; 2 Cor. 4:5; Phil. 2:11). Anyone who was able to make this declaration was regarded as being a Christian. The Christian is thus someone who "receives Jesus Christ as Lord" (Col. 2:6).

To declare that "Jesus Christ is Lord" involves two related claims. In the first place, it declares the believer's loyalty and commitment to Jesus Christ. For someone to confess that "Jesus Christ is Lord" is to declare that Jesus is the Lord of his or her life. To recognize that Jesus is Lord is to seek to do his will. The refusal of the first Christians to worship the Roman emperor reflects this belief: You can serve only one master, and for the Christian that is, and can only be, none other than Jesus himself. Much the same situation arose in Nazi Germany, eventually giving rise to the Barmen Declaration (p. 239), perhaps one of the most powerful modern statements of the Lordship of Christ over his church.

In the second place, "Jesus is Lord" declares certain things about Jesus, especially his relation to God. "Let all Israel be assured of this: God has made this Jesus, whom you crucified, both Lord and Christ" (Acts 2:36). With these words, Peter echoes the common teaching of the New Testament— through the resurrection of Jesus, God has established his credentials as both Messiah and the Lord. The Old Testament frequently uses the term "Lord" to refer to God (e.g., Gen. 12:1; 15:6; 17:1; 39:2; Ex. 3:2). When the Old Testament scriptures were translated from Hebrew into Greek, the Greek word *kyrios*—"the Lord"—was used to translate the sacred name of God. But an astonishing new development takes place in the New Testament: It is now *Jesus* who is regularly referred to as "the Lord" (e.g., Phil. 2:11; 3:8; Col. 2:6). A word which was once used to refer to God has now come to refer to Jesus.

As time went on, however, it became necessary to explain what Christians believed about Jesus Christ in more detail. The full implications of declaring that "Jesus is Lord" needed to be spelled out. What did Christians believe about God? About Jesus? About the Holy Spirit? By the fourth century, the Apostles' Creed as we now know it had assumed a more or less fixed form; what variations did exist were slight, and were finally eliminated in the seventh century. Although it was not actually written by the apostles, the Apostles' Creed is a splendid summary of the apostolic teaching concerning the gospel. It lists a series of central doctrines, which may be regarded as fundamental to the Christian faith. The Nicene creed includes important additional material relating to Christ and the Holy Spirit, allowing certain misunderstandings to be avoided. The creeds are the classical expression of what Christians believe about God and Jesus Christ. In short, they provide a shorthand account of the central doctrines of the Christian faith.

In an earlier chapter, we pointed out that a distinction could be made between "fundamental" or "essential" doctrines, and those which were of lesser importance. Many writers have suggested that the doctrines of the creed are the fundamental doctrines of the Christian faith—the doctrines which bind Christians together down the ages and across the world, and which must be defended in the face of an external or internal threat. Others, however, have suggested that other doctrines need to be added to provide a more complete picture of the Christian faith—for example, a doctrine of original sin, or a more explicit doctrine of redemption, or a more detailed account of the identity and status of the sources of Christian doctrine (such as scripture).

THE PURPOSE OF THE CREEDS

The Apostles' Creed had its origins in the early church as a profession or confession of faith made by converts at their baptism. The early church placed great emphasis upon the importance of the baptism of converts. During the period of Lent (the period from Ash Wednesday to Easter), those who had recently come to faith were given instruction in the Christian faith. Finally, when they had mastered the basics of faith, they would recite the Apostles' Creed together, as a corporate witness to the faith in which they believed, and which they now understood. Faith had now been reinforced with understanding. These converts would then be baptized with great ceremony and joy on Easter Day itself, as the church celebrated the resurrection of its Lord and Savior. In this way, the significance of the baptism of the believer could be fully appreciated: He or she had passed from death to life (Rom. 6:3–10). Baptism was a public demonstration of the believer's death to the world, and being born to new life in Jesus Christ.

A central part of the baptism celebration was the public declaration of faith by each candidate. Anyone who wished to be baptized had to declare publicly his faith in Jesus Christ. At many times in the history of the Christian church, this was exceptionally dangerous: To admit to being a Christian could mean imprisonment, victimization, suffering, or even death. (The English word "martyr" derives from the Greek word meaning "witness." To be a martyr was seen as the finest witness possible to Jesus Christ and his gospel.) The believer did not, however, merely recite the creed; he was also asked, as an individual, whether he *personally* believed in the gospel, before he could be baptized. Here is part of a sermon preached in the fourth century to those who had just been baptized, in which this practice is described. (Incidentally, note the important references to Romans 6:3–4; those who have died to their past have risen to new life in Christ.)

> You were asked, "Do you believe in God the father almighty?" You replied, "I believe," and were immersed, that is, were buried. Again, you were asked, "Do you believe in our Lord Jesus Christ and his cross?" You replied, "I believe," and were immersed. Thus you were buried with Christ, for he who is buried with Christ rises again with him. A third time you were asked, "Do you believe in the Holy Spirit?" You replied, "I believe," and were immersed for a third time. Your three-fold confession thus wiped out the many sins of your previous existence.

Historically, then, the Apostles' Creed was the profession of faith made by converts at their baptism, and formed the basis of their instruction. As more and more individuals now come to discover Christianity as adults, the Apostles' Creed can once more serve this historic purpose. Since then, it has served other purposes—for example, as a test of orthodoxy for Christian leaders, or as an act of praise in Christian worship. In our own day and age, the creed serves three main purposes.

In the first place, the creed provides *a brief summary of the main doctrines of the Christian faith*. A creed is not, and was never meant to be, a substitute for personal faith: It attempts to give substance to a personal faith which already exists. You do not become a Christian by reciting the creed; rather, the creed provides a useful summary of the main doctrinal points of your faith. There are certain items which are not dealt with. For example, there is no section which states "I believe in scripture." This is not strictly necessary, in that the doctrines of the creed are basically a distillation or summary of the main points of the scriptural teaching concerning the gospel. The importance of scripture is assumed throughout; indeed, most of the creed can be shown to consist of direct quotations from scripture.

In the second place, the creed allows us to *recognize and avoid inadequate or incomplete versions of Christianity*. Some might insist that Christianity is mainly (or perhaps even entirely) about the Holy Spirit. Others might be alarmed by this, replying that Christianity is primarily about God the Father. A further group might maintain that the gospel centers upon Jesus Christ himself. The creed reminds us that there is actually much more to the gospel than any of these on their own. By providing a balanced and biblical approach to the doctrines of the Christian faith, the creed allows us to recognize deficient versions of the gospel. Many people have found their faith immeasurably strengthened and matured by being forced to think through areas of faith which they would otherwise not have explored. See the creed as an invitation to explore and discover areas of the gospel which otherwise you might miss or overlook.

Many people who have come to faith recently want to be baptized, in order to make a public declaration of their faith. A central part of that celebration of your new birth will probably be the congregation declaring their corporate faith, using the words of the creed. Let that be a stimulus to you! See the creed as setting the agenda for your personal exploration of the doctrines of the Christian faith. See it as mapping out areas for you to explore, on your own or with others. Some of its statements may remind you of those ancient maps, where vast areas of the world were marked as *terrae incognitae,* "unknown territory." But see this as a challenge! It may take you some time to fathom the depths of your faith; nevertheless, the result is well worth the time and effort.

In the third place, the creed emphasizes a point noted earlier (chapter 5), that *to believe is to belong.* To become a Christian is to enter a community of faith, which stretches right back to the upper room (John 17:20–21). By putting your faith in Jesus Christ, you have become a member of his body, the church, which uses this creed to express its faith. By accepting and studying its doctrines, you are reminding yourself of the many men and women who have used it before you. It gives you a sense of history and perspective. It emphasizes that you are not the only person to put your trust in Jesus Christ. It draws attention to the fact that its doctrines unite you with Christians down the ages and throughout the world. Think of how many others recited those words at their baptism down the centuries. Think of how many others found in the doctrines of the creed a superb statement of their personal faith. You share that faith and those doctrines, and you can share the same words that they used to express it.

USING THE CREEDS

The creeds provide an outstanding opportunity for wrestling with individual Christian doctrines, and thinking through their importance. In particular, it is helpful to ask the following questions:

1. What scriptural passages does the doctrine integrate?
2. What does it tell us about God? Jesus Christ? Ourselves?
3. How can we apply it to our Christian living?
4. How does belief in this doctrine distinguish us from non-Christians?

Grappling with the doctrines of the creed is thus an excellent way of deepening our understanding of the Christian faith, and seeing how its various aspects relate. It invites us to consider the foundations of doctrine in scripture, the manner in which it affects the way in which we live and think, and marks us off from non-Christians around us. It is an excellent subject for a study group, at an elementary or advanced level, allowing contributors to pool their ideas and insights, in order that all may come away enlightened and stimulated.

In order to encourage this process of engagement with the creeds, a worked example will be given. A relatively obscure section of the creed will serve our purposes well: "He [Jesus Christ] suffered under Pontius Pilate." In what follows, we shall consider the doctrinal implications of this statement of the creed, using the four questions noted above as a framework for discussion. Unfortunately, there is only space to give some samples of what might be said about this section of the creed; what follows is intended to illustrate the sort of wrestling with matters of Christian doctrine that the creed allows.

1. What Biblical Passages Does It Integrate?

A number of key passages, centering upon the passion of Christ, should be noted: Matthew 27:11–26; John 19:1–16. Note the way in which the gospel is firmly anchored to history: Pontius Pilate was a real historical individual. There are also a number of passages, scattered throughout the Epistles, which affirm that Jesus suffered, before explaining the relevance of this for believers: Romans 8:17; Hebrews 2:9, 18; 1 Peter 2:21.

2. What Insights Does It Allow?

First and foremost, it stresses the humanity of Jesus Christ. He really did suffer, as we suffer. The New Testament stresses the humanity of Christ in other ways—for example, by noting that he became tired (John 4:6) and wept when deeply moved (John 11:35). Here is no divine figure taking on human form externally, as one might put on a coat—here is someone who really is human, who shares the experiences of our human life.

Second, the fact that he suffered under Pilate points to the tragic rejection of Jesus Christ by his world—a major theme of the New Testament. The disowning of Jesus is seen as representing the rejection of the creator by his creation. The New Testament portrays that rejection in many ways: Jesus is rejected by those who had known him from his youth at Nazareth (Luke 4:16–30). He was condemned as a blasphemer by the leaders of the Jewish people (Matt. 26:59–66).

Third, it points to the mysterious link between suffering and salvation. Jesus had to suffer in order that we might be redeemed. The doctrine of the atonement serves to remind us of the reality of sin, and the power and purpose of God to deal with it. The close relation between suffering and redemption is clearly brought out in Isaiah 52:13–53:12. This powerful and moving passage describes a mysterious suffering servant. He was innocent;

he suffered on behalf of the guilty. Through his sufferings, others will be healed:

> He was despised and rejected by men, a man of sorrows and familiar with suffering.... Surely he took up our infirmities and carried our sorrows, yet we considered him stricken by God, smitten by him and afflicted. But he was pierced for our transgressions, he was crushed for our iniquities; the punishment that brought us peace was upon him, and by his wounds we are healed. We all, like sheep, have gone astray, each of us has turned to his own way; and the Lord has laid on him the iniquity of us all.... For he bore the sin of many, and made intercession for the transgressors.

The New Testament writers saw this passage fulfilled in the suffering of Jesus Christ (see 1 Peter 2:21–25). His sufferings on the cross were not pointless or accidental, but the mysterious and wonderful way in which God was working out the salvation of the world. In this terse statement of the creed lie the beginnings of a doctrine of redemption.

3. How Can We Apply It to Our Christian Living?

One point may be made. Christianity has always held that it is the suffering of Christ upon the cross which is the culmination and fulfillment of his ministry. Here is the incarnate God suffering alongside us and for us. In the suffering of Jesus Christ, God shares in the darkest moments of his people. God can be found in suffering. There is a famous saying about the medical profession worth remembering here: "Only the wounded physician can heal." The God who offers to heal the wounds of our sin has himself been wounded by sinners.

The suffering of Jesus Christ upon the cross at Calvary does not explain suffering. It does, however, reveal that God himself is willing and able to allow himself to be subject to all the pain and suffering which his creation experiences. We are not talking of a God who stands far off from his world, aloof and distant from its problems. We are dealing with a loving God who has entered into our human situation, who became man and dwelt among us as one of us. We know a God who, in his love for us, determined to experience at firsthand what it is like to be frail, mortal, and human, to suffer and to die.

We cannot explain suffering, but we can say that, in the person of his Son Jesus Christ, God took it upon himself to follow this way. God became the man of suffering, so that we can enter into the mystery of death and resurrection. This is a deeply comforting thought to those who are suffering. It speaks to them of a God who knows what they are going through, who can sympathize with them. God understands their situation, and their anguish. He has been through it himself. And seen in this light, suffering assumes a new meaning. This brief statement of the creed, when fully explored, opens up a new perspective on one of the darkest sides of human life—and brings hope through the comfort of knowing that God has been through it as well.

4. How Does This Belief Distinguish Us from Non-Christians?

Suffering is a mystery for everyone. It seems to serve no purpose. It denies human ability to control our situation. It is deeply threatening. The non-Christian has little to say in the face of human suffering. Socrates may have taught us how to die with dignity; Jesus Christ enables us to die in hope. The suffering of Jesus Christ allows Christians to take an attitude toward suffering which marks them off from others. Four main answers have been given to the mystery of suffering in the history of the world. First, suffering is an illusion. It is not really there, but is a product of our imaginations. Once this has been recognized, it can be dismissed. Second, suffering is real, but ends with death, leading to final peace. Third, suffering is real—but we ought to be able to rise above it, and recognize that it is of little importance. We are asked to maintain a stiff upper lip in the face of suffering, and not allow it to gain the upper hand. The Christian has the fourth, and very different, answer: God suffered in Christ. God knows what it is like to suffer. The letter to the Hebrews talks about Jesus being our "sympathetic High Priest" (Heb. 4:15)—someone who suffers along with us (which is the literal meaning of both the Greek word *sympathetic* and the Latin word *compassionate*). This thought does not explain suffering, although it may make it more tolerable to endure. For it is expressing the deep insight that God himself suffered at firsthand as we suffer. We are thus given a new perspective on life, which marks us off from the world.

There is much more that could be said. But this is intended to illustrate how useful the creeds can be in helping individuals and study groups to wrestle with matters of doctrine. See the creeds as an invitation to wrestle with the richness of the Christian faith. See them as an opportunity to explore some of its less familiar aspects. To wrestle with the doctrines of the creeds is to probe deeper into the Christian faith, and discover how rich and deep it really is.

To help individuals and study groups to wrestle more closely with some central matters of doctrine, the final part of this work will examine three key doctrines in some detail—the doctrine of the person of Jesus Christ (often referred to as the doctrine of the incarnation), the doctrine of the work of Jesus Christ (sometimes referred to as the doctrine of the atonement), and the doctrine of the Trinity. Each of these doctrines deals with central insights of the Christian faith, and they are ideally suited to the needs of those wishing to deepen their grasp of their faith.

PART THREE

Some Key Doctrines
Examined

11

The Person of Jesus Christ

The Christian doctrine of the person of Jesus Christ is often discussed in terms of "incarnation." "Incarnation" is a difficult yet important word, summarizing the basic Christian belief that Jesus Christ is both God and man. Time after time, the New Testament represents Christ as acting as and for God in every area of crucial relevance to Christianity. When we worship Jesus Christ, we worship God; when we know Christ, we know God; when we hear the promises of Christ, we hear the promises of God; when we encounter the risen Christ, we encounter none other than the living God. The idea of the incarnation is the climax of Christian reflection upon the mystery of Christ—the recognition that Jesus Christ reveals God; that he represents God; that he speaks as God and for God; that he acts as God and for God; that he is God. In short, we must, in the words of a first-century writer, learn to "think about Jesus as we do about God" (2 Clement 1.1–2). We are thus in a position to take the crucial step which underlies all Christian thinking on the incarnation—to say that, as Jesus Christ acts as God and for God in every context of importance, we should conclude that, for all intents and purposes, he is God.

Far from being an optional extra, something which had accidentally been added and which now requires removal, this doctrine is an essential and integral part of the authentically Christian understanding of reality. But some modern writers (such as the radical English religious critic, Don Cupitt) have laid down two fundamental challenges to this view. First, they say, it is *wrong*. Our growing understanding of the background to the New Testament, the way in which Christian doctrine has developed, the rise of the scientific worldview, and so on, force us to abandon the idea that Jesus Christ was God in any meaningful sense of the word. Second, they argue, it is *unnecessary*. Christianity can get on perfectly well without the need for such obsolete and cumbersome ideas as God becoming man, traditionally grounded in the resurrection of Jesus Christ and expressed in the doctrine of the incarnation. In a world come of age, Cupitt suggests, Christianity must learn to abandon these ideas as archaic and irrelevant if it is to survive. In fact, however, it seems to this writer that just about the only way in which Christianity is likely to survive in the future is by reclaiming its incarnational heritage as the only proper and legitimate interpretation of the significance of Jesus Christ.

Many recent criticisms of the incarnation, such as those expressed in the classic work of English radical religious thought, *The Myth of God Incarnate* (1977), demonstrate a tendency to concentrate upon objections to the *idea* of incarnation, rather than the *basis* of the idea itself. After all, the idea of God incarnate in a specific historical human being was quite startling within its first-century Jewish context, whatever may have been made of it in the later patristic period, and the question of what caused this belief to arise requires careful examination. Of central importance to this question is the resurrection itself, a subject studiously ignored (along with the major contributions to the incarnational discussion by Pannenberg, Moltmann, Rahner, Kasper and others) by most of the contributors to *The Myth of God Incarnate*. The idea of incarnation is easy to criticize: It is paradoxical, enigmatic, and so on. But everyone already knows this, including the most fervent advocates of the idea! And it is simply absurd, even to the point of being offensive, to suggest that those who regard the incarnation as legitimate and proper are mentally deficient, intellectually hidebound or trapped in their traditions, unable to think for themselves. The question remains, as it always has been: Is the incarnation a proper and legitimate interpretation of the history of Jesus of Nazareth? Objections to the doctrine have tended to center on its alleged illogicality: How can one person be two things—God and man—at one and the same time?

THE INCARNATION AS ILLOGICAL?

A serious charge against the principle of the incarnation is developed by the radical theologian John Hick who asserts ("argues" is hardly an appropriate word to use, given Hick's style of writing) that the idea of Christ being both God and man is logically contradictory. Quoting Spinoza, Hick asserts that talk of one who is both God and man is like talking about a square circle. Hick's sensitivity at this point is difficult to follow, as he is already committed to the belief that all the concepts of God to be found in the world religions— personal and impersonal, immanent and transcendent—are compatible with each other. Indeed, such is the variety of the concepts of divinity currently in circulation in the world religions that Hick seems to be obliged to turn a blind eye to the resulting logical inconsistency between them—only to seize upon and censure this alleged "inconsistency" in the case of the incarnation. But Hick cannot be allowed to make unchallenged this robust assertion concerning the logical incompatibility of God and man, and his less than adequate knowledge of the development of Christology in the medieval period is clearly demonstrated in this matter. The fact that there is no *logical* incompatibility between God and man in the incarnation was demonstrated, and then theologically exploited, by that most brilliant of all English theologians, William of Ockham, in the fourteenth century. Ockham's discussion of this point is exhaustive and highly influential, and has yet to be discredited.

More seriously, Hick seems to work on the basis of the assumption that we know *exactly* what God is like, and on the basis of this knowledge are in a position to pass judgment on the logical niceties of the incarnation. But this is obviously not the case! Hick may be saying that there is a logical problem involved with classical theism (a *philosophical* system) in relation to the incarnation—but this is merely to suggest that classical theism is not necessarily compatible with Christianity, a point which has been made with increasing force by theologians such as Jürgen Moltmann and Eberhard Jüngel in recent years. It is not to discredit the incarnation! Hick may be in a position to say that God is totally unable to come amongst us as a human being, and that the incarnation is impossible on account of who and what God is—but if he can do so, he would seem to have access to a private and infallible knowledge of God denied to the rest of us! And do we really fully understand what is meant by that deceptively familiar word "man?" Do we really have a total and exhaustive grasp of what it is to be human? Many of us would prefer to say that the incarnation disclosed the true nature of divinity and humanity, rather than approaching the incarnation on the basis of preconceived ideas of divinity and humanity.

The fact that something is paradoxical and even self-contradictory does not invalidate it, as many critics of the incarnation seem to think. Those of us who have worked in the scientific field are only too aware of the sheer complexity and mysteriousness of reality. The events lying behind the rise of quantum theory, the difficulties of using models in scientific explanation—to name but two factors which I can remember particularly clearly from my own period as a natural scientist—point to the inevitability of paradox and contradiction in any except the most superficial engagement with reality. Our apprehension of reality is partial and fragmentary, whether we are dealing with our knowledge of the natural world or of God. The Enlightenment worldview tended to suppose that reality could be totally apprehended in rational terms, an assumption which still persists in some theological circles, even where it has been abandoned as unrealistic elsewhere. All too many modern theologians cry "Contradiction!" and expect us all to abandon whatever it is that is supposed to be contradictory there and then. But reality just isn't like that.

We have sketched one of the most important objections raised recently against the doctrine of the incarnation of Jesus Christ, and indicated briefly the way in which it can be met. It has not been possible to do justice to this objection or the responses to it, and all that we have had the opportunity to do is to note how resurrection and incarnation alike are "bloodied but unbowed" through recent criticisms. But one final point may be made before moving on. All too often, we are given the impression that something dramatic has happened recently, which suddenly forces everyone of any intellectual respectability to abandon faith in these matters. We are told that in a world come of age, ideas such as resurrection and incarnation are to be discarded as premodern, perhaps as vestiges of a cultic idol. We are children of the modern period, and must abandon the doctrinal heritage of the past. Many critics of the doctrine of the incarnation appear to envisage their criticisms as establishing a new, more relevant and universal version of Christianity.

But what might this new version of Christianity be like? The inclusion of the word "new" is deliberate and weighed: Historically, Christianity has regarded the doctrines of the resurrection and incarnation as essential to its identity, and any attempt to eliminate or radically modify them would seem to lead to a version of Christianity which is not continuous with the historical forms it has taken in the course of its development. In the following section, we shall look at the result of the elimination or radical modification of these two traditional ideas.

THE INCARNATION AND THE LOVE OF GOD

On the basis of a number of important works reflecting the spirit of Enlightenment modernism, it is clear that a central idea congenial to the modern spirit is that Christ reveals to us the love of God. It is frequently pointed out that the modern age is able to dispense with superstitious ideas about the death of Christ (for example, that it represented a victory over Satan or the payment of a legal penalty of some sort), and instead get to the real meat of the New Testament, so movingly expressed in the parable of the Prodigal Son, and modern Christianity—the love of God for humanity. In what follows, I propose to suggest that abandoning the ideas of resurrection and the incarnation means abandoning even this tender insight.

This may seem an outrageous suggestion to make, but I cannot see how this conclusion can be avoided. How may the death of Jesus Christ upon a cross at Calvary be interpreted as a demonstration of the love of God for humanity? Remember, the idea that Jesus Christ *is* God cannot be permitted, given the presuppositions of modernism. Once modernism dispenses with the idea of incarnation, a number of possible alternative explanations of the cross remain open.

1. It represented the devastating and unexpected end to the career of Jesus, forcing his disciples to invent the idea of the resurrection to cover up the totality of this catastrophe.
2. It represents God's judgment upon the career of Jesus, demonstrating that he was cursed by the Law of Moses, and thus disqualified from any putative messianic status.
3. It represents the inevitable fate of anyone who attempts to lead a life of obedience to God.
4. It represents the greatest love which one human being can show for another (cf. John 15:13) inspiring Jesus' followers to demonstrate an equal love for others.

5. The cross demonstrates that God is a sadistic tyrant.
6. The cross is meaningless.

All of these are plausible, within the framework of modernism. The idea that the cross demonstrates the love of God for man cannot, however, be included among this list. It is not *God* who is dying upon the cross, who gives himself for his people. It is a man—an especially splendid man, who may be ranked with others in history who have made equally great sacrifices for those whom they loved. The death of an innocent person at the hands of corrupt judges is all too common, even today, and Jesus Christ cannot be singled out for special discussion unless he *is* something or someone qualitatively different from us.

A critic might, of course, immediately reply that Jesus Christ is a higher example of the kind of inspiration or illumination to be found in all human beings, so that he must be regarded as the outstanding human being—and for that reason, his death assumes an especial significance. But this is a remarkably dogmatic assumption—that Jesus Christ is unique among human beings in this respect! The uniqueness of Christ was established by the New Testament writers through the resurrection (Rom. 1:3–4) and the subsequent recognition that Christ was none other than the living God dwelling among us. But this insight is given and guaranteed by two doctrines which some radical modern writers cannot allow—the resurrection and incarnation. It would seem that modernists are prepared to retain insights gained through the traditional framework of resurrection and incarnation—and then declare that this framework may be dispensed with. It is as if the traditional framework is treated as some sort of learning aid, which may be dispensed with once the ideas in question are mastered.

But this is clearly questionable, to say the least. If the traditional framework is declared to be wrong, the consequences of this declaration for each and every aspect of Christian theology must be ascertained. Discard or radically modify the doctrines of resurrection and incarnation, and the idea of the "uniqueness" or the "superiority" of Christ becomes a dogmatic assertion without foundation, an assertion which many of more humanist inclinations would find offensive. We would be equally justified in appealing to other historical figures—such as Socrates or Gandhi—as encapsulating the desiderata of Christian moral behavior.

This point becomes more important when we return to the question of how the death of Christ can be interpreted as a self-giving divine act, demonstrating the love of God for humanity. It is not God who is upon the cross: It is a human being. That point must be conceded by those who reject the incarnation. It may then be the case that God makes his love known indirectly (and, it must be said, in a remarkably ambiguous manner) through the death of Jesus Christ, but we have lost forever the insight that it is God himself who shows his love for us on the cross. What the cross might conceivably demonstrate, among a number of other, more probable, possibilities, is the full extent of the love of one human being for others. And as the love of human beings can be thought of as mirroring the love of God, it would therefore be taken as an indirect demonstration of what the love of God is like, in much the same way that countless other individuals throughout history have given up their lives to save their friends or families. But who did Christ die to save? None, save possibly Barabbas, can be said to have benefited directly from his death, and it would seem that modernism would like us to understand Christ's death as making some sort of religious point which will enrich our spiritual lives. But this is not how the New Testament writers understood his death (not least because they insisted upon interpreting that death in the light of the resurrection, a procedure regarded as illegitimate by modernists), and it is certainly difficult to see how it would have cut much ice in the hostile environment in which Christianity had to survive and expand in the first period of its existence.

The traditional framework for discussion of the revelation of the love of God in the death of Christ is that of God humbling himself and coming among us as one of us, taking upon himself the frailty and mortality of our human nature in order to redeem it. To deny that the lonely dying figure upon the cross is God is to lose this point of contact, and to return to the view which Christianity overturned in its own day and age—that "God is with us only in his transcendence" (Don Cupitt). A divine representative—not God himself—engages with the pain and suffering of this world. It is his love, not God's, which is shown. And to those who might think that this difficulty may be eliminated by developing the idea of God allowing himself to be identified with the dying Christ, it may be pointed out that the exploration of this idea by Moltmann and Jüngel leads not merely to an incarnational, but to a *Trinitarian*, theology. In order to do justice to the Christian experience of God through Jesus Christ, a higher profile of identification between Christ and God than function is required—we are dealing with an identity of being, rather than just an identification of function. Jesus Christ acts as and for God precisely because he *is* God.

THE INCARNATION AND SUFFERING

A similar point may be made in relation to suffering. Twentieth-century apologetics has recognized that any theology which is unable to implicate God in some manner in the sufferings and pain of the world condemns itself as inadequate and deficient. The twentieth century witnessed previously unimagined horrors of human suffering in the trenches of the First World War, in the extermination camps of Nazi Germany, and the programs of genocide established by Nazi Germany and Marxist Cambodia. The rise of "protest atheism"—perhaps one of the most powerful sentiments to which modern theology must address itself—reflects human moral revulsion at these acts. Protest atheism has a tendency to select soft targets, and there are few targets softer in this respect than a non-incarnational theology.

An incarnational theology speaks of God subjecting himself to the evil and pain of the world at its worst, in the grim scene at Calvary, bearing the brunt of that agony itself. God suffered in Christ, taking upon himself the suffering and pain of the world which he created. In her essay "Creed or Chaos" (1940), Dorothy L. Sayers wrote:

> It is only with the confident assertion of the creative divinity of the Son that the doctrine of the Incarnation becomes a real revelation of the structure of the world. And here Christianity has its enormous advantage over every other religion in the world. It is the *only* religion which gives value to evil and suffering. It affirms—not, like Christian Science, that evil has no real existence, nor yet, like Buddhism, that good consists in a refusal to experience evil—but that perfection is attained through the active and positive effort to wrench a real good out of a real evil.

A non-incarnational theology is forced, perhaps against its basic instincts, to speak of a God who may send his condolences through a representative, but who does not (or cannot, for fear of being accused of logical contradiction?) enter into and share his people's suffering at first hand. And for a modernist, highly critical of substitutionary theories of the atonement, God can hardly be allowed to take responsibility for the suffering of the world vicariously, through a human representative, who suffers instead of and on behalf of God. In 1963, the English *Sunday Observer* publicized John Robinson's book *Honest to God* with the Headline "Our image of God must go." The image that Robinson had in mind was that of an old man in the sky. But the "image of God that must go" in the face of the intense and deadly serious moral criticisms of protest atheism is that of a god who does not experience human suffering and pain at firsthand—in short, a non-incarnational image of God. Many of those who criticize the incarnation seem to realize the force of this point, and attempt to retain it, despite their intellectual misgivings. Perhaps in the end, it will not be the protests of orthodoxy which destroy non-incarnational theologies, but protest atheism, which wisely and rightly detects the fundamental weakness of such a theology in precisely this respect.

THE INCARNATION AND REDEMPTION

A further vital consideration concerns the whole doctrine of redemption, the fulcrum of the Christian faith. If God has not redeemed us through Jesus Christ, the entire gospel is false, and the Christian hope little more than a cruel illusion. The electrifying declaration that God has redeemed us through Jesus Christ has as its central presupposition that he *is* God. This point was made with great force by the third-century writer Athanasius, who argued along the following lines.

Athanasius insists that it is only God who can save. God, and God alone, can break the power of sin, and bring us to eternal life. In doing this, Athanasius takes up a great Old Testament tradition (see, for example, Isa. 45:21–22). There is no point in looking to horses, armies, princes or any worldly authorities for salvation: God alone can save. Athanasius builds his argument on this important premise. No creature can save another creature—only the creator can redeem his creation.

Having emphasized that it is God alone who can save, Athanasius then makes the logical move which Arius found difficult to counter. The New Testament regards Jesus Christ as the proper savior of humanity. New Testament texts making this suggestion would include Matthew 1:21 (which speaks of Jesus saving his people from their sins), Luke 2:11 (the famous Christmas message of the angels: "Today in the town of David a Savior has been born to you"), Acts 4:12 (which affirms that salvation comes through Jesus), Hebrews 2:10 (which calls Jesus the "author of salvation"). According to the New Testament, it is Jesus who is the Savior. Yet, as Athanasius emphasized, only God can save. So how are we to make sense of this?

The only possible solution, Athanasius argues, is to accept that Jesus is God incarnate. The logic of his argument goes something like this:

Only God can save.
Jesus saves.
Therefore Jesus is God.

This sort of logic seems to underlie some New Testament passages. For example, Titus 1:3–4 speaks of "God our savior" at one point, and "Christ Jesus our Savior" at another. Now Athanasius is able to strengthen his argument by pointing out that no creature can save another creature. Salvation involves divine intervention. Athanasius thus draws out the meaning of John 1:14 by arguing that the "word became flesh": In other words, God entered into our human situation, in order to change it. To use Athanasius' own words: "God became man so that we might become God." If Jesus Christ was just a creature like the rest of us, he would be part of the problem, rather than its solution. He would share our dilemma, rather than being able to liberate us from it.

THE INCARNATION AND THE SIGNIFICANCE OF JESUS CHRIST

A final point which may be made concerns the permanent significance of Jesus Christ. Why is he of such importance to the Christian faith here and now, some twenty centuries after his death? The traditional answer is that his significance lay in his being God incarnate; that in his specific historical existence, God assumed human nature. All else is secondary to this central insight, deriving from reflection upon the significance of his resurrection. The fact that Jesus was male; the fact that he was a Jew; the precise nature of his teaching—all these are secondary to the fact that God took upon himself human nature, thereby lending it new dignity and meaning.

But if Jesus Christ is not God incarnate, his significance must be evaluated in terms of those parameters which traditional Christianity has treated as secondary or accidental (in the Aristotelian sense of the term). Immediately, we are confronted with the problem of historical conditioning: What conceivable relevance may the teachings and lifestyle of a first-century male Jew have for us today, in a totally different cultural situation? The maleness of Christ has caused offense in radical feminist circles: Why should women be forced to relate to a male religious teacher, whose teaching may be compromised by his very masculinity, as well as by the patriarchal values of his cultural situation? And why should modern Western humanity pay any attention to the culturally conditioned teaching of such an individual, given the seemingly insuperable cultural chasm dividing first-century Palestine and the twentieth-century West? And even the concept of the "religious personality" of Jesus has been seriously eroded, as much by New Testament scholarship as by shifts in cultural expectations. For reasons such as these, a non-incarnational Christianity is unable convincingly to anchor the person of Jesus Christ as the center of the Christian faith. He may be the historical point of departure for that faith, but its subsequent development involves the leaving behind of the historical particularity of his existence in order to confront the expectations of each social milieu in which Christianity may subsequently find itself. Jesus Christ says *this*—but we say *that. This* may be acceptable in a first-century Palestinian context—but *that* is acceptable in a modern Western culture, in which we live and move and have our being. Jesus Christ is thus both relativized and marginalized. Many non-incarnational versions of Christianity accept and welcome such insights—but others find them disturbing, and perhaps unconsciously articulate an incarnational Christianity in order to preserve insights which they intuitively recognize as central.

In this chapter, we have briefly summarized the case for defending the doctrine of the incarnation as a proper and legitimate interpretation of the history of Jesus of Nazareth, and rejecting alternative explanations as inadequate. In no way whatsoever can it be said that this matter has been discussed adequately: The volumes this demands are just not available. Nevertheless, it is hoped that the contours of the case for arguing that the doctrine of the incarnation is a proper and necessary element of the Christian faith have been sketched in sufficient detail to allow the reader to take his or her own thinking further. We end this chapter with some final reflections.

Critics of doctrines such as the incarnation tend to work on the basis of two presuppositions. First, that there exists a theological equivalent of precision surgery, which allows certain elements of the Christian faith to be excised without having any detrimental effect whatsoever upon what remains. Second, that by eliminating logical and metaphysical difficulties, a more plausible and hence more acceptable version of Christianity will result. Both these assumptions are clearly questionable, and must be challenged.

As C. S. Lewis wrote to Arthur Greaves on December 11, 1944: "The doctrine of Christ's divinity seems to me not something stuck on which you can unstick but something that peeps out at every point so that you'd have to unravel the whole web to get rid of it." For C. S. Lewis, the coherence of Christianity was such that it was impossible to eliminate the idea of the divinity of Christ without doing such damage to the web of Christian doctrine that the entire structure of the Christian faith would collapse.

To return to our surgical analogy, we are not talking about the removal of an appendix (a vestigial organ apparently serving no useful purpose), but of the heart, the life pump of the Christian faith. Faith in the resurrection and incarnation is what kept and keeps Christianity growing and spreading. The sheer vitality, profundity, and excitement of the Christian faith ultimately depends upon these. In a day and age when Christianity has to fight for its existence, winning converts rather than relying upon a favorable cultural milieu, a non-incarnational theology despoiled of the resurrection has little to commend it. It is perhaps significant that many critics of the resurrection and incarnation were themselves originally attracted to Christianity through precisely the theology they are now criticizing. And what, it must be asked in all seriousness, is the *converting power* of an incarnationless Christianity?

The history of the church suggests that such a version of Christianity is a spiritual dead end. In the fourth century, as has been discussed, such a version of Christianity temporarily developed, associated with the writer Arius. To its critics, incarnationless Christianity seems to be scholarly, bookish, and devoid of passion, without the inner dynamism to challenge and conquer unbelief in a world in which this is essential for its survival. In the characteristically pithy words of Dorothy L. Sayers: "If Christ was only man, then he is entirely irrelevant to any thought about God; if he is only God, then he is entirely irrelevant to any experience of human life." But this is where history will pass its own judgment, in that only a form of Christianity which is convinced that it has something distinctive, true, exciting, and relevant to communicate to the world in order to transform it, will survive.

In this chapter, we have examined the doctrine of the incarnation, in order to illustrate some aspects of the nature of Christian doctrine. Even in doing so, the coherence of Christian doctrine became evident. In discussing the person of Christ (specifically, the doctrine of the incarnation), we were unable to avoid discussing its implications for the work of Christ (specifically, the demonstration of the love of God in the death of Christ). In the following chapter, we shall pursue this second area of Christian doctrine.

12

The Work of Jesus Christ

A central area of Christian theology focuses on the question of what Jesus Christ achieved through his death and resurrection. In older textbooks, especially those written in the nineteenth century, this area of Christian doctrine is often referred to as "the atonement." The origins of the word "atonement" can be traced back to 1526, when the English writer William Tyndale was confronted with the task of translating the New Testament into English. There was, at that time, no English word which meant "reconciliation." Tyndale thus had to invent such a word—"at-one-ment." This word soon came to bear the meaning "the benefits which Jesus Christ brings to believers through his death upon the cross." This unfamiliar word is rarely used in modern English, and has a distinctively archaic flavor to it. Rather than convey the impression that Christian thought it totally out of date, theologians now prefer to speak of this area as "the doctrine of the work of Christ."

Throughout the New Testament, we find stress on the fact that God has acted, has achieved something, through the death and resurrection of Jesus Christ. Something has happened through Jesus Christ, which otherwise would not and could not have taken place. The New Testament uses a wide range of images and ideas to attempt to express what it is that God has done through Christ. In an attempt to integrate the richness of the scriptural affirmations concerning the work of Jesus Christ, a number of ways of approaching this vast subject have been developed. Occasionally, these are still referred to as "theories of the atonement," although this expression is not especially helpful. In what follows, we shall look at the three most influential ways of approaching the meaning of the cross and resurrection. Each of these integrates a range of biblical ideas and emphasis, and has considerable implications for human experience of ourselves and of God.

A VICTORY OVER SIN AND DEATH

The first way of approaching the meaning of the cross integrates a series of biblical passages focusing upon the notion of a divine victory over hostile forces. The New Testament declares that God has given us a victory through the resurrection of Jesus Christ (1 Cor. 15:57). But in what way may this victory be understood? Who is it who has been defeated? And how?

The Christian writers of the first five centuries (often collectively designated "the fathers") were captivated by the imagery of Christ gaining a victory through the cross. It was clear to them that Christ had defeated death, sin, and the devil. Just as David killed Goliath with his own weapons, so Christ defeated sin with its weapon—death. Through an apparent defeat, victory was gained over a host of hidden forces which tyrannized humanity.

The fathers spelled out this tyranny, using a number of central images. We were held in bondage by the fear of death. We were imprisoned by sin. We were trapped by the power of the devil. With great skill, these writers built up a coherent picture of the human dilemma. Human beings are held prisoner by a matrix of hostile forces, and are unable to break free unaided. Someone was required who would break into their prison, and set them free. Someone from outside the human situation would have to enter into our predicament, and liberate us. Someone would have to cut the bonds which held us captive. Time and time again, the same theme is restated: We are trapped in our situation, and our only hope lies in liberation from outside.

The great and thrilling news of the Christian gospel is therefore that God has entered into the human situation in his Son, Jesus Christ. Through his death and resurrection, Christ confronted and disarmed the host of hostile forces which collectively held us in captivity. The cross and resurrection represent a dramatic act of divine liberation, in which God delivers his people from captivity to hostile powers, as he once delivered his people Israel from bondage in Egypt. The second-century writer Irenaeus of Lyons put it like this. "The Word of God was made flesh in order that he might destroy death and bring us to life. For we were tied and bound in sin, we were born in sin, and we live under the dominion of death."

A number of the great hymns of the medieval church make this point. For example, the hymn *Panga lingua* stresses the triumph of the cross through the paradox that its victim was actually its victor:

> Sing my tongue the glorious battle!
> Sing the ending of the fray!
> Now above the cross the trophy,
> Sound the loud triumphal lay!
> Tell how Christ the world's redeemer,
> As a victim won the day!

(Incidentally, note the importance of Christian hymns and songs as means of making doctrinal statements. The hymn books of the Christian church are often its most important and most memorable statements of doctrine.)

In dealing with this theme of Christ's victory through the apparent defeat of the cross, the fathers were especially attracted to the scriptural image of a "ransom." The New Testament talks about Jesus giving his life as a "ransom" for sinners (Mark 10:45; 1 Tim. 2:6). What does this analogy mean? The everyday use of the word "ransom" suggests three ideas.

1. *Liberation.* A ransom is something which achieves freedom for a person who is held in captivity. When someone is kidnapped, and a ransom demanded, the payment of that ransom leads to liberation.
2. *Payment.* A ransom is a sum of money which is paid in order to achieve an individual's liberation.
3. *Someone to whom the ransom is paid.* A ransom is usually paid to an individual's captor, or his agent.

These three ideas seem to be implied by speaking of Jesus' death as a "ransom" for sinners.

The fathers thus developed the idea that the death of Jesus Christ upon the cross was a payment made to the devil, in order to persuade him to liberate humanity from its bondage to him. In extending this theory, the fathers argued that, on account of human sin, we are all subject to the power and authority of the devil. There was no way that we could break free from this serfdom. However, God provided a payment, by which the devil was induced to hand over humanity to God their creator. They were thus ransomed.

This idea will probably seem deeply disturbing to many readers. But to the fathers, it was a perfectly proper doctrine, based upon the three elements of the scriptural analogy of ransom. But are all of these three actually present in scripture? There is no doubt whatsoever that the New Testament proclaims that we have been liberated from captivity through the death and resurrection of Jesus. We have been set free from captivity to sin and the fear of death (Rom. 8:21; Heb. 2:15). It is also clear that the New Testament understands the death of Jesus as the price which had to be paid to achieve our liberation (1 Cor. 6:20; 7:23). Our liberation is a costly and a precious matter. In these two respects, the scriptural use of "redemption" corresponds to the everyday use of the word. But what of the third aspect?

There is not a hint in the New Testament that Jesus' death was the price paid to someone (such as the devil) to achieve our liberation. Some of the writers of the first five centuries, however, assumed that they could press this analogy to its limits, and declared that God had delivered us from the power of the devil by offering him Jesus as the price of our liberation. But this idea is without scriptural warrant, and actually amounts to a serious distortion of the New Testament understanding of the meaning of the death of Jesus Christ. It is therefore important to consider how far we are allowed to press analogies before they break down, and mislead us.

The idea of Christ's death and resurrection as a victory over hidden forces which oppress us continues to be enormously helpful to many Christians.

Many African Christians, for example, find it very helpful to think of the cross and resurrection of Jesus Christ as breaking the baleful influence of malevolent ancestors and evil spirits upon their lives. The Second World War in Europe also brought new relevance to the idea, and also allowed new insights to be gained concerning the Christian life. One central question thus illuminated is the following: If Christ gained a victory over sin, why do Christians still experience a continuing conflict with sin in their lives?

In his work *Christ and Time*, the distinguished New Testament scholar Oscar Cullmann showed how events of the Second World War cast light upon the great scriptural theme of the victory of Christ over sin, and also addressed the question just noted. Cullmann suggested that it was helpful to think of a pattern of events which the war had made only too familiar to many Europeans: A long period of occupation by a foreign power. A country is occupied by an invading force, and its people held captive. There is no hope of liberation from within. A sense of despondency and hopelessness begins to creep in.

Then the situation is dramatically altered. Liberating forces establish a bridgehead on occupied territory. A great battle is won, and the course of the war is irreversibly altered. Yet the battle goes on. It is only when the last of the foreign forces have been defeated that victory is finally complete. (Cullmann has in mind the events of D-Day, which gave Allied forces a foothold in occupied Europe, and VE-Day, when the German armies finally surrendered.) Looking back on events from after VE-Day, it is clear that the war entered a decisive new phase at D-Day. Victory was given with that strategic struggle. And yet, in another sense, victory was not given, in that the war in Europe would continue for the best part of another year. But the will of the Nazi armies to resist had been broken at that decisive moment.

Similarly, the cross and resurrection represent a decisive battle, in which God confronts the age-old enemies of humanity through the cross of Christ. Their power is broken. They are defeated. Yet they have yet to be utterly conquered. Mopping-up operations must go on. The power of sin over us may be broken, but it continues to fight a rearguard action, however hopeless. The doctrine of the work of Christ assures us of final victory over sin and death, despite the fact that they are still at work in the world around us.

A PENALTY FOR HUMAN SIN

A second approach to the meaning of the death of Christ integrates a series of biblical passages dealing with notions of judgment and forgiveness. The understanding of the work of Christ outlined above has enormous attractions, not least on account of its highly dramatic character. It also, however, has some serious weaknesses. For the eleventh-century writer Anselm of Canterbury, two weaknesses were of particular importance. In the first place, it failed to explain why God should wish to redeem us. And, in the second, it was of little value in understanding how Jesus Christ was involved in the process of redemption. Anselm felt that more explanation was required.

To meet this need, he developed an approach to the work of Christ which centers upon the rectitude of the created order. God created the world in a certain way, which expresses his divine nature. He also created human beings in order that they might have fellowship in eternity with him. This purpose, however, would seem to have been frustrated by human sin, which comes as a barrier between us and God. A fundamental disruption has been introduced into creation. Its moral ordering has been violated. The redemption of humanity is thus called for, in order that the natural rectitude of the created order may be restored. In this sense, Anselm understands redemption as a restoration of humanity to its original status within the creation.

How, then, can we be redeemed? Anselm stresses that God is obliged to redeem us in a way that is consistent with the moral ordering of the creation, reflecting the nature of God himself. God cannot create the universe in one way, as an expression of his will and nature, and then violate its moral order in the redemption of humanity. He must redeem us in a way that is consistent with his own nature and purposes. Redemption must be moral, and be seen to be moral. God cannot employ one standard of morality at one point, and another later on. He is therefore under a self-imposed obligation to respect the moral order of the creation. His personal integrity demands that he be faithful to his own moral principles in redeeming us (see pp. 283–85).

Having established this point forcefully, Anselm then considers how redemption is possible. The basic dilemma can be summarized as follows. God cannot restore us to fellowship with him, without first dealing with human sin. Sin is a disruption of the moral ordering of the universe. It represents the rebellion of the creation against its creator. It represents an insult and an offense to God. The situation must be made right before fellowship can be restored. God must "make good" the situation. Anselm thus introduces the concept of a "satisfaction"—a payment or other action which compensates for the offense of human sin. Once this satisfaction has been made, the situation can revert to normal. But this satisfaction *must* be made first.

The problem, Anselm then observes, is that human beings do not have the ability to make this satisfaction. It lies beyond their resources. They need to make it—but cannot. Anselm thus reaches a crucial stage in his argument. Humanity ought to make satisfaction for its sins, but cannot. God himself is under no obligation to make satisfaction—but he could, if he wanted to. Therefore, Anselm argues, if God were to become a man, the resulting God-man would have both the obligation (as man) and the ability (as God) to make satisfaction. Thus the incarnation leads to a just solution to the human dilemma. God can redeem us, while maintaining his personal integrity. The death of Jesus Christ upon the cross demonstrates God's total opposition to sin, while at the same time providing the means by which sin could be really and truly forgiven, and the way opened to renewed fellowship between humanity and God.

But how does Christ's achievement upon the cross affect us? In what way do we share in the benefits of his death and resurrection? Anselm felt that this point did not require discussion, and so gave no guidance on that matter. Later writers, however, felt that it needed to be addressed. Three main ways of understanding how believers relate to Christ in this manner may be noted.

1. Participation

Through faith, believers participate in Jesus Christ. They are "in Christ," to use Paul's famous phrase. They are caught up in him, and share in his risen life. As a result of this, they share in all the benefits won by Christ, through his obedience upon the cross.

2. Representation

Christ is the covenant representative of humanity. Through faith, we come to stand within the covenant between God and humanity. All that Christ has won for us is available to us, on account of the covenant. Just as God entered into a covenant with his people Israel, so he has entered into a covenant with his church. Christ, by his obedience upon the cross, represents his covenant people, winning benefits for them as their representative. By coming to faith, individuals come to stand within the covenant, and thus participate in all its benefits, won by Christ.

3. Substitution

Christ is here understood to be our substitute. We ought to have been crucified, on account of our sins; Christ is crucified in our place. God allows Christ to stand in our place, taking our guilt upon himself, in order that his righteousness—won by obedience upon the cross—might become ours.

Each of these three approaches has merits in explaining how the believer comes to benefit from the death and resurrection of Christ.

A DEMONSTRATION OF THE LOVE OF GOD

If these two accounts of the meaning and inner dynamic of the cross of Christ are flawed at any point, it is perhaps most obviously in their failure to do justice to the love of God. Peter Abelard, a near-contemporary of Anselm of Canterbury, gently chided him for this apparent omission. How could one speak of the cross of Christ without also wanting to speak of the love of God for us?

The third approach to the death of Christ integrates a cluster of biblical passages which relate the death of Christ to the tender love of God for sinners. The New Testament affirms that the death of Jesus Christ demonstrates the love of God for us (John 3:16; Rom. 5:8). There can be no doubt that this insight is essential to any complete and balanced Christian account of the meaning of the death of Christ. As we saw earlier, this insight is safeguarded by a cluster of doctrines—above all, that of the incarnation (pp. 323–25). We are enabled to avoid abstract and vague ways of thinking about the love of God, and can begin to say precisely what form it takes. The love of God is like the love of a man, who voluntarily lays down his life for his friends (John 15:13). In the tragic scene of Jesus trudging his lonely and painful road to the cross, there to die for those whom he loved, we are given a vivid and deeply moving picture of what the love of God is like. The commitment and pain of that love are brought home to us every time we read the passion stories of the Gospels. To realize that God loves us—and loves us so much—is a devastating insight.

There is, however, a real danger here. Salvation can be reduced simply to a change in our perception of the situation. Nothing has changed—except that we realize that God loves us. We remain sinners. We remain trapped within our sinful situation. The death of Christ is like a catalyst, or a particularly powerful learning aid, which triggers off our recognition of the fact that God loves us. Up to this point, we may have been laboring under the delusion that God is wrathful, and liable to punish sinners. From that point onward, we rejoice in the recognition that God actually (whatever we may have though earlier) loves us. And this insight changes our lives. We are liberated by this knowledge.

The difficulty I have with this theory is perhaps best explored with reference to the writings of Karl Marx, especially the *Economic and Philosophical Manuscripts* of 1844. In these papers, Marx considers the question of human alienation. He distinguishes two broad senses of the term: A psychological sense, in which human beings are subjectively alienated from their true being; and an economic sense, in which they are objectively alienated from their property rights. Marx argues powerfully that a subjective feeling of alienation arises from an objective state of alienation. You feel alienated because you are alienated—alienated from your proper social, political, and economic rights. No amount of tinkering around with the human subjective consciousness is going to change this situation. So long as humans are socially alienated, they will continue to be psychologically alienated.

Marx thus argues that the proper way of achieving psychological tranquillity is through improvement of the social, political, and economic situation of individuals and society. Marx's point can be made with reference to a common problem in modern urban society. Many people are depressed. They suffer from a psychological condition, which can be treated, at least to some extent, by psychological techniques. But if these people then have to go and live in appalling social conditions, in bad housing, under constant threat of violence, and permanently short of money, they become depressed again. There is an objective cause to their subjective state of depression.

With this analogy in mind, let us return to our discussion of the work of Jesus Christ. Our subjective feeling of alienation from God is grounded in our objective state of alienation from God. We *feel* alienated because we *are* alienated from God. It is not just as if we *think* that we are sinners; we *are* sinners. It is not just that we *think* we are cut off from God; we *are* cut off from God. Our situation must be changed. We must be brought into a new relationship with God. To think of Christ dying on the cross just to change the way we think is dangerously shallow. Rather, Christ's death upon the cross changes our situation, in both its objective and subjective aspects. We are brought into a new relationship with God, in which the threat posed by sin is neutralized. And we respond to God, in the knowledge that he loves us and that we are free to love him.

In 1915, Hastings Rashdall delivered a series of Bampton Lectures at Oxford University. In these lectures, Rashdall argued forcefully that Jesus Christ was a moral example whom we are called to imitate. Having realized that God loves us, through contemplation of the death of Christ, we are moved to echo that love within our hearts—and thus to imitate Jesus, as an expression of our love for God. There is nothing, Rashdall asserted, fundamentally wrong with human nature, except that we fail to appreciate that God loves us.

Unfortunately, there were not that many present to hear Rashdall's lectures. Most of Oxford's young men were at the front, involved in some of the worst carnage the human race has ever seen. Even as Rashdall spoke, the First World War had plumbed new depths of human depravity. It was obvious to all that there was something fundamentally wrong with human nature—an impression to be confirmed by the shocking episodes of the Second World War, such as Auschwitz. Human beings needed more than education—they needed transformation. An understanding of the cross of Christ as moral education is inadequate, precisely because it rests upon an inadequate and unrealistic view of human nature. A deficient understanding of the human predicament leads to a defective understanding of the nature of the solution offered.

Having considered these three main ways of approaching the doctrine of the work of Christ, we may briefly explore some of its implications. One of the more important aspects of the Christian doctrine of salvation is its logical implication—original sin. Christianity proclaims that Christ is the savior of all human beings. If this is the case, then all human beings must require redemption. The presupposition of the doctrine of universal redemption of humanity through Christ is the universal sinfulness of humanity. "All have sinned and fall short of the glory of God" (Rom. 3:23).

What does this imply about human nature? Two points may be made. First, it does not imply that God made humanity with in-built defects. The doctrine of the fall asserts that human nature, having been created by God, fell into sin. Sin is a consequence of the independent action of God's creatures, rather than of any defective action on the part of the creator himself. Classical Christian theology locates the origins of sin in the human desire to be God, to usurp the place of God, to play at being the creator rather than accepting the status of being a creature. Second, it allows us to draw an important distinction between *fallen* and *redeemed* human nature. Although fallen, we remain the creation of God. We are still God's, even though we have sinned against him. In the process of redemption, however, we are brought into a new relationship with God. We become the children of God, with inheritance rights. A new status results. We may be sinners—but we are forgiven sinners.

How are we to think of original sin? In practice, original sin tends to be thought of as the antithesis of salvation. In other words, the way that you understand salvation affects the way you understand original sin. If you understand salvation as forgiveness, original sin is understood as legal or moral guilt. If you understand salvation as reconciliation to God, original sin is conceived as alienation from God. If salvation is understood as liberation from hostile forces, original sin is understood as enslavement to those forces. The basic function that the doctrine serves is to define the state from which we are redeemed. Many people find this doctrine puzzling; seen in its proper context, however, it can be seen as setting the scene for the great drama of redemption, which culminates in the work of Jesus Christ.

In this chapter, we have sketched various doctrinal approaches to the meaning of the death of Jesus Christ on the cross. Each of these approaches is complementary. Each integrates a different series of biblical passages. The full depths of the biblical understanding of the death of Christ are only to be appreciated by bringing together these three approaches, and the scriptural passages upon which they are based. For the death of Christ does not just involve a divine victory over sin, death, and evil—it *also* involves the gaining of real forgiveness, and the demonstration of the full extent of God's love for us.

With this point in mind, we may turn to think about how doctrines of the work of Christ relate to human experience. The three ways of thinking about the death of Christ we have just considered address themselves to—with a view to transforming—three different areas of human experience.

1. The Cross as Victory over a Fear of Death

Many people are frightened of death. Contemporary existentialist philosophers point out how humans try to deny death, try to pretend that they aren't going to die. We like to think that death is something which happens to somebody else. It is very difficult for us to come to terms with the fact that our personal existence will one day be terminated. It is a very threatening and disturbing thought. People are afraid of death. How often has it been said that death is a forbidden subject in the modern world?

It is here that the gospel has a decisive contribution to make. The New Testament points to the death and resurrection of Jesus Christ as God's victory over sin and death (1 Cor. 15:55–56). Christ "shared in their humanity so that by his death he might destroy him who holds the power of death—that is, the devil—and free those who all their lives were held in slavery by their fear of death" (Heb. 2:14–15). The gospel invites those who are afraid of death to look at what God has achieved through the cross and resurrection of Jesus. So long as human beings walk the face of this earth, knowing that they must die, the gospel will continue to be relevant and powerful. A feeling of fear and despair in the face of death can be changed into a sense of hope—*real* hope—in the light of the death and resurrection of Christ. A fundamental human experience (the fear of death) is addressed, in order to be transformed.

2. The Cross and a Feeling of Guilt

Many people have a deep sense of personal inadequacy and guilt. "How," they may ask, "can someone like me ever enter into a relationship with God? After all, he is so holy and righteous, and I am so sinful and wretched." This is a very important question, and Christianity has a very powerful answer to give. The cross demonstrates God's determination to deal with human sin. It shows just how serious and costly a thing real forgiveness is—and reassures us that our sins really have been forgiven. God doesn't say something like, "Never mind, let's pretend that sin doesn't exist." Instead, God brings together in the cross of Jesus his total condemnation of sin and his tender love for the sinner. We see in the death of Jesus on the cross the full impact of human sin, the full cost of divine forgiveness, and the full extent of the love of God for sinners. God hates the sin and loves the sinner. Christ endured the cross for our sakes, and bore the full penalty for sin. As a result, sin is forgiven—really forgiven. We are able to come to God, as forgiven sinners, as men and women whose sin has been condemned and forgiven. We must learn to accept that we have been accepted by God, despite being unacceptable.

So the cross is indeed good news to those who feel that they could not possibly come to God on account of their sin or inadequacy. The gospel gloriously affirms that God has forgiven that sin, has overcome that inadequacy. The words of 1 Peter 2:24 are very helpful and important here: "He himself bore our sins in his body on the tree, so that we might die to sins and live for righteousness; by his wounds you have been healed." Through the great events which centered on Calvary, God has wiped out our past sin and, at enormous cost, given us a fresh start. He has smoothed out every difficulty in order that we might go forward with him into eternal life. We are able to turn our backs on our past (which is what the idea of "repentance" basically means) in order to go forward into the future with the God who loves us. Once more, a human experience (a sense of guilt or inadequacy) is addressed, in order to be transformed into a sense of forgiveness and acceptance by God.

3. The Cross and the Human Need for Love

Many people feel lost in the immensity of the universe. We all need to feel loved, to feel that we are important to someone else. Yet at the root of the lives of many, there is a virtual absence of any meaning. President John F. Kennedy once remarked that "modern American youth has everything—except a reason to live." And the words of Jean-Paul Sartre express this point with force: "Here we are, all of us, eating and drinking to preserve our precious existences—and yet there is nothing, nothing, absolutely no reason for existing." We could even give a name to this feeling of meaninglessness—we could call it an "existential vacuum." But that doesn't solve the problem. We still feel lonely and lost, in a vast universe which threatens to overwhelm us.

It is this feeling of meaninglessness which is transformed through the electrifying declaration that God—the same God who created the universe—loves us. Love gives meaning to life, in that the person loved becomes special to someone, assumes a significance which he otherwise might not have. Christianity makes the astonishing assertion—which it bases upon the life, death, and resurrection of Jesus Christ—that God is profoundly interested in us and concerned for us. We mean something to God; Christ died for us; we are special in the sight of God. Christ came to bring us back from the "far country" to our loving and waiting father. In the midst of an immense and frightening universe, we are given meaning and significance by the realization that the God who called the world into being, who created us, also loves us and cares for us, coming down from heaven and going to the cross to prove the full extent of that love to a disbelieving and wondering world. Once more, a human experience (a sense of loneliness and meaninglessness) is addressed, and transformed into a sense of being dearly loved and given a sense of purpose.

The doctrine of the work of Christ, in addition to being an important area of Christian thought in its own right, is also of significance in that it illustrates the manner in which doctrine seeks to integrate scripture and interpret and transform experience. Much the same is true of the doctrine of the Trinity, to which we now turn.

13

The Trinity

For many Christians, the doctrine of the Trinity is perhaps one of the most obscure aspects of Christian theology. Many read the puzzling words of the Athanasian Creed—"The Father incomprehensible, the Son incomprehensible, and the Holy Spirit incomprehensible"—and feel sorely tempted to add, "the whole thing incomprehensible!" In this closing chapter, it is not my intention to explain this doctrine. My main concern is to show how this specific doctrine casts light on the nature and purpose of doctrine in general. We begin by considering how the doctrine of the Trinity arises as a response to Christ.

THE TRINITY AND THE INCARNATION

In an earlier chapter (chapter 11), we considered the doctrine of the incarnation—the recognition that Jesus Christ is none other than God himself. We noted that this crucial insight can be justified on both the basis of the New Testament evidence and the Christian experience of God in the risen Christ. We also noted how the doctrine of the incarnation is essential to the fabric of the Christian faith. Remove or deny this insight, and the Christian faith, like a knitted garment, begins to unravel, lose its shape, and become of no significance. To abandon the idea of the incarnation is to end up with an understanding of Jesus as little more than an academic moralist, incapable of *understanding*, let alone *redeeming*, our situation. But for Christianity, God meets people precisely where they are—because he has already been there himself.

If Jesus *is* God, something very important about God himself is being implied. Is God to be identified with Jesus? How can we avoid suggesting that Jesus is a second God? After all, did not Jesus pray to God? And did not God remain in heaven during the earthly ministry of Jesus? In one sense, Jesus is God; in another, he isn't. Thus Jesus is God incarnate—but he still prays to God, without giving the slightest indication that he is talking to himself. Jesus is not *identical* with God, in that it is obvious that God continued to be in heaven during Jesus' lifetime—and yet Jesus may be *identified* with God, in that the New Testament has no hesitation in ascribing functions to Jesus which, properly speaking, only God could do. One way of dealing with the problem was to refer to God as "Father," and Jesus as "Son," or "Son of God" (e.g.,

Rom. 1:3; 8:32; Heb. 4:14; 1 John 4:15)—thus indicating that they had the common bond of divinity, but that they could in some way be distinguished, with the Father being thought of as being in some way prior to the Son.

If Jesus Christ is God, the conclusion would seem to follow that God is to be identified totally with Jesus Christ. And yet it is obvious from Jesus' own teaching that he thought that God was still very much in heaven. The paradox we are beginning to wrestle with is expressed well by St. Germanus, in his famous seventh-century Christmas hymn:

The Word becomes incarnate
And yet remains on high!

The doctrine of the incarnation affirms that it really is God whom we encounter in Jesus Christ—but that this does not allow us to assert that Jesus and God are identical. It does not mean that God is *localized* in this one individual, Jesus Christ. Rather, it is stating that, because Jesus *is* God, he allows us to find out what God is like, to have a direct encounter with the reality of God. And because God is not totally identical with Jesus, he remains in heaven. God is just too big, too vast, for us to handle—and so God, knowing our weakness and accommodating himself to it (to use a helpful phrase due to John Calvin), makes himself available for us in a form which we can cope with. The doctrine of the incarnation affirms that it really is God whom we encounter directly in Jesus Christ—just as it affirms that God remains God throughout.

Recognizing the divinity of Christ is one of the central pressures which leads to the doctrine of the Trinity. In asking questions like those just noted, we begin to travel down the path which leads to the distinctively Christian understanding of God—the doctrine of the Trinity. We have a long way to go before we arrive there—but by recognizing that Jesus Christ is none other than God incarnate, we have set our feet firmly upon the road that leads to this most enigmatic of all Christian doctrines.

The relationship between the doctrines of the incarnation and the Trinity neatly illustrates a central theme of this book—the *coherence of Christian doctrine*. Individual Christian doctrines do not exist in noninteracting watertight compartments. They interact with, and modify, each other. They build up to give a coherent whole. Thus the recognition that Jesus is God immediately modifies any view of God which is incapable of coping with this insight. The history of the development of Christian doctrine shows this pattern clearly: Once the full divinity of Jesus Christ was accepted as normative in the fourth century, the process of rethinking the doctrine of God began in earnest. The culmination of this process is the doctrine of the Trinity.

Both historically and theologically, the doctrine of the Trinity can be shown to be a direct result of insights concerning the identity and significance of Jesus Christ. The doctrine of the Trinity is the end product of a long process of wrestling with two questions: "Who and what must God be, if he was able to become incarnate in Jesus Christ? What must be true about God, if it is true that Jesus Christ is divine?" In coming to consider these questions, theologians were able to integrate certain key scriptural passages within this Christological context. In the following section, we shall examine these passages, with a view to demonstrating how doctrine integrates scripture.

THE DOCTRINE OF THE TRINITY AND THE INTEGRATION OF SCRIPTURE

In one sense, there is no *doctrine* of the Trinity in the New Testament. Although the common work of the Father, Son, and Holy Spirit is evident throughout the New Testament, there is no developed and comprehensive account of the precise manner in which these relate to one another. That this is the case should be the occasion for neither surprise nor disquiet. The New Testament is primarily concerned to witness to the *reality* of the Father, Son, and Spirit; the doctrine of the Trinity is primarily reflection upon that reality by believers, as they attempt to make sense of it. The doctrine of the Trinity may not be present within the New Testament—but the saving revelation and action of God in Jesus Christ, which that doctrine attempts to interpret, is unquestionably at the heart of the New Testament proclamation.

Even within the New Testament itself, however, there are to be found clear hints of a Trinitarian way of thinking. A number of key passages develop a triadic approach to God. The doctrine of the Trinity aims to integrate these passages, bringing out their common features and establishing their central insights concerning God. What sort of passages are we talking about? The most important are the following.

Matthew 28:19: "Go and make disciples of all nations, baptizing them in the name of the Father and of the Son and of the Holy Spirit." Although baptism was initially performed in the name of Jesus (Acts 8:16; 19:5), this passage clearly indicates the implications of this practice. To be baptized in the name of Jesus is to be baptized in the name of the "God and Father of our Lord Jesus" (1 Pet. 1:3).

Second Corinthians 13:14: "May the grace of the Lord Jesus Christ, and the love of God, and the fellowship of the Holy Spirit be with you all." This formula (which is echoed elsewhere in the New Testament—such as Rom. 16:20–21; 1 Cor. 16:23; 1 Thess. 5:28; 2 Thess. 3:18) is thought to be (or perhaps to echo) a very early Christian liturgical formula. This formula summarizes the central aspects of the Christian understanding of God, clearly anticipating the later development of the formula into the doctrine of the Trinity.

Second Thessalonians 2:13–14: "From the beginning God chose you to be saved through the sanctifying work of the Spirit and through belief in the truth. He called you to this through our gospel, that you might share in the glory of our Lord Jesus Christ." This verse shows clearly how Paul's thought revolves around three sources of grace and salvation. Here, as elsewhere, Paul links these three sources together: Grace and salvation derive from these three sources, which cannot be regarded as independent agencies. All three are involved in the same common work.

A series of such passages could be produced, all making the same fundamental point: Salvation is the work of the Father, the Son, and the Spirit. All three are involved, perhaps in different manners, in the process of salvation. The following texts are worth study in this respect: 1 Corinthians 12:4–6; 2 Corinthians 1:21–22; Galatians 4:6; Ephesians 2:20–22; 3:14–17; Titus 3:4–6; Hebrews 6:4; 1 Peter 1:2; Jude 20–21; Revelation 1:4–6. The doctrine of the Trinity aims to identify the central point being made by such passages, state it in a coherent and systematic form, and explore its implications.

THE DOCTRINE OF THE TRINITY IDENTIFIES THE CHRISTIAN GOD

One of the most important tasks facing early Christian writers was that of identifying the God they worshiped and adored. "What God are you talking about?" was a frequent question put to them. A Jewish questioner would want to know how the "God of the Christians" related to the "God of Abraham, Isaac, and Jacob." Do Christians worship the same God as the Jews—or someone else?

As Christianity expanded into the Mediterranean world of the second century, it began to encounter religious rivals, which again forced Christian theologians to identify their God, and distinguish him from potential alternatives. A powerful threat to Christianity was posed by Gnosticism in the second century. Gnosticism, as we have seen, represented a complicated and diverse bundle of beliefs, many very similar to those of the Christian church. For example, it laid great stress on the importance of personal salvation. But it also differed from Christianity at a number of crucial points, including the notion of God. Gnosticism argued that there were *two* gods. The first was responsible for the creation of the world; the second was responsible for its redemption. Most Gnostics treated the creator god as a second-rate deity, and gave priority to the redeemer god.

This alarmed Christian theologians, who saw a real danger in these beliefs. For example, they might suggest that the God of the Old Testament was simply responsible for creating the world, while the God of the New Testament was responsible for the much more important and prestigious work of redemption. To confuse the Christian and Gnostic gods could lead to a serious perversion of the gospel. Accordingly, Christian theologians—such as the second-century writer Irenaeus of Lyons—insisted that the God of the Old and New Testaments was one and the same. It was one and the same God who created the world, who redeemed it through Jesus Christ, and who is now present through his Spirit. As Robert Jenson has stressed in his *Triune Identity*, the doctrine of the Trinity thus served to distinguish Christianity from its rivals, by identifying the God whom Christians knew, worshiped, and adored.

The Trinity thus came to be seen almost as something approaching a proper name. There are obvious parallels between the Christian phrase "Father, Son, and Holy Spirit" (Matt. 28:19; 2 Cor. 13:14) and its Old Testament predecessor "the God of Abraham, Isaac and Jacob." Both *identify* the God in question. Question: What God are you talking about? Answer: The God who raised Jesus Christ from the dead, and is now present through the Spirit. The Trinitarian formula is a shorthand way of identifying exactly what God we are talking about. Christianity packs into this one neat phrase the high points of the history of God's redeeming work, the big moments (resurrection and Pentecost) when God was so clearly present and active. It specifically linked God with the Exodus from Egypt. It focuses our attention on events, events in which God's presence and activity were to be found concentrated and publicly demonstrated.

The doctrine of the Trinity thus identifies the God of Christianity, and clarifies his relation to potential rivals. (Thus, to give but one example, the "God and Father of our Lord Jesus Christ" is the same as the "God of Abraham, Isaac, and Jacob," but is to be distinguished from Gnostic concepts of God.) And by identifying God in this way, the doctrine of the Trinity also identifies the Christian church. It marks it off from religious rivals—such as Unitarianism (the denial of the divinity of Christ and the Holy Spirit)—which might otherwise seem very similar to Christianity.

THE DOCTRINE OF THE TRINITY INTERPRETS THE SCRIPTURAL NARRATIVE

Scripture tells the story of God's dealings with humanity, reaching its climax in the history of Jesus Christ. The story neither begins nor ends with the coming of Christ; nevertheless, his coming divides that story in two. For Christians, Christ is the center of time. Yet God was active before the coming of Christ, and remains active afterwards. Scripture tells the story of the actions of God in history.

Yet that story is complex. God acts in different ways at different points. One of the central themes of the New Testament is that it tells the story of the same God as the Old Testament. The "God of Abraham, Isaac, and Jacob" is the same as the "God and Father of our Lord Jesus Christ." The doctrine of the Trinity gives us a framework for making sense of the acts of God in history, as they are told in the scriptural narrative. How is the Exodus from Egypt related to the resurrection of Jesus Christ? Or to the coming of the Holy Spirit at Pentecost? The doctrine of the Trinity interprets the great scriptural story, making it clear that it is one and the same God who is present and active throughout the story of our redemption.

Tertullian, the third-century Christian writer, gave us a particularly helpful way of beginning to make sense of the scriptural narrative. He suggested that we think of "one God in three persons." For Tertullian, the word "person" seems to have meant "a role in a drama." (The Latin word *persona* originally meant "mask," and by a process of transference, came to mean "the role played in a theater." Roman actors wore masks to represent the different characters which they played.) The phrase "one God in three persons" could be interpreted along the following lines. In the great drama of human redemption, three different roles are played out. These are the roles of the creator, the redeemer, and the sanctifier. All these three roles are played by the same actor—God. The roles of Father, Son, and Spirit are not played by three independent actors. "Three persons, but one God" means "three roles, but one actor." Behind the richness of the scriptural account of redemption is to be discerned the action of one and the same God.

THE DOCTRINE OF THE TRINITY INTERPRETS CHRISTIAN EXPERIENCE

As we stressed earlier, one of the classic functions of Christian doctrine is to interpret Christian experience. For example, we noted how the doctrines of the fall and redemption gave new meaning to the deep sense of "longing" within human nature, which proves incapable of being satisfied by any finite object (pp. 260–62). The doctrine of the Trinity brings new meaning and depth to the whole area of Christian experience, especially in the specific areas of worship and prayer.

Christians pray to God almost as a matter of instinct—it seems to come to them naturally. As they kneel down to say their prayers, they are aware that in some way (which is very difficult to express in words) God is actually *prompting* them to pray. It is almost as if God is at work within them, creating a desire to pray, or to turn to God in worship and adoration. Yet God is also the one to whom they are praying. A similar situation arises in worship. Although it is God whom we are praising, we are aware that it is somehow God himself who moves us from within to praise him. And theologians have captured this mystery in the formula "to the Father, through the Son and in the Holy Spirit." In prayer and worship alike, we seem to be brought before the presence of the Father, through the mediation of the Son, in the power of the Holy Spirit.

And that, in conclusion, is the function of doctrine itself—to bring us and others safely into the presence of God, and hold us there.

CONCLUSION

The present work has aimed to examine and explain the purpose and place of Christian doctrine. it is responsible and obedient reflection on the part of the church on the mysteries of faith. Doctrine preserves the Christian church from woolly and confused understandings of its identity and calling, and provides believers with a framework for interpreting the ambiguities of human experience in the world to be interpreted and transformed. It opens the way to the construction of a worldview, through which Christian attitudes and approaches to a range of matters—social, spiritual, ethical, and political—can be developed.

The idea of "Christianity without doctrine" will doubtless continue to tantalize those who, for one reason or another, find doctrine pedantic, petty, or pointless. The present work is written in the conviction that doctrine, rightly understood, is nothing of the sort. Inadequate, weak, and unsympathetic accounts of the nature of doctrine may indeed create this impression. Doctrine may at times seem to be something of an irrelevance—but on closer inspection it holds the key to the future of the Christian faith in the modern world. The church cannot think, let alone act, without basing its thoughts and actions upon a doctrinal foundation. Doctrine must continue to be, and to be *allowed and recognized to be*, a central resource in Christian education. Christianity is irreducibly doctrinal in its foundations, upon which a considerable experiential, social, and political superstructure may be erected. The foundation must be capable of supporting this structure. To neglect—still worse, to repudiate—this foundation is to deny the Christian church the critical resources it needs if it is to retain its identity and mission in the third millennium of its existence.

BIBLIOGRAPHY

The list of books and articles below is intended to allow the reader to develop at least some of the ideas found in this work to whatever level seems appropriate. A common difficulty encountered by many readers concerns the level at which works are written. Some of the more severely academic works are written with the needs of specialists in mind and make no allowance for the general reader. Those marked with an asterisk (*) are especially suitable as introductory texts and are generally easier to read than the present work. Those marked with a dagger (†) are somewhat technical and may prove considerably more difficult to read than this book. The extra effort required, however, should be found to be merited.

This bibliography includes all those works cited in the text itself.

Atkinson, James, and Rowan Williams. "On Doing Theology." In *Stepping Stones*, edited by C. Baxter (London: Hodder and Stoughton, 1987): 1–20.

Avis, Paul. *Ecumenical Theology and the Elusiveness of Doctrine*. London: SPCK, 1986.

Barth, Karl. *Evangelical Theology: An Introduction*. New York: Holt, Rinehart, & Winston, 1968.

Bauckham, Richard. "The Worship of Jesus in Apocalyptic Christianity." *New Testament Studies* 27 (1980): 322–41.

————, and Rowan Williams. "Jesus—God with Us." In *Stepping Stones*, edited by C. Baxter (London: Hodder and Stoughton, 1987): 21–41.

Berkhof, Hendrikus. *Christian Faith: An Introduction to the Study of Faith*. Grand Rapids: Eerdmans, 1980.

Boff, Leonardo. *Trinity and Society*. New York: Orbis Books, 1988.

Brown, David. *The Divine Trinity*. London: Duckworth, 1985.

Brown, Harold O. J. *Heresies: The Image of Christ in the Mirror of Heresy and Orthodoxy*. Garden City: Doubleday, 1984.

Carson, D. A., and John D. Woodbridge, eds. *Scripture and Truth*. Grand Rapids: Zondervan, 1983.

†Christian, W. A. *Doctrines of Religious Communities: A Philosophical Study*. New Haven: Yale University Press, 1987.

Curran, Charles E. *Themes in Fundamental Moral Theology*. Notre Dame: University of Notre Dame Press, 1977.

†Dunn, J. D. G. *Christology in the Making*. Philadelphia: Westminster, 1980.

Forsyth, P. T. *The Person and Place of Jesus Christ.* London: Independent Press, 1909.

France, R. T. "The Worship of Jesus: A Neglected Factor in the Christological Debate?" In *Christ the Lord*, edited by H. H. Rowdon (Leicester: InterVarsity, 1982): 17–36.

Gore, Charles. *The Incarnation of the Son of God.* London: John Murray, 1922.

†Jenson, Robert. *The Triune Identity: God According to the Gospel.* Philadelphia: Fortress, 1982.

Kelly, J. N. D. *Early Christian Creeds.* 3d edition. New York: Longman, 1982.

†Lash, Nicholas. *Easter in Ordinary: Reflections on Human Experience and the Knowledge of God.* Charlottesville: University Press of Virginia, 1988.

Lewis, C. S. *Surprised by Joy.* San Diego: Harcourt, Brace & Jovanovich, 1956.

_____. *Till We Have Faces.* San Diego: Harcourt, Brace & Jovanovich, 1980.

_____. "The Weight of Glory." In *Screwtape Proposes a Toast* (London: Collins, 1965): 94–110.

_____. "The Language of Religion." In *Christian Reflections* (Grand Rapids: Eerdmans, 1974): 164–79.

†Lindbeck, George. *The Nature of Doctrine.* Philadelphia: Fortress, 1984.

†McGrath, Alister E. *The Making of Modern German Christology.* Cambridge, MA: Basil Blackwell, 1986.

*_____. *Understanding Jesus: Who Jesus Christ Is and Why He Matters.* Grand Rapids: Zondervan, 1987.

*_____. *Understanding the Trinity.* Grand Rapids: Zondervan, 1990.

†_____. *The Genesis of Doctrine: A Study in the Foundations of Doctrinal Criticism.* Cambridge, MA: Basil Blackwell, 1990.

*_____. *The Basics of Faith: A Study Guide to the Apostles' Creed.* Leicester: InterVarsity, 1991.

†MacIntyre, Alasdair. *Whose Justice? Which Rationality?* Notre Dame: University of Notre Dame Press, 1988.

†Mahoney, John. *The Making of Moral Theology.* Oxford: Oxford University Press, 1989.

Marshall, I. Howard. *The Origins of New Testament Christology.* Downers Grove: InterVarsity, 1976.

_____. "Incarnational Christology in the New Testament." In *Christ the Lord*, edited by H. H. Rowdon (Leicester: InterVarsity, 1982): 1–16.

Mitchell, Basil. "Is There a Distinctive Christian Ethic?" In *How to Play Theological Ping-Pong* (London: Hodder & Stoughton, 1990): 42–56.

Moule, C. F. D. *The Origin of Christology.* Cambridge: Cambridge University Press, 1978.

†O'Donovan, Oliver. *Resurrection and Moral Order.* Grand Rapids: Eerdmans, 1986.

Reid, J. K. S. *The Authority of Scripture*. Westport, CT: Greenwood Press, 1981.

Sayers, Dorothy L. "Creed or Chaos?" In *Creed or Chaos?* (London: Methuen, 1947): 25–46.

Stott, J. R. W. *The Cross of Christ*. Downers Grove: InterVarsity, 1989.

†Stout, Jeffrey. *Ethics after Babel*. Boston: Beacon Press, 1988.

Taylor, A. E. *The Faith of a Moralist*. 2 volumes. London: Macmillan, 1930.

Thielicke, Helmut. *Theological Ethics*. 3 volumes. Grand Rapids: Eerdmans, 1978.

Torrance, T. F. *The Trinitarian Faith*. Minneapolis: Augsburg Fortress, 1988.

†Williams, Rowan. *Arius: Heresy and Tradition*. London: Darton, Longman & Todd, 1987.

————. "The Incarnation as the Basis of Dogma." In *The Religion of the Incarnation*, edited by R. Morgan (Bristol: Bristol Classical Press, 1989): 85–98.

JUSTIFICATION
—by—
FAITH

PREFACE

For the Reformers of the sixteenth century, the doctrine of justification by faith was the center of the Christian faith, the foundation of their program of reform and renewal. The doctrine was no innovation introduced by the Reformers but a call to renovation, a call to grasp and proclaim the gospel of grace, to restore to the church the theological basis of her mission to the world. I hope that this introductory book will help a new generation of readers wrestle with the ideas that so stirred individuals such as Paul and Luther, in order that they may grasp and proclaim to a disbelieving world the astonishing and thrilling truth of what God has done for us through the death and resurrection of Jesus Christ.

Like every primer, this book makes no claim to be exhaustive or definitive but merely aims to guide the reader through a series of complex biblical, historical, and theological questions that are an inevitable part of the study of the doctrine of justification by faith. It will be clear that this little book is not intended as a substitute for serious study of the major works on the subject. I hope, however, further study will be made easier and more fruitful by this introduction to the themes and problems associated with the doctrine.

The work falls into two main parts. After an introduction, the first part deals with the biblical and historical background of the doctrine. The second part considers the contemporary relevance of the doctrine and in particular deals with the suggestion that the doctrine is out of date and irrelevant in the modern period. It is hoped that the reader will be stimulated to develop these ideas in his or her own thinking and personal ministry. An appendix deals with the difficult question of the theological significance of the doctrine, assessing its place within systematic theology as a whole.

Finally, the reader has a right to know why this book was written. Some ten years ago, I began work on a study of the development of the doctrine of justification.[1] As I worked on that study, I began to realize how important the ideas in question are and how vital the doctrine of justification is to the life of the Christian church and the believer. I therefore decided that I would, as soon as I had time, attempt to explain and defend these ideas in a day and age when the doctrine of justification is often treated as a relic of a bygone age.[2] This book is the result, and any shortcomings it may have are a reflection on my weakness as an author rather than on my subject. For there can be no greater subject than what God has done for us in Jesus Christ and how this may be actualized in a new relationship in which he and we are together—a relationship that not even death itself can destroy.

—ALISTER MCGRATH

1

Introduction

Contemporary theologians generally tend to treat the doctrine of justification as some sort of theological dinosaur—something that was of great importance in its own day and age but has now become extinct as a burning theological issue. They see it as something that survives only in fossil form, embodied in confessional documents dating from the sixteenth century but without contemporary relevance. One modern theologian who adopts this negative attitude is Paul Tillich:

> Protestantism was born out of the struggle for the doctrine of justification by faith. This doctrine is strange to the man of today, and even to Protestant people in the churches; indeed, as I have over and over again had the opportunity to learn, it is so strange to the modern man that there is scarcely any way of making it intelligible to him.[1]

But is Tillich really right? Is not what Tillich is describing simply the failure of theologians to *explain* what the doctrine of justification by faith really means? It is certainly true that the term "justification" today is more associated with word processing than with our relationship with God. But to say that "justification" seems strange as a theological idea to many today is certainly not equivalent to saying that the *truths and insights* which the doctrine of justification by faith expresses are strange or incomprehensible. It is the responsibility of theologians, who know what the doctrine means, to translate its significance into terms their readers and hearers may understand. The wise words of C. S. Lewis express this point perfectly:

> We must learn the language of our audience. And let me say at the outset that it is no use laying down *a priori* what the "plain man" does or does not understand. You have to find out by experience .... You must translate every bit of your theology into the vernacular. This is very troublesome ... but it is essential. It is also of the greatest service to your own thought. I have come to the conclusion that if you cannot translate your own thoughts into uneducated language, then your thoughts are confused. Power to translate is the test of having really understood your own meaning.[2]

If the doctrine of justification by faith is "unintelligible," it is because we have made it so and have failed to *explain* its power and relevance for the human situation. The failure lies with us, and not with the doctrine.

This book is intended to be an introduction to this central and neglected doctrine of the Christian faith. There is much that the reader needs to know about it—what its background in Scripture is, how it has been understood in the history of the Christian church, and what was at stake in the Reformation controversies over the matter. But above all, the reader needs to be stimulated to translate the insights of this doctrine into the language of a world which, we are told, has "come of age."

One of the reasons why the doctrine of justification by faith has lost its impact is the tendency of preachers to discuss the doctrine in general terms or in terms appropriate to a bygone age—without addressing it to the specific situation of their audience. Because it was in the sixteenth century, in the period of the Reformation, that the doctrine assumed prominence, preachers have all too often proclaimed the great theme of justification in terms drawn from the sixteenth century, fondly imagining that this is the *only* way of approaching it and that the doctrine must be taught and proclaimed in precisely this form! But, as the history of Christian thought shows, generations of theologians constantly have sought to apply the theme of justification by faith creatively to their own day and age. They were aware that their interpretation of the theme might not have cut much ice several centuries earlier and would do so even less several centuries later. They knew, however, that their task was to proclaim this great theme to their hearers *in terms they could understand.* We all too easily assume that the theme of justification was preached in exactly the same way from the first through the nineteenth centuries, only to fail us in the twentieth. But the truth is that the preachers of every age recognized the need to apply the theme to their specific situation—with the apparent exception of the modern period. For Augustine, the theme was to be proclaimed in neo-Platonist terms; for Anselm of Canterbury, in feudal terms; for Thomas Aquinas, in Aristotelian terms; for Calvin, in legal terms—in short, they proclaimed the doctrine in terms that drew upon the experience, hopes, and fears of their own day and age.

The theme of "justification by faith" is the fulfillment of human existence through the removal of the barriers that get placed in its path. To the individual who is preoccupied with guilt and knows that he cannot draw near to a holy and righteous God, the word of forgiveness is spoken: through your faith in the death of Jesus Christ and his resurrection from the dead your sins are forgiven—rise, a forgiven sinner, and go forward into life in fellowship with your God! To the individual who is overwhelmed by a fear of death, the gospel speaks the word of life: he who raised Christ Jesus from the dead will do the same for you—rejoice in that victory over death which is ours through Jesus Christ! In short, there is a need to particularize the theme of justification in terms of the specific situation of those to whom it is proclaimed. The gospel "sameness" is not being eroded by doing so—we are merely drawing on the fullness of its remarkable resources.

But this is precisely the problem—the fullness of those resources has *not* been fully drawn upon. The doctrine of justification, if it is to regain the place it rightly should hold, must be treated for what it is and not as a museum piece or as a fossil from the past that must be preserved in exactly the same form it had in the fourth, eleventh, or sixteenth century. It must be liberated from this prison and allowed to confront with its full force the expectations, hopes, and fears of the modern period. The church cannot be kept in bondage to the forms of theological expression used in the sixteenth century! Christian theology is concerned with the application of the history of redemption, which culminates in the death and resurrection of Jesus Christ, to the situation of the moment. It was this application that Augustine attempted in his day and age, and Luther and Calvin in theirs. And now, in turn, it is we who have to link the two horizons of the witness to God's redeeming actions recorded in scripture on the one hand and the specific context of our own situation on the other.

If twentieth-century Westerners think of human destiny primarily in terms of ideas like "purpose," "existence," and "meaning," then the gospel must be particularized in these terms. By doing this, these concerns may be directly addressed and thence transformed. To do this is not to capitulate or surrender to the preoccupations of modern humanity; it is rather to recognize that the gospel needs to be addressed to points of contact with human beings in each and every age if it is to gain a hold and transform them. It is to exploit a means by which authentically Christian insights may be established, not to endorse contemporary concerns. We cannot argue twentieth-century people back into a sixteenth-century way of thinking if we are to communicate the vital truths embodied in the theme of justification by faith! The gospel meets people right where they are in order to move them on from there—and we cannot dictate where they should start from; rather, we must simply meet them *where they already are*. This is an essential precondition for the reappropriation of the doctrine of justification by faith and its reinstatement where it rightly belongs.

Another stumbling block theologians have put in the way of recovering the vitality and relevance of this doctrine stems from a mixture of Cartesianism and Platonic idealism. This is the concept of a universal abstract truth that is valid for all people and for all time. For some theologians, the doctrine of justification embodies exactly this sort of universal abstract truth. But is this really right? Is it not actually the case that the doctrine of justification by faith points to a central theme of both the Old and New Testaments—namely, that God wants and intends the restoration of a lost world to himself and to its true nature and destiny by breaking down whatever barriers are placed between it and him, and that in Jesus Christ he actually makes this possible? What we are talking about here is the mediation and manifestation of God's determination to restore his lost world through Jesus Christ *from whatever specific historical forms the human predicament takes at any given moment in time*.

It may be that the lostness that is experienced in one moment in human history is that of being held captive in slavery in an alien land—in which case the theme of justification by faith points to God's gracious act of liberation in the Exodus. It may be that the lostness experienced at another moment in that history is a profound sense of guilt at moral inadequacy—in which case the same theme points to God's gracious act of a real and costly forgiveness through the cross of Christ, in which all is squarely faced and all is fairly forgiven. It may be that the lostness experienced at another time is a deep and genuine desire for meaningful and purposeful existence—and once more there is a need to *particularize* the gospel by demonstrating how such an authentic way of existing is made available as a gift through the death and resurrection of Jesus Christ. Like any good preacher, the theologian must know the hopes and fears of his audience if he is to ground the gospel in their experience in order to transform it.

A further point that must be made concerns the intimate relationship between *doctrine* and *experience*.[3] Doctrines are fundamentally concerned with experience rather than with abstract conceptual truths! In other words, doctrines are attempts to preserve something that is all too easily lost through misunderstanding, namely, an experience. To use a famous analogy that goes back to Augustine, doctrine is like a hedge that protects a field. The field is the richness of the Christian's redemptive encounter with the living God through Jesus Christ, here and now—and the doctrine is simply an attempt to ensure that this experience can be *verbalized*, put into words, so that it can be passed down from one generation to another. And yet what is passed down from one generation to another is not merely a doctrine, a formula, a form of words, but the living reality and the experience that lie behind them. The doctrine of justification by faith is concerned with the Christian's experience of a redemptive encounter with the living God. It affirms that this encounter really can and does take place and attempts to explain how it may take place—what it is that we must do if we are to have this experience. It cannot adequately describe this experience any more than any of us could put our experience of God into words, but it points to the reality of the experience and describes how it may be actualized.

Some famous words of T. S. Eliot should be remembered here: "We had the experience, but missed the meaning, but approach to the meaning restored the experience." In other words, we need not only an encounter with God, we also need, if this encounter and experience is to be passed down to our children, an intellectual framework within which the redeeming and liberating encounter with and experience of the living God takes place. The doctrine of justification establishes this framework. But it is the *experience*, the *encounter*, rather than this framework the preacher is primarily concerned with! It is possible to misunderstand the doctrine of justification by faith as simply an obscure verbal formula—when it is in fact concerned with transmitting and preserving the experience of an encounter with none other than the living God. The doctrine expresses and conserves this experience and encounter, but it is not identical with it. What the doctrine of justification by faith offers is not truth concerning God but the possibility of encountering God. The preacher must explain how that experience may be had and how it is grounded in the life of his hearers.

The general principle at issue is that of *contextualization*—or, to put it in plain English, of taking the trouble to think through what the gospel proclamation might mean to the specific situation faced by your hearers. The gospel is perfectly capable of being accommodated within every human culture and every human situation—even the situation faced by a "world come of age." If the gospel does not speak to people today, the fault lies not in the gospel but in ourselves. The New Testament bears eloquent witness to the power and vividness of contemporary images and analogies to convey the theme of justification by faith—and places us under an obligation to do the same in our own day and age. Paul felt free to "become all things to all men so that by all possible means [he] might save some" (1 Cor. 9:19–23), in order that the power of the gospel might make its full impact felt in the specific and unique cultural context of each historical situation. While cultural matters are relativized by the gospel's absolute claims, these claims must still be communicated and articulated in and to those specific life situations and contexts.

How might this be done? In a later section of this book we shall be looking at several points of contact with modern Western thought that allow the doctrine of justification by faith to be grounded in our contemporary culture. The general principles of such a procedure are set out by David Shank, who provides the following analysis of some of the many dimensions of justification as they relate to a variety of felt needs and cultural themes.[4]

TABLE 1

Context of Experience	From	To	Through Jesus
Acceptance	Rejection	Acceptance	Love
Direction	to err about	to aim at	Call
Festival	Boredom	Joy	Feast-giver
Meaning	the absurd	the reasonable	Word
Liberation	Oppression	Liberation	Liberation
Becoming	Nobody	Somebody	Invitation
Fellowship	Solitude	Community	Presence

Here, the theme of justification by faith is stated in a number of specific forms, each of which may be grounded in a given cultural situation. For example, we are not acceptable—but God accepts us as we are and where we are, through Jesus Christ. We have no meaning—but we are given meaning as a free gift of God through Jesus Christ. And so forth. And it is the task of the preacher, the missionary, and the theologian to ground this doctrine in the situation of their hearers, to unpack the relevance of that affirmation, and apply it.

It is at this point that a further difficulty must be noted. It is a difficulty known already to most, yet all too often overlooked. This is the danger of using technical theological vocabulary without explaining what it means, often without attempting even to restate or rephrase it. One of the gentle ironies of much of the contemporary attempt to preach justification by faith is a failure to realize that, as used by Paul in the New Testament, the term and the cluster of ideas it embraced had a freshness, an immediacy, and a vividness that are missing today. That vividness must be resupplied and refreshed. An illustration may help bring out the problem and perhaps point to one way of dealing with it.

A friend of mine had been feeling tired and weak for some time and had gradually come to believe that this was normal for someone his age. However, something he had heard someone say had made him suspect that there was actually something wrong with him—that he wasn't meant to be this tired and low. So he went to see his doctor. The doctor examined him and told him that there was indeed something wrong with him. He used lots of complicated technical terms such as "metabolism" and "calcium deficiency" to describe the problem. He referred my friend to a medical textbook in which his condition was described. But it still didn't make much sense to my friend.

Eventually, he gave up trying to understand the doctor. "Look, doctor, you and I just seem to speak different languages! How about explaining this to me in plain English? Can you tell me what's wrong with me without all these technical words?" And so the doctor finally really *explained* his problem to him. He told him how the human body normally works efficiently, breaking down food in order to extract the energy from it and changing it into a form that can be used for everyday activities. To do this, however, it needs certain substances. If these substances aren't there, the body can't work efficiently, and tiredness and lethargy set in. My friend's problem was that he didn't have enough of these substances. My friend now finally *understood* what was wrong with him, and the doctor proceeded to treat the problem.

This story probably falls within the experience of most of us. All of us know the tendency of the medical profession to talk their own private language. They use words every medical practitioner understands yet only relatively few people outside the profession are familiar with. It is a highly specialized form of shorthand, which allows a lot to be said in a very few words to those who already know the language—but which needs to be *explained* to those not familiar with it. The fact that most of us can't understand it doesn't mean that it's not true—just that it needs to be explained, translated into plain English, with a few homely analogies to help bring out the meaning.

Of course, it's not just the medical profession that uses jargon in this way. Anyone who tries to read computer or automobile manuals knows how any area of life develops its own specialized language—including theology. The vocabulary of the Christian preacher and teacher is littered with technical terms such as "sin," "grace," and "justification"—all of which make perfect sense to those who know what they mean but are unintelligible to the rest of the world. There is a need for the preacher or teacher to explain what these terms mean; to use plain English to convey their sense; to find analogies and illustrations to bring out their force and relevance; to *contextualize* them, explaining what they mean in the specific case of the person we're talking to.

In dealing with the doctrine of "justification by faith" we are handling a technical term that has become unfamiliar to many of our hearers. This does not for one moment mean that the doctrine is irrelevant—it means that there is an urgent need that it be explained, interpreted, and illustrated to meet the needs of a new generation.

To continue with our medical analogy, we could begin to illustrate the relevance and meaning of the doctrine like this. The gospel declares that we are like ill people who need the attention of a doctor (Mark 2:17). This comes as news to many of us, who weren't aware that there was anything wrong with us in the first place! The "world come of age" is rather like my friend who was ill but refused to believe it. The gospel declares that the name of this illness is sin, something that threatens to wreck our full potential as human beings. It is like a deficiency—something is missing from our system and needs to be added if we are to be whole. It is like a short in a complex electronic circuit—it throws the whole equipment into confusion. It is like a bug in a computer program—it turns an intelligent operation into chaos. And as the symptoms of this illness—such as being lost in the world, a sense of being far from God, of meaninglessness and guilt—are explained, we begin to realize that it is our own situation that is being described. We realize that there is little point in tinkering with the symptoms of this illness—the important thing is to deal with the illness itself. It is the root cause that must be identified and dealt with. The gospel passes judgment on us in the same way as a medical practitioner gives a diagnosis—declaring that something *is* wrong, and identifying precisely what the nature of the problem is.

And it is at this point that the gospel can be recognized as good news. It affirms the reality of sin but also the power and purpose of God to deal with it. It affirms that our human nature has been wounded by sin, that something essential to its well-being is absent, that we have been invaded by some hostile force, just as the body may be invaded by a viral infection. It insists on the seriousness of the problem while declaring that something can be done to remedy the situation.

As a younger man, I spent two years at Cambridge University, carrying out theological research at St. John's College. One of my great delights was to visit the chapel of nearby Kings College, a magnificent building, famous for its choral tradition. One of the great attractions of the chapel was an Old Master—a beautiful painting at one end of the main chapel building. One day, a protester made some sort of political gesture and, to the horror of all watching, produced a knife and slashed the painting. Within a short time, a notice was placed alongside the ruined painting: "It is believed that this masterpiece can be restored." Much of the same is true of human nature, according to the gospel. Standing at the height of God's creation, human nature has been seriously wounded by sin—and the gospel declares that this, the masterpiece of God's creation, can be restored by its loving creator.

"Justification by faith" summarizes the glorious affirmation that God is able and willing to deal with sin. An illness which we ourselves could not cure (sin) has been diagnosed by God, and a cure (justification) is offered. The futility of half measures, such as merely relieving symptoms, is affirmed. And we, like the invalid at the pool of Bethesda, are given the privilege of accepting or rejecting the cure: "Do you want to get well?" (John 5:6). The theme of justification by faith, as we shall see, speaks of our restoration to wholeness, of the recapturing in the garden of Gethsemane of what was lost in the garden of Eden.

To realize the full power of this good news, we need to try to think ourselves into a situation like that described in Arthur Hailey's *Strong Medicine*. A young woman is dying in the hospital. The attending doctor does everything he can, but the illness is incurable. He knows that within a matter of hours his young patient will be dead, with devastating results for her family. With remarkable skill, the author builds up a picture of the hopelessness and helplessness of the situation. And then, unexpectedly, a drug is rushed in. It has just been developed, and no one is quite sure what its effects will be. As the medical staff watch anxiously, the drug is administered to the patient. Then suddenly, what all had been hoping for, but none dared believe, takes place—the patient rallies and then slowly but surely recovers.

In many ways, this story illuminates the thrilling dimension of the gospel proclamation of justification by faith. The human situation has been transformed through the death and resurrection of Jesus Christ. As the first-century writer Ignatius of Antioch declared, the gospel proclamation is like "the medicine of immortality." The hopelessness and helplessness of our weak and mortal natures, trapped in the rut that leads only to death and decay, is transformed. What we could not do for ourselves has been done for us—and done well. In the famous words of Martin Luther, "We are like ill people under the care of a physician—we are ill in fact, but healthy in hope." The same sense of excitement, of realization of hope, can be found in the famous old Christmas hymn of St. Germanus:

> A great and mighty wonder!
> A full and holy cure!

PART ONE

The Background of the Doctrine

2

The Biblical Foundation

The primary source of both Christian faith and Christian theology is the Bible. Scripture witnesses to the self-revelation of God in human history, beginning with the call of Abraham, continuing through the call of Israel out of the land of Egypt, and culminating in the life, death, and resurrection of Jesus Christ. The central theme of scripture could be said to be God's dealings with his people.

But how do we enter into a relationship with God? How are we distinguished from those outside this relationship? And what obligations does this relationship place upon us? Questions such as these are raised throughout the Old and New Testaments. In the present chapter we propose to identify some of the more important aspects of the scriptural witness to God's gracious dealings with his people, which converge in the doctrine of justification by faith.

Many operas open with an orchestral prelude or overture. The original reason for these introductions was that the audience tended to arrive late, and the overture allowed the action to be postponed for about ten minutes until everyone had arrived. However, by the nineteenth century the orchestral prelude to an opera was well established as an integral part of the work (and the audience now had to arrive on time!). The prelude introduces the musical themes that will dominate the remainder of the opera, allowing the audience to get used to them and recognize them when they occur. Richard Wagner's operas, such as *Lohengrin*, are excellent examples of this development. And in many ways it is helpful to regard the first eleven chapters of Genesis as a prelude, introducing the themes that will dominate the rest of scripture—themes such as human sinfulness, the rebellion of humanity against God, the graciousness of God, and the covenant between God and man. The scene is set for the great drama of divine redemption that follows. And then the curtain rises upon human history to reveal God calling Abraham and promising to make him into a great people (Gen. 12:1–3). In effect, Abraham is called in order to reverse the sin of Adam. And the response to that promise is faith. This point is developed in a famous passage, referred to several times by Paul: Genesis 15:1–6.

In this passage, God promises Abraham a son and descendants who will outnumber the stars of heaven—and Abraham believes this seemingly impossible promise. "Abraham believed the Lord, and [the Lord] credited it to [Abraham] as righteousness" (Gen. 15:6). Here we encounter a central biblical theme of direct relevance to the doctrine of justification—the idea of *righteousness*. What does it mean? Clearly it does not mean that God considered Abraham's faith to be a moral virtue which he was under some kind of obligation to reward (after all, the promise had already been made!). The difficulty is that the Hebrew word which most English versions translate as "righteousness" has no exact English equivalent.[1] In modern Western thought, "righteousness" tends to be thought of in terms of absolute, impersonal standards of justice and morality, and it is important to realize that this is not what the Old Testament writers had in mind. In the Old Testament, righteousness is a *personal* concept: it is essentially the *fulfillment of the demands and obligations of a relationship between two persons*.[2] The Old Testament sees each individual as set within a complex network of relationships. For example, a given individual will as a father have a relationship to his children; as a husband, to his wife; as a citizen, to his king as well as to the poor and needy; as an employer, to his employees; and so on. Each of these relationships is governed by obligations on the part of both parties, and fulfillment of these obligations constitutes "righteousness."

The most important relationship, the relationship that underlies all others, is the covenant relationship between God and his people. And "righteousness" in the Old Testament most often refers to the fulfillment of the conditions of that all-important covenant. When God or man fulfills the conditions imposed upon them by that covenant relationship, then God or man is, according to the Old Testament, righteous.

This recognition of the covenantal framework within which the concept of "righteousness" is set also allows us to gain important understandings of related concepts—such as "sin." Just as "righteousness" is primarily concerned with faithfulness, so "sin" is primarily concerned with faithlessness. While the biblical concept of sin has many aspects that could rightly be described as forensic or legal (such as the ideas of "missing the mark" or "falling short of what is required"), the idea of the betrayal of a personal relationship is fundamental to a biblical understanding of sin. Sin is about failing to trust God, challenging his authority, or failing to take his promises seriously (see Ps. 106:24–27)—in short, a failure to trust in God. We shall return to this grounding of the concept of sin in a personal relationship in chapter 7.

With this point in mind, let us go back to Genesis 15:6. We can now see that the basic idea is that faith in God's promises is regarded as "righteousness"—in other words, Abraham's relationship with God is "right" when he puts his trust in God's promises. The righteousness that is demanded of

Abraham is faith in the *faithfulness* of God. Similarly, the Old Testament prophets emphasize that the condition required of the people of Israel if the covenant with God is to continue is righteousness—not primarily *moral virtue*, but rather *faithfulness* to God. This point helps us understand why the prophets protest against Israel's flirtations with foreign gods as much as—if not more than!—against their moral shortcomings. To worship a foreign god is not so much an act of *immorality* as an act of *infidelity* that breaks a relationship of personal trust and mutual commitment between God and his people. The close connection between "righteousness" and "covenant" in the Old Testament is evident. Indeed, so close is the relationship that it might be suggested that for either God or an Israelite "to act righteously" is "to act in accordance with the covenant."

Let us now consider the Old Testament idea of *justification*. It is interesting to note that the abstract noun "justification" is not found in the Old Testament—the verb "to justify" is found instead. It is evident that justification is understood as something active rather than as some abstract idea. "Justifying" is something God *does*. It is something dynamic rather than static. The basic sense of the Old Testament idea of "justifying" is probably best expressed as "declaring to be within the covenant." Throughout the Old Testament we find witness to the divine desire to redeem sinful humanity by initiating actions directed towards this end. God brings individuals into a relationship with himself despite their unfitness. The calling of Israel illustrates this point: God declares that he chose Israel to be his unique and exclusive possession, not on account of her merit or greatness (Deut. 7:7; 9:4–6), but because of his own loving, saving initiative. Then as now, God chose what the world thought weak and foolish. Indeed, if the Old Testament is viewed from the standpoint of God's gracious activity towards sinful humanity, particularly as expressed in the covenant-relationship, the New Testament appears as its perfect fulfillment.

The New Testament bears witness to the belief of the first Christians that believers were "right with God" (perhaps the most helpful translation of the term "justified") because of the death and resurrection of Jesus Christ (see Rom. 3:24–26; 4:24–25; 1 Cor. 1:30; 6:11; 1 Peter 3:18; 1 Tim. 3:16). The conviction that God had dealt justly and properly with human sin—rather than just ignored it or treated it as insignificant—is evident, particularly in the Pauline writings. We could say that the New Testament understands justification to be based upon the objective foundation of the death and resurrection of Jesus Christ.

Occasionally the term "justification" also has a clearly *forensic* dimension in the New Testament, implying the image of a court of law. "Justification" then assumes the meaning "declared to be right, or in the right, before God as judge." The verdict in question is basically about the individual's *status before God*, rather than his or her *moral character or virtues*. The New Testament, particularly the Pauline writings, thus seems to take up the Old Testament concept of righteousness as right relationship, so that "justification" comes to have the root meaning "being in a right relation with God," or "being right with God." The New Testament understanding of justification has thus primarily to do with how human beings enter into a right relation with God—a point that can be brought out by translating the Greek verb *dikaioun*, which is usually rendered "to justify," as "to rectify," stressing the relational aspect.

The New Testament, of course, uses other ideas to develop what is to be understood by being "right with God." Being right with God involves the expiation of sin (Rom. 3:25), being reconciled to God (2 Cor. 5:18–20), being adopted (Rom. 8:15, 23; Gal. 4:5), being transformed (Rom. 12:20; 2 Cor. 3:18), being sacrificed or consecrated (1 Cor. 1:20, 30), and so forth. All these ideas give flesh to the framework established by the basic idea of being right with God. God's gift brings with it transformation—and recent New Testament scholarship has noted how the basic Pauline idea of "the righteousness of God" conveys both the notion of a *gift from God* and *the transforming power of God*.[3]

These insights have gone some way towards allowing us to appreciate the brilliance with which Paul developed the "righteousness" and "justification" language of the Old Testament in order to describe what Jesus Christ has achieved for sinful humanity through his cross and resurrection. Salvation is given to us as a gift, bringing with it the transformation of the individual. God's gracious justification of sinners is offered to all through faith in Jesus Christ, a justification accomplished once and for all through the death and resurrection of Jesus Christ. It is not simply a past or present event but embraces the future: the verdict to be pronounced on the last day is brought forward into the present, in that God declares in advance that those who believe in Jesus Christ are in the right. The believer is justified and may live at peace in Christ (Rom. 5:1), having in effect heard the judgment of God and his justifying word (Rom. 5:1–2; 8:28–37; Gal. 2:15–20).

Perhaps the most significant contribution of Paul to the New Testament understanding of justification by faith concerns the manner in which we are put in the right with God. For Paul, justification takes place by the grace of God, through faith, not through the law (Rom. 3:22–24; Gal. 2:21). Of particular importance in Paul's exposition of this crucial point is the story of Abraham, which he recounts in Galatians 3:1–4:31 and in Romans 4:1–25. For Paul, faith in Christ is a response to the gospel: it comes from hearing the gospel (Rom. 10:17; Gal. 3:2, 8) and results in obedience. Of particular interest, however, is Paul's understanding of the relation of Christian believers to the covenant made by God with Abraham, which we must explore further.

Earlier, we noted the importance of Genesis 15:6 for an understanding of the concept of "the righteousness of faith." Abraham trusted in the promises of God—and by doing so placed himself in a right relationship with God. To be "right with God" is to trust in his gracious promises and to act accordingly. The call of Abraham is a call to enter into a covenant relationship with God (Gen. 15:7–11 is a description of the ritual of covenant-making). The theme of the covenant between God and Abraham and his successors is further developed in Genesis 17, where circumcision is established as the "sign of the covenant" (signifying that the individual stands within the sphere of the redemptive promises of God) and the full extent of the scope of the covenant in time and space is indicated.

In taking up the theme of the calling of Abraham, Paul clearly regards the patriarch as exemplifying the right relationship of the individual to God: faith in the divine promises and faithfulness. But it also seems that Paul sees a far deeper meaning in the call of Abraham—the establishment of the covenant people of God, based on the gracious promises of God and human faith in them. "All people on earth will be blessed through you" (Gen. 12:3). While there will always be elements of "understanding" and "assent" in any Christian definition of faith, the element of "trust" (relationship!) must never be minimized. Faith is understood as a humble, obedient, and trusting response of the individual to the promises of God. Faith is, in its passivity, an active readiness to receive from God. Grace gives and faith receives. Put very simply, faith says "Amen!" to God. And Paul clearly envisages that anyone who stands in this relationship to God stands within the covenant established with Abraham. Justification is by grace through faith—in other words, it is God who graciously gives and we who trustingly receive.

This obviously raises the question of the general relationship between faith and the Old Testament law, as well as the more specific issue of the relationship between faith and works. Paul's polemic against "justification within the law" and "justification by works" appears to be aimed primarily against the Jewish claim that Jews, and Jews alone, may be justified. Paul's emphatic declarations that *all* have sinned and that the "righteousness of God has now been revealed *apart from the law*" (Rom. 3:21–23) are directed against any claim on the part of a Jew to have the exclusive privilege of standing within the covenant with Abraham, to the exclusion of Gentiles. The theme of a "national righteousness," or of the Old Testament law as a charter of Jewish national privilege, is certainly one of the things Paul argues against by his emphatic insistence that *obedience* to the Old Testament law establishes an individual's right to stand within the covenant with Abraham.[4] Romans is of central importance to Paul's argument in that he argues in this letter that being a Jew is neither necessary (Rom. 4:1–25) nor sufficient (9:1–33) for justification. The sole condition, open to all, is faith.

The Old Testament law defines the people of God, those who stand within the covenant made between God and Abraham—and Paul clearly understands that faith in Jesus Christ fulfills the Old Testament law and establishes the believer's claim to stand within that covenant. Thus when Paul speaks of the "law of faith" (Rom. 3:27), he indicates that Christian believers are actually the true people of God, standing within the same covenant defined by the Old Testament law—the covenant made with Abraham. And in Galatians Paul argues forcefully that converted Gentiles have no need to become circumcised, since they already stand within the covenant made with Abraham on account of their faith.

This is not to say, of course, that Paul's doctrine of justification by faith was only relevant when the influence of Judaizers, who wanted Gentile Christian believers to observe the Old Testament law, posed a serious threat to the early church. Every age has its spurious concepts of justification, inadequate or misleading ideas of what we must do if we are to be "right with God." Justification does not take place on the basis of human works, nor does man's justification excuse him from the subsequent performance of good works. The Pauline emphasis upon God's gracious activity and man's trusting passivity in justification transcends the controversies of the Jewish and Gentile Christians and has direct and immediate relevance to our own day and age.

Furthermore, Paul's appeal to the constancy and faithfulness of God to his covenant is of considerable importance. According to Paul, God's justification of humanity through faith demonstrates his faithfulness to the promises once made to Abraham and to the covenant pledged to Abraham, revealed to Moses, and finally sealed with the blood of Christ. The great theme of the saving purposes of God throughout human history is proclaimed by the doctrine of justification by faith. The death and resurrection of Jesus Christ and the mission of the Christian church are not to be seen as a departure from God's original intentions, but rather as their climax and culmination. The covenant made with Abraham is renewed and revitalized through the death and resurrection of Jesus Christ.

There is not enough space here even to sketch the importance of the doctrine of justification by faith in the remainder of the New Testament. There is, however, one passage that has occasionally been held to contradict Paul's doctrine of justification by faith. This is James 2:14–26, which argues that justification is not by faith alone but by works that make it complete. It has frequently been suggested, with excellent support, that James's views are not directed against Paul's doctrine of justification by faith but against a distortion or caricature of it—and indeed, there are points in Paul's letters which seem to indicate that he himself had to contend with just such a distortion (for example, Rom. 3:8; 6:1, 15). "You see that a person is justified by what he does and not by faith alone" (James 2:24) might seem to contradict Paul's vigorous assertion that we "are justified by faith, and not by observing the law" (Rom. 3:28; Gal. 2:16). However, it is obvious that no such contradiction exists or was intended. By "faith," James explicitly means "acceptance of revelation without corresponding behavior" (James 2:19), a dead orthodoxy that bears no relation to Paul's concept of faith. For Paul, faith involves the reorientation of the individual towards obedience to Jesus Christ—note the important phrase "the obedience that comes from faith" (Rom. 1:5) and the assertion that both the *faith* and the *obedience* of the Roman Christians were widely known (1:8; 16:19). Paul and James merely state in different ways, and with different emphases, the basic meaning of the doctrine of justification by faith: we are graciously offered our salvation as a gift, which we receive by faith, and which transforms our natures (Rom. 12:20; 2 Cor. 3:18) so that good works result.

Two famous slogans sum up these important insights. The first dates from the time of the Reformation: "Faith is pregnant with good works." In other words, the gift of faith contains within itself the seeds of our new nature and our new desire for obedience to God, both out of gratitude for what he has done for us and as a result of the changes that are brought about within us through the transformative nature of faith. The second dates from the new interest in Paul, particularly in Pauline ethics, evident in the present century: "Become what you are!" In other words, through justification we are made children of God—and we must learn to act accordingly. Through justification, we are refashioned after the image of God—and we must learn to show this in our lives. The basic idea is that justification involves a declaration of our new status and relationship with God—and we must learn to accept this new status and relationship and refashion our lives and attitudes accordingly. God's gift brings with it obligations, just as it brings with it the ability to meet them.

In this chapter, we have looked briefly at the main themes of the biblical understanding of justification by faith. We have noted the two crucial themes of grace and faith: on the one hand the completely unconditional, loving, and gracious promises of God directed towards us in his actions, beginning with the promises to Abraham and culminating in the death and resurrection of Jesus Christ; and on the other hand the need for us to receive and appropriate these promises, with empty, open, and trusting hands. We have seen the remarkable scope of these themes, embracing the saving purposes of God from the calling of Abraham onwards. In the calling of Abraham, in the calling of the people of Israel, and in the calling of the Christian church—in each of these we find the same two themes developed. We are what we are by the grace of God. God chooses us without respect to our merits (and overlooking our obvious *de*merits!) in order that he may make of us what we ourselves could never achieve (1 Cor. 3:5; 4:7; Phil. 2:13). It is a deeply humbling and inspiring insight—and one that is all too easily forgotten. In the next chapter we shall consider the first major controversy in the church over this theme. Although the Pelagian controversy belongs to the distant past, the same ideas continue to threaten to this day the gospel of justification by grace through faith.

FOR FURTHER READING

E. R. Achtemeier. "Righteousness in the Old Testament." In *Interpreter's Dictionary of the Bible*. Nashville: Abingdon, 1962. 4:80–85.

C. Brown et al. "Righteousness, Justification." In *New International Dictionary of New Testament Theology*. Grand Rapids: Zondervan, 1976. 3:352–76. It has an excellent bibliography.

E. Käsemann. "The 'Righteousness of God' in Paul." In *New Testament Questions of Today*. Philadelphia: Fortress, 1969. 168–82.

_____ . *Commentary on Romans*. Grand Rapids: Eerdmans, 1980.

B. Przybylski. *Righteousness in Matthew and His World of Thought*. Cambridge: Cambridge University Press, 1980.

J. Reumann. *Righteousness in the New Testament*. Grand Rapids: Eerdmans, 1983.

K. Stendahl. "The Apostle Paul and the Introspective Conscience of the West." In *Paul among Jews and Gentiles*. Philadelphia: Fortress, 1976. 78–96.

J. A. Ziesler. *The Meaning of Righteousness in Paul*. Cambridge: Cambridge University Press, 1972.

3

Augustine and the
Pelagian Controversy

In September 386, a clever young North African teacher of rhetoric had an experience that was to prove to be of momentous importance for the future development of Christianity in the Western world. Attracted to the Christian faith by the preaching of Bishop Ambrose of Milan, Augustine underwent a dramatic conversion experience. Having reached the age of thirty-two without satisfying his burning wish to know the truth, Augustine was agonizing over the great questions of human nature and destiny when he thought he heard some children nearby singing *Tolle, lege* ("take up and read"). Feeling that this was divine guidance, he took the book nearest to hand—Paul's letter to the Romans, as it happened—and read the fateful words "clothe yourselves with the Lord Jesus Christ" (Rom. 13:14). This was the final straw for Augustine, whose paganism had become increasingly difficult to maintain. As he later recalled, "A light of certainty entered my heart, and every shadow of doubt vanished."[1] From that moment on, Augustine dedicated his enormous intellectual abilities to the defense and consolidation of the Christian faith, writing with a style that was both passionate and intelligent, appealing to both heart and mind.

Augustine left Italy to return to North Africa and was made bishop of Hippo (in modern Algeria) in 395. The remaining thirty-five years of his life witnessed numerous controversies of major importance to the future of the Christian church in the West, and Augustine's contribution to the resolution of each of these was decisive. His careful exposition of the New Testament, particularly of the Pauline letters, gained him a reputation, which continues today, as the "second founder of the Christian faith" (Jerome). The first four centuries of the Christian era had seen intensive discussion of the identity of Jesus Christ and the nature of God, while the doctrine of justification had remained largely unexplored.[2] The onset of the Pelagian controversy in the early fifth century forced urgent consideration of this question—and Augustine's carefully weighed statements on the relationship between nature and grace and on the human and divine roles in justification have come to be regarded as perhaps the most authentic and reliable exposition of the biblical insights on these questions. In this chapter we will consider the issues at stake in this important controversy and the shape of Augustine's highly influential doctrine of justification.

As with any historic theological debate, it is important to distinguish between the actual course of the debate and the issues involved. While the former is of interest primarily to the historian, the latter are of continuing relevance to the Christian church. The historical course of the Pelagian controversy centers on Pelagius, a British (probably Scottish) layman living in Rome in the early fifth century, who was distressed by the questionable moral character of some Roman Christians.[3] By this time Augustine had already developed an understanding of justification that was much closer to the Pauline concept than that of Augustine's predecessors; he laid considerable emphasis on the human inability to achieve justification and the need for divine grace. Augustine's consciousness of his total dependence on divine grace seemed outrageous to Pelagius, because it appeared to deny human responsibility and the need for human exertion to become holy. It is certainly true that some Christians at the time regarded Christianity as a convenient way of obtaining salvation in the next world without undue effort in this one! In order to give his campaign for moral reform a theological basis, however, Pelagius developed a theology of justification that is generally regarded as at least compromising, and almost certainly contradicting, the crucial insights of the doctrine of justification by faith.

We shall summarize the main points of the controversy under four headings: (1) the understanding of the "freedom of the will," (2) the understanding of sin, (3) the understanding of grace, and (4) the understanding of the grounds of justification.

1. The Understanding of the "Freedom of the Will"

For Augustine, both the total sovereignty of God and genuine human responsibility and freedom must be upheld at one and the same time if justice is to be done to the richness and complexity of the biblical statements on the matter. To simplify the issue, denying either the sovereignty of God or human freedom is to seriously compromise the Christian understanding of the way in which God justifies man. Augustine in his own lifetime was obliged to deal with two heresies that simplified and compromised the gospel in this way. *Manichaeanism* (to which Augustine himself was initially attracted) was a form of fatalism that upheld the total sovereignty of God but denied human freedom, while *Pelagianism* upheld the total freedom of the human but denied the sovereignty of God. Before developing these points, it is necessary to make some observations concerning the term "free will."

The term "free will" (which is a translation of the Latin *liberum arbitrium*) is not a biblical term but derives from Stoicism. It was introduced into

Western Christianity by the second-century theologian Tertullian, who borrowed this Latin term to translate the Greek word *autexousia*, which meant something rather different: "responsibility for one's own actions" is probably the most helpful translation. What Augustine had to do, therefore, was to keep the term "free will" (which during the two centuries since Tertullian had become so well established that its elimination was impossible) but to try and bring its meaning back into line with teaching of the New Testament, especially that of Paul.

Augustine says that the term *liberum arbitrium*, if it *must* be used, is not to be understood as meaning that human beings have complete freedom in every area of their existence. The basic elements of Augustine's teaching are the following:

1. We are responsible for our own actions, even after the Fall (notice how this goes back to the real meaning of the Greek word *autexousia*, which Tertullian translated in such a poor way).

2. We are not puppets trapped in a web of fate, but we have real freedom of action in a number of spheres of our lives. It must be remembered that Augustine's opponents included the Manichaeans, who had a strongly fatalistic or deterministic outlook on life—everything happens through fate, and the individual has no control over things. Augustine insists that human beings have a real, if limited, freedom of choice.

3. This freedom is, however, compromised by sin, which biases our judgment to the extent that we are unable to break free from it. Like Paul, Augustine often regards sin as a power that needs to be broken—and sees the grace of God as the only way in which we can be liberated from its baleful influence.

Augustine developed a helpful analogy to explain the relationship between free will and sin. Consider a pair of scales, with two balance pans. One balance pan represents good and the other evil. If the pans are properly balanced, the arguments in favor of doing good or doing evil could be weighed and a proper conclusion drawn. The parallel with the human free will is obvious: we weigh up the arguments in favor of doing good and evil, and act accordingly. But what, asks Augustine, if the balance pans are loaded? What happens if someone puts several heavy weights in the balance pan on the side of evil? The scales will still work, but they are seriously biased towards making an evil decision. Augustine argues that this is exactly what has happened to humanity through sin. The human free will is biased towards evil. It really exists, and really can make decisions—just as the loaded scales still work. But instead of giving a balanced judgment, a serious bias exists towards evil.

Of course, critics of Augustine's theology of grace have pointed out that there are several logical flaws in his scheme. Augustine, however, was not concerned with logical rigor—his prime concern was to do justice on the one hand to the clear teaching of the New Testament concerning human bondage to sin and, on the other, to the human experience of being trapped by evil. While Pelagianism was admirably logical and consistent, it bore little relation to the teaching of the New Testament or to human experience. For Augustine, theology was not a matter of logical explanation; rather, it was about wrestling with the mystery of the nature and character of God—something that defies the neat categories of human logic and cannot be allowed to be subordinated to it.

Augustine thus argues that the human free will really exists in sinners, but that it is compromised by sin. Indeed, the human free will is so seriously compromised by sin that it is incapable of wanting to come to God. How then, he asks, can we ever come to God? And so Augustine develops the crucial insight that the grace of God is both necessary and sufficient to overcome the negative influence of sin. Two main images are used to explain how this happens.

First, grace is understood as the *liberator* of human nature. Augustine uses the term "the captive free will" (*liberum arbitrium captivatum*) to describe the free will that is so heavily influenced by sin and argues that grace is able to liberate the human free will from this bias and make it the "liberated free will" (*liberum arbitrium liberatum*). As we suggested above, sin is seen as a hostile power within us, which is fought and gradually overwhelmed by grace. To go back to the scales analogy, grace removes the weights loading the scales towards evil and allows us to recognize the full weight of the case for choosing God. Thus Augustine is able to argue that grace, far from abolishing or compromising the human free will, actually establishes it!

Second, grace is understood as the *healer* of human nature. One of Augustine's favorite analogies for the church is that of a hospital full of sick people. Christians are those who recognize that they are ill and seek the assistance of a physician, in order that they may be healed. Thus Augustine appeals to the parable of the Good Samaritan (Luke 10:30–34) and suggests that human nature is like the man who was left for dead by the roadside, until he was rescued and healed by the Samaritan (who represents Christ as redeemer, according to Augustine). On the basis of illustrations such as these, Augustine argues that the human free will is unhealthy and needs healing. Again, grace is understood as establishing, rather than destroying, human free will, as the obstacles that prevent the free will from functioning properly are removed. Our eyes are blind and cannot see God—grace heals them in order that we may see him. Our ears are deaf to the gracious calling of the Lord—until grace heals them.

One of the more persuasive features of Augustine's account of the influence of sin upon the human free will is its faithfulness to our experience. All of us have experienced being torn between *knowing* that something is good and *not being willing* to do it. It is this tension that Paul recognizes: "What I do is not the good I want to do; no, the evil I do not want to do—this is what I keep on doing!" (Rom. 7:19). Augustine's own prayer before his conversion also reveals this tension: "Give me chastity and continence—but not yet!" This inbuilt human tendency to want to do what is wrong—with such profound theological consequences!—is well summarized in the story about a visitor to a European monastery. This visitor was shown to his room and told that he could do anything he liked—provided he didn't look out of one of the windows. Unable to control his curiosity, he eventually gave in to the desire to find out what was so wrong about looking out of this window—and was horrified to find all the monks there, waiting for him! "They always look out!" was their final word. This little story illustrates the profound tension arising from a divided human will, which defies the neat classification of the Pelagian system. In fact, many Pelagian writers recognized that individuals are easily trapped by evil—and found this very difficult to reconcile with their dogmatic assumption of the total autonomy and freedom of human beings.

For Augustine, then, sin traps humanity within the sphere of nature. It allows us freedom within this sphere of activity—but it prevents us from breaking free from this sphere to encounter and respond to the living God. Through grace, God enables us to break free from the limitations of our natural condition and to recognize and respond to his gracious call. For Augustine, we are blind to God and our eyes must be opened by grace; we are deaf to his word, and our ears must be opened in the same way.

According to Pelagius and his followers, however, humanity possesses total freedom of the will and is totally responsible for its own sins. Human nature is essentially free and not compromised or incapacitated by some mysterious weakness. According to Pelagius, any imperfection in man would reflect negatively upon the goodness of God. For God to intervene in any direct way to influence human decisions is equivalent to compromising human integrity. Going back to the analogy of the scales, the Pelagians argued that the human free will is like a pair of balance pans in perfect equilibrium, not subject to any bias whatsoever. There is no need for divine grace in the sense understood by Augustine (although Pelagius did have a quite distinct concept of grace, as we shall see later). In many ways, Pelagius resembles the subject of William Ernest Henley's poem "Invictus," a favorite with the Victorians:

> It matters not how strait the gate,
> How charged with punishment the scroll,
> I am the master of my fate:
> I am the captain of my soul!

In 413 Pelagius wrote a lengthy letter to Demetrias, a woman who had just decided to turn her back on wealth in order to become a nun. In this letter, Pelagius spelled out with remorseless logic the consequences of his views on human free will. God has made humanity and knows precisely what it is capable of doing. Hence all the commands given to us are capable of being obeyed and are meant to be obeyed. It is no excuse to argue that human frailty prevents them from being fulfilled—God has made human nature and only demands of it what he knows it can achieve. Human perfection is possible, and Pelagius thus makes the uncompromising assertion that "since perfection is possible for humanity, it is obligatory." The moral rigorism of this position, and its unrealistic understanding of human nature, served only to strengthen Augustine's hand as he developed the rival view of a tender and kindly God attempting to heal and restore wounded human nature.

2. The Understanding of Sin

For Augustine, humanity is universally affected by sin as a consequence of the Fall. The human mind has become darkened and weakened by sin and is unable to recognize God for what he is or to discern his glory. Sin makes it impossible for the sinner to think clearly, and especially to understand higher spiritual truths and ideas. Similarly, as we have seen, the human will has been weakened (but not eliminated) by sin. For Augustine, the simple fact that we are sinners means that we are in the position of being seriously ill and unable to diagnose our own illness adequately—let alone cure it. It is through the grace of God alone that our illness (sin) is diagnosed and a cure (grace) made available.

The essential point Augustine makes is that we have no control over our sinfulness. It is something that contaminates our lives from birth and dominates our lives thereafter. We could say that Augustine sees human nature as having an inborn sinful disposition with an inherent bias towards acts of sinning. In other words, sin causes sins: the *state* of sinfulness causes *individual acts* of sin. Augustine develops this point with the help of three important analogies.

The first analogy treats sin as a *hereditary disease*, which is passed down from one generation to another. As we saw above, this disease weakens humanity and cannot be cured by human agency. Christ is thus the divine physician by whose "wounds we are healed" (Isa. 53:5), and salvation is understood in essentially sanative or medical terms. We are healed by the grace of God, so that our minds may recognize God and our wills may respond to him.

The second analogy treats sin as a *power* that holds us captive and from whose grip we are unable to break free by ourselves. The human free will is captivated by the power of sin and can only be liberated by grace. Christ is thus seen as the liberator, the source of the grace that breaks the power of sin.

The third analogy treats sin as essentially a judicial or forensic concept: *guilt*, which is passed down from one generation to another. This was a particularly helpful way of understanding sin in a society that placed a high value on law such as the later Roman Empire in which Augustine lived and worked. Christ thus comes to bring forgiveness and pardon.

These analogies of sin have, of course, been taken up and developed since Augustine. For example, consider the following lines in A. M. Toplady's famous hymn "Rock of Ages":

> Let the water and the blood,
> From thy riven side which flowed,
> Be of sin the double cure,
> Cleanse me from its guilt and power.

The "double cure" of sin refers to the need for sin to be forgiven and its power to be broken (note the appeal to the death of Christ as the source of this cure). Or consider the famous hymn by Charles Wesley, "O for a Thousand Tongues to Sing," which has the following profound verse:

> He breaks the power of cancelled sin,
>   He sets the prisoner free
> His blood can make the foulest clean;
>   His blood availed for me.

The reference to breaking the power of "cancelled sin" is particularly important, since it incorporates the idea of liberation and forgiveness: "cancelled sin" is basically *forgiven* sin.

Pelagius, however, understood sin very differently. The idea of a human disposition towards sin has no place in Pelagius' thought. For Pelagius, the human capacity for self-improvement could not be thought of as being compromised. It is always possible for an individual to discharge his obligations towards God and his neighbors, and failure to do so cannot be excused on any grounds. Sin is to be understood as an act committed wilfully against God. Pelagianism thus appears as a rigid form of moral authoritarianism—an insistence that humanity is under obligation to be sinless and an absolute rejection of any excuse for failure. Humanity is born sinless, and people only sin through deliberate actions (Pelagius insisted that many Old Testament figures actually remained sinless). Only those who were morally upright could, according to Pelagius, be allowed to enter the church—whereas Augustine, with his concept of fallen human nature, was happy to regard the church as a hospital where fallen humanity could recover and grow gradually in holiness through grace.

3. The Understanding of Grace

One of Augustine's favorite biblical texts is John 15:5, "Apart from me you can do nothing." He sees us as totally dependent upon God for our salvation, from the beginning to the end of our lives. Augustine draws a careful distinction between the *natural human faculties*—given to humanity as its natural endowment—and *additional and special gifts of grace*. God does not leave us where we are by nature, incapacitated by sin and unable to redeem ourselves, but he gives us his grace in order that we may be healed, forgiven, and restored. Augustine's view of human nature is that it is frail, weak, and lost, and needs divine assistance and care if it is to be restored and renewed. Grace, according to Augustine, is God's generous and quite unmerited attention to humanity by which this process of healing may begin. Human nature requires transformation through the grace of God, so generously given.

Pelagius uses the term "grace" in two different ways. First, grace is to be understood as the *natural human faculties*. For Pelagius, these are not corrupted or incapacitated or compromised in any way. They have been given to humanity by God, and they are meant to be used. When Pelagius asserts that humanity can, through grace, choose to be sinless, what he means is that the natural human faculties of reason and will should enable humanity to choose to avoid sin. As Augustine was quick to point out, of course, this is not what the New Testament understands by the term!

Second, Pelagius understands grace to be *external enlightenment* provided for humanity by God. Pelagius gives several examples of such enlightenment—for instance, the Ten Commandments and the moral example of Jesus Christ. Grace informs us what our moral duties are (otherwise, we would not know what they were), but it does not assist us in the performance of these duties. We are enabled to avoid sin through the teaching and example of Christ. But, as Augustine was quick to point out, "this locates the grace of God in the law and in teaching"—whereas what the New Testament envisages is grace as divine assistance to humanity, rather than just some sort of moral advice. For Pelagius, grace is *external and passive*, something outside us, whereas Augustine understands grace as the real and redeeming presence of God in Christ within us, transforming us—something *internal and active*.

According to Pelagius, then, God created humanity and provided information concerning what is right and what is wrong—and then ceased to take any interest in humanity, apart from the final day of judgment. On that day, individuals will be judged according to whether they have fulfilled *all* their moral obligations. Failure to have done so leads to eternal punishment—and Pelagius' exhortations to moral perfection are characterized by their emphasis upon the dreadful fate of those who fail in this matter. For Augustine, however, humanity was created good by God and then fell away from him—but God, in his grace, came (and comes) to rescue fallen humanity from its predicament. God assists us by healing us, enlightening us, strengthening us, and continually working within us in order to bring us back to him. For Pelagius, humanity merely needs to be shown what to do and can then be left to achieve it unaided; for Augustine, humanity needs to be shown what to do and then must be gently aided at every point if this objective is even to be approached, let alone fulfilled.

4. The Grounds of Justification

For Augustine, humanity is justified as an act of grace: even human good works are the result of God's working within fallen human nature. Everything leading up to salvation is the free and unmerited gift of God, given out of love for his people. All too often Augustine's views on grace are regarded as threatening—whereas they are in fact deeply reassuring! Weak and feeble though we are, and prone to sin, God is at work within us, achieving something we ourselves could never do. Through the death and resurrection of Jesus Christ, God is enabled to deal with fallen humanity in this remarkable and generous manner, giving us what we do not deserve (salvation), and withholding from us what we do deserve (condemnation).

Augustine's exposition of the parable of the laborers in the vineyard (Matt. 20:1–10) is of considerable importance in this respect. As we shall see, Pelagius argued that God rewards each individual strictly on the basis of merit, of the *work* which that individual has performed. Augustine, however, points out that this parable indicates that the basis of the reward given to the individual is the *promise made to* that individual. Augustine emphasizes that the laborers did not work for equal periods in the vineyard, yet the same wage (a denarius) was given to all. The owner of the vineyard had promised to pay each individual a denarius, provided that he worked from the time when he was called till sundown—even though this meant that some worked all day and others only for an hour. And so Augustine draws the important conclusion that the basis of our justification is the divine promise of grace made to us. God is faithful to his promises, and justifies sinners. Just as the laborers who began work in the vineyard late in the day had no claim to a full day's wages, except through the generous promise of the owner, so sinners have no claim to justification and eternal life, except through the gracious promises of God, received through faith.

For Pelagius, however, humanity is justified on the basis of its merits: human good works are the result of the exercise of the totally autonomous human free will, in fulfillment of an obligation laid down by God. A failure to meet this obligation opens the individual to the threat of eternal punishment. If an individual is to be justified, he must meet the full rigor of the demands God makes of him. Jesus Christ is involved in salvation only to the extent that he reveals, by his actions and teaching, exactly what God requires of the individual. If Pelagius can speak of "salvation in Christ" it is only in the sense of "salvation through imitating the example of Christ."

In comparing Augustine and Pelagius on these four points, the totally different perspectives of their understandings of the way in which God redeems humanity are obvious. Through the centuries, the church has always regarded Augustine as by far the more reliable exponent of Paul—which explains why Augustine is often referred to as "the doctor of grace" (*doctor gratiae*). Augustine's gospel is that of a gracious God passionately concerned for the salvation of sinful humanity. Pelagius' gospel initially seems to be sweet reasonableness itself but on closer inspection turns out to be a fanatical moral rigorism. Yet Pelagius' ideas are revived in every age of the church. Perhaps the most celebrated of these revivals is generally thought to have been the occasion for the movement that is the subject of the next chapter—the Reformation.

FOR FURTHER READING

For basic material, see:

Alister E. McGrath. *Iustitia Dei: A History of the Christian Doctrine of Justification*. 2 vols. Cambridge: Cambridge University Press, 1986. 1:17–36, 51–54, 71–75.

On Augustine, see further:

Gerald Bonner. *St. Augustine of Hippo: Life and Controversies*. Philadelphia: Westminster, 1963.

Peter Brown. *Augustine of Hippo: A Biography*. Berkeley: University of California Press, 1967.

On Pelagius, see further:

Robert F. Evans. *Pelagius: Inquiries and Reapprisals*. New York: Seabury, 1968.

The Reformation

A lthough there was extensive discussion of the doctrine of justification during the Middle Ages, it is generally recognized that the doctrine proved to be of conclusive importance in the Reformation debates of the sixteenth century.[1] The present chapter will deal with the main contributions of those debates to our understanding of the doctrine. First, we must consider the views on justification that were in circulation in the Middle Ages.

Augustine died in 430, shortly before the barbarians invaded his city of Hippo in North Africa. Although they destroyed the city, they preserved Augustine's writings. It was almost as if they sensed that Western Christianity would need to rely upon his words as the ancient world died away and the Dark Ages were born. When the clouds of the Dark Ages began to lift from Europe in the eleventh century, it was to the writings of Augustine that medieval theologians turned for guidance and inspiration. The result was that all medieval theologians were influenced to a greater or lesser degree by Augustine, and all medieval theology may be thought of as "Augustinian" to at least some extent. However, as the fourteenth and fifteenth centuries dawned, it became increasingly clear that some of these medieval interpretations of Augustine were open to question.

By the late medieval period, all sorts of questionable popular practices had developed that reflected a lack of theological clarity. It was widely held that salvation was something that could be earned by good works, which included fulfilling the moral law and observing a vast range of ecclesiastical rules. The sale of indulgences—which so outraged Luther—shows that it was widely thought possible to avoid purgatory by paying the appropriate amount of money. The famous words of the indulgence dealer Johannes Tetzel sum up this attitude:

> As soon as the coin in the coffer rings
> The soul from purgatory springs!

For a substantial sum of money, it was possible for an individual to buy forgiveness for every sin committed in a lifetime and thus guarantee a direct entry into heaven. And so forgiveness of sins was treated as a marketable commodity. Although Augustine may have continued to influence at least some academic theologians, popular Pelagianism was rampant. For this reason, the Reformers recognized that it was necessary to rediscover both the academic and the pastoral elements of the doctrine of justification by faith— and the reform program associated with Martin Luther represents an attempt to do precisely this.

To begin with, we must understand that the late medieval church was seriously confused over the doctrine of justification. There was a bewildering variety of answers to the crucial question that was being asked by so many at the dawn of the sixteenth century: "What must I do to be saved?" Indeed, there was such confusion that the question simply could not be answered with any degree of confidence, as is reflected in Luther's early struggle with the problem of how he could find a gracious God.

To fully appreciate Luther, we need to understand his theological background. All of us know how "schools of thought" get established. Someone presents some exciting new ideas, and a group of followers builds up around him and develops his teachings. This happens in almost every area of human thought. Think of the influence of Sigmund Freud in the field of psychoanalysis, for example. A famous example in the area of theology is the development of Liberal Protestantism in Germany in the nineteenth century, based on the ideas of F. D. E. Schleiermacher and Albrecht Ritschl. But every now and then a thinker arises *within* an established school of thought who initially accepts its ideas and then comes to find them unacceptable. A good example from the present century is the great Swiss theologian Karl Barth. Initially Barth stood within the Liberal Protestant school—but on rethinking his ideas in the light of both Paul's letter to the Romans and the First World War, he recognized that Liberal Protestantism was based on a totally inadequate view of God and of humanity. And so the "rediscovery of God"— which has had enormous influence on twentieth-century theology—began.

The latter is what took place in the case of Martin Luther, in the early sixteenth century. The theological school that became dominant in many northern European universities in the late fifteenth and early sixteenth centuries was the *via moderna* ("the modern way"), also known as "nominalism."[2] This school came to exercise considerable influence over many leading theologians of the late medieval period, including the young Luther, who studied at the University of Erfurt before entering the Augustinian monastery in the same town in 1505. Both university and monastery were dominated by the *via moderna*, and all the evidence available indicates that Luther followed the teaching of this school until the 1510s. After a period of study, teaching, and traveling, Luther became professor of biblical studies at the University of Wittenberg in 1512, where he delivered lectures on the Psalms (1513–15), Romans (1515–16), Galatians (1516–17), and Hebrews (1517–18). At some point during these lectures, Luther broke free from the theology of justification of the *via moderna* and forged his own reforming theology based on his new understanding of the doctrine of justification.

In view of the historical importance of the development of Luther's doctrine of justification, this chapter focuses on the two most common questions concerning Luther's breakthrough. First, what were Luther's original views on justification and in what way did they change? Second, when did this change take place?

Luther's early views on justification (up to about 1514) can be summarized as follows. God has entered into a covenant or contract (the Latin word *pactum* is used to express this idea) with humanity. This contract lays down certain conditions that must be met before it is possible to be justified.[3] God has promised that he will justify anyone who meets the precondition that the individual turn to God in faith and humility. Both faith and humility are human works, which the individual may achieve without the assistance of divine grace. Once this precondition has been met, God is under a self-imposed obligation (because of his promise) to justify the individual in question. God is gracious towards humanity in that he has established a framework within which an individual may be justified through a minimum effort. Nevertheless, a definite and specific human effort is required.

This brings us to the concept of the "righteousness of God," of such central importance to Luther's development. At this early stage, Luther understood the "righteousness of God" (*iustitia Dei*) to refer to an impersonal attribute of God, which stands over and against us and judges us with complete impartiality on the basis of whether or not we have met the basic precondition for justification. If we have, God's verdict is justification; if we have not, the verdict is condemnation. God is completely fair in his dealings with humanity: whoever meets the basic precondition of faith and humility has a right to demand justification on the basis of the divine promise to justify anyone who fulfills the precondition. The same demand is made under both the Old and New Testaments. For the theologians of the *via moderna*, it was unthinkable that God should give the sinner any special assistance in this matter—to do so would amount to favoritism. The same condition had to be met by everyone, without any divine aid. To Luther, and to many others at the time, this seemed remarkably like Pelagianism—the assertion that an individual could justify himself without divine grace. Indeed, one important work written in the fourteenth century against this theology of justification was entitled *The Cause of God against the Modern Pelagians*.

But what happens if it is impossible to meet this precondition through one's own efforts? The young Luther was intensely aware of his own sinfulness, and as time progressed became increasingly uncertain whether he could meet these demands. The demand for faith—which seemed so simple and easy—proved to be more than he thought he could fulfill and drove the young Luther to near-despair. The central question that burdened him was this: "How can I find a gracious God" (*Wie kriege ich einen gnädigen Gott?*). For Luther, the twin conditions of faith and humility made justification impossible: it was as if God promised a blind man a million dollars, provided that man could see, or as if someone who could not speak was promised the contents of Fort Knox if he recited aloud the works of Shakespeare. The promise was real enough—but the conditions laid down made it impossible that it could ever be fulfilled. Luther became increasingly persuaded that an individual needed the assistance of the grace of God if justification was to be a real possibility.

Luther reflected constantly on Romans 1:17: "In the gospel a righteousness of God is revealed," but he could not see how the revelation of the "righteousness of God" was gospel, "good news." And then at some point— we are not exactly sure when—he seems to have had a breakthrough. Fortunately, we have his own account of what happened. In the final year of his life, Luther published a brief account of his theological reflections as a young man.[4] Luther recalls that he was taught to interpret the "righteousness of God" as that righteousness by which God himself is righteous and punishes sinners, so that the revelation of the "righteousness of God" in the gospel was nothing other than the revelation of the wrath of God directed against sinners. How could this be good news for *sinners?* Luther continues:

> At last, by the mercy of God, meditating day and night, I gave heed to the context of the words, namely "In it the righteousness of God is revealed," as it is written, "He who through faith is righteous shall live." There I began to understand that the righteousness of God is that by which the righteous lives by a gift of God, namely by faith. And this is the meaning: the righteousness of God is revealed by the gospel, namely the passive righteousness with which merciful God justifies us by faith, as it is written, "He who through faith is righteous shall live." Here I felt that I was altogether born again and had entered paradise through open gates.

This passage vibrates with the excitement of discovery as Luther relates how he came to realize that the righteousness of God that is revealed in the gospel is *a gift of God given to sinners.* The God who is revealed in the gospel is not a harsh judge who judges us on the basis of our merits, but a merciful and gracious God who gives his children something they could never attain by their own unaided efforts.

What, then, did Luther come to understand by the "righteousness of God"? In a series of images, Luther builds up a picture of a righteousness, given to us by God, which remains outside us. Just as a mother hen covers her chicks with her wing, so God clothes us with an "alien righteousness." It is something that is given to us, something that we ourselves could never obtain. We stand as justified sinners before God, clothed with a righteousness that is not our own but is given to us by God himself. Our righteous standing with God, the fact that we are "right with God" through the faith he gives us, is ultimately due to the overwhelming grace of God rather than to our efforts to make ourselves righteous in his sight. The great theme of "justification by faith alone," so characteristic of Luther, extols the graciousness and generosity of God as much as it affirms the impotence of sinful humanity to justify itself. We are passive, and God is active, in our justification. Grace gives, and faith gratefully receives—and even that faith must itself be seen as a gracious gift of God. "Justification by faith" affirms that it is *God* who justifies us in an act of grace, by means of a gift which he himself gives us—faith. To suggest that Luther teaches that we are justified by a human work (faith) is to miss the entire point of his doctrine of justification. Even the faith through which we are justified is a gift of God!

Luther develops this understanding of the "righteousness of God" in terms of a "wonderful exchange" between Christ and the believer. Using the analogy of a human marriage, Luther argues that Christ and the believer are united through faith: Christ bestows his righteousness upon the believer, and the believer's sin is transferred to Christ. Luther thus speaks of "a grasping faith" (*fides apprehensiva*), a faith that grasps Christ and unites him to the individual believer, in order that this wonderful exchange of attributes may take place. Luther insists that justification involves a change in an individual's *status* before God, rather than a fundamental change in his *nature*: although the individual believer is righteous by faith, he remains a sinner. It is this insight that underlies Luther's famous assertion that the believer is "righteous and a sinner at one and the same time" (*simul iustus et peccator*).

In many ways, the Reformation may be regarded as a rediscovery of the Pauline writings, and especially of the doctrine of justification by grace through faith. Although the Reformation insights into justification are often summarized in the slogan "justification *sola fide*" (by faith alone), they are probably better represented in the slogan "justification *per fidem propter Christum*" (through faith on account of Christ). For the Reformers, our justification does not rest on anything we ourselves do, but rather on the work of Christ—we are justified when we receive this passively, through faith. Faith is the earthen vessel that conveys the treasure of Christ, as Calvin put it. God is active and we are passive in justification. Even the faith through which we believe and receive Christ is a work of God.

This point is of importance in connection with one of the leading features of Protestant spirituality—the concept of *assurance*. For Luther and Calvin alike, the question of how the believer can rest assured that he is justified was of central importance. The living of the Christian life, with all the ethical and spiritual consequences this entails, is dependent on the knowledge that this Christian life *really has been begun*. The believer is able to rest secure in the knowledge that he *has* been justified because justification does not depend on him in any way. It is God who establishes the basis of the Christian life, and the believer may build on this as he explores the ethical, political, and spiritual consequences of his new life in Christ. In short, the doctrine of justification by faith is a *security doctrine* for the Reformers—and the concept of forensic justification was seen as establishing the foundation of the Christian life far more reliably than the Augustinian concept of justification by infused, imparted, or inherent righteousness.

A popular misunderstanding of the Reformation doctrine of justification by faith is that we are justified *because we believe*, that it is our decision to believe that brings about our justification. Here faith is understood as a human work, something which we do—and so we are justified on the basis of our works! This is actually the later doctrine, especially associated with seventeenth-century Arminianism, of "justification *propter fidem per Christum*," justification on account of faith through Christ (rather than "justification *per fidem propter Christum*," justification by faith on account of Christ). The Reformation doctrine affirms the activity of God and the passivity of humanity in justification. Faith is not something human we do, but something divine that is wrought within us. "Faith is the principal work of the Holy Spirit" (Calvin), and it is through faith that Christ and all his benefits are received. Calvin summarizes these benefits as "being reconciled to God through Christ's sinlessness" and "being sanctified by the spirit of Christ."

Perhaps one of the most famous passages in which this recognition is described was written by John Wesley in his journal entry for 24 May 1738. After a long period of wrestling with the question how he could ever come to a living faith in God, he describes how the realization that faith is something God gives to us, rather than something we must achieve, changed his outlook on existence:

> In the evening I went very unwillingly to a society in Aldersgate Street, where one was reading Luther's preface to the Epistle to the Romans. About a quarter before nine, while he was describing the change which God works in the heart through faith in Christ, I felt my heart strangely warmed. I felt that I did trust in Christ, Christ alone for salvation, and an assurance was given me that he had taken away my sins, even mine, and saved me from the law of sin and death.[5]

Luther's total emphasis on the gift-character of salvation led him to call into question any theology that failed to do justice to this aspect of the gospel. Initially, Luther seems to have directed his criticisms chiefly against the theological school to which he once belonged, the *via moderna*—but his conviction that it was not just this theological school but the entire church of his day that had fallen into the Pelagian heresy led him to mount a campaign for doctrinal reform that would prove to be unstoppable. The central theme of the Reformation—affirmed in slogans such as *sola gratia, sola fide*, and *soli Christo*—was the graciousness of God. For Luther, to compromise the gospel of the grace of God was to destroy the central element of Christianity. It is for this reason that Luther's views have been summarized by designating the doctrine of justification by faith as "the article by which the church stands or falls." In the Schmalkald Articles of 1535, Luther wrote thus of the doctrine of justification: "Nothing in this article may be given up or compromised.... On this article rests all that we teach and practice against the pope, the devil, and the world." By compromising this central element of the gospel, the church had lost the right to call itself "the church of God"—and thus Luther felt justified in breaking away from this "church" in order to restore to it its theological basis. Thus it is important to notice that Luther did not criticize the church of his day on the basis of a direct *ecclesiological* argument (in other words, an argument about the nature of the church), but on the basis of his conviction that the church, by compromising the gospel of free grace, had fallen into the Pelagian heresy.

This conviction led to the German Reformation. Initially, it was restricted to the theology faculty at the University of Wittenberg, but by the 1520s it was enjoying considerable popular support. However, Luther was no systematic theologian; he preferred to write in response to particular needs, rather than writing theological textbooks, and the task of consolidating his doctrine of justification was left to others, most notably Philip Melanchthon, who was responsible for drawing up the famous Augsburg Confession of 1530. It seems that Luther's doctrine of justification was modified somewhat by his followers, such as Melanchthon,[6] and one aspect of this development needs to be noted carefully.

Earlier we noted Luther's idea of the "alien righteousness of Christ:" the righteousness we gain in justification is not part of our being but is something that is and remains external to us. Charles Wesley's famous lines express this idea well:

No condemnation now I dread:
Jesus, and all in Him, is mine!
Alive in him, my living head,
And clothed in righteousness divine.

Luther's understanding of "righteousness" as external to us led him to criticize Augustine, who understood the righteousness in question to be part of our being. Luther and Augustine agreed that the righteousness through which we are justified is given to us by God and not something which we ourselves can acquire—but they did not agree on the *nature* of that righteousness. For Augustine, justifying righteousness is an *internal* righteousness, something God works *within* us; for Luther, it is *external*, something God works *outside* us. And it is the development of this idea of an "external" or "alien righteousness" that led to the establishment of the characteristically Protestant idea of *forensic justification*. We shall consider this idea, as developed by Melanchthon and John Calvin.

Melanchthon gives the following definition of justification: "To be justified does not mean that an ungodly man is made righteous, but that he is *pronounced righteous in a forensic manner*." Augustine had interpreted the Latin verb *iustificare* ("to justify") as *iustum facere* ("to make righteous"), but Melanchthon eliminates this idea: justification is about being *declared or pronounced righteous*, not being *made righteous*. Similarly, Calvin defines justification as "the remission of sins and the imputation of the righteousness of Christ." A distinction is made between *justification* and *sanctification* (or *regeneration*): the former is the work of God outside us, the latter his work within us. In effect, Melanchthon and Calvin distinguish two aspects of the process that both Augustine and the young Luther had treated as a single unit. Thus Augustine taught that justification embraces all of Christian existence, including both the *event* of being treated as righteous and the *process* of becoming righteous. For Melanchthon and Calvin, however, the event (justification) and the process (sanctification) could be and should be distinguished. The forgiveness of sins and the renewing gift of the Holy Spirit are to be treated as logically distinct.

Why should this distinction have been introduced and what is its significance?[7] To understand this, we need to consider the doctrines of justification associated with Zwingli and Bucer, two early Reformed theologians who rose to prominence before John Calvin. It is often overlooked that early Reformed theology was strongly moralistic. Zwingli's chief concern was with reforming the morals, structures, and practices of the church of his day and bringing them in line with Scripture. Zwingli argued that Christian morality consists in following the example of Jesus Christ, and that justification took place as a result of this imitation of Christ (an idea already found in the writings of Erasmus of Rotterdam). *The moral regeneration of the individual was thus the cause of his justification.*

The early Reformed theologians therefore viewed Luther's teaching on justification with alarm, as it seemed to them (quite wrongly, as it happened) to break the link between morality and religion. Luther had insisted that the sinner is justified without any reference to his works, regeneration, or moral character. On the other hand, it seemed to the critics of Zwingli's teaching (rightly!) that it was simply works-righteousness: individuals were justified on the basis of their works (in this case "moral regeneration," which was obviously a human achievement). Furthermore, it seemed to the critics (again, rightly) that Christ was only involved in Zwingli's theology of justification in an external manner: Christ provides the moral example we are supposed to imitate, and when we do this, we are justified. But according to Luther, Christ comes to dwell within the believer and is involved with his existence internally. And so it became essential to clarify the Reformed teaching on justification to ensure that several elements were preserved:

1. The total gratuity of our reconciliation with God had to be upheld.
2. The necessity of regeneration and good works had to be upheld.
3. Christ had to be involved *internally* in the process.

It was due to the genius of John Calvin that this difficulty was completely overcome—in fact, so successful was Calvin's solution that it was adopted by just about every Lutheran theologian as well, despite Luther's somewhat different views on the matter. Calvin argued like this. The gospel concerns our encounter with Jesus Christ and our union with him. What we receive from God is not a series of gifts, but one supreme gift—the gracious indwelling of Jesus Christ himself. In making this assertion, Calvin clearly develops the authentic New Testament insight that the believer is incorporated into the life of the risen Christ. Calvin thus integrates Christ into the life of faith in an *internal*, rather than a purely *external*, manner. To meet Christ in this way is to be born again as a new creation (2 Cor. 5:17).

This union with Christ has two main consequences. Calvin, basing himself on 1 Corinthians 6:11, refers to them as the "double grace" of *justification* and *sanctification*. These two are given to us simultaneously as aspects of our union with Christ. They cannot be separated from that union, nor from one another. In other words, apart from union with Christ there can be no justification and no sanctification. And justification cannot exist without sanctification, since both are given together, simultaneously. The following extended quotation from Calvin makes this point perfectly:

Christ "is made unto us wisdom and righteousness, and sanctification and redemption" (1 Cor. 1:30). Christ, therefore, justifies no man without also sanctifying him. Those blessings are joined by a perpetual and inseparable tie. Those whom he enlightens by his wisdom, he redeems; whom he redeems, he justifies; whom he justifies, he sanctifies. But as the question relates only to justification and sanctification, to them let us confine ourselves. Though we distinguish between them, they are both inseparably comprehended in Christ. Would you then obtain justification in Christ? You must previously possess Christ. But you cannot possess him without being made a partaker of his sanctification: for Christ cannot be divided. Since the Lord, therefore, does not grant us the enjoyment of these blessings without bestowing himself, he bestows both at once, but never the one without the other. Thus it appears how true it is that we are justified not *without*, and yet not *by* works, since in the participation of Christ, by which we are justified, is contained not less sanctification than justification.[8]

In other words, although justification and sanctification may be *distinguished*, they cannot be *separated*. In that our redemptive encounter and union with Christ are totally free and unmerited, the gratuity of justification is upheld—just as the unbreakable link between the union with Christ and sanctification upholds the necessity of both regeneration and sanctification. Justification is still treated as the external pronouncement of God that we are right in his sight—but the pronouncement is made on the basis of the presence within us of the living Christ.

This distinction between justification and sanctification has led to considerable confusion. What the first fifteen hundred years of the Christian church had called "justification" now had to be split into two parts, one of which was still called "justification!" In practice, the reader may use the term "justification" *either* to mean the creative and redemptive encounter of the individual with the risen Christ (the sense used by Augustine, the young Luther, and in the systematic sections of the present work) *or* in the sense of the declaration that the believer is in the right, linked to (but distinct from!) sanctification and regeneration. The important point is that the reader must be clear which understanding is being used, especially when discussing such matters with anyone else. It may be that differences of opinion arise because different definitions of the same term are used!

A further point of importance concerns the grounds of assurance and is best seen by comparing Zwingli and Calvin. For Zwingli, the individual is justified on account of his moral regeneration. In effect, God endorses his moral regeneration. The grounds of assurance are thus located in the individual, who is under obligation to ensure that he is sufficiently regenerated to merit his justification (the use of the word "merit," by the way, is deliberate—Zwingli teaches a doctrine of justification by works). For Calvin, however, the key right-making maneuver takes place outside the believer by an act of God's grace. The believer may therefore rest assured—in a manner not permitted by Zwingli—that all that needs to be done to initiate the Christian life has been done by God, allowing the believer to concentrate upon *living* his Christian life.

The concept of the "imputation of the righteousness of Christ," mentioned above, needs further discussion. For the later Reformers, such as Melanchthon and Calvin, the basis of our justification is the righteousness of Christ, earned through his obedience to God in his life and death. This righteousness, however, is always alien and external to us: we do not possess in ourselves sufficient righteousness upon which the verdict of divine justification may be based. The righteousness of Christ is thus "imputed" to us—in other words, it is treated as if it were ours, or reckoned to us, without ever *becoming* ours. Shielded by this aura of divine righteousness, the process of sanctification (in which we are gradually made righteous) may begin and develop. The Reformation doctrine of assurance, already noted above, is linked with this understanding of both justification and justifying faith: Because it is God who supplies both the righteousness on the basis of which we are justified and the faith through which it is imputed to us, we may rest assured that all that needs to be done for our justification has been done—and has been done well.

A helpful way of distinguishing the Reformed understanding of the nature of justifying righteousness from that of Augustine or the Council of Trent is by using the concepts of *analytic* and *synthetic* divine judgment. For Augustine, the righteousness on the basis of which we are to be justified is already present within us, through the gracious action of God—and God therefore *analyzes* what is already there in order to justify us. But for Melanchthon and Calvin, there is no righteousness within us which could function as the basis of the divine verdict of justification—and God must therefore *synthesize* this righteousness himself.

An important factor in this sixteenth-century discussion was the new awareness of the forensic background of the Old Testament concept of justification, an awareness that resulted from new insights into the Hebrew language. Augustine and the medieval theologians had to rely upon Latin translations of the Old Testament texts, whereas the Reformers of the sixteenth century had direct access to the original Hebrew. It was largely for this reason that the distinction between "justification" (being *declared* righteous) and "sanctification" (being *made* righteous) was made. Of course, the Reformers were not suggesting that these two were separable, so that it was possible to be declared righteous without being made righteous! What they were doing was to draw attention to the misleading interpretation given to the term "justification" by Augustine and to try to correct him on this point. However, the Roman Catholic opponents of the Reformation misunderstood the Reformers to be suggesting that it was not necessary for a justified sinner to be regenerated, and they criticized the doctrine of forensic justification as a result.

The fierce controversy surrounding the views of Andreas Osiander— who argued for a doctrine of justification by inherent righteousness—served to consolidate Protestant opinion on the nature of justification and justifying righteousness, with the result that the following four characteristics of the Protestant doctrines of justification were established by the year 1540.

1. Justification is the forensic *declaration* that the Christian is righteous, rather than the process by which he or she is *made* righteous. It involves a change in *status* rather than in *nature*.

2. A deliberate and systematic distinction is made between justification (the external act by which God declares the believer to be righteous) and sanctification or regeneration (the internal process of renewal by the Holy Spirit).
3. Justifying righteousness is the alien righteousness of Christ, imputed to the believer and external to him, not a righteousness that is inherent within him, located within him, or in any way belonging to him.
4. Justification takes place *per fidem propter Christum*, with faith being understood as the God-given means of justification and the merits of Christ the God-given foundation of justification.

FOR FURTHER READING

For the development of the doctrine of justification at the time of the Reformation, see:

Alister E. McGrath. *Iustitia Dei: A History of the Christian Doctrine of Justification*. 2 vols. Cambridge: Cambridge University Press, 1986. 2:1–53.

For more general reading:

Paul Althaus. *The Theology of Martin Luther*. Philadelphia: Fortress, 1966.
Roland H. Bainton. *Here I Stand: A Life of Martin Luther*. New York: Scribner, 1950.
Wilhelm Dantine. *The Justification of the Ungodly*. St. Louis: Concordia, 1968.
Gerhard O. Forde. *Justification by Faith—A Matter of Death and Life*. Philadelphia: Fortress, 1982.
Alister E. McGrath. *Luther's Theology of the Cross: Martin Luther's Theological Breakthrough*. New York: Basil Blackwell, 1985.
_____ . *The Intellectual Origins of the European Reformation*. New York: Basil Blackwell, 1987. 32–122.
_____ . *Reformation Thought: An Introduction*. New York: Basil Blackwell, 1988. 67–94.
Jaroslav Pelikan. *The Christian Tradition: A History of the Development of Doctrine: 4. Reformation of Church and Dogma (1300–1700)*. Chicago and London: University of Chicago Press, 1984. 127–82.

5

Denominational Differences

Since the European Reformation of the sixteenth century, a significant number of Christian denominations have developed. In this chapter we will survey the opinions of the main Christian denominations on the doctrine of justification by faith. This survey is not intended to be exhaustive but merely to sketch and compare highlights.

First, it should be noted that it is the Western churches who have chosen to pay most attention to the doctrine of *justification*. The Eastern churches—such as the Greek and Russian Orthodox churches—have always preferred to discuss the redemption of humanity in terms of the image of *deification*.[1]

A second point that should be noted is the general agreement among most Protestant denominations concerning the doctrine of justification. Although there are indeed differences between the Lutheran and Reformed positions,[2] these differences either are somewhat technical or else are tied in with the related doctrines of predestination and election. Similarly, there are some areas of divergence between Lutheran and Reformed theology on the one hand and Pietist versions of these on the other; again, these disagreements tend to be somewhat technical.[3] The most important historical disagreement on justification has, of course, been between the Protestant churches on the one hand and the Roman Catholic church on the other. Yet even between these there exists a large measure of agreement, as will be shown at the end of this chapter.

With this in mind, we now proceed to a point-by-point comparison of the views of Protestant denominations and Roman Catholicism on a number of points on which disagreement exists. These are:

1. What is understood by "justification"?
2. What is understood by "justification by faith"?
3. What is the nature of justifying righteousness?
4. May an individual be said to merit justification?

We shall consider these questions individually, basing our analysis on the historical confessional documents of the respective denominations. It is, of course, necessary to note that some modern Protestants do not feel themselves bound by these documents (for example, modern Anglicans tend to pay little attention to the Thirty-Nine Articles). This analysis will, however, clarify the respective *historical* positions adopted by the various denominations on the matters in question. With this point in mind, we may turn to the first question.

1. What Is Understood by "Justification"?

The Council of Trent defined the Roman Catholic understanding of justification as follows: "The movement from the state in which man is born a son of the first Adam to the state of grace and adoption as sons of God through the second Adam, our savior Jesus Christ." Justification is thus understood as involving the entire transition from nature to grace, involving both the event by which the Christian life is begun and the process by which it is developed and finally consummated. In many ways, this understanding of justification parallels that of Augustine of Hippo.

The Protestant denominations have defined justification primarily in forensic terms, as the act of God by which the sinner is declared to be righteous. The *event* of justification (by which God declares the individual to be righteous) is to be distinguished from the *process* of sanctification (in which the individual is regenerated and renewed through the action of the Holy Spirit). Justification is thus an act of God external to the sinner, and sanctification is the action of God within him. Although justification and sanctification can be distinguished in theory, in practice they are inseparable: whoever is justified is also sanctified. In the previous chapter (p. 394), we noted Calvin's emphatic statements on this matter. The words of John Wesley are also helpful here, despite the old-fashioned English:

> Though it be allowed that justification and the new birth are, in point of time, inseparable from each other, yet they are easily distinguished, as not being the same, but things of a widely different nature. Justification implies only a relative, the new birth a real, change. God in justifying does something *for* us; in begetting us again, he does the work *in* us. The former changes our outward relation to God, so that of enemies we become children; by the latter, our inmost souls are changed, so that of sinners we become saints.[4]

It will therefore be obvious that the Roman Catholic understands by "justification" what the Protestant understands by "justification" *and* "sanctification" linked together. The same word is used by both—but it has a different meaning in each case. This has led to enormous confusion. Consider the following two statements.

A. We are justified by faith alone.
B. We are justified by faith and works.

The former broadly corresponds to the Protestant, the latter to the Roman Catholic position. But what do they mean?

For the Protestant, statement A means that the Christian life is begun through faith, and faith alone, which appears to be the New Testament teaching on the question. For the Roman Catholic, however—who understands "justification" in a different way—statement A means that the Christian life *as a whole* is begun and continued by faith alone, which seems to exclude any reference to regeneration or obedience. For the Roman Catholic, statement B means that the Christian life is begun in faith, but is continued and developed through obedience and good works—which appears to be the general position of the New Testament. But the Protestant—who understands "justification" to refer only to the *beginning* of the Christian life—would regard this as a totally unacceptable doctrine of justification by works. In fact, there is general agreement between Protestant and Roman Catholic that the Christian life is *begun* through faith and *continued and developed* through obedience and good works—the Reformation slogan "faith is pregnant with good works" embodies this principle.

Protestants are often accused by their opponents of developing a totally fictitious concept of justification—of suggesting that the believer lives in a sort of Walter Mitty world in which he is treated as righteous when he is actually nothing of the sort. The phrase "legal fiction" is often used to describe or discredit this concept of justification. But the forensic understanding of justification merely highlights the fact that sinners have nothing to contribute to their own justification—an insight shared with even those who do *not* adopt a forensic understanding of justification! There is nothing within the sinner that can ever be said to constitute the basis or grounds of his justification—those must be provided by none other than God himself. Justification does not depend upon, or follow, transformation and regeneration—only if justification is understood to follow, or to be based on, transformation or regeneration is there any substance to this criticism. In fact, the view that justification is based on and contingent on moral regeneration is associated with the Enlightenment and represents an abandonment of the idea of justification by grace in favor of justification by merit. The Protestant understanding of the nature of both justification and justifying righteousness is simply one way of emphasizing that it is God who both establishes the grounds for our justification and provides the means by which that justification may be appropriated, which is in agreement with the strongly forensic overtones of the Hebrew verb "to justify."

2. What Is Meant by "Justification by Faith"?

The basic point is that it is *God* who justifies us. The slogan *sola fide* ("by faith alone") emphasizes the total incapacity of humanity for any kind of self-justification. The grounds of our justification lie in the gracious promises of

God, and not in any moral actions or works of any kind which we may perform. *All* our salvation comes to us by faith. This faith is not a blind, dogmatic obedience or an arrogant boasting, but is a firm and humble trust in which we look to God as the gracious and faithful author of our salvation and believe in his promises of mercy—recognizing that even our faith, through which we come to trust in God, is nothing other than a gracious gift given to us, rather than something which we ourselves accomplish.

In recent years, there has been a growing awareness that Roman Catholics and Protestants have several important insights into this doctrine in common. Thus the Council of Trent insisted upon the priority of faith over everything else in justification. "Faith is the beginning of human salvation, the foundation and root of all justification, without which it is impossible to please God." Similarly, the Reformers insisted upon faith as the sole instrument of justification. In justification, we receive by faith the effects of the work of Christ on our behalf, appropriating it and making it our own. Justifying faith is not just historical knowledge (which the English Reformer William Tyndale called a "story-book faith") or intellectual conviction, but a trustful, self-involving response to the gospel. We are justified *per fidem propter Christum* (through faith on account of Christ): The objective basis of our justification is the person and work of Jesus Christ, and the means by which we appropriate this justification and make it our own is faith. To repeat: justification by faith does *not* mean that we are justified *on account* of our faith, but that we are justified on account of *Christ* through the grace of God. Faith must always be acknowledged as the work of God within us.

3. What Is the Nature of Justifying Righteousness?

Just as a major historical difference exists between Protestants and Roman Catholics concerning the nature of justification, so a corresponding difference exists with regard to the question of justifying righteousness. For the Protestant, justifying righteousness is the alien righteousness of Christ which is imputed to the believer. It never becomes part of the believer or can be said to belong to him; it is "reckoned" or "imputed" to him. The believer remains a sinner, but he is counted as righteous in the sight of God: he is *simul iustus et peccator* (righteous and a sinner at one and the same time). Indeed, it is God's justification of the sinner that fully demonstrates the extent of his sinfulness. The Heidelberg Catechism states this as follows:

Q. How are you righteous before God?
A. Only by true faith in Jesus Christ. In spite of the fact that my conscience accuses me that I have grievously sinned against all the commandments of God, and that I have failed to keep any of them, and that I am still ever prone to all that is evil, yet God, without any merit of my own, out of pure grace, grants me the benefits of the perfect expiation of Christ, imputing to

me his righteousness and holiness, as if I had never committed a single sin or had ever been sinful, having fulfilled myself all the obedience which Christ has carried out for me, if only I accept such favor with a trusting heart.[5]

For the Roman Catholic, however, justifying righteousness is inherent in the believer, part of his person. Although it is a gift of God bestowed upon the sinner, it may be said to be part of the sinner's being. The sanctifying action of the Holy Spirit removes the guilt of sin and renders the believer righteous in the sight of God. To use a distinction introduced earlier (p. 396), Protestants understand justification to be based on a *synthetic* divine judgment, whereas Roman Catholics understand it to be based on an *analytic* divine judgment.[6]

Protestants tend to be suspicious of the concept of an inherent justifying righteousness, which they fear may cause the believer to become either complacent or anxious and thus fail to rely completely upon the mercy and grace of God. In addition, the possibility that this "inherent righteousness" might be confused with a *human* righteousness gained by good works has caused serious anxieties in Protestant circles in that this misunderstanding immediately opens the way for a doctrine of justification by works. Roman Catholics, on the other hand, tend to be suspicious of the concept of an external or alien justifying righteousness, fearing that the idea could lead to the neglect of good works and Christian obedience. It is clear that these anxieties may be based on misunderstanding. It is important to realize that Roman Catholics as well as Protestants teach that the righteousness of the individual, upon which his justification is based, is itself provided by God. For both, justification remains an act of God based upon an objective foundation provided and established by God himself. The Protestant understanding of the nature of justifying righteousness has the advantage of bringing out the forensic and declaratory overtones of the Old Testament idea of "justifying," while emphasizing that the righteousness in question is not a human righteousness, acquired through the performance of good works— but properly understood, this is not what the Roman Catholic view implies.

4. May an Individual Be Said to Merit Justification?

There is general agreement between Roman Catholics and Protestants that justification is a totally free and unmerited act of God that is not the result of our works or achievements. Justification will always remain an act of divine graciousness. To suggest that an individual can earn his justification is Pelagian and quite incompatible with the Christian gospel. The suggestion that an individual can merit his justification is actually associated with the rationalistic Enlightenment, rather than with Roman Catholicism.

Yet the Roman Catholic teaching on merit is open to a number of misunderstandings, in part because of the slightly confusing terms used by Roman Catholic theologians to discuss it. Some Roman Catholic theologians make a distinction between two types of merit: merit in the strict sense of the word, meaning something God is under obligation to reward ("condign" merit), and merit in a weak sense of the word, meaning something to which it is appropriate that God should respond ("congruous" merit).[7] All Roman Catholic theologians insist that it is impossible that an individual should *in the strict sense of the word* merit justification, although some allow that justification may be "merited" *in the weak sense of the term.* The idea of "congruous" merit has been viewed with intense suspicion by Protestants, who tend to regard it as having Pelagian overtones.

The Council of Trent taught that individuals gain merit in the strict sense of the term *after justification.* Although this doctrine is understood to be an attempt to express the New Testament's views on the rewards given to believers as a result of their good works, this doctrine has been criticized by Protestants as tending to undermine trust in God alone for salvation. Even though the Council of Trent emphasized that these rewards are the consequence of divine generosity rather than human endeavor, its critics pointed out that it tends in practice to lead to the individual believer coming to trust in his own efforts as the basis of salvation. The real problem here, however, lies in the use of the term "merit" in the first place.

In an earlier chapter (pp. 377–78), we pointed out how Tertullian was responsible for introducing the rather unhelpful translation *liberum arbitrium* into the theological vocabulary of the Western church. It may not come as much of a surprise, therefore, to learn that it was this same person who introduced the Latin term *meritum* as a translation for the Greek word for "reward." *Meritum* came from the field of Roman law (Tertullian, remember, was a lawyer) and had legal overtones that came to pass into theology. Once more, it was Augustine who managed to rescue the Western church from a serious misunderstanding of the idea. While the word "merit" had become so well established that it was virtually impossible to stop using it, Augustine managed to recover a more authentic biblical insight. For Augustine, "merit" is not something we may claim because of what we have achieved, but *something God gives to us on account of who he is.* The initiative is always understood, by Augustine and by the New Testament, as coming from God (who *gives*), rather than from human individuals (who *claim*).

Protestants and Roman Catholics, therefore, are united in asserting that we have no claim whatsoever upon God for our justification: it is something *God gives us,* something *God does for us.* However, it must be noted that a difference develops concerning the role of merit in the Christian life itself. While Protestants are content to speak of God rewarding our efforts as believers, Roman Catholics speak of believers gaining merit. The Catholic approach is regarded with some suspicion by Protestants, in that it appears to place an unhealthy emphasis upon achievements and the claim they allow us to make upon God, instead of emphasizing the divine generosity towards us.

On the basis of the above analysis, it will be clear that there exist real differences between Protestants and Roman Catholics over the matter of justification. The question remains, however, as to the significance of these differences. How important, for example, is the distinction between an alien and an intrinsic justifying righteousness? In recent years, there appears to be increasing sympathy for the view that these differences, although of importance in the Reformation period, no longer possess the significance that they once had. This is not to say that the Christian denominations are agreed on the matter of justification, for it is obvious that their respective teachings have a very different "feel" or "atmosphere" to them. It seems that in the modern period the Christian denominations have preferred to concentrate on their points of agreement, rather than draw attention to their historical disagreements!

This may be due in part to an increasing recognition that today the real threat to the gospel of grace comes from the rationalism of the Enlightenment rather than from other Christian denominations. The Enlightenment promoted the idea that God can only justify morally renewed individuals; the idea that God justifies *sinners*, just as they are here and now, was rejected as contrary to both reason and morality. In many ways, the Enlightenment marked the rebirth of Pelagianism, with a new emphasis upon human moral capabilities and responsibilities.[8] Before an individual may be accepted by God, he must first make himself acceptable by becoming a good person. And so the Enlightenment, like the Pelagianism of the fifth century, developed a doctrine of the "justification of the *godly*," which was totally opposed to the gospel concept of the "justification of the *ungodly*."

The following points of agreement among the Christian denominations, including both the Protestant and Roman Catholic churches, are now widely recognized.

1. As a result of original sin, all human beings—whoever they are and whenever and wherever they live—stand in need of justification.
2. Christians have no hope of final salvation and no basis for justification before God other than through God's free gift of grace in Christ, offered to them through the Holy Spirit. Our entire hope of justification and salvation rests on the promises of God and the saving work of Jesus Christ, expressed in the gospel.
3. Justification is a completely free act of God's grace, and nothing we can do can be said to be the basis or ground of our own justification. Even faith itself must be recognized as a divine gift and work within us. We cannot turn to God unless God turns us first. The priority of God's redeeming will and action over our own actions in bringing about our salvation is expressed by the doctrine of predestination.
4. In justification we are declared righteous before God, and the process of making us righteous in his sight through the renewing

action of the Holy Spirit is begun. In that justification, we receive by faith the effects of the death and resurrection of Jesus Christ as we respond personally to the gospel, the power of God for salvation, as we encounter the gospel through scripture, the proclamation of the word of God, and the sacraments, and as it initially awakens and subsequently strengthens faith in us.

5. Whoever is justified is subsequently renewed by the Holy Spirit and motivated and enabled to perform good works. This is not to say that individuals may rely upon these works for their salvation, because eternal life remains a gift offered to us through the grace and mercy of God.

FOR FURTHER READING

For a general survey of the doctrines of justification associated with Lutheran, Reformed, and Anglican churches, the Council of Trent, and also Puritans and Pietists, see:

Alister E. McGrath. *Iustitia Dei: A History of the Christian Doctrine of Justification.* 2 vols. Cambridge: Cambridge University Press, 1986. 2:1–53, 63–86, 98–134.

For a point-by-point comparison of Lutheran, Reformed, and Roman Catholic views, see:

Wilhelm Niesel. *The Gospel and the Churches.* Philadelphia: Westminster, 1962.

For a classic comparison of the views of the Council of Trent and Karl Barth, see:

Hans Küng. *Justification: The Doctrine of Karl Barth and a Catholic Reflection.* 2nd ed. Philadelphia: Westminster, 1981.

For criticism of this book, see:

Alister E. McGrath. "Justification: Barth, Trent and Küng." *Scottish Journal of Theology* 34 (1981): 517–29.

For two recent documents recording at least a degree of agreement between Protestants and Roman Catholics, see:

"Justification by Faith" [Report of the Lutheran-Roman Catholic Dialogue Group in the United States], *Origins* 13/17 (1983): 277–304.

Salvation and the Church: An Agreed Statement by the Second Anglican-Roman Catholic International Commission, London: Church House Publishing/ Catholic Truth Society, 1987.

PART TWO

The Contemporary
Significance of the Doctrine

6

The Existential Dimension

Modern Western humanity tends to judge its spiritual state in terms of categories such as "meaning," "fulfillment," and "purpose." Where the theologians of the sixteenth-century Reformation or the eighteenth-century Great Awakening directed their preaching towards "law" and "guilt," the modern preacher must learn to direct his proclamation of the gospel to the felt needs of modern humanity. He must become receptor-oriented, sensitive to the needs, fears, and aspirations of his audience, in order to gain a point of contact, a toehold by which his proclamation may be grounded in the existential situation of hearers. What he has to proclaim must be seen to relate to modern human existence.

As we emphasized earlier (p. 361), this does not mean compromising or distorting the gospel proclamation to suit the preoccupations of modern Western humanity—rather, it means taking the trouble to determine how the gospel, with its richness and multifaceted character, impinges upon modern humanity. *The transformation of human existence depends upon prior correlation with that existence.* It is the task of the theologian to aid and support the work of the preacher by becoming the translator and interpreter of the gospel of justification by faith into contemporary Western categories. It is necessary for the theologian to wrestle with the religious, cultural, social, and political realities of his own situation, *in order to be relevant to that situation*— just as he must also wrestle with the scriptural witness and history of scriptural interpretation *if he is to be faithful to the gospel.* The theologian must engage in a dialectical and dialogical approach, moving back and forth from the gospel center of free justification in Jesus Christ to the context and situation to which it is to be proclaimed. The gospel both addresses and challenges the presuppositions of that context—but before the process of criticism may begin, it is necessary that a real engagement between gospel and context takes place and a real connection between the two is established.[1]

Contemporary existentialist philosophies offer the modern Western theologian a point of contact with the existential concerns of modern Western humanity and a possible means of bridging the gap between the Christian proclamation of justification by faith and modern ways of thinking about ultimate concerns. In this chapter, we propose to illustrate how this may be done by considering the structures of human existence as uncovered by contemporary existentialist analysis. We begin by briefly outlining some aspects of existentialist thought.

1. The Basics of Existentialism

Who are we? Why are we here? Why do we exist? What does it *mean* to exist? All of us exist in the world—yet we are often aware of an uncomfortable sense of not being quite at home there, of being anxious about our existence, of feeling threatened and worried by the inevitability of death. We feel that our existence is threatened by forces over which we have little or no control—forces such as social pressures and political manipulation on the one hand, and mortality, death, and finitude on the other.

A human being, a stone, and a tree all *exist* in that they are all unquestionably part of the same world. And yet, ever since human beings began to think, they have been aware of some fundamental, though perhaps undefinable, distinction between themselves on the one hand and all other forms of life on the other. But what *is* this difference? The entire career of human philosophy has concerned itself with trying to cast light on this crucial question.

Perhaps the most important thing that distinguishes human beings from other forms of life is the fact that human beings are aware of their own existence and ask questions about it. The rise of existentialist philosophy is ultimately a response to this crucial insight.[2] We not only exist—we *are aware* and we *understand* that we exist, and we are aware that our existence will one day be terminated by death. The sheer fact of our existence is important to us and we find it difficult, probably impossible, to adopt a totally detached attitude towards it. Existentialist philosophy is basically a protest against the view that human beings are "things" and a demand that we take the personal existence of the individual with full seriousness. Each of us is an individual and defies general classification. We cannot be defined just in terms of our social security number—we are individuals, and our individuality is important to us.

This distinction between ourselves and objects or things is brought out with special clarity by the highly influential German existentialist philosopher Martin Heidegger in his analysis of the structures of human existence. Heidegger draws a distinction between the mode of existence of a human being, aware of his own existence (*Dasein*), and the mode of existence of an inanimate object, a thing (*Vorhandenheit*—literally, "being at hand"). And Heidegger emphasizes that there is every danger that *Dasein* will become *Vorhandenheit*—in other words, that our existence will be reduced to the level of things. We can get so tied up and concerned with things, with the world, that we lose our distinctive identities as individuals. We become a member of a crowd, as our individual identity is swallowed up and lost.

This point is also expressed in terms of the difference between "objective" and "subjective" knowledge. "Objective" knowledge involves knowing about something in a theoretical or detached manner, rather like a scientist examining samples of blood or a statistician analyzing consumer trends. Although these impersonal figures and statistics are ultimately based on individuals, those individuals are lost in a mass of impersonal data. Individuals just don't matter here. More importantly, the scientist or statistician must *eliminate* his own personal feelings from his work, so that he can adopt a totally neutral and detached approach to the subject. There is no doubt that this is important—but, as we shall emphasize later (p. 461), there is no real possibility of a neutral, disinterested, or objective knowledge *of God*, simply because we realize that we ourselves, our own personal existence, are bound up with his existence. Subjective knowledge involves knowing something which is of importance to our own personal existence. The distinction between "objective" and "subjective" knowledge is probably best brought out in relation to the knowledge of death.

Death may be treated objectively as a biological phenomenon, as the termination of the life-process. The physiological changes in humans associated with the phenomenon may be objectively described and recorded. But this is dealing with *somebody else's death*. To treat death as an existential phenomenon, however, is to recognize that the future event of *our own death* already enters into our way of thinking and exercises influence over us. To be born is already to be on the way to death. There is no way we can avoid it. And every now and then something happens to remind us of the fact that we must die—perhaps a relative or close friend dies, and we are forced to reflect on the fact that we too must die. This is subjective knowledge—the awareness of something that affects our individual existence (in this case, by bringing home to us that it won't go on forever!). This recognition of the inevitability of death, of the fact that existence as we know it will one day be terminated, causes us anxiety (the German word *angst* is often used to refer to this "existential anxiety").

It is for this reason that contemporary existential philosophy has placed great emphasis upon "subjective" knowledge—an approach exemplified by the Danish philosopher Kierkegaard in his famous affirmation "truth is subjectivity." By "subjective" he did not mean "prejudiced," "unreliable," or "biased," as the usual sense of the word would imply. Rather, he meant that the personal concerns of the individual cannot be ignored in the search for truth. "Truth" is not just about intellectual theories or concepts, involving just the human mind, but it is about the whole person, the whole of human existence. Our emotions and our wills, our passions as well as our intellects, must be caught up and involved in our search for truth. Truth must be personally relevant if it is to transform us and our existence. For this reason, existentialism—while not having any quarrel with objective scientific truth!—has emphasized the need for the subjective relevance of truth if it is to affect the way we are, the way we exist. If we are to encounter the "truth that sets us free," that truth must be something that grasps us and changes us inwardly, rather than something we just know with our minds. Head knowledge must become heart knowledge. A distinction often made by existentialist thinkers is between *knowing about the truth* (in other words, objective truth) and *being grasped by the truth* (in other words, subjective truth). And it is with this latter that the doctrine of justification is concerned—*subjective knowledge of God as redeemer through Jesus Christ.*

2. The Existential Analysis of Human Existence

Existentialism draws a careful distinction between two modes of existence, two ways of existing in the world, that are open to individuals. Following Heidegger, these ways of existing are usually referred to as "authentic existence" and "inauthentic existence." An individual who exists authentically may be said to be existing in such a way as to fulfill his potential as a human being. In this state, he may be said to have fulfillment, purpose, and meaning. In inauthentic existence, on the other hand, an individual loses his distinctive capacities and identity. He is trapped by forces he cannot master and is a slave to illusions about the nature of existence. He refuses to face up to the realities of life, such as death and finitude. His whole life is a sham, and he probably knows it.

Unlike animals, human beings know at the cognitive or intellectual level that they must die, but they are reluctant to accept this fact existentially. In other words, they know that one day they will die (and may even joke about it!), but find it difficult—and even distressing—to reflect seriously on the fact that one day they, as individual human beings, will cease to exist. Individuals cannot bear the thought of death. It is threatening to think of the world going on without them. The thought of finitude is deeply distressing to many individuals, who tend to make the denial of this eventuality their life projects. The seductiveness of the words of the serpent to Eve lie in the fact that they suggest that death is *not* inevitable: "You will not surely die . . . you will be like God" (Gen. 3:4–5). And so humanity becomes trapped within its own lie, as it tries to deny death and protect itself against it. Fallen humanity is tempted to base its entire existence upon a delusion and a lie, and feels threatened by the possibility of the exposure of this lie. And yet the way to authentic existence is through facing the realities of human existence—such as our death and finitude.

Heidegger speaks of individuals "falling" away from a state of authentic existence, or being "alienated" from authentic existence. For Heidegger, this "fallenness" or "alienation" can come about through obsession with transitory things or through becoming absorbed into a crowd and losing individual identity. Conversely, this fallenness and alienation may be overcome by adopting a correct attitude towards existence. And the first step in this process, according to Heidegger, is the *disclosure of inauthenticity*. In other words, something happens to make you aware that you're living a lie, that you are running away from the realities of existence. Existential anxiety (*angst*) is perhaps the most important of these realities, and this is often grounded in the fear of death.

The anticipation of death brings home to us the fact that our existence is transitory, and that we are living in a state of delusion, of inauthentic existence, if we base our existence upon this world and its goods. Fallen humanity is tempted to overlook death, despite its importance, precisely because it *wants* to overlook it. Heidegger thus emphasizes that existential anxiety in the face of death discloses to individuals that they are living a lie if they cannot cope with it, that their whole existence is based upon a delusion unless they face up to its reality and inevitability and reorient themselves accordingly. And because *angst* is so threatening, much of Western society prefers to ignore death or marginalize it, if it cannot be denied completely.

This brief analysis of the two categories of human existence—authentic and inauthentic—allows us to take the next step in our discussion. We may now ask how the gospel links up with these categories and how it may be articulated and explained in their terms.

3. Existence and the Gospel

The New Testament recognizes two quite distinct modes of human existence: an unbelieving, unredeemed form of existence, based on illusions and lies; and a believing and redeemed existence, in which the human existential potential is brought to its fullness. Similarly, the New Testament recognizes the need to disclose to humanity that its unbelieving and unredeemed mode of existence is inauthentic, in order that the way may be opened to authentic existence—life in all its redeemed fullness.

These two modes of human existence are both developed at great length in scripture. For example, it is clear that a major element in the story of the Fall (Gen. 3) concerns the desire on the part of humanity to dispense with God in order to become self-sufficient. Here, the individual refuses to recognize himself for what he really is—a creature of God, dependent on him for his well-being and salvation. The individual seeks to justify himself by trying to secure his existence through moral actions or material prosperity. He tries to gain his essential nature, his authentic way of existence, through his own powers. His entire way of life is bound up with what is transitory, and so his life is subject to transitoriness and death. This individual lives in dependence upon the world, upon things that must ultimately pass away. And it is this attempt at self-sufficiency on the part of humanity that both the Old and New Testaments designate as "sin."

Over against this inauthentic mode of human existence the New Testament sets the mode of believing, redeemed existence, in which we abandon all security created by ourselves and place our trust in God. We recognize the illusion of our self-sufficiency and trust instead in the sufficiency of God. Instead of denying that we are God's creatures, we recognize and exult in this fact and base our existence upon it. Instead of clinging to transitory things for security, we learn to abandon faith in this transitory world in order that we may place our trust in something eternal—God himself. Instead of trying to justify ourselves, we learn to recognize that God offers us our justification as a free gift. Instead of denying the reality of our human finitude and the inevitability of death, we recognize that these have been faced and conquered through the death and resurrection of Jesus Christ, whose victory becomes our victory through faith. Christ shared in our humanity "so that by his death he might destroy him who holds the power of death—that is, the devil—and free those who all their lives were held in slavery by their fear of death" (Heb. 2:14–15).

It is God who has the "knowledge of good and evil" (Gen. 2:16–17), and by attempting to gain this knowledge for itself, humanity demonstrates its perennial tendency to seek after self-sufficiency—to "be like God, knowing good and evil" (Gen. 3:5). Similarly, the Pelagian heresy (see pp. 376–385) is perhaps the most natural of all heresies in that it involves the suggestion that we are the masters of our own destiny. Humanity has always been tempted to believe in the seductive suggestion that it possesses the resources necessary for salvation and need not rely upon God for assistance. The temptation to boast in ourselves is continually countered by Paul, who points out that the only grounds for boasting we possess are Jesus Christ and his cross (1 Cor. 1:31; 2 Cor. 10:17; Gal. 6:14). Authentic human existence is only achieved through abandoning faith in ourselves and the world as the basis of our salvation, and by grounding our faith in God instead.

Similarly, the New Testament emphasizes the illusion of security created by material goods and human moral actions, in order to emphasize instead the promises of God as the only adequate basis for our security. Two famous affirmations from the Sermon on the Mount make this point with brilliance:

> Do not store up for yourselves treasures on earth, where moth and rust destroy, and where thieves break in and steal. But store up for yourselves treasures in heaven, where moth and rust do not destroy, and where thieves do not break in and steal. For where your treasure is, there your heart will be also (Matt. 6:19–21).

Two modes of existence are contrasted: the inauthentic mode of existence, based upon this world, which is transitory and temporary; and the authentic mode of existence, based on God himself, which involves rejection of any basis of trust in this world in order to place trust in God himself. The same point is made very forcefully by contrasting the man who built his house on the rock with the man who built his house on the sand (Matt. 7:24–27).

Both the New Testament and existentialism condemn the human tendency to conceal the ever-present possibility of death. Thus the parable of the rich fool (Luke 12:13–21) illustrates with some brilliance the human desire to flee from facing the reality of death and to rely on plans that exclude or overlook death. The perennial temptation is to justify ourselves by basing existence on human self-sufficiency or upon worldly goods—but death and decay show the temptation up for what it is: the allurement of an illusion. Instead, we are invited to base our existence upon God himself, the rock that nothing—not even death itself—can destroy or remove. The constantly repeated biblical emphasis upon God himself as the only basis for authentic human existence is accompanied by an equally persistent emphasis upon the inability of humanity to achieve authentic existence through its own efforts or through what the world has to offer.

At this point, we need to note one very important difference between the New Testament understanding of inauthentic existence and that associated with existentialist philosophers such as Heidegger. For Heidegger, inauthentic existence is *something we choose*. It is one of several options open to us. But for the New Testament, inauthentic existence is a *given*, not a choice. Whether we like it or not, we must all recognize that we enter the world already in a state of inauthentic existence, alienated from our true way of being.

The gospel reports the universal sinfulness of humanity. It is not primarily concerned with the question of *why* this should be the case: it simply declares that this *is* the case and that recognition of this fact is the starting point from which rectification of the situation can proceed. When a physician diagnoses an illness, his first concern is to establish what is wrong with his patient. His interest in how the condition arose is generally more academic. The same point may be made about the New Testament, which has relatively little interest in *how* we came to be sinners: the important thing is that God has addressed our condition directly in Jesus Christ. But there are some individuals—as there always have been, and probably always will be—who refuse to come to terms with the reality of universal human sinfulness unless it is explained and justified to them precisely how this situation arose. "*Why* are we sinful and alienated from our true mode of existence? Unless you explain to me why God allowed this situation to happen, I won't accept it or act upon it." The following point may prove useful in dealing with this objection.

There are a number of facts about human existence which we have to learn to accept, even if we don't understand why they are so in the first place. We may ask the question *why*, but a failure to give an answer to this question doesn't alter the situation. All of us must die. But why? Why were we created in such a way that we must die? Why can't we just go on living forever? But the fact that there aren't any especially convincing answers to these questions does not mean that we don't have to die! The fact that I can't explain why you're going to die won't keep you from dying! It doesn't *alter* the situation! It is simply a fact of life. Another fact of life is that humans reproduce sexually, and that this exercises an enormous influence over human behavior. But why should humans reproduce in this way? Why aren't we all hermaphrodites, able to reproduce without the need for a partner? Why don't we reproduce asexually, like an amoeba? And again, the answers given to these questions are not especially convincing. The simple answer is that this is the way things are, and no amount of refusing to accept that this is the way things are is going to alter the situation. The important thing—which we all *do* in the end—is to accept that this is the way things are and to get on with life. And so it is with sin. It's just the way things are, and no amount of arguing about it is going to alter the situation. The important thing is how this situation may be altered, rather than quibbling about how it arose in the first place!

The Christian proclamation addresses our present existence and discloses (or confirms) its inauthenticity—and names it "sin." Just as we may come to know about the existence of God through contemplating the night sky and afterward have our views confirmed by scripture and the Christian proclamation, so we may come to know about the inauthenticity of our existence through contemplating the inevitability of death and then have our views confirmed by scripture and the Christian proclamation. Alternatively, just as we may come to realize through reading scripture that God exists and then find our views confirmed by contemplating the night sky, so we may learn of the inauthenticity of our way of being through reading scripture and then find our views confirmed through reflecting on the inevitability of death. In both cases, the same fundamental realization takes place. We realize that our natural mode of existence, which is tied up with the world and things that are temporal and transitory, is inauthentic, and we are moved to ask how our alienation from our true way of being may be abolished and overcome.

4. The Gospel and Authentic Existence

The New Testament proclaims that the universal human predicament of inauthentic existence can be transformed to a state of authentic existence. It is this insight that is encapsulated in the doctrine of justification by faith. The main elements of the New Testament proclamation of the possibility of authentic human existence are the following:

1. The recognition of the fallenness of humanity, of the alienation of humanity from its authentic existence.

2. The realization that we are offered authentic existence as a gift through the death and resurrection of Jesus Christ.
3. The embodiment of this authentic existence in the life of faith.

We shall consider each of these points individually.

The gospel affirms that humanity was created in the image of God (Gen. 1:26), with the intention that they would be the children of God. But by worshiping the creation instead of the creator, humanity has lost that possibility. We have become enslaved to the world—our being and concerns have become tied up with things that are transitory and material. We have become alienated from our true way of being, our authentic mode of existence. It will be clear that existentialism casts valuable light on the concept of original sin, which is understood as alienation from our true way of existence and being. The constant threat of death and extinction discloses to us the inauthenticity of this existence, and this *angst* is the point of contact addressed by the Christian proclamation.

The doctrine of original sin is fundamentally an assertion that humanity is trapped in its existential situation and unable to extricate itself. If extrication from this situation is to take place, it must take place from outside the human situation. The idea of being trapped by forces we recognize as irrational but appear unable to break free from is only too familiar to us all. The streets of our cities bear depressing witness to the human tendency to be trapped by alcohol, drugs, gambling, and pornography, to name but the more obvious. We *know*, at the cognitive level, that it is absurd for a rational being to be trapped in this way—and yet we find it difficult to break free. Addiction provides a model of the more general human enslavement and bondage to sin.

Just as the individual who is hooked on cocaine may recognize that he is addicted, yet still remain unable to break free from the habit, so we may recognize that we are trapped within our human existential predicament—and yet that recognition does not bring liberation with it. For many theologians of the older liberal school, the recognition of one's predicament was virtually identical with liberation from it: by being enlightened with the truth it was possible to break free from delusions. You might think you were in a prison, but you were actually free—and once you realized this, you were able to live as a free individual. How shallow and naïvely optimistic an understanding of human nature underlies such a view! The streets of our cities bear witness to the grim realities of the human predicament, of human enslavement to forces lying beyond our control. The doctrine of justification proclaims that the human existential situation can be transformed through action from outside humanity, as God himself breaks into that situation and offers us authenticity as a gift. Although we ourselves are powerless to transform the fundamental cause of our predicament, God offers us precisely this transformation through the death and resurrection of Jesus Christ.

The gospel proclaims that fallen humanity is offered authentic existence *as a gift* through the death and resurrection of Jesus Christ. Authentic existence is not something that we can achieve, but is something that is offered to us by God himself. The gospel judges our present existence, condemns it as inauthentic in much the same way as a physician diagnoses an illness, and then offers us the possibility of abolishing our alienation from our true way of being. We are invited to abandon our attempts at self-sufficiency, to abandon our reliance upon things that are transitory, and instead to base our existence upon the promises of the eternal and living God.

For the New Testament, the achievement of our true nature is not something that *we* can attain, something that is at our disposal—that would be the way of self-justification, of justification by works. Every attempt on the part of fallen human individuals to justify themselves fails, since it is based upon the illusion of self-sufficiency. Human beings need to be liberated from their own situation by one who stands outside it. This liberation from the human situation thus takes place from outside humanity itself, in the life, death, and resurrection of Jesus Christ. It is God himself who intervenes in human history in order to make the attainment of authentic existence a genuine possibility for fallen humanity. We are set free to become ourselves, to become what we really are, through the grace of God, who does for us what we could never do for ourselves.

The word of justification is thus both the word of judgment and the word of life. It exposes and destroys our illusions about ourselves, revealing us as inadequate creatures of sin who must die. It also offers us the word of life in that it proclaims that death—the final event and boundary of finite human existence—has been confronted and overcome through the death and resurrection of Jesus Christ. The final event and boundary of believing and redeemed human existence is now the resurrection, not the event of death. Although the road to resurrection passes under the shadow of the cross, which cannot be avoided, we are reminded and reassured that Christ has trodden this road before us and promised eternal life to all who follow in his path. Death is not eliminated as an event in human existence—but it is shown to be the *penultimate* event, the gateway to resurrection, allowing human beings to transcend the bounds of their finite and mortal human existence through claiming by faith the power of the one who raised Christ Jesus from the dead. Inauthentic existence, characterized by the desire to deny sin, death, and mortality, gives way through faith to authentic existence, characterized by the willingness to confront the reality of death and claim Christ's victory over it as our own.

The New Testament proclaims this decisive alteration in the human situation in a number of images. The fallen and inauthentic mode of existence is designated as the way of darkness and death, and the way of authentic, believing, and redeemed existence as the way of light and life. It is helpful to remember that there are two Greek words that may be translated into English as "life." The Greek word *bios* corresponds to mere biological existence, the fact that we are alive and exist upon the face of the planet earth. The Greek word *zoe* is used by John's gospel to mean "life in all its fullness," or "the full and authentic human existence" that transcends mere biological existence. Thus John declares that Jesus Christ has come into the world in order that we might have "life in all its fullness" (John 10:10; 20:31). It is Jesus Christ who brings life to the world. It is Jesus Christ who is the bread of life (John 6:35); it is he who is the resurrection and the life (John 11:25). Through the life, death, and resurrection of Jesus Christ, the authentic mode of existence which God intends for us becomes a present real possibility. That which we could never attain for ourselves is made available for us by God as a gift. The gospel promises eternal life to those who believe (John 6:40, 51, 53–58), and that eternal life manifests itself in the present as authentic, believing, and redeemed existence, a foretaste of what is yet to come.

A further point of interest may be made at this point. As is well known, John's gospel emphasizes that God's judgment is not some totally future event but is inaugurated here and now. Judgment is *now*, in order that eternal life may begin *now* (John 12:31). The gospel proclamation passes judgment on our inauthentic existence, showing it up for what it really is. Just as the "light of the world" illuminates and thus exposes human sin (John 3:19–21), so Jesus Christ judges our mode of existence and condemns it as inauthentic—in order that we may act upon this judgment and seek authentic existence. But where is this authentic existence to be found? And how is it to be obtained? And then we realize that the same one who confronts us with the word of judgment is also the one who offers us the word of life. It is through the coming of Jesus Christ into the world and into our personal existence that sin is exposed for what it really is, and that our existence is transformed through his real and redeeming presence. It is through judgment (in other words, through exposure of our condition for what it really is) that we are saved. Jesus did not come merely to judge us, but to save us (John 12:44–47).

A similar point is made by Paul, particularly in his dialectic between "flesh" (*sarx*) and "spirit" (*pneuma*). Fallen inauthentic human existence is defined as existence "according to the flesh" (*kata sarka*), while authentic existence is defined as existence "according to the spirit" (*kata pneuma*).[3] The word "flesh" is not being used to refer to the human body or any specifically sexual aspects of human existence, but to a mode of human existence that is oriented away from God, towards the world and things that are tangible, temporary, and transitory. Similarly, the word "spirit" is not used to refer to some spiritual substance, but to a mode of human existence that is oriented towards faith in God and his promises of eternal life.

The individual who lives "according to the spirit" realizes the futility of the values of existence "according to the flesh" and devalues them. We are delivered from the tyranny and oppression of the world and the flesh, in order to gain the freedom of becoming children of God. Living "according to the flesh" is living in the world, for the world, and in rebellion against God; living "according to the spirit" is living in the world but for God. Inauthentic existence involves treating the world both as the place in which we live and as the bounds and norms of our existence; authentic existence involves treating the world as the place in which we live and God as the reason and basis of our existence. In other words, Christians are in the world but not of the world (John 17:6–19).

This point may be developed further with reference to John's gospel. We have noted how "the world" can have two senses in relation to human existence: a *neutral* sense, meaning simply "the place in which we live" or "other human beings"; and a *negative* sense, meaning "a threat to our existence." In its negative sense, "the world" stands for the forces that threaten to overwhelm us and trap us through shackling us to things that are temporary, transient, and temporal. It is interesting to note that we find the same word used in these two senses in John's gospel. Often, "the world" is used in its neutral sense—for example, in the famous affirmation, "God so loved the world that he gave his one and only Son, that whoever believes in him shall not perish but have eternal life" (John 3:16). More often, however (especially towards the end of the gospel), "the world" assumes a negative sense, meaning "a threat to authentic Christian existence" (for example, John 15:18–19; 16:33). The world is increasingly seen as exerting a sinister influence upon faith, threatening to overwhelm it and pull the believer back into the world of tangible and material things from which he was called. The great theme of "victory over the world," which is so characteristic a feature of the later chapters of this Gospel, is primarily a victory over the threat to faith which the world poses. Similarly, Christians may be said to be in the world yet not of the world—meaning that Christians live in the world (the neutral sense of the term), but do not share the inauthentic existence which the world (in its negative sense) offers. This negative aspect of the world, however, is only fully recognized from the standpoint of faith, which recognizes the judgment passed upon that world by Jesus Christ.

The doctrine of justification by faith thus proclaims the possibility of the abolition of our alienation from our authentic mode of existence. It declares that we are offered as a gift an authentic mode of existence which we cannot attain by our own efforts. It offers to transform our existence so that, although we continue to remain in the world (for the time being), we are no longer oppressed by its values and threatened by the fear of death. God has overcome the world through Jesus Christ, and by overcoming it has set us free from its oppression (John 16:33), in order that we may live *in* it without being *of* it. The question of the authenticity of human existence troubles modern Western humanity as it has probably never troubled humanity before—and it is important to realize that the Christian doctrine addresses this question directly and offers its own characteristic solution. This is no outdated idea belonging to the museum of the history of ideas—it is an affirmation about the meaning and destiny of human existence that is as relevant today as it ever was.

5. The Existential Point of Contact for the Gospel

For generations, thinkers have tried to account for the strange and unhappy history of humanity—for the intractable fact of sin and human unhappiness. The less perceptive accounts of this problem attempt to externalize it by blaming the human predicament upon political and economic structures and other factors that are external to us. The more thoughtful and persuasive accounts of human misery, however, point to human nature itself as being the root of the problem—a problem that no amount of tinkering with economic and social structures will eliminate. The great French existentialist Albert Camus identified this problem in human nature as a profound alienation in our nature, a sense of lost innocence—in almost biblical terms he talks about the Fall and about a sense that we have been expelled from a homeland and are now unhappily wandering through history, trying to find a way to return. Where is that homeland? And how may we find it? Here we find a point of contact at the deepest level of human existence—the sense of *lostness*, of alienation, of inauthenticity.

The gospel proclamation is addressed to those who want their existence to be fulfilled and meaningful. It analyzes the existential situation of humanity, and then proceeds to describe the means by which the individual's situation may be transformed. Not very far from the surface of an individual's existence lie deep and dark fears about the threat of death and extinction and about the seeming meaninglessness of life. The gospel exposes these, bringing them to the surface in order that they may be faced and dealt with. For the gospel confronts the human fear of death and meaninglessness by speaking of someone who faced and conquered death, lending dignity and meaning to it. More importantly, the gospel treats the natural human desire to avoid dying and death and to seek refuge in the world as the symptom of human alienation from an authentic way of existence—in other words, fear of death and its corollaries are regarded as an aspect of the fundamental and global human alienation from God.

The gospel thus confirms what human *angst* suggests—that there is something wrong with the way in which humanity exists. It also affirms that the human existential situation is capable of being transformed through acceptance and appropriation of what God has done for us in Jesus Christ. Something we could not achieve ourselves is offered to us. Earlier (p. 361) we noted an analysis of the human situation of value in contextualizing the gospel:

TABLE 1

Context of Experience	From	To	Through Jesus
Acceptance	Rejection	Acceptance	Love
Direction	to err about	to aim at	Call
Festival	Boredom	Joy	Feast-giver
Meaning	the absurd	the reasonable	Word
Liberation	Oppression	Liberation	Liberation
Becoming	Nobody	Somebody	Invitation
Fellowship	Solitude	Community	Presence

The gospel addresses each of these areas of existence. For example, the gospel addresses our feeling of existential rejection—the deep-seated feeling of "not being at home in the world" (Heidegger)—in order to tell us that we are accepted elsewhere by someone else. It teaches us to accept that we have been accepted by God, despite the fact that we are unacceptable. Our rejection by the world is thus transformed into our acceptance by God. The gospel addresses, and finds a point of contact in, our sense of not being right with or at home in the world—and interprets this in terms of our fulfillment, purpose, and destiny lying elsewhere. It speaks affirmatively of being accepted by God, of fulfillment and meaning being gained through responding to his love demonstrated in Jesus Christ. It speaks of us being *in* the world, but not *of* the world—identifying the world as our "playroom" (Heidegger), the area in which we exist, while locating the grounds of our fulfillment elsewhere.

This analysis could be extended to each of the remaining items on the above list. The category of "becoming" is of particular interest. The threat to human existence posed by death is that of ceasing to exist in any meaningful sense. We lose our identities. We become nobodies. Christianity doesn't talk about our individual identities being swallowed up into the absolute (like the Buddhist Nirvana), but about God affirming our identities in order to fulfill and perfect them. We become somebody. We stop living at the purely biological level (*bios*) and embrace life in all its fullness (*zoe*). The threats to our individual existence are overcome and disarmed. The Christian understanding of resurrection is of particular interest here, because of its emphasis on the continuity of personal identity after death. God affirms that we are somebody, that we mean much to him, and that to him our individual identity is distinct from everybody else's. The reader may like to extend this analysis to other items on the list.

Earlier we noted the important distinction between "objective" and "subjective" knowledge. The doctrine of justification by faith does not concern objective knowledge of "God in himself" (*Deus in se*), but the subjective knowledge of "God for us" (*Deus pro nobis*). The Christian proclamation, founded upon and embodying this doctrine, concerns *Deus iustificans* (Luther), a God who apprehends us, enters into our experience and transforms it, abolishing our alienation from our true existence in order that we might have and hold the glorious liberty of the children of God. "It is not we who handle these matters, but we who are handled by God" (Luther). Something that is beyond ourselves and our resources is *given* to us through grace and accepted by us through faith. So long as human beings walk the face of this earth, knowing that they must die, the gospel of authentic existence, of life in the midst of death, through the death and resurrection of Jesus Christ will continue to be exciting and relevant. Through the gospel proclamation we are presented with the possibility—as a gift!—of authentic human existence, living with God and for God, being forgiven and renewed through our acceptance of the crucified and risen Christ. This is indeed good news for humanity—and it is *intelligible* good news for modern Western humanity!

7

The Personal Dimension

Personal growth, personal development, personal relationships, and personal fulfillment are important items on the life agendas of many today. Some of the major preoccupations of contemporary society are linked with the idea of "the person"—preoccupations such as purpose and meaning. But what does it mean to speak of a "person"? In what way does a "person" differ from an "individual"? And in what way can the Christian doctrine of justification by faith address this interest in "the person"?

First, let us recall that Christians have found it natural and helpful to think and speak of God as a person. The Old and New Testaments alike continually ascribe to God attributes—such as love, compassion, mercy, kindness, purpose, and anger—that we naturally associate with persons. The idea of a personal relationship between God and the individual believer, established through the death and resurrection of Jesus Christ, has long been recognized as an exceptionally helpful way of understanding the way in which God deals with us. Thus Paul is able to use the same verb ("to reconcile") to refer to both the restoration of a wife to her estranged husband (1 Cor. 7:11) and the restoration of the relationship between God and ourselves through Jesus Christ (2 Cor. 5:18–20). Indeed, many contemporary Christian writers have gone further than this, emphasizing that to think of God in abstract, rather than personal, terms (such as "power") is to lose sight of an essential aspect of the nature of God.[1]

In an earlier chapter, we pointed out (p. 369) that the Old Testament concept of "righteousness" is now generally regarded as being grounded in personal relationship: to be righteous is to be faithful to a personal relationship. It implies acting upon the obligations, responsibilities, and privileges this relationship brings with it. For the Old Testament writers, the relationship in question was primarily the relationship between God and his people Israel. The related term "justification" can also bear this personal meaning and refer to the *rectification* of a personal relationship. To justify a person is to place him in the right relation to another person. It is this personal dimension of the doctrine of justification by faith that we shall explore in this chapter.

1. The Basics of Personalism

In recent years, there has been renewed interest in the idea of God as a "person." This interest may be traced to the writings of Martin Buber and the personalist philosophy he developed, usually referred to as "dialogical personalism."[2] This philosophy has proved to be of considerable importance in modern attempts to explain the nature of God and his dealings with humanity,[3] and in this chapter we propose to indicate its relevance for a contemporary understanding of the doctrine of justification by faith.

Buber points out that there are two basic ways in which we experience things, and designates one *experience* and the other *encounter*. To illustrate "experience," imagine a stone lying on a table, awaiting our inspection. We can look at the stone, we can pick it up and handle it, we can weigh it, and even send bits of it off to a laboratory for chemical analysis. The stone remains there, completely passive. It contributes nothing by way of self-disclosure, and it is we who have to engage in activity in order to gain a knowledge and understanding of it. First, we have to find the stone—it doesn't come looking for us! Then, once we have found it, we have to begin a long process of investigation to discover what it is like. The stone doesn't disclose this to us. We are active and the stone is passive throughout the relationship. Much the same is true of our relationship with most other living things—a tree, for example, or a fish. We *experience* them, in that they do not actively contribute to our attempts to know and understand them. Furthermore, the stone isn't changed by being experienced by us. It is still there, unchanged (unless, of course, a bit has been removed for chemical analysis). Because it does not *participate* in the relationship, it is not affected by it. As Buber pointed out, "The world does not participate in experience. It allows itself to be experienced, but it is not concerned, for it contributes nothing, and nothing happens to it."[4]

This point can be developed by making a distinction between an *object* and a *subject*. An object is something that is passive, that is available for our inspection, but that does not initiate disclosure. A subject, however, is someone who is active, who takes the initiative in knowing or understanding. Thus, going back to the example of the stone lying on the table, the stone can be said to be an *object*, while the person trying to gain knowledge of it can be said to be a *subject*. Buber designates this type of experience as an "I-It" relation—the sort of relationship which we have with a passive object.

Let us now contrast this with a very different example. Let us suppose that you are at a party, and you find yourself introduced to another person. What difference is there between that person and a stone? Four main areas of difference are immediately obvious. First, with the stone you had to take the initiative in knowing or understanding it—but with another person you may find that they take the initiative away from you! They may start trying to find out about *you* before you have a chance to start finding out about them. They may come looking for you before you start looking for them! Second, the stone was passive, and didn't disclose itself to you—you had to do all the hard work. But with another person, you may find that they start disclosing themselves to you. While you are still wondering how to start finding out about them, they may begin to tell you all about themselves. Third, there was no way that the stone would start trying to find out what you were like, but there is every chance that this other person may start quizzing you. You are addressed by someone else. With the stone, you were in the position of asking all the questions—but with another person, you may find that they are quizzing you while you are trying to quiz them. Fourth, the "It" is not changed by being experienced by us. The stone just remains the same. But a "You" may be changed by the encounter with an "I," just as the "I" may be changed by the encounter with a "You." The relation is potentially mutually transformative and creative. Both "I" and "You" contribute to and participate in the relationship: it is something reciprocal and mutual.

These four areas help define what Buber calls an "I-You" relationship. (English translations of Buber's works often designate this an "I-Thou" relationship, to emphasize that the "You" is singular rather than plural. This archaic phrase can be avoided, so long as it is remembered that the "You" in an "I-You" relationship is always a singular.) An "I-You" relationship is an *encounter* between two subjects, each of which actively contributes to the relationship. It is the fact that both subjects are active that distinguishes this relationship from an "I-It" experience in which only one of the two participants is active. The "You" can thus (1) take the initiative away from the "I"; (2) disclose himself to the "I"; (3) force the "I" to disclose himself; and (4) be changed by the "I"—and none of these are possibilities within the context of an "I-It" experience. Whereas we have control over an "It" and can dictate the course of our relationship with it, our relationship with another "You" is unpredictable, creative, and open. It can develop and change, and become something new and exciting.

2. God as a Person

As Buber pointed out, God must be treated as a "You," a subject we encounter rather than an object we experience. Many theologians have tended to treat God as some sort of object that human beings could discover by thinking hard or by studying culture, the world, or the stars. He was something over which we had control and whom we could seek out. To use Buber's terms, God was being treated as an "It"—while he should be treated as a "You." This point was developed by theologians such as Emil Brunner, who showed that the idea of "a personal God" embodies many of the essential biblical insights concerning the being and nature of God. The following points will help bring this out.

First, God must be recognized as having taken the initiative away from us by disclosing himself to us before we began to seek him. From beginning to end, Scripture witnesses to the gracious self-revelation of God rather than to human discovery of God or to rational proofs of his existence. God is known first and foremost as the God who reveals himself, who makes himself known, who discloses himself. God encounters us by addressing us, and this encounter with him is his gift (we shall return to this point shortly). We are not required to discover God but to respond to him as he has made himself known.

Second, "God" is not something we can examine at leisure under conditions of our own choosing. He is no stone on a table awaiting our examination and study. Rather, we must recognize that—like any other person—God is independent, with a will of his own, who allows us to encounter him on his own terms. As Buber pointed out, every "I-You" relationship is a *relationship of grace*, in that it presupposes that both the "I" and the "You" are *willing* to relate to each other. In order for a relationship to develop, both parties to that relationship must be willing to disclose themselves, and each must be prepared to allow the other to encounter him or her. God encounters us and discloses himself to us in a relationship of grace in that he is willing and prepared to disclose himself to us. To seek God elsewhere than in his gracious self-disclosure is to lose that encounter altogether and to treat God as an object.

Third, God has revealed himself primarily in personal form. God addresses us as persons in the form of a person. It is in the person of Jesus Christ, the "Word become flesh" (John 1:14), that we encounter the definitive self-revelation of God—and as that revelation is embodied in a person, it is both inevitable and right that we should think of God in personal terms. To those who suggest that this represents some sort of primitive anthropomorphism unsuitable for modern sophisticated humanity, it may be pointed out that this insight is far more sophisticated than the philosophical concepts of God they would have us adopt in its place. It points to personal relationships—the arena of the highest human values and most profound human feelings—as a model for our encounter with God. To speak of God as "love" is immediately to speak of the supreme human experience of love as giving insights into the nature of God. And if the idea of "love" is too unsophisticated for some, it may surely be reasonably suggested that their sophistication is preventing them from encountering the deepest experience of reality open to us in this life!

It will therefore be clear that to speak of God as a person is to remain faithful to a number of central and essential biblical insights into the nature of God. It is now appropriate to ask how the insights of dialogical personalism may be applied to the doctrine of justification by faith.

The essential point that must be made is that the doctrine of justification may be recast in terms of personal relationships. Whereas some of the language traditionally used in connection with the doctrine of justification (such as "imputation," "forensic," and so forth) is unfamiliar to many, the idea of a personal relationship is familiar to everyone from their own experience. All of us are involved with other persons and relate to them. All of us are familiar with the way in which relationships begin and develop (and end), whether from our own experience, from reading books, or from watching the latest television soap opera. An immediate point of contact is established with human experience. To drop into jargon for a moment: the categories of personal experience are receptor-oriented towards Western culture, and the perceptive theologian, teacher, or preacher is in an excellent position to exploit this point of contact in order to convey the insights of the gospel in this way.

3. Personal Relationships

It will be clear from the discussion so far that a *person* is basically an *individual who is involved in relationships*. In other words, the idea of a person suggests a network of relationships with other persons. An individual is solitary, but a person exists in relationships with others. Now let us ask how a relationship between two persons begins. First, we note the point made by Buber—both these persons are *subjects*. In other words, they are both active in their relationships with the world and other persons and are able to exercise near-total control over their relationships with passive objects, and a certain degree of control over their relationships with other active subjects. With this point in mind we may consider how a personal relationship is initiated. Let us consider John and Mary. Initially, they do not know each other. Then they meet, and John takes the initiative in introducing himself to Mary. What happens next? A number of possibilities exist.

1. John and Mary interact, and get to know something about each other. They discover that they have a common interest in the novels of Betty McDonald. John would like this relationship to develop further, but Mary feels that she would like to keep the relationship on the Betty McDonald level.
2. John and Mary interact, and get to know something about each other. They discover that they have a mutual interest in flowers: John runs a seed import business and Mary has earned a master's degree in flower arranging at an until recently famous midwestern university. Mary indicates that she would like "a meaningful ongoing relationship to develop," at which point John decides that he isn't into academics. The relationship does not develop.
3. John and Mary interact, and get to know something about each other. They discover that they have no particular interests in common, but that they *are* interested in each other. A relationship develops as a result.

In situations (1) and (2), no relationship results, although in both cases moves are initiated that might lead to a relationship. But in neither case are John and Mary prepared to allow this to take place. They are both able to exercise control over the situation to the extent that they prevent any relationship from developing. They come to learn *about* each other, but not to *know* each other. In effect, they treat each other as an "It." Essential to the idea of the person is the freedom to enter into a relationship with other persons: to deny this freedom is to stop treating this individual as a *person* and start treating him as a *thing*—an *object* that has no say in its destiny. Only in situation (3) are both John and Mary willing to allow a relationship to develop.

The theological application of this is obvious. God takes the initiative in encountering us through the word of proclamation, disclosing himself to us. This is an act of sheer grace—God is under no obligation to us to do any such thing, yet he does so out of his love for us. God makes himself available to us in a personal manner, entering into our experience and meeting us where we are. He addresses us, he calls us, he offers us his friendship. God proclaims his love for us, in word and in deed. God condescends to enter into a relationship with his creatures. But it takes two to make a personal relationship, and unless we say "Yes!" to God, that relationship remains unfulfilled. God has given us the immense privilege of saying "No!" to him. God treats us as persons, not as objects. Our decisions, our feelings, matter to him and are respected by him.

This point is of particular importance in relation to the doctrine of universal salvation, which has gained some following in modern theological circles but is, in fact, based on a sub-Christian view of God.

4. Universalism and Personalism

One challenge to the relevance of the doctrine of justification by faith arises from the suggestion that *all* human beings will eventually be saved—a doctrine usually known as *universalism*. According to this doctrine, the love of God for humanity is such that every human being will eventually be saved. God expresses his love for humanity by condemning none and saving all. In many respects, this is an appealing doctrine, particularly to those attracted by the Enlightenment view that all religions possess essentially the same validity. It will be obvious that if this doctrine is correct, the doctrine of justification by faith loses its power and relevance: since all will be saved anyway, there is not much point in proclaiming salvation and the conditions upon which it is made available. But is this doctrine *right*? Although superficially attractive, the doctrine is in fact deeply offensive and harsh. It parallels Pelagianism in this respect (see pp. 377–385): although seeming to be reasonable and positive, it is actually intensely authoritarian and continually threatens to compromise humanity's God-given integrity. Let us consider why this is the case.

Such is the respect that God has for us, that we are given the enormous privilege of being able to say "No!" to God. It is this, after all, that distinguishes a person from an object, a "You" from an "It." The offer of forgiveness, renewal, and transformation is there, waiting for us to accept it—but we are not coerced to accept it. In John's gospel, we read of Jesus encountering an invalid and taking pity upon him. "Do you want to get well?" he asked this unfortunate individual (John 5:56). The offer was there, but the decision to accept or reject it remained the invalid's.

This privilege of saying "No!" to God must be respected. One of the greatest travesties of this privilege—indeed, one of the greatest travesties of human dignity—is precisely this doctrine of "universalism." According to this doctrine, everyone will eventually be saved. They may not wish to be saved, but they have no say in the matter. Whether they like it or not, everyone will receive eternal life. Those who hold this doctrine usually protest against what they term the "exclusivism" of the gospel—the suggestion that some are deliberately excluded from eternal life—as compromising human dignity. And, totally unwittingly, they thus compromise the very human dignity that they treat with such respect. What happens, we may reasonably ask, if someone doesn't want to be saved? After all, it is perfectly obvious that at least a substantial part of the human population would regard the idea of being cooped up with God for eternity as something to be avoided at any cost!

But let us develop this point further. Let us suppose that one individual does not want to be saved. Unless the universalist denies human free will, this possibility must be acknowledged as genuine. *At least one* individual, and almost certainly a number several orders of magnitude greater, will not wish to be saved. What will God do about it? According to traditional Christian teaching, as expressed in the New Testament and elsewhere, God will respect that decision. God wants everyone to be saved—but, in the end, will not force himself upon an individual who, through exercise of his God-given freedom, decides that he does not wish to fulfill his relationship with his creator and redeemer. But for the universalist, God must *force* this individual to be saved. He must violate this individual's freedom and integrity. The same free will God gave to this individual is overruled as God gets his way and ignores the wishes of the individual. In an insulting display of paternalism, universalism represents God as brushing aside and overruling the wishes of the individual on the grounds that he knows best what is right for that person. To put this very crudely, but accurately: where traditional Christianity speaks of God seeking a free response of love on the part of the individual towards him, universalism is obliged to represent God as *raping* this individual. No choice is offered, and the integrity of that individual is totally compromised. Rape involves treating a *person* as an *object*—and that is precisely what is happening in this unthinkable scene.

This is not the view of traditional Christianity, which knows of a God who offers himself to us and is deeply wounded by our rejection of him—but who nevertheless respects our decision. God continually treats us as *persons*, not as *objects*. For the decision to accept or reject God remains *our* decision, a decision for which we and we alone are responsible. God gives us every assistance possible to make the decision he wants us to make, but he cannot make that decision for us. God enables us to accept his offer of forgiveness and renewal by removing or disarming every obstacle in its path—obstacles such as spiritual blindness, arrogance, confusion, a compromised freedom of the will, and so forth. But, in the end, God cannot and does not make that decision for us. To affirm human dignity is to affirm our ability to say "No!" to God—an affirmation the New Testament and the Christian tradition have no hesitation in making. Universalism perverts the gospel of the love of God into an obscene scene of theological rape quite unworthy of the God whom we encounter in the face of Jesus Christ.

God offers us a personal relationship with him through grace—and if that relationship is to be fulfilled, we must accept it. The doctrine of justification by faith affirms that it is God who takes the initiative and we who respond to that initiative. But personal relationships are not static—they are dynamic, they *develop*, they *change individuals*. And so our relationship with God, once established, forms the context within which we develop. It is the starting-point for becoming more like the God who has entered into this gracious relationship with us. All of us know how the two parties in a relationship become closer as that relationship matures and develops. And so it is with our personal relationship with God. It is a transformational relationship, in which our knowledge of God deepens and we become more like him. There is no such thing as a "legal fiction" in the area of personal relations! Saying "Yes!" to God is opening the way to a dynamic and transforming relationship in which God meets us where we are and takes us on from there to become like him.

5. Original Sin and Personalism

This personalist approach to the doctrine of justification by faith is particularly helpful in relation to two areas: the doctrine of original sin, and the relationship between creation and redemption. Scripture does not see the relationship between God and humanity established through the death and resurrection of Jesus Christ as being the initiation of a new relationship, but rather as the restoration of an old one. The relationship established between God and his creations in the action of creation and broken through the Fall is reestablished through the death and resurrection of Christ. Yet even in its fallen state, humanity remains the creature of God. How are we to distinguish between the fallen and redeemed states, since humanity remains the creature of God in both cases?

The personalist answer to this important question can be illustrated particularly well from the parable of the prodigal son (Luke 15:11–32). Of the three parables linked together in Luke 15 to illustrate the idea of lostness it is this one that has captured the imagination of generations. Perhaps we all know this parable too well to appreciate its vividness and clarity. Perhaps we all too easily concentrate upon the wayward son and overlook the tender picture of the waiting father, watching for the return of his son. Every age has its "distant country" (Luke 15:13), its own form of lostness, and can see its own predicament poignantly reflected in the narrative of the proud adventurer turned into repentant refugee. The son journeys to the distant land, there to be treated and exploited as an object. His assertion of his independence from his father eventually leads to the loss of his identity as a person, as he becomes merely a lost individual in a foreign land. And then he remembers his relationship with his father, in which he was treated and loved as a person.

Throughout the moving narrative, however, the son remains what he is—the son of his father. Nothing can destroy that relationship: it is something that is "given," something the son tries to cast off but eventually reclaims. The son may act as if he were *not* the son of his father, the relationship may be purely *nominal*; nevertheless, it remains. The son has no other father. Nothing will alter the fact that the father has this specific and unique relation to his son. As the son journeys into that distant country, his father becomes a memory, a past event; he is experienced as an "It," rather than a "You." But the relationship remains there, as real as it is unacknowledged. The great turning point in that parable (Luke 15:18–19) is when the son reclaims the relationship, making once again actual what had become nominal, and recognizing his father as a "You" rather than an "It": he arises and goes back to encounter his father, to reclaim and restore that relationship. The relation of the father to the son is still there, as it was before and would be after—but the son is now prepared to make that relation real and vital, rather than nominal and dead.

The theological significance of this point will be obvious. All of humanity are the children of God, but that relationship is experienced in purely nominal terms, if it is experienced at all. God is experienced as an "It," if at all. Humanity may be created in the image of God, just as the prodigal son is created after the likeness of his father—but humanity, like that prodigal son, experiences God as little more than a haunting and distant memory, a faint melody from a distant and unreachable land, the scent of a strange and far-off blossom. But the relationship is there. It can be reclaimed and restored. God can become a "You" and not an "It." God can be encountered as we return to meet him, not merely experienced in a distant and ambiguous manner.

To put this in more theological terms, we can say that humanity has fallen and is alienated from God—but through the death and resurrection of Jesus

Christ the possibility of reconciliation to God is proclaimed. Whether alienated from God or reconciled to him, humanity remains the creature of God. But in the former case the relationship is purely nominal—in all that humanity says and does it denies that it is the creature of God. Genesis 3 makes it clear that the fundamental sin of humanity lies in denying its creaturely status and attempting to become self-sufficient, placing itself in the place of God its creator. But through the reconciling death and resurrection of Jesus Christ, appropriated by faith, humanity is able to transform that nominal relationship into a real relationship, acknowledging the fact that it is God's creature and joyfully accepting the rights and responsibilities this brings with it, as humanity "is brought into the glorious freedom of the children of God" (Rom. 8:21).

This discussion illustrates the deficiency of the view that humanity is adequately defined *theologically* in terms of being "the creature of God." It will be obvious that the distinctively *Christian* understanding of humanity is that of "a creature of God *who requires redemption through Jesus Christ*." To say that an individual is a "creature of God" says nothing about the actual status of that relationship. It is as meaningful as defining the prodigal son as "the son of the father": this is *true*, but inadequate—it does not allow us to make the crucial distinction between the *alienated* and *reconciled* states of that son! To be unable to distinguish between the son as he tends to pigs on a distant foreign soil and that same son as he rushes to embrace his waiting and forgiving father is not merely to miss the point of a splendid parable—it is to miss the point of the gospel altogether!

It will also be clear that the concept of original sin may be illuminated by thinking of it in personalist terms, in terms of a broken personal relationship. Original sin is the state of existing in a broken relationship, alienated from the true way of existence. It is to live in a distant land, with only the haunting and fading memory of the homeland. It is like living in the aftermath of the break-up of a personal relationship. It is the state of being alienated from a friend. So deep is that alienation and so distant is the memory of him that, to all intents and purposes, God might as well not exist. And it is to *this* situation that the gospel proclamation of the possibility of restoration is addressed. God has taken the initiative in offering us reconciliation, offering to restore the relationship to what it once was and what it was always meant to be. The sense of joy is similar to that which greeted the news that Jerusalem's period of Babylonian captivity was to be ended, as God restored his people to their former relationship with him:

> How beautiful upon the mountains are the feet of those who bring good news, who proclaim peace, who bring good tidings, who proclaim salvation, who say to Zion, "Your God reigns!" Listen! Your watchmen lift up their voices; together they shout for joy. When the Lord returns to Zion, they will see it with their own eyes. Burst into songs of joy together, you ruins

of Jerusalem, for the Lord has comforted his people, he has redeemed Jerusalem (Isa. 52:7–9).

The gospel proclamation interprets *human experience of the absence of God* as *experience of alienation from God* and proclaims that this alienation may be abolished through accepting the offer of reconciliation and forgiveness that God extends to us. This offer remains an offer of sheer grace—nothing that we could do or have done deserves what God chooses to do out of his overwhelming love for us. Unilaterally, God takes the initiative in coming to us, in entering into our history and our experience, in order to meet us and address us with the word of forgiveness and reconciliation. To use Buber's terms, God ceases to be an "It" and becomes a "You." We cease to *experience* him as absent or far away and *encounter* him as our Lord and Savior.

6. The Personalist Point of Contact for the Gospel

How may these personalist insights help us address the doctrine of justification by faith to the contemporary Western human situation? The modern Western preoccupation with personal relationships and categories such as "personal fulfillment" allows a gospel that speaks of a personal encounter with God, of the fulfillment of human personality, to be grounded in the contemporary situation. As we shall see in a moment, human relationships are not fulfilling in themselves but point beyond themselves to the ground of their fulfillment—and the Christian doctrine of justification asserts that the ground of their fulfillment is none other than the living God, who makes himself available to us. We begin reflecting upon the curious sense of bittersweet longing associated with human personal relationship by considering a musical analogy.

Suppose you are listening to a remarkable musical work—perhaps Beethoven's *Eroica* symphony, or a Wagner opera. As you listen to it, you are aware that through the medium of the music comes a person—the person of the composer, who is reaching you and involving you in his personal engagement with the forces of fate and destiny. You are caught up with his passions and concerns as you listen to his music and attempt to understand it. The music mediates the person—it points beyond itself to its ground and basis in the person of its composer. Something—such as the sense of *Sturm und Drang* in a Brahms symphony, or the deep sense of melancholy in Tchaikovsky's *Pathétique*—comes *through* the music even though it is not actually *in* the music. And as we try to capture that sense, we find that it eludes us: it lies beyond our reach—something has been evoked but cannot be grasped. This same sense of something that is so nearly captured and yet eludes us is a characteristic feature of human relationships.

In human personal relationships is to be found a parable of our need for God. In love, the deepest human relationship of all, we encounter the strange longing to lose ourselves in another—to enter into a relationship that, paradoxically, simultaneously heightens and obliterates our own identity. We do not just love something *about* another—such as an interest in the literary works of Betty McDonald or flower arranging—but we love *another*. We love them for what they are, as persons. This is the stuff of personal relationships, the need for another person, a "You" whom we may encounter. Yet somehow in personal relationships there is to be found a bitter-sweet longing—something that comes *through* the relationship but is not *in* that relationship. It is as if a personal relationship points to something beyond itself, something that Buber calls "the eternal You." The paradox of hedonism—the simple yet stultifying fact that pleasure cannot satisfy—is another instance of this curious phenomenon. Pleasure, beauty, personal relationships—all seem to promise so much, and yet when we grasp them we find that what we were seeking was not located in them, but lies beyond them. The great English literary critic and theologian C. S. Lewis captured this insight perfectly:

> The books or the music in which we thought the beauty was located will betray us if we trust in them; it was not *in* them, it only came *through* them, and what came through them was longing. These things—the beauty, the memory of our own past—are good images of what we really desire; but if they are mistaken for the thing itself they turn into dumb idols, breaking the hearts of their worshippers. For they are not the thing itself; they are only the scent of a flower we have not found, the echo of a tune we have not heard, news from a country we have not visited.[5]

Our existence and experience as persons—whether it be of other persons, of beauty, or of pleasure—point beyond, like signposts, to something they themselves can never capture or encapsulate.

One of the most sensuously stimulating works of recent English literature is Evelyn Waugh's novel *Brideshead Revisited*, which captures the frustration of so much personal experience, whether in the quest for love or the quest for beauty. Somehow that quest always fails to find its object. Even when the search seems close to its end, we find another corner to turn:

> Perhaps all our loves are merely hints and symbols; vagabond-language scratched on gateposts and paving-stones along the weary road that others have tramped before us; perhaps you and I are types and this sadness which sometimes falls between us springs from disappointment in our search, each straining through and beyond the other, snatching a glimpse now and then of the shadow, which turns the corner always a pace or two ahead of us.[6]

And have we not been told, and probably discovered to our cost, that "it is better to journey in hope than to arrive," a theme so beautifully crafted into story form in John Master's classic novel *Coromandel*?

It is here that we may begin to ground the Christian doctrine of justification: in the experience of longing, of the constant failure to capture something that seems to be there in a personal relationship, pointing beyond it, but that seems to be forever beyond our grasp. As Buber points out, every human "You" points beyond itself to "the eternal You," to God. The unfulfilled dimension of a human relationship points to God: what is conveyed through human relationships, but not in them, makes itself—makes *himself*—available to us as a gift.

This curious feature of longing, of reaching out for what seems to be within our grasp, parallels the situation of the prodigal son. Even in the distant country he remembers the homeland. Its distant echo reverberates within him. It is as if we were born in a distant country, yet remembering our homeland. Traces and hints of that homeland are all around us, beckoning us, inviting us to grasp them—and yet we can never reach out and possess them. We see and hear them through, but not in, others. It is this point of contact that the gospel of justification addresses. The "It" we know intuitively to lie through and beyond our quests and hopes discloses himself as a "You." We learn that our longings point to something, to some*one*, whom we were longing for. "What you worship as something unknown, I am going to proclaim to you" (Acts 17:23).

The gospel thus complements and develops such insights by proclaiming the astonishing insight that a *person* lies behind and under our personal existence—and more than that: it is possible to *relate* to this person, to the "You" who lies beyond and behind every human "I-You" relationship. God discloses himself in personal form, in order to enter into a relationship with us, in which our own personality is both heightened and obliterated—as in any deep personal relationship. God takes the initiative in the process that leads to the fulfillment of our personal potential—by relating to the person, "the eternal You," who underlies our personal experience. To encounter God is to encounter what every personal relationship seems to promise yet fails to deliver.

The doctrine of justification by faith addresses the human need for the fulfillment of personality and affirms that God has made himself available for us, as a person, in order that we might become the persons we are destined to be. Justification is about the transformation and fulfillment of our persons through an encounter with *the* Person who underlies personality itself. It affirms a right and a wrong way in which this may be done: "Seek God—or, rather, recognize that he has sought you out and found you—and you will find personal fulfillment and purpose. But seek personal fulfillment and purpose, and you will find that they elude you, slipping through your fingers when you thought you had found them." For the doctrine of justification by faith reminds us that these are things that we ourselves cannot achieve but are graciously given to us by God, who asks us to receive them from his hands. True personality and authentic existence—which judge our ideas of "true" personality and "authentic" existence and find them wanting—are both offered to us by God through Jesus Christ.

The personalist approach to the doctrine of justification by faith thus makes a direct appeal to our experience of personal relationships and shows how these may be transformed. It speaks to us of a God who takes the initiative in addressing us and in offering us the possibility of a renewed and restored personal relationship with us. It remains faithful to the central biblical insights into the personal nature and purposes of God, and to the simple fact, so eloquently witnessed to in scripture and so powerfully confirmed through Christian experience, that God does not encounter us as an idea, concept, or argument—but as a person.

8

The Ethical Dimension

The Christian church and the Christian believer exist in the world and are required to live and act within it. But what principles and presuppositions should govern and guide the way in which Christians act within both the believing community and society? The Christian can hardly be expected to behave in exactly the same manner as his non-Christian neighbor and endorse each and every moral belief of secular society. In recent decades there has been a growing interest in the field of Christian ethics, and this growth shows no sign of abating. Ethics is widely regarded as embodying the practical or pragmatic aspect of Christian theology, with a contemporary relevance denied to Christian theology itself. But what is the relationship between ethics and theology in particular, and ethics and Christian faith in general? In this chapter we propose to demonstrate how the doctrine of justification by faith lays a sound foundation for the development of a distinctively and authentically *Christian* ethical system. It is at the point of ethical decision-making that Christian theology is seen by outsiders as coming out of the ghetto of the church and taking root in the world in which others live, thus establishing the interface between faith and unbelief.

For those who feel that the Christian church should establish its identity and relevance in the eyes of the world by its actions, the temptation is thus always there to treat ethics as the chief or sole aspect of Christianity. The rapid growth of "secular Christianity" prior to its equally rapid fall was marked by the belief that the secular justification of Christianity lay in the field of concrete political and social action, while matters of doctrine were seen as being at best peripheral and at worst a positive hindrance to establishing the relevance of the gospel in the modern period. Much was made of "Christianity come of age"—a faith without religion and belief, which was committed to socially acceptable political action. Inevitably, however, a critical attitude developed towards these trends. On what basis could the acceptability of such actions be judged? The church could hardly be expected to say "Amen!" to each and every contemporary attitude! The increasing recognition of the ethical shallowness and superficiality of secular "undogmatic" Christianity led to a growing concern to establish the basis upon which responsible, critical, *Christian* ethical decision-making could proceed. One of the most remarkable indicators of this change in mood was the increasing interest shown in Europe in the theology of Karl Barth, which, it was realized, established a basis for a Christian ethics—whereas the thought of Paul Tillich, once thought so relevant, was increasingly recognized as devoid of ethical significance.[1]

1. Theology and Ethics

Christian ethics must not be regarded as that compartment or division of Christian theology which attempts to work out the practical consequences of that theology. Christian faith is the root and ground of both Christian theology and Christian ethics. The question addressed by Christian theology is how our faith expresses itself in the way we think, while the question addressed by Christian ethics is how our faith should express itself in the practical affairs of human life. Just as theology deals with the question of how Christian faith affects the way we think about God, ourselves, and the world, so Christian ethics deals with the question of how we should act in that world. Ethics and theology are thus concerned with the unfolding of faith, and both must be regarded as essential to the life of the Christian church.[2] The Christian church must *think* and must *act* on the basis of its faith—and that thinking and acting are not independent of each other, but are related in the closest of manners. Both derive from faith in Jesus Christ as Lord and Savior, and this faith must find its expression in thought and deed.

It is as impossible to reduce Christian faith to matters of ethics as it is to suggest that ethics are irrelevant to Christian life: precisely because believers think and act, the permanent relevance and mutual relationship of Christian theology and ethics must be recognized. It may be, of course, that at certain moments in history it proves necessary to emphasize the ethical dimension of Christianity, just as at others it may prove necessary to dwell upon its doctrinal aspects—but this must be recognized as a tactical development, based upon the perceived needs of the moment, rather than as a permanent and irreversible development within Christianity. The mistake made with such astonishing ease by "secular Christianity" was to treat a short-term shift in attitudes as if it were a permanent development.

2. The Transformation of the Situation of the Moral Agent

The doctrine of justification by faith establishes the mutual relationship of faith, theology, and ethics in terms of the redeeming and transforming encounter of the living God with the sinner as an individual. The *gift* of our justification lays upon us the *obligation* to live in accordance with our new status.[3] We are *made* children of God through our justification as an act of free grace—and now we must act in accordance with this transformation. The slogan "Become what you are!" neatly summarizes this situation and encapsulates the essence of Pauline ethics with some brilliance. In justification we are made to be the light of the world (Matt. 5:15–16): therefore we must shine out as lights in a dark world, as a city on a hill (v. 14; Phil. 2:15). Our justification brings about a new obedience—an obedience that would not be conceivable before our justification and that ultimately rests on the grace of God.

The significance of the gospel for ethics lies not so much in its answers to the focal questions of secular ethics (What must I do? And how can I know what I am meant to do?) as in its transforming of the situation of the moral agent. The focus and emphasis are shifted from what is to be done (the *agendum*) to the agent, to the one who is required to act. The presupposition of Christian ethics is precisely this transformation of the moral agent in conversion, and the inauguration of the "new obedience" through the renewing and regenerating action of the Holy Spirit. It is this alteration in the life and existence of the individual that establishes the point of departure for any authentically *Christian* ethical thinking; a failure to recognize and uphold this intimate relation between conversion and the new obedience opens the way to the reduction of the glorious liberty of the children of God to a mere external observance of rules and regulations.

In what sense is Christian ethics dependent upon Jesus Christ? Are Christians obliged to imitate the example of Christ in each and every area of life? The New Testament does not seem to understand Christian ethics as an "imitation of Christ." Jesus is not understood as an ethical pioneer who hacked his way through a moral jungle in order to make it easier for those who followed him. Rather, it is the cross and resurrection of Jesus Christ that are understood to constitute the very basis of the Christian life and Christian ethics alike. To follow Jesus is not so much to imitate his example in every respect as to participate in the salvation he accomplished for us. We do not become the children of God by imitating the Son of God, but we imitate the Son of God because we already *are* the children of God on account of what Jesus Christ accomplished through his death and resurrection, which we appropriate by faith. What God has done for us in Jesus Christ assumes a specific form in history that gives some shape, expression, and form to what human purposes and actions are appropriate expressions of "following Christ," but our interest in the example of Christ must ultimately be recognized to be a *consequence* rather than a *cause* of our justification by faith.

The New Testament is dominated by the proclamation of the transformation of sinful human beings through a redeeming encounter with the living God. This transformation is understood to be partial rather than total—something is initiated, or *inaugurated*, within us that will eventually be completed and fulfilled on the last day, but that has effects upon us here and now. A new situation in our personal existence is inaugurated through the gracious action of God. And this alteration in our situation leads to a new desire to obey God. It is God's gift that leads to the obligation on our part: the death and resurrection of Jesus Christ are the acts of God that bring into being a new covenant with consequential obligations for us as the covenant partners of God. This new desire to obey God, which before our conversion was either absent or present only to a diminutive extent, is now stimulated and catalyzed by the action of God within us, as a transformation in our outlook upon and understanding of life takes place. The New Testament uses helpful biological analogies to bring this point out.

In the Sermon on the Mount, Jesus points out that a good tree bears good fruit, and a bad tree bad fruit (Matt. 7:16–18). The nature of the fruit is biologically determined: grapes don't grow on thornbushes, nor do figs grow on thistles. These are the biological facts of life—if you want to get figs, you must grow a fig tree. Underlying this remarkably simple analogy is a profound theological insight: The transformation of humanity is a prerequisite for its reformation. Or, as Martin Luther put it, "It isn't good works which makes an individual good, but a good individual who does good works."

Luther develops this point with a number of useful analogies. For example, consider an apple tree in an orchard in the spring. We could go to that orchard and read numerous learned botanical textbooks to the tree, which inform it that it ought to bear apples in the fall. But the reason why the apple tree finally bears those apples in the fall is simply that it is an apple tree, and this is what apple trees do naturally. Similarly, Luther points out, Christians do not need to be told to do good works, because they do them naturally. Secondly, Luther points out that doing the sorts of things a bishop does— like dedicating churches or confirming children—doesn't make someone a bishop! The office precedes the function—otherwise an actor could dress up as a bishop and make himself into a bishop by doing the sorts of things a bishop usually does. *Because* an individual is a validly ordained bishop he may dedicate churches. And so Luther points out that it is the transformation of the situation of the moral agent through his justification by faith that initiates a process that leads to the performance of good works as a matter of course. To exhort a sinner to become good through his own works is about as realistic as telling a thornbush to bear grapes or a thistle to bear figs.

A contemporary illustration of this insight may be found in the Oxford Group, founded in England in the 1920s by Frank Buchman and subsequently renamed Moral Rearmament (MRA). Buchman's emphasis on the Four Absolutes (absolute honesty, absolute purity, absolute unselfishness, and absolute love) made a deep impression on many and challenged them to undertake a personal moral revolution. Thus at the University of Cambridge, especially in the years 1929–32, the movement emphasized the distinction between "orthodoxy" and "life." What they had to offer was not any orthodox theology but the promise of new life through personal moral renewal.

In practice, that personal moral renewal tended to be ephemeral. It had nothing to sustain it and in itself seemed incapable of giving new life. Indeed, the history of thought suggests that such moral renewal movements are remarkably short-lived; they tend to spring up like seed on rocky ground, only to die for lack of firm roots. The Christian affirms that new life leads to personal moral renewal, inverting the MRA order.

There is simply no point in informing sinful humanity that the world would be a better place if everyone stopped doing things that are wrong! What is required is a transformation of the human situation so that the motivation for doing wrong is reduced or eliminated. Humanity doesn't need moral education—it has had plenty over the last several thousand years and cannot really be said to be much the better off as a result. It seems to be a universal fact of human experience that when we attempt to live up to our moral ideals, we find ourselves failing in the attempt. We all recognize the claims of morality, and we find ourselves failing in the attempt to live up to them. Underlying both the view that the human predicament arises from ignorance and the view that Jesus Christ is nothing more than a good teacher is a remarkably shallow understanding of the nature of humanity itself. As the great American moral theologian Reinhold Niebuhr emphasized, all too many modern thinkers have tended to work with a remarkably naive view of human nature—probably reflecting the fact that their middle-class intellectual backgrounds tend to inhibit them from encountering and experiencing the darker side of human nature.

Of the many remarkable works relating to practical matters written by English Puritans, one of the most fascinating is William Romaine's tract *A Method for Preventing the Frequency of Robbers and Murders*, published in London in 1770. In this work, Romaine pointed out that the law of the land was inadequate to deal with the root cause of robbery and murder. At best, it could inhibit them by prescribing severe penalties for those who were apprehended. Romaine pointed out that these measures were simply means of containing, rather than eliminating, the problem. The real problem lay in the sinful condition of humanity, which the legislature could merely control, rather than cure. The real solution lay in the transformation of human nature so that the individual was enabled to exercise at least some degree of control over that nature. And it is the gospel alone that holds the cure for the sinful condition of humanity:

> Thro' the merits of our Lord Jesus Christ, the divine grace and influence are offered unto us again, and whoever seeks them by humility and prayer, until he receive them, is then made a partaker of the Spirit of God, who first makes the heart faithful and penitent, and afterwards sanctifies it by the blood of Jesus Christ. . . . And whoever is renewed after the image of the second Adam, he has a clean and pure heart, and a sweet fountain might as

soon send forth poisonous water, as this sanctified heart can produce murder, adultery, fornication, or any of the filthy works of the flesh.[4]

While we may find ourselves slightly amused at Romaine's optimism in trying to persuade the English legislature to encourage the preaching of the gospel, we must allow that he was making a serious and valid theological point. The law curbs human sinfulness by making it more difficult for it to indulge itself—but it does not cure it. Human regeneration, which brings about at least a partial transformation of our sinful nature, is required if the root cause is to be dealt with. As an Irishman, I can still remember hearing stories of a local Irish religious revival in the year 1859. One of its most significant side effects was that the local police force found themselves without a job to do, due to the sudden decline in the local crime rates!

There is thus an "automatic" or "natural" connection between the justification of the sinner and his desire and ability to perform good works. The New Testament analogy of the tree and its fruits expresses the fundamental idea that the radical transformation of the individual ("radical" comes from the Latin *radix*, meaning "root") is prior to his ability to produce good works. The New Testament, particularly the Pauline writings, emphasizes that this is to be understood as *God's transformation of us*, rather than as our own attempt to transform us. Thus Paul speaks of the "fruit of the Spirit" (Gal. 5:22), drawing attention to the fact that this "fruit" is the result of God's action within us, rather than our action independent of God. Therefore, whereas secular ethical systems tend to discuss moral acts in terms of their goal (in other words, what they achieve or are intended to achieve), a theological ethical system based on the doctrine of justification will discuss moral acts in terms of what they *presuppose* or *are intended to express*—the individual's radical transformation through his conversion. The starting point of an authentically *Christian* ethics is the recognition that the conversion of the individual inaugurates a new obedience, a new lifestyle, and a new ethic that is at least potentially different from secular ethical systems.

3. Ethics and Original Sin

The doctrine of justification forces us to acknowledge a determinative aspect of human nature that secular ethical systems tend to ignore, play down, or deny: sin. The fact that we are made in the image and likeness of God (Gen. 1:26–27) is a starting-point for any discussion of our relationship with and responsibility towards God—and functions as precisely such a starting-point in Jewish, Islamic, and Deist ethical systems. But for the Christian it is *only* a starting-point in that it is necessary to recognize that, although we are created in the image of God, this image has become obscured, corrupted, and tarnished through sin. We are sinners—and any ethical system that fails to take the sinfulness of humanity with full seriousness must have its right to call itself "Christian" challenged.

The radical realism of the biblical view of sin and its devastating consequences for our understanding of human beings as moral agents are captured in the words of Robert Browning in "Gold Hair":

> 'Tis the faith that launched point-blank its dart
> At the head of a lie; taught Original Sin,
>   The corruption of man's heart.

The bland assumption of the natural and fundamental goodness of human nature, so characteristic of much Western liberal thought, is called into question by this doctrine. The myth of human perfectability and inevitable progress has been shown up for what it is by the savagery and cruelty of the twentieth century. If ever there has been a period in human history when human evil was evident, it is the twentieth century. How many outrages such as Auschwitz must we experience before the naïve assumption that all human beings act out of the best of intentions is exposed for what it is—a cruel and seductive lie? Reason is so often used as a tool for human ends, rather than a guide to those ends. As Reinhold Niebuhr so provocatively stated this point: "The will to power uses reason, as kings use chaplains and courtiers, to add grace to their enterprises."[5]

4. Towards a Pragmatic Ethics

As we saw in connection with Augustine and the Pelagian controversy (pp. 376–85), the concept of original sin entails a human bias towards sin. In other words, there is something about human nature that inclines it to commit sin. It is not simply a matter of committing sin without knowing that we are doing so—it is, rather, *knowing* as we do so that we are sinning. We know what is right and what is required of us—and yet there is an inherent tendency to fail to live up to these ideals. All too many ethical systems adopt a very shallow and superficial approach to the human dilemma, precisely because they are based on the assumption that the basic human problem is simply the need to be told what is right and what is wrong—whereas this is only *part* of the problem! The real problems arise when we try to put into action what we know to be right and find ourselves failing to meet up to our ideals. Any ethical system that fails to recognize this dialectic between obligation and ability must be regarded as failing to encapsulate adequately a fundamental Christian insight into the nature of the human ethical agent. The congenital weakness of human nature is the submerged rock on which the naïve claims of optimistic liberal thought founder so cruelly and so totally. The history of social ethics is littered with confident plans that have been wrecked through the stubborn intractability of human nature: the simple fact that human beings have a disquieting and deeply disturbing tendency to say "Yes, if we all behaved like that, the world would be a better place"—only to go and do something totally different.

It would be quite unrealistic to expect social intellectual visionaries to be diverted by the contradiction between the way humanity is and always has been, and the way they would like it to be. The great pagan myth of the "Golden Age," when people were rational and unselfish, is ultimately an expression of weariness with people as they are now. We must not allow the rhetoric of great social visionaries to distract us from the dreadful gulf fixed between rhetoric and reality. The doctrine of justification by faith sounds a note of somber realism, places a question mark against the confident declarations of the visionaries, and raises doubts about the fundamental perfectability (or even reformability!) of human nature. It is, however, a critical, not a negative, approach to ethics, whether personal or social. It warns us of the false prophets of naïve moral optimism, insisting that human nature in its totality—from the highest to the lowest of human faculties—is permeated by sin. Even those who are reluctant to call this inborn and inbuilt discord "sin" are prepared to recognize its reality—witness the famous words of the atheist poet A. E. Housman:

> The troubles of our proud and angry dust
> Are from eternity, and shall not fail.

This insight, however, does not of necessity lead to some form of cynical pessimism, as some ethical writers appear to suggest. The Reformers stressed that—viewed from the *theological*, but not the *ethical*, standpoint—human virtue and morality are "like filthy rags" (Isa. 64:6). In the face of the moral optimism of much Renaissance thought, the Reformers insisted that there is a flaw in human nature that prevents people from achieving their true destiny and renders them impotent to come unaided to that saving knowledge of God for which they are created. They asserted that man, considered from the ethical standpoint, is a mixture of good and evil. (Luther's famous phrase *simul iustus et peccator*, "at one and the same time both righteous and a sinner," is often cited in this connection.) But only a third-rate student of the Reformation would suggest that the Reformers had no interest in ethics, law, or morality! The writings of the Reformers abound with such concerns! But these concerns are always informed by the insight that human ethical actions cannot redeem the fallen human situation; that even the highest human virtue is tainted and compromised by sin; that even the purest ideals and most disinterested actions of individuals and societies are stained by self-interest and pride.

The doctrine of justification by faith results in a realist approach to Christian ethics, which recognizes that the pursuit of self-interest is an inevitability because of the total permeation of human nature by original sin. The liberal vision of the elimination of such self-centeredness and self-interest by education remains an illusion: education may broaden an individual's horizons, but it still keeps that individual at the center of the panorama. How often have we been reminded that the center of "sin" is "I"? Reinhold Niebuhr—perhaps the most distinguished recent exponent of "Christian realism" in ethics—argues that "where there is history at all, there is freedom; and where there is freedom, there is sin."[6] Original sin finds its ethical expression in ineradicable human self-interest—and any ethical system that overlooks or denies this fact threatens to degenerate into utopian idealism, losing any point of contact with the real human situation. It will, however, be clear that the assertion of the universality of sin does not eradicate moral distinctions within human existence. If sin itself is an inevitability, the actual extent of that sin is open to control.

Although it is often suggested that human social problems are a consequence of human *society*, rather than of human *nature*, the realist approach to ethics suggests that the fallenness of human nature infects the society in which we live. Individual self-interest becomes the corporate egoism of contending groups. These insights suggest that a "perfect society" is impossible in history, simply because of the individuals who compose such a society. Thus the goal of Christian social moral action is not the *perfection* of society but its *amelioration*—to make society better in the realization that it cannot be perfect because of human fallenness. If such insights are right, Christians who wish to be involved in politics and social action must realize that they, like everyone else, must operate within the context of the fallen system of human groups.

It is insights such as these that underlie Martin Luther's famous statement, "Be a sinner and sin boldly—but even more strongly have faith and rejoice in Jesus Christ." In other words, the world is fallen, and if the Christian acts within it, he will sin—but he must act *in faith* that he is doing what is best in the situation, under God's guidance, and rejoice that his sin may be forgiven. To put it crudely, but accurately: the world is fallen, and anyone who acts within it will get his hands dirty—but the only other option available is to retreat from that world altogether. Luther's doctrine of justification governs his thinking on social action: *given* that society is sinful because of human sin, the Christian has a right and a duty to try to make bad things better, recognizing that by becoming involved in this fallen world he cannot avoid being associated with its sin. He must act *in faith*, trusting that his assessment of the situation is as realistic as can be hoped for. And if this seems like blundering around in the darkness, it must be remembered that the human apprehension of ethical situations is notoriously inaccurate. Peter Berger speaks persuasively of the "ethics of ignorance": we are unable to assess complex moral situations accurately, and even less able to make sure that the consequences of our acts are what we expect them to be.

On the basis of this discussion it will be clear that we are placed under obligation to God through our redemptive encounter with him in the act of justification. But what form should that obligation take? There is a real danger that talk about our obligation towards the living God will remain abstract and formal unless we are able to ground it in the concrete realities of human existence. It remains an idea, whereas what is required is action. It will be obvious that a discussion of the *nature* of such action must lie far beyond the scope of this work: what we have been primarily concerned with is establishing the foundation upon which any responsible Christian ethics must be based. The doctrine of justification forces us to adopt a critical, but not a negative, attitude towards ethical systems. We learn to ask whether an ethical system is capable of coping with both the transformation of the situation of the moral agent and the sheer intractability of human sinfulness. The doctrine of justification does not stipulate any specific ethical system—it establishes the framework by which such ethical systems are to be judged.

Earlier we noted that the ethical concept of the "imitation of Christ" must be treated cautiously and critically. All too often, the concept is based on serious deficiencies in both Christology (Christ is treated simply as an example) and soteriology (the actions of the Christian believer are regarded as causing, or contributing to, his salvation, rather than expressing what has already been accomplished in Christ). Nevertheless, the concept of the "imitation of Christ" may be allowed a positive role in Christian ethics as long as these deficiencies are avoided. The "shape" of the life of Christ maps out the shape of the believer's life, in that the believer's existence is understood to be broadly patterned after that of Jesus Christ. But, in the end, the doctrine of justification reminds us that the very existence of that believing life constitutes the supreme significance of Jesus Christ for Christian ethics.

FOR FURTHER READING

James Gustafson. *Theology and Ethics*. Chicago: University of Chicago Press, 1981.

Oliver O'Donovan. *Resurrection and Moral Order: An Outline for Evangelical Ethics*. Grand Rapids: Eerdmans, 1986.

Paul Ramsey. *Basic Christian Ethics*. New York: Scribner, 1950.

_____ . *Deeds and Rules in Christian Ethics*. New York: Scribner, 1967.

Helmut Thielicke. *Theological Ethics*. 3 vols. Grand Rapids: Eerdmans, 1978.

John B. Webster. "Christology, Imitability and Ethics." *Scottish Journal of Theology* 39/3 (1986): 309–26.

9

Conclusion

We conclude by summarizing the importance and relevance of this doctrine under five headings.

1. Justification by Faith Concerns an Experience

Underlying the Christian faith is first and foremost an experience, rather than the acceptance of a set of doctrines. The New Testament bears powerful witness to the experience of the first Christians—an experience of the presence and power of the risen Christ in their lives, charging them with meaning and dignity. The experience of being crucified, having died to the world, and being caught up in the life of the risen Christ runs through the fabric of the New Testament as its golden thread. Christ was experienced and known as the risen Lord. This strongly experiential aspect of Christianity tends to be played down by academics, who understandably wish to concentrate on the intellectual framework of the faith—but this must not allow us to overlook the importance of religious experience in the Christian life.

The essential purpose of Christian doctrine is to provide a framework within which the experience of the first Christians may become ours. Just as engineers may construct a channel to bring water from a reservoir to a parched and arid desert area in order that it might flourish and blossom, so Christian doctrine provides the intellectual framework by which the experience of the first Christians may be passed down to us. It must never be forgotten that the great patristic debates about the incarnation and the Trinity were not undertaken for want of something better to do in the long hot Syrian afternoons! It was felt, and felt rightly, that certain doctrines of God and Christ—in other words, certain intellectual frameworks—were inadequate to convey the Christian experience of redemption in Christ. There was a contradiction between the intellectual framework and experience. Let us illustrate this briefly before passing on to the main point.

In the case of Arianism, an important fourth-century Christological heresy, the intellectual framework made it impossible to allow that the Christian experience, mediated through the risen Christ, was of *God*. Arius' views on the identity of Jesus—whom he treated as a quasi-divine figure, but *not* as God—made it impossible for doctrine and experience to be held together.

The two would have drifted apart. As Thomas Carlyle observed, "If the Arians had won, Christianity would have dwindled to a legend." Nazareth and Calvary would have no greater significance for us than Long Island or Tower Hill. It was the recognition of the need to ensure that the intellectual framework and the experience it mediated were consistent with each other that forced the clarification of doctrines upon the church. Just as a channel has to be dredged in order to allow the current to flow, so the intellectual framework had to be overhauled to ensure that the Christian experience of God in Christ could be mediated through it.

The importance of the doctrine of justification by faith relates to precisely this point. This doctrine constitutes the intellectual framework by which the Christian experience is transmitted from one generation to another. It creates the expectation that an encounter with God *is* possible and indicates how obstacles to this experience (such as self-righteousness) may be removed. It is the channel through which the Christian experience is passed down. The Reformation period in particular represents an instance of the recognition of the need to dredge this channel, to remove obstacles to this experience. The doctrine affirms that that which so excited and moved the first Christians—the experience of the risen and redeeming Christ—is available today, and it lays the foundation for the appropriation of this experience.

Our interest in the doctrine concerns what it points to, what it *makes available*—a reality that is sometimes obscured by the unfamiliarity of the technical term "justification by faith" both to laypeople and to those outside the Christian church. Many technical terms are unfamiliar and seem to be irrelevant to everyday life—and yet they describe something that is actually vital to our way of life. This is as true in law as it is in theology. The "Fifth Amendment to the Constitution" is a technical term that refers to a fundamental principle of American democracy. Even if the term is unfamiliar, the ideas it expresses are not. The same point can be made about many medical terms, hopelessly technical in themselves, which nevertheless refer to fundamental aspects of the way in which the human body works—to realities upon which our lives may ultimately rest. The important point—whether in law, medicine, or theology—is to *explain* the reality that underlies the terminology. And it is the task of the Christian preacher and teacher to *explain* just what the doctrine of "justification by faith" means to us as human beings in the sight of God.

2. Justification by Faith Concerns a Paradox

Any attempt to speak about God involves paradox for the simple reason that God cannot be comprehended in human words or, indeed, in any categories of our finite thought. Our experience of God—who he is, and how he is present and active in the world—cannot be reduced to simple logical statements. To try to do this is to treat God as if he were an "It" rather than a "You" (using Martin Buber's terms; see pp. 425–36). We cannot study God as if he were an object—if we did, theology would certainly make far more sense, but the price paid for this enhanced intelligibility would be a total loss of the *real* God and the substitution of an *idea of God* we felt we could handle! The difficulty lies simply in *expressing in words* what we *experience*. As we emphasized a moment ago, Christianity is primarily about an experience of God through Christ—and when we try to state that experience in words, we find ourselves groping about for ways of trying to express something that is virtually inexpressible.

The doctrine of justification by faith is an excellent example of the inevitability of paradox in conceptualizing, or putting into human language, an experience. The paradox concerns the relationship between ourselves and God in our justification. Christian experience points to the conclusion that every good thing about us, every good thing we do, is somehow not done by us, but is done by God. This is particularly well expressed by Paul, who captures this paradox perfectly. "By the grace of God I am what I am, and his grace to me was not without effect. No, I worked harder than all of them— yet not I, but the grace of God that was with me" (1 Cor. 15:10). On the one hand it was unquestionably Paul who was working hard—but Paul interpreted his experience in terms of God being at work within him. We remain morally responsible and free individuals—and yet we recognize that, somehow, our very freedom is grounded in something God did first.

We noted this paradox in the case of Augustine's controversy with Pelagius (p. 380). Although it is, according to Augustine, the believer who responds to God at conversion, the believer recognizes that God has prepared the way for that conversion and even has taken the upper hand *in* that conversion. Yet the individual makes the choice freely. It is not as if one part of the process could be ascribed to God and the other to the human agent—rather, God's grace evokes the response of faith, and even in that human response the hand of God must be seen. In fact, the only thing we could really be said to contribute to our justification is the sin God so graciously forgives.

It is this same paradox that underlies the conversion of those who, like Saul of Tarsus, seem to be permanently opposed to the gospel and far removed from God. The story of the conversion of Augustine is yet another instance of the importance of the doctrine of justification by faith—the astonishing fact that God will confront those who are hostile to him and far removed from him, in order to bring them home to himself. As Paul himself knew, reconciliation to God is a possibility held out even to those who seem to have permanently turned their back on God. Perhaps one of the most famous instances of this principle in action is the conversion of the slave-trader John Newton (1725–1807). Aware that he was trapped in his own sinful situation and unable to extricate himself, Newton was overwhelmed by the fact that God still met him in Jesus Christ and brought him home. His famous autobiographical opening lines from *Faith's Review and Expectation* make his awareness of "grace abounding unto the chief of sinners" exceptionally clear:

> Amazing grace! (how sweet the sound!)
> That saved a wretch like me;
> I once was lost, but now am found;
> Was blind, but now I see.

In practice, many evangelistic preachers find it difficult to cope with this paradox. When they are praying, they will gladly ask God to convert their hearers (working on the assumption that it is God who does the converting). When they are preaching, they will give their hearers the impression that it is *they* who have the choice to respond to God (working on the assumption that it is a free human response). It is this situation that has given rise to the famous jibe that they are "Calvinists on their knees, and Arminians in the pulpit."

Why is this paradox, so characteristic a feature of the doctrine of justification, so important? Simply stated, it is important because it deliberately excludes two inadequate understandings of the way in which God and human beings interact in justification: On the one hand the view that we are mere puppets in the hands of the Almighty, who are coerced into salvation whether we like it or not (the universalist position); on the other hand the view that it is we, and we alone, who decide whether or not to respond to God. In this latter case, "election" means that we choose God, rather than the other way round. The paradox of grace—which is ultimately safeguarded by the doctrine of predestination—affirms that it is just not this simple. In some way, God is involved in our justification, even in the response we make to his offer of grace. It is best to see this paradox as a safety check against dangerous simplifications of the gospel, particularly against those that present the gospel as an option that we are totally autonomous in accepting or rejecting. While there is a human side to every action, the Christian gains the impression—an impression that is difficult to put into words—that there is a divine side as well, and that this divine side is actually prior to the human side. For Augustine, this was the mystery of prevenient grace—grace that "goes before" us, preparing the way for us. It cannot be explained—but it must be recognized if we are to remain faithful to the Christian understanding of the way in which God is at work in his world.

3. Justification by Faith Concerns Personal Humility

The doctrine of justification by faith affirms that we are what we are by grace through faith—God gives, and we receive. The gospel portrayal of the believer's childlike trust in God, his Father, perfectly captures the attitude towards God which the doctrine of justification by faith suggests. As Calvin pointed out, we come to God with empty open hands, knowing that we have nothing to give and everything to receive. It is to God that we pray for the gifts he gives, knowing that we are ultimately dependent on God for our spiritual existence and development. We are totally dependent on God—a dependence we must recognize and incorporate into our understanding of ourselves and our relation to God. Whereas the Pelagian theologian Julian of Eclanum declared that we are "emancipated from God" and are free to live in our own strength and freedom, the doctrine of justification by faith affirms that we are weak and frail, requiring God's support and grace throughout our existence.

Augustine of Hippo likened the Christian church to a hospital full of people who are ill and have recognized the need for the assistance of a physician if they are to recover. The doctrine of justification by faith diagnoses our spiritual illness (sin) and offers us an effective cure (grace), made available through the death and resurrection of Jesus Christ. We are offered that cure, but must receive it if it is to heal us. Thus Augustine interprets the parable of the good Samaritan (Luke 10:25–37) as illustrating the compassion of Jesus Christ for sinful humanity. We are wounded and left half-dead through sin, and Christ the physician comes to our aid to make us whole. The two silver coins (Luke 10:35) represent the sacraments of baptism and the eucharist, by which God gives us grace. When we receive communion, we usually kneel with empty open hands to receive the bread, just as we come before God himself with empty open hands, with nothing to offer or give except ourselves, and everything to receive from a gracious God. It is this attitude of dependence on God that the doctrine of justification affirms as essential to an authentically Christian existence. In the words of Augustus Toplady,

> Nothing in my hand I bring,
> Simply to thy Cross I cling;
> Naked come to thee for dress,
> Helpless, look to thee for grace;
> Foul, I to the fountain fly,
> Wash me, Savior, or I die.

4. Justification by Faith Concerns an Overturning of Secular Values

The doctrine of justification establishes and upholds a central insight that both the Old and New Testaments proclaim with force: that God chooses those who are weak or foolish in the eyes of the world—indeed, even in their own eyes!—in order to work through them. "Brothers, think of what you were when you were called. Not many of you were wise by human standards; not many were influential; not many were of noble birth. But God chose the foolish things of the world to shame the wise; God chose the weak things of the world to shame the strong" (1 Cor. 1:26–28). It is not what they *are* that matters—it is what they are prepared to allow God to *do through them*. Let us illustrate this point to bring out its full importance.

The Old Testament frequently draws attention to the fact that the great men of faith were not called by God on account of their status, position, or wealth. Thus God called Abraham, not because he *was* great, but in order to *make* him great (Gen. 12:1–3). God did not choose Israel because she was powerful or mighty, but because he loved her (Deut. 7:7–10). Similarly, God chose Gideon to deliver Israel from the Midianites, despite the fact that Gideon's position within Israel was insignificant. As Gideon himself protested, "How can I save Israel? My clan is the weakest in Manasseh, and I am the least in my family" (Judg. 6:15). And yet, once more, the pattern is set: God chooses the weak, the lowly, the humble, and the insignificant in order to make them great. Perhaps the most striking—and certainly the most famous!—illustration of this principle is to be found in the story of Samuel's search for the Lord's anointed one (1 Sam. 16:1–13). Knowing that one of Jesse's sons is to be anointed king of Israel, Samuel assumes that Eliab has been chosen, because of his obvious great stature. But the word of the Lord comes to him, "Do not consider his appearance or his height, for I have rejected him. The Lord does not look at the things man looks at. Man looks at the outward appearance, but the Lord looks at the heart" (v. 7). And so Samuel eventually recognizes the youngest son, David, who has been sent off to look after the sheep, as the Lord's anointed one. And as the story of David and Goliath makes clear (ch. 17), David is able to conquer in weakness where others were defeated in their strength, because he trusted in the Lord.

The same principle is developed in the New Testament, especially by Paul. Paul himself was acutely aware that in choosing him as an apostle, God has picked someone who was totally unworthy of this high office. In the eyes of the world, Paul was virtually excluded from becoming an apostle. However, God was able to take this unpromising material, and make of it what he wanted. "For I am the least of the apostles, and do not even deserve to be called an apostle, because I persecuted the church of God. But by the grace of God I am what I am" (1 Cor. 15:9–10). It is this theme which Paul expounds with some force in his "theology of the cross" (1 Cor. 1:18–2:5), in which the great theme of God's choosing what the world regards as weak and foolish is developed with considerable skill. God takes those who know that they are nothing, in order to make them into something which they otherwise could not be. God chooses the humble, in order to elevate them (Luke 2:52; 18:9–14). The great theme here developed is that of God taking something small, in order to make it into something great and significant in his eyes which he may use to good effect in his plans for the world—and it is this theme that is grounded in and expounded by the doctrine of justification by faith.[1]

5. Justification by Faith Concerns the Future of Christianity

How will Christianity survive in the future? In the past, the Christian church in Europe and North America alike has relied too much on a favorable cultural milieu for its survival, knowing that its existence was safeguarded by social patterns of behavior. While this state of affairs continued, the doctrine of justification by faith was neglected, because it was seen as lacking relevance and urgency. But this state of affairs may not continue. How will the Christian faith and the Christian church survive if social factors favoring church membership are reversed?

It is here that the doctrine of justification by faith assumes its specific and peculiar importance. The doctrine underlies all evangelism, the proclamation of Christ to the world. As we have seen, the doctrine affirms that the same experience that stamped its powerful impression upon the New Testament is available today, here and now. It affirms that individuals may here and now be caught up in the Christian experience of the risen Christ. It exults in the sheer *attractiveness* of Christianity, motivating individuals to *want* to become Christians. In a day and age when belief must be won, rather than assumed, the doctrine of justification fulfills a crucial role. It is the *articulus stantis et cadentis ecclesiae*, the "article by which the church stands or falls." The Christian church takes its stand against a disbelieving world on the basis of the firm and constant belief that God *acted* in the death and resurrection of Jesus Christ to achieve something that will remain of permanent significance to human beings, so long as they walk the face of this planet knowing that they must die. We are exposed for what we really are—sinners—and are offered the possibility of transformation as a free gift of God. The life of the Christian church—its doctrine, worship, and proclamation—is based on the knowledge that God has established a new relationship between himself and sinful humanity through the death and resurrection of Jesus Christ, and that this relationship constitutes the only basis for authentic human existence on the face of this earth. The great themes of authenticity, of forgiveness, of eternal life, of meaningfulness, of purpose—all these are affirmed and expounded by the doctrine of justification by faith. This is the spiritual heritage that has been passed down from one generation of believers to another, like the torch of liberty, and we must pass it on to those who follow. For the gospel of the gracious justification of sinful humanity by a living and loving God is the pearl of great price of which we are the temporary stewards, and we must safeguard, defend, and *use* this vital doctrine on their behalf. A generation is waiting to be born, to discover the graciousness of the living God, and to respond to it—and we, like the runners in a relay race, must be poised and ready to hand over to them what has been entrusted to us for a time— the doctrine of justification by faith.

APPENDIX:
The Dogmatic Significance of the Doctrine

At the center of the Christian faith stands the person of Jesus Christ. To each and every generation, the same fundamental question is addressed: "Who do *you* say that I am?" (Matt. 16:15). The answers which the Christian faith proclaims to the fundamental and central questions of life—who God is, and what he is like; our own nature and destiny—all center upon the figure of Jesus Christ. Who is this remarkable figure? And why is he judged to be so important? The question of who Jesus *is* cannot, however, be divorced from the question of what Jesus *does for us*.[1] Jesus' identity and function—who he is and what he does—are simply the two sides of the same coin. Perhaps the most famous statement of this general principle comes from the German Reformer Philip Melanchthon: "This is to know Christ: to know his benefits." Who Jesus Christ is becomes known through his saving action—and Jesus Christ's saving action is only possible in the first place because of who he is. Thus our interest in the person of Jesus Christ is primarily motivated by our interest in the salvation that is proclaimed in his name. The growing agreement among theologians that Christology (the question of the *identity* of Jesus Christ) cannot be considered in isolation from soteriology (the question of what Jesus Christ *does for us*) has led to a growing interest in and concern for the latter.[2]

The assumption that reconciliation to God through Jesus Christ is a present reality for those inside the church and a present possibility for those outside it underlies the Christian proclamation of the gospel. To proclaim Christ is to proclaim his benefits. The essence of the Christian proclamation is that, sinners though we are (and sinners though we will remain!), we really may be reconciled to the living God through the death and resurrection of Jesus Christ. How can this be so? we naturally ask. We find it difficult to accept that we have been accepted, despite being unacceptable. How can it be that the holy and righteous God should enter into a relationship with sinners like us? Theories about how this might be possible are, however, secondary to the simple fact that it *is* possible! It is through the proclamation of this astonishing fact that the church takes her stand against a disbelieving world. The Christian church proclaims the possibility of transforming the human situation, of resolving the human dilemma, through confrontation with the crucified and risen Christ.

The central feature of the Christian proclamation is that God offers us salvation *as a gift* through the death and resurrection of Jesus Christ. Moral or religious renewal is not a precondition of forgiveness—forgiveness is offered to us unconditionally, as a gift of God. We come to God empty-handed, having nothing to offer except that which we receive by the grace of God. That gift, however, brings with it our transformation. Just as the planting of the seed leads to the bearing of fruit, so forgiveness leads to renewal and regeneration. To invert this order, and to suggest that forgiveness is conditional, depending upon renewal and regeneration, is to abandon a crucial insight of the gospel and to degenerate into some form of moralism, such as that associated with the Enlightenment of the eighteenth century. The gift of God precedes his demands and brings with it renewal and transformation.

Having recognized that something remarkable and astonishing, of permanent relevance to the human situation, was achieved by God through the death and resurrection of Jesus Christ, the first Christians were obliged to try and put this into words. This proved difficult: how could the richness and vitality of their experience of a redeeming encounter with the living God ever be expressed in mere words? The New Testament documents, particularly the letters of Paul, show how various ideas were used to try to express what had been accomplished through the death and resurrection of Jesus Christ. Redemption, salvation, forgiveness, justification, reconciliation[3]—all these ideas illuminated one or more aspects of the greater reality of what God has done for us in Jesus Christ. Although none of these ideas was adequate in itself to describe exhaustively what the "benefits of Christ" are, they combined to build up an overall picture of what is involved. Just as the individual pieces of a jigsaw, or an artist's individual brush-strokes, build up to reveal a picture, so these ideas combined to reveal the overall shape of the experience of the first Christians when they encountered the living God through the crucified and risen Christ. And their experience has become our experience—just as their difficulties in adequately describing it have become our difficulties!

As theologians wrestled with the richness of the biblical conception of God's redeeming action in the cross and resurrection of Jesus Christ, one idea began to emerge as the most convenient summary of the nature and purpose of that action—"justification by faith."[4] This leading idea of the gospel, particularly as expressed in the letters of Paul (see, for example, Rom. 5:1), came to be seen as encapsulating the essence of the New Testament proclamation: We are offered forgiveness, redemption, and salvation as a gift through the death and resurrection of Jesus Christ and are transformed through this creative encounter with the living God. As we indicated in the first part of this work, this central insight has constantly come under threat during the history of the Christian church. It is for this reason that the doctrine of justification by faith has often assumed a polemical, or controversial, role—challenging inadequate or inaccurate understandings of how we are reconciled to the living God.

In fact, the doctrine of justification by faith has now come to have a meaning that is virtually independent of its Pauline origins. In systematic theology, the doctrine of justification by faith has come to refer to the gracious restoration of man's broken relationship with God through the crucifixion and resurrection of Jesus Christ. It is this assumption that underlies the proclamation of the church—the fact that a real, genuine, and authentic personal relationship with the living God is possible, here and now. It is on the basis of this firm and certain belief that the church of God takes its stand against a disbelieving world. The doctrine of justification by faith proclaims the possibility of a total alteration of the human situation through accepting this gift. It declares that peace may be concluded between a holy and righteous God and sinful humanity. It asserts that a transition is possible between a dead and godless human existence and the living and vital relationship with the God and Father of our Lord Jesus Christ. The church of God stands or falls with the truth of this assertion—and it is for this reason that the doctrine of justification is often designated "the article by which the church stands or falls (*articulus stantis et cadentis ecclesiae*)."[5]

It is clear that both the Old and the New Testament regard justification as a transformational experience—in other words, justification changes us, initiating a new relationship with God that is charged with a creative power to transform us. As we saw in earlier chapters, Christian theology has expressed this important insight in a number of ways. For Augustine, justification included both the *event* of being *declared* to be righteous and the *process* of being *made* righteous. For Calvin, two aspects of this one entity could be distinguished—the *event* of *justification* (in which we are declared to be righteous) and the *process* of *regeneration or sanctification*, in which we are made righteous. As Calvin emphasizes, justification and sanctification are to be regarded as two aspects of the same divine act (1 Cor. 6:11)—indeed, Calvin refers to them together as "the double grace." It will, of course, be obvious that Augustine and Calvin use the term "justification" to mean different things (Augustine meaning by "justification" what Calvin means by "justification" and "sanctification" together). Obviously, this has given rise to considerable confusion, as we saw (pp. 393–97). It is a matter for debate which of these two positions is more faithful to the biblical witness—but in each case, the basic idea remains the same: something happens that initiates a creative encounter with the risen Christ, an encounter through which we are both forgiven and renewed. God meets us where we are, but he doesn't just leave us there! The offer of pardon and forgiveness carries with it the promise of transformation and renewal. When God promises the removal of our condemnation, thus giving us a new status before him, he also begins to refashion us and renew us through grace. Underlying all these related themes is the basic content of the doctrine of justification by faith: that God offers himself to us in Jesus Christ, and that the resulting union with Jesus Christ through faith brings about our inner renewal and transformation. The gift that God offers to us in justification is nothing other than himself. In justification, God offers to dwell within us as his temple and do for us what we could never hope to achieve for ourselves. It is this idea that underlies the most difficult verse of John Henry Newman's famous hymn "Praise to the Holiest in the Height":

> And that a higher gift than grace
> Should flesh and blood refine
> God's presence and his very self
> And essence all-divine.

It is helpful to make a distinction at this point between the *concept of justification* and the *doctrine of justification*. The concept of justification is one of several such concepts used by the New Testament (and especially Paul) to build up a comprehensive picture of what the "benefits of Christ" involve. The concept of justification speaks to us of the removal of condemnation and the establishment of a new relationship and status with God (Rom. 3:22–27; 4:5; 5:1–5). The idea of adoption points to our new identity as children of God (Rom. 8:15–17). The concepts of reconciliation and forgiveness point to the restoration of broken relationships (2 Cor. 5:18–21; Eph. 2:13–18). The concepts of redemption and liberation point to rescue from bondage and slavery, and the price paid by God in Christ for this (Mark 10:45; Eph. 1:7). Here, justification is an important, but not exhaustive, description of what the "shape" of our new life in Jesus Christ is like.

The *doctrine* of justification, however, is concerned with the fundamental question of how the "benefits of Christ" may be appropriated. How may this new life in Jesus Christ be begun? What must the individual *do* if he is to meet God in Christ in this transforming encounter? The doctrine of justification is the thin end of the wedge of Christian theology in that it is this doctrine that confronts an individual with the means by which he may enter the community of faith. It is this doctrine that controls the gateway to the church. It is this doctrine that controls the Christian preaching of Jesus Christ. Even if it could be shown that the *concept* of justification is not central to Christian theology, this would not allow us to draw the conclusion that the *doctrine* of justification lacks this centrality. In a day and age when the Christian church has to win the hearts and minds of men and women, rather than rely upon a favorable cultural milieu for church membership, the doctrine of justification assumes a new importance—because it is concerned with the winning of men and women for Christ by setting before them what Christ has done for them and how they may make this their own.

The doctrine of justification by faith has thus, for both theological and historical reasons, come to designate the astonishing affirmation that God meets us where we are through Jesus Christ, embraces us, and takes us home. It affirms both human sinfulness and the graciousness of God. Without sin, there is no need for justification—and without grace, there is no possibility of justification. The doctrine of justification by faith asserts that the real personal and transforming presence of Christ within believers is given as a gift. It is conceivable that this emphasis upon justification goes beyond the New Testament statements on the matter. But even if this is the case, it does not affect the importance of the doctrine. "Justification by faith" is best regarded as a slogan, a cipher, a shorthand way of affirming a crucial insight of the Christian faith: that we come to God empty-handed and broken, to receive a gift which far exceeds anything we can imagine and anything we deserve—the real and redeeming presence of the crucified and risen Christ within us, and the promise of forgiveness, renewal, and eternal life.

A similar situation has arisen within English-language theology in relation to the word "atonement," and it will be instructive to compare the two cases. The term "atonement" has come to be treated as equivalent to "the work of Jesus Christ." If you pick up one of the many books with the phrase "the atonement" in its title, you can be sure that its subject matter is what Christ achieved through his death upon the cross. The origins of this development are historical. In the early sixteenth century, the English Reformer William Tyndale translated the New Testament into English. Tyndale translated the Greek word *katallage* (now generally translated as "reconciliation") as "atonement." It is obvious that Tyndale took "at-one-ment" to mean what we understand by "reconciliation." The term "atonement," however, rapidly acquired a developed meaning—"the grounds on which reconciliation to God is possible." And just as one of Paul's soteriological terms has come to mean "the grounds on which reconciliation to God is possible," so another (justification) has come to mean "the free gift of salvation in Jesus Christ."

At this point it may be helpful to distinguish two related areas of Christian doctrine that are often confused. It is necessary to draw a careful distinction between the following:

1. *The grounds of justification.* This deals with the question how justification is actually *possible* in the first place. Why can a holy and righteous God enter into fellowship with a sinner? With this question, we are asking about the objective basis of our justification, the grounds upon which it is ultimately possible. This question is dealt

with by the area of theology often referred to as either "the doctrine of the work of Christ" or "the doctrine of the Atonement."

2. *The doctrine of justification.* This *assumes* the objective grounds of justification—in other words, that it really is possible for God to justify sinners—and moves on to ask a more pressing and practical question: What must we do if we are to make this relationship a reality? How do we actualize this exciting possibility?

We could say that the doctrine of the atonement, or of the work of Christ, deals with the question *why justification is possible*, and the doctrine of justification with the question *what must be done if we are to be justified*. The former is a little theoretical, but the latter is very practical and of enormous importance to Christian preaching, counseling, and evangelism. An analogy may bring this point out.

Let us suppose that you are in your automobile in a parking lot and want to get across town to an important meeting. You need to get the motor started. What do you do? You insert the key in the ignition, and turn it—and the motor turns over and starts. Why does this happen? Well, turning the key completes an electrical circuit, which energizes a motor, which turns the engine over, while at the same time generating a high tension discharge at the spark plugs, which ignites the gasoline, causing controlled explosions, which force the pistons down.... And so on. We are dealing with two questions, one very practical one (what do I do to get going?) and one much more theoretical (how come all this happens when I do that?). The doctrine of justification is basically about what you need to do to get going in the Christian faith, while the doctrine of Christ is about why this is possible in the first place. And, to take this analogy just a little further, the work of Christ is what powers our justification, just like the motor powers the automobile.

Another way of illuminating the relationship between the doctrines of the atonement and of justification is the following. Imagine an enormous hydroelectric plant, with thousands of tons of water pouring down every second to be turned into electrical power—or a coal or oil-fired furnace generating an enormous amount of heat to drive the great turbines powering the generators. You can sense the power, the energy of these plants, through the roar of the machinery and whine of the generators. Now imagine you're in a workshop, with an electrically powered lathe. You throw a switch, and the lathe comes to life—the electric motor builds up speed and momentum, ready for action. The power of that vast amount of water, the energy of those great furnaces, is now available for your use. In many ways, this illustrates the relationship between atonement and justification. Atonement is the powerhouse of the Christian faith, the source of the new life of the Christian and the basis on which the power of God becomes ours. But we still have to make the connection by appropriating that power, by switching in to it. And justification is rather like throwing a switch: It is through justification that the "benefits of Christ" become ours, are actualized in our lives. They are both essential links in the same chain—one deals with the "why," the other with the "how."

The Christian faith itself stands or falls with the fundamental declaration that God has in Christ established a new relationship between himself and sinners, and the life of faith stands or falls with the knowledge of this decisive action on the part of God. If this belief is false, the Christian faith must be recognized as a delusion—a deeply satisfying delusion, to be sure, but a delusion none the less. But if it is true, it is of central and decisive importance to the Christian understanding of the meaning of life, human nature and destiny, and the nature and purposes of God. The doctrine of justification by faith touches human existence at its heart, at the point of its relation to God. It defines the preaching of the Christian church, the establishment and development of the life of faith, the basis of human security and our perspective for the future. So important was the doctrine for Martin Luther that he stated it to be "the master and ruler, lord, governor and judge over all other doctrines, which preserves and governs every Christian doctrine and upholds our conscience before God." Once grasped, the importance of the doctrine for every aspect of Christian life—theology, spirituality, and ethics—must be explored and acted on.

Like many college students, I once had to study mathematics. One of the areas of that subject which I found particularly interesting was vectors. A vector is basically a force acting in a certain direction, and one of the problems we were usually asked to solve was to work out its relative strength in other directions. This was referred to as "resolving a vector into its components" along the three-dimensional axes x, y, and z. And just as a vector V may be transformed around the x, y, and z axes to give the components V_x, V_y, and V_z, so the doctrine of justification requires transformation about the theological, spiritual, and ethical axes in order to allow its theological, spiritual, and ethical components to be identified. We must ask what the implications are of the remarkable assertion that God offers us our salvation as a gift through the death and resurrection of Jesus Christ.

The doctrine of justification by faith contains within itself the germs of the leading doctrines of the Christian faith. It contains certain concepts of God, Christ, and human nature which assume a specifically *Christian* meaning when properly interpreted. By declaring that this doctrine stands at the center of the Christian faith, we are actually defining both the real center and the actual limits of its theological system. This has four important results:

1. The saving action of God in the death and resurrection of Jesus Christ is declared to be at the center and heart of the Christian faith.

2. Any necessary presuppositions or consequences of this doctrine must be regarded as essential to the Christian faith.
3. Any opinions that are necessarily excluded by the doctrine must be regarded as non-Christian or anti-Christian, allowing a provisional definition of the limits of the Christian faith.
4. Any matters on which the doctrine has no direct bearing must be regarded either as *adiaphora*, "matters of indifference," or else as matters that may be resolved by the application of other, secondary, criteria.

We shall consider the first three of these points individually.

1. By affirming that God's saving action in Jesus Christ lies at the heart of the Christian faith, we are suggesting that responsible theological speculation must begin with, be based upon, and be governed by, that action. It is this action that brought the Christian faith and the Christian church into being, and gives it its grounds for existence. For Martin Luther, this recognition led to the formulation of the "theology of the cross" (*theologia crucis*)—the assertion that theology is not concerned with abstract speculation about metaphysics but with the concrete event of the cross and resurrection of Jesus Christ.[6] It is at this point that the central concerns of the Christian faith converge, just as the spokes that support the rim of a wheel converge upon the central hub.

Martin Luther took this point with full seriousness, making the following statement about the nature of Christian theology: "The proper subject of theology is man as a thing of sin and the justifying God, the savior of sinful man." Luther's statement is of considerable importance in the face of the perennial tendency on the part of much academic theology to see its task in terms of philosophical speculation rather than reflection upon the self-revelation of God in the death and resurrection of Jesus Christ. Theology doesn't set its own agenda—it has its agenda set for it by the Christian proclamation. For Luther, God is to be conceived as the one who justifies sinners, rather than as an abstract concept. Similarly, the idea that we can have "objective knowledge" of God is to be rejected: our knowledge of God is never disinterested but is a response to God's faithfulness to his promises of salvation. God addresses us as the one who justifies us, who calls us to stand within his covenant of grace, who offers us eternal life through the death and resurrection of Jesus Christ. This is no objective historical knowledge of God—it is a creative and redeeming knowledge that promises to transform our existence.

The "truth that sets us free" (John 8:32) is not some form of abstract knowledge—it is Jesus himself (John 8:36), the concrete expression of the saving will and actions of God. It is in Jesus Christ that we have knowledge of ourselves as sinful and God as our redeemer. It is the death and resurrection of Jesus Christ that brought the Christian faith and the Christian church into being, and gives it its grounds for existence. The "theology of the cross" is diametrically opposed to our natural tendency to want to conceptualize God and insists that God is not some idea or concept which we can just play around with in some seminar room, but that he is none other than the living God who acts in our history in order to transform it. God takes the initiative away from us by moving first, by acting to justify and redeem us in Jesus Christ.

A similar point was made by John Calvin. In his famous *Institutes of the Christian Religion*, Calvin pointed out that knowledge of God is of two types—"knowledge of God the creator" (*cognitio Dei creatoris*) and "knowledge of God the redeemer" (*cognitio Dei redemptoris*). The former is open to anyone who bothers to look at the night sky or reflect on the beauty and orderliness of creation. The knowledge of God the redeemer, however, is a specifically Christian form of knowledge and is concentrated in and focused on the crucified and risen Jesus Christ and the witness to him in Holy Scripture. Thus for Calvin the distinctively Christian insight into God concerns the fact that he acted to redeem us in Christ. This is not to deny that he created us in the first place—Christianity shares this belief with Islam, Judaism, and deism. But Christianity comes into its own through the recognition that God acted to redeem his creation, to re-create it, through Jesus Christ.

The historical relevance of this point is obvious. The first Christians had no hesitation in worshiping Jesus Christ as their Savior and their Lord, and the early patristic christological and trinitarian debates were primarily concerned with upholding the fundamental belief that it was only through Jesus Christ that mankind could be redeemed. Historically, there are excellent reasons for suggesting that it was the recognition of the fact that "God was reconciling the world to himself in Christ" (2 Cor. 5:19) that led to the recognition of the divinity of Jesus Christ. Even in the Arian controversy of the fourth century, the conviction that Christ was the sole redeemer of mankind constituted the common ground between the two opposing views of Christ.

The importance of this point for a correct understanding of the nature and task of Christian theology will also be evident. There has been a tendency in much recent academic theology to drive a wedge between preaching and theology—yet it is evident that the two are closely related. Preaching is basically the re-presentation of the saving act of God in Jesus Christ to the present generation, an attempt to confront humanity with the possibility, the actuality, and the necessity of being reconciled to the living God through the death and resurrection of Jesus Christ. It is through responding to this call, through coming to the crucified and risen Christ, that faith is born. The

Christian proclamation is basically the distillation or summary of the significance of Jesus Christ for the human situation, linked with an invitation and challenge to make this significance our own. And it is unthinkable that Christian theology should drive a wedge between what is perhaps the most important task of the Christian church—the proclamation of Christ as Savior and Lord to the world—and the church's reflection upon its nature and identity.

This point was fully appreciated by Karl Barth, who regarded theology as a critical and positive tool for the undergirding of the Christian proclamation. Theology is about proclamation—the preaching of Jesus Christ. And an essential presupposition of that preaching is that God *has* achieved something through Jesus Christ. Barth's comments are full of insight:

> The Christian community and Christian faith stand or fall with the reality of the fact that in confirmation of the covenant broken by man the holy God has set up a new fellowship between Himself and sinful man, instituting a new covenant which cannot be destroyed or even disturbed by any transgression on the part of man. The community rests and acts on this basis. Faith lives by the certainty and actuality of the reconciliation of the world with God accomplished in Jesus Christ.[7]

In other words, the Christian church and faith *exist*, and the Christian proclamation of Jesus Christ *proceeds*, on the basis of the belief that God has altered the human situation through Jesus Christ. This is an essential presupposition of Christian theology and must be recognized as such.[8]

Anselm of Canterbury, the famous eleventh-century archbishop and theologian, defined theology in words that have gained wide acceptance: theology is "faith seeking understanding" (*fides quaerens intellectum*). In other words, theology is basically concerned with *understanding* what has already been *believed*. And central to that faith—indeed, the *immediate cause* of that faith—is the recognition of the crucifixion and resurrection of Jesus Christ as the saving act of God. Whatever interests the theologian may develop, priority is claimed by the need to explore and explain the consequences of the justification of sinful humanity for Christian theology (the way we think), spirituality (the way we pray), and ethics (the way we act). The gospel brings before us the free gift of God and challenges us to make this gift the basis of every aspect of our life—and it is the task of the theologian to work out what bearing our justification has upon the way in which we think and act. For justification brings transformation—and part of that transformation is rethinking every aspect of our existence.

The recognition that the saving action of God in Jesus Christ stands at the center of the gospel proclamation also allows us to assign priorities to certain doctrines. An excellent example of this is provided by the doctrine of predestination. In the New Testament, this doctrine is overshadowed by the proclamation of the divine right-making maneuver in the death and resurrection of Jesus Christ. It is seen as part of the substructure of that maneuver. It is, however, very easy to distort the relative priority the New Testament assigns to the doctrines of predestination and salvation in Christ. To illustrate this point, let us consider the positions of John Calvin and Theodore Beza (a later Reformed theologian) on this matter.[9]

For Calvin, the doctrine of predestination is an aspect of the doctrine of salvation. In the *Institutes*, Calvin does not assign the doctrine of predestination to any particular place of importance—it is one aspect, and certainly not the most important aspect, of our salvation through the death and resurrection of Jesus Christ. Calvin tends to treat the doctrine as a safety check, emphasizing the mysteriousness of divine election, and also cutting the ground from under any suggestion that it is we who choose God. The doctrine of predestination affirms that God has the upper hand in our salvation. Calvin's theological method at this point is *inductive* and *analytic*: he begins with the specific and unique event of the saving death and resurrection of Jesus Christ as the center of his doctrine of salvation, and then sets out from that point to explore its implications. The event is considered first—and only then the theological framework within which it is set. One of those implications is the mystery of predestination and election. But it is the saving event of Jesus Christ himself that is the center of Calvin's thought at this point—not the doctrine of predestination! This point becomes all the more important when the very different approach of Theodore Beza is considered.

For Beza, Christian theology should not begin with the saving event of the death and resurrection of Jesus Christ, but with the theological framework within which this event is set. Beza thus begins with the divine decision to predestine and redeem the elect in Jesus Christ, and then proceeds to deduce the actuality of this redemption of the elect in Christ. Beza thus employs a *synthetic* and *deductive* approach, quite distinct from that of Calvin, which assigns priority to the doctrine of predestination. The logical consistency of Beza's scheme is achieved through replacing the New Testament emphasis upon an *event* with a quite different emphasis (foreign to the New Testament) on a conceptual framework. Furthermore, in keeping with the logical rigor of his theological framework, Beza draws conclusions that are dictated by *logic*, but not by *theology*—for example, that Jesus Christ died only for the elect, a view that is not found in the New Testament itself.

By assigning priority to the doctrine of justification in this way, we are thus able to retain the characteristic New Testament emphasis upon Jesus Christ, upon something that happened in history which is charged with meaning and significance for us. The developments associated with theologians such as Beza take us far away from this concrete event, into the obscure and abstract realms of intra-trinitarian debates. The Christocentricity of the New Testament is preserved and consolidated through the recognition of the priority of the doctrine of justification, in both Christian preaching and theology.

2. As theologians, we are also obliged to consider the presuppositions and consequences of the fact that God has justified us in Jesus Christ. The affirmation that God has acted in this way is like the center of a spider's web—it is supported by a complex structure. It is like the rhododendrons Betty McDonald tried to uproot and transplant on her chicken ranch (what reader of *The Egg and I* can forget that description?)—the little bushes were discovered to have enormous tap roots, not visible from the surface, thrusting deep into the ground. The roots of the Christian proclamation run deep and wide into the rich soil of Christian theology. The part of the Christian proclamation which we encounter—the free justification of humanity through the death and resurrection of Jesus Christ—is supported by a considerable substructure, whose presence is real and vital, even if it is not immediately obvious.

The proclamation of the justification of sinful man through the death and resurrection of Jesus Christ presupposes certain things, and also has certain things as its necessary consequences. As we suggested above, it is necessary to explore these and to recognize them as authentically Christian. We shall illustrate this point with reference to two areas of theology: anthropology (the Christian understanding of human nature) and Christology (the understanding of the identity and significance of Jesus Christ).

For Paul, the "message of the cross" (1 Cor. 1:18) was the foundation of his mission to Gentiles and Jews alike—the proclamation that everyone, irrespective of their origins or importance, could be reconciled to God through the death and resurrection of Jesus Christ. It will be clear that this extremely positive assertion has a negative presupposition—that everyone, irrespective of their origins or importance, *stands in need of reconciliation to God*. The negative presupposition of justification is therefore sin. Through reflection upon the proclamation of our restoration to fellowship with God through Christ, we are forced to reflect upon the presupposition of this proclamation—that we are alienated from God and require reconciliation to him. The theological understanding of human nature begins with the recognition that we are the object of God's justification.

This point may be developed further. According to Genesis 1:26 we are made in the image of God—and some theologians have suggested that this is an adequate theological understanding of human nature. But as we noted earlier, the characteristically Christian insight into human nature is based upon the knowledge of God as redeemer rather than just as creator. The insight that God created humanity is important, but it is very far from being all that needs to be said about human nature! The doctrine of justification forces us to recognize humanity as a creation of God requiring redemption. The image of God in humanity is real, but tarnished and obscured, and requires renewal and regeneration. The doctrine of justification points not merely to the fact that humanity is created in the image of God but also to the necessity and possibility of the renewal of that divine image by redemption through Christ. It forces us to recognize a tension, a dialectic, between nature and grace. This tension is evident both in individual humans and in human culture. "Because man is God's creature, some of his culture is rich in beauty and goodness. Because he is fallen, all of it is tainted with sin, and some of it is demonic."[10]

It will therefore be clear that one of the presuppositions of the doctrine of justification is a doctrine of original sin. Perhaps the term "original sin" is not particularly helpful in understanding what is involved. The basic idea is that humanity is naturally alienated from God. We enter the world as creatures of God, and are confronted with the possibility of *becoming* children of God. "Original sin" may be defined as the natural human state, the state in which we are born into the world. It is not a moral concept but refers to the human state with only a nominal relation to God (that of being his creatures), rather than a real relationship (that of being his children). The doctrine of justification affirms that the possibility of that relationship is there. Man is "created in the image of God"—suggesting that there is an inbuilt possibility for exactly that relationship. There is a certain "likeness," a point of contact, between God and us that allows this relationship to be established. Some modern theologians, such as Emil Brunner, have analyzed this in terms of "addressability" (*Ansprechbarkeit*): human beings are capable of being addressed by God and of responding to that gracious address. Although we are born into the world alienated from God, the possibility of being reconciled to God remains open. As the French philosopher Blaise Pascal observed: "There is a God-shaped gap within man." In other words, human nature is unfulfilled until that gap is filled by God—and the doctrine of justification both highlights this deficiency in the natural human state and proclaims the possibility of this situation being radically altered.

The doctrine of justification by faith brings together an important cluster of ideas concerning the *identity and nature* of humanity. It affirms that we are creatures who are elevated above all other creatures by being made in the image of the God who created us and who subsequently addresses us through Jesus Christ. That address discloses to us that we are not what we could and should be, that we are lost and that God has journeyed into the distant country to find us. Our true destiny and fulfillment lie in our restoration to fellowship to God. Justification discloses what we *now are*, what we *are called to be*, and how the transition between these two states may be effected.

As we saw earlier, this point is illuminated by the parable of the prodigal son (Luke 15:11–32). Throughout this story, nothing the son does alters the fact that he is his father's son. But his action in leaving home for the distant country points to this relation existing in name only. He does not act as if he is his father's son. Then, of course, the situation changes: the son returns home to be reconciled to his father and to assume the responsibilities which the relation with his father involves. While he is in the far country, he is his father's son in name only—but on his return, reconciled to his father, that relation ceases to be nominal and becomes real. So it is with God. We enter the world with a *nominal* relation to God—and the possibility of this being converted to a *real* relationship is proclaimed in the gospel.

This does not, of course, mean that the doctrine of original sin has the same importance as the doctrine of redemption through Jesus Christ! We proclaim redemption in Christ as something that is purely positive and exciting, rather than as something that is negative. The doctrine of original sin, like the doctrine of predestination, is part of the theological framework within which the event of the death and resurrection of Jesus Christ is set. It is part of the substructure of the proclamation of the redemption of humanity in Jesus Christ. In affirming the reality and actuality of that redemption we are also affirming a cluster of related, but less important ideas—ideas such as original sin and predestination. The proclamation of redemption is positively good news—but, as we begin to reflect on it, we realize that it has certain negative presuppositions, one of which is that we *need* redemption. And it is this presupposition of our redemption which is expressed in the doctrine of original sin.

Let us take this matter a little farther. As we have seen, the doctrine of justification by faith is a shorthand way of referring to the fact that God freely offers us, as a gift, redemption through the death and resurrection of Jesus Christ. It is clearly presupposed that we are incapable of redeeming ourselves. That which we could never achieve is offered to us as a gift by God. Fallen and rebellious humanity is utterly impotent to come unaided to the saving knowledge of God for which we were created. It is not a question of asking how we shall reconcile ourselves to God, but rather of receiving the reconciliation God has accomplished and is still accomplishing, in order that a new relationship may result. One of the more humbling aspects of the doctrine of justification is the insight that we contribute little to our own justification apart from accepting all that has already been done on our behalf.

3. As "judge over all other doctrines" (Luther), the doctrine of justification allows us to give a provisional definition of the limits of the Christian faith. We have already seen how the doctrine of justification allows us to define the saving work of God in Jesus Christ as standing at the heart of the Christian

faith—but the doctrine of justification by faith also allows us to clarify the limits of that faith. How this may be done is of particular interest in relation to a perennial difficulty—the problem of defining heresy, and of distinguishing this from simple unbelief.

The problem of defining heresy has confronted the church from the earliest of times. If the distinctive essence of Christianity consists in the fact that God has redeemed us through Jesus Christ, it must follow that the Christian understanding of God, Jesus Christ, and humanity be consistent with this understanding of redemption. Thus the Christian understanding of God must be such that he can effect the redemption of humanity through Christ; the Christian understanding of humanity must be such that redemption is both possible and genuine. In other words, it is essential that the Christian understanding of God, Christ, and humanity be *consistent with* the doctrine of justification by faith. Let us develop this point.

First, let us note that the rejection or denial of the principle that God has redeemed us through Jesus Christ is nothing less than the rejection of Christianity itself. In other words, to deny that God has redeemed us through Jesus Christ is to deny the most fundamental truth claim the Christian faith dares to make. This isn't heresy—it is simply unbelief, a flat rejection of what Christianity has to say. In the early fifth century, the theologian Vincent of Lérins developed a test to determine whether something was authentically Christian or not—the so-called "Vincentian Canon."[11] According to Vincent, it was necessary to ask three crucial questions before deciding whether something was authentically Christian. First, was it believed everywhere? If there was a significant section of the Christian church that refused to accept a certain doctrine, it could not be regarded as authentic. Second, was it always believed? If it was a recent innovation, there were excellent reasons for questioning its authenticity. Third, was it believed by everyone? In other words, did the doctrine command widespread support among ordinary believers? Once more, the authenticity of any doctrine only believed by a small section of the Christian church down through the ages had to be challenged. Yet it is obvious that the basic principle encapsulated in the doctrine of justification satisfies all three conditions. The belief that God has redeemed humanity through Jesus Christ is probably the most central and characteristic feature of the Christian faith down through the ages—and to deny this is to step outside the limits of the Christian faith. The distinction between what is Christian and what is not lies in whether this doctrine is accepted: the distinction between what is orthodox and what is heretical, however, lies in how this doctrine, once conceded and accepted, is understood.

Heresy arises through accepting the basic principle but interpreting its terms in such a way that internal inconsistency results. In other words, the principle is granted, but it is inadequately understood: (1) It is interpreted in such a way that Christ cannot effect the redemption of humanity; and (2) it is interpreted in such a way that humanity—the object of justification—cannot be justified, properly speaking. Let us examine each of these possibilities.

Who is the redeemer? The answer given to this question must be able to account for the uniqueness of his office and for his ability to mediate between God and humanity. There must therefore be an essential similarity between Christ and ourselves if he is to be able to mediate between us and God, and yet at the same time there must be something fundamentally different about him—every human being is not, after all, a redeemer! Heresy can arise simply by failing to uphold these two points simultaneously, so that the affirmation of one amounts to the denial of the other. If the *difference* of Jesus Christ from us is emphasized without maintaining his essential similarity to us, his ability to reconcile us to God is lost, in that he no longer has a point of contact with those whom he is supposed to redeem. On the other hand, if his *similarity* to us is emphasized, without acknowledging that in at least one respect he is fundamentally different, then the redeemer himself requires redemption! If the redeemer is treated as being similar in every respect to us, he must be acknowledged to share our need for redemption. Therefore *either* all of us are actually redeemers, to a greater or lesser extent, or else the redeemer cannot redeem!

Two ways of approaching this may be noted. In the patristic period, two fundamental assumptions governed thinking on the redemption of mankind in Christ. First, only God can save. Unless Jesus Christ *is* God in some sense of the word, redemption is impossible. Second, "the unassumed is the unhealed."[12] In other words, if human nature is to be redeemed, it is essential that the redeemer (God) comes into contact with what is to be redeemed (human nature). Therefore, the patristic period was virtually unanimous in declaring that Jesus Christ, as the redeemer of mankind, had to be both God and man. In the modern period, however, the personalist philosophies, noted earlier, have laid emphasis on the need for a personal encounter of the reconciler (God) with those who are to be reconciled to him. God must meet us in a personal manner within history—in other words, he must meet us as a person. Once more, the traditional "two-natures" doctrine proves to preserve a crucial insight—that God meets us where we are through Jesus Christ. If it is not God who meets us in Jesus Christ, no reconciliation to God is possible. And if Jesus Christ is not a human being like us, the personal point of contact with us is lost.

It will be obvious that the doctrine of justification by faith requires that Jesus Christ shares our common humanity, except our need for redemption. After all, Christianity has always insisted that Jesus is a solution to the human dilemma, rather than part of the problem! Traditional Christianity has upheld this crucial insight by insisting that Jesus Christ is at one and the same time both God and man. It would be much simpler to suggest that Jesus was just God, or just man—but if we are to uphold the possibility and actuality of our justification, it is necessary to insist that they are both true. From the above discussion, it will be obvious that two heresies may arise when, though the principle of redemption through Christ is upheld, the person of Christ is interpreted in such a way that this redemption becomes impossible. On the one hand, Jesus Christ loses his point of contact with those he is meant to redeem—this heresy is generally known as *Docetism*.[13] On the other, he loses his essential dissimilarity from those whom he came to redeem, and comes to be treated simply as a particularly enlightened human being—a heresy generally known as *Ebionitism*.[14]

Who are the redeemed? The answer to this question must be capable of explaining why redemption is necessary from outside humanity itself—in other words, why we cannot redeem ourselves. The doctrine of justification affirms that we cannot *achieve* redemption, but that if someone else obtains that redemption for us we are in a position to *receive*. The object of redemption—we, ourselves—must both require redemption and be capable of accepting that redemption when it is offered to us. These two aspects of the question must be maintained at one and the same time, just like the humanity and divinity of Christ. If our need for redemption is granted, yet our impotence to redeem ourselves is denied, the conclusion follows that we would be the agents of our own redemption. This is not necessarily to say that each individual could redeem himself, but rather to suggest that individual A could redeem B, and individual B could redeem A. Reconciliation could then be effected by at least some individuals, if not by all, to varying degrees—which immediately contradicts the principle of redemption through Jesus Christ alone. And if our impotence to accept redemption, once it is offered to us, is denied, that redemption again becomes an impossibility. Broadly speaking, these two positions correspond to the Pelagian and the Manichaean heresies discussed in chapter 3.

The four positions we have just outlined are to be rejected as inadequate as much as false, in that they maintain the central principle of the doctrine of justification by faith—that we are redeemed through Christ alone—while interpreting its terms in such a way that inconsistency results. It is in this sense that the doctrine of justification by faith defines both the center and the limits of the Christian faith. It defines the center of the Christian faith as the gratuitous redemptive activity of God in Jesus Christ. It defines the limits of the Christian faith by regulating the interpretation of that redemptive activity. To bring this point out, let us develop a geometrical analogy.

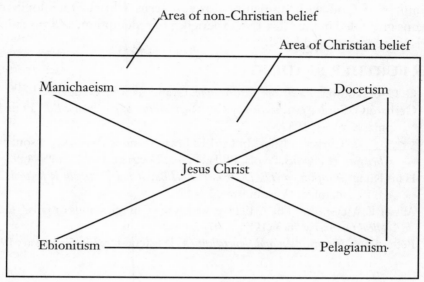

Figure 1

The area of authentically *Christian* teaching on man and Christ can be compared with a square or rectangle, whose diagonals intersect at the center: the saving work of God in Jesus Christ. The limits of the Christian faith are defined by the four corners of that figure, corresponding to the Docetic and Ebionite heresies at the ends of one diagonal, and the Pelagian and Manichaean heresies at the end of the other. The area encompassed within that figure may be regarded as authentically Christian, in that redemption through Christ is asserted to be both *necessary* and *possible* in the terms stated.

The four heresies described above may be regarded as the four natural heresies of the Christian faith, each of which arises through an inadequate interpretation of the doctrine of justification by faith. It is no accident that these were by far the most important heresies to be debated in the early church, just as it is no accident that all four, under different names, are still encountered in the modern period. The doctrine of justification by faith gives us a way of demonstrating how these views arise, as well as an important means of dealing with them by helping us define both the center and the limits of the Christian faith.

On the basis of the above discussion, it will be clear that the doctrine of justification by faith provides an important method of ensuring the connection and continuity between Christian preaching and Christian theology. It provides a valuable cluster of checks and balances to ensure that theological speculation never gets out of hand but remains wedded to the creative saving encounter of God with humanity through Jesus Christ. Theology thus remains grounded in the Christian experience of redemption, and worship of Christ as redeemer and Lord.

FOR FURTHER READING

G. C. Berkouwer. *Faith and Justification*. Grand Rapids: Eerdmans, 1954.

Gerhard O. Forde. *Justification by Faith—A Matter of Death and Life*. Philadelphia: Fortress, 1982.

_____ . "Christian Life." In Carl E. Braaten and Robert W. Jenson, eds., *Christian Dogmatics*. 2 vols. Philadelphia: Fortress, 1982. 2:395–469.

Hans Küng. *Justification: The Doctrine of Karl Barth and a Catholic Reflection*. 2nd ed. Philadelphia: Westminster, 1981.

Alister E. McGrath. "The Article by which the Church stands or falls." *Evangelical Quarterly* 58/3 (1986): 207–28.

Peter Toon. *Justification and Sanctification*. Westchester, Ill.: Crossway, 1983.

NOTES

PREFACE

1. *Iustitia Dei: A History of the Christian Doctrine of Justification*, 2 vols. (Cambridge: Cambridge University Press, 1986).

2. Initially, the present work was modeled on Gerhard Müller's excellent college textbook *Die Rechfertigungslehre: Geschichte und Probleme* (Gütersloh: Mohn, 1977), but it soon became apparent that modifications to this model were necessary.

CHAPTER 1: INTRODUCTION

1. Paul Tillich, "The Protestant Message and the Man of Today," in *The Protestant Era* (Chicago: University of Chicago Press, 1948), 196–98.

2. C. S. Lewis, *God in the Dock* (Grand Rapids: Eerdmans, 1970), 96.

3. For a discussion of the point at issue in relation to the Christological doctrines, see Alister E. McGrath, *Understanding Jesus: Who Jesus Christ Is and Why He Matters* (Grand Rapids: Zondervan, 1987), 29–36.

4. David A. Shank, "Towards an Understanding of Christian Conversion," *Mission Focus* 5 (1976): 5. See further Harvie M. Conn, *Eternal Word and Changing Worlds: Theology, Anthropology and Mission in Trialogue* (Grand Rapids: Zondervan, 1984), for a stimulating analysis.

CHAPTER 2: THE BIBLICAL FOUNDATION

1. For an analysis of the problem, see Alister E. McGrath, *Iustitia Dei: A History of the Christian Doctrine of Justification*, 2 vols. (Cambridge: Cambridge University Press, 1986), 1: 4–16.

2. The full implications of the Hebrew idea of "righteousness" have probably only been fully realized since the publication of H. Cremer, *Die paulinische Rechtfertigungslehre im Zusammenhang ihrer geschichtlichen Voraussetzungen* (Gütersloh, 1899) ["The Pauline Doctrine of Justification in the Context of Its Historical Presuppositions"]. For a summary of Cremer's views, see Walther Eichrodt, *Theology of the Old Testament*, 2 vols. (Philadelphia: Westminster, 1975), 1: 240–41.

3. See especially Ernst Käsemann, *Commentary on Romans* (Grand Rapids: Eerdmans, 1980).

4. This point is argued by E. P. Sanders, *Paul and Palestinian Judaism* (Philadelphia: Fortress, 1977), and more recently in his *Paul, The Law and the Jewish People* (Philadelphia: Fortress, 1983). For a response to Sanders' views, see W. D. Davies, *Paul and Rabbinic Judaism*, 2nd ed. (Philadelphia: Fortress, 1980).

CHAPTER 3: AUGUSTINE AND THE PELAGIAN CONTROVERSY

1. For details, see Peter Brown, *Augustine of Hippo: A Biography* (Berkeley: University of California Press, 1967), 101–14.

2. See Alister E. McGrath, *Iustitia Dei: A History of the Christian Doctrine of Justification*, 2 vols. (Cambridge: Cambridge University Press, 1986), 1: 17–23.

3. For the course of the controversy, see Brown, *Augustine of Hippo*, 340–735.

CHAPTER 4: THE REFORMATION

1. For details of the medieval and Reformation debates, see Alister E. McGrath, *Iustitia Dei: A History of the Christian Doctrine of Justification*, 2 vols. (Cambridge: Cambridge University Press, 1986), 1: 37–187.

2. For details of this school, see Alister E. McGrath, *The Intellectual Origins of the European Reformation* (New York: Basil Blackwell, 1987), 69–85.

3. For details see Alister E. McGrath, *Luther's Theology of the Cross: Martin Luther's Theological Breakthrough* (New York: Basil Blackwell, 1985), 53–63; 85–92.

4. *Luther's Works*, 54 vols. (Philadelphia: Muhlenberg, 1956–76), 34: 336–38; McGrath, *Luther's Theology of the Cross*, 95–98.

5. As quoted in Charles W. Carter, ed., *A Contemporary Wesleyan Theology* (Grand Rapids: Zondervan, 1983), 344.

6. See McGrath, *Iustitia Dei*, 2: 20–32, for details.

7. See McGrath, *Iustitia Dei*, 2: 32–39, for a discussion.

8. John Calvin, *Institutes of the Christian Religion*, trans. Henry Beveridge, 2 vols. (Grand Rapids: Eerdmans, 1975), 2: 99.

CHAPTER 5: DENOMINATIONAL DIFFERENCES

1. For the reasons why, see Alister E. McGrath, *Iustitia Dei: A History of the Christian Doctrine of Justification*, 2 vols. (Cambridge: Cambridge University Press, 1986), 1: 2–4.

2. For a detailed analysis, see ibid., 2: 44–51.

3. See ibid., 51–53, for the five main points of divergence.

4. John Wesley, *Sermons on Several Occasions* (London: Epworth, 1944), 174.

5. Heidelberg Catechism, Q.60, in Arthur C. Cochrane, *Reformed Confessions of the 16th Century* (Philadelphia: Westminster, 1966), 315. Questions 61–64 (pp. 315–16) are also relevant to this discussion.

6. The term often used in connection with discussions of the nature of justifying righteousness is *the formal cause of justification*—in other words, the *immediate* cause of justification. Although it is possible to distinguish various causes of our justification (for example, the grace of God, the merit of Christ, and so forth), the Protestant–Roman-Catholic debate has tended to center on the immediate (that is, formal) cause of justification. For the Protestant, the formal cause of justification is imputed righteousness; for the Roman Catholic, it is inherent righteousness.

An interesting theology of justification, which attempts to mediate between the Roman Catholic and Protestant positions, is known as *double justification*. This view, associated with Girolamo Seripando at the Council of Trent and several theologians of the Church of England in the later seventeenth century, holds that there is a double or two-fold formal cause of justification: the imputed righteousness of Christ and inherent righteousness. In practice, this doctrine has had little influence and is of purely historical interest.

7. For the development of this distinction and its significance, see McGrath, *Iustitia Dei*, 1: 109–19; 2: 80–9 (esp. 83–89).

8. For the doctrines of justification associated with the Enlightenment, see McGrath, *Iustitia Dei*, 2: 136–48.

CHAPTER 6: THE EXISTENTIAL DIMENSION

1. See, e.g., James O. Buswell, III, "Contextualization: Theory, Tradition and Method," in David J. Hesselgrave, ed., *Theology and Mission* (Grand Rapids: Baker, 1978), 93–99; Bruce J. Nichols, *Contextualization: A Theology of Gospel and Culture* (Downers Grove: InterVarsity, 1979).

2. See David E. Roberts, *Existentialism and Religious Belief* (New York: Oxford University Press, 1959).

3. Thus Romans 8:4, which states that believers do not live according to the flesh, but according to the Spirit: the New International Version translates, . . . "do not live according to the sinful nature, but according to the Spirit," correctly identifying "flesh" with "sinful nature."

CHAPTER 7: THE PERSONAL DIMENSION

1. Such as C. S. Lewis; see his *Letters to Malcolm: Chiefly on Prayer* (New York: Harcourt Brace Jovanovich, 1955), 63–65. At this point, we must note a difficulty in terminology. The term "person" is used in two slightly different senses in connection with the doctrine of God: in one sense, God is one person; in another, he is three persons. For a demonstration that the trinitarian doctrine of God as *three* persons is implicitly contained in the idea of a personal God, see Alister McGrath, *Understanding the Trinity* (Grand Rapids: Zondervan, 1988).

2. His most influential work is *I and Thou*, which should be read in the translation by Walter Kaufmann (New York: Scribner, 1970).

3. For example, in the field of Christology: see Alister E. McGrath, *The Making of Modern German Christology: From the Enlightenment to Pannenberg* (New York: Basil Blackwell, 1986), 101–3.

4. Buber, *I and Thou*, 56.

5. C. S. Lewis, *The Weight of Glory* (New York: Macmillan, 1949), 8.

6. Evelyn Waugh, *Brideshead Revisited* (New York: Dell, 1968), 288.

CHAPTER 8: THE ETHICAL DIMENSION

1. The most famous exposition of the political relevance of Barth's thought remains Friedrich-Wilhelm Marquardt, *Theologie und Sozialismus: Das Beispiel Karl Barths* [Theology and Socialism: The Example of Karl Barth], 3rd ed. (Munich: Kaiser Verlag, 1985).

2. The most distinguished and reliable discussion of this question may be found in Helmut Thielicke, *Theological Ethics*, 3 vols. (Grand Rapids: Eerdmans, 1978), vol. 1, esp. pp. 27–38.

3. German-speaking theologians like to play with the words *Gabe* ("gift") and *Aufgabe* ("task"). Another relevant play on words is between *Angebot* ("invitation") and *Gebot* ("commandment"). Unfortunately, this word-play can't be translated into English!

4. William Romaine, *A Method for Preventing the Frequency of Robbers and Murders* (London, 1770), 17.

5. Reinhold Niebuhr, *Moral Man and Immoral Society* (New York: Scribner, 1932), 44.

6. Reinhold Niebuhr, *The Nature and Destiny of Man*, 2 vols. (New York: Scribner, 1941–43), 2: 82.

CHAPTER 9: CONCLUSION

1. It is interesting to note the close connection in Luther's thought between the doctrine of justification by faith and the "theology of the cross." See Alister E. McGrath, *Luther's Theology of the Cross: Martin Luther's Theological Breakthrough* (New York: Basil Blackwell, 1985), 149–751, esp. 153–61.

APPENDIX

1. For a more detailed discussion of this question see Alister E. McGrath, *Understanding Jesus: Who Jesus Christ Is and Why He Matters* (Grand Rapids: Zondervan, 1987).

2. For the relationship between Christology and soteriology, see Alister E. McGrath, "Christology and Soteriology: A Response to Wolfhart Pannenberg's Critique of the Soteriological Approach to Christology," *Theologische Zeitschrift* 42/3 (1986): 222–36.

3. For a brief discussion of these terms, see McGrath, *Understanding Jesus*, 123–36.

4. For the reasons underlying this selection, see Alister E. McGrath, *Iustitia Dei: A History of the Christian Doctrine of Justification*, 2 vols. (Cambridge: Cambridge University Press, 1986).

5. See Alister E. McGrath, "The Article by which the Church stands or falls," *Evangelical Quarterly* 58/3 (1986): 207–28.

6. For a detailed study of this theme, see Alister McGrath, *The Mystery of the Cross* (Grand Rapids: Zondervan, 1988). See also Walter von Loewenich, *Luther's Theology of the Cross* (Minneapolis: Augsburg, 1976), 17–24.

7. Karl Barth, *Church Dogmatics* (Edinburgh: T. & T. Clark, 1956), IV/1, 518.

8. For a fuller discussion, see Alister E. McGrath, "Justification and Christology: The Axiomatic Correlation between the Proclaimed Christ and the Historical Jesus," *Modern Theology* 1/1 (1984): 45–54.

9. For further discussion of what follows, see Alister E. McGrath, "Reformation to Enlightenment," in P. D. L. Avis, ed., *The History of Christian Theology I: The Science of Theology* (Grand Rapids: Eerdmans, 1986), 105–229, esp. 154–60.

10. Lausanne Covenant, para. 10.

11. This is often stated as "what has been believed everywhere, always and by everyone" (*quod ubique, quod semper, quod ab omnibus creditum est*).

12. Gregory of Nazianzen, *Epistle* 101. See further M. F. Wiles, "The Unassumed Is the Unhealed," *Religious Studies* 4 (1968): 47–56.

13. From the Greek word meaning "to appear." Docetism held that Christ's humanity and sufferings were apparent, rather than real. In other words, Jesus Christ was God disguised as a human being: God never knew at first hand what it was like to be human.

14. The name derives from a small sect of Jewish Christians in the first two centuries, who held that Jesus Christ was the human son of Mary and Joseph, singled out for special favor by God. In no meaningful sense of the word could he be said to *be* God.

BIBLIOGRAPHY

The articles and books listed below will enable the reader to develop some of the historical and theological themes encountered during the course of this work. It is not intended to be exhaustive, but simply to allow the reader to take further any ideas that have been found stimulating in the present work.

Achtemeier, E. R. "Righteousness in the Old Testament." In *Interpreter's Dictionary of the Bible*. Nashville: Abingdon, 1962. 4:80–85.

Atkinson, J. "Justification by Faith: A Truth for Our Times." In David Field, ed., *Here We Stand: Justification by Faith Today*. London: Hodder & Stoughton, 1986. 57–83.

Berkouwer, G. C. *Faith and Justification*. Grand Rapids: Eerdmans, 1954.

Bray, G. "Justification and the Eastern Orthodox Churches." In David Field, ed., *Here We Stand: Justification by Faith Today*. London: Hodder & Stoughton, 1986. 103–19.

Brown, C. et al. "Righteousness, Justification." In *New International Dictionary of New Testament Theology*. Grand Rapids: Zondervan, 1976. 3:352–76. This work has an excellent bibliography.

Forde, Gerhard O. *Justification by Faith—A Matter of Death and Life*. Philadelphia: Fortress, 1982.

_____ . "Christian Life." In Carl E. Braaten and Robert W. Jenson, eds., *Christian Dogmatics*. 2 vols. Philadelphia: Fortress, 1982. 2:395–469.

Käsemann, E. "The 'Righteousness of God' in Paul." In *New Testament Questions of Today*. Philadelphia: Fortress, 1969. 168–82.

_____ . *Commentary on Romans*. Grand Rapids: Eerdmans, 1980.

Küng, H. *Justification: The Doctrine of Karl Barth and a Catholic Reflection*. 2nd ed. Philadelphia: Westminster, 1981.

Lampe, G. W. H., ed. *The Doctrine of Justification by Faith*. London: Mowbrays, 1954.

McGrath, A. E. "The Anti-Pelagian Structure of 'Nominalist' Doctrines of Justification." *Ephemerides Theologicae Lovanienses* 57 (1981): 107–19.

_____ . "'Augustinianism'? A Critical Assessment of the So-called 'Mediaeval Augustinian Tradition' on Justification." *Augustiniana* 31 (1981): 247–67.

_____ . "Justification: Barth, Trent and Küng." *Scottish Journal of Theology* 34 (1981): 517–29.

_____ . "Justice and Justification. Semantic and Juristic Aspects of the Christian Doctrine of Justification." *Scottish Journal of Theology* 35 (1982): 403–18.

_____ . "Humanist Elements in the Early Reformed Doctrine of Justification." *Archiv für Reformationsgeschichte* 73 (1982): 5–20.

_____ . "Forerunners of the Reformation? A Critical Examination of the Evidence for Precursors of the Reformation Doctrines of Justification." *Harvard Theological Review* 75 (1982): 219–42.

_____ . "'The Righteousness of God' from Augustine to Luther." *Studia Theologica* 36 (1982): 63–78.

_____ . "Mira et nova diffinitio iustitiae. Luther and Scholastic Doctrines of Justification." *Archiv für Reformationsgeschichte* 74 (1982): 37–60.

_____ . "John Henry Newman's 'Lectures on Justification.' The High Church Interpretation of Luther." *The Churchman* 97 (1983): 112–22.

_____ . "Karl Barth and the *articulus iustificationis*. The Significance of His Critique of Ernst Wolf within the Context of His Theological Method." *Theologische Zeitschrift* 39 (1983): 349–61.

_____ . "Justification and Christology. The Axiomatic Correlation between the Proclaimed Christ and the Historical Jesus." *Modern Theology* 1 (1984–85): 45–54.

_____ . "ARCIC II and Justification. Some Difficulties and Obscurities relating to Anglican and Roman Catholic Teaching on Justification." *Anvil* 1 (1984): 27–42.

_____ . "The Emergence of the Anglican Tradition on Justification 1600–1700." *The Churchman* 98 (1984): 28–43.

_____ . "Justification in Earlier Evangelicalism." *The Churchman* 97 (1983): 217–28.

_____ . "The Influence of Aristotelian Physics upon St Thomas Aquinas' Discussion of the 'Processus Iustificationis.'" *Recherches de théologie ancienne et médiévale* 51 (1984): 223–39.

_____ . *Luther's Theology of the Cross: Martin Luther's Theological Breakthrough*. New York: Basil Blackwell, 1985.

_____ . "The Moral Theory of the Atonement. An Historical and Theological Critique." *Scottish Journal of Theology* 38 (1985): 205–20.

_____ . "The Article by which the Church Stands or Falls." *Evangelical Quarterly* 58 (1986): 207–28.

_____ . "Christology and Soteriology. A Response to Wolfhart Pannenberg's Critique of the Soteriological Approach to Christology." *Theologische Zeitschrift* 42 (1986): 222–36.

_____ . *Iustitia Dei: A History of the Christian Doctrine of Justification*. 2 vols. Cambridge: Cambridge University Press, 1986.

Packer, J. I. "Justification in Protestant Theology." In David Field, ed., *Here We Stand: Justification by Faith Today*. London: Hodder & Stoughton, 1986. 84–102.

Przybylski, B. *Righteousness in Matthew and His World of Thought*. Cambridge: Cambridge University Press, 1980.

Reumann, J. *Righteousness in the New Testament*. Grand Rapids: Eerdmans, 1983.

Stendahl, K. "The Apostle Paul and the Introspective Conscience of the West." In *Paul among Jews and Gentiles*. Philadelphia: Fortress, 1976. 78–96.

Thielicke, H. *Theological Ethics*. 3 vols. Grand Rapids: Eerdmans, 1978.

Tiller, John. "Justification by Faith and the Sacraments." In Gavin Reid, ed., *The Great Acquittal: Justification by Faith and Current Christian Thought*. London: Fount, 1980. 38–61.

Toon, P. *Justification and Sanctification*. Westchester, Ill.: Crossway, 1983.

Wright, T. "Justification: The Biblical Basis and Its Relevance for Contemporary Evangelicalism." In Gavin Reid, ed., *The Great Acquittal: Justification by Faith and Current Christian Thought*. London: Fount, 1980. 12–37.

Yarnold, E. J. *The Second Gift: A Study of Grace*. London: St Paul Publications, 1974.

Ziesler, J. A. *The Meaning of Righteousness in Paul*. Cambridge: Cambridge University Press, 1972.